REA's Test Prep Books Are The Best!

(a sample of the <u>hundreds of letters</u> REA receives each year)

" I did well because of your wonderful prep books... I just wanted to thank you for helping me prepare for these tests. "

Student, San Diego, CA

" My students report your chapters of review as the most valuable single resource they used for review and preparation. "

Teacher, American Fork, UT

" Your book was such a better value and was so much more complete than anything your competition has produced (and I have them all!). "

Teacher, Virginia Beach, VA

" Compared to the other books that my fellow students had, your book was the most useful in helping me get a great score. "

Student, North Hollywood, CA

" Your book was responsible for my success on the exam, which helped me get into the college of my choice... I will look for REA the next time I need help. "

Student, Chesterfield, MO

" Just a short note to say thanks for the great support your book gave me in helping me pass the test... I'm on my way to a B.S. degree because of you! "

Student, Orlando, FL

(more on ne...

D1383598

(continued from front page)

" I just wanted to thank you for helping me get a great score
on the AP U.S. History exam... Thank you for making great test preps! "

Student, Los Angeles, CA

" Your Fundamentals of Engineering Exam book was the absolute best
preparation I could have had for the exam, and it is one of the major
reasons I did so well and passed the FE on my first try. "

Student, Sweetwater, TN

" I used your book to prepare for the test and found that the advice and the
sample tests were highly relevant... Without using any other material, I earned
very high scores and will be going to the graduate school of my choice. "

Student, New Orleans, LA

" What I found in your book was a wealth of information sufficient to shore up
my basic skills in math and verbal... The section on analytical ability was
excellent. The practice tests were challenging and the answer explanations most
helpful. It certainly is the Best Test Prep for the GRE! "

Student, Pullman, WA

" I really appreciate the help from your excellent book. Please keep up
the great work. "

Student, Albuquerque, NM

" I am writing to thank you for your test preparation... your book helped me
immeasurably and I have nothing but praise for your GRE preparation."

Student, Benton Harbor, MI

(more on back page)

The Best Test Preparation and Review

GMAT CAT

Graduate Management Admission Test
Computer-Adaptive Test

Anita Price Davis, Ed.D.
Chairperson of Education Department
Converse College, Spartanburg, SC

Ellen H. Davis, M.A.
English Instructor
Clearlake High School, Houston, TX

Roger C. Fryer, M.A.T.
Mathematics Instructor
Cosumnes River College,
Sacramento, CA

Thomas C. Kennedy, Ph.D.
Professor of English
Washburn University, Topeka, KS

Elaine M. Klett, M.S.
Assistant Professor
Brookdale Community College, Lincroft, NJ

Alexander Kopelman, M.B.A.
Educational Consultant
New York, NY

James S. Malek, Ph.D.
Chairperson and Professor of English
DePaul University, Chicago, IL

Marcia Mungenast, B.A.
Educational Consultant
Upper Montclair, NJ

Vijay K. Rohatgi, Ph.D.
Professor of Mathematics
Bowling Green State University,
Bowling Green, OH

Ernest Woodward, Ed.D.
Professor of Mathematics
Austin Peay State University, Clarksville, TN

Tefera Worku, M.S.
Mathematics Instructor
State University of New York, Albany, NY

Research & Education Association
61 Ethel Road West
Piscataway, New Jersey 08854

The Best Test Preparation and Review for the
GMAT CAT

Year 2000 Printing

Copyright © 1999 by Research & Education
Association. All rights reserved. No part of this
book may be reproduced in any form without
permission of the publisher.

Printed in the United States of America

Library of Congress Catalog Card Number 98-66855

International Standard Book Number 0-87891-236-3

Research & Education Association
61 Ethel Road West
Piscataway, New Jersey 08854

REA supports the effort to conserve and
protect environmental resources by
printing on recycled papers.

CONTENTS

ABOUT RESEARCH & EDUCATION ASSOCIATION

Research & Education Association (REA) is an organization of educators, scientists, and engineers specializing in various academic fields. Founded in 1959 with the purpose of disseminating the most recently developed scientific information to groups in industry, government, high schools, and universities, REA has since become a successful and highly respected publisher of study aids, test preps, handbooks, and reference works.

REA's Test Preparation series includes study guides for all academic levels in almost all disciplines. Research & Education Association publishes test preps for students who have not yet completed high school, as well as high school students preparing to enter college. Students from countries around the world seeking to attend college in the United States will find the assistance they need in REA's publications. For college students seeking advanced degrees, REA publishes test preps for many major graduate school admission examinations in a wide variety of disciplines, including engineering, law, and medicine. Students at every level, in every field, with every ambition can find what they are looking for among REA's publications.

While most test preparation books present practice tests that bear little resemblance to the actual exams, REA's series presents tests that accurately depict the official exams in both degree of difficulty and types of questions. REA's practice tests are always based upon the most recently administered exams, and include every type of question that can be expected on the actual exams.

REA's publications and educational materials are highly regarded and continually receive an unprecedented amount of praise from professionals, instructors, librarians, parents, and students. Our authors are as diverse as the fields represented in the books we publish. They are well-known in their respective disciplines and serve on the faculties of prestigious high schools, colleges, and universities throughout the United States and Canada.

ACKNOWLEDGMENTS

In addition to our authors, we would like to thank Dr. Max Fogiel, President, for his overall guidance, which brought this book to completion; Carl Fuchs, director of Educational Software Publishing, for his guidance and management of the editorial staff through every phase of development; John Paul Cording, Manager of Educational Software Publishing, for coordinating the editorial phases of the project; Larry B. Kling, Quality Control Manager of Books in Print, for his supervision of revisions; Kristin Massaro, Editorial Assistant, for her editorial contributions; Jeff LoBalbo, Senior Graphic Designer, for the design of the book cover; and Wende Solano, for typesetting the book.

GMAT CAT STUDY SCHEDULE

This study schedule will help you become thoroughly prepared for the GMAT CAT. *Although the schedule is designed as a 12-week study program, it can be condensed into six weeks if less time is available by combining each two-week period into one.* Be sure to set aside enough time each day for studying purposes. If you choose the 12-week program, you should plan to study for at least one hour per day. If you choose the six-week program, you should plan to study for at least two hours per day. Depending on your personal time schedule, you may find it easier to study during the weekend. Keep in mind that the more time you devote to studying for the GMAT CAT, the more prepared and confident you will be on the day of the exam.

Week	Activity
1	Read and study our introduction to the GMAT CAT.
2	Take and score Practice Test 1 to determine your strengths and weaknesses. Be sure to record your scores on the Scoring Worksheet. Any areas in which you score low are the ones you will need to study most thoroughly. For example, if you obtain a low number of correct answers on the Verbal Section, then you will need to study carefully each part of the Verbal Review. Your performance on the Quantitative and Analytical Writing Assessment sections should be treated in the same manner, and you should study the corresponding reviews.
3	Study the math, algebra, and geometry refresher courses of the Quantitative Review. Complete all practice drills and check your answers. Become comfortable with the material presented before proceeding to the next review.
4	Study all sections of the Verbal Review: reading comprehension, sentence correction, and critical reasoning. Be sure to complete all drills and check your answers.
5	Study the Analytical Writing Assessment Review. For practice, write at least one essay each for the "Analysis of an Issue" and "Analysis of an Argument" essay topics. Compare your essays to the sample scored essays provided.

Week	Activity
6	Skim through each of the reviews to refresh your memory of newly-acquired information or skills. Address any weaknesses you perceive with extra review in just those areas.
7	Take Practice Test 2. After scoring the exam, record your total on the Scoring Worksheet to keep track of your progress. Make sure to review thoroughly all of the explanations to the items you answered incorrectly. This will help to strengthen your command of areas in which you need work. Restudy the reviews of the areas in which you are still weak.
8	Take Practice Test 3. Score the exam and record your total on the Scoring Worksheet to keep track of your progress. Make sure to review thoroughly all of the explanations to the items you answered incorrectly. Again, this will help to strengthen your command of areas in which you need work. Restudy the reviews of the areas in which you are still weak.
9	Take Practice Test 4. Score the exam and record your score. Then, thoroughly review all of the explanations to the questions you answered incorrectly. Restudy the reviews of the areas in which you are still weak.
10	Take Practice Test 5. Score the exam and record your score. Continue to review thoroughly all of the explanations to the questions you answered incorrectly. Restudy the subject areas in which you are still weak.
11	Take Practice Test 6. Score the exam and record your score. Review all of the explanations to the questions you answered incorrectly. Restudy any areas in which you are still weak.
12	In this final week of prepping, cover any areas in which you still need help by continuing to study the reviews. You may want to retake Practice Test 1 as a confidence builder.

GOOD LUCK ON THE GMAT CAT!

GMAT CAT

Graduate Management Admission Test
Computer-Adaptive Test

CHAPTER 1:
Achieving a
Top GMAT Score

Chapter 1

ACHIEVING A TOP GMAT SCORE

PREPARING FOR THE GMAT CAT

By reviewing and studying this book, you can achieve a top score on the computer-adaptive Graduate Management Admission Test. The GMAT CAT is probably different from any exam you have taken in college. First, it is administered only on computer, whereas most of the tests you have taken in your collegiate life have likely been of the paper-and-pencil variety. Second, it does not test prior knowledge of facts specific to any subject or field of study; rather, it tests quantitative and verbal skills. Perhaps the tests most similar to the GMAT CAT were your general college entrance exams, which also tested verbal and quantitative skills, rather than prior knowledge of facts specific to any subject or field of study.

The exams included in this book contain more questions than the computer-adaptive GMAT, in order to provide a score that is roughly comparable to the actual computer-adaptive test. The practice exams and drills we provide include every type of question that can be expected on the GMAT CAT. Accompanying each practice exam is an answer key, complete with detailed explanations and solutions designed to clarify the material. Our objective is not only to provide the answers, but also to explain why the answer to a particular question is more acceptable than the other possible choices. By completing all the practice exams and studying the explanations that follow, you can discover your strengths and weaknesses. This will allow you to concentrate on the sections of the exam that you find most difficult.

ABOUT OUR TEST EXPERTS

To ensure that our GMAT CAT practice exams provide you with both score comparability and the proper degree of difficulty, every exam section has been carefully prepared by test experts in the various fields correlating to the content areas of the GMAT. Our authors have taken care to examine and research the mechanics of the actual GMAT CAT. Having studied at the master's and doctoral level and taught in their respective fields at competitive colleges and universities throughout the United States, our experts are highly regarded in the educational community. In this book they bring to bear the weight of their research and classroom experience.

ABOUT THE TEST

Who Takes the Test and What is its Purpose?

The GMAT is required by graduate business and professional schools, as it is considered a critical criterion for admission to a graduate program. Applicants for graduate business schools submit GMAT test results together with undergraduate records, references, and work experience as part of the highly competitive admission process associated with a Master of Business Administration (M.B.A.) program. The exam tests verbal, quantitative, writing, and critical reasoning skills and abilities that have been found to contribute to successful achievement in a graduate program. It does not test prior knowledge of data or facts specific to any field of study. Approximately 230,000 students take the GMAT each year.

Who Needs an M.B.A.?

Some people dismiss the necessity of an M.B.A., believing that only business majors can benefit from the program. It turns out, however, that those with non-business backgrounds often need management training as much as business majors. Engineers find that increased management skills are more valuable than technical training as they become more successful, and liberal arts majors enter a graduate management program to make up for a lack of practical, on-the-job skills. In fact, almost half the GMAT test-takers worldwide majored in the sciences, humanities, and social sciences.

In addition to careers in business and industry, students with an M.B.A. are in demand in the fields of government, education, healthcare, arts, and non-profit management. Students with the vision to see where management skills will be needed can make their own opportunities in almost any business.

With an increase in competition for fewer jobs, graduates with the ability to manage resources, time, and people will have an advantage over those with only technical training. Those already employed can use an M.B.A. to advance beyond their current level.

Who Administers the Test?

The GMAT is developed and administered by the Educational Testing Service under the direction of the Graduate Management Admission Council (GMAC), a not-for-profit organization of graduate business schools worldwide.

When and Where is the Test Given?

The GMAT is offered year-round during the last three weeks of each month, generally on a six-day-a-week cycle. For exact dates and test center locations, contact ETS at the number and/or address listed below.

How Can I Apply?

To receive an application or information about the application process, including test dates, locations, fees, and registration, request the GMAT CAT registration bulletin by contacting ETS at:

GMAC Publications
P.O. Box 6108
Princeton, NJ 08541-6108
Phone: (609) 771-7330
Website: www.ets.org

WHAT IS A COMPUTER-ADAPTIVE TEST (CAT)?

The GMAT is a computer-adaptive test (CAT), which means that you will use a computer to take the test. The software will determine the questions based on your performance on the previous questions. In this way, the test will customize itself to your level of ability. A correct response will be followed by a more difficult question; an incorrect response will be followed by an easier question. You get more points for correctly answering difficult questions than you do for correctly answering medium or easier questions.

In the traditional paper-and-pencil test, every examinee sees the same questions. Because of the adaptive nature of the GMAT CAT, and the large pool of questions that are available, different examinees will be asked different questions. Nonetheless, the questions have been designed to meet content and difficulty specifications that allow an equitable comparison of scores.

Pros and Cons of Computer-Adaptive Testing

There are several advantages to computer-adaptive testing. First, you will receive your unofficial scores for the multiple-choice sections on the day you take your test, rather than several weeks later. Second, the CAT is offered much more frequently than the paper-and-pencil version, and you may register just a few days in advance. Third, you may choose to take the test in the morning or afternoon. In addition, the testing venue is quieter and more orderly than traditional testing locations. Finally, there are generally fewer questions on the GMAT CAT than on traditional paper-and-pencil tests.

Unfortunately, there are also some important disadvantages to the CAT. People who are unfamiliar with computers may find the testing environment intimidating. While no computer skills are required, an unusual environment may have a psychological impact on your preparedness. In addition, you must answer the questions in the order in which they are presented, one at a time. You cannot skip a question and return to it later—or return to an earlier question to change your answer, as you could with a paper-and-pencil test. This is significant because it eliminates the important test-taking strategy of answering the easier questions first and returning to the more difficult questions if you have time. Finally, because of the nature of adaptive testing, the majority of the questions you encounter will be challenging.

Taking the Test

The CAT testing environment is based on a point-and-click interface. You will be presented with a question, and you will use a mouse to choose your answer. When you have chosen your answer and clicked "Next," you will click on the on-screen "Answer Confirm" button to verify your choice. When you have confirmed your answer, the computer will select the next question. The first question asked in each multiple-choice section will be of medium difficulty. Subsequent questions will be more or less difficult, depending on your answer to the preceding question. The CAT software will continue to adjust throughout the test until it reaches your ability level.

At any time during the test, you may choose to quit an individual section, or the entire test. You may wish to exercise this option if you feel that you are ill-prepared for the exam. However, you must not take this decision lightly. Once you quit a section or the entire test and confirm your desire to do so, you will be unable to reverse your decision. Note that you will not be able to take the GMAT CAT again for 30 days, *even if you do not complete the exam.*

When you complete the exam, you will receive your unofficial scores for the multiple-choice sections, as well as a total score for those sections. Your official score report, which will include your score on the Analytical Writing Assessment, will be mailed to you within ten days of the test date.

When Should I Start Studying?

It is never too early to start studying for the GMAT CAT. The earlier you begin, the more time you will have to sharpen your skills. Do not procrastinate! Cramming is *not* effective since it does not allow you the time needed to learn the material.

FORMAT OF THE GMAT CAT

The GMAT CAT contains three distinct sections with various types of questions:

1. **Quantitative**: One section of 37 mathematical Problem Solving and Data Sufficiency questions.

2. **Verbal**: One section of 41 Sentence Correction, Critical Reasoning, and Reading Comprehension questions.

3. **Analytical Writing Assessment**: One section of two essay questions.

The Graduate Management Admission Test consists of multiple-choice questions contained in two timed sections and one timed essay-writing section. The total testing time is three and one-half hours, including time for preliminary instructions. Each multiple-choice question presents five answer choices. On the actual exam, experimental questions (included to allow ETS to try out new questions) will be mixed in throughout the multiple-choice sections. In all, about one-quarter of the questions are experimental, but you won't be able to identify them and they won't count toward your score.

TEST FORMAT*

Section	Number of Questions	Minutes
Quantitative	37	75
Verbal	41	75
Analytical Writing Assessment	2 Essay Questions	30**

*Note: The test sections do not necessarily appear in the order shown above. This test format refers to the actual GMAT CAT. The practice tests in this book are longer, in order to provide a score comparable to that which you would achieve on the actual GMAT CAT. These tests are intended to provide scoring information, to pinpoint strengths and weaknesses, and to familiarize you with the types of questions you will encounter on the GMAT CAT. They are not intended to provide an accurate depiction of the CAT format.

**For each essay.

TYPES OF GMAT CAT QUESTIONS

QUANTITATIVE

Problem Solving

The GMAT CAT Problem Solving questions are designed to test basic mathematical skills, the comprehension of elementary mathematical concepts, and the ability to reason quantitatively.

Data Sufficiency

Each Data Sufficiency question is usually accompanied by initial information, as well as statements (1) and (2), which contain more information. To answer the question, you must decide whether there is sufficient information in either (1), (2), or both.

VERBAL

Reading Comprehension

You will be asked interpretive, applicative, and inferential questions regarding reading passages. The passages may be as long as 450 words; they discuss the social sciences, the physical or biological sciences, and/or business-related fields. The questions measure your ability to analyze, understand, and apply information that is presented in written form.

Critical Reasoning

These questions test the reasoning skills involved in formulating and evaluating arguments. Questions are based on an argument or set of arguments. The arguments come from a variety of sources and cover a multitude of topics.

Sentence Correction

Sentence Correction questions present you with five choices, and you must determine which choice best expresses an idea or relationship. Knowledge of stylistic conventions, grammatical rules of written English, and the ability to improve incorrect or ineffective expressions will be tested. An effective sentence expresses both a relationship and an idea in a grammatically and structurally sound manner.

WRITING

Analytical Writing Assessment (AWA)

The Analytical Writing Assessment section of the GMAT CAT tests your ability to communicate ideas and to write effectively. The two essay questions in this section test your ability to analyze an issue and an argument. Scoring is based upon organization, critical reasoning, and proper use of the English language and its conventions. A variety of general subjects, in addition to business-related topics, appear as test questions. Previous knowledge of the essay topics is not assumed.

ABOUT THE REVIEW SECTIONS

The Quantitative, Verbal, and Analytical Writing Assessment Reviews are written to help you understand the concepts behind GMAT CAT test questions. They will help prepare you for the test by teaching you what you need to know. By using the reviews in conjunction with taking the practice tests, you will be able to sharpen your test-taking skills.

Quantitative Review

This review includes strategies for the two quantitative ability question types: Problem Solving and Data Sufficiency. To help you cover these sections thoroughly, the review is split into three parts:

1) The first portion of the review consists of refresher courses in basic math, algebra, and geometry.

2) Mastering Problem Solving and Mastering Data Sufficiency, the second part of this review, contains strategies for solving the most commonly found problems on the GMAT CAT.

3) The last section of the review is designed to help you evaluate your performance after you have taken our practice tests.

Verbal Review

Reading Comprehension, Sentence Correction, and Critical Reasoning are the three question types covered in this review. The review summarizes each of these in detail, focusing on the specific skills you need to practice. Strategies for improving your performance are provided; test-taking strategies for each are given and explained in detail.

Analytical Writing Assessment (AWA) Review

This review includes strategies for the two types of essay questions that appear in the GMAT exam: Analysis of an Issue and Analysis of an Argument. The strategies cover the general pre-writing and organizational skills necessary to perform well on this section. It also includes sample scored essays and evaluations of the essays for both types of questions.

There are three sample essays given for each essay topic; each essay is judged as falling within a range on the GMAT scoring scale. On the actual GMAT, only one score is given per essay, i.e., 6, 5, 4, 3, 2, 1, or 0.

HOW THE GMAT CAT IS SCORED

In traditional, paper-and-pencil tests, every question is equal in value. The CAT is scored quite differently, since more difficult questions add more to your score than easier questions. For this reason, you should not be concerned if the test seems very difficult to you. Because the software is continuously refining its estimate of your ability level, nearly all of the questions should seem difficult to you.

The Analytical Writing Assessment score is based upon the average of four scores, given by four different readers—two of whom are human, two of whom are in fact computer programs. As there are two essay topics, each essay is given two scores, both of which are averaged together to acquire one score for each essay. One score is provided by ETS's *e-rater*™, an electronic reader; the other score is determined the old-fashioned way, by a human professor. These two scores are then averaged together to give you your AWA score, ranging from 0 to 6, 6 being the highest.

It is possible to receive half-point scores: for example, if one reader gives a score of 4 and the other scores the essay as a 5, your grade would be 4.5. In the event that the computer and the professor disagree with each other by more than a point, a second professor is called in. If the third reader scores the essay with the higher number, the low number is discarded. If the reader scores it with a lower number, the average of the three is used.

The GMAT test results consist of four scores: a total score (which is the combined Verbal and Quantitative scores), a separate Verbal score (Reading Comprehension, Critical Reasoning, and Sentence Correction), a separate Quantitative score (Problem Solving and Data Sufficiency), and an Analytical Writing score. The total score is reported on a scale from 200 to 800. The Verbal and Quantitative scores are reported on a scale from 0 to 60. The Analytical Writing score is reported on a scale of 0 to 6.

Refer to the chart below to find the percentile into which your scaled score falls.

For instance, according to the chart, a scaled score of 655 would fall between the 89 and 93 percentile. This means that 89% to 93% of examinees scored below 655 and 7% to 11% scored above 655.

Use the provided scoring worksheet to track your progress from test to test. Watch your scores improve with the use of our test-taking strategies and practice.

Percentiles Based on Recent GMATs			
Scaled Scores	Percentage Below	Scaled Scores	Percentage Below
740	> 99	460	32
720	98	440	26
700	97	420	20
680	95	400	15
660	93	380	11
640	89	360	8
620	85	340	6
600	80	320	4
580	74	300	2
560	68	280	1
540	61	260	1
520	53	240	1
500	46	220	0
480	39		

CALCULATING YOUR RAW AND SCALED SCORES

For the purpose of scoring the six written practice tests in this book, use the directions and tables that follow. Taking Practice Test 1 as an example[†]:

To determine your Verbal raw scores, you will use sections 2 (Reading Comprehension), 5 (Critical Reasoning), and 6 (Sentence Correction).

To determine your Quantitative raw scores, you will use sections 1 (Problem Solving), 3 (Data Sufficiency), and 4 (Problem Solving). To determine your total raw score, you will use all the sections of a test.

To obtain your raw score (Verbal, Quantitative, total), count the number of correct answers for the sections you are scoring, and then subtract one-fourth of the incorrect answers from the number of correct answers.

[†]Sections fall differently in different practice tests.

DO NOT DEDUCT POINTS FOR ANSWERS LEFT BLANK. Then, add .5 to the total and drop all the digits to the right of the decimal point. This gives you the raw score for each section.

The following example will aid you in finding your Verbal raw score. (The process is the same for determining your Quantitative raw score.)

IF YOU GET: 50 correct answers

AND YOU GET: 8 incorrect answers

YOU DID NOT ANSWER: 12 questions — these will not be calculated into your score.

Take 1/4 of the number of incorrect answers, in this case, 8

YOU GET: 2

SUBTRACT 2 from your CORRECT answers

YOU GET: 48

ADD .5 = 48.5

DROP ALL NUMBERS TO THE RIGHT OF THE DECIMAL POINT.

YOU GET: 48.

This would be your Verbal raw score.

Conversion Table for Verbal and Quantitative Scores—GMAT

Corrected Raw Score	Verbal	Quant.	Corrected Raw Score	Verbal	Quant.	Corrected Raw Score	Verbal	Quant.
61	60		40	42	48	19	24	27
60	59		39	41	47	18	23	26
59	59		38	40	46	17	22	25
58	58		37	40	45	16	21	24
57	57		36	39	44	15	20	23
56	56		35	38	43	14	19	22
55	55		34	37	42	13	18	21
54	54		33	36	41	12	17	20
53	53		32	35	40	11	16	19
52	52	60	31	34	39	10	16	18
51	51	59	30	34	38	9	15	17
50	50	58	29	33	37	8	14	16
49	50	57	28	32	36	7	13	15
48	49	56	27	31	35	6	12	14
47	48	55	26	30	34	5	11	13
46	47	54	25	29	33	4	10	12
45	46	53	24	28	32	3	9	11
44	45	52	23	27	31	2	9	10
43	45	51	22	26	30	1	8	9
42	44	50	21	25	29	0	7	8
41	43	49	20	25	28			

Take your raw score of 48 and find this number in the Raw Score column (on left) in the table above. Looking to the right of this number in the "Verbal" Scaled Score column, you will find that your scaled score is 49.

Conversion Table for Total Scores—GMAT

Corrected Raw Score	Total Scaled Score	Corrected Raw Score	Total Scaled Score	Corrected Raw Score	Total Scaled Score
113	800	75	613	37	403
112	800	74	607	36	398
111	800	73	602	35	392
110	800	72	596	34	387
109	800	71	591	33	381
108	795	70	585	32	376
107	789	69	580	31	370
106	784	68	574	30	365
105	778	67	569	29	359
104	773	66	563	28	354
103	767	65	558	27	348
102	762	64	552	26	343
101	756	63	547	25	337
100	751	62	541	24	332
99	745	61	536	23	326
98	740	60	530	22	321
97	734	59	525	21	315
96	728	58	519	20	310
95	723	57	514	19	304
94	718	56	508	18	299
93	712	55	503	17	293
92	707	54	497	16	288
91	701	53	492	15	282
90	696	52	486	14	277
89	690	51	481	13	271
88	684	50	475	12	266
87	679	49	470	11	260
86	673	48	464	10	255
85	668	47	459	9	249
84	662	46	453	8	244
83	657	45	448	7	238
82	651	44	442	6	233
81	646	43	437	5	227
80	640	42	431	4	222
79	635	41	426	3	216
78	629	40	420	2	211
77	624	39	414	1	205
76	618	38	409	0	200

When Will I Receive My Score Report?

Your official score report for the GMAT will arrive within ten days after the test. You can also elect to receive *unofficial* verbal, quantitative, and total scores on site as soon as you complete the GMAT. The summary report will list your total Verbal and Quantitative scores. Remember, your Verbal and Quantitative score will range from 0 to 60, while the total score will range from 200 to 800.

The summary score report sent to score users is one page in length. The Analytical Writing Assessment report is seven pages in length. Your AWA score, ranging from 0 to 6, will be listed here. Copies of the essay topics and your responses are also included in this report.

As previously mentioned, a percentile ranking will also be given for each score. The percentile figure is actually the percentage of three years' test scores that were lower than the score you received.

SCORING WORKSHEET

	Test 1	Test 2	Test 3	Test 4	Test 5	Test 6
Number of Correct Verbal Responses (Reading Comprehension + Critical Reasoning + Sentence Correction)	___	___	___	___	___	___
Minus 1/4 of the Incorrect Responses (# Incorrect)	___	___	___	___	___	___
Equals Raw Score	___	___	___	___	___	___
Scaled Score	___	___	___	___	___	___
Number of Correct Quantitative Responses (Problem Solving + Data Sufficiency)	___	___	___	___	___	___
Minus 1/4 of the Incorrect Responses (# Incorrect)	___	___	___	___	___	___
Equals Raw Score	___	___	___	___	___	___
Scaled Score	___	___	___	___	___	___
Total Raw Score (Verbal Raw Score + Quantitative Raw Score)	___	___	___	___	___	___
Total Scaled Score	___	___	___	___	___	___
Percentile	___	___	___	___	___	___

STUDYING FOR THE GMAT

It is very important for you to choose the time and place for studying that works best for you. Some students may set aside a certain number of hours every morning to study, while others may choose to study at night before going to sleep. Other students may study during the day, while waiting on a line, or even while eating lunch. Only you can determine when and where your study time will be most effective. But, be consistent and use your time wisely. Work out a study routine and stick to it!

When you take the practice exams, try to make your testing conditions as much like the actual test as possible. Turn your television and radio off, and sit down at a quiet table free from distraction. Make sure to time yourself.

As you complete each practice exam, thoroughly review the explanations to the questions you answered incorrectly; however, do not review too much at any one time. Concentrate on one problem area at a time by reviewing the question and explanation, and by studying the review until you are confident that you completely understand the material.

Use scratch paper for working out problems and practicing drills, since scratch paper will be provided when you take the actual exam.

Keep track of your practice exam scores. By doing so, you will be able to gauge your progress and discover general weaknesses in particular sections. You should carefully study the reviews that cover your areas of difficulty, as this will build your skills in those areas.

THE DAY OF THE TEST

Before the Test

On the day of the test, you should wake up early and have a good breakfast. Make sure that you dress comfortably, so that you are not distracted by being too hot or too cold. Also, plan to arrive at the test center early. This will allow you to collect your thoughts and relax before the test, and will also spare you the anguish that comes with being late. As an added incentive to make sure you arrive early, keep in mind that NO ONE WILL BE ALLOWED INTO THE TEST SESSION AFTER THE STATED STARTING TIME. If you arrive late, you will not receive credit or a refund.

Before you leave for the test center, make sure that you have your admission ticket and two other forms of identification, one of which must contain a recent photograph (e.g., driver's license, student identification card, passport, department of public safety identification card, current alien registration card, etc.). You will not be admitted to the test center if you do not have proper identification, and you will not be refunded or credited in any way.

If you would like, you may wear a watch to the test center; however, only ordinary watches will be permitted. Watches with alarms, calculator functions, flashing lights, beeping sounds, etc., will not be allowed. You also cannot bring a calculator, slide rule, or any written material (such as a dictionary, textbook, or notebook) into your testing room. In addition, you will not be permitted to have briefcases or packages with you. Drinking, eating, and smoking are prohibited.

During the Test

When you arrive at the test center, you will be assigned a cubicle. If you need to use the rest room, you may leave the testing room, but you will not be allowed to make up any lost time. Procedures will be followed to maintain test security.

Once you enter the test center, follow all of the rules and instructions given by the test supervisor. If you do not, you risk being dismissed from the test and having your GMAT scores canceled.

After the Test

When you have completed the last section of the GMAT, go home and relax!

CAT TEST-TAKING STRATEGIES

Computer-adaptive testing has eliminated many of the traditional test-taking strategies, such as answering the easier questions first and returning to the more difficult questions later. However, new strategies have evolved that take the place of traditional ones. The most important of these strategies are listed below:

- **Take the Tutorial**

  Even if you have some computer experience, pay attention to the tutorial that introduces the GMAT CAT. This tutorial will teach you how to use the features and characteristics of the computer system to your advantage. As with any software package, there are some aspects of the testing system that are unique to the CAT environment. It is not in your best interest to learn about these features in the middle of a timed test.

- **Use Your Time Wisely**

  Keep in mind that this is a timed test, and check your time regularly. As with any standardized test, you should not spend too much time on any one question. If you do not know the answer to a question, try to make an educated guess by eliminating as many of the answer choices as possible, and move on to the next question.

- **Answer Every Question in Each Section**

  Because the number of questions answered is calculated into your overall score, it is in your best interest to answer every question. If you are running out of time, you will be better served by guessing (even random guessing) than by leaving the last questions unanswered.

- **Pay Particular Attention to the First 10 Questions of Each Section**

  The adaptive testing engine makes major score adjustments based on your answers to the first 10 questions of each section, and uses subsequent questions to "fine-tune" your score. While you should not spend an undue amount of time on these questions, you should be aware that they are potentially more important than later questions, and treat them accordingly.

- **Use the "Answer Confirm" Button To Your Advantage**
  It is very easy to get into the habit of choosing an answer and automatically clicking on the "Answer Confirm" button. This is a dangerous tendency. Be absolutely sure that you have clicked on the appropriate answer choice before confirming.

- **Make Effective Use of Scratch Paper**
  You will be given scratch paper at the testing center to be used on the mathematical and analytical sections. Drawing diagrams can be very helpful in working out the complex analytical and mathematical problems.

- **Make Effective Use of Break Periods**
  You will generally be given an optional five minute break between test sections. Use this time to rest and take a well-deserved break.

GMAT CAT

Graduate Management Admission Test
Computer-Adaptive Test

CHAPTER 2:
Quantitative
Review

Chapter 2

GMAT QUANTITATIVE REVIEW

OVERVIEW OF THE QUANTITATIVE SECTION

The quantitative sections of the GMAT are designed to test basic mathematical skills and to evaluate your ability to reason and solve problems in a mathematical setting. A working knowledge of basic arithmetic, algebra, and geometry is required, as well as the ability to read and solve word problems. In addition, you must be able to analyze data and determine the relevancy and sufficiency of data in order to solve problems.

There are two types of GMAT quantitative ability sections: Problem Solving and Data Sufficiency. Each Problem Solving section consists of 16 questions to be completed in 25 minutes; each Data Sufficiency section consists of 20 questions to be completed in 25 minutes. The questions in both sections are ordered according to difficulty. Most people find the first seven or so questions in a section to be quite easy, and the last seven or so questions to be quite difficult. Questions in the middle of a section are usually of average difficulty.

HOW TO PREPARE FOR THE GMAT QUANTITATIVE

As a person applying to business school, you may be using math in your work or studies right now. This gives you an advantage, because you are used to thinking quantitatively and to using mathematical skills quickly and accurately. Be aware, however, that some of the math you will encounter on the GMAT may not be the math that you are using every day. In order to do well on the GMAT, you must review basic arithmetic (including properties of numbers), algebra, and geometry. As you do this, you will probably find that there are certain definitions and formulas that you have forgotten. You may also find that certain skills—such as solving quadratic equations or adding fractions—have become rather rusty from lack of use. It is important that you bring *all* of your basic math skills up to a maximum level of proficiency before you take the test. This way, you can concentrate on the strategy needed to solve each problem without having to worry about the mechanics of basic math.

If you have been away from math for several years, or if you have a weakness in a particular area, you may find that the explanations in this Review are not adequate for your needs. If this is the case, you should supplement this Review with a textbook or study guide in arithmetic, algebra, or geometry. These books can give you the detailed explanations and additional practice questions that you need.

Once you have reviewed arithmetic, algebra, and geometry, you will be ready to focus on the specific skills and strategies that you need to solve GMAT problems. While a few questions may require nothing more than a simple calculation or the application of a formula, most questions require more than that. Most GMAT questions require not only knowledge and basic skills—they require *insight* as well. Insight is the ability to look at a problem and determine what mathematical principles are required to solve it and how these principles should be applied. In problems requiring several steps, insight is the ability to see how parts of a problem are related and how these relationships can be used to find a solution.

Although insight may sound like a mysterious quality (and you may be worried that you don't have it), insight can be learned. Like most standardized tests, the GMAT is constructed according to a predictable pattern. Certain types of questions appear on the test over and over again, year after year. Certain mathematical principles tend to be applied in certain ways. By studying the types of questions that appear often on the GMAT, you will gain insight into the way the test is constructed. This insight will enable you to recognize specific problem types and know the kinds of solutions they require. It will also enable you to spot shortcuts and perceive important relationships among key elements in a problem.

USING THIS REVIEW

This Review is designed to provide you with the knowledge, skills, and strategy tactics that you need in order to do well on the GMAT. It is also designed to help you set goals and maximize the effectiveness of your study time.

The first portion of the Review consists of Refresher courses in basic math, algebra, and geometry. You will find these sections extremely valuable, because they include *only* the math that you need to know for the GMAT. Too often, test review books overload you with more basic math than you will ever need to know for the test. By summarizing the most essential math in an easy-to-reference format, these Refresher sections will enable you to review basic skills easily and efficiently.

You will notice in the Refresher sections items labeled TEST BREAKER. TEST BREAKERS are powerful strategy tips that will help you save time, spot shortcuts, avoid traps, and zero in on what the test makers are seeking. When you see a TEST BREAKER, you will probably find it helpful to mark it with a highlighter pen. This way, you can review these strategy tips frequently so they become a part of your thought processes.

Once you have worked through the Refresher sections, you will be ready to use the second portion of this Review. This portion consists of two sections: Mastering Problem Solving and Mastering Data Sufficiency. These sections contain specific strategies for solving the types of problems most commonly found on the GMAT. They also show you how basic principles of arithmetic, algebra, and geometry are applied in GMAT questions.

The final section of this Review is designed to help you evaluate your performance after you have taken a practice test. You will learn how to analyze your wrong answers and use your insights to coach yourself. You will also learn how to develop a plan and set goals to improve your performance on the next test.

BASIC MATH REFRESHER

The basic math that you will need to know for the GMAT includes definitions, properties of numbers, and arithmetic. Arithmetic topics include fractions, decimals, percents, averages, ratios and proportions, powers, and roots.

It is important to remember that you will not be able to use a calculator when you take the GMAT. This means that you must be able to add, subtract, multiply, and divide quickly and accurately. If you find yourself less than proficient in these skills, you should practice arithmetic calculations daily as part of your test preparation.

COMMON SYMBOLS

Some standard symbols that appear frequently on the GMAT are listed below. You will find additional symbols listed in the Geometry Refresher.

SYMBOL	DEFINITION
=	is equal to
≠	is not equal to
<	is less than
>	is greater than
≤	is less than or equal to
≥	is greater than or equal to

1. PROPERTIES OF NUMBERS

INTEGERS

An integer is any of the whole numbers {1, 2, 3, ...} or their opposites {− 1, − 2, − 3, ...} or 0. Integers can be represented on a number line:

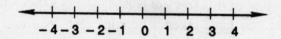

ABSOLUTE VALUE

The absolute value of a number is its distance from 0 on the number line. The symbol for absolute value is | |. This means that the absolute value of − 5, which is written | − 5 |, is 5, and the absolute value of +5, which is written | +5 | or | 5 |, is also 5.

POSITIVE AND NEGATIVE NUMBERS

Numbers to the right of 0 on the number line are positive numbers and numbers to the left of 0 are negative numbers. (The number 0 is neither positive nor negative.) Numbers commonly referred to as fractions or decimals fall between the integers on the number line. For example, $1/2$ would fall between 0 and +1; − 6.37 would fall between − 6 and − 7. Numbers on the number line increase in value from left to right.

TEST BREAKER

Always remember that negative numbers get *smaller* in value as they move away from 0. This means that − 5 is smaller than − 4, and − 20 is smaller than − 1.

OPERATIONS WITH POSITIVE AND NEGATIVE NUMBERS

To add numbers with the same sign, add the numbers and keep the same sign in the answer.

Examples

$$19 + 8 = 27; -5 + (-13) = -18$$

To add numbers with unlike signs, subtract the number with the smaller absolute value from the number with the larger absolute value. Then take the sign of the larger number.

Examples

$$-28 + 32 = +4; 6 + (-20) = -14$$

To **subtract** positive and negative numbers, follow this rule: The minus sign changes the sign of the number being subtracted. Once you change the sign, you can add the numbers according to the rules for addition.

Examples

$$-8 - (+7) = -8 + (-7) = -15$$

$$-3 - (-6) = -3 + 6 = +3$$

To **multiply or divide** positive and negative numbers, multiply or divide as usual, then sign the answer according to the following rules:

Positive ($\times$ or $\div$) positive = positive: $6 \times 7 = 42$

Negative ($\times$ or $\div$) negative = positive: $-10 \div (-5) = 2$

Positive ($\times$ or $\div$) negative = negative: $(-9) \times 3 = -27$

TEST BREAKER

GMAT questions often require you to apply the rules for positive and negative numbers in order to come to a conclusion about an algebraic expression. For example, if the expression xy is negative, you can conclude that either x or y must be negative.

DIGITS AND PLACE VALUE

In the decimal number system, there are ten digits: 0, 1, 2, 3, 4, 5, 6, 7, 8, and 9. The value of a digit is determined by its position relative to a decimal point. For example, in the number 345, 3 is in the hundreds place,

4 is in the tens place, and 5 is in the units place. In the number 1.891, 1 is in the units place, 8 is in the tenths place, 9 is in the hundredths place, and 1 is in the thousandths place.

ODD AND EVEN NUMBERS

Numbers that can be divided evenly by 2 are even; numbers that cannot be divided evenly by 2 are odd. Zero is considered an even number.

Adding:

> even + even = even
>
> odd + odd = even
>
> even + odd = odd

Multiplying:

> even × even = even
>
> even × odd = even
>
> odd × odd = odd

PRIME NUMBERS

Whole numbers that can be divided evenly only by themselves and 1 are called **prime numbers**. The numbers 0 and 1 are **not** prime numbers. The smallest prime number is 2, which is also the only even prime. Some other examples of prime numbers are: 3, 5, 7, 13, 41, and 79.

DIVISIBILITY, FACTORS, AND MULTIPLES

A number is **divisible** by another number if it can be divided evenly by that number. For example, 28 is divisible by 7 and 4, but it is not divisible by 3.

A number that divides another number evenly with no remainder is a **factor** of that number. For example, 6 is a factor of 24. The factors of a number are all of those numbers that divide it evenly; for example, the factors of 18 are 1, 2, 3, 6, 9, and 18.

The **prime factors** of a number are all of its factors that are prime numbers. For example, the prime factors of 18 are 2 and 3. A whole number can always be written as the product of its prime factors:

> 18 = 2 × 3 × 3.

A **multiple** of a number is that number multiplied by any non-zero number. For example, some multiples of 6 are 12, 18, 36, and 60.

TEST BREAKER

Learning the properties of numbers is a quick way to earn points on the GMAT. Some easier questions require nothing more than the application of a definition or rule.

☞ Practice Drill 1

1. Circle the statement(s) that could be true if xy is positive.

    I. x or y is negative.

    II. x or y is zero.

    III. x and y are negative.

2. List all the even integers between 0.5 and 17.2.

3. Write the number 56 as a product of its prime factors.

4. Compute.

    (a) $|6| - |-7|$ (c) $2 - 5 + |6 - 14|$

    (b) $|-8 + 5| + |-4|$ (d) $|-5| \times 4 + \dfrac{|-12|}{4}$

5. If ab is even, which of the following cannot be true?

    I. a or b is zero.

    II. b is odd.

    III. a and b are odd.

6. Name the digits that appear in the thousands place and the hundredths place.

    7,890.34

7. List all of the prime numbers between 14 and 26.

8. Name a whole number that is divisible by 4 and has 7 and 3 as factors.

9. List all of the multiples of 5 between 0 and 50 that are divisible by 3.

2. FRACTIONS, DECIMALS, AND PERCENTS

SUMMARY OF RULES FOR FRACTIONS

Equivalent fractions are fractions that have the same value:

$$\frac{4}{5} = \frac{8}{10}; \frac{2}{3} = \frac{6}{9}; \frac{1}{3} = \frac{12}{36} = \frac{100}{300}$$

To add or subtract fractions with the same denominators, add or subtract the numerators and keep the same denominator.

Examples

$$\frac{4}{7} + \frac{1}{7} = \frac{5}{7}; \frac{6}{13} - \frac{2}{13} = \frac{4}{13}$$

To add or subtract fractions with unlike denominators, first change the fractions to equivalent fractions with common denominators. Then add or subtract the numerators.

Examples

$$\frac{1}{5} - \frac{2}{15} = \frac{3}{15} - \frac{2}{15} = \frac{1}{15}$$

$$\frac{6}{11} + \frac{1}{2} = \frac{12}{22} + \frac{11}{22} = \frac{23}{22}$$

To multiply fractions, multiply the numerators and then multiply the denominators.

Example

$$\frac{2}{5} \times \frac{3}{4} = \frac{6}{20}$$

To divide fractions, invert the divisor, then multiply.

Example

$$\frac{4}{5} \div \frac{1}{2} = \frac{4}{5} \times \frac{2}{1} = \frac{8}{5}$$

SUMMARY OF RULES FOR DECIMALS

To add or subtract decimals, line up the decimal points, adding zeros if necessary. Place the decimal point in the answer in line with the other decimal points.

Example

$$57.98 + 6.2 + 34 \rightarrow$$

$$
\begin{array}{r}
57.98 \\
6.20 \\
+\ 34.00 \\
\hline
98.18
\end{array}
$$

To multiply decimals, multiply the numbers, then place the decimal point in the answer according to the total number of decimal places in the numbers being multiplied.

Example

$$
\begin{array}{r}
56.2 \text{ — 1 decimal place +} \\
\times \quad 1.3 \text{ — 1 decimal place =} \\
\hline
73.06 \text{ — 2 decimal places}
\end{array}
$$

To divide decimals, move the decimal point in the divisor until it shows no decimal part; then move the decimal point in the dividend the same number of decimal places, adding zeros if necessary. The decimal point in the answer is placed directly above the decimal point in the dividend.

Example

$$0.25\overline{)62.5} \qquad 25.\overline{)6250.}^{\,250.}$$

RULES FOR CONVERTING FRACTIONS, DECIMALS, AND PERCENTS

To convert a decimal into a fraction, look at the place value of the last digit in the decimal part to determine the denominator. If the last digit is in the tenths place, the denominator will be 10; if the last digit is in the hundredths place, the denominator will be 100, and so on.

Examples

$$0.03 = \frac{3}{100}; \; 0.9 = \frac{9}{10}; \; 0.993 = \frac{993}{1,000}$$

To convert a fraction into a decimal, divide the denominator into the numerator.

Examples

$$\frac{4}{5} = 4 \div 5 = 0.80 \qquad \frac{1}{3} = 1 \div 3 = 0.\overline{3}$$

Note that $0.\overline{3}$ is a **repeating decimal**. Certain fractions never divide evenly, but repeat the same digit in the quotient over and over again:

$$\frac{1}{3} = 0.3333333\ldots$$

To convert a percent into a fraction, remove the percent sign and write the number over 100.

Example

$$99\% = \frac{99}{100}$$

To convert a fraction into a percent, write the fraction as an equivalent fraction with a denominator of 100. Then take the numerator of the fraction as the percent.

Example

$$\frac{3}{5} = \frac{60}{100} = 60\%$$

To convert a percent into a decimal, remove the percent sign and move the decimal point two places to the left.

Example

$$34\% = 0.34$$

To convert a decimal into a percent, move the decimal point two places to the right and add a percent sign.

Example

$$0.08 = 8\%$$

☞ Practice Drill 2

1. Which fractions are equivalent to $\dfrac{3}{7}$?

   (A) $\dfrac{9}{63}$ (D) $\dfrac{27}{63}$

   (B) $\dfrac{24}{56}$ (E) $\dfrac{12}{96}$

   (C) $\dfrac{9}{14}$

2. What are the decimal and fractional equivalents of 5%?

3. Express

   (A) 1.65 as a percentage.

   (B) 0.7 as a fraction.

   (C) $-\dfrac{10}{20}$ as a decimal.

4. Perform the indicated operation.

   (A) $\dfrac{9}{10} - \dfrac{2}{5}$ (D) $\dfrac{7}{20} \div \dfrac{1}{4}$

   (B) $\dfrac{5}{6} \times \dfrac{3}{4}$ (E) $\dfrac{6}{7} \div \dfrac{2}{9}$

   (C) $\dfrac{9}{10} \div \dfrac{1}{5}$ (F) $\dfrac{1}{8} \times \dfrac{2}{3}$

5. Compute.

    (A) $0.98 + 1.5$

    (B) $78.9 \div 0.3$

    (C) 44.4×0.88

    (D) $345.04 - 9.9$

    (E) $506 \div 0.004$

    (F) 1.234×5

6. Write $\dfrac{2}{7}$ as a repeating decimal.

---

3. AVERAGES, RATIOS, AND PROPORTIONS

RULES AND DEFINITIONS

The **average**, or **mean**, is the sum of all the numbers in a set divided by the number of elements in the set.

Example

The average of $\{4, 5, 6\} = \dfrac{15}{3} = 5.$

The **median** is the middle value in a set of numbers. If there are an even number of items in a set, the median is the average of the two middle values.

The **mode** is the value that appears most often in a data set.

Example

The median of $\{3, 3, 5, 7, 9, 11, 12, 12, 12\}$ is 9; the mode is 12.

A **ratio** compares two numbers. A ratio can be written as two numbers separated by a colon or as a fraction.

Example

The ratio of 1 to 2 = $1:2 = \dfrac{1}{2}.$

A **proportion** describes two ratios that are equal.

Example

2 is to 4 as 5 is to 10; $\dfrac{2}{4} = \dfrac{5}{10}.$

☞ Practice Drill 3

1. Find the mean, median, and mode:

    $\{1, 2, 2, 2, 3, 5, 6, 6, 7, 9, 11\}$

2. Express each ratio as a fraction.

    (A) 8 is to 10

    (B) 6:12

    (C) 4:7

    (D) 1 is to 5

3. What is the sum of 8 numbers if the average is 14?

4. Write as a proportion the following statement:

    7 is to 9 as 14 is to 18.

5. Find the missing term in each proportion.

    (A) $\dfrac{4}{5} = \dfrac{20}{x}$

    (C) $\dfrac{6}{36} = \dfrac{x}{18}$

    (B) $\dfrac{x}{12} = \dfrac{1}{4}$

---

4. EXPONENTS AND RADICALS

SUMMARY OF RULES

$$(a^n)(a^m) = a^{n+m}$$

$$\frac{x^n}{x^m} = x^{n-m}$$

$$(a^n)^m = a^{nm}$$

$$\sqrt{\frac{a}{b}} = \frac{\sqrt{a}}{\sqrt{b}}$$

$$x^{-n} = \frac{1}{x^n}$$

$$(ax)^n = a^n x^n$$

$$\left(\frac{a}{b}\right)^n = \frac{a^n}{b^n}$$

$$\sqrt{ab} = \sqrt{a} \times \sqrt{b}$$

$$x^{a/b} = \sqrt[b]{x^a}$$

TEST BREAKER

Remember that any number raised to the 0 power equals 1:

$$x^0 = 1; \quad 4^0 = 1; \quad 58^0 = 1$$

Also remember that a negative number raised to an even power is positive, while a negative number raised to an odd power is negative:

$$(-2)^2 = 4; \quad (-2)^3 = -8$$

☞ **Practice Drill 4**

1. $(3^2)^3 =$

2. $\left(\dfrac{2}{5}\right)^2 =$

3. $(4y)^4 =$

4. $a^6 \times a^3 =$

5. $\sqrt{\dfrac{1}{49}} =$

6. $\sqrt{36x^4} =$

7. $\dfrac{y^8}{y^4} =$

8. $\sqrt{\dfrac{x^6}{16}} =$

9. $-3^{-2} =$

10. $\dfrac{-3}{4^{-1}}$

ALGEBRA REFRESHER

Basic high school algebra is required for the GMAT. You will need to know how to factor and rearrange algebraic expressions and how to solve equations (linear and quadratic), systems of equations, and inequalities. You will also need to know order of operations, which is used in both arithmetic and algebra problems.

It is important to remember that algebraic skills are essential in solving many types of geometry problems and word problems. The use of algebra in word problems will be covered in detail in the Mastering Problem Solving section.

5. ALGEBRAIC EXPRESSIONS

USEFUL PROPERTIES

The **associative property** allows you to regroup numbers and variables as you add or multiply.

Examples

$$(a + b) + c = a + (b + c);$$

$$(ab)c = a(bc)$$

The **commutative property** allows you to reverse the order as you add or multiply.

Examples

$$x + 3 = 3 + x;$$

$$ab = ba$$

The **distributive property** enables you to multiply out an expression or find a common factor.

Examples

$$4x + 4 = 4(x + 1);$$

$$a(b + c) = ab + ac$$

TEST BREAKER

> Sometimes, the answer to a GMAT problem appears like magic when you rearrange an algebraic expression. For example, if you are asked to compare
>
> $$3z + 2x + 4y + 6$$
>
> and
>
> $$2(x + 2y) + 3(z + 2),$$
>
> you can see by rearrangement that the two expressions are equal.

FAMILIAR PATTERNS

Differences of Squares

$$a^2 - b^2 = (a + b)(a - b)$$

Examples

$$x^2 - 4 = (x + 2)(x - 2)$$
$$9 - 25y^2 = (3 + 5y)(3 - 5y)$$

Binomial Squares

$$(a + b)^2 = (a + b)(a + b) = a^2 + 2ab + b^2$$
$$(a - b)^2 = (a - b)(a - b) = a^2 - 2ab + b^2$$

TEST BREAKER

> Difference of squares and binomial squares appear so often on the GMAT that you should learn to recognize them in every possible form. The solution to a problem often comes to light when you multiply out the factored expression or factor the unfactored expression.

MULTIPLYING BINOMIALS

$$(a + b)(c + d) = ac + ad + bc + bd$$

If you forget how to multiply binomials, think FIRST-OUTSIDE-INSIDE-LAST: first, multiply the first terms in each parentheses; then, multiply the terms on the outside; next, multiply the inside terms; last, multiply the last terms in each parentheses.

FACTORING TRINOMIALS

To factor a trinomial expression, you must find two factors that, when multiplied, will produce the expression.

Examples

$$x^2 - 5x + 4 = (x - 4)(x - 1)$$

$$2n^2 + 3n + 1 = (2n + 1)(n + 1)$$

ORDER OF OPERATIONS

Sometimes it is necessary to simplify an expression by performing several different operations. It is essential that you perform these operations in the following order:

1. Parentheses—do operation in ( ) first

2. Exponents

3. Multiplication

4. Division

5. Addition

6. Subtraction

If a problem contains brackets [ ] and parentheses, work from the inside out. For example,

$$10 - [2 + (8 \times 9) + 12]$$

becomes

$$10 - [2 + 72 + 12],$$

which then becomes

$$10 - [2 + 6] = 10 - 8 = 2.$$

☞ Practice Drill 5

1. Multiply.

    (A) $(x + 5)^2$

    (B) $(x + 2)(5x - 1)$

    (C) $(8 - 6x)(8 + 6x)$

    (D) $4x(x - 3 + y)$

2. Factor.

   (A) $16y^2 - 9$ (C) $a^2 + 6a + 9$

   (B) $10x^2 - x - 2$

3. Which of the following expressions is equal to

   $(a + b)^2 + 7$?

   (A) $a^2 + 2ab + b^2 - (4 + 3)(4 - 3)$

   (B) $2ab + a^2 + b^2 + (4 + 3)(4 - 3)$

   (C) $(a + b)(a - b) + (4 + 3)^2$

4. Simplify

   $8 \times 2 + 1 - 3[(4^2 + 9) + 5] - 10.$

---

6. EQUATIONS AND INEQUALITIES

GENERAL RULES FOR SOLVING EQUATIONS

1. You can add or subtract the same number from both sides of an equation.

2. You can multiply or divide both sides of an equation by the same number.

LINEAR EQUATIONS

In a linear equation, the highest power of any variable is one. You can solve a linear equation by isolating a variable on one side of the equation.

Example

$$8 - 3x = 11$$
$$8 = 11 + 3x$$
$$-3 = 3x$$
$$x = -1$$

QUADRATIC EQUATIONS

In a quadratic equation, at least one variable is raised to the second power. To solve a quadratic equation for a particular variable, follow these steps:

1. Set one side of the equation equal to zero.

2. Factor the non-zero side.

3. Set each factor equal to 0 and solve for the variable. You will obtain two solutions.

Example

$$a^2 + 5a = 6$$

1. $a^2 + 5a - 6 = 0$

2. $(a + 6)(a - 1) = 0$

3. $a + 6 = 0;$ $a - 1 = 0$

     $a = -6;$ $a = 1$

SYSTEMS OF EQUATIONS

Systems consist of two or more equations that contain the same variables. There are several methods for solving systems of equations, but the easiest one to use on GMAT problems is usually substitution. To solve by substitution, you solve one equation for a particular variable, then substitute that value into another equation to solve for the second variable. If a system consists of more than two equations, you repeat this process until you have solved for all variables.

Example

$$a + b = 5 \text{ and } 4a = 7 - b$$

$$a = 5 - b$$

$$4(5 - b) = 7 - b$$

$$20 - 4b = 7 - b$$

$$13 = 3b$$

$$\frac{13}{3} = b$$

$$a = 5 - \frac{13}{3}$$

$$a = \frac{2}{3}$$

Solution

$$a = \frac{2}{3}; b = \frac{13}{3}$$

GENERAL RULES FOR SOLVING INEQUALITIES

1. As with equations, you can add or subtract the same number from both sides of an inequality.

2. You can multiply or divide both sides of an inequality by the same number provided that number is positive. *However, if you multiply or divide by a negative number, the inequality sign is reversed.*

Example

$$x < 1; -x > -1$$

☞ Practice Drill 6

1. Solve for x.

    (A) $qrt = rx + 2q$

    (B) $x - 7 = 3x - 1$

    (C) $\frac{1}{2} + \frac{(x-4)}{3} = x$

    (D) $5(2 + x) = 2x + 1$

2. Solve for a and b.

    $$9a + b = 20$$

    $$3 + b = -a - 1$$

3. Solve for y.

    (A) $5 - y < -1$

    (B) $\frac{y}{2} > 6 - y$

    (C) $ay + by > 10$

4. Solve for the variable.

    (A) $x^2 + 3x = 4$

    (B) $16x^2 = 25$

    (C) $6a^2 - a = 1$

GEOMETRY REFRESHER

When was the last time you solved a 30–60–90 right triangle? Do you know how to compute the volume of a cylindrical tank? If you are like many people taking the GMAT, geometry is not something that you use everyday. Yet, about 25% of GMAT math problems involve geometry, and all of these problems require the application of rules and formulas.

Geometry questions on the GMAT tend to be more difficult than algebra and arithmetic questions. One reason for this is that the geometry problems usually require you to apply several concepts simultaneously— for example, knowledge of parallel lines and triangles. In addition, the ability to work a problem is dependent upon knowing the correct formulas.

This Refresher provides a review of the geometry rules and formulas that you need to know for most GMAT questions. *You should memorize these rules and formulas absolutely.* By doing so, you will pick up quick points on the easier questions and have a good head start on the difficult questions.

COMMON SYMBOLS

SYMBOL	DEFINITION
‖	is parallel to
⊥	is perpendicular to
∠	angle
∟	right angle
Δ	triangle

7. LINES AND ANGLES

RULES AND DEFINITIONS

A **line** can be identified by two points on the line or by a single lowercase letter.

A   B

line *AB*   *m*

line *m*

A **line segment** is a portion of a line named by its two endpoints: line segment *AB*, also written *AB*.

An **angle** can be named by: (1) three letters, with the vertex letter in the middle; (2) the letter at the vertex; or (3) a lowercase letter inside the angle.

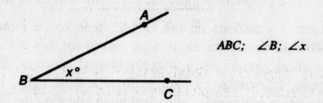

ABC; ∠*B*; ∠*x*

A **bisector** divides a line or angle into two equal parts.

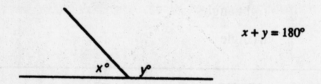

AB = *BC*   ∠*ABO* = ∠*OBC*

A **straight line** = 180°.

Angles that add to 180° are called **supplementary**.

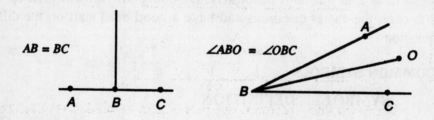

x + *y* = 180°

A **right angle** = 90°.

Angles that add to 90° are **complementary**.

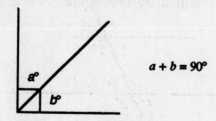

a + *b* = 90°

Lines that intersect at right angles are **perpendicular**.

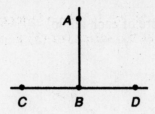

TEST BREAKER

Because diagrams in GMAT Problem Solving sections are usually drawn to scale, it is helpful to know what certain common angles look like:

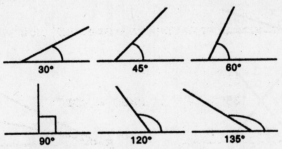

When two lines intersect, opposite angles are called **vertical angles**. Vertical angles are equal.

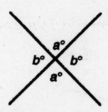

Two **parallel lines** cut by a third line (transversal) form equal angles as shown. Supplementary angles are formed by $x + y = 180°$.

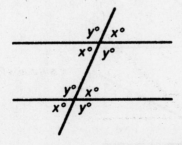

☞ **Practice Drill 7**

1. Determine the measure of each angle.

    (A)

    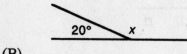

    (B)

    (C)

    (D)

2. Which of the following is closest to 31°?

    (A)

    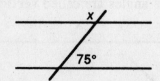

    (B)

    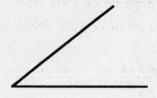

    (C)

8. TRIANGLES

DEFINITIONS

An **equilateral triangle** has three equal sides and three equal angles.

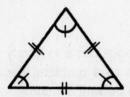

An **isosceles triangle** has two equal sides. The angles opposite the equal sides are equal.

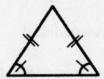

A **right triangle** has one right angle.

The **hypotenuse** is the side opposite the right angle. The other two sides are called legs.

The **altitude** of a triangle is a line drawn from a vertex perpendicular to the side opposite that vertex. The side to which the altitude is drawn is called the **base**.

In a right triangle, two of the altitudes are sides of the triangle.

In an equilateral triangle, any altitude bisects the vertex angle and the base.

In an isosceles triangle ABC, with $\angle A = \angle C$, an altitude drawn from vertex B bisects angle B and base AC.

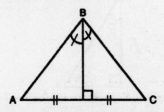

RULES AND FORMULAS

The **sum of the angles** of a triangle = 180°.

The **sum of the lengths of any two sides** must be greater than the length of the third side.

TEST BREAKER

Rules such as the ones above come in handy when you are eliminating obvious wrong answers to a problem. For more on this strategy, see the Mastering Problem Solving section.

Perimeter of a triangle = sum of the three sides.

Area of a triangle = $\frac{1}{2}$ (base) (altitude).

Pythagorean theorem: For a right triangle, the square of the length of the hypotenuse is equal to the sum of the squares of the other two sides:

$a^2 + b^2 = c^2$.

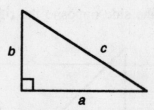

45–45–90 Triangle: For a triangle with angles 45°, 45°, and 90°, the lengths of the sides are related as shown:

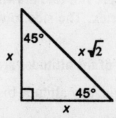

30–60–90 Triangle: For a triangle with angles 30°, 60°, and 90°, the lengths of the sides are related as shown:

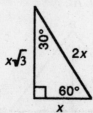

TEST BREAKER

The radicals $\sqrt{2}$ and $\sqrt{3}$ show up so often in GMAT problems that you should memorize their decimal approximations:

$\sqrt{2} = 1.4$ and $\sqrt{3} = 1.7$.

This will help you estimate sizes better.

☞ Practice Drill 8

1. Determine the measure of each lettered angle or side.

(A)

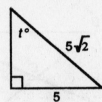

(C)

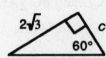

(B)

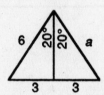

2. Which of the following cannot be the lengths of the sides of a triangle?

(A) 2, 3, 4

(c) 1, 1, 3

(B) 7, 9, 14

3. Find the area of each triangle.

(A)

(B)

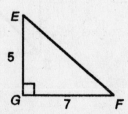

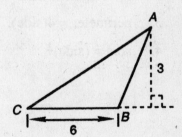

4. Which is longer— 4.5 meters or $3\sqrt{3}$ meters?

9. PARALLELOGRAMS AND OTHER FOUR-SIDED FIGURES

DEFINITIONS AND FORMULAS

A **parallelogram** is a four-sided figure in which

1. opposite sides are parallel.
2. opposite sides are equal in length.
3. opposite angles are equal.
4. the diagonals bisect each other.
5. area = (altitude) (base).

In parallelogram *ABCD*,

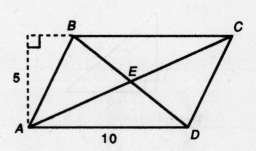

$AB \parallel CD$ and $BC \parallel AD$;

$AB = CD$ and $BC = AD$;

$BE = DE$ and $AE = CE$;

$\angle A = \angle C$ and $\angle B = \angle D$;

Area = 5 × 10 = 50.

A **rectangle** is a parallelogram in which

1. all angles are right angles.
2. the diagonals are equal.
3. perimeter = 2(length) + 2(width).
4. area = (length) (width).

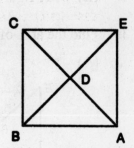

A **square** is a rectangle in which

1. all sides are equal.
2. the diagonals intersect at right angles.
3. perimeter = 4(side).
4. area = (side)².

A **trapezoid** is a four-sided figure in which two sides are parallel. These sides are called bases.

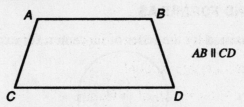

AB ∥ CD

When the base angles of a trapezoid are equal, the sides opposite the angles are equal.

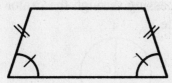

Area of a trapezoid = $\dfrac{\text{(sum of the bases) (height)}}{2}$

Area of trapezoid $ABCD = \dfrac{(4+8)\,(6)}{2} = 36$

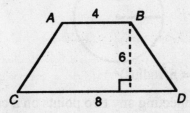

☞ Practice Drill 9

1. Solve the figure below for the angles and lengths indicated by lower-case letters. Assume that *PQ* is parallel to *TR* and *PT* is parallel to *QR*.

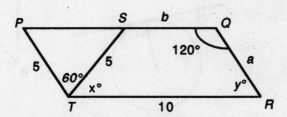

10. CIRCLES

DEFINITIONS AND FORMULAS

A circle is **named** by the letter of its center; for example, circle *O*.

A **diameter** is a line passing through the center of a circle that connects two points on the circle.

A **radius** is a line from the center of the circle to any point on the circle. The radius is $1/2$ the diameter.

The **area** of a circle = $\pi(\text{radius})^2$.

A **chord** is a line connecting any two points on a circle.

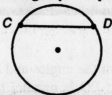

A **tangent** is a line that intersects a circle at one point. A tangent is perpendicular to a radius or diameter at the point of tangency.

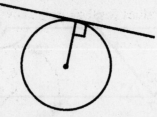

The **circumference** of a circle is the distance around the circle.

Circumference = $\pi(\text{diameter})$

An **arc** is a portion of the circumference, named by three letters: for example, *ABC*.

The **number of degrees** in a complete circle = 360°.

A **central angle** has its vertex at the center of the circle. For a central angle of measure $x°$, the length of the corresponding arc is equal to $x/360$ of the circumference.

Example

If $x = 60°$, the length of arc $ABC = \dfrac{1}{6}$ the circumference of the circle.

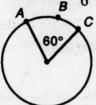

The area of a portion of a circle defined by central angle x is equal to $x/360$ of the total area.

TEST BREAKER

You should know the approximate value of π, which is 3.14 or $^{22}/_7$. By knowing the approximate value, you can estimate measurements on the test.

☞ Practice Drill 10

1. Fill in the missing values for the circle shown below.

   (A) diameter =

   (B) circumference =

   (C) $\angle x =$

   (D) area =

   (E) area of sector *AOB* =

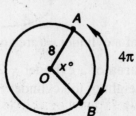

11. SOLIDS

RECTANGULAR SOLIDS

A rectangular solid consists of six rectangular surfaces called **faces**.

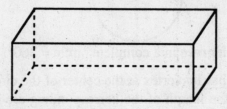

The intersection of any two faces is called an **edge**.

The intersection of any three faces is called a **vertex**.

Opposite faces are parallel and have equal dimensions.

The **surface area** of a rectangular solid is equal to the sum of the areas of all the faces.

The **volume** of a rectangular solid is equal to the product (length) (width) (height).

A **cube** is a rectangular solid in which all edges are equal in length. A cube has six identical square faces.

The **volume** of a cube is equal to $(edge)^3$.

CYLINDERS

A **cylinder** is a solid figure that consists of two circular bases of equal size and a height perpendicular to the bases.

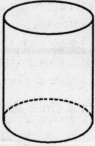

Volume of a cylinder = (area of base) (height).

Surface area of a cylinder = $2(\pi r^2) + 2\pi rh$, where r = radius of the base and h = height of the cylinder.

☞ **Practice Drill 11**

1. Compute the volume and surface area of each figure.

(A)

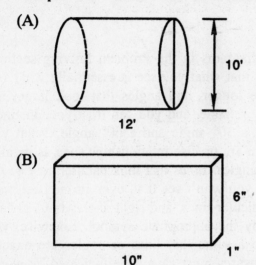

10'

12'

(B)

6"

10"   1"

MASTERING PROBLEM SOLVING

The Problem Solving sections of the GMAT test basic mathematical skills and evaluate your ability to apply mathematical concepts, reason quantitatively, and solve quantitative problems. About half of the questions in this section are "straight math" problems, while the other half are what are commonly known as "word problems."

All of the questions are multiple choice, with five answer choices. Inherent in multiple-choice math questions are certain advantages and disadvantages. The most obvious advantage is that the right answer is there for you to see, whether you know how to solve the problem or not. You have the opportunity to work backwards from the answer, estimate, or—if all else fails—guess. The greatest disadvantage is that the most tempting wrong answers are also there for you to see. The test makers seem to know what careless errors, incomplete solutions, and mistakes in interpretation are most common among test takers. If you make one of these "famous" errors, you can bet that the answer will be there for you to choose.

The purpose of this coaching section is to give you the skills and insights that you need in order to solve the types of problems most often found on the GMAT, and to help you cope with the advantages and disadvantages of a multiple-choice math test. By avoiding traps and obvious wrong answers and by taking advantage of the clues that the answer choices offer, you can maximize your score and use your math skills to your greatest advantage.

INTERPRETING DIAGRAMS

Unless stated otherwise, diagrams in the Problem Solving sections are drawn to scale. This means that what you see is essentially what you get. Lines that look longer are longer, and angles that look larger are larger. The shape of a figure is reliable, and you can trust your instincts when discerning between, say, a 30° angle and a 60° angle. What you *cannot* tell from a scale diagram are precise relationships such as parallel lines, equal lengths, and equal angles. Lines that look parallel may be off by a fraction of a degree—and you won't see that, even in the best scale drawing. Parallel lines, perpendicular lines, and right angles must always be stated, either in words or by the appropriate symbol. Likewise, you should never use a drawing to assume that lines or angles are exactly equal. To be precise, equal measures must always be indicated by words or by numbers.

SOLVING WORD PROBLEMS

Translating Words into Math

Word problems can be difficult because they require two sets of skills. First, you have to set up the problem. Then, you have to solve the problem. For most people, setting up the problem is the hard part.

Setting up word problems can become much easier if you follow these steps:

1. List the information given.

2. Assign variables to unknown quantities.

3. Look for keywords that tell you how various items in the problem are related.

4. Look for keywords that refer to familiar formulas.

5. Write equations that describe the relationships that you found in steps 3 and 4.

TEST EXAMPLE

A rectangular container with a square base has a volume of 54 cubic feet. The height of the container is twice the width of the base. How many feet high is the container?

(A) 3   (D) 8

(B) 6   (E) 9

(C) 7

Solution

Step 1: List the information.

rectangular solid with square base

volume = 54 cubic feet

height = twice the width of the base

Step 2: Assign variables to unknown quantities.

height = h

width of base = w

Step 3: Look for keywords.

"twice" means "times 2"

Step 4: Recognize a familiar formula.

volume of a rectangular solid = (length) (width) (height)

Step 5: Write equations based on steps 3 and 4.

from step 3: $h = 2w$

from step 4: since the base is a square, length = width,

so volume = (width) (width) (height), or

$V = w^2h$; $54 = w^2h$

Now you have two equations that you can solve as a system:

$h = 2w$; $54 = w^2h$

By substitution,

$$54 = h\left(\frac{h}{2}\right)^2$$

$$54 = h\frac{3}{4}$$

$$216 = h^3$$

$$h = 6$$

COMMON TYPES OF WORD PROBLEMS

Distance Problems

Distance problems relate distance traveled, rate of travel, and the amount of time the travel required. You can solve distance problems by using this formula:

rate × time = distance or $r \times t = d$.

TEST EXAMPLE

Susan walked 10 kilometers in $2^1/2$ hours. What was Susan's rate in kilometers per hour?

(A) 4   (D) 25

(B) 5   (E) 30

(C) 20

Solution

r = rate

$$t = 2\frac{1}{2} \text{ hrs} = \frac{5}{2} \text{ hrs}$$

$d = 10$ km

Plugging the values into $r \times t = d$, you obtain

$$r \times \frac{5}{2} = 10$$

$$r = 10\left(\frac{2}{5}\right)$$

$$r = 4$$

Mixture Problems

In a mixture, or combination, problem, different items are combined in definite amounts. The characteristics of the resulting combination are related to the characteristics of the original items. You can solve a mixture problem by using these general formulas:

(value item$_1$) (number$_1$) + (value item$_2$) (number$_2$)

= total value (number item$_1$) + (number item$_2$)

= total number

TEST EXAMPLE

Tina has 20 stamps that are worth a total of 72¢. If some of the stamps are 3¢ stamps and some are 4¢ stamps, how many 4¢ stamps does she have?

(A) 3   (D) 10

(B) 4   (E) 12

(C) 8

Solution

Let x = the number of 3¢ stamps and let y = the number of 4¢ stamps.

$$3x + 4y = 72$$

$$x + y = 20$$

Solving the system of equations for x:

$$x = 20 - y$$

$$3(20 - y) + 4y = 72$$

$$60 - 3y + 4y = 72$$

$$y = 12$$

Notice that answer choice (C) is waiting for the person who solves for the number of 3¢ stamps instead of the number of 4¢ stamps.

Work Problems

Work problems relate the time it takes two or more workers to do a job together to the time it takes each worker to do the job alone. The general formula for work problems is:

$$\frac{1}{a} + \frac{1}{b} = \frac{1}{t},$$

where a and b are the rates of the individual workers and t is the time it takes them to do the job together.

TEST EXAMPLE

A certain copy machine can make 100 copies in 10 minutes, while another copy machine can make 100 copies in 6 minutes. If both machines work simultaneously, how many minutes will it take to make 100 copies?

(A) $1\frac{1}{2}$

(D) $6\frac{1}{4}$

(B) 2

(E) 8

(C) $3\frac{3}{4}$

Solution

$$10 = \text{rate of copy machine 1}$$

$$6 = \text{rate of copy machine 2}$$

$$\frac{1}{10} + \frac{1}{6} = \frac{1}{t}$$

$$(30t)\frac{1}{10} + (30t)\frac{1}{6} = (30t)\frac{1}{t}$$

$$3t + 5t = 30$$

$$8t = 30$$

$$t = 3\frac{3}{4}$$

Age Problems

Age problems relate the ages of two or more people. Age problems usually include references to future or past ages as well as present ages.

TEST EXAMPLE

Art is 3 times as old as Peter. In 13 years, Art will be 1 year younger than twice Peter's age. How old is Art now?

(A) 12   (D) 40

(B) 24   (E) 49

(C) 36

Solution

A = Art's age now

P = Peter's age now

$A + 13$ = Art's age 13 years from now

$P + 13$ = Peter's age 13 years from now

Set up equations:

$$A = 3P$$

$$A + 13 = 2(P + 13) - 1$$

By substitution, $P = 12$ and $A = 36$.

Notice that if you solved for Peter's age instead of Art's age, answer choice (A) is waiting for you. If you added 13 to Art's present age, choice (E) is there to tempt you.

Percent Problems

There are three basic types of percent problems:

1. What is $p\%$ of n?

2. m is what percent of n?

3. m is $p\%$ of what number?

You can solve the first type by changing the percent to a fraction or a decimal, then multiplying by n:

Type 1: What is 14% of 20?

$$14\% = 0.14; 0.14 \times 20 = 2.8$$

You can solve the second and third types by using this general formula:

$$\frac{m}{n} \times 100 = p\%$$

Type 2: 8 is what percent of 40?

$$\frac{8}{40} \times 100 = p; p = 20\%$$

Type 3: 15 is 60% of what number?

$$\frac{15}{n} \times 100 = 60; n = \frac{1,500}{60}; n = 25$$

TEST EXAMPLE

The number 65 is 6.5% of which of the following?

(A) 10

(D) 255

(B) 25.5

(E) 1,000

(C) 100

Solution

65 is 6.5% of what number?

$$\frac{65}{n} \times 100 = 6.5; n = \frac{6,500}{6.5}; n = 1,000$$

Percent Change Problems

In addition to the three basic types of percent problems, you will need to know how to solve percent increase and decrease problems. Percent increase and decrease problems describe the change in a value as a percent of that value. The general formula for solving percent increase or decrease problems is:

$$\% \text{ change} = \left(\frac{\text{change in value}}{\text{original value}} \right) \times 100$$

TEST EXAMPLE

A pair of jeans is reduced in price by 25%. If the jeans now cost $24, what was the original price of the jeans?

(A) $18

(D) $49

(B) $25

(E) $96

(C) $32

Solution

Let p = the original price.

$$25\% = \left(\frac{p-24}{p}\right) \times 100$$

$$25p = 100p - 2{,}400$$

$$75p = 2{,}400$$

$$p = 32$$

Notice that the wrong answer choices anticipate several common errors. Choice (A) is waiting for someone who takes 25% off the sale price. Choice (E) is anticipating the person who thinks that $24 represents 25% *of* the original price, rather than a 25% *discount* on the regular price. Choice (D) is a tempting answer to someone who is guessing, because it is the sum of two numbers in the problem—24 and 25.

Profit Problems

Profit is equal to selling price minus cost, or income minus expenses:

$$s - c = p,$$

where s is the selling price, c is the cost, and p is the profit.

TEST EXAMPLE

A cake costs a baker $3.50 to make. At what price should the baker sell the cake in order to make a profit that is 50% of the cost?

(A) $1.75   (D) $5.25

(B) $2.50   (E) $7.00

(C) $4.50

Solution

$$s - 3.50 = (0.5)\,(3.50)$$

$$s = 1.75 + 3.50 = 5.25$$

Interest Problems

Interest problems ask you to calculate the amount of money earned on invested capital. The invested capital is called the principal. There are two basic types of interest, and you must read a problem carefully to determine which is involved. If a problem states that money is invested at a *simple annual interest,* you compute interest on the principal only. If a problem states that interest is *compounded,* then interest is computed on the principal and on any interest that has already been earned.

TEST EXAMPLE

Ms. White invested $10,000 in an account with an annual interest rate of 12% compounded monthly. If she made the deposit on April 1, 1990, and no additional deposits or withdrawals were made, how much money was in the account on June 1, 1990?

(A) $10,200

(B) $10,201

(C) $10,500

(D) $11,200

(E) $12,100

Solution

The key words in this problem are *compounded monthly.* To find the monthly interest rate, divide the annual rate by 12:

$$12\% \div 12 = 1\%$$

To find the interest earned the first month, compute 1% of the total amount of money in the account, which is $10,000 and add it to that amount:

$$1\% \text{ of } \$10,000 = \$100; \$10,000 + \$100 = \$10,100$$

To find the interest earned for the second month, compute 1% of the amount of money in the account, which is now $10,100, and add it to that amount:

$$1\% \text{ of } \$10,100 = \$101; \$10,100 + \$101 = \$10,201$$

Notice that choice (A), which is very close to the correct answer choice (B), is the result that you would have obtained if you had incorrectly computed simple annual interest instead of compound interest.

SKILLS AND STRATEGIES

ELIMINATING OBVIOUS WRONG ANSWERS

Very often, GMAT questions will have one or two answer choices that are "out of the ballpark." These answers will be obviously wrong for one of several reasons: they may be impossible given the conditions of the problem; they may violate a mathematical rule or principle; or they may be illogical. Being able to spot obvious wrong answers before you finish a problem is a great advantage—first, because you won't be tempted by those answers, and second, because you will be able to make an intelligent guess if you run out of time or don't know how to complete the problem.

TEST EXAMPLE

Of the management level employees in Corporation X, 75% have attended graduate school and 80% of those who attended graduate school have an MBA. If 300 management level employees in Corporation X have MBAs, how many management level employees are in Corporation X?

(A) 500

(D) 225

(B) 400

(E) 180

(C) 250

Solution

The problem tells you that 300 management level employees have MBAs. The problem also tells you that the management employees who have MBAs represent only a portion of the total number of management employees. Therefore, the total number of management level employees must be greater than 300. This logical observation immediately eliminates choices (C), (D), and (E)—meaning that you have a 50-50 chance of getting the question right if you guess (A) or (B). Working out the problem with x equal to the total number of management employees yields:

$$300 = (0.80)(0.75)x$$

$$300 = 0.6x$$

$$x = 500$$

WORKING BACKWARDS

One of the advantages of a multiple-choice test is that the correct answer is given to you as one of the answer choices. There are times when working backwards from the answer choices is a useful strategy—for example, when you don't know how to solve a problem or when a direct method of solution seems complicated or time-consuming.

TEST EXAMPLE

A bank teller counted out $120 in cash. If each of the bills he counted was either a $5 bill or a $10 bill, which of the following cannot be the number of $5 bills?

(A) 2   (D) 16

(B) 8   (E) 20

(C) 15

Solution

Look at the five answer choices. Does one answer look different from the rest? Choice (C) stands out because it is the only odd number in the group. Start by testing this choice: $15 \times \$5 = \$75$. Subtracting $75 from $120, you see that the remaining amount of money is $45. Since $45 is not a multiple of 10, it could not be made up of $10 bills. Thus, the number of $5 bills cannot be 15.

TACKLING MULTIPLE-STEP PROBLEMS

There are three basic types of multiple step problems that you will encounter on the GMAT:

1. Problems in which the same step or similar steps are repeated several times in order to arrive at a solution.

2. Problems in which several different steps are performed in sequence in order to arrive at a solution.

3. Problems in which the various steps are "layered" and you must discern a solution without an obvious order of steps.

The best way to approach types 1 and 2 is to map out a plan of action before you begin. Determine what your first step will be and what your final step will be, and then decide how you will get from the first step to the last step.

The best way to approach a type 3 problem is to look at the problem and determine what mathematical concepts are involved. Think of rules or formulas that are associated with these concepts; also look for ways in which these concepts are related. If you don't see a clear course of action for solving the problem, begin working the problem on a trial-and-error basis. Quite often, the solution will present itself as you do this.

TEST EXAMPLE

Of the members of a business organization, 75% are self-employed, and 40% of the self-employed members are women. If a total of 300 people belong to the organization, how many members are self-employed women?

(A) 30   (D) 225

(B) 90   (E) 345

(C) 120

Solution

This problem requires several applications of finding the percent of a number. First, you must find out how many of the members are self-employed:

75% of 300 = 0.75 × 300 = 225

Next, you must find out how many of the self-employed members are women:

40% of 225 = 0.40 × 225 = 90

The solution to the problem is that 90 members of the organization are self-employed women. Notice that the answer to the first step—225—shows up as wrong answer choice (D).

TEST EXAMPLE

The brick shown below is to be covered with gold foil. Which of the following sheets of foil would cover the brick completely and have the least amount of foil left over?

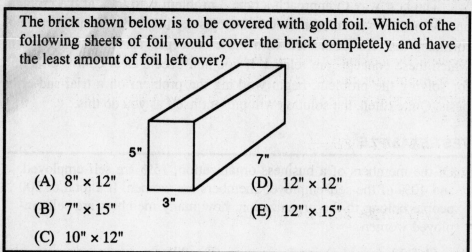

(A) 8" × 12"

(B) 7" × 15"

(C) 10" × 12"

(D) 12" × 12"

(E) 12" × 15"

Solution

This problem requires three distinct steps. First, you must compute the surface area of the brick. Next, you must determine the area of each sheet of foil. Finally, you must compare the surface area of the brick to the area of each sheet of foil.

Surface Area = 2(5 × 7) + 2(5 × 3) + 2(3 × 7) = 142 square inches

Area of foil: A = 96 square inches; B = 105 square inches; C = 120 square inches; D = 144 square inches; E = 180 square inches

By comparison, (D) would cover the brick with only 2 square inches left over.

TEST EXAMPLE

The figure below shows square *ABCD*. If the area of *ABCD* = 9 and

$$AY = YZ = ZD,$$

what is the length of *XZ*?

(A) $\sqrt{6}$

(B) $2\sqrt{2}$

(C) $\sqrt{10}$

(D) 4

(E) $3\sqrt{2}$

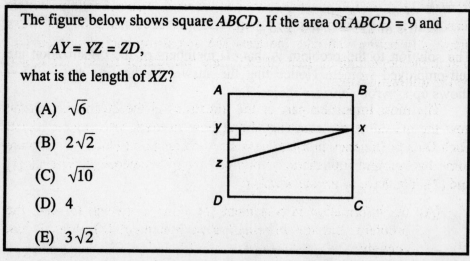

Solution

This problem is typical of GMAT geometry problems in which the steps are "layered" and you must be aware of several concepts simultaneously. By looking at square *ABCD* and using the information given in the problem, you can determine that: the area of the square = 9 and so the side of the square = 3; *XY* is perpendicular to the sides of the square and so *XY* = 3.

$$AY + YZ + ZD = 3;$$

since

$$AY = YZ = ZD, YZ = \frac{1}{3} \text{ of } 3 = 1$$

Since *XYZ* is a right triangle, length *XY* can be computed by using the Pythagorean theorem. Putting all of this information together, you have

$$3^2 + 1^2 = (XZ)^2; \ 10 = (XZ)^2; \ XZ = \sqrt{10}$$

MASTERING DATA SUFFICIENCY

Data Sufficiency questions test your ability to analyze a quantitative problem and determine whether the information given is sufficient to solve the problem. Unlike Problem Solving questions, Data Sufficiency questions do not ask you to solve the problem per se. Instead, they ask you to determine whether you *could* solve the problem given certain information.

UNDERSTANDING THE DIRECTIONS

GMAT Data Sufficiency questions are probably different in format from the kinds of test questions that you are used to encountering. For this reason, it is important that you memorize and understand the directions thoroughly before you take the test. The actual directions that you will find at the beginning of each GMAT Data Sufficiency section are shown on the following page.

The most important part of the directions is the information about how the questions are constructed and how to mark your answer sheet. Each Data Sufficiency problem consists of a question (which may include some background information) followed by two statements, labeled (1) and (2). You have to decide whether:

(A) the information in Statement (1) alone is enough to solve the problem, but the information in Statement (2) alone is not enough;

DATA SUFFICIENCY SAMPLE TEST SECTION 1

TIME: 25 Minutes

   20 Questions

DIRECTIONS: Each of the data sufficiency problems below consist of a question and two statements, labeled (1) and (2), in which certain data are given. You have to decide whether the data given in the statements are <u>sufficient</u> for answering the question. Using the data given in the statements <u>plus</u> your knowledge of mathematics and everyday facts (such as the number of days in July or the meaning of <u>counterclockwise</u>), you are to fill in oval

   A   if Statement (1) ALONE is sufficient, but Statement (2) alone is not sufficient to answer the question asked;

   B   if Statement (2) ALONE is sufficient, but Statement (1) alone is not sufficient to answer the question asked;

   C   if BOTH Statements (1) and (2) TOGETHER are sufficient to answer the question asked, but NEITHER statement ALONE is sufficient;

   D   if EACH statement ALONE is sufficient to answer the question asked;

   E   if Statements (1) and (2) TOGETHER are NOT sufficient to answer the question asked, and additional data specific to the problem are needed.

<u>Numbers</u>: All numbers used are real numbers.

<u>Figures:</u> A figure in a data sufficiency problem will conform to the information given in the question, but will not necessarily conform to the additional information given in Statements (1) and (2).

   You may assume that lines shown as straight are straight and that angle measures are greater than zero.

   You may assume that the positions of points, angles, regions, etc., exist in the order shown.

   All figures lie in a plane unless otherwise indicated.

<u>Example</u>:

In $\triangle PQR$, what is the value of x?

(1) $PQ = PR$

(2) $y = 40$

<u>Explanation:</u> According to Statement (1), $PQ = PR$; therefore, $\triangle PQR$ is isosceles and $y = z$. Since $x + y + z = 180$, $x + 2y = 180$. Since Statement (1) does not give a value for y, you cannot answer the question using Statement (1) by itself. According to Statement (2), $y = 40$; therefore, $x + z = 140$. Since Statement (2) does not give a value for z, you cannot answer the question using Statement (2) by itself. Using both statements together, you can find y and z; therefore, you can find x, and the answer to the problem is C.

(B) the information in Statement (2) alone is enough to solve the problem, but the information in Statement (1) alone is not enough;

(C) the information in Statements (1) and (2) together is enough to solve the problem, but neither statement alone can solve the problem;

(D) either Statement (1) or (2) alone provides enough information to solve the problem;

(E) neither statement nor the two statements together provide enough information to solve the problem.

You can better understand these choices by looking at some simple examples.

TEST EXAMPLE

What percentage of Golo Company's yearly advertising budget is spent on direct mail?

(1) Golo Company spends $12,000 per year on direct mail.

(2) Golo Company's advertising budget is $60,000 per year.

Solution

In order to answer the question, you must know the amount of the company's yearly advertising budget and the amount per year spent on direct mail. Statements (1) and (2) *together* provide this information, but neither statement alone provides the information. Thus, the answer is (C).

TEST EXAMPLE

What is the value of x in $x + y = 20$?

(1) $x > 5$

(2) $y = 8$

Solution

By knowing the value of y (Statement (2)), you can easily solve the equation for x. However, you cannot determine the value of x just by knowing that $x > 5$. Thus, the answer is (B).

INTERPRETING DIAGRAMS

Unlike the diagrams found in the Problem Solving sections, diagrams in the Data Sufficiency section are not intentionally drawn to scale. This means that you cannot rely on a diagram to show you accurate shapes or relative sizes. What you can determine from a diagram is that: (1) straight lines are straight and closed figures are closed; (2) all angle measures are greater than zero; and (3) the position of points, lines, angles, etc. exist in the order shown.

SKILLS AND STRATEGIES

Identifying the Question

In order to determine the sufficiency of data, it is important that you know what type of answers a problem requires. Once you have identified this, you should immediately ask yourself, "What information do I need in order to answer this question?" By knowing in advance what information you need, *before you look at the data statements,* you will be in a better position to judge whether or not the data is sufficient.

TEST EXAMPLE

Is $\triangle ABC$ an isosceles triangle?

   (1) $\angle A = \angle B$

   (2) $AB = 6$

Solution

It is not necessary to know the actual dimensions of triangle *ABC* in order to answer this question. What matters is whether the triangle conforms to the definition of an isosceles triangle. Before looking at the data statements, you might say to yourself, "In order to answer this question, I must know if two angles or two sides of the triangle are equal." Looking at Statement (1), you can see that the information is sufficient to answer the question. The information in Statement (2), however, is insufficient, because it describes only one side of the triangle. Thus, the correct answer is (A).

TEST EXAMPLE

What fraction of her weekly salary does Meg spend on child care?

   (1) Meg's weekly salary is $500.

   (2) Meg spends 5% of her salary on child care.

Solution

Before looking at the data statements, you might say to yourself, "I am going to need to know the amount that Meg spends on child care and the amount of her weekly salary, or I am going to need to know something specific about the relationship between these two amounts." Looking at statement (1), you see part of the information you need, but this data alone is not sufficient to answer the question. Looking at Statement (2), you see that 5% describes the relationship between Meg's salary and the amount she spends on child care. Since 5% can be converted into a fraction, the information in Statement (2) is sufficient, and the answer is (B).

Isolating Each Statement

One of the most difficult aspects of solving Data Sufficiency problems is determining whether Statement (1) or (2) *alone* can solve a problem without being influenced by the other statement once you have read it. A technique that you may find helpful is to cover up one statement with the edge of your answer sheet while you read the other statement. Another technique is to go back and read a problem a second time, but this time read Statement (2) before you read Statement (1). This will help clarify whether the information in Statement (2) alone is sufficient.

Keeping Track of Your Responses

As you isolate each statement and evaluate its contents, it is a good idea to mark the statement according to your conclusion. For example, you may want to write "y" next to a statement that is sufficient and "n" next to a statement that is not sufficient. This way, you can determine your final answer quickly, simply by tallying your responses. Marking each statement is also helpful if you run out of time and have to guess at the answer—at least you will have some information on which to base your guess.

Sufficient or Insufficient?

The question of whether or not data is sufficient can be answered by considering these two criteria:

(1) Is the data complete?

(2) Is the data relevant?

Data is complete when you have all the information that you need in order to solve a problem. When a question is based on a definition or formula—such as finding the percent of a number or determining if a figure is a right triangle—it is usually quite obvious when you have enough information.

Data is relevant when it provides useful information. Data can be relevant and still not be sufficient, but irrelevant data can never be sufficient.

TEST EXAMPLE

> How much money will Sam receive in commissions on his sales for February?
>
> (1) Sam sold $5,000 worth of merchandise in February.
>
> (2) Wendy's commission on sales is 15%.

Solution

You can answer this question if you know the amount of Sam's sales and his rate of commission. One of these facts is given in Statement (1), but this fact alone is not enough to solve the problem. Thus, the data in (1) is relevant, but not sufficient. Statement (2) tells you Wendy's rate of commission, but Wendy's commission has nothing to do with Sam. The data in Statement (2) is irrelevant, and irrelevant data is always insufficient. Since neither statement alone nor the statements combined can solve the problem, the answer is (E).

When the Answer is Yes or No

The two basic types of questions that you will encounter in Data Sufficiency problems are those that ask for a specific value and those that ask for a yes or no answer. When a question requires a yes or no answer, there are several things that you should keep in mind. First, see if the data enables you to base your conclusion on something specific, such as a number or definition. For example, if a question asks, "Is x larger than y?" and you can determine that x is 6 and y is 2, then you have a clear answer to the question. If, however, you are given only general information, such as $x > 5$ and $y > 1$, you have to be more careful. You must ask yourself, "Can I *always* tell if x is larger than y? In this case, x could be 6 and y could be 2, but x could also be 8 and y could be 20. Because you can draw two different conclusions from the information given, the data is insufficient to answer the question.

Another factor to keep in mind when answering yes or no questions is that a "no" is just as valid as a "yes" when determining if data is sufficient.

Do not fall into the trap of thinking that the problem is a true-or-false question.

TEST EXAMPLE

Is $\triangle ABC$ a right triangle?

(1) The degree measure of $\angle A$ is twice the degree measure of $\angle C$.

(2) The degree measure of $\angle C$ is 40.

Solution

According to the data in Statement (1), $\angle A = 2\angle C$.

Adding the information from Statement (2), $\angle C = 40°$, so $\angle A = 80°$.

Since $\angle A + \angle B + \angle C = 180°$, $\angle B = 60°$, and the triangle is not a right triangle.

The combined data from Statements (1) and (2) was sufficient to arrive at this conclusion and answer the question, but there is a temptation to reason, "Since the triangle is not a right triangle, the answer is no, so I'll mark (E)"—rather than marking the correct answer, which is (C).

Guessing Intelligently

Sometimes, you may come across a Data Sufficiency question in which you are quite certain about the sufficiency or insufficiency of one data statement, but you are unsure about the other statement. When this happens, you can make an intelligent guess by eliminating certain answer choices. For example, suppose that you are considering the problem:

What is the value of x?

(1) $x - 9 = 10$

(2) $x^2 + 2x = 1$

Also, suppose that you are sure that Statement (1) is sufficient, but you really don't know if statement (2) is sufficient. Based on the fact that (1) is sufficient, you know that:

1. The correct answer could be (A), if Statement (2) is not sufficient.

2. The correct answer could be (D), if Statement (2) is also sufficient.

3.   The correct answer cannot be (B), since Statement (1) is sufficient.

4.   The correct answer cannot be (C), since Sstatement (1) alone is sufficient.

5.   The correct answer cannot be (E), since at least one statement is sufficient.

You have narrowed your choices down to two possible answers, (A) or (D). You have a 50-50 chance of getting the question right if you guess. The same line of reasoning follows if you are sure that Statement (2) is sufficient but you are unsure about Statement (1). In this case, the correct answer would have to be (B) or (D).

If you are sure that one statement is not sufficient, but are uncertain about the other statement, you can narrow your answer choices down to three. For example, consider the problem:

What is the value of n?

(1) $0 < n$

(2)   The smallest prime factor of n is less than 4.

If you are sure that Statement (1) is insufficient, you know that:

1.   The correct answer cannot be (A).

2.   The correct answer could be (B), if Statement (2) is sufficient.

3.   The correct answer could be (C), if (1) and (2) together are sufficient.

4.   The correct answer cannot be (D), since (1) is not sufficient.

5.   The correct answer could be (E), if neither (2) nor the combined statements are sufficient.

Based on this reasoning, your possible choices are (B), (C), or (E). You have a 1/3 chance of getting the question right if you guess. If you know that Statement (2) is insufficient but you are uncertain about Statement (1), your possible choices are (A), (C), and (E).

Dangerous Assumptions—Avoiding Traps and Pitfalls

Inherent in Data Sufficiency questions are traps and pitfalls that come from making incorrect assumptions. One of these assumptions has already been discussed, and that is the tendency to confuse yes-no questions with true-and-false questions. Two other dangerous assumptions include reading into a problem and confusing sufficiency with compatibility.

Reading into a problem is assuming that something is true even though it is not stated. Most people read into a problem something that seems logical to them based on the way the problem is worded.

TEST EXAMPLE

A blue car and a green car are in line at the drive-in bank. How many cars are in the line?

(1) There are 4 cars between the green car and the blue car.

(2) There are 6 cars ahead of the green car and 4 cars behind the blue car.

Solution

The obvious assumption is that the green car is ahead of the blue car. However, the problem does not say that. It is just as possible that the blue car is ahead of the green car. If the blue car is ahead of the green car, there are only 6 cars in line. If the green car is ahead of the blue car, there are 14 cars in line. The answer is (E), because the data is not sufficient to answer the question.

Confusing sufficiency with compatibility is a common pitfall when one data statement is clearly sufficient while the other statement is relevant but insufficient.

TEST EXAMPLE

What is the value of n?

(1) n is negative

(2) $5n = -10$

Solution

Statement (2) is clearly sufficient, since $n = -2$. Since Statement (1) "fits in" by stating that n is negative, the temptation is to say, "The correct answer must be (C), since both statements together answer the question." The trap in this reasoning is that while Statement (1) is compatible with the solution, it is not necessary. The correct answer is (B), because Statement (2) alone is sufficient, and Statement (1) alone is not sufficient.

EVALUATING YOUR PERFORMANCE

This section is designed to help you evaluate your performance after you have taken a practice GMAT test. The best way to evaluate your performance on a practice test is to analyze your wrong answers. You should note the types of questions that you got wrong and *why* you got them wrong. You should also look for a pattern in your wrong answers. For example, do you often get word problems wrong? Do you tend to miss questions because you don't know a rule or formula? Do most of your wrong answers involve a particular subject area, such as geometry? Are you decidedly weak in solving one general type of quantitative problem, such as Data Sufficiency? Do you tend to get the harder questions wrong because you make false assumptions or fall into traps? Do you often misread or misinterpret a question?

You should also analyze your use of time. Do you miss a lot of questions in a section because you run out of time? Do you spend a lot of time on questions that you end up getting wrong anyway? Is it possible that you could pace yourself better in order to make time for the types of questions that you are likely to get right?

The chart below provides a model that will help you organize your test results. You should make a similar chart for each quantitative ability section of the GMAT that you take. Under the heading "Type of Question," you can describe a question both in terms of the math involved and the type of problem: for example, "geometry—word problem," "percent decrease problem," or "algebra problem involving difference of squares." Under the heading "Reason," you should tell why you got the problem wrong. Possible reasons might include the following: did not know how to do the problem; forgot the formula for ____; made a false assumption; misread or misunderstood the problem; ran out of time; made a careless mistake.

ANALYZING WRONG ANSWERS

Section: ____ (Problem Solving or Data Sufficiency) _____

Question #	Type of Question	Reasons

Once you have analyzed your wrong answers, you should also analyze your right answers. You can do this with a similar chart using the following headings:

Question #	Type of Question	Knowledge

Under the heading "Knowledge," you can indicate whether you got a question right because (1) you were sure of how to solve the problem; (2) you were somewhat aware of how to solve the problem and made an intelligent guess; or (3) you didn't really know how to solve the problem but made a lucky guess. You should also note in this column if a particular problem-solving strategy worked for you—for example, working backwards or eliminating obvious wrong answers.

By analyzing your right and wrong answers, you will be able to identify many of your strengths and weaknesses. With this information, you can develop a plan for improving your performance. Look at your strengths and decide how to maximize them. Study your weaknesses and find ways to lessen their impact. Make special note of those things that you can correct easily—such as careless errors or forgotten formulas—and set goals for improvement. By setting goals, making a plan, and analyzing your results, you will not only improve your GMAT score, but sharpen the kinds of problem-solving skills that you'll need for a successful business career as well.

PRACTICE DRILLS

ANSWER KEY

Drill 1

1. III only
2. 2, 4, 6, 8, 10, 12, 14, 16
3. $2 \times 2 \times 2 \times 7$
4. (A) -1 (B) 7   (C) 5   (D) 23
5. III only
6. 7; 4
7. 17, 19, 23
8. 84
9. 15, 30, 45

Drill 2

1. (B) $\dfrac{24}{56}$ (D) $\dfrac{27}{63}$

2. 0.05; $\dfrac{5}{100}$

3. (A) 165%   (B) $\dfrac{7}{10}$ (C) -0.5

4. (A) $\dfrac{5}{10}$ (B) $\dfrac{15}{24}$ (C) $\dfrac{9}{2}$ (D) $\dfrac{28}{20}$

    (E) $\dfrac{27}{7}$ (F) $\dfrac{1}{12}$

5. (A) 2.48   (B) 263   (C) 39.072   (D) 335.14
    (E) 126,500   (F) 6.17

6. $0.\overline{285714}$

Drill 3

1. mean = 4.91; median = 5; mode = 2

2. (A) $\dfrac{8}{10}$ (B) $\dfrac{6}{12}$ (C) $\dfrac{4}{7}$ (D) $\dfrac{1}{5}$

3. 112

4. $\dfrac{7}{9} = \dfrac{14}{18}$

5. (A) 25   (B) 3   (C) 3

Drill 4

1. 3^6

2. $\dfrac{4}{25}$

3. $256y^4$

4. a^9

5. $\dfrac{1}{7}$

6. $6x^2$

7. y^4

8. $\dfrac{x^3}{4}$

9. $-\dfrac{1}{9}$

10. -12

Drill 5

1. (A) $x^2 + 10x + 25$ (B) $5x^2 + 9x - 2$
   (C) $64 - 36x^2$ (D) $4x^2 - 12x + 4xy$

2. (A) $(4y + 3)(4y - 3)$ (B) $(5x + 2)(2x - 1)$
   (C) $(a + 3)^2$

3. (B) $2ab + a^2 + b^2 + (4 + 3)(4 - 3)$

4. -8

Drill 6

1.　(A) $x = qt - \dfrac{2q}{r}$　　　　　　(B) $x = -3$

　　(C) $x = -\dfrac{5}{4}$　　　　　　　(D) $x = -3$

2.　$a = 3,\ b = -7$

3.　(A) $y > 6$　　　　　　　　(B) $y > 4$

　　(C) $y > \dfrac{10}{a+b}$

4.　(A) $x = 1;\ x = -4$　　　　(B) $x = -\dfrac{5}{4};\ x = \dfrac{5}{4}$

　　(C) $a = -\dfrac{1}{3};\ a = \dfrac{1}{2}$

Drill 7

1.　(A) $x = 160°$　　　　　　(B) $x = 58°$
　　(C) $x = 135°$　　　　　　(D) $x = 105°$

2.　c

Drill 8

1.　(A) $t = 45$　　　(B) $a = 6$　　　(C) $c = 2$
2.　(C)　1, 1, 3

3.　(A) $\dfrac{35}{2}$　　　　(B) 9

4.　$3\sqrt{3}$ meters

Drill 9

1.　$a = 5;\ b = 5;\ x = 60;\ y = 60$

Drill 10

1.　(A) diameter = 16　　　　　(B) circumference = 16π
　　(C) angle $x = 90$　　　　　(D) area = 64π
　　(E) area $AOB = 16\pi$

Drill 11

1.   (A) Volume = 300π cubic feet; surface area = 170π sq. ft.

     (B) Volume = 60 cubic inches; surface area = 152 sq. in.

GMAT CAT

Graduate Management Admission Test
Computer-Adaptive Test

CHAPTER 3:
Verbal
Review

Chapter 3

GMAT VERBAL REVIEW

OVERVIEW OF THE VERBAL SECTION

The GMAT is designed to measure your verbal and quantitative abilities. To quote from the GMAT Bulletin, "The verbal sections . . . measure the ability to understand and evaluate what is read and to recognize basic conventions of standard written English." These abilities are tested by three question types: Reading Comprehension, Sentence Correction, and Critical Reasoning. Each one tests a different aspect of your verbal ability.

Reading Comprehension measures your ability to understand, analyze, evaluate, and apply written information. Each passage is approximately 400–600 words in length.

Sentence Correction tests your knowledge of grammar, English usage, and your ability to distinguish good writing from bad writing. Each question is based on a different, individual sentence.

Critical Reasoning tests your ability to evaluate the arguments and reasoning presented in what you read. The questions are based on arguments presented in short paragraphs.

We will discuss each of these question types in detail, focusing on the specific skills you need to practice, and recommending strategies for improving your performance. We will also recommend test-taking strategies for each.

The tips and strategies we will discuss will help you prepare for the GMAT. **Practice these techniques**. The drills in the chapters and the tests in the second half of the book will help you sharpen your skills and develop your test-taking technique.

READING COMPREHENSION

The Reading Comprehension section tests your ability to read and understand written material. The section consists of three passages of approximately 400–600 words each and 18–23 questions based on the passages (six to eight questions per passage).

The passages are taken from several subject areas: the biological and physical sciences, the social sciences, and business. Prior knowledge of these subjects is not assumed or required, however. The questions are based exclusively on the content of the passages. There are six types of questions designed to test different aspects of your ability to read and evaluate written material. The questions focus on

(1) the main idea of the passage,

(2) specific details,

(3) inferences that can be made from the information in the passage,

(4) the logical organization of the passage,

(5) possible application of the information in the passage, and

(6) the author's tone.

We will discuss each type of question and ways to approach them in detail below.

You should first read the directions for the section. Get to know the directions for all the sections as part of your preparation for the GMAT. If you become familiar with the directions now, you will avoid wasting time reading them during the exam.

DIRECTIONS: Each passage in this group is followed by questions based on its content. After reading a passage, choose the best answer to each question and fill in the corresponding oval on the answer sheet. Answer all questions following a passage on the basis of what is *stated* or *implied* in that passage.

Why is it emphasized that you should answer the questions based only on what is stated or implied in the passage? The point is that you are being tested on your ability to read and understand written material, not on your prior knowledge of the subjects with which the passages deal. You do not need knowledge of any subject to do well on Reading Comprehension. In fact, if you use your outside knowledge to answer the questions instead of what is stated in the passages, you will probably not do as well as if you simply concentrate on reading and understanding the passages.

All of this might sound rather intimidating; but if you understand what the test-makers are really seeking, you will see that there is no reason to be overly concerned. You are not expected to gain a deep understanding of the subject that any particular passage explores. The test-makers are trying to determine how well you can do the following: (1) sift through written material of varying degrees of difficulty to grasp the central idea being presented, (2) locate important supporting information, and (3) understand the author's attitude toward the subject. In other words, the test-makers are trying to determine how **efficient** a reader you are.

THE EFFICIENT READER

Every day, each of us is confronted with a tremendous amount of information. We read newspapers, magazines, memos, and reports; we talk with people, attend meetings, watch the news, and so on. If we were to try to absorb all of the information we encounter, we would quickly become overloaded. Instinctively, we focus on only those pieces of information that are of special interest to us.

This principle of selective focus is particularly important in dealing with written material. To one degree or another, we are all limited by the rate at which we read. Even if you read very, very quickly, you may not need to understand and absorb every word you read. However, you do want to grasp the central idea of what you are reading—the important supporting information and the logic of the argument—so you can evaluate the information. (Of course, when you read for pleasure, you take the time to enjoy the words, the rhythm of the writing, the flow of the story, and so on.) How well you can focus on the important parts of the information being presented determines how efficient a reader you are. And that is exactly what the GMAT measures.

The ability to read efficiently is not innate; it is a skill that is relatively easy to develop with some practice. The following section presents a basic approach to efficient reading and offers specific strategies for reading the passages in the Reading Comprehension section.

READING STRATEGIES

As we have said above, the key to reading efficiently is the ability to focus on the important elements of the information being presented. Here is a basic approach that will help you focus in this selective way when you read:

Identify the Main Idea of the Passage

Most written pieces are designed to communicate some central idea. The author may be expressing an opinion, proposing a new hypothesis, describing a theory, criticizing an opponent's viewpoint, or praising the work of a colleague. The main idea is the unifying theme of the passage. You can identify the main idea by asking yourself the following: Why is the author writing? What is the purpose of this passage? What is the one thing the author would want me to take away from reading this?

Locate Supporting Evidence

After the author expresses the main idea, he or she goes on to provide evidence that supports that idea. In order to read efficiently, identify the details that are important as evidence and note their location in the text. Do not be concerned with terms you do not understand. Do not waste time trying to grasp the meaning of specific details.

Note the Author's Logic

Once you locate the evidence, note how the passage is organized. Paragraphs are useful for this purpose. Each paragraph is a step in the argument. By following the steps, you can see how the whole passage is constructed.

Determine the Author's Tone

The tone of the passage reveals the author's attitude toward the subject about which he or she is writing. You can determine the attitude by asking yourself whether the author's feelings toward the subject are positive, negative, or neutral.

Now we need to adapt this basic approach to reading the passages in the Reading Comprehension section of the GMAT. Timing is of great importance here. You have ten minutes for each passage and set of questions; therefore, you should take approximately three to four minutes to read each passage. The following step-by-step reading strategy is designed to maximize your efficiency and speed.

STEP-BY-STEP STRATEGY FOR GMAT READING COMPREHENSION

1. Select a passage.

2. Read the first paragraph very carefully.

3. Identify the main idea of the passage.

4. Determine the author's tone.

5. Scan the rest of the paragraphs for the location of details.

6. Note the author's logic.

Select a Passage

The passages in the Reading Comprehension section of the GMAT vary in difficulty. Furthermore, you may find certain topics more accessible than others. Therefore, it is important that you take a look at all the passages and select the one with which you are most comfortable. Be careful to mark the answer sheet correctly if you do the passages out of order.

Read the First Paragraph Very Carefully

The main idea of the passage is usually stated in the first paragraph. By paying close attention to the first paragraph, you will grasp the main idea of the passage and be able to go through the rest of the passage confidently and quickly. In most cases, the author's tone is also evident in the first paragraph.

Identify the Main Idea of the Passage

Use the method discussed above to identify the main idea. It is very useful to restate the idea plainly, in your own words. You may also find it helpful to jot down the main idea.

Determine the Author's Tone

The first paragraph usually clarifies the author's attitude toward the subject of the passage. At this point, you should determine whether the general tone is positive, negative, or neutral.

Scan the Rest of the Paragraphs for the Location of Details

Once you have identified the main idea, scan the rest of the passage to locate the details that act as supporting evidence. Note where these details are in the text, so you can quickly find each of them if a question about it comes up.

Note the Author's Logic

Look to see how each paragraph fits into the organization of the passage. The purpose of each paragraph and its role in the passage make clear the structure of the passage.

Remember that your goal in reading the passages is to get just enough information to answer the questions. Do not get trapped into trying to understand complex concepts or trying to remember minute details. And do not be intimidated by the passages. Be confident. By keeping in mind the principles of efficient reading and by practicing the step-by-step strategy presented earlier, you can sharpen your skills and improve your performance.

THE QUESTIONS

The six types of questions on the Reading Comprehension section of the GMAT CAT focus on

(1) the main idea of the passage,

(2) specific details,

(3) inferences that can be made from the information in the passage,

(4) the logical organization of the passage,

(5) possible application of the information in the passage, and

(6) the author's tone.

We will look at each type of question and ways to approach it in the context of the example given below. We will then discuss an overall strategy for answering the questions.

Example

The words "organic," "chemical," "natural," and "health" are among the most misunderstood, misused, and maligned in our vocabulary, especially when they are applied to our food.

All organic materials are complex combinations of chemicals and contain one chemical element in common—carbon. But not all chemicals occur in the form of organic material. All of our food supply is in organic form because it has come from animal or plant sources. Most man-made foods are also in organic form.

Today, our chief concern about things organic and chemical relates to how foods are grown and processed. Our greatest concern is about the substances used in growing and processing our food.

Organic fertilizers used in growing the plants we eat directly, or which are fed to the animals that furnish our meat, are all made by the living cells in animal or plant tissues. They contain nutrients such as nitrogen, phosphorus, potassium, sulfur, magnesium, and other essential minerals in complex combinations with carbon, hydrogen, and usually oxygen.

Inorganic or commercial fertilizers contain the same chemical nutrients, but in simpler forms, and not always in combination with carbon. It is inaccurate to refer to inorganic fertilizers as "artificial" just because they have not been made by living cells.

A plant is unaware of the type of fertilizer—organic or inorganic—that is furnishing the chemicals for its growth. It does demand that these building blocks be in inorganic form. Plant cells synthesize the complex materials needed for growth rather than absorbing them ready-made from the soil.

Organically-raised animals are fed on organically grown grasses and feed. They are not given growth hormones, antibiotics, or synthetic materials. But it is unlikely that an animal's cells are aware of whether the many essentials for their growth are being furnished by feed in the organic or inorganic form.

Main Idea Questions

Test Example

The primary purpose of the passage is to

(A) analyze a frequent source of disagreement.

(B) define terms.

(C) explain a theory.

(D) eliminate misunderstanding by defining.

(E) explore the implications of a finding.

The above is an example of a main idea question. These questions ask you to identify the central theme of the passage. They are usually worded in one of the following ways:

The primary purpose of the author is to . . .

The main purpose of the author is to . . .

The author is mainly concerned with . . .

The key to answering main idea questions correctly is to select answer choices that fully and precisely describe the main idea of the passage. Incorrect choices fall into three categories: totally wrong or irrelevant, too broad, or too narrow.

In our example, choices (C) and (E) are totally wrong; neither a theory nor a finding is discussed in the passage. Choice (B) is too narrow; terms are defined, but only as part of an effort to clear up a misunderstanding. Choice (A) is too broad, and it asks us to make the assumption that the subject of the passage is a source of disagreement. Never make assumptions on the GMAT. Work only with the given information. Finally, choice (D) fully and precisely describes the author's primary purpose.

Detail Questions

Test Example

> According to the passage, nearly all of man's food supply
>
> (A) has been organically-processed.
>
> (B) has been organically-grown.
>
> (C) is both organic and inorganic because it comes from both plants and animals.
>
> (D) has been contaminated by artificial additives.
>
> (E) is in organic form because it is the product of living cells.

Detail questions test your ability to locate supporting details in the text. Most detail questions ask directly about a specific detail. For instance, the example above asks about man's food supply.

Test Breaker

To answer a detail question, locate the relevant detail in the passage and carefully read the sentence concerning the detail and one or two surrounding sentences to determine the context. Then, select the answer choice that correctly restates the detail.

In our example, man's food supply is mentioned in the third sentence of the second paragraph. You should have noted this as you read the passage. Read one sentence above and one sentence below the third sentence. Now look at the answer choices. Choice (E) restates the third sentence of the second paragraph almost word for word. Choice (E) is the right choice.

In addition to the detail questions that ask about one specific detail, there are two forms of detail questions that test your ability to locate several details in the text. These are the EXCEPT questions and the Roman numeral questions.

EXCEPT questions ask you to identify a detail that is not in the passage. The following is a typical EXCEPT question based on our example.

TEST EXAMPLE

The passage contains information that would answer all of the following questions EXCEPT

(A) Why is organic fertilizer superior to inorganic fertilizer?

(B) What are organic materials?

(C) Do plants require nutrients in organic or inorganic form?

(D) What is the common chemical in all organic materials?

(E) Why is it inaccurate to call inorganic fertilizers "artificial?"

Choice (A) is correct since there are no details in the passage to support the claim that organic fertilizer is superior to inorganic fertilizer. (In fact, the author would probably disagree with such a statement.) Remember, in EXCEPT questions the "wrong" answer is the right choice.

Roman numeral detail questions test the same ability as EXCEPT questions, but in a different format. Here is an example.

TEST EXAMPLE

According to information in the passage, plants

I.   can be used as a source of organic fertilizer in growing other plants.

II.   can absorb complex growth chemicals directly from the soil.

III. need inorganic chemicals for growth.

(A) II only.   (B) I and II.

(C) I and III.   (D) II and III.

(E) I, II, and III.

The elimination technique is the best approach to Roman numeral questions. (The Roman numeral format comes up in other sections of the GMAT; use the elimination technique throughout.) The basics of the technique are as follows: (1) Decide which statement in the question to read first. Your goal is to read as few statements as possible. If by eliminating one of the statements you can narrow the choices to one, read that statement. (2) Read the statement. If the statement is true, eliminate all answer choices that do not contain that statement. If the statement is false, eliminate all choices that do contain the statement. (3) Now decide which statement to read next. In the majority of cases, you will need to read only two statements.

Look at our example. All answer choices except (C) contain Statement II. Statement II is incorrect and can be eliminated. Therefore, the correct choice is (C).

Inference Questions

TEST EXAMPLE

It can be inferred from the passage that

(A) animals must convert synthetic fertilizers to organic form to benefit from them.

(B) organically-raised animals are more likely to be disease-free than those raised inorganically.

(C) organically-raised animals process chemical nutrients in the same way as organically-raised plants.

(D) organically-raised animals tend to be smaller than animals raised inorganically.

(E) animals can use chemical nutrients for growth in either organic or inorganic form.

Inference questions test your ability to recognize information that is not explicitly stated in the passage, but that is strongly implied. Inference questions can refer to specific details or more general ideas and are usually worded in one of the following ways:

It can be inferred . . .

The passage suggests . . .

The author probably considers . . .

The author implies that . . .

TEST BREAKER

To answer inference questions, look for answer choices that present information that can be deduced directly from the passage. Do not make assumptions. The majority of wrong answer choices in inference questions try to draw you into making unwarranted assumptions. Do not assume anything. Do not use your outside knowledge. Use only the information in the passage.

In our example, the question deals with a detail—namely, organically-raised animals. When an inference question asks about a detail, follow the procedure for locating details that we discussed in the Reading Strategies section on page 87. The discussion of organically-raised animals is found in the last paragraph. Reread the paragraph.

Now look at the answer choices. Choice (A) has two problems: It claims that synthetic fertilizers are necessarily inorganic—which is not true—and it contradicts the author's implicit point, made in the last sentence, that animals can use both organic and inorganic nutrients. Choice (B) tries to get you to make the assumption that organically-raised animals are healthier because they are not given antibiotics. Choice (C) contradicts the information implicit in the paragraph. Choice (D) asks you to assume that since organically raised animals are not given growth stimulants, they tend to be smaller than those raised inorganically. Finally, choice (E) explicitly states the author's implicit point that animals can use organic and inorganic nutrients. Choice (E) is the right choice.

Logic Questions

TEST EXAMPLE

Which of the following statements best describes the organization of the passage?

(A) A dispute is presented and resolved.

(B) A problem is outlined, and a solution is proposed.

(C) A misunderstanding is underscored, and clarifying definitions are presented.

(D) A critique is made, and supporting evidence is presented.

(E) A current hypothesis is examined, and an alternative is suggested.

Logic questions test your ability to analyze the organization of the author's argument. These questions focus on the organization of the passage as a whole, the organization of a paragraph, or the role played by a particular detail in the structure of the argument.

TEST BREAKER

As with main idea questions, the key to answering logic questions is to select the answer choice which fully and precisely describes the structure of the passage or paragraph, or the role of the detail in question.

Look at our example. The question asks about the organization of the passage as a whole. Logic questions of this type are closely connected to main idea questions. Use the work you have done on earlier questions to help you. Here, refer to the main idea question we looked at above. We said that the primary purpose of the passage is to eliminate a misunderstanding by providing definitions. Keep that in mind as you look at the answer choices in our logic question.

Choices (A), (D), and (E) are wrong since the passage does not present a dispute: no critique is made and no hypothesis is examined. Choice (B) has to be rejected—even if we accept that the author outlines a problem—since no solution is proposed. Choice (C) fully and precisely describes the organization of the passage and is therefore the right choice.

Application Questions

TEST EXAMPLE

The passage most likely appeared in a(n)

(A) nutrition textbook.

(B) encyclopedia.

(C) popular science magazine.

(D) medical journal.

(E) college chemistry textbook.

Application questions ask you to relate the information in the passage to a larger context or one that is different from that of the passage. These questions primarily appear in one of the following forms:

The passage most likely appeared in a . . .

The passage is most relevant to which field of study . . .

TEST BREAKER

> To answer application questions, think about the main idea of the passage, the scope of supporting evidence, and the author's style. Select the answer choice that puts the passage into the most suitable context.

Look at the above example. Now, consider the passage. The main idea is to clear up the misunderstanding about the terms "organic" and "chemical" by providing definitions. The evidence provided is in the form of an explanation of how animals and plants get the nutrients they need for growth. The style is explanatory; the author uses very accessible language and does not get overly technical. With all this in mind, look at the answer choices.

A nutrition textbook would be more technical and more detailed on the subject of organic and inorganic substances in our foods; therefore, choice (A) is incorrect. Choice (D) can be rejected for the same reasons.

The purpose of an encyclopedia is to provide facts, not to clear up misunderstandings. Furthermore, the style of an encyclopedic entry would be more scholarly. Choice (B) is wrong.

Choice (C) presents a suitable context for the passage. A popular science magazine would be likely to publish an article clarifying the terms "organic" and "chemical" as they relate to our foods. The level of detail and the style of the passage would also be appropriate for this type of publication. There, choice (C) is the right choice.

A college chemistry text would probably not deal with the subject of the passage. In addition, the style is inappropriate for a textbook. Choice (E) is incorrect.

Tone Questions

TEST EXAMPLE

> The author's attitude toward inorganic fertilizers can best be described as
>
> (A) hostile.
>
> (B) mildly critical.
>
> (C) objective or neutral.
>
> (D) defensive and supportive.
>
> (E) enthusiastically supportive.

Tone questions test your ability to gauge the author's attitude toward his or her subject. There are two types of tone questions: those concerning the tone of the passage as a whole and those concerning the author's attitude toward a particular detail. The example above illustrates the second type of tone question.

To answer general tone questions, follow the procedure described in the Reading Strategies section on page 87 to determine whether the tone is positive, negative, or neutral. Several answer choices will obviously be wrong. Once you have narrowed down your choices, consider the intensity of the author's tone. Is the author's attitude very or only mildly negative or positive? Select the answer choice that best reflects the author's tone and its intensity.

To answer tone questions regarding specific details, reread the part of the passage in which the detail is discussed. Pay special attention to the context in which the detail occurs. Consider how the detail relates to the main idea of the passage. Look for key words—especially adjectives—that relay the author's attitude. Determine whether the tone is positive, negative, or neutral. Eliminate wrong answer choices. Consider the intensity of the tone. Select the appropriate answer choice.

Look at our example. The question asks about the author's attitude toward inorganic fertilizer. Inorganic fertilizer is discussed in the fourth paragraph. Reread the paragraph. The author's point is that inorganic fertilizers contain the same nutrients as organic ones, and, therefore, it is inaccurate to call them artificial. It is clear that the author's attitude toward inorganic fertilizers is not negative. We can eliminate choices (A) and (B). But now we need to decide whether the author is neutral, positive, or very positive. Look at the language of the paragraph. It is very objective, with no strong adjectives. If the last sentence were something like, "It is a travesty to refer to these fine products as 'artificial' . . . ," we would have to decide between choices (D) and (E). But as the paragraph is written, it is objective and neutral. Choice (C) is correct.

COACHING TIPS FOR GMAT READING COMPREHENSION

- Quickly look over the questions after reading the passage.

- While reading the passage, try to pick out the main idea, and get a feel for the essay's structure and tone.

- To answer questions concerning specific details, find the detail in the passage and reread it in context. Many questions on the GMAT provide line references; do not get trapped into reading only the lines that are specified.

- Do not make assumptions. Use only the information provided—explicitly or implicitly—in the passage to answer the questions.

- If you cannot decide which choice is correct, eliminate as many choices as you can and guess.

- Do not spend too much time on any one question.

- Do not second-guess yourself. Be confident.

☞ Practice Drill 1

Not long after the founding of Virginia, other Englishmen established another colony to the north. In 1620, a shipload of religious dissenters, later known as Pilgrims, debarked from the Mayflower on the western shore of Cape Cod Bay, on the coast of Massachusetts. The nucleus of the group were Puritan separatists, part of a congregation of nonconformists of Scrooby parish in Nottinghamshire, England. Because of the strict enforcement of religious laws by James I, in 1608-9 the entire congregation of about 100 had moved to Holland seeking toleration. In 1620, they received permission from the Crown and financial backing from the London Company to migrate to Virginia. About 35 members of the congregation chose to do so; they first traveled to England, where they joined another group of dissenters. The Mayflower carried 101 passengers and a crew of 48. They were the first Englishmen—but by no means the last—to escape Stuart prosecution in the New World.

The religious situation in England had grown complicated since Henry VIII separated the established church from Rome and placed himself at its head. In the last years of his reign, pressure from Protestant reformers forced him to modify much of the ecclesiastical code. After his death, the regents of his young son stimulated the Protestant movement. Queen Mary then had attempted to reverse the tide, but Elizabeth I wisely chose the middle course. She instituted moderate reforms in the Church of England and, though not disposed to tolerance of Protestants, did not rigorously enforce the regulations that restricted them.

A large group arose that wanted to continue the process of reform. Gradually, they came to be called Puritans. Those Anglicans, who would "purify" the church from within, were known as conforming Puritans; those favoring stronger measures were known as nonconformists, dissenters, or separatists. Religious disputation was the rage of the day when translations of the Bible were first beginning to reach the hands of the people, who were also stimulated by the controversies that the Reformation had fostered. Interestingly enough, the version on which the Scrooby Puritans based their dissent was probably the Bishops' Bible, not the King James translation used today by most Protestant sects.

By authorizing this magnificent translation, James I undoubtedly hoped to put an end to dissent; instead, he only quickened it. His other religious policies, which grew harsher toward the end of his reign, were also designed to stamp out the heresy that was budding all over England. The King increased the pressure on nonconformists and separatists, and churchmen grew more and more intolerant, even of the conforming Puritans. But the more vigorous the pruning, the healthier the plant became. After James died in 1625, his son Charles I (1625-49) proved to be even less tolerant. A bloody revolution cost Charles his throne and his life, while the Puritan colonies in New England grew rapidly.

1. The main purpose of the passage is to

   (A) provide a brief outline of seventeenth-century English history.

   (B) summarize the chief political problems in the reign of James I.

   (C) define the various terms applied to Protestant dissenters.

   (D) provide background information elucidating the authorization of the King James Bible.

   (E) provide a context for understanding the establishment of Massachusetts settlements.

2. The passage provides information that would answer which of the following questions?

   I. Why did the Pilgrims settle in Massachusetts rather than Virginia?

   II. Why didn't the Scrooby Puritans seek reform within the Church of England?

   III. Why did the Scrooby nonconformists leave England?

   (A) I only.   (B) II only.

   (C) III only.   (D) II and III only.

   (E) I, II, and III.

3. The author suggests that

   (A) Henry VIII welcomed revision of the ecclesiastical code.

   (B) the Reformation weakened the fabric of intellectual life in England.

   (C) the Scrooby Pilgrims left Holland chiefly for economic reasons.

   (D) James I had at least some political motives in authorizing a new translation of the Bible.

   (E) the controversies fostered by the Reformation led to a new spirit of increased tolerance in the Church of England.

4. The author's attitude toward the King James Bible is

   (A) mildly critical.   (B) skeptical.

   (C) indifferent.   (D) laudatory.

   (E) optimistic.

5. Which of the following statements most accurately describes the second paragraph?

    (A) It describes the "persecution" alluded to in the last sentence of the first paragraph.

    (B) It describes the religious situation in England in the years prior to the events discussed in the first paragraph.

    (C) It places English religious dissent in the context of the European Reformation.

    (D) It makes clear that the Pilgrims began a movement that was becoming more influential in England.

    (E) It outlines the Church of England's position in regard to dissenting sects.

6. In the metaphor in the last paragraph, the "plant" refers to

    (A) the colonies.   (B) religious dissent.

    (C) the Reformation in general. (D) the Church of England.

    (E) James I.

7. Which of the following would be the most appropriate title for the passage?

    (A) James I and the Reformation

    (B) The Church of England in the 17th Century

    (C) The Pilgrims: Seeking Religious Freedom in the New World

    (D) Religion in Virginia

    (E) The Origin of the King James Bible

8. It can be inferred from the passage that which of the following was most politically astute in dealing with religious dissent?

    (A) James I   (B) Charles I

    (C) Henry VIII   (D) Queen Mary

    (E) Elizabeth I

SENTENCE CORRECTION

The Sentence Correction section of the GMAT is designed to measure your knowledge of grammar, English usage, and your ability to distinguish good writing from bad writing. The section consists of 22 questions, each based on one sentence.

The directions for the Sentence Correction section are very important. Read them carefully and learn them well for the exam. As we have said before, you should familiarize yourself with the directions for all the sections before the exam, so you do not waste time reading them during the exam.

DIRECTIONS: In each of the following sentences, some part of the sentence or the entire sentence is underlined. Beneath each sentence, you will find five ways of phrasing the underlined part. The first of these repeats the original; the other four are different. If you think the original is better than any of the alternatives, choose answer A; otherwise, choose one of the others. Select the best version and fill in the corresponding oval on your answer sheet.

This is a test for correctness and effectiveness of expression. In choosing answers, follow the requirements of standard written English; that is, pay attention to grammar, choice of words, and sentence construction. Choose the answer that expresses most effectively what is presented in the original sentence; this answer should be clear and exact, without awkwardness, ambiguity, or redundancy.

A lot of information is packed into these directions. We will analyze the information one piece at a time.

Each question presents a sentence, with a part of the sentence or the whole sentence underlined. You are then given five versions of the underlined part. Choice (A) repeats the original. The other four choices give you rewritten versions of the underlined part. Several observations have to be made here.

First, although in the majority of the questions only a part of the sentence is underlined, you have to read the whole sentence very carefully. Very often the problem with the sentence is in how the underlined part fits in with the rest. Do not try to save time by reading only the underlined portions of the sentences. This will only hurt your score.

Second, in giving you the choice to select the original as the best version of the sentence, the test-makers imply that not all of the sentences contain mistakes. In fact, choice (A) will be the correct answer as frequently as any of the other choices. Do not assume that something must be wrong with the original. Check for mistakes; if you do not find any, choose (A) and move on.

Finally, since choice (A) repeats the underlined part of the original sentence, there is no reason to read (A) when you are considering the answer choices. Reading choice (A) for any question in the Sentence Correction section is a waste of time. Learn to skip (A) and to begin reading the choices with (B).

Continuing with our review of the directions, we need to focus on the statement that instructs you to "select the best version" of the sentence. Notice that the directions do not say that you should select the correct version. In fact, in some questions, the original sentence is not wrong but is written poorly; and one of the answer choices presents a better version. Below, we will discuss in detail the standards used by the test-makers to judge writing. You should learn what these standards are and practice recognizing sentences that meet them.

Another point has to be made here. Sometimes, the original sentence and all of the answer choices will seem unacceptable. However, since none of the questions have a "none of the above" option, one of the choices must be better than the rest according to the test-makers' standards. Always remember that the correct answer is the one considered best by the test-makers.

The directions go on to say that the Sentence Correction section "is a test of correctness and effectiveness of expression." This means that your ability to recognize sentences that are grammatically correct and well-written is being tested.

We then come to the statement that you should "follow the requirements of standard written English" in choosing answers. Here, the test-makers are defining what standards they use for judging sentences. But what exactly is standard written English? It is a way of writing that rigidly adheres to the rules of grammar and to conventions for choosing words and constructing sentences. Standard written English, as defined on the GMAT, is more formal than the way most of us write and is much more formal than the way we speak. In fact, it is so formal that sometimes sentences will sound awkward. Therefore, it is important you get used to the way standard written English sounds.

At this point, you may be feeling somewhat intimidated by the prospect of being tested on your knowledge of grammar. It is a very broad and sometimes complicated subject. Do not be concerned, however. The GMAT covers only a few relatively simple rules of grammar, which we will discuss in detail in the following section. For instance, there are no questions on punctuation or capitalization. Furthermore, you do not need to know the terms used in grammar.

Finally, we need to consider the last sentence of the directions, which states that the answer you choose should be exact. This is a very important point. In selecting an answer, you have to make sure that the meaning of the original sentence is not changed. A choice that alters the meaning of the sentence even slightly is not acceptable. To safeguard against making such a mistake, reread the whole sentence, substituting the version you think is correct for the original. In fact, this technique will also help you ensure that the new version works with the whole sentence and does not introduce new errors.

We now move on to discuss the topics that are covered on the Sentence Correction section of the GMAT. In discussing the rules of grammar, we will use some simple grammatical terms. However, as we stated above, you do not need to know these terms for the test. Do not concern yourself with them; concentrate on understanding the concepts.

GRAMMAR REFRESHER FOR THE GMAT

THE SENTENCE

A sentence is a group of words that communicates a complete thought.

NO: The dogs in my neighborhood.

YES: The dogs in my neighborhood bark all night.

The first example is not a sentence because it does not present a complete thought. The second example completes the thought and is a sentence.

To be a sentence—to communicate a complete thought—a group of words must have both a subject and a predicate. The subject is a word (or combination of words) that represents the person or thing upon which the sentence focuses. The predicate is a word (or group of words) that states what the subject is doing or what is being done to the subject. The predicate is the part of the sentence that contains the verb.

My dog   **does not bark.**

subject   **predicate**

On the Sentence Correction section of the GMAT, two types of sentence errors are tested: (1) sentence fragments and (2) run-on sentences.

Sentence Fragments

A sentence fragment is a group of words that does not express a complete thought—missing either a subject or a predicate—but that is punctuated as a sentence. In other words, a sentence fragment is an incomplete sentence posing as a complete one.

TEST EXAMPLE

Trying his best not to wake his parents, but finding it difficult to see in the dark, <u>Bobby finally the house to go fishing</u> after bumping into several pieces of furniture in the living room and breaking a glass in the kitchen.

(A) Bobby finally the house to go fishing

(B) Bobby finally the house in a rush to go fishing

(C) Bobby finally left the house

(D) Bobby eventually to go fishing

(E) Bobby finally left the house to go fishing

The problem with the sentence is that while it gives us a lot of information about Bobby, it does not tell us what he finally does. The verb is missing, and therefore the thought is incomplete.

Looking at the answer choices, we see that choices (B) and (D) repeat the mistake made in the original sentence. Furthermore, (D) inserts *eventually* in place of *finally*, thus altering the meaning of the sentence.

Choices (C) and (E) correct the original's mistake by inserting the verb *left*. However, (C) does not communicate the original's exact meaning since it omits the phrase "to go fishing." The correct choice is (E).

Run-on Sentences

A run-on sentence is one that is formed when two or more complete sentences are combined in one of the following ways:

(1) Without punctuation

  e.g., The candidate finished his speech the crowd cheered.

(2) With a comma, but without a conjunction

   e.g.,   The candidate finished his speech, the crowd cheered.

(3) With a conjunction, but without a comma

   e.g.,   The candidate finished his speech and the crowd cheered.

A run-on sentence can be corrected in three ways.

(1) It can be rewritten as two sentences.

   e.g.,   The candidate finished his speech. The crowd cheered.

(2) The two parts of the sentence can be joined by a semicolon, without a conjunction.

   e.g.,   The candidate finished his speech; the crowd cheered.

(3) The two parts can also be joined by a comma and a conjunction.

   e.g.,   The candidate finished his speech, and the crowd cheered.

The method used to correct any particular run-on sentence depends largely on the context and the author's style. On the GMAT, you will never have to decide which is a better method. All you need to know is how to recognize a run-on sentence and how to fix one.

TEST EXAMPLE

A sudden gust of wind filled the sails, the masts groaned, Jones gripped the wheel tighter and hoped that they could outrun the pirate.

(A) A sudden gust of wind filled the sails, the masts groaned, Jones gripped the wheel tighter and hoped that they could outrun the pirate.

(B) A sudden gust of wind filled the sails; the masts groaned, Jones gripped the wheel tighter and hoped that they could outrun the pirate.

(C) A sudden gust of wind filled the sails; the masts groaned. Jones gripped the wheel tighter and hoped that they could outrun the pirate.

(D) A sudden gust of wind filled the sails and the masts

> groaned. Jones gripped the wheel tighter and hoped that they could outrun the pirate.
>
> (E) A sudden gust of wind filled the sails. The masts groaned. Jones gripped the wheel tighter, and hoped that they could outrun the pirate.

The sentence is a run-on sentence. It is composed of three complete sentences spliced together with commas. Choices (B) and (D) provide only partial solutions and, therefore, are incorrect. Choices (C) and (E) fix the problem. However, (E) introduces a new error. In (E), a comma is inserted after *tighter* in the second sentence. This comma separates the two predicate verbs—*gripped* and *hoped*—of the compound predicate. The verbs of a compound predicate are joined by a connecting word, such as *and*, and are never separated by a comma. Choice (C) is the correct answer.

SUBJECT-VERB AGREEMENT

A verb and its subject must agree in number and person. If the subject is singular, the verb must be singular. If the subject is plural, the verb must be plural.

> NO: The girls (plural) stands (singular) in the rain.
>
> YES: The girls stand in the rain.

Similarly, if the subject is in the first person (I, we), second person (you), or third person (he, she, it, they), the verb must agree.

> NO: My parrot do not speak.
>
> YES: My parrot does not speak.

Subject-verb agreement is the basis for many questions in the Sentence Correction section. The questions usually focus on one of the following special cases.

Intervening Phrases

Often the subject and the verb in a sentence are separated by a group of words. The intervening phrase might be a parenthetical comment, a description, and so on. The intervening phrase might be very short or quite long. The point is that no matter what comes between the verb and its subject, the two must agree.

> NO: The passengers, who had watched in amazement as the

train sped through the station, was told that another train would arrive within the hour.

YES: The passengers, who had watched in amazement as the train sped through the station, were told that another train would arrive within the hour.

Compound Subjects

We have mentioned that sentences can have compound predicates. Sentences can also have compound subjects. Compound subjects are formed when two or more simple subjects are joined by connecting words, such as *and, or, nor, either . . . or,* and *neither . . . nor.*

If the subject of a verb is a compound joined by *and,* the verb must be plural.

e.g., Mary **and** John *are* in the same class.

If the subject is a compound formed by two singular subjects joined by *or, nor, either . . . or,* or *neither . . . nor,* the verb is always singular.

e.g., Dave **or** Sam *has* to mow the lawn.

If the subject is a compound formed by a singular and a plural subject joined by *or, nor, either . . . or,* or *neither . . . nor,* the verb must agree with the subject closest to it. If both subjects are plural, however, the verb must also be plural.

e.g., **Neither** soothing words **nor** a hug *was* enough to console the crying child.

e.g., **Either** apples **or** oranges *were* always served after dinner.

Collective Nouns

Words such as *group, committee, crowd,* and so on, are called collective nouns because they represent a number of people or objects considered as a unit.

TEST BREAKER

On the GMAT, collective nouns appear only in contexts where they are singular in meaning. When the subject of a sentence is a collective noun that is singular in meaning, the verb must be singular.

e.g., The theater group was thrilled by the critics' enthusiastic reviews.

Inverted Sentence Structure

The subject of a sentence does not always precede the verb. Take special care to identify the subject—the person or thing the sentence concerns. Then make sure that the verb agrees with the subject.

NO: In the street were not a single person.

YES: In the street was not a single person.

TEST EXAMPLE

<u>Among the passengers on the ship was</u> a film critic from New York, a retired couple from Michigan, a college student from California, and a Florida real-estate developer.

(A) Among the passengers on the ship was

(B) The passengers on the ship were

(C) Among the passengers on the ship were

(D) On the ship was

(E) There was among the passengers on the ship

Did you spot the problem in the example? We have a compound subject—the list of people who are among the passengers on the ship. However, the verb is incorrectly singular.

Choices (D) and (E) repeat the mistake. Therefore, we can eliminate them without further consideration. We now have to choose between (B) and (C). Both these choices correct the error. Choice (B), however, changes the meaning of the sentence. Therefore, (C) is the correct choice.

VERBS

The verb is the most important part of any sentence. It tells us what is happening to the subject or what the subject is doing. Furthermore, the verb lets us know the time of the action. Many questions on the GMAT test your knowledge of verb tenses and verb forms. The following discussion focuses on the topics that most often appear on the exam.

Tenses

Tenses are unique to verbs. They indicate the time of the action. There are three simple tenses and three perfect tenses.

Present: I see the dog.

The present tense is used when the action in the sentence is taking place in the present.

Past: I saw the dog.

The past tense is used when the action took place in the past.

Future: I shall (will) see the dog.

The future tense is used when the action will take place in the future.

Present Perfect: I have seen the dog.

The present perfect tense is used when the action is completed at the time of writing. It can also be used to indicate that the action is continuing into the present.

Past Perfect: I had seen the dog.

The past perfect tense is used when the action was completed before some definite time in the past.

Future Perfect: I shall (will) have seen the dog.

The future perfect tense is used when the action will be completed at some definite time in the future.

Each of the six tenses also has a progressive form. Progressive forms are used when the action is continuing at the time indicated by the tense.

Progressive:

Present	You are reading.
Past	You were reading.
Future	You will (shall) be reading.
Present Perfect	You have been reading.
Past Perfect	You had been reading.
Future Perfect	You will (shall) have been reading.

(**Note:** With certain exceptions, *shall* is used in the first person, and *will* in the second and third persons. This distinction is not tested on the GMAT.)

TEST BREAKER

Many questions on the GMAT measure your ability to use tenses to communicate the sequence of events. If two events happen at the same time, the same tense must be used.

NO: Mary fell asleep just as the movie starts.

YES: Mary fell asleep just as the movie started.

If events happen at different times, the tenses must reflect the difference. This is easy to do with the simple tenses.

e.g., Bob and I ate lunch together, and now I am going to meet with Beth.

If events happened at different times in the past, the past perfect must be used for the event that happened first, and the past tense for the event that happened later.

NO: The dinosaurs died out before the mammals came to dominate the Earth.

YES: The dinosaurs had died out before the mammals came to dominate the Earth.

Similarly, if events take place at different times in the future, the future perfect must be used for the event that will happen first, and the future tense for the event that will happen later.

NO: I will play tennis tomorrow, when the rain will pass.

YES: I will play tennis tomorrow, when the rain will have passed.

TEST EXAMPLE

The mission to Mars was planned for the end of the first decade of the twenty-first century, although scientists are not yet certain of the effects such a prolonged space flight will have on the astronauts.

(A) The mission to Mars was planned

(B) The mission to Mars will be planned

(C) The mission to Mars had been planned

(D) The mission to Mars is planned

(E) The mission to Mars will have been

There is a problem with the tenses in the example. "Was planned" is in the past tense, while "are not yet certain" is in the present tense. Notice the word *yet* here. It is an additional clue that the action is taking place in the present. Look for such words to help you determine the sequence of events.

Since the action is taking place now, the whole sentence has to be in the present tense. Therefore, choice (D) is correct.

Mood

In addition to tenses, verbs also change to reflect mood. The mood indicates the speaker's (or writer's) attitude toward the action. There are three moods in English. The indicative is used for factual statements. The imperative is used to command. And the subjunctive is used to communicate doubts, wishes, and requirements.

TEST BREAKER

The subjunctive is the only mood that is tested on the GMAT. The subjunctive is used to express conditions that are not true, as well as needs, suggestions, doubts, and wishes.

The two characteristics of the subjunctive that you should know are as follows: The subjunctive form of *to be* in the past tense is *were* in the first, second, and third persons, singular and plural.

> e.g., I wish I were a baseball star.
>
> If he were taller, he could reach the top shelf.

For all other verbs in the present tense, third person, singular, the "s" is omitted.

> e.g., If the generator should fail, we will need candles.
>
> The doctor suggested that Lillian take a trip.

TEST EXAMPLE

It is essential that Bob leave immediately.

(A) It is essential that Bob leave immediately.

(B) It is essential that Bob leaves immediately.

(C) It is essential that Bob should leave immediately.

(D) Bob's leaving immediately is essential.

(E) It is essential that Bob go immediately.

Is anything wrong with the sentence? No. Remember that at least some of the questions on the exam will give you sentences that are correct. Do not be afraid of selecting choice (A).

Verbals

Verbals are words that are derived from verbs. They retain certain characteristics of verbs and can function as adjectives, adverbs, or nouns. However, verbals can never function as predicate verbs in a sentence. This is a rule that is often tested on the GMAT.

There are three verbals in English: participles, gerunds, and infinitives.

Participles: Participles are verbals that are used as adjectives.

> e.g., Susan found the lecture **interesting.**
>
> The puppy, **woken** by the bell, ran to the door.
>
> **Having recovered fully**, Janet left India.

Gerunds: Gerunds are verbals used as nouns.

> e.g., **Writing** is Carla's calling.
>
> Jill's **being** promoted took her by surprise.

(**Note**: In constructions such as this, the modifying noun or pronoun always takes the possessive form.)

Infinitives: Infinitives are verbals used as nouns, adjectives, or adverbs. Infinitives are usually preceded by the word *to*. Split infinitives—such as, "to better understand"—are considered incorrect in standard written English.

> e.g., **To compete** in the Olympics was Peter's dream.
>
> Ellen asked for water **to drink**.
>
> The dog cocked his ears **to listen**.

TEST EXAMPLE

> The campers having lost the canoe and cut the trip short.
>
> (A) The campers having lost the canoe and
>
> (B) The campers, having lost the canoe,

(C) The campers have lost the canoe and

(D) The campers, losing the canoe,

(E) The campers, having lost the canoe, and

We have a tense problem here which stems from the improper use of the participle phrase "having lost the canoe" as part of the predicate. We have to either correct the sentence to have the participle serve as an adjective, or change the tenses.

In choice (B), the participle serves as an adjective. Choice (C) attempts to change the tenses. However, the sentence ends up sounding as if the trip were cut short prior to the loss of the canoe. Choices (D) and (E) unsuccessfully attempt to get the participle into its adjective role. The correct choice is (B).

MISPLACED MODIFIERS

An element in a sentence that describes another element of that sentence is called a modifier. Adjectives and adverbs are modifiers. Adjectives describe nouns, and adverbs describe verbs. Phrases and even relative clauses can also be modifiers. For example, in the sentence "Jim, who is a very fast runner, won the race," the relative clause "who is a very fast runner" modifies the subject, "Jim."

Because English depends primarily on word order for the meaning of sentences, modifiers have to come immediately before or after the elements they modify. Misplaced modifiers—modifiers that are placed away from their antecedents (the things they modify)—cause a lot of confusion.

> e.g., Frustrated with the two-party system, the independent candidate was favored by many voters.

In the above example, "Frustrated with the two-party system" is a modifier, and "candidate" is its antecedent. The sentence does not make a lot of sense, however. The author means that the voters are frustrated. The modifier is in the wrong place, and the meaning is confused.

We can correct the mistake in three different ways.

> e.g., Frustrated with the two-party system, many voters favored the independent candidate.
>
> Many voters, frustrated with the two-party system, favored the independent candidate.

The independent candidate was favored by many voters who were frustrated with the two-party system.

Notice that all of the rewritten sentences place the modifier right next to *voters*. That is the key to correcting modification errors. The closer the modifier is to its antecedent, the less likely is the sentence to be confusing.

TEST EXAMPLE

Cold, numb Ellen took off her shoes and rested her feet near the fireplace.

(A) Cold, numb Ellen took off her shoes and rested her feet near the fireplace.

(B) Ellen, cold and numb, took off her shoes and rested her feet near the fireplace.

(C) Ellen took off her shoes and rested her cold, numb feet near the fireplace.

(D) Ellen took off her shoes and rested her feet near the fireplace, cold and numb.

(E) Resting her cold, numb feet near the fireplace, Ellen took off her shoes.

In the example, you have to decide what the author meant to say. This is often the case with sentences that have modification problems. The sentence would make the most sense if the adjectives *cold* and *numb* modified *feet*. Ellen's feet are cold and numb; therefore, she takes off her shoes and rests her feet near the fireplace.

In choice (B), *cold* and *numb* modify *Ellen*. In (D), *fireplace* becomes the antecedent. Choices (C) and (E) place the modifiers in the right place, before *feet*. In (E), however, a new error is introduced; the sequence of events is disrupted. Choice (C) is the correct choice.

PRONOUNS

A pronoun is a word that stands in for a noun or another pronoun. There are five classes of pronouns in English: personal, interrogative, demonstrative, indefinite, and relative. For the purpose of preparing for the GMAT, you only need to concern yourself with personal, indefinite, and relative pronouns. Following are examples of these three classes of pronouns.

Personal Pronouns

I, you, he, she, we, they, it

Indefinite Pronouns

one, anybody, everything, each

Relative Pronouns

who, whom, whose, which, that, what

Reference

Since the role of the pronoun is to stand in for another word, there must be no confusion as to which word the pronoun is replacing. The pronoun must clearly refer to one antecedent.

> NO: Barry asked Jon to be on the softball team because **he** is a good hitter.

> YES: Because **Jon** is a good hitter, Barry asked **him** to be on the softball team.

In the first sentence, the pronoun *he* can refer to either Barry or Jon. Therefore, the sentence is confusing. In the second sentence, on the other hand, the pronoun *him* clearly refers to Jon.

Another reference error to watch out for involves a pronoun that refers to an unspecified antecedent. This is particularly common with the pronoun *they*.

> NO: They expect rain this evening.

> YES: Rain is expected this evening.

An exception to this rule is the pronoun *it*, which can be used to refer to an indefinite antecedent.

> e.g., It might rain this evening.

Agreement

As is the case with verbs and their subjects, pronouns must agree with their antecedents in number and person.

> NO: The **houses** on our block are smaller than **that** on the next block.

YES: The **houses** on our block are smaller than **those** on the next block.

Some pronouns are always singular. A pronoun that refers to one of these indefinite pronouns must also be singular.

e.g., Neither of the candidates had met his opponent.

Below is a list of indefinite pronouns that are always singular.

anybody	somebody	everybody	nobody
anyone	someone	everyone	no one
one	each	either	neither
other	another		

Conversely, some pronouns are always plural. Pronouns that refer to them must also be plural.

e.g., Few imagined the greatness their futures held.

The following are pronouns that are always plural.

both   few   many   others   several

Pronouns that refer to compound antecedents follow the same rules as verbs that refer to compound subjects. If the parts of the compound antecedent are joined by *and*, the pronoun must be plural. If the parts are joined by *either . . . or* or *neither . . . nor* and are both singular, the pronoun must be singular. If the parts are plural, the pronoun must be plural. And if the parts of the antecedent are different in number, the pronoun must agree with the one closest to it.

e.g., The dog and the cat have marked their territories.

Either Greg or Mark left his mitt on the field.

Neither the men nor the women left their chairs.

Neither Dave nor his brothers own their tuxedos.

Pronouns that refer to collective nouns, such as *group, band* etc., must be singular. (There are cases when this is not so. However, you do not have to concern yourself with these for the GMAT.)

e.g., The party nominated its candidate at the convention.

As we have said, pronouns must agree with their antecedents in person. A very common mistake in English—and one that comes up on the

GMAT—is to start a sentence in the third person and then use a second person pronoun to refer to the antecedent. This is especially true when *one* and *you* are used. *One* is third person. *You* is second person. These pronouns must not be mixed in one sentence.

> NO: When one studies, you do better on exams.

> YES: When one studies, one does better on exams.
> When you study, you do better on exams.

In addition to number and person, pronouns must agree with their antecedents in gender. In grammar, gender means the classification of nouns and pronouns according to sex. There are four genders in English.

Masculine: he, him, uncle, actor

Feminine: she, her, aunt, actress

Common: parent, cousin, friend

Neuter: it, candle, chair

The pronoun must be the same gender as its antecedent. Such agreement rarely presents problems except in the cases of common gender and indefinite pronouns.

If the antecedent of a pronoun is common gender, the pronoun can be either masculine or feminine. However, if the sentence clearly indicates that the antecedent refers to a specific gender, the pronoun of that gender must be used.

> NO: My uncle took her children to Florida.

> YES: My uncle took his children to Florida.

> My uncle took Amanda's children to Florida.

In cases where the antecedent of a pronoun is an indefinite pronoun, the masculine pronoun has been used traditionally. Many authors now use *his or her* in such cases, however.

> e.g.,   Everyone is entitled to his opinion.

> Everyone is entitled to his or her opinion.

Furthermore, if a sentence indicates clearly that the indefinite pronoun refers to members of one sex, the pronoun of appropriate gender should be used.

e.g.,   Anyone in the Boys' Choir could invite his family and friends to the performance.

Relative Pronouns

As we have said, the relative pronouns are *who, whom, whose, which, that,* and *what. Who* is used when the antecedent is a person. *That* is used for persons or things. And *which* is used when the antecedent is anything other than a person.

TEST BREAKER

Questions on the GMAT that involve relative pronouns usually focus on the distinction between *who* and *whom. Who* is used when the antecedent of the pronoun is the subject of the sentence.

e.g.,   Dan is a teacher who is respected by his students.

Whom is used when the antecedent is the object of the sentence.

e.g.,   Dan is a teacher whom his students respect.

TEST EXAMPLE

<u>The boy, whose mother was away on a business trip, had the run of her house during the day</u>, when his father was at work.

(A) The boy, whose mother was away on a business trip, had the run of her house during the day

(B) The boy's mother was away on a business trip and had the run of the house during the day

(C) The boy, whose mother was away on a business trip, had the run of their house during the day

(D) The boy's mother was away on a business trip and he had the run of his house during the day

(E) The boy, whose mother was away on a business trip, had the run of his house during the day

We have a pronoun agreement problem in this example. *The boy*, the subject of the sentence, is masculine. *Her*, on the other hand, is feminine. It is possible to interpret the sentence as meaning that the boy had the run of his mother's house. However, it is unlikely that the author meant that. Therefore, we have to change the *her* to *his*.

Choice (B) completely changes the meaning of the sentence and makes it nonsensical. Choice (C) uses *their* instead of *her*. This is unacceptable since we have a singular antecedent. Choice (D) corrects the pronoun agreement error. However, the sentence in (D) is a run-on sentence. Choice (E) corrects the original mistake and is the correct choice.

PARALLEL STRUCTURE

When similar ideas are expressed in one sentence, they should be in similar grammatical form. This is true of items in a list, elements of a compound subject or predicate, compared ideas, and parallel clauses of a compound sentence.

The following are illustrations of several common parallelism errors.

Lists

NO: Last summer, Mark traveled to New Mexico, Texas, and to Colorado.

YES: Last summer, Mark traveled to New Mexico, Texas, and Colorado.

Last summer, Mark traveled to New Mexico, to Texas, and to Colorado.

NO: Doris wanted to study French, Italian, or learn Spanish.

YES: Doris wanted to study French, Italian, or Spanish.

Compounds

NO: Industrial pollutants, car emissions, and the use of aerosols contribute to global warming.

YES: Industrial pollutants, car emissions, and aerosols contribute to global warming.

NO: The astronauts had orbited the Earth, deployed a satellite, and had conducted several biological experiments.

YES: The astronauts had orbited the Earth, deployed a satellite, and conducted several biological experiments.

Correlative Conjunctions

NO: Mary not only enjoyed camping but also fishing.

YES: Mary enjoyed not only camping but also fishing.

Compared Ideas

NO: Drinking alcohol can be as dangerous to your health as to smoke cigarettes.

YES: Drinking alcohol can be as dangerous to your health as smoking cigarettes.

To drink alcohol can be as dangerous to your health as to smoke cigarettes.

TEST EXAMPLE

To see Rome is having history come alive.

(A) To see Rome is having history come alive.

(B) Seeing Rome is to have history come alive.

(C) Seeing Rome is having history come alive.

(D) To see Rome is like history coming alive.

(E) To see Rome is to live history.

The example presents us with a parallelism problem. The infinitive *to see* is paired with the gerund *having*. This is incorrect. An infinitive must be paired with an infinitive, a gerund with a gerund.

Choice (B) reverses the problem. Choices (D) and (E) change the meaning of the sentence. Choice (C) is the correct choice.

COMPARISONS

For a sentence that makes a comparison to be correct, there must be no ambiguity about what is being compared. In addition, the comparison must be logical. In other words, you cannot compare people with objects, groups with individuals, and so on.

NO: Jim enjoyed the play more than Sally.

YES: Jim enjoyed the play more than Sally did.

NO: Many doctors claim that the benefits of walking are greater than running.

YES: Many doctors claim that the benefits of walking are greater than those of running.

TEST EXAMPLE

Key West is farther south than <u>any town in the continental United States</u>.

(A) any town in the continental United States

(B) any other town in the continental United States

(C) all towns in the continental United States

(D) most other towns in the continental United States

(E) any other town in the United States

The sentence in the example does not make sense. If Key West is farther south than **any** town in the continental United States, it is farther south than itself. What the sentence is trying to say is that Key West is the southernmost town in the continental United States.

Choice (B) achieves this by inserting *other*. Choice (C) repeats the original error. Choices (D) and (E) change the meaning of the sentence. Therefore, the correct choice is (B).

STYLE

Although grammar is the focus of the majority of questions in the Sentence Correction section, some questions do measure your sense of effective style. In considering questions and answer choices, therefore, always check the grammar first, but then check the style.

The three types of stylistic problems that most often appear on the GMAT are the following:

(1) passive-voice constructions,

(2) redundancy, and

(3) wordiness.

In active-voice constructions, the subject of the sentence is acting.

e.g., I shall always remember this trip to Alaska.

In passive-voice constructions, the subject of the sentence is the receiver of the action expressed by the verb.

e.g., This trip to Alaska will always be remembered by me.

The active voice is always more direct and crisp. On the GMAT, the active voice is invariably preferred to the passive. Therefore, given the choice, always select the active-voice sentence.

Redundancy is the use of words or phrases that are identical in meaning in the same sentence.

> e.g., The international buffet featured foods from many countries.

Such errors are easily corrected by removing the redundant element. In doing so, however, be careful not to change the meaning of the sentence.

> e.g., The buffet featured foods from many countries.

Finally, wordiness is the use of unnecessary words. It is always preferable to use a sentence that expresses a thought more concisely. On the GMAT, select the most concise choice, as long as the meaning of the sentence is not altered.

> NO: Wild animals that are domesticated do not lose their instincts but adapt to their environments.

> YES: Domesticated wild animals do not lose their instincts but adapt to their environments.

TEST EXAMPLE

It was not long before I realized that Michael had tricked me.

(A) It was not long before I realized that Michael had tricked me.

(B) Michael had tricked me, I realized not long before.

(C) It was not long after Michael had tricked me that I realized it.

(D) I realized, not long before, that Michael had tricked me.

(E) I soon realized that Michael had tricked me.

The sentence is grammatically correct. In fact, it does not even seem to be stylistically problematic. However, if you examine the answer choices, (E) stands out as expressing the same thought as the original, but more concisely and vigorously. Making *I* the subject of the sentence in place of the indefinite *it* changes the passive voice to active. Choice (E), therefore, is preferable and is the correct choice.

WORDS AND IDIOMS COMMONLY MISUSED

A few questions on the Sentence Correction section test your ability to recognize diction and idiomatic errors. A diction error is the use of a word in an inappropriate context. An idiomatic error is the incorrect use of a commonly accepted expression.

Below is a list of some words and idioms that are commonly misused. Questions on the Sentence Correction section involving diction and idiomatic errors are likely to focus on these words and expressions.

Affect, Effect

Affect is a verb which means "to influence." *Effect* is usually used as a noun which means "result." As a verb, *effect* means "to bring about."

> e.g., The rain did not affect our outing.
>
> The rain had no effect on our outing.

Among, Between

Among is used when more than two people or things are involved. *Between* is used when two people or things are involved, or if more than two are involved but each is considered individually.

> e.g., I could not choose between the cake and the pie.
>
> The candy was divided among all the children.

Amount, Number

Amount is used to refer to a collective. *Number* is used to refer to a quantity that can be counted.

> e.g., The amount of money I have is rather small.
>
> I have a rather small number of bills in my wallet.

As good or better than

The correct idiom is "as good as." Therefore, the expression should be "as good as, or better."

> NO: My dog is as strong or stronger than yours.
>
> YES: My dog is as strong as your dog, or stronger.

Compare to, Compare with

To *compare to* is to point out a resemblance between essentially different things. To *compare with* is to point out a difference between essentially similar things.

> e.g., Writing has sometimes been compared to boxing.
>
> New York has often been compared with London.

Different from

Since one thing differs from another, the expression is *different from*.

> NO: Huskies are different than Labradors.
>
> YES: Huskies are different from Labradors.

Each other, One another

Each other is used to refer to two things. *One another* is used to refer to three or more things.

> e.g., Dolly and John really like each other.
>
> The members of the group got along with one another.

Fewer, Less

Fewer is used to refer to number. *Less* refers to quantity.

> e.g., Fewer people are interested in soccer than in baseball.
>
> People now have less time to relax.

Hopefully

This is an adverb meaning "with hope." It is wrong to use it to mean "I hope" or "it is to be hoped."

> NO: Hopefully, you will be accepted by the school of your choice.
>
> YES: I hope you will be accepted by the school of your choice.

Lay, Lie

Lay means to put something down. The verb *lie* means to recline, to rest, or to remain in a reclining position. (The other verb *lie* means to tell a falsehood.)

e.g.,   I lay my hat on the table.

My hat lies on the table.

Like, As

Like should be followed by a noun or a pronoun. *As* introduces phrases and clauses.

e.g.,   My dog looks like a German shepherd.

That dog looks as if he is going to attack.

Not only . . . but also

Not only must always be used with *but also*.

NO: Ted not only dances and sings.

YES: Ted not only dances but also sings.

Regard as

The correct idiom is *regard as*.

NO: I regard Chaucer to be the greatest poet.

YES: I regard Chaucer as the greatest poet.

I consider Chaucer to be the greatest poet.

That, Which

That is the restrictive pronoun. A phrase or subordinate clause introduced by *that* limits the meaning of the word that it modifies. A restrictive phrase or clause is essential to the meaning of the sentence and is not set off by commas. *Which* is nonrestrictive.

e.g.,   The bus that stops near my house just left.

The bus, which stops near my house, just left.

EVALUATING SENTENCES

The most effective approach to the questions in the Sentence Correction section is as follows. Read each sentence. Evaluate it to see whether it contains an error. If it does, think about how the mistake is best corrected. Then, look through the answer choices (starting with (B)) to find the one that fixes the error.

Below is a step-by-step guide for evaluating sentences. Use it to practice recognizing sentences that contain grammatical, stylistic, or diction errors.

STEP-BY-STEP STRATEGY FOR GMAT SENTENCE CORRECTIONS

1. Check whether the sentence is complete by finding the subject and the predicate.

2. In compound sentences, make sure clauses are properly connected to avoid run-ons.

3. Make sure that the subject and the predicate agree in number and in person.

4. Check the tenses of the verbs. The sequence of events should be properly expressed.

5. Make sure there are no misplaced modifiers. Is there any ambiguity in the sentence?

6. Check the pronouns. Does each pronoun have one clear antecedent? Do they agree with their antecedents in number, person, and gender?

7. Make sure that there are no problems with parallel structures or comparisons.

8. Is the active voice used? Is the sentence too wordy or redundant?

9. Are there diction or idiomatic errors?

COACHING TIPS FOR GMAT SENTENCE CORRECTIONS

— Read the whole sentence, not just the underlined section.

— Try to determine what, if anything, is wrong with the sentence before looking at the answer choices.

— Do not be afraid to choose choice (A) if you think the original is the best version of the sentence.

— Do not read choice (A) since it merely repeats the question.

— Scan the choices and eliminate the ones that repeat the original mistake.

— In deciding between two choices, select the one that is more concise and effective.

— If you cannot decide which choice is correct, eliminate as many responses as you can and guess.

☞ Practice Drill 2

1. <u>His arm has been injured,</u> the team's best relief pitcher will miss the rest of the season.

    (A) His arm has been injured,

    (B) Having an arm that was injured,

    (C) Having injured his arm,

    (D) Having an arm that had been injured,

    (E) His injured arm made it necessary that

2. It would have been better for everyone concerned in this situation if <u>Bill would have sent a more detailed letter to the other company in question.</u>

    (A) Bill would have sent a more detailed letter to the other company in question.

    (B) Bill would have sent a more detailed letter to the company he has been discussing.

    (C) a more detailed letter would have been sent to the aforementioned company.

    (D) a more detailed letter had been sent to the other company.

    (E) Bill had sent a more detailed letter to the other company.

3. Although talent is crucial to a professional athlete, many other factors, such as <u>remaining injury-free, getting enough playing time, and effective coaching, is also important.</u>

    (A) remaining injury-free, getting enough playing time, and effective coaching, is also important.

    (B) remaining injury-free, getting enough playing time, and effective coaching, are also important.

    (C) remaining injury-free, getting enough playing time, and an effective coaching staff, are also important.

    (D) no injuries, playing time, and an effective coaching staff, is also important.

    (E) remaining injury-free, getting enough playing time, and a coaching that is effective, are also important.

4. <u>Yesterday, there were fewer members of the legislature who talked like they were in favor of a tax increase for the public citizens.</u>

   (A) Yesterday, there were fewer members of the legislature who talked like they were in favor of a tax increase for the public citizens.

   (B) Yesterday, less members of the legislature talked to the public like they were in favor of a tax increase.

   (C) Yesterday, there were fewer members of the legislature who talked as if they were in favor of a tax increase for citizens.

   (D) Publicly, there were less members of the legislature talking like they were in favor of raising taxes.

   (E) For the public, fewer members of the legislature talked yesterday about raising taxes.

5. <u>The candidate was sure that if his opponent did not propose an economic plan, he would win the election.</u>

   (A) The candidate was sure that if his opponent did not propose an economic plan, he would win the election.

   (B) The candidate was sure that he would win the election if his opponent did not propose an economic plan.

   (C) If his opponent did not propose an economic plan, the candidate was to win the election.

   (D) If his opponent did not propose an economic plan, he would win the election, the candidate was sure.

   (E) The candidate was sure to win the election if his opponent did not propose an economic plan.

CRITICAL REASONING

The Critical Reasoning section of the GMAT measures your ability to understand and evaluate arguments. The section consists of 16 questions based on arguments presented in short paragraphs. In most cases, each argument is followed by one question. Sometimes, two or more questions are based on one argument. The arguments are taken from a variety of fields. However, no specialized knowledge of any subject is required to answer the questions.

The questions focus on specific skills, such as analyzing arguments, recognizing assumptions, drawing inferences, strengthening or weakening arguments, and evaluating the logic of arguments. You are not expected to have any knowledge of formal logic. The questions are designed to test your ability to understand the point the author tries to prove, to determine the evidence the author uses to support the argument, to trace how the author gets from the evidence to the conclusion, and to judge the effectiveness of the argument.

The directions for the Critical Reasoning section are short and not very informative.

DIRECTIONS: For each question in this section, select the best of the answer choices given.

You are told to select the "best" of the answer choices. But what is the "best" choice? To answer this question we need to consider what the test-makers are seeking.

The Critical Reasoning section measures your ability to think logically and to evaluate the reasoning of others. In this context, the structure of an author's argument and the soundness of the method he or she uses are of primary importance. The actual idea or opinion the author expresses is essentially irrelevant. Do not base your answers on whether the author's point is true or false. A strong argument can be made to support a false conclusion; conversely, a weak argument may support a conclusion that is true. Concentrate on how the argument is made, not on its content.

In the following sections, we will discuss in detail the structure of an argument and common methods of argument. We will also explain how to evaluate arguments. And finally, we will discuss the types of questions you will encounter in the Critical Reasoning section and the skills you need to practice for these questions.

THE ARGUMENT

An argument is a line of reasoning designed to prove a point. Arguments can be simple, expressed in a few lines, or very complex, taking up whole books. Regardless of length and complexity, all arguments have the same basic framework: The author wants to communicate some central idea, to do so, the author presents supporting evidence, laying it out in a logical pattern.

The central point of an argument is called the **conclusion**. Each piece of evidence used by the author is called a **premise**. And the way in which the premises are fitted together is called **reasoning**.

Premise: My dog is black.

Premise: My dog is a Labrador retriever.

Conclusion: All Labrador retrievers are black.

The above example presents a simple argument. The conclusion is based on two premises. The argument is very weak since the premises do not really support the conclusion.

Note that a premise does not have to be objective, factual evidence for the conclusion. A premise is any statement that the author uses to support the conclusion.

The first skill you need to practice for Critical Reasoning is identifying the conclusions and premises of arguments. The majority of arguments in the section are of two basic patterns: (1) the conclusion follows the premises and (2) the premises follow the conclusion. The ability to locate the conclusion and the premises quickly is very important in order to do well on Critical Reasoning.

To identify the conclusion of an argument, ask yourself what central point the author is trying to make. What is the author trying to prove? Think about the one idea the author would want you to take away after reading the argument. That idea is the conclusion of the argument.

TEST BREAKER

Certain structural words can help you locate the conclusion. Look for words such as:

therefore	thus	hence	consequently
accordingly	so	as a result	it follows
suggests	indicates		

The premises of an argument are statements made by the author to support the conclusion. A statement, as we have said above, does not have to be factually true to be a premise.

TEST BREAKER

Structural words that indicate a premise include the following:

since	because
for	inasmuch as
insofar as	due to

Consider the following example and identify the conclusion and the premises.

Benson is not a professional tennis player. He has not played in a single professional tournament, whereas the majority of professional tennis players have extensive tournament experience.

What is the central point of the argument? The author wants to prove that Benson is not a professional tennis player. Do not be fooled by conclusions that are phrased as statements of fact, as is the case in this example.

We can rewrite the argument as follows:

Premise: Professional tennis players have extensive tournament experience.

Premise: Benson has not played in a single professional tournament.

Conclusion: Benson is not a professional tennis player.

With the argument in this form, it becomes clear how the author proceeds from the premises to the conclusion. Note that the actual sequence is not important: The logic of the argument is the same whether the conclusion follows the premises or precedes them.

There are few questions in the Critical Reasoning section that directly ask you to identify the conclusion of an argument. These questions are usually worded as follows:

— Which of the following best summarizes the author's main point?

The ability to identify the conclusions and the premises of arguments, however, is essential in order to answer almost all of the questions in the Critical Reasoning section.

ASSUMPTIONS

In an argument, an assumption is a premise that is not explicitly (directly) stated. These unstated premises are very important since the validity of an argument is determined by the validity of its assumptions.

Many questions in the Critical Reasoning section deal with assumptions, either directly or indirectly. Therefore, the second important skill you need to practice is recognizing assumptions in arguments.

Assumptions are the missing links of arguments. You can think about assumptions in visual terms. Imagine the premises of an argument as spans of a bridge leading to the conclusion. An assumption—an unstated premise—is a missing span. The author takes for granted that it is there, but we cannot see it. In considering an argument to find the underlying assumption, look for such missing links.

TEST EXAMPLE

> Since Governor Simpson is a member of the Blue Party, which endorses higher government spending on social programs, he will surely raise taxes.
>
> Which of the following does the argument assume?
>
> (A) Elected officials always enact policies endorsed by their parties.
>
> (B) The only way to increase government spending on social programs in Governor Simpson's state is to raise taxes.
>
> (C) The Blue Party does not tolerate dissent.
>
> (D) The Blue Party has the majority in the legislature of the state.
>
> (E) An increase in government spending always leads to an increase in taxes.

What is the underlying assumption in the example? Note that we are interested in the major assumption in the argument—the unstated premise without which the argument would not work.

To make it easier to see how the author proceeds from the premises to the conclusion and to see which premise is not explicitly stated, we can rewrite the argument as follows, clearly identifying the premises and the conclusion:

Premise: The Blue Party endorses higher government spending on social programs.

Premise: Governor Simpson is a member of the Blue Party.

Conclusion: Governor Simpson will raise taxes.

It is evident that the conclusion does not follow from the premises. In order for this argument to work, there must be another premise, which is assumed by the author. The most important missing link here is the connection between increased government spending on social programs and increased taxes. If we insert a premise that connects the two, the argument works.

Premise: Governor Simpson is a member of the Blue Party.

Premise: The Blue Party endorses higher government spending on social programs.

Assumption: The only way to increase government spending on social programs in Governor Simpson's state is to raise taxes.

Conclusion: Governor Simpson will raise taxes.

It is a good idea to formulate an answer to the question before considering the answer choices. If you cannot identify the major assumption, however, use the answer choices to help you. Take the choices one at a time and negate the statements they provide. Then look to see what happens to the argument. If the argument is not affected, the statement is not the major assumption. If the argument falls apart or stops making sense, you have found the major assumption.

We can test the technique on Example 1. Choice (A) says that elected officials always enact the policies endorsed by their parties. To negate this statement, we would say that elected officials do not always enact the policies of their parties. The argument is not affected by this; Governor Simpson may still raise taxes. Notice that since the argument is specifically about the Blue Party and Governor Simpson, it need not assume anything about parties and elected officials in general.

By negating the statement in choice (B), we get a claim that there are other means of increasing government spending on social programs in Governor Simpson's state besides raising taxes. If this is so, the connection between government spending and taxation is broken, and the argument falls apart. The statement in (B), therefore, is the major assumption (as we have stated above).

In (C) we are told that the Blue Party does not tolerate dissent. The argument is unaffected by this statement or its opposite.

Choice (D) states that the Blue Party has the majority in the state legislature. The opposite of this is that the Blue Party does not have a majority. Does this affect the argument? No, it does not. Therefore, this is not a major assumption.

Finally, choice (E) states that an increase in government spending always leads to an increase in taxes. This choice is tempting since, like (B), it establishes a connection between government spending and taxation. The opposite of the statement is that an increase in spending does not always lead to taxation. The specific argument about Governor Simpson's state, however, is not affected by this general claim. Therefore, the statement in (E) is not a major assumption.

The logic of an argument largely depends on the validity of its major assumption. For instance, in Example 1, if the assumption that the only way to increase spending on social programs is valid, the argument makes sense. However, if there are other ways to increase spending, the argument is shaky. But to judge whether the assumption is valid or not, we would need additional information.

On the Critical Reasoning section, you will see questions which ask you to state which piece of information would be relevant (or useful) to evaluating the logic of an argument. These questions, in fact, provide information which enables you to evaluate the validity of the arguments' assumptions. In dealing with such questions, identify the major assumption and then determine which piece of information would be most useful in evaluating that assumption.

TEST EXAMPLE

Doctors recommend a diet low in fat and high in fiber as the best preventative measure against heart disease. People concerned with their health should take fiber pills as a regular dietary supplement.

In order to evaluate the logic of the above argument, which of the following questions would be most relevant?

(A) How expensive are fiber pills?

(B) Do doctors recommend fiber pills to their patients?

(C) Do all doctors agree that a low-fat, high-fiber diet prevents heart disease?

(D) Are fiber pills effective in lowering dietary fat?

(E) How effective are fiber pills in providing the necessary dietary fiber compared to foods that are high in fiber?

The major assumption made in the argument is that fiber pills are the best source of dietary fiber. If this assumption is valid, the argument is logical. If, on the other hand, there is a better source of fiber than fiber pills, the argument does not make sense. Therefore, the answer to the question in choice (E) would be most relevant in order to evaluate the argument.

Choice (A) is of minor relevance since the cost of fiber pills would only be important in comparing them to other sources of fiber. Choice (B)—whether doctors recommend fiber pills to their patients—is not relevant to the logic of the argument. The answer to the question in (B) would add to a comparison of fiber sources, but it would not either validate or negate the argument. Choices (C) and (D) are not relevant since neither addresses the effectiveness of fiber pills as a source of dietary fiber.

STRENGTHENING AND WEAKENING ARGUMENTS

Questions that ask you to strengthen or to weaken an argument play a very important role in the Critical Reasoning section. These questions test your understanding of how arguments work and your ability to validate the logic of an argument or to undermine it.

Assumptions are central in strengthening and weakening arguments. As we have said, the validity of the major assumption made in an argument largely determines whether that argument is logical. Therefore, if you want to strengthen an argument, you should support its major assumption. If, on the other hand, you want to weaken an argument, you should undermine its major assumption.

TEST EXAMPLE

> The rate of unemployment has risen for the past five years. Some economists assert that the best way to combat this trend is to reduce capital gains taxes.
>
> Which of the following, if true, would most weaken the argument?
>
> (A) Reductions in capital gains taxes have been shown to stimulate investment.
>
> (B) The additional corporate profits which result from reduced capital gains taxes are usually distributed as stock dividends.
>
> (C) Reductions in personal income taxes have been shown to have a positive effect on the rate of savings.
>
> (D) Major government investments in infrastructure projects reduce unemployment rates.
>
> (E) The loss of tax revenue which would result from a cut in capital gains taxes offsets any gain from reduced unemployment benefit payments.

To weaken the argument, we must first identify the underlying assumption. The missing premise in the argument is one that connects a reduction in capital gains taxes to lower unemployment. The argument assumes that lower capital gains taxes lead to an increase in investment, which, in turn, creates more jobs.

Now we can consider the answer choices to see which one undermines this assumption. Choice (A) states that there is a connection between capital gains taxes and levels of investment. This supports the assumption made by the argument and, therefore, the argument itself.

Choice (B) tells us that capital gains taxes do not stimulate investment, but increase the dividends distributed to stockholders. This clearly invalidates the assumption underlying the argument.

Choices (C), (D), and (E) are essentially irrelevant since none of them addresses the major assumption of the argument.

TEST BREAKER

Although assumptions appear in a great number of questions, not all arguments employ assumptions in their reasoning. In looking to strengthen or to weaken an argument without a major underlying assumption, concentrate on the connection between the evidence and the conclusion. To strengthen an argument, select the answer choice which provides additional evidence for the conclusion. To weaken an argument, look for an alternative conclusion, which can be made based on the given evidence.

TEST EXAMPLE

The average temperature during the last three months has been two degrees lower than normal. The drop in temperature has been attributed to unusually high volcanic activity during the course of last year.

Which of the following, if true, best supports the argument?

(A) Temperature fluctuations of less than five degrees are not statistically significant.

(B) The cyclical El Niño, which greatly affects world temperatures, was at its lowest point last year.

(C) Volcanic ash in the upper atmosphere has been shown to reflect sunlight.

(D) There has been no volcanic activity over the last three months.

(E) Scientists have detected increased levels of elemental carbon, a by-product of volcanic eruptions, in the atmosphere.

Since we are asked to strengthen the argument, we need to find evidence to support the connection between volcanic activity and temperature. We can immediately eliminate choices (A) and (B).

Of the remaining three choices, only (C) provides evidence that supports the conclusion. Volcanic ash in the atmosphere reflects sunlight, allowing less solar radiation to reach the surface of the Earth. Since there has been unusually high volcanic activity, it is safe to assume that there is an increased concentration of volcanic ash in the atmosphere. Therefore, we can conclude that the lower temperatures are a result of the volcanic activity.

Choice (D) provides no evidence to support or to invalidate the argument. And choice (E) only provides evidence of increased volcanic activity.

METHODS OF ARGUMENT

There are no questions on the Critical Reasoning section that directly ask you to identify specific methods of argument. Two types of questions in the section do, however, test your familiarity with certain common methods of argument and your understanding of the reasoning used in these methods.

We will first discuss the methods of argument that appear on the GMAT and then look at the questions that involve them.

ARGUMENTS ON THE GMAT

Deductive Arguments

Deductive arguments are designed to prove definitively the author's conclusion. In a deductive argument, the conclusion necessarily follows from the premises. If the premises are true, the conclusion must be true. Deductive arguments use generalizations as premises to prove specific conclusions.

Premise: All dogs know how to swim.

Conclusion: My dog knows how to swim.

This example is a valid deductive argument. The conclusion follows necessarily from the premise: If all dogs know how to swim, my dog must know how to swim. The argument is valid, but untrue—it is unsound—because the premise is false.

Inductive Arguments

Inductive arguments use limited specific experience to support the probability of a generalized conclusion. In an inductive argument, if the premises are true, the conclusion is probably true.

Premise: The mail has been delivered to my new house by noon every day since I moved in three months ago.

Conclusion: The mail will be delivered to my new house by noon today.

In the example above, the conclusion does not follow from the premise. The argument is a relatively strong one, however, since the conclusion is probably true if the premise is true.

Causal Arguments

Causal arguments usually appear in explanations. An example of a causal argument is a scientific hypothesis that explains a natural event.

> e.g., Global warming is caused by the build-up of carbon dioxide in the atmosphere.

Quite often, causal arguments confuse correlation—coincidental occurrence—and causality. Do not assume that if X happened right before Y, X caused Y. Always consider alternative causes.

Statistical Arguments

Statistical arguments use statistics in their premises.

> Premise: Four out of five people surveyed preferred Meltdown detergent.
>
> Conclusion: Use Meltdown detergent.

Statistical arguments are often invalid because they use samples that are too small or are not representative of the group upon which the conclusion focuses. Be especially wary of arguments that make conclusions about the whole based on the attributes of its parts, or vice versa.

Analogous Arguments

Analogous arguments use analogies in their premises.

> Premise: Cigarette smoking has been shown to cause a number of diseases.
>
> Conclusion: Cigars, which are also made of tobacco, cause the same diseases as cigarettes.

The strength of analogous arguments depends on the similarity between the elements of their analogies. These arguments can never prove their conclusions, however; they can only support them.

Parallel Reasoning Questions

Parallel reasoning questions most directly test your grasp of different methods of argument. These questions follow one basic format. An argument is presented to you, and then you are asked to select an argument that uses similar logic.

You have to be careful to select arguments that parallel the ones given in the question as closely as possible. For instance, if the argument in the question is an unsound deductive argument (one whose premises are not true), you have to select the answer choice which also presents an unsound deductive argument. In other words, answers to parallel reasoning questions should reflect the argument completely, including logical flaws.

TEST EXAMPLE

Students who do well in science must also do well in mathematics. If they did not do well in mathematics, they would not do well in science.

Which of the following is logically most similar to the argument above?

(A) John received straight A's in math, chemistry, biology, and physics. People who do well in math must also do well in science.

(B) Baseball pitchers who injure their arms must retire. If they do not retire, they may be in danger of a permanent injury.

(C) Nine out of ten high-school dropouts find it difficult to support themselves. A diploma increases one's earning potential.

(D) Government must act to protect the environment. If the environment is not protected, the ecosystem will be irrevocably damaged.

(E) Criminals must have a history of antisocial behavior. If they were not antisocial, they would not have turned to crime.

To answer the question we must first identify the method of argument used. If you look carefully at the argument, however, you will notice that it is impossible to tell which of the two statements is the conclusion, and which is the premise. In fact, both statements say essentially the same thing. This is an example of circular reasoning.

We must, therefore, look for an answer choice that presents a circular argument. Choice (A) presents a weak inductive argument. Choice (B) presents an unsound deductive argument. In (C) we have a statistical argument. Choice (D) presents an invalid deductive argument. And finally, choice (E) presents a circular argument.

Inference Questions

Another group of questions that tests your understanding of methods of argument is comprised of several varieties of questions that ask you to draw inferences from given information. These questions are usually worded in one of the following ways:

– Which of the following can be inferred from the passage?

– Which of the following conclusions can most properly be drawn from the passage?

– If the above information is true, which of the following must also be true?

– If the above statements are true, which of the following is probably also true?

Notice that these questions focus on the connection between the premises and the conclusion. Pay particular attention to whether the question asks for the conclusion that must be true or the one that is probably true. Remember the difference between deductive and inductive arguments. Do not insert your own knowledge. And most importantly, do not make assumptions.

TEST EXAMPLE

Barry is shorter than Jim.
Dave and Jim are the same height.
Lon is taller than Dave.
Robert is taller than Barry.

If the above statements are true, which of the following must also be true?

(A) Robert is taller than Dave.

(B) Robert is taller than Lon.

(C) Jim is shorter than Robert.

(D) Dave is shorter than Barry.

(E) Lon is taller than Barry.

The question asks which of the statements must be true. In other words, we have to find the statement that necessarily follows from the given information.

To make things clearer, we can symbolize the information. Below are the four original statements in mathematical notation.

B < J

J = D

D < L

B < R

We can derive further information from these four statements. If Jim and Dave are the same height and if Jim is taller than Barry, then Dave is also taller than Barry.

B < D

If Dave is taller than Barry and if Lon is taller than Dave, then Lon is also taller than Barry.

B < L

Now consider the answer choices. Choice (A) says that Robert is taller than Dave. Both are taller than Barry. We have no way to compare the two to each other, however. The statement does not necessarily follow from the given information.

The statement in choice (B) claims that Robert is taller than Lon. Again, we have no grounds for comparison except for the fact that both are taller than Barry. Therefore, no definitive statement can be made.

Choice (C) repeats the same scenario. We cannot compare Jim and Robert directly.

The statement in (D) asserts that Dave is shorter than Barry. We know that this is wrong from the additional information we derived from the original statements.

Choice (E) states that Lon is taller than Barry. Again, from the additional information we derived, we know that this must be true. This statement follows necessarily from the given information. Therefore, the correct answer is (E).

STEP-BY-STEP STRATEGY FOR GMAT CRITICAL REASONING

1. Read the questions before reading the argument. This will help you focus your attention and get more out of your reading.

2. In reading the argument, identify the premises and the conclusion. Look for major assumptions. Think about whether the connection between the premises and the conclusion is logical.

3. After reading the argument, try to formulate an answer in your own words before considering the answer choices.

4. Do not make assumptions.

5. If you cannot decide which choice is correct, eliminate as many choices as you can and guess.

6. Do not second-guess yourself.

☞ Practice Drill 3

1. Research indicates that individuals who have served in the army tend to be more physically fit than other citizens of the same age. Obviously, the experience of serving in the army has an influence on the physical conditioning of these individuals.

    Which of the following, if true, would most strengthen the conclusion?

    (A) Individuals who volunteer for the army are more knowledgeable than other citizens about the benefits of exercise.

    (B) Individuals who have served in the army are more aware of the need to maintain good eating habits than are other citizens.

    (C) The research also indicated that those who did not serve in the army were more likely to smoke cigarettes.

    (D) The research results have been criticized as unreliable because of a bias in the recruiting of individuals for the research.

    (E) Individuals who volunteer for the army are not more physically fit than other people prior to serving in the army.

2. Bob: Johnson's batting average improved when he joined the Gray Sox. Obviously, the Gray Sox's hitting coach is better than the one the Cougars have.

   Jim: I read an interview with Johnson in which he said that his hitting started to improve when he got new glasses, right before he was traded to the Gray Sox.

   Which of the following best describes the weak point in Bob's argument on which Jim's response focuses?

   (A) Bob uses evidence from one case to make a general conclusion.

   (B) Johnson's batting average might decrease again.

   (C) Bob does not give exact figures to support his claim.

   (D) Bob assumes that the improvement in Johnson's batting average was a result of his being traded to the Gray Sox.

   (E) Bob does not mention the contribution of the Gray Sox's manager to overall coaching.

3. Public governments govern behavior, regulate businesses, set standards, and define certain acts as crimes. Private governments (a corporation, a school, a labor union, a family) may fine, suspend, or expel a disobedient member.

   Which of the following can be most reliably inferred from the passage above?

   (A) Private governments take their authority from public governments; so, in this, private governments may be empowered to execute offenders.

   (B) Only a public government can legally use force, imprison, or execute an offender.

   (C) Private governments may legally execute an offender on occasion in our country.

   (D) The jurisdiction of private government is all the individuals within a certain geographical area—a nation, a state, a province, a town.

   (E) Public government rules only the members of a particular group, like a corporation.

4. Leash laws should be strictly enforced. Last year, over 100 people were attacked by dogs.

Which of the following is assumed by the argument above?

(A) Leash laws are more effective in preventing attacks than bans on vicious breeds of dogs.

(B) Leashed dogs do not attack people.

(C) Government is responsible for ensuring the safety of its citizens.

(D) Dog owners resist leash laws.

(E) Dogs are naturally vicious.

5. Some research indicates that aluminum may be a cause of Alzheimer's disease, a disease that afflicts older people and that is characterized by a progressive loss of memory. According to one explanation, aluminum cookware could be the principal source of the aluminum causing the disease.

Which of the following, if true, would tend to weaken the above explanation?

(A) Aluminum cookware is not the only possible source of aluminum in the immediate environment.

(B) It is not always possible to know whether a patient is suffering from Alzheimer's disease or a stroke.

(C) There is no known cure for Alzheimer's disease.

(D) According to some research, there is a genetic factor that contributes to Alzheimer's disease.

(E) Alzheimer's disease occurs as frequently among those who have not used aluminum cookware as it does among those who have used aluminum cookware.

PRACTICE DRILLS

ANSWER KEY

Drill 1

1. (E) Main Idea Question

Choice (A) is too broad; the passage deals with only one aspect of seventeenth-century English history. Choice (B) is also too broad; undoubtedly religious dissent was only one of the political problems encountered by James I. Choice (C) is too narrow; the terms applied to Protestants are mentioned, but their definition is a minor point in the passage. Choice (D) is also too narrow. The authorization of the King James Bible is cited only as part of the evidence in the passage. Choice (E) fully and precisely describes the main idea of the passage.

2. (C) Detail Question

Statements II and III appear in three of the answer choices. Statement III is shorter; therefore, it should be read first. Paragraph one provides a clear answer to Statement III: The Scrooby nonconformists left England "because of the strict enforcement of the religious laws...." Since Statement III is acceptable, choices (A) and (B) are eliminated. Statement II appears in two of the remaining choices; it should be read next. The passage does not provide an answer to the question in Statement II. Therefore, choices (D) and (E) are eliminated.

3. (D) Inference Question

Choice (A) is wrong since paragraph two clearly states that Henry VIII was pressured into changing the ecclesiastical code. Choice (B) is contradicted in the third paragraph, where the author describes the religious debate fostered by the Reformation. The economic conditions of the Scrooby Puritans are not discussed in the passage; choice (C) is incorrect. The controversies fostered by the Reformation led to greater intolerance, as stated in paragraph four. Therefore, choice (E) is wrong.

4. (D) Tone Question

The King James Bible is discussed at the end of the third paragraph and in the beginning of the fourth. The author calls it a "magnificent translation." Clearly, the attitude is positive. We eliminate choices (A), (B), and (C). Now we have to choose between "laudatory" and "optimistic." "Optimistic," while positive, implies looking toward the future, which does not apply in this case. The author praises the King James Bible. Therefore, "laudatory" is the appropriate choice.

5. **(B) Logic Question**
This question asks you to describe the role of the second paragraph in the passage. The paragraph gives a brief summary of religious history in England in the years prior to the establishment of the Massachusetts settlements. The other choices present statements that are incorrect.

6. **(B) Detail Question**
This is a perfect illustration of why it is essential to read details in context. The sentence immediately preceding the one in question makes it clear that the "plant" is religious dissent.

7. **(C) Application Question**
Choice (A) is too narrow; James I and the Reformation are part of the supporting evidence, but are not at the center of the passage. Choice (B) is likewise too narrow. Choice (D) is irrelevant since life in Virginia is not even mentioned in the passage. While one of the reasons for the authorization of the King James Bible is alluded to by the author, there is no discussion of the translation's origin.

8. **(E) Inference Question**
In paragraph two, the author states that Elizabeth "wisely chose a middle course." Elizabeth instituted moderate reforms in the Church of England and was lenient in enforcing laws restricting dissenters. From this information and from the author's assertion that this course was wise, we can infer that it was the most effective—and therefore, most politically astute—approach to dealing with religious dissent.

Drill 2

1. **(C) Run-on Sentence**
The sentence is composed of two independent clauses joined by a comma. All the answer choices except (A) correct the structural error. However, we need to decide which one is the best choice. Choices (D) and (E) introduce new grammatical errors. In (D), the past perfect is used incorrectly. In (E), the construction requires the subjunctive "he miss." Both (B) and (C) are grammatically correct. However, (C) is preferable since it is more concise.

2. **(E)   Verb Tense**

Two actions are expressed in this sentence: "would have been better" and "would have sent." Since one action occurred before the other, both verbs cannot be in the same tense. Choices (B) and (C) repeat the original mistake. In addition, (C) uses the passive voice. Choice (D) also uses the passive voice.

3. **(B)   Subject-Verb Agreement**

The subject of the sentence is the plural *factors*. The predicate verb *is* is singular. Choice (D) repeats the mistake. Choices (C) and (E) introduce parallelism errors; all of the items in the list should be in the gerund form.

4. **(C)   Diction Error**

Like cannot introduce a clause. Choices (B) and (D) repeat the original error. Choice (E) alters the meaning of the sentence.

5. **(B)   Pronoun Reference**

The pronoun *he* refers to an ambiguous antecedent. Choice (D) repeats the error. Choices (C) and (E) change the meaning of the sentence.

Drill 3

1. **(E)**

The argument assumes that the better physical condition of the army volunteers resulted from their experiences in the army. To strengthen this argument, we need information that affirms this assumption. Choice (E) provides such information. Choices (A), (B), and (C) provide information that is essentially irrelevant to the argument. Choice (D) weakens the argument since it states that the evidence is unreliable.

2. **(D)**

Jim focuses on Bob's assumption that the improvement in Johnson's batting average is the result of his being traded to the Gray Sox. Jim presents evidence that contradicts this assumption. Choice (D) presents the weakness of Bob's argument that Jim addresses. The other choices present points upon which Jim does not focus.

3. **(B)**

Only choice (B) correctly reflects the information in the passage. Both (A) and (C) misrepresent the power of private governments. Such governments can never legally execute offenders. Choices (D) and (E) present erroneous definitions of private and public governments. In fact, each choice gives the direct opposite of the correct definition.

4. **(B)**

The argument assumes that dog attacks on people would be minimized if leash laws were enforced. In other words, it assumes that leashed dogs do not attack people. The other choices are essentially irrelevant to the argument.

5. **(E)**

To weaken this argument, we would need to demonstrate that there is no connection between the use of aluminum cookware and Alzheimer's disease. Choice (E) provides exactly such evidence. Choice (A) suggests that there might be another source of aluminum responsible for Alzheimer's disease. It does not, however, disprove the connection between the disease and aluminum cookware. Choices (B) and (C) are irrelevant. Choice (D) suggests that genetic factors may also play a role in causing Alzheimer's disease. This, in itself, however, does not break the connection between aluminum cookware and the disease.

GMAT CAT

Graduate Management Admission Test
Computer-Adaptive Test

CHAPTER 4:
Analytical Writing Assessment Review

Chapter 4

GMAT ANALYTICAL WRITING ASSESSMENT REVIEW

OVERVIEW OF THE ANALYTICAL WRITING ASSESSMENT (AWA)

The Analytical Writing Assessment (AWA) will be administered by a computer, but will not be computer-adaptive. You will compose and type the essays on the computer using basic word-processing functions. The essays will be scored at a later time—by both a computer program and a professor—and the scores will be sent to you as part of the official score report, approximately 10 days after your test date. You should bear in mind that the computer scorer may be less forgiving of structural, spelling, and grammatical errors—if only because these things simply will not escape its notice. By the same token, the computer will tend to look favorably on the use of transitional words and phrases like *first*, *consequently*, *as a result*, and *nonetheless*, and will likewise reward the essayist for accurate use of synonyms. The former is interpreted as evidence of a well-structured argument, the latter as indicative of a strong vocabulary.

This review includes sample essays, which you may use as a guide to score your own essays. Try to be as objective as possible when comparing your essays to those in this review, and base your score estimate on what you wrote, not on what you *assumed* or *meant* to write.

If you are unfamiliar with computers, or have difficulty typing, it is extremely important that you compose your practice essays on a computer using only simple word-processing techniques. In many ways, composing an essay on a computer is easier than paper-and-pencil composition, because it allows you to revise as you write without unsightly erasures or insertions. However, you should practice your typing skills so that the unfamiliar environment does not interfere with your ability to express your ideas clearly and fluently.

The AWA section of the GMAT CAT consists of two essay questions.

The essay responses will be used to inform score recipients of their prospective applicants' writing skills.

Each essay is scored by the computer and a human reader on a scale of 0 to 6, with 6 being the highest score. The readers take a number of criteria into account, based upon the particular essay section in question. (For more information on scoring, see Chapter 1.) The computer, called *e-rater*™ by ETS, is now considered one of the two expert readers who score the essay independently. Should the readers differ by more than a single point in their assessment, the essay is passed to a third reader who determines the final score. In the rare instances where the readers still disagree, a third professor is called in to referee the score.

What follows is a detailed guide to formulating your thoughts and executing your ideas when preparing for the AWA section of the GMAT.

STRATEGIES FOR ESSAY COMPOSITION

Before we examine the particular characteristics of each of the two essay types, it is important to review some general strategies for essay composition. Because you will have only one half-hour to write each essay, each minute will be precious. You must try to allocate your time to gain specific ends. You should not simply begin writing your draft without forethought or planning because design and organization are important facets of your score. Although time schedules will vary from person to person, you should budget your time more or less in accordance with the following schedule:

> ➤ Step 1   *First five minutes:* Carefully read the topic, then write down some ideas on paper. Try to develop an angle, perspective, and direction through which you can filter your ideas. This will help you subsequently to jot down a rough outline of your paragraph order.

> ➤ Step 2   *Next 20 minutes:* Work through your draft, paragraph by paragraph, trying as much as possible to follow the paragraph outline you had initially sketched.

> ➤ Step 3   *Final five minutes:* Reread your draft, correcting spelling, punctuation, or grammatical errors.

Adjust the schedule to your personal writing style and needs. To do this, practice before the exam with a clock to see where you need to expand or limit certain time periods.

Pre-Writing

Because you will not have time to revise extensively and/or rewrite your essay, the first five to ten minutes of your time will be the most important. The first thing you must do is carefully read through the topic at least twice, making sure you are clear on the precise nature of the assignment. Then comes the more difficult part: brainstorming for an approach. The worst thing you can do at this stage of the game is panic. You must concentrate on the task. Do not allow yourself to be distracted by the elapsing time. On the other hand, you must learn to think quickly and make firm decisions, for once a certain amount of time has elapsed, you have no choice but to continue with your original design. The only way to learn to plan carefully, quickly, and without nervous fear of the clock is to practice. Once you have honed your planning skills, you will be more prepared to work in this very limited time constraint.

In order to make the actual draft-writing segment of your task easier, you must first establish your direction, purpose, or thesis. After reading the topic, you must decide what unique perspective you will adopt to shape your essay. For example, for an "Analysis of an Argument" essay, you must decide whether you will predominately agree or disagree with the argument. Secondly, you must establish reasons why you will agree or disagree with the argument.

After you have established your perspective or angle, you must set up a rough outline to help ease the draft-writing segment that will follow. Your first paragraph will serve as both an introduction to the essay and as a statement of the direction you will take during the course of your work. A number of paragraphs will follow, each of which will contain a special purpose in the process of relating your essay's overall message. Finally, a conclusion paragraph is necessary to sum up your ideas and generally round out the essay.

Without an outline, you will be forced to pause before writing each new paragraph in order to think out your next step. With an outline, you merely need to glance at the ideas allotted for a particular paragraph and then express those ideas through your writing. An additional purpose for the outline is to ensure that all of the crucial elements required to score well on the essay are present in your composition. For example, the "Analysis of an Issue" essay requires examples to illustrate your ideas. Even if you cannot develop ideas for all of your examples during the planning stages, you can at least devote specific paragraphs to the development of illustrations. This way, you need not fear that you will overlook a crucial element in the midst of your hurried writing.

The Introductory Paragraph

Once you have decided on a direction for your essay, and sketched out a brief outline, you will need to begin the second-most difficult task: the opening paragraph and the statement of thesis. The thesis statement usually appears at the end of the introductory paragraph. This sentence allows your reader to understand both the point and the direction of your essay. While the introductory paragraph provides background information and prepares your reader for your discussion, the topic or thesis sentence will clearly state the issue you will argue during the essay, along with your stance on that issue. The thesis is not an accepted fact; it must be proven or argued. A good thesis takes a stand and challenges the writer to provide credible evidence, while stimulating the reader to think.

Supporting Paragraphs

Once you have established both the direction you will take and the point you are trying to prove in the essay, you must use logic to organize premises that support your argument. In order to do this, you must develop a step-by-step formula that defines the validity of your conclusion. For example, let us assume you are attempting to prove that rapid business expansion can often result in bankruptcy. In order to prove this assertion, you would need to provide concrete, specific reasons why unchecked growth in business might produce financial instability. These would be the basic premises of your argument.

In addition to listing the ideas that support your premises, you would have to make sure your many ideas are clear and understandable to your audience. Some useful devices to achieve this end are *definition, illustration,* and *analogy.* It might prove useful to define initially the precise meaning of "rapid business expansion" as it pertains to your argument. This would be a *definition* paragraph.

It would also be helpful if you provided examples that make your points clearer. For these purposes, you might refer to a specific case of which you are aware, or, if this fails, you can create a hypothetical business whose rise and fall you could invent on the spot to suit your purposes. These would be *illustration* paragraphs.

If you prefer to relate your ideas to examples that do not connect directly to the nature of your subject, you might create an *analogy* to suit your needs. In a very famous essay entitled "The 'Roast Pig' Problem," Rosabeth Moss Kanter focuses on the inability of expanding small businesses to recognize the elements contributing to their initial success. She relates the phenomenon to a village that accidentally discovered roast pork when a pig was trapped in a burning house; the unwise villagers then burnt down an entire house every time they wished to dine on roast pig. While this example has no direct correlation to the business world, as an *illustration* would, the situation represents a metaphoric parallel that proves useful to the reader.

You should also pay close attention to your transitions from paragraph to paragraph. In order for your essay to flow smoothly from one premise or example to the next, you must be careful to introduce your paragraph with words that connect your ideas. Simple transitions are words such as "first, second, next, in addition, also, therefore, in contrast, on the other hand, but, for example, as a result" and the like. Like signposts or signals, simple transitions help the reader move from one idea to the next, and provide linkages among both key and minor points. Complex transitions repeat or echo key phrases or ideas from above. These transitions keep the reader on track, unify the essay, and give it a sense of smoothness and flow. Without transitions, you will jar the reader and distract him or her from your own good ideas.

The Conclusion

Your final paragraph serves two purposes: to generally sum up what has gone before, and to leave the reader on a note of thought and future reflection. While a new topic should not be introduced in the final paragraph, it is important to leave the reader with a sense that the ideas in the essay merit future consideration; therefore supplying solutions to a problem or suggesting future prospects is a useful way to finish the essay. Also, be sure not to repeat every point over again in your conclusion's summary; simply restate the general premises of the argument in their relation to the essay's overall thesis.

Revision

Because you will be allotted only a half-hour to write each essay, there will not be enough time to revise your composition extensively. However, you should leave yourself at least five minutes to reread the essay carefully in order to pick out spelling, punctuation, or grammatical errors, as well as gross errors in syntax (such as leaving "not" out of a negative sentence). If time allows, you can even rewrite awkward sentences and attempt to smooth out transitions. But you should not feel compelled to rewrite the essay entirely, because the scorers will be well aware of your time constraints, and will be expecting merely a first draft, not a polished masterpiece.

Analysis of an Issue Essay

While you will find the above building blocks of essay composition useful for both essays in the AWA section of the GMAT, there are significant differences between the two. The purpose of the first essay, "Analysis of an Issue," is to respond to a given topic in such a way that expresses your opinion on the matter. You must take a stand on the topic, justifying your position with concrete reasons, and clarifying your argument with examples. The following is a sample essay topic for "Analysis of an Issue":

> Many new businesses are finding it difficult to survive in modern times without an enormous amount of financial backing. Many people recall "the good old days," when a person with a smart head, an ambitious heart, and a pocketful of change could start a potentially prosperous business. Today, however, larger companies continually swallow up smaller companies, or offer the type of competition against which no small business could ever hope to survive. However, larger corporations provide the country with a certain economic stability that would be lost if the nation were overrun solely with tiny businesses struggling to keep themselves alive.

The topic would be followed by suggestive questions such as:

> Which type of business described above, the small business or the large corporation, do you feel is most beneficial to both consumers and the business community at large? Explain your position, using relevant reasons and/or examples drawn from your own experience, observations, or reading.

This type of essay demands that you consider the two sides of a given issue. You must take a firm stand in expressing your opinion concerning the matter. When preparing for such an essay, write down any examples or ideas that come to mind on a piece of paper. Make sure that your introductory paragraph clearly defines both sides of the issue, and asserts your own position. Use supporting paragraphs to explain the elements that helped you to shape your opinion. Don't merely state your thesis statement. Instead, dissect your position into smaller parts, and devote individual paragraphs to explaining these component premises. It is important for you to provide examples that clarify either your position as a whole or individual steps that lead to your conclusion.

The essay will be scored primarily on the basis of the following criteria:

1) Willingness to explore ideas and develop a stance on the issue

2) Use of convincing reasons and clarifying illustrations

3) Clear and precise organization

4) Stylistic command of language skills

5) Grammar, punctuation, and spelling

Use the sample essays that follow this review to obtain a clearer idea of the differences among diversely scored essays. The first three essays respond to the sample essay topic introduced above.

Analysis of an Argument Essay

There are significant differences that separate the two essay types. Unlike the "Analysis of an Issue" segment of the AWA, the "Analysis of an Argument" requires you to evaluate the effectiveness of a particular idea or proposition. You must carefully analyze the line of thought followed in the argument. You must employ logic to dissect the argument, focusing on evidence and reasoning found in its thesis. In addition, you must add to the argument by making suggestions that would improve or clarify it further. The following is a sample essay topic of "Analysis of an Argument":

Television is about to become one of the most important resources of Americans today. With new cellular technology, hundreds of stations from around the world will be available at a user's fingertips. In addition, cellular television users will be able to call specific programs (movies, documentaries, etc.) onto their screens at the touch of a button. An entire world of information will be available to the modern television viewer, who will no longer be a passive "couch potato," but an active student of a global society.

The topic would be followed by suggestive statements such as:

Discuss how logically convincing you find this argument. In explaining your point of view, be sure to analyze the line of reasoning and the use of evidence in the argument. Also discuss what, if anything, would make the argument more sound and persuasive or would help you to better evaluate its conclusion.

When preparing for this essay segment, you must pay strict attention not so much to your opinion of the argument's ideas but to the logical framework that expresses those ideas. You must criticize the argument solely on the basis of the essay's contents. You are not judging the passage based upon your own outside knowledge of the situation. Instead, you are following the line of reasoning inherent in the argument and examining its internal strengths and weaknesses.

Your introductory paragraph should express your opinion of the argument's persuasiveness and logical effectiveness. Your supporting paragraphs should analyze the individual elements, reasons, and examples found in the argument. You should also include a paragraph that suggests what might be done to improve the argument and make it more convincing to a reader.

The essay will be scored primarily on the basis of the following criteria:

1) Ability to identify and analyze the most significant parts of the argument

2) Logical and clear organization and development of ideas

3) Use of smooth and clear transitions

4) Ample explanation for each criticism of the argument

5) Stylistic command of language skills

6) Grammar, punctuation, and spelling

Use the sample essays that follow this review to obtain a clearer idea of the differences among diversely scored essays. The second three essays respond to the sample essay topic introduced in this section.

ANALYSIS OF AN ISSUE SAMPLE ESSAYS

Each of the two essays will receive two scores that will be averaged together. The mean of all four scores will be your mark for the AWA portion of the GMAT. The scores run as follows: 6 (Outstanding), 5 (Strong), 4 (Adequate), 3 (Limited), 2 (Seriously Flawed), 1 (Fundamentally Deficient), and 0 (Unscorable). What follows are three sample essays (5-6; 3-4; 1-2) from each of the two essay sections. The sample essay topics were introduced in the previous sections.

Sample Analysis of an Issue Essay Topic

Many new businesses are finding it difficult to survive in modern times without an enormous amount of financial backing. Many people recall "the good old days," when a person with a smart head, an ambitious heart, and a pocketful of change could start a potentially prosperous business. Today, however, larger companies continually swallow up smaller companies, or offer the type of competition against which no small business could ever hope to survive. However, larger corporations provide the country with a certain economic stability that would be lost if the nation were overrun solely with tiny businesses struggling to keep themselves alive.

Which type of business described above, the small business or the large corporation, do you feel is most beneficial to both consumers and the business community at large? Explain your position, using relevant reasons and/or examples drawn from your own experience, observations, or reading.

Sample Essay Scoring 5 to 6

Despite the illusion of financial security offered by large corporations, this country's economy will crumble unless small businesses are given a chance. The fundamental flaw of large corporations' advocates is that they ignore the overwhelmingly negative consequences of the demise of small businesses. The formulating principle of this nation and all capitalistic societies is that every man and woman can pursue a prosperous life without bounds or limitations. However, the rise of the large corporation is turning this country into a place where ambition is discouraged, and competition unthinkable.

Advocates of large corporations ignore the fact that these businesses did not simply spring out of nowhere. Most of them began as small businesses that, through initiative and sweat, built themselves up into something far beyond their original expectations. Enterprising individuals, in an attempt to better themselves, found in this nation avenues for financial improvement.

America was famous for being a land of opportunity. For the first time, immigrants from countries with restrictive caste systems could choose their social standing for themselves; they were no longer forced to adopt a role imposed upon them at birth. Now, however, freedom for personal expansion and growth has become extremely limited by the presence of larger corporations. It is much more financially stable and lucrative to become an employee in a large company, and next to impossible to strike out on one's own. The very premises of this country's existence have been undermined by its own successes.

Let us imagine that an enterprising individual, Mr. Smith, is very ambitious and eager to make a comfortable living. He lives in a remote neighborhood where there is a need for a grocery store. Years ago, he might have simply found a backer to help him get started or borrowed enough capital from the bank to start a prosperous business. Now, however, in order to start a business with any chance of competing with the larger food store chains, Smith would have to pay a considerably larger fee to become part of a grocery store chain. If he were to strike out on his own, his business would always be jeopardized by the possibility that a Foodtown or an A&P would open up in his area. The only way he could compete with such a store would be to drastically reduce his prices, and this would turn his enterprising skills into a mere struggle for survival.

Of course, there are also advantages to large corporations. Job security and market stability are two important factors that they offer. However, a chain reaction has begun that will certainly end in disaster for this country. If the most ambitious individuals in this country are forced to be underlings in larger corporations, or, at best, buy into large corporations for the sake of competition, then more and more of our nation's outstanding individuals will vanish in the system. The successful ones will be those without initiative, those only willing to take the smooth road laid out by large corporations. Because of this, these corporations will suffer. Top executives will be those "smart" enough to play the game by the rules and squelch ambition in the process.

It is therefore imperative that small businesses be given a fairer chance. We have seen how large corporations stifle ambition and initiative, and how they are on the way to creating a society where conformity is the key to success. Perhaps the government can step in and create charters that will lend more advantages to people starting businesses. State budgets should devote portions of tax money to aid small businesses in peril. If not, our country will be sold to corporate giants that will turn our land of promise and dreams into a living nightmare.

Analysis of Sample Essay Scoring 5 to 6

This essay scores highly because of several factors. The writer shows a willingness to take a bold stand and support his or her position with concrete reasons and examples. There is a serious attempt on the writer's part to use descriptive phrases and vary sentence structure to avoid monotony. While his or her views are sometimes generalized and could use some additional support or evidence, they are presented clearly and consistently. There is an overall flow and direction to the essay; each paragraph follows the next in a specific order.

The first paragraph states the writer's perspective and suggests some of his or her reasons for maintaining that position. The second paragraph introduces the premise that large corporations owe their success to having been able to begin as small businesses. The third paragraph provides a reason why smaller businesses are having difficulty surviving in a world filled with large corporations. The fourth paragraph provides a hypothetical example, using "Mr. Smith" to illustrate that ambitious individuals were in a much greater environment in previous years than they are now. The fifth paragraph admits the advantages provided by large corporations but expresses the overwhelming penalties that they impose on society. The sixth paragraph reiterates the writer's position and suggests possible solutions to avert a potential catastrophe.

Sample Essay Scoring 3 to 4

It all boils down to this: is this a country about making money or isn't it? It's quite clear to me that if you aren't making money one way, you should be making it another. If small businesses are failing, then so be it. If they are doing well, then so be it. You've got to go with the flow. There's no question about it.

Large corporations have been around for a long time. They provide the nation with many excellent things. If it weren't for large corporations, we would find it very difficult to find the many things that we require in our daily lives. For example, fast food chains. If it weren't for fast food chains, everyone would have only two choices: cook at home or eat out at an expensive restaurant. But fast food chains all over the country (and all over the world for that matter) allow us to choose to pay cheap for a quick meal. Then you can go to the movies, or anywhere else, on time if you have to.

Small businesses are becoming a thing of the past. This is kind of sad, especially if you are fond of nostalgic general stores and such. But in order to survive in a capitalistic society, you've got to do what you must. And that could mean that large corporations are the only way to go for a career. It's just become too hard to survive it on your own.

There's been a lot of bad press lately about large corporations. But all we have to do is consider the facts. Thousands of jobs are provided by big companies, and now, with all the unions, high salaries come with the job. And you can strike if things are unfair or make you unhappy. This kind of thing would be a little silly in a small business. They'd just rehire your position, but that's not so easy in a large corporation.

Therefore, large corporations are the key to the future. Small businesses, however nostalgic and cultural, are sinking steadily into the depths of the past. In order to survive in today's world, you have to find a job working for someone else. If you don't find a job, you can try to survive on your own, but you won't find it easy. This isn't a good thing, but there's absolutely nothing that can be done about it. And besides, large corporations provide us with all sorts of things that small companies could never dream of doing, not by a long shot. And in order for a small business to become a large business, they have to go against the big shots, the "corporate giants" as it were. And unless they have the luck that David had with Goliath, they don't stand a chance.

Analysis of Sample Essay Scoring 3 to 4

This essay attempts to establish a firm position: "We have to accept the realistic fact that large corporations are the way of the future. Therefore, to start your own business is brave and praiseworthy, but pointless in today's society." However, it takes the writer a long time to get this message across. There are many vague and unclear statements that can only be deciphered after a good deal of interpretation. The essay often rambles on, restating the same point continually without offering new insight into the idea. It is often difficult to interpret the meaning of certain phrases because of the writer's frequent use of vague pronouns such as "it" and "this," as well as his or her pervasive use of the word "things." The essay demonstrates an effective command of spelling and punctuation, but sentence structure is sloppy, confusing, and monotonous.

The first paragraph attempts to establish the writer's position, but the execution is vague and ambiguous: it is difficult to determine just where the essay is going. The second paragraph demonstrates some of the advantages of large corporations, but uses a very poor example ("fast food chains") to illustrate the point that large corporations provide "the many things that we require in our daily lives." The third paragraph establishes an important point: the writer acknowledges the advantages of small businesses. He or she asserts, however, that the futility of starting such a business outweighs its potential merits. The fourth paragraph again states some of the advantages, such as unions, that are offered by large corporations. The final conclusion offers us no additional insight, and, for the most part, simply repeats the points that have been made previously in the essay.

Sample Essay Scoring 1 to 2

Busness. That's all we see and hear on T.V. nowadays. It's getting so you can't hear yourself think anymore. It don't matter whether the busness is small or big instead we should wonder whether its good or not good to worry about any of this. lets be frank, there are times when its good to where a shirt and tie and there's times when its good to kick back and just be yourself.

This country is too concerned with all this stuff; we should be concerned instead with moral issues. When a big company swallows a little company its a moral dilemma, not a social, political, economic dilemma. All those bigwigs in their big desks pushing papers and saying "sign this, sign that; buy this, sell that" when there's a lot of people starving to death on the sidewalks of wall street. Its like I said, its a moral dilemma.

If I had to make a choice it would be small busnes 99% of the time. No question. Big busness dont care about employees or thier famlys. Small busness is run by famlys most of the time. Familys care about each other, big busness don't care about nobody else but thier money. If they have to lay off everybody in the whole city, they'd do it in a flash if it would save them a couple of bucks.

So what do I think about the whole thing? Well, if you must know, I think that we shouldnt worry about these sorts of things. We should just live life happy and not worry about money. Then all those busness, big and little, would be up the creek without a paddle. Thats all I have to say about it.

Analysis of Sample Essay Scoring 1 to 2

This essay is extremely incoherent and difficult to follow. The inconsistent spelling, punctuation, and grammatical errors are only part of the problem. The more serious flaw of this essay is that it has no direction or flow. It seems, at times, as if the writer is favoring small businesses over large corporations; at other times, he or she seems to be attacking the very idea of organized businesses. There are scattered appeals to contemporary issues to provide emotional support, such as the mention of "people starving to death on the sidewalks of [W]all [S]treet," or the representation of small businesses as primarily family businesses. However, emotional appeals are lost when there is no structure or organization to the essay. The paragraphs drift from one point to the next with no sense of transition or unity. The colloquial expressions that pervade the essay ("good to kick back and just be yourself") also become distracting; their common use in society blinds the reader from what could have been an original and valid argument.

ANALYSIS OF AN ARGUMENT SAMPLE ESSAYS

What follows are sample essays for the "Analysis of an Argument" section of the AWA. The sample essay topic was introduced in a previous section.

Sample Analysis of an Argument Essay Topic

Television is about to become one of the most important resources of Americans today. With new cellular technology, hundreds of stations from around the world will be available at a user's fingertips. In addition, cellular television users will be able to call specific programs (movies, documentaries, etc.) onto their screens at the touch of a button. An entire world of information will be available to the modern television viewer, who will no longer be a passive "couch potato," but an active student of a global society.

Discuss how logically convincing you find this argument. In explaining your point of view, be sure to analyze the line of reasoning and the use of evidence in the argument. Also discuss what, if anything, would make the argument more sound and persuasive or would help you to better evaluate its conclusion.

Sample Essay Scoring 5 to 6

This passage makes a number of interesting points about the future of video technology in America. The author anticipates a vast array of resources available "at the touch of a button" for future users of cellular television. There are, however, a few assumptions made by the writer that require additional support. He or she assumes first of all that cellular technology will be marketed as an educational tool, and not solely commercialized as a supreme entertainment center. Even granting the assumption that a significant amount of cellular technology users will pool their new resources for the sake of research, we must question whether there is enough activity involved in the process to free these television viewers from the title of "couch potato."

The author identifies two principle uses for cellular television. He or she notes primarily that users will be able to access "hundreds of [television] stations from around the world." There is little doubt that this could indeed be a significant source of educational research. However, it would be ridiculous to assume that this is the avenue that will be pursued by most television viewers. This is clear to anyone with seventy cable stations filled with mindless drivel. The writer might have suggested that some sort of selection process be employed to choose a substantial percentage of research-oriented programming. Without this selection process, there would be "hundreds of stations from around the world" that provided the same commercialistic, mind-wasting rubbish.

Users will also be able to call up "specific programs (movies, documentaries, etc.)"; in effect, they will be able to view any known program at any time. This, on the surface, certainly seems to conform to the idea that cellular television users will become "active student[s] of a global society." It would be pointless to once again drill the point that such resources could be abused by those with no educational purposes in mind. A more serious concern involves those who would indeed be using this technology for proper research needs. What frightens me is that an unlimited supply of research "at the touch of a button" is not really "research" at all.

This can only be explained by redefining the connotations of the word "research." There is a certain quality of initiative and ambition that builds itself around the "research" conducted by an archaeologist in ancient Egypt as opposed to a high school student examining an encyclopedia to write a history report. It is for this reason that instructors send students to the library to quest for data rather than simply photocopy all the data their students could possibly require. The very act of searching for resources is a significant exercise in our mental development. If all we need do is punch in a few keys, there will be no challenge to the affair.

Seen in this way, we realize that something of the backbone of humanity will be lost if the connotations of "research" change this drastically. Faced with a seemingly infinite array of information before them, young students of the future will no longer be motivated by that drive which would compel them to seek out and find what humanity has yet to even imagine. Students of the next generation will be blinded by the illusion that all things are already known. Untold discoveries will be lost because that primal urge to explore and discover will be permanently extinguished by this cellular technology.

It would therefore be imperative that this technology be carefully utilized. The writer of this passage should have stressed the potential dangers of cellular television, as well as its benefits. For there is no denying that this will indeed be a supreme source of information. But it must be regarded solely as a tool, a way to rediscover that which has already been discovered. Its chief purpose should be to help those in the midst of researching matters unknown to humanity, not simply to appear as a source of infinite knowledge. For there will never be a time that we will know all. Unfortunately, with the rise of cellular technology, there may be a tragic time when we *think* we know all.

Analysis of Sample Essay Scoring 5 to 6

This essay scores strongly for a number of reasons. Its main strength is that it directly interacts with the passage. The essay shows a distinct understanding of the points made by the author, and reveals a lack of support in the author's assertions that: 1) cellular technology will be used primarily for educational reasons; 2) cellular research will be an active, not a passive, enterprise. The essay is clear, structurally sound, and easy to follow. Its various criticisms of the main passage are also clearly and firmly supported.

The introductory paragraph clearly states the two assertions with which the essay will contend. The second paragraph explores the first premise (entertainment vs. research) with regard to the author's mention of the many television stations that will be available to users of cellular technology. The third paragraph introduces the second premise (active vs. passive) with regard to cellular television's ability to call up "any known program at any time." The fourth paragraph continues this premise by defining some connotations of the word "research." The fifth paragraph continues this point even further by projecting the dark future that will result if cellular technology is abused in this manner. The sixth paragraph concludes by suggesting that cellular technology can indeed be an excellent source of productive research, as long as it is clearly labelled as a "tool" and not "as a source of infinite knowledge." This conclusion is weakened by the fact that the essayist has lost track of that other, less significant premise (entertainment vs. research). However, the depth of interaction between the essay and the passage more than makes up for this minor flaw.

Sample Essay Scoring 3 to 4

There's no doubt that this will be an excellent part of our society. We will be able to watch any television programs and movies that we desire. We will also be able to watch T.V. in Russia, China, or any other country that we want. This will put video technology into a new place. We will be able to trash our VCR's and rip out our cable wires. Cellular technology is here to stay.

I couldn't agree more with the writer that "television is about to become one of the most important resources of Americans today." Just imagine coming home from a long day at work and flipping on the television for a little entertainment. You'll be able to call up anything at all, and it will be there in seconds. Or if your a student, and you have to write a report on economics or literature or anything else, and you don't have time to go to the library or you don't have time to go thumbing through your books, then all you have to do is punch some buttons and call up some documentaries or the Discovery channel and you'll have everything before you, right at the proverbial "fingertips."

This will also free television viewers from that abominable label of "couch potato." No will have time to just sit around all day watching the same old boring stuff. Instead, they'll be punching keys like crazy, calling up all kinds of information and research. They'll be calling up the news from other countries, learning different languages, and just generally using their cellular technology for good things.

There is only one very important critique I can make about the passage. It states that a "world of information will be available to the modern television viewer." If you look at that word, "world," you realize how shallow the idea is. We can't expect the world to be contained in a television screen. This ignores the importance of the outside world, and the experiences that we have outside of our living rooms. The writer of the passage is implying some sort of virtual reality that will be contained in this cellular technology. She seems to be saying that our entire existence will consist of sitting in front of the television and pressing buttons. Whether she meant to sound that way or not, she should have stressed the fact that cellular technology will only be a part of our lives, not our entire lives in itself.

In conclusion, we have a lot to expect out of the cellular technology of the not too distant future. We'll be able to do all kinds of things that we never even dreamt of before. We'll be able to watch television all over the world, and call up movies and programs whenever we want to. But we must also remember that television, no matter how powerful it becomes, can never be allowed to dominate our lives completely.

Analysis of Sample Essay Scoring 3 to 4

This is a borderline essay for a number of reasons. Although the essayist does make occasional references to the passage, he or she spends too much time on personal tangents. The essayist is more concerned with the general concept of cellular technology than he or she is with the applications for that technology that are implied by the author of the passage. The essayist also fails to make a clear, firm stand regarding the premises of the passage's argument. It merely comments here and there without making definitive assertions. Paragraph order is arbitrary and without direction. Overall, the essay lacks design. It drifts from point to point without a dominating perspective. Key references to the passage are often vague and ambiguous due to a heavy use of vague pronouns such as "it" and "this," and a frequent use of the word "thing."

The first paragraph asserts the essay's overall agreement with the use of cellular technology, but does not even hint at the later misgivings that the essay's writer will portray. The second paragraph states some of the potential advantages and uses of cellular technology. The third paragraph agrees with the passage's assertion that cellular television viewers will be active users, not passive "couch potatoes." The fourth paragraph offers a critique of the argument; it notes that this technology will be abused if it takes the place of all other human experience. The fifth paragraph roughly sums up the essay's main points, offering no additional insight or direction to the essay.

Sample Essay Scoring 1 to 2

First it was celullar telephones. Now its cellullar TV. What will they think of next?

This is where I think the tecknology thing has gotten so out of hand. They keep coming up with new things day in and day out and never once do they think about using that mony for other things. its obvious to me that what we're in for is a bunch of spaced out monkeys sitting in front of the boob tube for the rest of their natural lives.

They may not be couch potatos any more, but that dont mean their not still lost to the good things in life, like taking walks and being with nature and going on hikes. These are the good things. Watching TV may be good for a little relaxation but its no good for expanding your mind. I dont care what they tell you.

Its just like this new virtual realty that they keep on making movies about. They want to replace the natural world with a fake one. I cant say I agree with that notion. Thats a bad thing to do. Anyone thats ever been to the beach and then come home to watch TV knows what that theres no comparison no matter whats on the set. It could be your favrite show but you still wish you where down on that beach.

I also dont buy the idea that it will be a good thing to have lots of TV stations to watch. There's never anything good on TV, not with 50 cable stations, not with 13 network stations, not with nothing. And it might be handy to be able to press a button and get any movie you want, and youll save yourself a trip to the video store, but that dont mean your not missing out, because you coulda been taking a healthy walk on the way to that video store.

To sum up, all I have to say is that this new technology could do us some good if we use it the right way. But we dont. Thats the plain and simple truth. We dont. Therefor we have to learn the rite way to use it or we're going to lose the one thing that really counts: Mother Erth.

Analysis of Sample Essay Scoring 1 to 2

This essayist makes very few references to the main passage. He or she barely grasps the general principles of the argument, and rambles continually on matters that are only peripherally related to the passage. There is no organized structure or flow to the essay. It often contradicts itself and makes statements that have nothing to do with its general topic. Spelling, punctuation, and grammar are seriously deficient throughout the essay. The essay is generally incoherent, difficult to follow, and makes very little sense. There are feeble attempts at using illustrations, such as that found in paragraph four, but these are too remote to lend any significant clarity to the essay's overall message.

GMAT CAT

Graduate Management Admission Test
Computer-Adaptive Test

Practice
Test 1

NOTE:

The following practice test contains more questions than the actual GMAT CAT. This is necessary to provide a score that is roughly comparable to the shorter computer-adaptive test. Although the format is different, this test will give you an accurate idea of your strengths and weaknesses, and provide guidance for further study.

PRACTICE TEST 1

Section 1

(Answer sheets are located in the back of the book.)

TIME: 25 Minutes
16 Questions

DIRECTIONS: Solve each problem using space on the page for scratchwork. Indicate the best answer from the choices given.

NUMBERS: All numbers used are real numbers.

FIGURES: Figures accompanying problems in this section provide information useful in solving the problems. They are drawn as accurately as possible; however, when a figure is not drawn to scale, more information will be provided. It is given that all figures lie in a plane unless otherwise stated.

---

1. In a particular state, the sales tax is $9^1/_2$ percent. In that state what will be the total cost of a $110 suit?

   (A) $116.35   (B) $117.85

   (C) $119.87   (D) $120.25

   (E) $120.45

2. $(3x)^2 - \dfrac{x^2}{9} =$

   (A) $\dfrac{8x^2}{9}$ (B) $2x^2$

   (C) $\dfrac{26x^2}{9}$ (D) $\dfrac{80x^2}{9}$

   (E) $9x^2$

3. $10^3 + 10^5 =$

    (A) 10^8 (B) 10^{15}

    (C) 20^8 (D) 2^{15}

    (E) 101,000

4. If x and 10 are relatively prime natural numbers, then x could be a multiple of

    (A) 9.   (B) 18.

    (C) 4.   (D) 25.

    (E) 14.

5. Evalute $10 - 5[2^3 + 27 \div 3 - 2(8 - 10)]$

    (A) -95 (B) 105

    (C) 65   (D) -55

    (E) -85

6. Bakery Z sells cookies for $7.20 a dozen. Bakery Y has a sale on the same cookies for $5.00 for the first 10 and $.80 a cookie after that. How many cookies could you buy from Bakery Y before the price exceeds that of Bakery Z?

    (A) 10   (B) 15

    (C) 18   (D) 20

    (E) 25

7. What is the area of the figure *ABCDE*?

    (A) 54

    (B) $54 + 9\sqrt{3}$

    (C) 63

    (D) $54 + 15\sqrt{5}$

    (E) 90

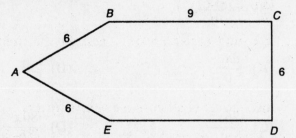

8. The mean (average) of the numbers 50, 60, 65, 75, x and y is 65. What is the mean of x and y?

(A) 67   (B) 70

(C) 71   (D) 73

(E) 75

9. A first square has a side of length x while the length of a side of a second square is two units greater than the length of a side of the first square. What is an expression for the sum of the areas of the two squares?

(A) $2x^2 + 4x + 4$ (B) $x^2 + 2$

(C) $x^2 + 4$ (D) $2x^2 + 2x + 2$

(E) $2x^2 + 3x + 4$

10. Mary got a 150 percent salary increase and is now earning $450 a week. What was her original weekly salary?

(A) $300   (B) $270

(C) $200   (D) $180

(E) $160

11. A room measures 13 feet by 26 feet. A rug which measures 12 feet by 18 feet is placed on the floor. What is the area of the uncovered portion of the floor?

(A) 554 sq. ft.   (B) 216 sq. ft.

(C) 100 sq. ft.   (D) 122 sq. ft.

(E) 338 sq. ft.

12. If a and b each represent a nonzero real number and if

$$x = \frac{a}{|a|} + \frac{b}{|b|} + \frac{ab}{|ab|}$$

then the set of all possible values for x is

(A) $\{-3, -2, -1, 1, 2, 3\}$.   (B) $\{3, -1, -2\}$.

(C) $\{3, -1, -3\}$.   (D) $\{3, -1\}$.

(E) $\{3, 1, -1\}$.

13. A man sold two-thirds of his pencils for 20 cents each. If he has 7 pencils left, how much money did he collect for the pencils he sold?

(A) $2.10   (B) $2.80

(C) $1.40   (D) $2.00

(E) $2.20

14. If $x = -3$, then $x^x =$

(A) $-\dfrac{1}{27}$.   (B) $\dfrac{1}{27}$.

(C) 27.   (D) -27.

(E) 9.

15. The area of $\triangle ADE$ is 12 square units. If B is the midpoint of $\overline{AD}$ and C is the midpoint of $\overline{AE}$, what is the area of $\triangle ABC$?

(A) 2 square units

(B) 3 square units

(C) $3\frac{1}{2}$ square units

(D) 4 square units

(E) 6 square units

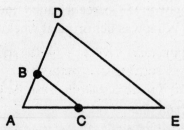

16. Louise leaves for a trip $1\frac{1}{2}$ hours before Larry and travels 50 miles per hour with a 30-minute lunch break. How many miles before Larry overtakes Louise driving 60 miles per hour?

(A) 300 miles   (B) 450 miles

(C) 500 miles   (D) 560 miles

(E) 750 miles

STOP

If time still remains, you may go back and check your work.
When the time allotted is up, you may go on to the next section.

Section 2

TIME: 25 Minutes
23 Questions

DIRECTIONS: Each passage is followed by questions based on its content. After reading the passage, choose the best answer to each question. Answer all questions based on what is indicated or implied in that passage.

The ocean is constantly in motion – not just in the waves and tides that characterize its surface but in great currents that swirl between continents, moving (among other things) great quantities of heat from one part of the world to another. Beneath these surface currents are others, deeply hidden, that flow as often as not in an entirely different direction from the surface course.

These enormous "rivers" – quite unconstant, sometimes shifting, often branching and eddying in a manner that defies explanation and prediction – occasionally create disastrous results. One example is El Niño, the periodic catastrophe that plagues the west coast of South America. This coast normally is caressed by the cold, rich Humboldt Current. Usually the Humboldt hugs the shore and extends 200 to 300 miles out to sea. It is rich in life. It fosters the largest commercial fishery in the world and is the home of one of the mightiest game fish on record, the black marlin. The droppings of marine birds that feed from its waters are responsible for the fertilizer (guano) exports that undergird the Chilean, Peruvian, and Ecuadorian economies.

Every few years, however, the Humboldt disappears. It moves out from the shore or simply sinks, and a flow of warm, exhausted surface water known as El Niño takes its place. Simultaneously, torrential rains assault the coast. Fish and birds die by the millions. Commercial fisheries are closed. The beaches reek with death. El Niño is a stark demonstration of man's dependence on the sea and why he must learn more about it.

There are other motions in the restless sea. The water masses are constantly "turning over" in a cycle that may take hundreds of years, yet it is essential to bring oxygen down to the creatures of the deeps, and nutrients (fertilizers) up from the sea floor to the surface. Here the floating phytoplankton (the plants of the sea) build through photosynthesis the organic material that will start the nutrient cycle all over again. Enormous tonnages of these tiny sea plants, rather than being rooted in the soil, are separated from solid earth by up to several vertical miles of saltwater. Sometimes, too, there is a more rapid surge of deep water to the surface, a process known as upwelling.

Internal waves, far below the surface, develop between water masses that have different densities and between which there is relative motion. These waves are much like the wind-driven waves on the surface, though much bigger: Internal waves may have heights of 300 feet or more and be six miles or more in length.

1. The primary purpose of the passage is to

   (A) criticize the general scientific community's lack of interest in oceanography.

   (B) explain the phenomenon known as El Niño.

   (C) describe various kinds of ocean movements.

   (D) call attention to the destructive nature of the ocean.

   (E) prove that subsurface ocean currents exist.

2. The passage contains information that answers which of the following questions?

   I.   How does "turning over" contribute to the nutrient cycle?

   II. Why does the Chilean guano industry suffer from the presence of El Niño?

   III. Why are the movements of under-surface "rivers" unpredictable?

   (A) I only   (B) I and II only

   (C) I and III only   (D) II and III only

   (E) I, II, and III

3. Which of the following best describes the organization of this passage?

   (A) Paragraphs two through five describe deep, hidden movements mentioned in paragraph one.

   (B) Paragraphs two and three describe harmful ocean movements, while paragraphs four and five describe beneficial ones.

(C) Paragraphs two through five describe movements that cannot be seen but whose effects are felt.

(D) Paragraphs two and three describe great surface currents, while paragraphs four and five describe deep, hidden movements.

(E) Paragraphs two through five describe various kinds of great surface currents.

4. According to the passage, all of the following result from the presence of the Humboldt Current EXCEPT

(A) abundant marine bird-life. (B) commercial fisheries.

(C) abundant rainfall. (D) fertilizer industries.

(E) game fish.

5. It can be inferred from the passage that oceanographers

(A) have spent little time studying El Niño.

(B) will eventually be able to convert El Niño's harmful effects to beneficial ones.

(C) do not yet understand why El Niño is as destructive as it is.

(D) will probably never be able to provide much help to the countries most affected by El Niño.

(E) cannot yet accurately predict or explain El Niño's periodic appearances.

6. The root cause of damage resulting from El Niño is

(A) a change in shoreline water temperature.

(B) the "turning over" of water masses.

(C) the surfacing of phytoplankton.

(D) the variation in rainfall.

(E) the absence of sea-floor nutrients.

7. Peruvian guano exports depend on

(A) El Niño's periodic appearance.

(B) the presence of internal waves in offshore water masses.

(C) occasional torrential rainfall.

(D) the presence of the Humboldt Current.

(E) an abundant black marlin population.

8. According to the passage, oceanic nutrient cycles depend primarily on which of the following?

(A) Internal waves   (B) Upwelling

(C) Swirling surface currents   (D) Subsurface rivers

(E) Turning over

9. Which of the following statements is best supported by information in the passage?

(A) El Niño could be eliminated with further study.

(B) Man will eventually harness the power generated by ocean movements.

(C) The behavior of oceanic subsurface movements can be reliably predicted by observing surface movements.

(D) Hidden ocean movements have enormous environmental impact.

(E) Though larger than surface waves, internal waves behave like surface waves because both are wind-driven.

Soon a canoe, with a little flag flying, was seen approaching, with one of the men in it washing the paint off his face. This man was poor Jemmy,—now a thin haggard savage, with long disordered hair, and naked, except a bit of a blanket round his waist. We did not recognize him till he was close to us; for he was ashamed of himself, and turned his back to the ship. We had left him plump, fat, clean, and well dressed;—I never saw so complete and grievous a change. As soon however as he was clothed, and the first flurry was over, things wore a good appearance. He dined with Captain Fitz Roy, and ate his dinner as tidily as formerly. He told us he had "too much" (meaning enough) to eat, that he was not cold, that his relations were very good people, and that he did not wish to go back to England: in the evening we found out the cause of this great change in Jemmy's feelings, in the arrival of his young and nice-looking wife. With his usual good feeling, he brought two beautiful otter-skins for two of his best friends, and some spear-heads and arrows made with his own hands for the Captain. He said he had built a canoe for himself, and he boasted that he could talk a little of his own language! But it is a most singular fact, that he appears to have taught all his tribe some English: an old man spontaneously announced "Jemmy Button's wife." Jemmy had lost all his property.

Jemmy went to sleep on shore, and in the morning returned, and remained on board till the ship got under weigh, which frightened his wife, who continued crying violently till he got into his canoe. He returned loaded with valuable property. Every soul on board was heartily sorry to shake hands with him for the last time. I do not now doubt that he will be as happy as, perhaps happier than, if he had never left his own country. Every one must sincerely hope that Captain Fitz Roy's noble hope may be fulfilled, of being rewarded for the many generous sacrifices which he made for the Tierra del Fuegians, by some shipwrecked sailor being protected by the descendants of Jemmy Button and his tribe! When Jemmy reached the shore, he lighted a signal fire, and the smoke curled up, bidding us a last and long farewell, as the ship stood on her course into the open sea.

10. The primary purpose of this passage is to

   (A) suggest that a good meal improved Jemmy Button's disposition.

   (B) argue that Jemmy Button had been forced to give up his property.

   (C) explain the effects of civilization on Jemmy Button.

   (D) show how Jemmy Button had changed.

   (E) detail ways for improving Jemmy Button's life.

11. According to information in the passage, which of the following is true?

   I.   Jemmy Button was an English sailor who preferred living in Tierra del Fuego.

   II. Jemmy Button was a missionary who had been adopted by the people of Tierra del Fuego.

   III. Jemmy Button was a native of Tierra del Fuego who had visited England.

   (A) I only   (B) II only

(C) III only   (D) I and II only

(E) II and III only

12. The author would most likely agree with which of the following statements about his feelings toward Jemmy Button?

(A) The author had admiration for Jemmy Button because he had managed to survive under such adverse conditions.

(B) The author showed Jemmy Button the respect he was due as the head of his tribe.

(C) The author was appalled by the degraded condition of Jemmy Button and did not understand why he would not improve himself.

(D) The author genuinely cared about Jemmy Button and wanted him to be content.

(E) The author felt contempt for Jemmy Button that he could be satisfied living in such terrible conditions.

13. According to the passage, Jemmy Button was presented as being an amiable sort of person according to all of the following evidence EXCEPT

(A) Jemmy washed the paint off his face when he came to greet the sailors.

(B) Jemmy gave presents to two of his friends and the Captain.

(C) Jemmy seemed concerned that his friends believed he had enough to eat and was happy.

(D) Jemmy had persuaded his tribe to learn some words of English.

(E) the sailors were sorry to leave Jemmy on Tierra del Fuego.

14. From information in the passage, it can be inferred that Jemmy Button held which of the following opinions about material possessions?

(A) He valued objects but was unable to protect himself from thieves.

(B) He felt that objects were appropriate to give to his white friends but not to keep for himself.

(C) He valued objects but lived in a society that shared with others.

(D) He felt that objects were useful only for utilitarian purposes.

(E) He thought the only use for objects was as a means of trade for food.

15. The passage suggests that Jemmy felt civilized society was

(A) admirable for others but not something he valued.

(B) the pinnacle of his success and he was ashamed that he could not carry on the tradition.

(C) something which had given him a valuable insight into the nature of the sailors.

(D) a wonderful blessing for everyone involved.

(E) appropriate for others but not something he wished to choose for himself.

16. It can be inferred from the passage that Jemmy Button

(A) was a particular friend of Captain Fitz Roy.

(B) ignored all but the most important people on board the ship.

(C) had known and lived with the people on the ship at some time in the past.

(D) felt degraded by having to board the ship and present himself to the others.

(E) did not hold Captain Fitz Roy in high esteem.

17. In the passage, the author is primarily concerned with

(A) predicting the consequences of a practice.

(B) recalling the results of an experiment.

(C) analyzing two sides of an opposing argument.

(D) proposing a solution to a problem.

(E) criticizing a point of view.

Legislative and regulatory efforts tend to reflect the concerns of franchisees, or potential franchisees, which fall generally within two broad groups. The first involves problems which arise prior to entering a franchise relationship, particularly deception or impropriety in the presentation, solicitation, or sale of a franchise opportunity. The second group involves problems arising within ongoing franchising relationships, generally involving contract performance, termination, or renewal of franchise agreements.

Federal authority to regulate franchise sales derives from the FTC's Trade Rule 436—"Disclosure Requirements and Prohibitions Concerning Franchising and Business Opportunities Ventures." This "Franchise Rule" is intended to provide prospective franchisees with the information necessary to make informed decisions by requiring franchisors or franchise brokers to disclose detailed information relating to twenty separate aspects of a franchise offering. Information to be disclosed includes all relevant facts about the identity, location, business experience and financial background of the franchisor, detailed descriptions of the franchise opportunity, including all initial and continuing fees and payments, and an explanation of all terms, obligations, conditions, and requirements of the franchise agreement.

Under the rule franchisors are not required to make claims regarding actual or potential sales, income, or profits of existing or proposed franchises. If a franchisor chooses to make such claims, however, the rule prescribes the manner in which claims can be made and requires that a reasonable basis exist to substantiate the accuracy of all claims. Failure to provide information required under the rule, or providing of false information or information inconsistent with that required under the rule, are considered violations of the FTC Act and subject to civil penalty actions with fines of up to $10,000 per violation.

To simplify disclosure and encourage compliance with both federal and state disclosure requirements, the FTC permitted franchisors to use either the disclosure format provided in its franchise rule or a similar set of detailed guidelines incorporated in the Uniform Franchise Offering Circular (UFOC).

In general, the FTC presumes the adequacy and accuracy of circulars submitted under state registration procedures, while reserving authority to determine compliance in non-regulation states and to enforce broad violations of its rule by national franchisors.

While claiming this broad authority, the FTC has often been reluctant to use it. For most of the period from 1979 through 1987, the agency's principal approach to rule enforcement involved monitoring compliance and encouraging franchisors to correct potential violations. While this approach was well-suited to the anti-regulation orientation of the Reagan Administration, it was severely criticized by state administrators and franchisee organizations. During this seven-year period, the FTC brought a total of fifteen enforcement actions—thirteen involving violations of the franchise rule and two involving misrepresentations by franchisors falling outside the scope of the rule. In contrast, state regulatory agencies commenced 1,026 enforcement actions during the three-year period between 1986 and early 1989.

18. The primary purpose of the passage is to

(A) demonstrate the need for reforms in the existing franchise laws.

(B) explain why businesses have so many complaints against regulations of franchises by the federal government.

(C) describe some of the problems in franchise laws and regulatory bodies.

(D) urge the federal government to ease the regulations on franchises.

(E) argue that many problems of franchises go unaddressed and unresolved.

19. The passage supplies information for answering which of the following questions?

(A) Why is the FTC so active in regulation of franchises?

(B) Which states are considered highly regulatory of franchises?

(C) Which FTC trade rule authorizes regulation of franchises?

(D) What penalties are involved in not fully disclosing business experience of the franchisor?

(E) Why has the FTC been reluctant to use its authority in determining compliance in non-regulation states?

20. The author mentions that there are two broad groups of legislative and regulatory efforts in order to

(A) expand on the regulatory efforts of groups of states.

(B) delineate the complexity of regulations dealing with franchises.

(C) describe problems with sales of franchises.

(D) argue for restructuring of enforcement responsibilities within the FTC.

(E) show how state and federal regulations mesh.

21. The passage supplies information to suggest that

    (A) most franchisors will not make claims regarding actual or potential sales unless required to by state regulations.

    (B) the FTC's Trade Rule 436 provides potential franchisees with a standard form with which to make informed decisions about purchasing a franchise.

    (C) the civil penalty actions and fines for violations of the FTC Act preclude any abuses of the figures in sales agreements.

    (D) the Uniform Franchise Offering Circular is a simplified form of the document provided by the FTC.

    (E) the FTC checks carefully the adequacy and accuracy of circulars submitted under state registration proceedings.

22. According to the article, the approach of the FTC has been most agreeable to which of the following groups?

    (A) Franchisors

    (B) Franchisees

    (C) Administrators of regulating states

    (D) Administrators of non-regulating states

    (E) Consumer advocacy groups

23. It can be inferred from the passage that

    (A) federal franchise disclosure requirements have been strongly enforced.

    (B) federal franchise laws are not uniform.

    (C) the FTC is stringent about sellers using correct forms during the sales proceedings.

    (D) information about potential profits of a franchise are irrelevant to its sale.

    (E) there is no federal law governing franchise relationships or practices.

STOP

If time still remains, you may go back and check your work.
When the time allotted is up, you may go on to the next section.

Section 3

TIME: 25 Minutes

20 Questions

DIRECTIONS: Each of the data sufficiency problems below contains a question and two statements, labeled (1) and (2), in which certain data are given. Decide whether the data given in the statements are sufficient for answering the question. Using the data given in the statements plus your knowledge of mathematics and everyday facts choose:

(A) if Statement (1) ALONE is sufficient, but statement (2) alone is not sufficient to answer the question asked;

(B) if Statement (2) ALONE is sufficient, but statement (1) alone is not sufficient to answer the question asked;

(C) if BOTH Statements (1) and (2) TOGETHER are sufficient to answer the question asked, but NEITHER statement ALONE is sufficient;

(D) if EACH Statement ALONE is sufficient to answer the question asked;

(E) if Statements (1) and (2) TOGETHER are NOT sufficient to answer the questions asked, and additional data specific to the problem are needed.

NUMBERS: All numbers are real numbers.

FIGURES: A figure in this section will conform to the information given, but will not necessarily conform to the additional information given in the numbered Statements (1) and (2).

NOTES: Lines are straight if shown as straight, and angle measures are greater than zero.

The position of points, angles, regions, etc., exist in the order shown.

All figures lie in a plane unless otherwise stated.

Sample Question:

In the figure, the two circles are concentric (have the same center O) with radius x and y, where $x < y$. What is the area of the shaded region?

(1) The sum of the two radii is 11 units.

(2) The area of the smaller circle is $1/2$ of the area of the larger one.

Sample Explanation:

(C) By Statement (1), $x + y = 11$. Since Statement (1) gives no other information about x and y, you cannot find the areas of the two circles. Since the area of the shaded region is the difference of the two areas, Statement (1) alone is not sufficient. According to Statement (2), $\pi y^2 = 2\pi x^2$; therefore, the area of the region is $2\pi x^2 - \pi x^2 = \pi x^2$. Since (2) does not give the value of x, it is not possible to find the area of the shaded region using (2) alone. However, if we use (1) and (2) together, we get the two equations

$$y = 11 - x \text{ and } \pi y^2 = 2\pi x^2$$

from which we can solve for x by writing the single equation $\pi(11 - x)^2 = 2\pi x^2$.

1. What is the distance from city A to city B?

   (1) Jane drives the trip at an average speed of 50 kilometers per hour.

   (2) Sally takes 3 hours to drive between the two cities.

2. A straight wire of length l is cut into two pieces and a ring is formed from one piece and a square from the other. If there was no overlap what is the width of the square?

   (1) The sum of the perimeters is 16 units.

   (2) The sum of the area of the circle and the area of the square is 21 square units.

3. In the figure, if $\triangle ABC$ is similar to $\triangle ADE$ and $AD = 2$, then what is the value of BC?

   (1) Area of $\triangle ABC$ = four times area of $\triangle ADE$.

   (2) $AC = 4$ units.

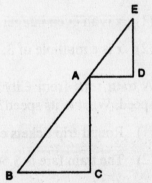

4. The figure shown represents what is left of a pizza. If O is the center, what is the radius of the pizza?

   (1) $\angle AOB = 60°$.

   (2) The length of $\overset{\frown}{ACB}$ is 20π inches.

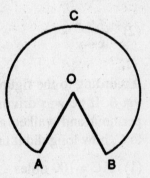

5. What is the value of z?

   (1) $z > 0$

   (2) $z^2 + z - 2 = 0$

6. The chart below shows how Jenny divides the money she saves. How much does Jenny have in her money market accounts?

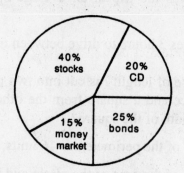

(1) She has $15,000 in bonds.

(2) She has $36,000 in stocks and CDs.

7. Is x a multiple of 4?

(1) x is an even integer.

(2) x is a multiple of 3.

8. A train runs from City A to City B, back and forth, at a constant speed. What is its speed?

(1) Round-trip tickets cost $81.25.

(2) The train fare is $.50 per mile.

9. If $y \ne x$, what is the value of y?

(1) $\dfrac{2y}{2x-1} = 1$

(2) $\dfrac{x+y}{x-y} = 1$

10. According to the figure, it took Michael one hour to get from A to C, via B. If he was driving from A to B at a constant speed of 25 miles per hour and walked at a constant speed of 5 miles per hour from B to C, how long did it take him to get from A to B?

(1) AC = 100 miles

(2) BC = .3 miles

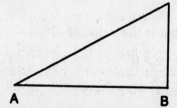

11. For a certain interview of students in New York State, x number of towns were selected, from each town x number of schools were selected and from each school x number of students were interviewed. Is x even?

    (1) The total number of students interviewed was even.

    (2) An even number of students were interviewed from each town.

12. A change machine takes only a $1 bill. How many quarters, dimes, and nickels did Joanna get in exchange?

    (1) Joanna changed $5.

    (2) Each time a $1 bill is inserted the machine releases three quarters and the rest in dimes and nickels.

13. In the 1988-89 academic year, 40 percent of the students in public schools are boys while 60 percent are girls. What percentage of the 10th graders are girls?

    (1) $\dfrac{1}{3}$ of the girls in public schools are 10th graders.

    (2) $\dfrac{3}{5}$ of the boys in public schools are 10th graders.

14. Paul ordered a certain number of books by mail from Academic Press publishers. If he had to enclose payment in the amount of $91.40, which includes sales tax and a payment for postage and handling, what was the price of each book?

    (1) The sales tax for each book was 8%.

    (2) Payment for postage and handling was $1.25 per book.

15. The average age of students in Classroom A is 15. If the number of students in Classroom B is higher than that of A by 5, what is the average age for Classroom B?

    (1) The average age for students in Classrooms A and B together is 20.

    (2) There are 20 students in Classroom A.

16. An open box is to be formed by cutting from the corners of a square piece of cardboard, along the dotted lines, and folding. What is the volume of the box to be formed?

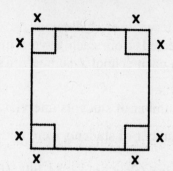

(1) The area of the cardboard was 49 square inches.

(2) The width of the cardboard is 7 inches.

17. If x, y are integers what is the value of xy?

(1) xy divides 336.

(2) x and y are prime numbers.

18. In the summer of 1989 there was only one economics course and one business course taught in a small college. If 3 girls dropped business and 4 boys added it, while 2 girls dropped and 3 boys added economics, how many girls are still taking the business course?

(1) There were 12 students in the economics class at the beginning.

(2) There are the same number of students in the two classes after adding and dropping.

19. What is the area of a triangle?

(1) Its base lies on the x-axis.

(2) The two sides lie on the graph of $y = 1 - |x|$.

20. Is $|x| < 1$?

(1) $x^4 - 1 > 0$

(2) $\dfrac{1}{1 - |x|} > 0$

STOP

If time still remains, you may go back and check your work.
When the time allotted is up, you may go on to the next section.

Section 4

TIME: 25 Minutes
22 Questions

DIRECTIONS: In each of the following sentences, some part of the sentence or the entire sentence is underlined. The five answer choices give various ways of phrasing the underlined part. The first choice repeats the given sentence. Pay attention to grammar, choice of words, and sentence construction in order to select the best version of the sentence. Choose (A) if you think the given sentence is correct.

---

1. It would have been better for everyone concerned in this situation if she would have sent a more detailed letter to the other company in question.

    (A) she would have sent a more detailed letter to the other company in question.

    (B) she would have sent a more detailed letter to the company she has been discussing.

    (C) a more detailed letter would have been sent to the aforementioned company.

    (D) a more detailed letter had been sent to the other company.

    (E) she had sent a more detailed letter to the other company.

2. Yesterday, there were fewer members of the legislature who talked like they were in favor of a tax increase for the public citizens.

    (A) Yesterday, there were fewer members of the legislature who talked like they were in favor of a tax increase for the public citizens.

    (B) Yesterday, less members of the legislature talked to the public like they were in favor of a tax increase.

    (C) Yesterday, there were fewer members of the legislature who talked as if they were in favor of a tax increase for citizens.

(D) Publicly, there were less members of the legislature talking like they were in favor of raising taxes.

(E) For the public, fewer members of the legislature talked yesterday about raising taxes.

3. A frequent problem <u>which is faced by homeowners</u> is the necessity of regular maintenance.

(A) which is faced by homeowners

(B) which a homeowner faces through his purchase

(C) not dealt with by apartment dwellers

(D) of the average homeowner

(E) homeowners face

4. <u>Totalling more than she had anticipated, the bride was shocked by the costs of flowers, food, and entertainment</u>.

(A) Totalling more than she had anticipated, the bride was shocked by the costs of flowers, food, and entertainment.

(B) The costs of food, flowers, and entertainment was shocking to the bride because it was more than she had expected.

(C) The costs of food, flowers, and entertainment were shocking to the bride totalling more than anticipated.

(D) Totalling more than she had anticipated, the costs of food, flowers, and entertainment shocked the bride.

(E) Shocking her, the bride had not anticipated the costs of food, flowers, and entertainment.

5. The state legislature is considering several bills, <u>among which is a bill making being behind the wheel of a powerboat drunk a misdemeanor</u> punishable by a fine and a jail sentence.

(A) among which is a bill making being behind the wheel of a powerboat drunk a misdemeanor

(B) among which is a bill that makes being drunk behind the wheel of a powerboat a misdemeanor

(C) among which is a bill that makes it a misdemeanor being drunk behind the wheel of a powerboat

(D) one bill a misdemeanor to be drunk behind the wheel of a powerboat

(E) among which is a bill making piloting in a drunken state a powerboat a misdemeanor

6. Surely you can see that this briefcase <u>greatly differs from the one over there in price and quality</u>.

(A) greatly differs from the one over there in price and quality.

(B) has a great difference from the one over there in price and quality.

(C) differs from the one over there greatly in price and quality.

(D) greatly differs with that one when taking into consideration things such as price and quality.

(E) differing greatly with the one over there in price and quality.

7. We asked Sandy Chen <u>to try and run the computer program as soon as possible</u> so we could check for problems.

(A) to try and run the computer program as soon as possible

(B) to try to run the computer program as soon as possible

(C) about trying to run the computer program possibly soon

(D) about trying and running the computer program as soon as possible

(E) when the computer program would possibly be run

8. Riding a bicycle is <u>in some ways like when you learn to roller skate in that once you learn how, you never forget</u>.

(A) in some ways like when you learn to roller skate in that once you learn how, you never forget.

(B) similar in some ways like when you learn to roller skate you never forget.

(C) is like never forgetting how to roller skate.

(D) similar to roller skating because once you learn how, you never forget.

(E) alike in some ways to roller skating in that once you learn how, you never forget.

9. <u>If you cut your scalp, you should</u> flush the wound with sterile water and apply a pressure dressing which consists of a sterile gauze or cloth bandage wound into a turban.

   (A) If you cut your scalp, you should

   (B) In cutting your scalp, you should

   (C) When you cut your scalp, you should

   (D) If one cuts his scalp, one should

   (E) If a person cuts his scalp, one should

10. People who have been knocked unconscious should be taken to a hospital immediately, especially if they <u>appear confused or sluggish, and a close watch should be kept if they have difficulty walking</u>.

    (A) appear confused or sluggish, and a close watch should be kept if they have difficulty walking.

    (B) appear to be sluggish or are confused, and a close watch should be kept if they have difficulty walking.

    (C) are sluggish, confused, or they should be watched closely if they have difficulty walking.

    (D) are sluggish, appear confused, or have been watched closely for difficulty in walking.

    (E) appear confused or sluggish, and they should be watched closely if they have difficulty walking.

11. An exceptionally good sport fish in the Bahamas and Florida Keys, <u>many fun hours can be spent challenged by muttonfish</u>.

    (A) many fun hours can be spent challenged by muttonfish.

    (B) muttonfish can be hourly challenging and fun.

    (C) muttonfish can provide hours of fun and challenge.

    (D) for many hours the muttonfish can be challenging and fun.

    (E) challenging and fun hours can be spent with muttonfish.

12. If pine trees are not available for tinder, birch bark is a good substitute <u>as it contains volatile oil and therefore will burn even when it is raining</u>.

(A) as it contains volatile oil and therefore will burn even when it is raining.

(B) containing volatile oil and will burn even when it is raining.

(C) for containing volatile oil and burning even when it is raining.

(D) to therefore burn even in the rain because it contains volatile oil.

(E) for burning even in the rain because it is known to certainly contain volatile oil.

13. I realized a fire started on damp ground will burn rapidly for a while, but <u>then it will not take long for it to be quickly smothered by steam rising from</u> the damp ground when it heats up.

(A) then it will not take long for it to be quickly smothered by steam rising from

(B) then it will not take long for rising steam to quickly smother the fire on

(C) it will not take long for it to be quickly smothered by steam rising from

(D) it will be smothered quickly by steam rising from

(E) then being smothered quickly by steam rising from

14. <u>The memories of when I last saw James and she are not ones I am proud of</u>.

(A) The memories of when I last saw James and she are not ones I am proud of.

(B) The memories I have of my last meeting with James and her are not ones of which I am proud.

(C) My last memories of James and her are not proud.

(D) My last meeting with James and she is not one of which I am proud.

(E) I am not proud of my memories of my last meeting with James and she.

15. <u>The less mistakes hunters make, the more it helps their chances of harvest game</u>.

(A) The less mistakes hunters make, the more it helps their chances of harvest game.

(B) The fewer mistakes hunters make, the better their chances of harvesting game.

(C) The fewer mistakes hunters make, the more chances they will have when it comes to being able to harvest game.

(D) The less mistakes hunters make, the best their chance is of harvesting game.

(E) The less mistakes, the better the chances of harvesting game.

16. Thanks in part to his boasting, Muhammed Ali ended up being criticized, although everyone recognized him to be one of the best fighters of all time.

(A) Thanks in part to his boasting, Muhammed Ali ended up being criticized

(B) Thanks in part to his boasting, Muhammed Ali was criticized for his talents

(C) Thanks in part for his boasting, Muhammed Ali was criticized

(D) Muhammed Ali was in the end criticized because of his boasting

(E) Because he boasted so much, Muhammed Ali's boastings ended up criticized

17. The skills required for the Winter Olympics biathlon is a combination of cross country skiing and shooting event.

(A) is a combination of cross country skiing and shooting event.

(B) combining the events of cross country skiing and shooting.

(C) is a combination of skiing and shooting event.

(D) combines cross country and skiing.

(E) are a combination of cross country skiing and shooting.

18. Although I think he was lying, he acted as if he knew the biathlon is won most often by countries with winter border patrols such as Finland and East Germany.

(A) was lying, he acted as if he knew

(B) had been lying, he acted as if he had known

(C) had been lying, he acted like he knew

(D) was lying, he acted like he knew

(E) was lying, he was acting like he knew

19. Many biathletes train during the summer with a five-kilometer run-and-shoot event <u>being now suggested as a sport meriting consideration to be an official sport</u> by the International Olympic Committee for the Summer Olympic Games.

(A) being now suggested as a sport meriting consideration to be an official sport

(B) now being suggested as meriting an official sport consideration

(C) now being suggested as meriting consideration as an official sport

(D) meriting consideration for being a sport officially part of

(E) meriting now consideration as being included as an official sport

20. We asked Gary Hunter, James Parrillo, and Bonnie Slupferling to help us design a better insurance package for the company, but <u>neither of them was willing</u> to meet until after lunch.

(A) neither of them was willing

(B) neither one of them were willing

(C) not a one of them were willing

(D) each one of them was willing

(E) not one of them was willing

21. <u>This kind of construction problems are difficult</u> to overcome in areas where earthquakes are frequent and severe.

(A) This kind of construction problems are difficult

(B) These kind of construction problems are difficult

(C) Those kinds of construction problems are difficult

(D) That kind of construction problem is difficult

(E) The kind of construction problem is difficult

22. <u>The woman who was the winner's voice had an excited tone, so</u> it made her sound shrill.

(A) The woman who was the winner's voice had an excited tone, so

(B) The woman as the winner had an excited-sounding tone, so

(C) Winning was an excited woman's voice and

(D) The woman winners' voice sounding excited and

(E) The woman winner's voice had an excited tone, so

STOP

If time still remains, you may go back and check your work.
When the time alloted is up, you may go on to the next section.

Section 5

TIME: 25 Minutes
16 Questions

DIRECTIONS: For each question in this section, select the best answer.

---

1. The town of Modern, USA, drinks Fizzy Pop after a hot day in the sun. Buy yours today!

    A reader who is not a resident of Modern, USA, would be most likely to purchase Fizzy Pop if he or she drew which of the following questionable conclusions invited by the advertisement?

    (A) Among many thirst quenchers, Fizzy Pop is the best after a day in the sun.

    (B) Many modern people use Fizzy Pop to quench their thirst; I should get on that bandwagon!

    (C) An entire town cannot be wrong; the numbers prove it.

    (D) Famous people in Modern use Fizzy; I should, too.

    (E) The advertisement is placed where those who have much leisure time can read it.

Questions 2–3 are based on the following.

The defeated candidate addressed her political party tonight at the final gathering of this election year. She talked to them about the platform of her opponent and pointed out many questions he left unanswered in their recent televised debate. She concluded by listing the many defeats suffered by Abraham Lincoln before he finally was elected President of the United States. She stated that she planned to pursue her political career despite this defeat.

2. The method of gaining support used by the defeated candidate was to

    (A) attack the character of the opponent by suggesting he equivocated by not answering questions.

    (B) imply an analogy between her experiences and those of Abraham Lincoln.

(C) point out that the opponent's claims imply a dilemma.

(D) show that the opponent's unanswered questions reflect an absurd lack of preparation and knowledge.

(E) show that the platform of her opponent was absurd.

3. The defeated candidate could effectively defend her platform against the newly elected candidate by pointing out that

(A) her expertise in answering the questions he avoided is outstanding.

(B) she is neither inept nor immoral.

(C) he avoided the truth in answering the questions asked.

(D) the defeats of Abraham Lincoln were caused by similar concerns and actions.

(E) point out that the opponent's platform leads to an absurd conclusion.

4. Students need to spend more time studying for standardized tests which colleges use in selection of students. With that test preparation scores could be raised and colleges would be likely to admit the students who apply. Such investment of study time could result in an improved student body at colleges and universities.

Which of the following conclusions can most properly be drawn from the information above?

(A) Increased study time could benefit both the students and the institutions of higher education.

(B) Increased enrollments in colleges and universities is likely to be accompanied by the creation of more jobs on campuses across the nation.

(C) Colleges and universities will decrease their enrollments unless students indicate that they are better prepared.

(D) The low test scores have been a cause of economic recession.

(E) Low test scores have caused a decline in education quality at colleges and universities across the nation.

5. Which of the following best completes the passage below?

    Educators today are putting emphasis on three different learning styles, or modalities. Most people actually have used all three modalities at different times in their learning, but generally they have a preference of one. Some people learn best what they hear (auditory learners); some learn best what they see (visual learners); some learn best what they do (kinesthetic learners). Good teachers are aware of these modalities so that they can _____ .

    (A) attempt to convert the students to auditory learners since the lecture method is most usually used in high school and college.

    (B) attempt to use the auditory method predominantly in their classroom since this is the method most usually used in high school and college.

    (C) attempt to get parents to use the method that the child prefers when the parent teaches the child at home.

    (D) provide for all three types of learners in their classrooms.

    (E) pass the National Teacher Examination, a test required for certification in many states.

6. Jules reads more than Kim.

    Millie reads less than Nurry.

    Leon reads more than Millie.

    Kim and Nurry read exactly the same amount.

    If the information above is true, which of the following must also be true?

    (A) Leon reads more than Nurry.

    (B) Leon reads more than Jules.

    (C) Kim reads less than Leon.

    (D) Jules reads more than Millie.

    (E) Kim reads less than Millie.

7. To conserve public lands, restrictions must be placed on the uses of this property.

   Which of the following statements provides support for the claim above?

   I. Since public lands belong to each citizen, each person should be able to use the lands as he/she wishes in order to recreate and relax.

   II. Vehicles which are made for off-the-road travel (two-wheelers, four-wheelers) must be prohibited from using the newly sown banks to halt erosion.

   III. Refreshment stand owners and workers were put out of work when they were prohibited from reopening their stands this morning; individuals are prohibited from using public lands to profit financially.

   (A) I only   (B) II only

   (C) I and III only   (D) II and III only

   (E) I, II, and III

8. Democracy means rule by the people. They have many rights, vote in secret, may seek public office, and may demand removing a public official who behaves improperly.

   Which of the following would most likely follow the above statements?

   (A) The people may also organize pressure groups to voice their opinions.

   (B) Legally, however, pressure groups which hold mass meetings or organize demonstrations are not allowable in a true democracy.

   (C) In most large democracies, however, public opinion is formed by legislators and does not really develop freely.

   (D) In democratic countries, the people are very limited in the opportunities they have to make the government truly representative.

   (E) Rival political parties, however, are discouraged in a true democracy because they tend to intimidate many persons.

9. The American school system is getting more children who are diverse and living in poverty. These children have more deficiencies; their needs are different and greater.

    Which of the following statements is not supported by the above conclusions?

    (A) Although the United States makes a tremendous dollar expenditure for education, the deficit in education seems to grow.

    (B) Many Americans remain ill-prepared for the real world.

    (C) It costs more to educate the children with many deficiencies and needs.

    (D) The needs of all these many children are not being met.

    (E) Education must be left to the schools and not interfered with by the home.

Questions 10–11 are based on the following.

Partly in response to consumer demand and partly to compete with foreign imports, car manufacturers produced more cars during the past two years than ever before. This production resulted in less steel being available for refrigerator manufacturing. So while the volume of car production has been increasing over the two year period, the volume of refrigerator production decreased.

10. Which of the following can be inferred from the passage?

    (A) Refrigerators are a profitable product only if they are produced on a large scale.

    (B) Production of refrigerators has been unusually high for the two year period.

    (C) Steel production will increase in the future.

    (D) Surplus stocks of refrigerators have been reduced in the two year period.

    (E) The profits that car manufacturers have made are unprecedented.

11. Which of the following conclusions is warranted from the above passage?

    (A) Refrigerator manufacturers foresaw how high the price of refrigerators would go.

(B) Car manufacturers made more profit in the two year period than they ever have or will again.

(C) Steel manufacturers preferred selling to refrigerator manufacturers rather than to car manufacturers even though the amount of steel might have been the same.

(D) The price of refrigerators has increased over the two year period.

(E) The price of refrigerators has declined over the two year period since there was no steel used in their production.

12. Dr. Harrison Faigel, convinced that student nervousness had affected their SAT scores, administered beta blockers to 22 students who (he believed) had low test scores because of nervousness; beta blockers interfere with the effects of adrenalin. The scores of the students administered the drug improved an average of more than 100 points as compared with 11 points for eight other students to whom he did not administer beta blockers to help control nervousness. Nationwide the second-time test takers improved their scores only an average of 28 points.

Which of the following, if true, would most strengthen the conclusion drawn by Dr. Faigel?

(A) The average scores of 4 of the 8 students in the control group increased by an average of 6 points as compared to an increase of an average of 22 points for the other four who were administered beta blockers in a later experiment.

(B) Nationwide the second-time test takers improved their scores an average of 38, rather than 28, points.

(C) When second-time test takers nationwide were administered adrenalin, their average test scores increased an average of 100 points.

(D) Faigel's study will be replicated; this time a control group will be used, an important factor Faigel overlooked.

(E) When Faigel's experiment was conducted on a larger scale, results similar to those he achieved were attained.

13. Paul: The South has made significant progress in reducing infant deaths since 1984. Nearly all Southern states reduced their infant mortality rate between 1983 and 1993. The statistics are very encouraging.

Paula: We need to wait until all the facts are in to be encouraged. The 1993 figures do not reflect the recent facts on infant deaths due to AIDS and drug abuse. Before we take heart, we need to remember the United States has one of the worst infant death rates of any industrialized country in the world.

Which of the following best describes the weak point in Paul's claim on which Paula's response focuses?

(A) The evidence Paul cites comes from only a single area of the United States, the South.

(B) The decrease may be a mathematical error.

(C) The 1993 statistics quoted are not current enough to reflect recent occurrences.

(D) No mention is made of Northern states in the report.

(E) No exact figures are given for infant mortality in 1984 through 1993.

14. Researchers in Florida, Texas, and Hawaii believe they are getting closer to the day when the oil substitute, hydrogen, is used as commonly as gasoline. Hydrogen will not pollute. It is one of the most abundant elements in the earth. The cost to consumers would eventually be reasonable, but now the cost is prohibitive. Skeptics prefer to keep gasoline as the major fuel for our vehicles.

Which of the following, if true, would tend to weaken the force of the skeptics' arguments?

(A) The threat of the greenhouse effect and acid rain from pollution is increasing.

(B) Hydrogen has never been used as an energy source.

(C) Future supplies of oil are guaranteed.

(D) A concerted national effort is needed.

(E) A gradual transition from gasoline to hydrogen is needed.

15. Women made up 45 percent of the work force in 1988, as compared with 38 percent in 1970. In a recent poll of women respondents 48 percent said that women had had to sacrifice too much to achieve their gains.

Which of the following conclusions can be properly drawn from the statements above?

(A) Their sacrifice was the financial cost to train for jobs; women could have come out just as well financially to have stayed at home.

(B) The sacrifices most working women make are too little time for children, family life, and themselves.

(C) Men do not have to sacrifice time for children, family life, and themselves when they work.

(D) If 48 percent of the women respondents said they had had to sacrifice too much for their career, then 52 percent (more than half) did not feel these concerns; sacrifices, therefore, do not affect most women in the work force.

(E) Because of these sacrifices, women can be expected to withdraw from the labor force.

16. The spoils system is the practice of awarding public offices for party services. When a new party comes to office, the elected leaders may find places for faithful followers.

Which of the following constitutes the most serious disadvantage for employing the spoils system?

(A) A major disadvantage of utilizing the spoils system is that it is illegal at all levels in our country.

(B) The victorious party must shape policies to satisfy its supporters and be held accountable.

(C) It is sometimes difficult to ascertain who is deserving of rewards for party services.

(D) Since the spoils system is less than ten years old in the United States, it has not had a chance to be proven good or bad.

(E) The chief disadvantage of the spoils system in the United States is that it is appropriate at times but not at other times.

STOP

If time still remains, you may go back and check your work.
When the time allotted is up, you may go on to the next section.

Section 6

TIME: 25 Minutes
16 Questions

DIRECTIONS: Solve each problem using space on the page for scratchwork. Indicate the best answer from the choices given.

NUMBERS: All numbers used are real numbers.

FIGURES: Figures accompanying problems in this section provide information useful in solving the problems. They are drawn as accurately as possible; however, when a figure is not drawn to scale, more information will be provided. It is given that all figures lie in a plane unless otherwise stated.

---

1. At a clothing store sale, Ms. Smith bought a coat marked $270 for $225. What rate of discount did she receive?

   (A) $83^1/_3$ percent   (B) $16^2/_3$ percent

   (C) $12^1/_2$ percent   (D) 20 percent

   (E) $16^1/_3$ percent

2. How many prime numbers are there between 0 and 40?

   (A) 9   (B) 12

   (C) 13   (D) 15

   (E) 17

3. An addition to a school is 90 feet by 150 feet. How many 18 inch tiles will be needed to do the flooring?

   (A) 6,000   (B) 7,500

   (C) 12,000   (D) 24,000

   (E) 30,000

4. If $\dfrac{x}{y} = 5$, then $\dfrac{x^2 - y^2}{y^2} =$

(A) – 25.   (B) – 24.

(C) 24.   (D) 25.

(E) 26.

5. $\dfrac{3}{4}$ is what percent of 1.5?

(A) 5 percent   (B) 50 percent

(C) $66^2/_3$ percent   (D) 75 percent

(E) 150 percent

6. Kathy is 2 times older than John. Five years ago she was 3 times older than John. How old is Kathy today?

(A) 5   (B) 10

(C) 15   (D) 20

(E) 25

7. Given $l_1 \parallel l_2$. Find y.

(A) 30°

(B) 60°

(C) 120°

(D) 150°

(E) 160°

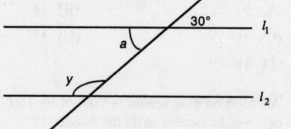

8. If the angles of a triangle are in the ratio of 2:3:5 then the degree measures of the angles must be

(A) 20°, 30°, 50°.   (B) 44°, 56°, 80°.

(C) 20°, 60°, 100°.   (D) 36°, 54°, 90°.

(E) It is not possible for the angles of a triangle to be in this ratio.

9. A VCR was advertised with successive discounts of 10 percent fol-
    lowed by another 10 percent. How much will it cost if its original
    price was $300?

    (A) $240   (B) $243

    (C) $253   (D) $207

    (E) $200

10. If $a + b = 3$ and $2b + c = 2$, then $2a - c =$

    (A) -4 (B) -1

    (C) 1 (D) 4

    (E) 5

11. A suit on sale at 40 percent off is now selling for the reduced price of
    $144. What was the original price of the suit?

    (A) $201.60   (B) $230.40

    (C) $240   (D) $360

    (E) $576

12. John, a salesman, traveled 2,000 miles during the month of June. He
    estimates that it cost him 27¢ per mile to run his automobile. His
    estimated average daily cost during June was

    (A) $5.40.   (B) $9.00

    (C) $10.00.   (D) $17.42.

    (E) $18.00.

13. If $x - y = 9$ then $3x - 3y - 1 =$

    (A) 23   (B) 24

    (C) 25   (D) 26

    (E) 28

14. The driving time for a 150-mile trip from Washington, D.C. to Phila-
    delphia was 3 hours. The return trip was made by the same route but
    at an average rate of speed that was 20 percent faster. The total
    amount of driving time for the round trip was

(A) 5 hours.

(B) 5 hours, 15 minutes.

(C) 5 hours, 30 minutes.

(D) 5 hours, 45 minutes.

(E) 6 hours.

15. Find the area of the isosceles trapezoid.

(A) $250\sqrt{3}$

(B) 150

(C) 250

(D) $125\sqrt{3}$

(E) Area cannot be found.

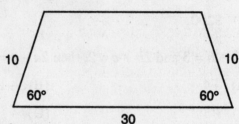

16. Joe and Bob were playing marbles. Bob said, "Give me two of your marbles and I'll have as many as you." Joe answered, "But if you give me two of yours, I'll have twice as many as you." With how many marbles did Bob start out?

(A) 14

(B) 12

(C) 6

(D) 8

(E) 10

STOP

If time still remains, you may go back and check your work.
When the time allotted is up, you may go on to the next section.

Section 7

ANALYSIS OF AN ISSUE ESSAY TOPIC

TIME: 30 Minutes

> **DIRECTIONS:** In an essay, develop a position on the issue be-low by investigating the different angles of the issue, and ex-plaining your thoughts on the topic. Remember, there is no one "correct" response to the essay topic.
>
> Before starting, read the essay topic and its question(s). You may make preliminary notes in your test booklet before writing the actual essay. Be sure to write your essay on the lined pages provided at the back of the book.

The assumption that the creation of responsible citizens is one of the main purposes of our school system raises complicated questions: what is a responsible citizen, and how can school-based practices be employed in the creation of one? There are many ideas about possible educational reforms which aim to answer these questions. At one extreme are those who demand a return to a more traditional education, who advise a study of more classical, scholarly subjects. At the other extreme are those who feel that any skill a student exhibits, from painting to auto mechanics, should be stressed as strongly as math or English.

Which educational method do you think would be the most effective? Why? What flaws do you find in the other theory? Explain your position using relevant reasons and examples drawn from your own experience, observations, or reading.

STOP

Do not go on until you are instructed to do so. Use any remaining time to check your work on this portion of the test.

ANALYSIS OF AN ARGUMENT ESSAY TOPIC

TIME: 30 Minutes

DIRECTIONS: In essay form, prepare a review on the position of the argument provided below. Before taking your own position on the argument's standpoint, it may be helpful to determine the method of thinking behind the argument itself. For example, consider alternative explanations to any assumptions the argument might make, and any evidence or examples that may strengthen or weaken the argument. Remember, there is no one "correct" response to the essay topic.

Before starting, read the essay topic and its question(s). You may make preliminary notes in your test booklet before writing the actual essay. Be sure to write your essay on the lined pages provided at the back of the book.

It has long been known that a lifestyle in which the diet consists predominantly of fruits, vegetables, and grains is the most healthy. Studies have shown that eating a lot of meat can contribute to heart disease and high cholesterol. A trip to the grocery store can verify that meat is a more expensive source of protein than tofu, eggs, cheese, nuts, and grains. Most importantly, it has become obvious that raising livestock is the least economically sound food production method available. The land used to raise food for livestock could be much more efficiently used to grow food that could feed the hungry people of the world. It may seem difficult to change the system, but we can certainly change our own lifestyle. How can we not when we see the pleading eyes of starving children staring at us in the pages of a magazine, and we realize that if everyone in the world was a vegetarian, no one would have to go hungry?

What is the main point of this argument? Do you think the author had a specific goal in mind when making this argument? Do you think this argument is effective? What are its strengths and what are its weaknesses?

STOP

If time still remains, you may go back and check your work.

PRACTICE TEST 1

ANSWER KEY

Section 1 — Problem Solving

1.	(E)	5.	(A)	9.	(A)	13.	(B)
2.	(D)	6.	(B)	10.	(D)	14.	(A)
3.	(E)	7.	(B)	11.	(D)	15.	(B)
4.	(A)	8.	(B)	12.	(D)	16.	(A)

Section 2 — Reading Comprehension

1.	(C)	7.	(D)	13.	(A)	19.	(C)
2.	(B)	8.	(E)	14.	(C)	20.	(B)
3.	(D)	9.	(D)	15.	(E)	21.	(A)
4.	(C)	10.	(D)	16.	(C)	22.	(A)
5.	(E)	11.	(C)	17.	(B)	23.	(E)
6.	(A)	12.	(D)	18.	(C)		

Section 3 — Data Sufficiency

1.	(E)	6.	(D)	11.	(D)	16.	(E)
2.	(C)	7.	(E)	12.	(E)	17.	(E)
3.	(A)	8.	(E)	13.	(C)	18.	(E)
4.	(C)	9.	(B)	14.	(E)	19.	(C)
5.	(C)	10.	(B)	15.	(C)	20.	(D)

Section 4 — Sentence Correction

1.	(E)	7.	(B)	13.	(D)	19.	(C)
2.	(C)	8.	(D)	14.	(B)	20.	(E)
3.	(E)	9.	(A)	15.	(B)	21.	(C)
4.	(D)	10.	(E)	16.	(C)	22.	(E)
5.	(B)	11.	(C)	17.	(E)		
6.	(A)	12.	(A)	18.	(A)		

Section 5 — Critical Reasoning

1.	(B)	5.	(D)	9.	(E)	13.	(C)
2.	(B)	6.	(D)	10.	(D)	14.	(A)
3.	(A)	7.	(B)	11.	(D)	15.	(B)
4.	(A)	8.	(A)	12.	(E)	16.	(E)

Section 6 — Problem Solving

1.	(B)	5.	(B)	9.	(B)	13.	(D)
2.	(B)	6.	(D)	10.	(D)	14.	(C)
3.	(A)	7.	(D)	11.	(C)	15.	(D)
4.	(C)	8.	(D)	12.	(E)	16.	(E)

DETAILED EXPLANATIONS OF ANSWERS

Section 1–Problem Solving

1. **(E)**
   Since .095 × 110 = 10.45 and since 110 + 10.45 = 120.45, the total cost is $120.45.

2. **(D)**

$$(3x)^2 - \frac{x^2}{9} = 9x^2 - \frac{x^2}{9}$$

$$= \frac{81x^2}{9} - \frac{x^2}{9}$$

$$= \frac{80x^2}{9}$$

3. **(E)**

$$10^3 + 10^5 = 10^3 \times 1 + 10^3 \times 10^2$$
$$= 10^3 (1 + 10^2)$$
$$= 10^3 (101) \qquad \text{or } 10^3 = 1,000 \text{ and } 10^5 = 100,000$$
$$= 1,000 \times 101 \qquad \text{and thus } 10^3 + 10^5 = 101,000$$
$$= 101,000.$$

4. **(A)**
   For two natural numbers to be relatively prime, their only positive common natural number divisor is 1. Then x could not be a multiple of 18 because then x and 10 have 2 as a common divisor. By a similar argument x could not be a multiple of 4, 25, or 14. However, the odd multiples of 9 do not contain factors of 2 and 5. Thus, x could be a multiple of 9.

5. **(A)**
   Remember the order of operation rules as PEMDAS, meaning parentheses, exponents, multiplication, division, addition, and subtraction. The

correct solution is

$$10 - 5[(8 + 9 - 2)(-2)] = 10 - 5(21) \Rightarrow 10 - 105 = -95.$$

Choice (B) comes from subtracting 10 and 5 before multiplying.

$$10 - 5 = 5 \text{ and } 5(21) = 105.$$

Choice (C) comes from $17 - 4$ instread of $17 + 4$ inside the parentheses and also the mistake of subtracting $10 - 5$ first. This gives

$$5(13) = 65.$$

Choice (D) comes from the mistake of $17 - 4$ without the additional mistake of subtracting $10 - 5$ first. This gives

$$10 - 5(13) = 10 - 65 = -55.$$

Choice (E) comes from making $2^3 = 6$ instead of 8. This gives

$$10 - 5(19) = 10 - 95 = -85.$$

6. **(B)**
    Let x = the number of cookies that Bakery Z and Bakery Y can make for the same price.

$$\left(\frac{x}{12}\right) 7.20 = 5 + .80 (x - 10)$$

$$.60x = 5 + .80x - 8$$

$$3 = .80x - .60x$$

$$3 = .20x$$

$$x = 15$$

7. **(B)**
    Draw a line from B to E to see that the area is the area of $\triangle ABE$ and rectangle $BCED$.
    Use the Pythagorean theorem to find the height of $\triangle ABE$.

$$3^2 + h^2 = 6^2$$

$$h^2 = 27$$

$$h = 3\sqrt{3}$$

The area of the rectangle and

triangle is

$$lw + \frac{1}{2}bh$$

$$(9)(6) + \frac{1}{2}(6)(3\sqrt{3})$$

$$54 + 9\sqrt{3}$$

8. **(B)**
    The mean of the six numbers if 65, so

    $$\frac{50 + 60 + 65 + 75 + x + y}{6} = 65$$

    or $\qquad 50 + 60 + 65 + 70 + x + y = 6 \times 65$

    $$x + y = 140$$

    but $\qquad \dfrac{x+y}{2} = 70.$

9. **(A)**
    The area of the first square is x^2 and the area of the second square is $(x + 2)^2$. Thus, the sum of the areas is

    $$x^2 + (x + 2)^2 = x^2 + (x^2 + 4x + 4)$$
    $$= 2x^2 + 4x + 4.$$

10. **(D)**
    Let x = the original salary

    $$x + 1.5x = 450$$
    $$2.5x = 450$$
    $$x = 180$$

11. **(D)**
    Since $26 \times 13 = 338$, the room area is 338 square feet and since $18 \times 12 = 216$, the rug area is 216 square feet, but $338 - 216 = 122$, so the area of the uncovered portion of the room is 122 square feet.

12. **(D)**

If a is positive and b is positive, then

$$x = \frac{a}{|a|} + \frac{b}{|b|} + \frac{ab}{|ab|}$$

$$= 1 + 1 + 1$$

$$= 3$$

If a is positive and b is negative, then

$$x = \frac{a}{|a|} + \frac{b}{|b|} + \frac{ab}{|ab|}$$

$$= 1 + (-1) + (-1)$$

$$= -1$$

If a is negative and b is positive, then

$$x = \frac{a}{|a|} + \frac{b}{|b|} + \frac{ab}{|ab|}$$

$$= 1 + 1 + (-1)$$

$$= -1$$

If a is negative and b is negative, then

$$x = \frac{a}{|a|} + \frac{b}{|b|} + \frac{ab}{|ab|}$$

$$= -1 + (-1) + 1$$

$$= -1$$

13. **(B)**

Let x = the number of pencils the man had. Then

$$x - \frac{2}{3}x = 7$$

$$\frac{1}{3}x = 7$$

$$x = 21$$

Since $\frac{2}{3} \times 21 = 14$, he sold 14 pencils. Since $14 \times 20 = 280$, he collected \$2.80.

14. **(A)**

$$-3^{-3} = \frac{1}{(-3)^3}$$

$$= \frac{1}{-27}$$

$$= -\frac{1}{27}$$

15. **(B)**

Let F be the midpoint of $\overline{DE}$. Then the four small triangles are congruent and have the same area. Thus, each small triangle (including $\triangle ABC$) has $1/4$ the area of the large triangle and $1/4$ of 12 is 3.

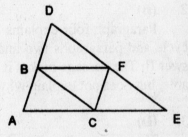

16. **(A)**

To solve the problem remember $d = rt$.
Let t equal the time it takes for Larry to overtake Louise.

$$50(1\tfrac{1}{2} + t - \tfrac{1}{2}) = 60t$$

$$50 + 50t = 60t$$

$$50 = 10t$$

$$t = 5 \text{ hours}$$

The question asked for the number of miles it would take Larry. Use the distance/time equation to find the number of miles.

$$d = rt$$

$$d = 60(5)$$

$$d = 300 \text{ miles}$$

Section 2–Reading Comprehension

1. **(C)**
   All of the phenomena discussed in the passage are ocean movements. (B) and (D) are true, but secondary. There is no need to prove something not in dispute (E), nor has there been a lack of interest in the subject matter of the passage (A).

2. **(B)**
   Paragraph four explains how turning over contributes to the nutrient cycle and paragraphs two and three provide sufficient information to answer II. The passage makes it clear that under-surface rivers are unpredictable, but does not explain why that is so.

3. **(D)**
   The passage describes the various kinds of ocean movements, including surface (paragraphs two and three) and under-surface (paragraphs four and five); hence (A), (C), and (E) are incorrect. (B) is incorrect because some movements described in paragraph two (the Humboldt Current, for example) are beneficial, and the passage does not indicate whether internal waves (paragraph six) are harmful or beneficial.

4. **(C)**
   The passage indicates that abundant marine bird-life, commercial fisheries, game fish, and fertilizer industries depend on the Humboldt Current. Abundant rainfall may also, but the passage does not indicate that; rather, it indicates that El Niño brings harmful, torrential rains.

5. **(E)**
   El Niño appears periodically, but the timing of its appearance cannot be accurately predicted, nor can the phenomenon be explained. Its destructiveness is no mystery (C); despite our knowledge of it (A), it is not yet clear what can be done to avert El Niño's destructiveness (B) and (D).

6. **(A)**
   All of El Niño's harmful effects ultimately are caused by the warming of shoreline water; (D) is a consequence of that. (B), (C), and (E) do not deal with El Niño.

7. **(D)**

The Humboldt Current supports sea life, including fish, on which marine birds feed. Their droppings, in turn, make possible Peruvian guano exports.

8. **(E)**

Paragraph four explains the role of "turning over" in the nutrient cycle.

9. **(D)**

The ocean's nutrient cycle, for example, depends on hidden movements. The passage supplies no information to support (A) or (B); (C) is mistaken, and (E) is incorrect because internal waves are not wind-driven.

10. **(D)**

The primary purpose of this passage is to show the change in Jemmy Button. The author comments that people on the ship had "left him plump, fat, clean, and well-dressed:—I never saw so complete and grievous a change." The change in Jemmy's appearance is shocking, for now he appears thin and ill-kept. Although a good meal (A) does improve his disposition, it is not the main reason for the passage. There is no evidence that Jemmy had been forced to give up his property (B). Choice (C) is directly contradicted by evidence in the passage, and there is no mention of methods (E) for improving his life.

11. **(C)**

All the evidence points to the fact that Jemmy was a native. He washes paint off his face, is called a "savage," is dressed like a native, brings native gifts of otter skins, spear-heads, and arrows, and has a canoe. However, Jemmy is ashamed of his current appearance, can speak English, has obviously known these men before, and states that "he did not wish to go back to England." Also, the author hopes that Jemmy will be as happy or happier than "if he had never left his own country," and that Captain Fitz Roy will be repaid for "the many generous sacrifices" he had made on behalf of "Jemmy Button and his tribe." Also, Jemmy boasts that he "could talk a little of his own language." It is not probable, in light of evidence in the passage, that Jemmy was an English sailor or missionary who preferred to live among the Fuegians.

12. **(D)**

The author appears to care genuinely for Jemmy, especially as he bemoans the "grievous" condition of Jemmy's thinness and lack of clothing. Indeed, Jemmy appears to be well-liked among all the sailors, as he departs loaded with gifts from them. There is no evidence to support that the author (A) admires Jemmy, nor does the author evidence (E) contempt for Jemmy. The author appears to care for Jemmy, but there is no evidence that he is respected as head of his tribe (B); in fact, although the author uses the phrase "his tribe," there is no information to indicate that Jemmy is anything but a member, instead of a chief. Although the author is appalled (C) by Jemmy's degraded condition, he understands why Jemmy wishes to remain on Tierra del Fuego at the appearance of Jemmy's "young and nice-looking wife."

13. **(A)**

Jemmy washes the paint off his face because he is ashamed to be seen as a savage to his former English friends. That he goes to some efforts to make the sailors comfortable with his current condition (C) leads us to believe he does not want his friends to worry about him. Giving handmade presents (B) and receiving presents, as well as the statement by the author that they are sorry to "shake hands with him for the last time" (E) are indications of goodwill. Jemmy is also perceived as friendly and outgoing by members of his tribe because he has taught them some English (D).

14. **(C)**

Jemmy realizes the values of objects because he gives valuable presents in the form of furs and weapons; also, he departs from the sailors "loaded with valuable property." However, the author states that "Jemmy had lost all his property." There are two logical conclusions—that the property had been stolen (A) or he had given it away (C). Because Jemmy gives away his property to the sailors and because Jemmy is not wearing the clothes he had been given earlier, it can be assumed he lives in a society that shares freely with others. If he did not feel it appropriate to keep objects (B), it is unlikely he would have bragged about having his own canoe or have kept the clothing or the other objects given to him. There is no evidence to support choice (D), although it is possible, and at no point in the passage does Jemmy trade for food (E).

15. **(E)**

Jemmy certainly knows the difference between his current condition and his former condition. He likes his friends and has been to England. However, at this time Jemmy makes it clear he is married, has his own canoe, and does not wish to return to England. He likes his friends, but to say that he thinks civilization is "admirable" (A), or the "pinnacle of success" (B), is too strong, as Jemmy obviously chooses to stay where he is. He does have enough insight into the nature of the sailors (C) to experience shame over his unusual appearance, but how valuable can that insight be which makes him ashamed to be like a member of his tribe? Certainly, it is no "blessing" (D) for Jemmy to be removed from his people long enough to forget his native tongue.

16. **(C)**

Jemmy was recognized by the sailors at the beginning of the passage, and he gives presents to his two "best" friends. Although Jemmy is invited to eat with Captain Fitz Roy, the author indicates that educating Jemmy to civilization was the Captain's noble experiment, not a particular act of friendship (A). Jemmy certainly is friendly to everyone, which refutes answers (B) and (E). He may feel ashamed, but he is too "degraded" (D) to come aboard and enjoy the company of his friends.

17. **(B)**

This question asks for the author's primary interest in writing this passage, or the main idea of the passage as a whole. In order to answer this question, it is necessary to look at the first word of each answer choice. The author is "recalling" (B) what has happened to Jemmy Button as a result of the experiment that took place in the past; Jemmy had obviously been taught to speak English and to imitate "civilized" manners of the Englishmen. Instead of inculcating his fellow natives with English habits and language, Jemmy has gone back to his native customs. "Predicting" (A) indicates a projection of the author's opinion into the future, which clearly does not happen here. Choice (C) "analyzing two sides of an opposing argument" or (D) "proposing a solution to a problem" could be applied to the choice of civilized versus native society, but the passage is clearly narrative. Choice (E) is the most probable of the incorrect answers as there appears to be an implicit criticism of meddling with another person's culture, but, again, the passage is so strongly narrative as to preclude this as the best choice.

18. **(C)**

The primary purpose of this passage is to describe some of the problems with franchise laws and differences of operation and opinions between the federal regulatory body, the FTC, and state regulatory bodies. Although (A) or (E) are possible secondary purposes, the author does not detail specific problems, call for reform, or suggest possible avenues of reform. It is apparent that businesses could have complaints (B) against federal regulations, but these complaints are not detailed here. From information in the article, it is obvious that the federal government needs to tighten up on regulatory activity, not ease it (D).

19. **(C)**

The article states that the FTC's Trade Rule 436—"Disclosure Requirements and Prohibitions Concerning Franchising and Business Opportunities Ventures," regulates franchises. Information in the article contradicts choice (A). Although it is apparent some states are highly regulatory (B), they are not named here. The article mentions that the franchisor should disclose his or her business experience (D), but the penalty for falsifying or not fully disclosing such information is not given. The article does not specifically state why the FTC has not been more active in determining compliance in non-regulating states (E), although the statement is made that this approach was "well-suited to the anti-regulation orientation of the Reagan Administration"; such non-action could therefore be attributable to any number of causes, such as budget shortfall or understaffing.

20. **(B)**

The author wishes to outline the two categories—federal and state—which regulate franchises in order to show the complexity of the problem. Regulatory efforts of some states (A) are not specifically mentioned by name or by problem. Choice (C) is an incomplete answer because the author describes both sales and day-to-day activities of franchises. Choice (D) is implied but not specifically addressed. Choice (E) is directly contradicted by arguments and information presented in the selection.

21. **(A)**

If the franchisors are not required to disclose information about actual or potential sales, income, or profit, and if there are fines for inaccuracies, then it is only reasonable to assume that franchisors will not make these claims unless required by state regulatory agencies. Information in the passage contradicts choice (B); it seems unlikely an "informed" decision is possible without information regarding profits. Choice (C) is incorrect because civil fines should not supersede federal fines, and, at any rate, people have been known to abuse the system in spite of penalties. The UFOC (D) is not a simplified form, but a detailed one. The FTC does not appear to check anything carefully (E).

22. **(A)**

According to the article, franchisors should have the least number of complaints as they appear to be quite loosely regulated by the FTC, and the article even mentions the "anti-regulation orientation of the Reagan Administration." Franchisees (B) should find buying a franchise without full financial disclosure a disconcerting procedure. State administrators (C) and (D) have complained about the lack of regulation. Consumer advocacy groups (E) stand to lose much without strict regulation of franchise practices, as this looseness encourages price gouging, misrepresentation, and perhaps outright fraud.

23. **(E)**

It can be inferred from the article that there is no federal law governing franchise relationships or practices. The only federal guidelines mentioned in the article cover sales of franchises, not daily operations. Federal franchise disclosure requirements have not been strongly enforced (A), and the FTC allows a variety of forms to be used (C). Federal franchise laws are uniform (B); state laws are not uniform. It would seem that information about potential profits would not be irrelevant to a sale (D), although it appears to be up to the buyer to find out such information.

Section 3–Data Sufficiency

1. **(E)**

Although a time and speed can be found in Statements (1) and (2) one cannot assume that the two people drive at the same speed. Therefore, neither statement is useful by itself, or together, for solving the problem.

2. **(C)**

Let x be the side of the square and y the radius of the circle. According to (1),

$$4x + 2\pi y = 16 \text{ units.}$$

Since Statement (1) does not give the value of y, you cannot find the value of x using (1) alone. According to Statement (2),

$$x^2 + \pi y^2 = 21 \text{ sq. units.}$$

Again, Statement (2) does not provide the value of y; you cannot find the value of x using (2) alone. But, using Statements (1) and (2) together, we get

$$\begin{cases} 4x + 2\pi y = 16 \\ x^2 + \pi y^2 = 21 \end{cases}$$

from which it is possible to solve for x: solving for y, in terms of x, from the first equation and substituting it in the second equation.

3. **(A)**

According to Statement (1) area of $\triangle ABC = 4 \times$ area of $\triangle ADE$. Since $\triangle ABC$ is similar to $\triangle EAD$, we have $BC/AD = a$ and $AC/ED = a$, i.e., $BC = a \times AD$ and $AC = a \times ED$; therefore,

$$\text{area of } \triangle ABC = \frac{1}{2} BC \times AC$$

$$= \frac{1}{2} \times a \times AD \times a \times ED$$

$$= \frac{1}{2} a^2 AD \times ED$$

$$= a^2 \times \frac{1}{2} AD \times ED$$

$$= a^2 \times \text{area of } \Delta ADE$$

So, $a^2 = 4$, i.e., $a = 2$. As a result, $BC = a \times AD = 2 \times AD = 4$ units. Hence, (1) alone is sufficient. According to Statement (2) $AC = 4$ units. Since Statement (2) does not suggest a way to find DE we cannot find the ratio of AC to DE. So, (2) alone is not sufficient to find BC.

4. **(C)**
    By Statement (1) $\angle AOB = 60°$ therefore, arc ACB is $\frac{5}{6}$ th of the circumference. Since (1) does not give us the circumference we cannot figure out the radius using (1) by itself. According to Statement (2) arc ABC is 20π inches long, but it does not tell us what portion of the circumference the arc is; we cannot figure out the radius using (2) alone. However, using Statements (1) and (2) together we can get the equation

$$\frac{5}{6} \times 2\pi r = 20\pi,$$

i.e., $r = 12$ inches.

5. **(C)**
    From Statement (1), we learn that z cannot be negative. From Statement (2), z can be equal to -2 or 1. Together the value of z can be determined to be 1.

6. **(D)**
    From Statement (1) the total amount of Jenny's savings can be determined by knowing that \$15,000 is 25 percent of the total (\$60,000); and therefore, we can determine the amount in her money market (15% of \$60,000). Likewise, Statement (2) can be used to determine Jenny's total savings, and subsequently, the money market account. Therefore, choice (D) is correct.

7. **(E)**
    Statement (1) is not sufficient since 4 is not a multiple of every even number. Statement (2) is also not sufficient since some numbers could be multiples of both 3 and 4 (such as 24) and others could not (such as 9). Using both statements is also not sufficient because the set of all numbers that are even integers and multiples of 3 (6, 12, 18, 24, ...) include some numbers that are multiples of 4, and others that are not. Therefore, the correct choice is (E).

8. **(E)**

According to (1), a round-trip ticket costs $81.25, according to (2) the train fare is $.50 per mile; therefore, the round trip is 162.5 miles long. Since (1) and (2) do not give the time the trip takes, you cannot find the speed. (1) and (2) taken together are not sufficient.

9. **(B)**

By Statement (1)

$$\frac{2y}{2x-1} = 1.$$

Since (1) does not give the value of x you cannot determine y using (1) alone. But, according to Statement (2)

$$\frac{x+y}{x-y} = 1.$$

In addition, we know that $x \neq y$; therefore,

$$\frac{x+y}{x-y} = 1$$

is the same as the equation $x + y = x - y$ or $y = 0$, so (2) alone is sufficient.

10. **(B)**

According to Statement (1) $AC = 100$ miles. Since (1) alone does not help to find the distance AB you cannot find the time it took to go from A to B using (1) alone. However, by Statement (2) $BC = .3$ miles; since we know the speed used to go from B to C, we can figure out the time it took to go from B to C. Moreover, the total time is known. So, (2) alone is sufficient to find the time it took to go from A to B.

11. **(D)**

The total number of students is x^3. According to (1) x^3 is even. Therefore, x is even and (1) alone is sufficient. According to Statement (2) x^2 is even, since the number of students interviewed in each town is x^2. Therefore, x is even. Hence, (2) alone is also sufficient.

12. **(E)**

By Statement (1) Joanna changed $5. Since (1) does not say how many quarters, dimes, and nickels are released each time a bill is fed into the machine, (1) alone is not sufficient. Moreover, if we use Statement (2) in addition to (1) we only know that of the $5 changed, $4 is in quarters while $1 is in dimes and nickels. Since (2) does not make it clear whether 3 quarters, 1 dime, and 3 nickels, or 3 quarters, 2 dimes, and 1 nickel are released it is not possible to figure out the number of dimes and the number of nickels using (1) and (2) together.

13. **(C)**

Statement (1) just says that ($1/3$) of the girls in public schools are 10th graders. (1) alone does not help to find the number of girls and boys in the 10th grade; you cannot find the percentage of girls in 10th grade using (1) alone. For similar reasons (2) alone is not sufficient. However, if we let x be the total number of students in public school, it is given that $.4x$ of them are boys, while the number of girls is $.6x$. Therefore, according to Statement (1), the number of girls in 10th grade is $1/3$ of $0.6x$, i.e., $0.2x$, and the number of boys in 10th grade is $3/5$ of $0.4x$, i.e., $0.24x$. As a result, the percentage of girls in 10th grade is

$$\frac{0 \times 2x}{0 \times 2x + 0 \times 24x} \times 100 \text{ percent.}$$

Hence, (1) and (2) together are sufficient.

14. **(E)**

Say the number of books he ordered is x and the price of each book is $y. According to Statement (1) the sales tax per book is 8 percent. According to Statement (2) payment for postage and handling was $1.25 per book. Therefore, based on the payment he enclosed the total expense per book is

$$y + \$0.08y + \$1.25.$$

Since the payment he enclosed is $91.40 we will have the equation

$$(\$y + \$0.08y + \$1.25)x = \$91.40.$$

Since neither Statement (1) nor (2) gives us the value of x we cannot solve for y (i.e., for the price per book). Hence (1) and (2) together are not sufficient.

15. **(C)**

By (1), the average age for the two classes together is 20. Since (1) does not give the number of students in Classroom B and the sum of their ages, you cannot find the average age in Classroom B. (2) tells us that the number of students in Classroom A is 20 therefore, the number of students in Classroom B is 25. Since (2) does not give the sum of the ages of students in Classroom B you cannot find the average using (2) alone. However, using (1) and (2) together you get the equations

the sum of ages in Classroom A: $15 \times 20 = 300$,

$$\frac{300 + \text{sum of ages in B}}{45} = 20,$$

and that there are 25 students in Classroom B and the average age

$$\frac{\text{sum of ages in B}}{25} = \frac{600}{25} = 24.$$

So, (1) and (2) together are sufficient.

16. **(E)**

According to (1) the area of the cardboard is 49 square inches; therefore, its width is 7 inches. (2) tells us the same information as (1). Since you cannot find the value of x from Statements (1) and (2), it is not possible to determine the height, width, and length of the box. So, (1) and (2) together are not sufficient to determine the volume.

17. **(E)**

Statement (1) says that xy divides 336. Statement (2) says x and y are primes. Since there are more than one pair of prine numbers x, y such that xy divides 336, (1) and (2) together are not sufficient to say exactly what xy should be.

18. **(E)**

According to (1) there were 12 students in economics class. Since 2 girls dropped and 3 boys added economics, there are 13 students enrolled in economics after adding and dropping courses. According to (1) and (2) there are 13 students in business class after adding and dropping courses. Since neither (1) nor (2) give the number of girls originally enrolled for the business course, you cannot find the number of girls still taking the business class. So, (1) and (2) together are not sufficient to answer the question.

19. **(C)**

According to Statement (1) the base of a triangle lies on the x-axis. Since Statement (1) does not say anything about the other sides it is not sufficient to find the area. Statement (2) tells where the two sides of the triangle lie but it is not helpful to find the dimensions of the triangle.

Therefore, Statement (2) alone is not sufficient to find the area. Using both Statements (1) and (2) together we get the picture of the triangle to be as shown below.

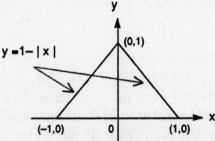

20. **(D)**

According to (1) $x^4 - 1 > 0$; therefore, by difference of two squares

$$x^4 - 1 = (x^2)^2 - 1 = (x^2 - 1)(x^2 + 1) > 0.$$

But $x^2 + 1 > 0$, and therefore $x^2 - 1 > 0$. So, (1) alone is sufficient. By Statement (2)

$$\frac{1}{1-|x|} > 0, \text{ but } \frac{1}{1-|x|} > 0$$

if and only if $1 - |x| > 0$, i.e., $|x| < 1$. Hence, (2) alone is also sufficient.

Section 4–Sentence Correction

1. **(E)**
Two actions are expressed in this sentence: WOULD HAVE BEEN BETTER and WOULD HAVE SENT. Since one action occurred before the other, both verbs cannot be in the same tense. The prior action should be expressed in past perfect, HAD SENT. Do not use WOULD HAVE in subordinate clauses which begin with IF and which express the prior of two past actions. Choices (A), (B), and (C) retain the WOULD HAVE construction in the subordinate clause. In addition, choice (C) introduces the weak passive voice. Choice (D) also introduces the weak passive voice.

2. **(C)**
LIKE introduces prepositional phrases, not clauses. Since the sentence continues with a subordinate clause, LIKE THEY WERE IN FAVOR OF A TAX INCREASE, AS IF should be used: AS IF THEY WERE. The adjective FEWER is correct before a plural noun. The wordy phrase FOR THE PUBLIC CITIZENS can be condensed. Choices (A), (B), and (D) are incorrect because they use LIKE. Choices (B), (D), and (E) change the meaning of PUBLIC.

3. **(E)**
The good writer should avoid wordiness; WHICH IS can be deleted because it inflates the sentence length and sets up the passive voice constructions in choices (A) and (B). Choice (C) still retains the passive, and choice (D) introduces a new concept, AVERAGE.

4. **(D)**
Choice (D) is correct because it has a correctly placed adjective participial phrase. TOTALLING MORE THAN SHE HAD ANTICIPATED is a participial phrase that modifies COSTS and not BRIDE, so the phrase must appear next to THE COSTS as in choice (D). The participial phrase cannot modify BRIDE, so choice (A) contains a dangling modifier. The rewording in choice (E) creates another dangling modifier, SHOCKING HER, THE BRIDE. Choice (C) places the participial modifier at the end of the sentence, next to BRIDE again; in addition, it has passive voice. Choice (B) lacks subject and verb agreement: COSTS…WAS should be COSTS…WERE.

5. **(B)**
     Choice (A) has a misplaced modifier: the concept of DRUNK appears too close behind POWERBOAT, making the boat seem to be drunk. Choices (C) and (D) would create another misplaced modifier. The end of the sentence, PUNISHABLE BY A FINE AND A JAIL SENTENCE, should modify MISDEMEANOR and not POWERBOAT. Choice (E) is awkwardly worded with three constructions in a row consisting of A plus a noun.

6. **(A)**
     Choice (A) correctly shows the contrast between the two briefcases. Choice (B) employed the awkward wording of A GREAT DIFFERENCE. Choices (C), (D), and (E) all use the incorrect idiom, DIFFER WITH. DIFFER WITH is used only with people in the sense of TO DISAGREE. DIFFER FROM is used with objects in the sense of TO BE UNLIKE. In addition, choice (C) has the modifier GREATLY misplaced, and the wording of choice (E) creates a fragment.

7. **(B)**
     Choice (B) correctly uses the phrase TO TRY TO accomplish something. Choice (A) uses the incorrect construction TO TRY AND accomplish something. Choice (D) mangles the phrase completely: ABOUT TRYING AND RUNNING. Choice (C) has the awkward phrasing, POSSIBLY SOON. Choice (E) changes the meaning of the sentence slightly by making it seem as if Sandy were not necessarily the one running the program and by deleting the idea of AS SOON AS POSSIBLE.

8. **(D)**
     Choice (D) is the only coherent, smoothly worded choice. Choice (A), besides being overly wordy, uses the incorrect construction IS...LIKE WHEN. Choices (A), (B), (C), and (E) lack parallelism. RIDING A BICYCLE must have the complementary parallel structure, ROLLER SKATING. Choices (B) and (E) are also too wordy. In choice (C), FORGETTING is not an idea equal in meaning with RIDING.

9. **(A)**
     Choice (A) uses the correct adverb to introduce the subordinate clause; IF indicates a possible problem, not a certain one. Choices (B) and (C) sound as if you intend to cut your scalp as a deliberate action. Choices (D) and (E) mix ONE and A PERSON with YOU, so they contain an incorrect shift in voice.

10. **(E)**

There are three ideas in the last part of this sentence. CONFUSED OR SLUGGISH are two equal modifiers; the third idea, AND THEY SHOULD BE WATCHED CLOSELY IF THEY HAVE DIFFICULTY WALKING is a subordinate clause parallel to the previous subordinate clause, ESPECIALLY IF THEY APPEAR CONFUSED OR SLUGGISH. Choice (E) is the only one that correctly pairs CONFUSED OR SLUG-GISH and correctly shows the parallelism of the two subordinate clauses. Choice (A) uses the passive voice. Choice (B), in addition to using the passive voice, unnecessarily uses two different forms of TO BE.

11. **(C)**

The introductory phrase, AN EXCEPTIONALLY GOOD SPORT FISH, must appear next to the word it modifies, MUTTONFISH. Choices (A), (D), and (E) make a dangling modifier out of the introductory phrase. Choice (B) changes the meaning of MANY HOURS to HOURLY.

12. **(A)**

Choice (A) correctly has compound verbs in the subordinate clause. The wording of choice (B) sounds as if pine trees also contain volatile oils and will burn when it is raining, but this idea is not contained in the original meaning of the sentence. Choice (C) makes birch bark seem to be some kind of a container for volatile oil. Choices (D) and (E) both have split infinitives: TO THEREFORE BURN and TO CERTAINLY CON-TAIN. Adverbs (THEREFORE and CERTAINLY) should not split the TO and the verb of an infinitive (TO BURN and TO CONTAIN).

13. **(D)**

Choice (D) is concise and accurate. Choices (A), (B), and (E) use the unnecessary word THEN. Choice (B) has a split infinitive: TO QUICKLY SMOTHER. Choices (A) and (C) have the adverb QUICKLY misplaced between TO BE and SMOTHERED. Choices (A) and (C) are redundant in their use of IT. In choices (A), (B), and (C) the phrase IT WILL NOT TAKE LONG can be deleted because it has the same meaning as QUICKLY. Choice (E) is incorrect because it is not an independent clause as required by the coordinating conjunction BUT.

14. **(B)**

The preposition OF requires a noun or a pronoun as a completer; an adjective subordinate clause (WHEN I LAST SAW JAMES AND HER) cannot follow a preposition. Therefore, Choice (A) is incorrect. In addi-tion, an objective case pronoun must follow an action verb (SAW HER) or a preposition (WITH HER and OF HER). The addition of another object of preposition or direct object (JAMES) does not change the case of the pronoun. Choices (A), (D), and (E) all use incorrect pronoun case. Choice (A) also incorrectly ends a sentence with a preposition. Choice (C) uses the correct pronoun case, but MEMORIES cannot be PROUD; only people can be proud.

15. **(B)**
    In standard English, FEWER is used before a plural noun; LESS is used before a singular noun. Choice (B) correctly uses FEWER before MISTAKES and continues the parallelism in the second half of the sentence: THE BETTER HIS CHANCES. Choices (A), (D), and (E) all incorrectly use LESS before MISTAKES. The second half of choice (C) is not parallel and is poorly worded, "when it comes to being able to."

16. **(C)**
    Choice (C) is correct because the second half of the sentence indicates that Muhammed Ali's talents were universally recognized; therefore, it was his personality that came under fire. Choices (A) and (E) are not properly worded; the phrase ENDED UP is incorrect because UP is redundant. Choice (B) indicates that Ali's talents were criticized, an idea directly contradicted by the rest of the sentence. Choice (D) changes the meaning of the sentence, adding IN THE END and inserting it awkwardly between the helping verb and the main verb.

17. **(E)**
    The subject of this sentence is SKILLS, a plural noun, so the verb also must be plural; the number of a subject does not change with an intervening prepositional phrase, FOR THE WINTER OLYMPIC BIATHLON. Choice (E) is the only one having a plural verb, ARE. The verb is followed by plural predicate nominatives, CROSS COUNTRY SKIING AND SHOOTING, so the sentence is logically completed by listing the two skills in the biathlon. Choice (A) uses a singular verb, IS, and completes the idea of skills by listing skiing and shooting as one event, an illogical completion to the plural subject. Choice (B) is a fragment and would be acceptable only if the verb form were changed to COMBINES. Choices (C) and (D) use a singular verb, and (D) changes the meaning of the events.

18. **(A)**
    LIKE can never be used to introduce a subordinate clause, so choices (C), (D), and (E) are all incorrect. In choice (B), two past perfect verbs,

HAD BEEN LYING and HAD KNOWN cannot be used together because the past perfect is used to indicate the previous of two past actions.

19. **(C)**
Choice (C) places the adverb NOW in front of BEING in order to correct the awkward wording of BEING NOW CONSIDERED. Choice (C) also eliminates the poor repetition of SPORT. Choice (A) contains the double us of SPORT and the awkward placement of NOW. Although choice (B) deletes one of the uses of SPORT, the resulting phrase is worse than the original. Choice (D) would leave the sentence with two prepositions in a row, OF and BY. Choice (E) inserts NOW in the incorrect place, as well as producing a sentence with unclear meaning and terrible wording.

20. **(E)**
The first part of the sentence introduces three people, and the second part of the sentence refers to each individual. Choices (A) and (B) use NEITHER, a word indicating a choice between two things. Choice (C) has an agreement problem with the singular pronoun ONE and the plural verb WERE. Choice (D) sounds as if all three were willing, a concept contradicted by the conjunction BUT.

21. **(C)**
Choice (C) has a plural construction for all the elements of this idea. THIS and THAT require singular constructions; THOSE and THESE require plural constructions. Choice (A) has a singular subject and a plural verb, THIS KIND...ARE. Choice (B) has a singular subject but other elements plural, THESE KIND...ARE. Choice (D) uses PROBLEMS with all other elements being singular. Choice (E) has all singular elements but creates a confusion with THE KIND.

22. **(E)**
Choice (E) eliminates awkward phrasing and problems with placement of modifier. In choice (A) the subject, THE WOMAN, and the subordinate clause WHO WAS THE WINNER'S VOICE, is poor phrasing because a woman cannot be a voice; in addition, it is the woman's voice—not the woman—that had AN EXCITED SOUND. Choice (B) contains two weak phrasings: THE WOMAN AS THE WINNER and EXCITED-SOUNDING. Choice (C) produces a fragment. Choice (D) is not a parallel simple sentence to balance the last half of the sentence following a coordinating conjunction.

Section 5—Critical Reasoning

1. **(B)**

    The advertisement does not suggest any comparison between Fizzy Pop and other thirst quenchers; (A) is not the best choice. (B) is the correct choice; the suggestion here is that a lot of "modern" residents use Fizzy Pop. People often want to follow the crowd and get on the bandwagon. This advertisement appeals to those individuals. (C) is a possibility, but it is certainly not the best choice. Numbers are only suggested in this ad. There are no numbers stated for the individual to use. (D) is not the correct choice since no famous people are alluded to in this advertisement. (E) is not the best choice because no indication is given as to where the advertisement appeared.

2. **(B)**

    There is no direct evidence to suggest that the defeated candidate attacked the character of the elected individual; therefore, (A) is not the appropriate choice. The candidate did make a comparison between her defeat and those of Lincoln; (B) is the correct choice. Little information is given about the opponents' claims so (C) is not the best choice. The reader is not given the reason for pointing out the unanswered questions. Perhaps he did not have the knowledge. Perhaps he was dishonest and avoided them. Perhaps he did not respond to the wishes of the people he is to serve. (D) is a possible choice, but it is not the best answer since there are so many unanswered questions about it. According to the passage, the defeated candidate did not directly show that the opponent's platform was absurd; hence, (E) is not the best choice.

3. **(A)**

    (A) is the best choice. Since the opponent failed to answer certain questions, she could demonstrate her expertise by answering the questions. The defeated candidate did not, according to the passage, make direct reference to her morality or capabilities; therefore, (B) is incorrect. Again, the truth may not have been avoided in the failure to answer questions by the opponent; (C) is not the correct choice. The concerns and actions which brought about Lincoln's defeats seem irrelevant at this point, so (D) is incorrect. It seems too late now to discuss the absurd conclusion to which the opponent's platform may lead. The passage does not even indicate that such is the case; therefore, (E) is not the best choice.

4. **(A)**

This passage (which has not been proven) suggests that increased study time could benefit both the students and the institutions of higher education. Therefore, (A) is the correct choice. (B) is not the best choice. The creation of more jobs on campuses is not a point covered in the passage. It is not likely that most colleges and universities will decrease their enrollments if test scores are lowered. It is more logical that the colleges and universities would lower their admission requirements to keep a certain number of students to meet necessary costs. Thus, (C) is not the best choice. The passage presents no evidence to suggest that low test scores have been a cause of economic recession; (D) is not the best choice. Since the passage does not suggest that low test scores have caused a decline in education quality at institutions of higher education across the nation, (E) is not the best choice.

5. **(D)**

A good teacher would not attempt to change a student's learning style; she might try to teach the child how to adapt, however, to a classroom which utilizes the auditory approach. Hence, (A) is not the best choice. Teachers who are aware of the differences in learning styles would not attempt to use just one teaching approach in their classrooms. Instead, they would use a variety of approaches; (B) is not the best choice. Most teachers do not encourage parents to teach children at home. Teaching is what they are paid to do. Since the word "teach" is employed, (C) is not a satisfactory choice. (D) is the best choice. Teachers who are aware of the learning styles of individual students will try to use approaches which accommodate all three styles at some time. (E) is not the best choice since most teachers would want to utilize the information on learning styles in their classes and not just to pass a test.

6. **(D)**

One cannot tell from the information given if Leon reads more than Nurry. One knows that Leon reads more than Millie, but the amount he reads could still be less than Nurry. On the other hand, it could be more than Nurry, so (A) is not the best choice. The answer cannot be determined from (B) either. One knows that Leon reads more than Millie, but one does not know how Leon ranks in relation to Jules. (C) cannot be stated as truth. One knows that Kim and Nurry read the same amount. One also knows that Millie reads less than Nurry and that Leon reads more than Millie; the reader, however, is not told for sure how Leon ranks in relation to the others. (D) is correct. Jules reads more than Kim; Kim and Nurry read the same amount. Since Millie reads less than Nurry, she also reads less than Kim. Therefore, Jules reads more than Millie. (E) is incorrect. Since the reader is told that Millie reads less than Nurry and since Kim and Nurry read exactly the same, Millie reads less than Kim. Choice (E), however, states that Kim reads less than Millie.

7. **(B)**
    Statement I does not support the claim that the land must be conserved. If each person uses the land as he/she wishes, there is no way that conservation can occur. II is correct. Restricting vehicles from traveling newly sown banks would support the conservation of land through rules. Restricting individuals from using public lands for financial advantage does not relate to conservation; therefore, III is incorrect. (B) is the correct choice since it includes II but not I and III.

8. **(A)**
    Pressure groups are an important privilege in democracy, (A) is correct. (B) is a false statement. In the United States and in a true democracy pressure groups can hold meetings and demonstrations. (C) is false since public opinion develops freely in a true democracy. People are not limited in the opportunities they have to make the government representative in a democracy; (D) is false. Rival political parties are important to a true democracy, hence (E) is incorrect.

9. **(E)**
    The deficit in education seems to grow in the United States (partially because the United States is educating children who would not have been in the school system some years ago). (A) supports the conclusion and should not be selected. It is true that many Americans remain ill-prepared for the real world; (B) does not refute the author's claim. Since it does cost more to educate the children with many deficiencies and needs, (C) should not be selected. As the article states, the needs of all these children are not being met; therefore, (D) is not the correct choice. (E) is the correct choice. It is not supported by the passage. The article does not suggest that the home should not interfere with the school system. In fact it seems to suggest that many of the problems the school faces are a result of the home.

10. **(D)**
    Refrigerators can be a profitable product when they are produced on a small scale if the demand is there; (A) is incorrect. The passage states that the production of refrigerators has been unusually low for the two year period since the steel has gone to automobiles; therefore, (B) is incorrect. (C) is not the best choice, since the passage does not speculate on whether steel production will increase in the future. (D) is the best choice;

with the decrease in refrigerator production, the surplus stocks of refrigerators have been decreased. (E) is not the best choice since the passage does not suggest whether the profits of car manufacturers are unprecedented.

11. **(D)**

It would have been impossible for refrigerator manufacturers to foresee how high the price of refrigerators would actually go; therefore, (A) is not the best choice. (B) cannot be ascertained from the passage. Just what the profit margin was for cars in the past or what it will be in the future was not discussed. Since there is not evidence in the passage to suggest that steel manufacturers would prefer selling to either the car or refrigerator producers (in some instances they may be one and the same). (C) is not the best answer. The price of refrigerators has increased since supply was down and the demand was there; (D) is the best choice. There is no evidence in the passage to suggest a less expensive substance was substituted for steel in refrigerators, which eliminates (E).

12. **(E)**

If the scores of those administered beta blockers in a later experiment increased only 22 points, this would not be a very impressive rate since nationwide the second-time test takers improved an average of 28 points; (A) would not be the best choice. If the scores nationwide improved from an average of 28 to an average of 38 points, this would not strengthen Dr. Faigel's conclusion. This nationwide improvement would not relate to Dr. Faigel's experiment in a direct way; therefore, (B) should not be chosen. Since Dr. Faigel believes that nervousness results in increased adrenalin, he administers beta blockers which interfere with the effects of adrenalin. If adrenalin were administered and the scores nationwide were increased 100 points, this would not strengthen Dr. Faigel's conclusion, thus (C) is incorrect. Dr. Faigel did not neglect to use a control group in his experiment. Replicating the experiment in order to use a control group would not be necessary; (D) is incorrect. If the experiment were conducted on a larger scale and similar results were achieved, it would strengthen Faigel's conclusion, so (E) is correct.

13. **(C)**

It is true that Paul is citing only a single area of the United States, but that was his explicit purpose. This is not the weak point that Paula is concerned about, thus (A) is incorrect. There is no indication made that the decrease is a mathematical error; (B) is not the correct choice. The fact that the 1987 statistics are not current enough to reflect recent occurrences is the weak point that Paula responds to at once; therefore, (C) is the best choice. Paula does not focus on the fact that Paul makes no mention of Northern states, (D) is not the best choice. Paula does not ask for exact figures for infant mortality for 1984–1987. She seems to be more concerned with the lack of current information, so (E) is not the correct choice.

14. **(A)**
The greenhouse effect and acid rain are both consequences of environmental pollution, much of which can be attributed to gasoline being used for vehicles. This threat to the environment could certainly be helped with the use of hydrogen fuel. Using hydrogen to help eliminate pollution would weaken arguments skeptics might have; (A) is the best choice. (B) should not be selected since hydrogen has been used as an energy source for rockets. Since future supplies of oil are **not** guaranteed, (C) is not the best choice. (D) is not the best choice. A concerted national effort is needed to utilize hydrogen as a fuel, but this is not an argument which would weaken the arguments of the skeptics. Certainly a gradual transition from gasoline to hydrogen is needed, but this does not serve to weaken the skeptics' arguments, (E) is not the best choice.

15. **(B)**
(A) is not the best choice; the cost that is implied here is not a financial cost. (B) (which refers to too little time for children, family, and themselves) is the sacrifice most women make when they work, this is the correct choice. Men, too, have to sacrifice time; (C), then, is not the correct choice. Since part of the 52 percent might include those who are undecided, the reader has no way of knowing that more than half of the women respondents did not feel these concerns; therefore, (D) is not the best choice. Women cannot be expected to withdraw from the work force; predictions are that the percentage of women working will increase in years to come; (E) is incorrect.

16. **(E)**
(A) is false, the spoils system is not illegal at all levels in our country. (B) is an advantage, not a disadvantage, of the spoils system. (C) should not be selected. It is sometimes difficult to ascertain who is deserving of rewards for party services, but this is not the most serious disadvantage listed for the spoils system. (D) is not the best choice. The spoils system dates back at least to the time of Thomas Jefferson; it is not a system that is less than ten years old. The chief disadvantage of the spoils system is that sometimes it is appropriate, but other times it is not; therefore, (E) is the correct choice.

Section 6–Problem Solving

1. **(B)**
    $270 - $225 = $45

    $$\frac{45}{270} = \frac{15}{90} = 0.1\overline{6} = 16\frac{2}{3}\%$$

Choice (A) comes from incorrectly dividing 225 by 270.

$$\frac{225}{270} = 0.8\overline{3} = 83\frac{1}{3}\%$$

Choice (D) comes from incorrectly dividing 45 by 225.

$$\frac{45}{225} = 0.2 = 20\%$$

2. **(B)**
    The easiest way is to write down the prime numbers and count them. Prime numbers between 0 and 40 are:

    2, 3, 5, 7, 11, 13, 17, 19, 23, 29, 31, 37.

3. **(A)**
    The area of the addition is equal to $l \times w$.

    $90 \times 150 = 13,500$ sq. ft.

The area of one tile is $1.5 \times 1.5 = 2.25$ sq. ft. and the number of tiles can be found by dividing the area of the room by the area of one tile.

$$\frac{13,500}{2.25} = 6,000 \text{ tiles}$$

4. **(C)**

    If $\frac{x}{y} = 5$, then $x = 5y$. Substitute in the equation to obtain

    $$\frac{x^2 - y^2}{y^2} = \frac{(5y)^2 - y^2}{y^2}$$

$$= \frac{(5y)^2 - y^2}{y^2}$$

$$= \frac{24y^2}{y^2}$$

$$= 24$$

5. **(B)**

Change $\frac{3}{4}$ to a decimal, .75, and solve.

$$\frac{.75}{1.5} \times 100 = 50\%$$

6. **(D)**

Let x = Kathy's age

y = John's age

From the information given the equation for their ages would be

$$2y = x$$

and their ages five years ago would be

$$x - 5 = 3(y - 5)$$

Substituting x with 2y

$$2y - 5 = 3y - 15$$

$$y = 10$$

Therefore, $2y = 2(10) = 20$, Kathy's age now.

7. **(D)**

Apply your knowledge of ∥ lines.

$\angle a = 30°$

$\angle y = 180° - 30°$

$\angle y = 150°$

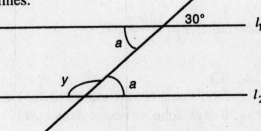

8. **(D)**

Let $2x, 3x, 5x$ = measures of the angles, then

$$2x + 3x + 5x = 180°$$

and

$$10x = 180°,$$

$$x = 18°.$$

Therefore, $2(18°) = 36°$ and $3(18°) = 54°$ and $5(18°) = 90°$.

9. **(B)**

The most common mistake in this kind of problem is to assume that two successive 10 percent discounts are equivalent to one 20 percent discount which is what is wrong with choice (A) because $300(.20) = 60$ so that $300 - 60 = 240$. The correct solution is:

$$300(100\% - 10\%) = 300(1 - .1) = 300(.9) = 270$$

after the first 10 percent discount. After the second 10 percent discount, the price is

$$270(.9) = 243.$$

10. **(D)**

If $a + b = 3$ and $2b + c = 2$, then

$$2(a + b) = 2(3) = 6$$

so that

$$2(a + b) - (2b + c) = 6 - 2.$$

Therefore, $2a - c = 4$.

11. **(C)**

If X is the original price of the suit, then

$$X(1 - .4) - 144.$$

Therefore, $X = \dfrac{144}{.6} = 240.$

12. **(E)**

John's cost for the month of June is $\$2,000(.27) = \$540$. Since June has 30 days, John's average daily cost is

$$\frac{540}{30} = \$18.$$

13. **(D)**

If $x - y = 9$ then

$$3(x - y) = 3(9)$$

and $\qquad 3x - 3y = 27$

and $\qquad 3x - 3y - 1 = 26.$

14. **(C)**

The average rate of speed from Washington to Philadelphia was

$$\frac{150}{3} = 50 \text{ miles per hour.}$$

Since the rate of speed on the return trip was 20 percent faster, the average rate must be $50(1.2) = 60$ miles per hour. At this rate it took

$$\frac{150}{60} = 2\frac{1}{2}$$

hours for the return trip. Hence, the total time it took for the round trip was

$$(3 + 2\frac{1}{2}) = 5 \text{ hours, 30 minutes.}$$

15. **(D)**

The height of the trapezoid must be drawn inside the figure in order to use the formula for the area of a trapezoid =

$$\frac{1}{2}h(a + b)$$

where a and b are the bases. When h is drawn, a $30°–60°–90°$ triangle is formed with the hypotenuse given as 10 (the side of the trapezoid). The side opposite the $30°$ is 5, making the height (the side opposite the $60°$) = $5\sqrt{3}$. Base $b = 30$ as given and base $a = 30 - 10 = 20$.

$$\text{Area} = \frac{1}{2}5\sqrt{3}(20 + 30)$$

$$= 25(5\sqrt{3})$$

$$= 125\sqrt{3}$$

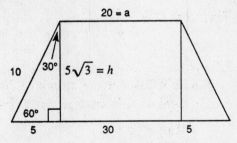

16. **(E)**

    Let x equal the number of Bob's marbles and let y equal the number of Joe's marbles. If Joe gives two of his marbles to Bob, then the equation

$$x + 2 = y - 2$$

is true. If Bob gives two of his marbles to Joe, then the equation

$$2(x - 2) = y + 2$$

is true. Simplifying both equations we have the following system:

$$x - y = -4$$

$$2x - y = 6$$

Subtracting the first equation from the second, gives $x = 10$. To check, we find that $y = 14$. If Bob gives 2 of his marbles to Joe, he will have 8 and Joe will have 16, which verifies Joe's comment that he will have twice the number Bob has.

Section 7—Analytical Writing Assessment

ANALYSIS OF AN ISSUE ESSAY TOPIC

Sample Essay Response Scoring 5 to 6

Americans are legally required to spend most of their childhood and young adulthood in school. Ideally, time so spent should be a valuable and enriching experience. When a person receives a high school or college diploma, they hopefully have become a responsible citizen, ready to enter society and give back some of what they have been given through their education. It is indeed difficult to define exactly what constitutes a "responsible citizen," or to decide the best way to create such an individual. However, I think it is important that we allow such a definition to change, and that we realize that our educational methods have to change as well. Ours is a complicated, fast-paced world, and new skills are necessary to survive in this environment. While I think that a broad range of knowledge is helpful and people should be required to learn about subjects they might not personally be motivated to explore, I also believe that all knowledge and skills are valuable, and that it is important to encourage a student in exactly the areas that interest him or her.

One advantage to teaching less traditional subjects is that it becomes increasingly likely that the student is learning because he or she wants to, and not because information is being forced upon them. It seems that all too often, students are seen as little more than computers who can be programmed with knowledge; no thought is given to whether or not that information is of interest or value to them. It seems that something which is learned merely because it may appear on a test is not likely to be remembered long after that test has been taken. If a study is encouraged to explore a skill or a subject that he or she finds interesting, however, it is probable that he or she will not only remember what was learned about that subject, but will be encouraged to learn more about other related subjects; furthermore, the student will be eager to share what he or she has learned.

This is not the case with an archaic curriculum which stresses skills and knowledge which are no longer of use to the student. It is unfair to assume that every student will have the same interests in school or the same needs once they leave school. If the canon of knowledge one must learn is prescribed from without for the entire country, it is probable that a large quantity of students will be left feeling neglected or apathetic. Such educational requirements will be seem as chores and eventually the students' discouragement will ensue.

If this is true for students whose family encourages their studies, how much more true must it be for those whose parents are uninterested or even abusive? The conflicts some children face are completely removed from the subjects held to be important in school. If a child is hungry or cold, unloved or abused, how can he or she be expected to connect algebra to the frightening realities of everyday life?

A genuine interest in a subject, when encouraged and nurtured, might give such a student a sense of hope that would help him or her to survive in school and would provide skills which would be useful once he or she graduated. Knowledge, when acquired through personal choice rather than as a chore, is one of the few things in this life that we can hold onto, that no one can take from us, and that we can build on throughout our lives. Knowledge could provide not only a good reason for a student to go to school, but on a deeper level, a good reason for him or her to live. It is further probable that a student with such a positive scholastic experience would graduate with more to offer society, and would be ready to begin a rewarding career and less likely to resort to crime or to be burdened with poverty.

A responsible citizen is one who shows concern for the welfare of the society in which he or she lives and tries to add something valuable to it. A positive scholastic experience which nurtures preexisting interests and practical applicable skills is the most likely to produce such a person. Of course, many subjects already being taught are important, but it is possible to incorporate a new emphasis in learning without removing the broad scope of knowledge. Schools could become a place to which most people will actively want to go, where they will learn to feel better about themselves and about their place in a community.

Analysis of Sample Essay Scoring 5 to 6

This essay analyzing an issue is considered a "six"-rated essay. The question asks the writer to choose one side of an issue, and effectively argue why they have chosen that position. In this essay, once the author has chosen one side, he or she clearly sets out several reasons for that choice. The specific question is about education; this essay examines many levels on which education is expected to work, taking into account both those students with supportive parents and those who difficult home lives. The essay is well-organized in that it arranges the various reasons it explores in such a way that they lead easily into one another, and they all tie back to the original theme.

ANALYSIS OF AN ARGUMENT ESSAY TOPIC

Sample Essay Response Scoring 5 to 6

In this argument, the author is compiling a list of reasons why it would be preferable for Americans to adopt a vegetarian diet. He or she has a definite goal in mind, which is to persuade the reader to undergo a change in lifestyle. In the process of setting forth her argument, she disparages our economic system and our food production system, and it is in this context that she calls upon the individual to change his or her own actions. The argument is extremely effective because it uses unusual lines of reasoning that might be convincing to people who ordinarily believe that they have no interest in vegetarianism. It is subtly persuasive in that it appeals to our emotions while appearing to be purely factual and intellectual.

Many arguments for vegetarianism tend to make it look like an unusual or strange lifestyle, suitable for only a fringe portion of the population. Traditional discussions on the subject might not appeal to a majority of the population, particularly in a country such as America where the raising and eating of meat is seen as a longstanding and valuable institution.

The strength of the argument set forth in this passage is that it does not seem to speak to a few strange people interested in an alternative lifestyle, but instead to everyone in America, with arguments which affect everyone, on many different levels, whether they are aware of it or not. It does this by discussing institutions upon which every citizen depends, namely the economic and the food production systems, and by showing how the long-term tradition of meat-eating might not be as practical as has been commonly believed.

One effective debating skill that this passage employs is to list a variety of arguments only to state that they are not as important as the main argument. In this way, the author manages to set forth these arguments, which are persuasive in their own right, and in so doing to lend even more cogency to her final point. In this passage, these are issues of health and money, two subjects which appeal to every individual, as nothing is more convincing than to speak to someone's pocketbook or to their very life. These subjects are so important that to follow them up by saying, "Most importantly...." makes what follows seem worthy of very close attention.

Another extremely effective technique that this passage employs is the subtlety with which it appeals to the emotions. Any argument which does so too directly is likely to cause suspicion. If the author had overtly tried to make the reader feel guilty in an effort to provoke a change in his or her lifestyle, she would instead have caused the reader to feel defensive. Instead, she appears to call upon the reader's common sense, to show how, as a country, we could all be healthier and richer if we adopted the eating practices she recommends. The one instance in which she does appeal directly to the emotions, and perhaps tries to cause a feeling of guilt, is in the final sentence when she mentions starving children. This is one of the few sections of the argument which does not seem as powerfully reasoned or as persuasive.

Although this passage is very strong, it might be made even more so with the addition of specific statistics or examples. If the author could have provided exact numbers to show how our food production system causes waste, or examples of a food production system which would be more cost-effective, it might have made the passage more convincing. If, for instance, she had provided a dollar figure for the money spent on meat production as opposed to that necessary to produce plant foods, or shown what that money could buy for the consumer, she might have appealed to a broader and more skeptical audience.

It is very difficult to make sweeping changes in the lifestyle of an entire country. This is particularly true if those changes involve something so basic as the production and consumption of food. The author makes her argument persuasive with a combination of vigorous conviction and subtle intellectual reasoning that does justice to the complexity of her task.

Analysis of Sample Essay Scoring 5 to 6

The above essay analyzing an argument is a "six"-rated or "outstanding" essay. The original argument is a complicated list of problems with our food production and economic system. Throughout the piece, the essayist correctly reads the main point of the argument—to try and persuade the reader to change his or her lifestyle and consume less meat. The essay proceeds to show how this is effectively set out in the argument, recognizing even subtle methods of persuasion. The organization helps the essayist to examine each element in as much depth as possible in a short space before moving on to the next, and the connections between the paragraphs are smooth and clear.

GMAT CAT

Graduate Management Admission Test
Computer-Adaptive Test

Practice
Test 2

NOTE:

The following practice test contains more questions than the actual GMAT CAT. This is necessary to provide a score that is roughly comparable to the shorter computer-adaptive test. Although the format is different, this test will give you an accurate idea of your strengths and weaknesses, and provide guidance for further study.

PRACTICE TEST 2

Section 1

(Answer sheets appear in the back of the book.)

TIME: 25 Minutes
20 Questions

DIRECTIONS: Each of the data sufficiency problems below contains a question and two statements, labeled (1) and (2), in which certain data are given. Decide whether the data given in the statements are sufficient for answering the question. Using the data given in the statements plus your knowledge of mathematics and everyday facts choose:

(A) if Statement (1) ALONE is sufficient, but Statement (2) alone is not sufficient to answer the question asked;

(B) if Statement (2) ALONE is sufficient, but Statement (1) alone is not sufficient to answer the question asked;

(C) if BOTH Statements (1) and (2) TOGETHER are sufficient to answer the question asked, but NEITHER statement ALONE is sufficient;

(D) if EACH statement ALONE is sufficient to answer the question asked;

(E) if Statements (1) and (2) TOGETHER are NOT sufficient to answer the questions asked, and additional data specific to the problem are needed.

NUMBERS: All numbers are real numbers.

FIGURES: A figure in this section will conform to the information given, but will not necessarily conform to the additional information given in the numbered Statements (1) and (2).

NOTES: Lines are straight if shown as straight, and angle measures are greater than zero.

The position of points, angles, regions, etc., exist in the order shown.

All figures lie in a plane unless otherwise stated.

Sample Question:

In the figure, the two circles are concentric (have the same center O) with radius x and y, where $x < y$. What is the area of the shaded region?

(1) The sum of the two radii is 11 units.

(2) The area of the smaller circle is $1/2$ of the area of the larger one.

Sample Explanation:

(C) By Statement (1), $x + y = 11$. Since Statement (1) gives no other information about x and y, you cannot find the areas of the two circles. Since the area of the shaded region is the difference of the two areas, Statement (1) alone is not sufficient. According to Statement (2), $\pi y^2 = 2\pi x^2$; therefore, the area of the region is $2\pi x^2 - \pi x^2 = \pi x^2$. Since (2) does not give the value of x, it is not possible to find the area of the shaded region using (2) alone. However, if we use (1) and (2) together, we get the two equations

$$y = 11 - x \text{ and } \pi y^2 = 2\pi x^2$$

from which we can solve for x by writing the single equation $\pi(11 - x)^2 = 2\pi x^2$.

1. In $\triangle ABC$, $AC = 2$. What is the length of BC?

    (1) $\angle B$ is 30°.

    (2) $AC \neq AB$.

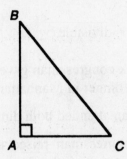

2. What is the value of x?

    (1) $\dfrac{x}{10} = \dfrac{y}{4}$.

    (2) $x = z + 6$.

3. A certain country took an $8 billion dollar loan from the World Bank. Under the agreement the debtor has to start paying a year later. If the debtor pays the agreed amount on schedule, when will the debtor finish paying?

    (1) There is a 5% annual interest on the unpaid part of the loan beginning at the time of borrowing.

    (2) The debtor has to pay $400 million, every year, deductible from what is left of the preceding payment and the interest on it.

4. What is the fraction?

    (1) If the numerator of the fraction is increased by 2, the fraction is $^{1}/_{4}$.

    (2) If the denominator is decreased by 6, the fraction is $^{1}/_{6}$.

5. In Iran 2% of the pre-war population have died during the war. What is the population of Iran right after the war?

    (1) One million people have died during the war.

    (2) The population right after the war is 103% of the pre-war population.

6. If x and $3x + y$ are integers, what is the value of y?

   (1) $0 \le y < 3$.

   (2) $3x + y$ is divisible by 3.

7. A New York congressman gave an x-a-plate dinner in Brooklyn and a y-a-plate dinner in Manhattan. What is the value of x and y?

   (1) Madigan attended both dinners and paid a total of $2,500.

   (2) The congressman raised the same amount of funds with 300 guests attending the x-a-plate dinner and 200 guests attending the y-a-plate dinner.

8. Each one of Boxes A and B contains basketballs, soccer balls, and tennis balls. How many tennis balls are there in Box A?

   (1) There are 10 basketballs, 12 soccer balls, and 14 tennis balls in the two boxes together.

   (2) There are 5 basketballs and 4 soccer balls in Box B.

9. There were 25,000 students at the University of Chicago in 1986. By what percent did the student population grow in 1988 from that of 1987?

   (1) The student population grew by 6% in 1987.

   (2) There were 28,620 students at the University of Chicago in 1988.

10. The Royal/Dutch Shell group of companies consists of 10 companies. If the Royal/Dutch Shell's after-tax profit soared 60%, to $1.64 billion, in the second quarter of 1988, how much profit did each company bring to the group in the first quarter?

    (1) Six of the companies made equal after-tax profit in the first quarter and each made twice as much profit in the second quarter.

    (2) Four of the companies made equal after-tax profit in the first quarter and each made the same profit in the second quarter as in the first one.

11. For a certain group of 10 people, what is their average income in 1988?

    (1) Their average income was $80,000 in 1987.

    (2) Five of the people had twice as much income in 1988 as in 1987; while the remaining five had the same income in 1988 as in 1987.

12. If x, y, and z are integers, is $x^2 + y^2 + z^2$ even?

    (1) x, y, and z are consecutive.

    (2) $x^2 + z^2$ is even.

13. In the figure shown what is the area of the rectangle *ABEF*?

    (1) $AF = 5$.

    (2) $AC = 6$; $DE = 3$.

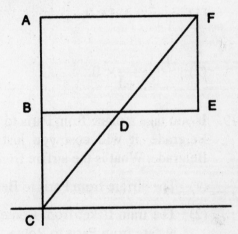

14. Lance and his 11 friends went to a snack bar where some had coffee, some had tea, and some had soda. If the price of coffee is $0.80, tea is $0.65, and soda is $0.90, and their check, not including tax, is $9.75, how many had coffee?

    (1) The number of those who had soda equals the number of those who had tea or coffee.

    (2) Six had soda.

15. If Liz works 60 hours a week, how many hours does she work on Wednesday?

    (1) She works Monday through Saturday.

    (2) Every day, other than Monday, she works one hour less than the preceding day.

16. Is $\dfrac{x^2 - 2x + 1}{x^2 + 1} = 0$?

    (1) $x^2 - 3x + 2 = 0$.

    (2) $x + y - 3 = 0$ and $2x - y = 0$.

17. For x and y integers, is xy even?

    (1) $x^2 + y^2$ is odd.

    (2) $x + y$ is even.

18. If $x \neq 0$, and $x \neq -1$, is $|x| < 1$?

    (1) $\dfrac{2}{1 + |x|} - 1 < 0$.

    (2) $\dfrac{1}{x} - \dfrac{1}{x+1} < 0$.

19. If you take a plane from Paris to Rome and take a train from Rome to Belgrade, it will cost you just 60% of the airfare from Paris to Belgrade. What is the airfare from Paris to Rome?

    (1) The airfare from Paris to Belgrade is $200.

    (2) The train ticket from Rome to Belgrade costs $40 less than the airfare from Paris to Rome.

20. How much profit did a store make on five pairs of shoes selling them at 15% off the original price?

    (1) The manufacturer of the shoes charged the store $3,000 for 40 pairs.

    (2) The original price was $130 a pair.

STOP

If time remains, you may go back and check your work.
When the time allotted is up, you may go on to the next section.

Section 2

TIME: 25 Minutes
22 Questions

DIRECTIONS: In each of the following sentences, some part of the sentence or the entire sentence is underlined. The five answer choices give various ways of phrasing the underlined part. The first choice repeats the given sentence. Pay attention to grammar, choice of words, and sentence construction in order to select the best version of the sentence. Choose (A) if you think the given sentence is correct.

---

1. Essentials of the golf swing include addressing the ball so that feet, knees, hips, and shoulders are parallel to one another, and to keep the wrists from breaking when on the upswing.

    (A) , and to keep the wrists from breaking when on the upswing.

    (B) and keeping the wrists from breaking on the upswing.

    (C) , and including an upswing that keeps the wrists from breaking.

    (D) ; and the wrists should not break when on the upswing.

    (E) and to upswing without breaking one's wrists.

2. Any allegations of <u>John being involved in that kind of a crime are</u> purely ridiculous.

    (A) John being involved in that kind of a crime are

    (B) John being involved in that kind of a crime is

    (C) John being involved in that kind of crime is

    (D) John's being involved in that kind of a crime are

    (E) John's being involved in that kind of crime are

3. <u>Being that our luggage had been sent on accident to our next destination</u>, the first two days of our tour were spent wearing the same clothes.

    (A) Being that our luggage had been sent on accident to our next destination

(B) Because our luggage had been sent on accident to our next destination

(C) Because our luggage had been sent by accident to our next destination

(D) By accident our luggage had been sent to our next destination

(E) Being sent to our next destination, our luggage by accident

4. Although parents and critics decry violence in modern films, <u>many of the persons who make up the audience</u> do not seem to notice all the gory details.

(A) many of the persons who make up the audience

(B) making up the audience are many persons that

(C) many people in the audience

(D) audiences composed of many people

(E) many audiences

5. <u>Irregardless of your views on a protestor</u> burning the American flag, any constitutional amendment is difficult to pass.

(A) Irregardless of your views on a protestor

(B) Irregardless of your views on a protestor's

(C) Your views regarding a protestor

(D) Regarding your protesting views on

(E) Regardless of your views on a protestor's

6. <u>The newspaper said on Monday that Paul Radous would receive a scholarship grant of $1,000.</u>

(A) The newspaper said on Monday that Paul Radous would receive a scholarship grant of $1,000.

(B) The newspaper indicated on Monday that Paul Radous would receive a scholarship grant of $1,000.

(C) On Monday the newspaper said that Paul Radous had received a scholarship grant of $1,000.

(D) On Monday the newspaper reported that Paul Radous would receive a scholarship grant of $1,000.

(E) That Paul Radous is receiving a $1,000 grant on Monday the newspaper reported.

7. <u>If you had seen</u> him cry, you would have been surprised, too.

(A) If you had seen

(B) If you saw

(C) If you would have seen

(D) If you would have saw

(E) If you see

8. Developing over a period of years, <u>Cindy Molina was finally able to present her novel to the publishers</u>.

(A) Cindy Molina was finally able to present her novel to the publishers.

(B) the novel was finally presented by Cindy Molina to the publishers.

(C) the publishers finally presented Cindy Molina with her novel.

(D) Cindy Molina finally presented to the publishers of her novel.

(E) a publisher's novel was finally presented by Cindy Molina.

9. No sooner did Kemper drive his new car off the lot <u>than</u> he was involved in an accident.

(A) than   (B) than when

(C) and   (D) but

(E) when then

10. Nearly all the band members showed for practice, every flag corps member came on time, and <u>also participating were the girls, all of the drill team</u>.

(A) also participating were the girls, all of the drill team.

(B) as well, the drill team girls were participating.

(C) of the drill team, all girls participated.

(D) of all the drill team girls participated.

(E) all of the drill team girls also participated.

11. <u>Here and there were walking participants of this morning's parade</u>.

(A) Here and there were walking participants of this morning's parade.

(B) Here and there was this morning's parade participants.

(C) The participants of this morning's parade was walking here and there.

(D) Walking participants of this morning's parade were here and there.

(E) The participants of this morning's parade were walking here and there.

12. <u>Much to our surprise</u>, we read that working women with children comprise about two-thirds of the entire temporary work force.

(A) Much to our surprise

(B) Surprising us

(C) When we were surprised

(D) Being as how we were surprised

(E) In order to surprise us

13. Finally apprehended by the police, Connie said <u>she only embezzled once in her life</u> and had already anonymously returned the money.

(A) she only embezzled once in her life

(B) only she embezzled in her life

(C) in her life that she would only embezzle once

(D) she embezzled only once in her life

(E) embezzling only once in her life

14. I <u>wish you would of told me</u> that the Mostly Mozart festival started yesterday.

   (A) wish you would of told me

   (B) wish you had told me

   (C) had wished you would of told me

   (D) wished you would have told me

   (E) , wishing that you had told me,

15. Tesfay did not leave suddenly because he was angry with us; <u>he was going to be late</u> for his interview.

   (A) he was going to be late

   (B) he left because he was concerned about being late

   (C) he realized about being late

   (D) realizing that he was running late

   (E) he left realizing his lateness

16. Boswell's biography of Johnson shows the influence these two talented men <u>had on each other</u>.

   (A) had on each other

   (B) had one for the other

   (C) had on one another

   (D) brought to bear on one another

   (E) showed one for the other

17. A Life Flight helicopter is routinely dispatched in cases of cardiac arrest, burns, and premature infants, <u>although they are used most often for the former</u>.

   (A) although they are used most often for the former

   (B) and they are used more often for the former

   (C) although it is used most often for the first type

   (D) and they are used most often for the number one

   (E) for being used most often for the first type

18. The main reason given for needing to purchase a Life Flight helicopter is <u>because the service extends</u> hospital care into the surrounding communities.

    (A) because the service extends

    (B) in extending the service

    (C) to extend the service

    (D) when the service is extended

    (E) by servicing the extended

19. Phi Delta Kappa, a professional organization for graduate students, presented a scholarship whose criteria included academic standing, fluency of written expression, and <u>to be involved in</u> community activities.

    (A) to be involved in   (B) be involved in

    (C) involving   (D) involvement in

    (E) involved with

20. <u>My son must convince me of need due to mechanical problems</u> before I will buy him a new car.

    (A) My son must convince me of need due to mechanical problems

    (B) A need must be shown by my son due to mechanical problems

    (C) In order to have need, my son must prove mechanical problems

    (D) Because he may have mechanical problems, my son

    (E) My son must convince me there are mechanical problems

21. The roof was leaking and the paint was peeling, so we decided to repair <u>it before we put it up for sale</u>.

    (A) it before we put it up for sale

    (B) the house before we put it up for sale

    (C) the roof and the paint before we put it up for sale

    (D) the roof and the paint before we put them up for sale

    (E) them before we put it up for sale

22. <u>Because</u> a summer sale was in progress, we stopped at Mona's Dress Store.

    (A) Because

    (B) So as

    (C) So that

    (D) Being that

    (E) Seeing as how

STOP

If time remains, you may go back and check your work.
When the time allotted is up, you may go on to the next section.

Section 3

TIME: 25 Minutes
16 Questions

DIRECTIONS: Solve each problem using space on the page for scratch work. Indicate the best answer from the choices given.

NUMBERS: All numbers used are real numbers.

FIGURES: Figures accompanying problems in this section provide information useful in solving the problems. They are drawn as accurately as possible; however, when a figure is not drawn to scale, more information will be provided. It is given that all figures lie in a plane unless otherwise stated.

1. A retailer originally had a coat priced at $125. Julie bought the coat on sale for $100. What is the percentage off that a retailer gave to Julie?

    (A) 20%   (B) 25%

    (C) $33^1/_3$%   (D) 50%

    (E) 80%

2. Fifteen percent of what number is 60?

    (A) 9   (B) 51

    (C) 69   (D) 200

    (E) 400

3. If $x - y = 10$ and $2x + 3y = 0$, what is x?

    (A) -6 (B) -4

    (C) 0   (D) 4

    (E) 6

4. How many square feet of carpeting are needed to cover the area pictured below?

   (A) 131

   (B) 145

   (C) 155

   (D) 195

   (E) 300

   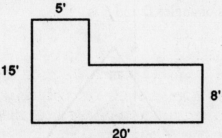

5. Jane wants to purchase a mixture of coffee equal to $12.50/lb. She has 2 pounds of coffee *A* at $14 per pound. How many pounds of coffee *B* at $12 per pound does she have to buy?

   (A) 3   (B) 4

   (C) 6   (D) 8

   (E) 10

6. Adam has to take four tests in his English class. After three tests his average is 87. What is the lowest score he can get on his last test and have an 85 point average for the class?

   (A) 59   (B) 79

   (C) 80   (D) 69

   (E) 85

7. Marie lives 6 miles east of Dave and 8 miles south of Joan. If you could fly from Joan's house to Dave's house, how far would you have to fly?

   (A) 4   (B) 5

   (C) 7   (D) 10

   (E) 12

8. If $X + Y = 8$ and $3X + Y = 12$, then $2X - Y$ is

   (A) -2.   (B) 2.

   (C) 4.   (D) 8.

   (E) 10.

9. In the diagram shown, *ABC* is an isosceles triangle. Sides *AC* and *BC* are extended through *C* to *E* and *D* to form triangle *CDE*. The sum of the measures of angles *D* and *E* is

    (A) 150°.

    (B) 105°.

    (C) 90°.

    (D) 60°.

    (E) 30°.

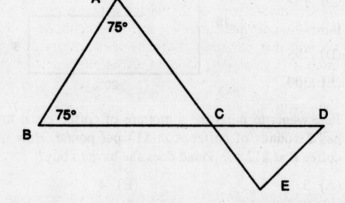

10. The ages of the students enrolled at XYZ University are given in the following table:

Age	Number of Students
18	750
19	1,600
20	1,200
21	450

    What percent of students is 19 and 20 years old?

    (A) 30%   (B) 40%

    (C) 50%   (D) 60%

    (E) 70%

11. Mr. Wheeler can purchase a television set for $395 cash or he can purchase it for $50 down and 12 monthly payments of $35 each. The cost of credit is

    (A) $25.   (B) $30.

    (C) $35.   (D) $50.

    (E) $75.

12. Sherry wishes to leave a 15% tip for her waiter. If she paid a total of $24.15 for her meal and the tip, how much was the cost of the meal?

(A) $20.00   (B) $21.00

(C) $22.00   (D) $23.00

(E) $24.15

13. Cyndi invests part of $2,000 in a certificate of deposit that pays simple annual interest of 9% and the remainder in a passbook savings account that pays 5% simple annual interest. If she receives $148 interest in one year, how much did she invest in the certificate of deposit?

(A) $800   (B) $1,000

(C) $1,200   (D) $1,500

(E) $1,800

14. A 26 gallon mixture of sulfuric acid and water contains 6 gallons of acid. If 4 more gallons of acid are added, what percent of the new mixture is water?

(A) 13.3%   (B) 33.3%

(C) 38.5%   (D) 66.7%

(E) 76.9%

15. An investor earns $930 from two accounts in a year. If she has three times as much invested at 8% as she does at 7%, how much does she have invested at 8%?

(A) $9,000   (B) $3,207

(C) $9,621   (D) $3,000

(E) $11,500

16. The average of 12 test scores is 55. When the two highest and two lowest scores are dropped, the average of the remaining scores is 50. The average of the scores dropped is

(A) 65.   (B) 60.

(C) 55.   (D) 52.5.

(E) 50.

STOP

If time remains, you may go back and check your work.
When the time allotted is up, you may go on to the next section.

Section 4

TIME: 25 Minutes
16 Questions

DIRECTIONS: For each question in this section, select the best answer.

1. Doctors in a recent survey recommended Swabby Cotton Swabs over Nifty Rayon Swabs. Try them today.

   A reader is likely to purchase the cotton swabs if he or she drew which of the following questionable conclusions invited by the advertisement?

   (A) Among swabs, cotton is better than rayon.

   (B) I should join the bandwagon and use Swabbies like most Americans.

   (C) The advertisement is placed where those with a high degree of education and status will be likely to read it.

   (D) The doctors mentioned were helped to become professionals by their using Swabbies.

   (E) If professional physicians use Swabbies, I should do so also.

2. In non-residential areas where increased funds have been allocated for night lighting, crime rates have declined dramatically. With this crime protection, individuals are more likely to frequent the businesses, and business owners are more likely to locate in the area. The establishment of businesses in many of these high crime areas can result in an improvement in the economic level of certain areas of our cities and states.

   Which of the following conclusions can most properly be drawn from the information above?

   (A) Allocations for lighting tend to benefit citizens as well as businesses.

   (B) Decreased profits are likely to result from the installation of adequate night lighting.

(C) Businesses will decline to locate in new areas unless adequate night lighting is provided.

(D) The absence of adequate night lighting has prevented the opening of many businesses and has resulted in economic recession.

(E) An increase in adequate night lighting would increase the opening of businesses and result in increased productivity for our nation as a whole.

3. Juarez is older than Korrie.

Lorenzo is older than Martin.

Martin is younger than Nedino.

Korrie and Nedino are twins.

If the information above is true, which of the following must also be true?

(A) Lorenzo is older than Nedino.

(B) Lorenzo is older than Juarez.

(C) Korrie is younger than Lorenzo.

(D) Juarez is older than Martin.

(E) Korrie is younger than Martin.

4. Pluralistic countries have both public and private governments to make and enforce rules of behavior. Individual and private groups provide most of the goods and services, but the regulation is achieved through public governments.

Which of the following conclusions can be properly drawn from the statements above?

(A) In the United States most citizens believe in individual freedom; they want as little control as possible from the government.

(B) In the USA firm limits are placed on individuals with much liberty being given to the government.

(C) Since American government has traditionally benefited those in authority, the trend is for private government to soon give way to the demands of public government in the USA.

(D) The above passage does not apply to America which is a democratic government.

(E) The above passage is typical of England, not the USA.

5. Many persons have advocated simplifying English words so that they are spelled exactly as they sound. For instance, <u>knock</u> would be spelled <u>nok</u>.

    The most serious disadvantage of modifying the English language to achieve this end would be which of the following?

    (A) Such modification would be confusing to people who do not speak the English language.

    (B) The modification may result in having to change the type on typewriters.

    (C) Pronunciations of words change over time and may vary from one region to another.

    (D) Most spelling modification programs have not been carefully thought out by the advocates.

    (E) Modification may be confusing to young children.

Questions 6 and 7 are based on the following:

Rudolf Flesch in his book *Why Johnny Can't Read* attributed Johnny's reading problem to the use of the sight word method in the schools. This method (often called the look-say method) focuses on the student's viewing the whole word rather than using word attack skills and breaking it down into individual parts. Flesch said that the number of students seen in remedial reading classes during this century could be attributed to the widespread use of the method since the 1920s.

6. The way of attacking the sight word method is to

    (A) attack the character of the school personnel who use the sight word method.

    (B) imply an analogy between the increase in numbers in remedial reading classes and the sight word method.

    (C) point out that more than one method implies a dilemma.

    (D) show that the sight word method leads to an absurd conclusion.

    (E) show that the word attack method is used more readily by students in the United States.

7. The proponents of the sight word method could effectively defend their position by showing that

    (A) the expertise of those employing the method is outstanding.

(B) they are neither inept nor immoral.

(C) other methods also attribute to remedial reading students.

(D) Flesch's advocation of the phonics method in preference to the sight word method poses a dilemma.

(E) there were other reasons (such as mandatory school attendance laws which kept everybody in school and which were passed at about the same time as the advent of the sight word method) for the increase in remedial reading cases.

Questions 8 and 9 are based on the following:

Georgia was once noted for its production of cotton. Almost all the people in the state grew the crop. Then cotton manufacturing (and other types of manufacturing) became more important than cotton growing. Today the state is the nation's leading producer of peanuts; it also ranks high in pecan, tobacco, and peach production. Service industries, like wholesale and retail trade, are still Georgia's chief source of income.

8. Which of the following can be inferred from the passage?

(A) Cotton was profitable to Georgia only when it was grown there.

(B) The growth of cotton in Georgia has been unusually high in the past few years.

(C) Farming is still important to Georgia.

(D) The initial cost involved in switching from cotton growing to cotton manufacturing was minimal.

(E) The profits from the farms are insignificant after Georgia switched from growing cotton to manufacturing.

9. Some observers have concluded that the production of goods in Georgia was possible only when cotton farmers became mill workers, but that the switch left the workers no better off. This conclusion, however, is unwarranted because it can be inferred to be likely that

(A) the growers foresaw how important the manufacturing industry would be to the state.

(B) the initial cost in switching from tenant farming to working in a factory was substantial.

(C) supplies of farm products would not be as low as they are if the growers had not switched crops.

(D) had the switch not been made, Georgia would not be the center of manufacturing it is today.

(E) manufacturing may cease to be important to the state soon.

Questions 10 and 11 are based on the following:

In July 1984 Richard Leakey and colleague Kamoya Kimeu found in Nairobi an almost entire *homo erectus* skeleton, the first recovered that was 1.6 million years old. The skeleton was that of a boy about 12 years of age. He was about five feet four inches tall and probably would have reached a height of six feet. His bones had been scattered and trampled in a swamp. In parts and proportion they were much like the human form today. Under him was volcanic material dating from 1.65 million years ago.

10. Which of the following hypotheses is best supported by the evidence above?

(A) This spectacular find confirms that the human form as we know it today only recently developed.

(B) The remains may have confused two different time periods.

(C) The body may not be as old as believed because it could have fallen through a large burrow dug by a gerbil in the area.

(D) The body could have been imported to the area by a religious group which used human sacrifices.

(E) This find confirms the antiquity of the human form.

11. The evidence from the find most seriously supports which of the following?

(A) The belief that humans did not exist 1.6 million years ago.

(B) The belief that people did not look like humans until 100 B.C.

(C) The belief that humans reached their present size more than a million and a half years ago, with some populations in poor areas becoming smaller recently.

(D) The belief that humans have grown larger through time.

(E) The belief that human life really began on the continent of Europe.

12. A recent study of data collected at sports events shows that spectator violence was a problem in 1988. The data shows, surprisingly, that there were more incidents of physical confrontations among fans at professional baseball games last year than at professional football games. Baseball seems to provoke more hostility among spectators than football.

Which of the following, if true, would most strengthen the opponents' theory that baseball attracts more aggressive fans?

(A) The climate affects behavior; hot summer weather when baseball is played contributes to temper flare-ups as much as the game.

(B) The baseball fans, as well as the football fans, were aware that they were being tested for aggressiveness.

(C) The same people who were summer baseball fans were winter football fans.

(D) Not only is there a greater number of incidents of fan violence at baseball games, but if the number of outbreaks of fan violence is divided by the number of games, the number of outbreaks per game at baseball games is higher than at football games.

(E) The research studies were designed to include no college athletes who participated in both sports.

13. Sammie: The grades of Jane improved when she entered private school. This is clear evidence that private schools are better than public schools.

    Johnnie: A close look at Jane's cumulative folder shows that Jane's grades improved after she was diagnosed as diabetic and proper treatment was begun. The "upturn" of her grades began while she was still in public school and insulin injections were started on her.

Which of the following best describes the weak point in Sammie's claim on which Johnnie's response focuses?

(A) The evidence that Sammie cites comes from only a single observed case, that of Jane.

(B) The "upturn" in grades might be only temporary.

(C) Sammie's statement leaves open the possibility that the cause he cites came after the effect he attributes to it.

(D) No mention is made of schools which have been public and then gone private.

(E) No exact figures are given from Jane's permanent records.

14. Which of the following best completes the passage below?

Depression afflicts nearly 10 million Americans. Dr. John E. Ware, Jr., states that depression is more commonly disabling than arthritis, ulcers, diabetes, or high blood pressure—all of which have been considered more serious in the past. As far as limiting people in their physical functioning or causing them to stay in bed, depression proved as bad as emphysema or back problems. The study is important because it shows _____.

(A) that arthritis is not as serious as was once thought.

(B) mental disorders can be avoided.

(C) emphysema may be psychosomatic.

(D) depression is a very costly affliction.

(E) sick benefits should not be assigned for depression.

15. Federal plans aimed at balancing the budget resulted in culling programs which helped some special groups within the country.

Which of the following statements refutes the claim above?

(A) With the special interest groups protected by elected officials, in a democracy one does not have to fear that individual or small group interests will go unnoticed or unprotected; looking at the number of new programs initiated, one finds that it is indeed rare for a program to be culled but that new programs are easily and frequently added.

(B) Individuals now have to assume responsibility for certain services normally paid for by the federal budget.

(C) Certain funded programs with a limited number of constituents have recently been discontinued.

(D) The USA market was saturated with wheat with a resulting decline in price when the monies given to farmers to encourage them to let their lands lie fallow were discontinued.

(E) By encouraging farm growers to allow their land to lie fallow, the federal government has helped to prevent grain from flooding the market, but milling companies and grain storage facilities in the area have had to close and many local residents now find themselves unemployed.

16. Americans save less of their earnings than citizens of any other major industrialized nation in the world. Legislators are looking at repealing the high capital gains tax.

Which of the following would be the main reason legislators might hesitate to announce their support of this repeal?

(A) Savings and investments would be encouraged.

(B) Consumption would become more economically attractive than investment.

(C) When capital is needed, the U.S. would have to borrow from other nations.

(D) The legislators might fear that they would appear to their constituents as favoring the rich over the poor.

(E) Spending would be cheaper than paying taxes on gains.

STOP

If time remains, you may go back and check your work.
When the time allotted is up, you may go on to the next section.

Section 5

TIME: 25 Minutes
16 Questions

> **DIRECTIONS:** Solve each problem using space on the page for scratch work. Indicate the best answer from the choices given.
>
> **NUMBERS:** All numbers used are real numbers.
>
> **FIGURES:** Figures accompanying problems in this section provide information useful in solving the problems. They are drawn as accurately as possible; however, when a figure is not drawn to scale, more information will be provided. It is given that all figures lie in a plane unless otherwise stated.

1. What is the area of the shaded region in the figure below?

   (A) $16\pi - 16$

   (B) $16 - 4\pi$

   (C) 2π

   (D) 4π

   (E) 16

   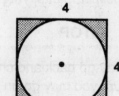

2. Find the product of the roots of $3x^2 + 3x - 6 = 0$.

   (A) -18 (B) -6

   (C) -3 (D) -2

   (E) 6

3. If a year which is not a leap year has two consecutive months with a Friday the thirteenth day, what are the months?

   (A) January and February

   (B) February and March

   (C) March and April

(D) April and May

(E) July and August

4. How many gallon cans of paint will be needed to give two coats of paint to the walls of a 15´ × 20´ room with 9´ ceilings? A gallon of paint covers 400 sq. ft.

(A) 2   (B) 4

(C) 7   (D) 8

(E) 14

5. Jim is twice the age of Betty. The sum of their ages is 18. How old is Betty?

(A) 2   (B) 4

(C) 6   (D) 8

(E) 12

6. The side of a square is increased by 40%. What percentage increase does the area have?

(A) 20%   (B) 40%

(C) 48%   (D) 80%

(E) 96%

7. $2x - (3y + x) + 5(x - y) =$

(A) $6x - 8y$ (B) $8x - 8y$

(C) $6x - 4y$ (D) $8x - 4y$

(E) $6x - 2y$

8. How many 6 inch by 6 inch square tiles would it take to cover the floor of an 8 feet by 9 feet room?

(A) 144   (B) 160

(C) 180   (D) 196

(E) 288

9. If $x^{64} = 64$, then $x^{32} =$

   (A) 8 or − 8.   (B) 12 or − 12.

   (C) 16.   (D) 32 or − 32.

   (E) 48.

10. What is the average of all the test scores shown in the figure below?

   (A) 5.6

   (B) 6.1

   (C) 6.2

   (D) 6.4

   (E) 6.7

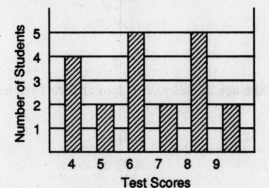

11. Quadrilaterals *ABCD* and *AFED* are squares with sides of length 10 cm. Arc *BD* and arc *DF* are quarter circles. What is the area of the shaded region?

   (A) 50 sq. cm

   (B) 100 sq. cm

   (C) 80 sq. cm

   (D) 40 sq. cm

   (E) 10 sq. cm

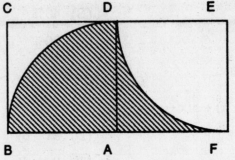

12. If $\sqrt{x-1} = 2$, then $(x-1)^2 =$

   (A) 4.   (B) 6.

   (C) 8.   (D) 10.

   (E) 16.

13. If $2^x = \dfrac{16^2 \times 8^3}{2^{19}}$, then $x =$

   (A) − 3.   (B) − 2.

(C) 1.   (D) 2.

(E) 3.

14. If peanuts sell for $1.80 per $1/2$ pound, what is the cost of 24 ounces of peanuts?

    (A) $4.20   (B) $4.60

    (C) $5.00   (D) $5.40

    (E) $5.60

15. A man works at a job for five days. His pay for each day is $1^1/_2$ times that of the previous day. If his total wages are $422 for the five days, what was his pay for the second day?

    (A) $12   (B) $36

    (C) $32   (D) $48

    (E) $66

16. Jean and Jim Jones have three children. The sum of the weights of the two smallest children is 71 lbs., the sum of the weights of the two largest children is 96 lbs., and the sum of the weights of the smallest and largest child is 87 lbs. What is the sum of the weights of all three children?

    (A) 125 lbs.   (B) 127 lbs.

    (C) 128 lbs.   (D) 130 lbs.

    (E) 135 lbs.

STOP

If time remains, you may go back and check your work.
When the time allotted is up, you may go on to the next section.

Section 6

TIME: 25 Minutes
23 Questions

DIRECTIONS: Each passage is followed by questions based on its content. After reading the passage, choose the best answer to each question. Answer all questions based on what is indicated or implied in that passage.

The bicycle, with a history that spans nearly two centuries, has frequently been looked upon in the United States as a child's plaything. Recent trends seem to indicate that America may come to follow the example of those other nations where the bicycle is an important means of transportation, extensively used by businessmen and workers traveling to and from their jobs. In the United States, during the late nineteenth century, the cycle's greatest use was likewise among adults, and this use sparked the early good-roads movement. Of equal importance was the role of the bicycle in demonstrating the possibilities of independent personal transportation, thus creating a demand that facilitated the introduction of the automobile.

The first known bicycle was shown by the Comte de Sivrac, who in 1791 was seen riding a two-wheel "wooden horse" in the gardens of the Palais Royal in Paris. Called a *célérifère,* the machine had two rigidly mounted wheels, so that it was incapable of being steered. To change direction, it was necessary to lift, drag, or jump the front wheel to one side. In 1793 the name was changed to *vélocifère,* and, as these machines became increasingly popular among the sporting set of Paris, clubs were formed and races were run along the Champs Elysées.

At some time during the first decade of the nineteenth century the *vélocifère* lost favor temporarily until, in 1816, Nicéphore Niepce of Chalons, better known as the "Father of Photography," demonstrated an improved type in the Luxembourg Gardens. Niepce's machine, still not steerable, was considerably lighter, and the larger wheels helped smooth the ride and permitted greater speed.

A revolutionary improvement in the *vélocifère* occurred in 1817, when Charles, Baron von Drais, of Sauerbrun, devised a front wheel capable of being steered. As chief forester for the Grand Duke of Baden, von Drais found the machine useful in traversing the forest land under his supervision. He also gave it a padded saddle, and an armrest in front of his body, which assisted him in exerting force against the ground. Granted a patent in 1818, he took his *Draisienne* to Paris, where it was again patented and acquired the name *vélocipède*, a term that was to continue in use until about 1869 when the word "bicycle" came into use.

The *vélocipède* gained rapid popularity in France, and almost immediately migrated to England, where it was known variously as a Draisine, Swiftwalker, Hobby Horse, Dandy Horse, or Pedestrian Curricle. In England one of its chief exponents was the London coachmaker, Denis Johnson, who not only added improvements, but even designed a woman's drop-frame model. Riding academies were established to teach the fine points of balance and management, and soon many riders were seen in the streets and parks about London; yet the pastime declined almost as rapidly as it had risen, and after the early 1820s *vélocipède* were rarely seen.

In the United States, W. K. Clarkson, Jr., of New York, was granted a patent for a *vélocipède* on June 26, 1819, but it is no longer known what this patent covered, for the records were destroyed in the Patent Office fire of 1836. There is no evidence that the sport gained much popularity here, yet it is known that Charles Wilson Peale, the noted American portrait painter, was an enthusiastic rider of one in 1819, at the age of 78.

1. The main purpose of the passage is to

    (A) argue for greater use of the bicycle in America.

    (B) explain the influence of Europe on the bicycling tastes of Americans.

    (C) trace the early history of the bicycle.

    (D) place the history of the bicycle in the context of European industrialization.

    (E) provide a detailed account of the chief improvements in the bicycle throughout its history.

2. The passage supplies information that answers which of the following questions?

    I. Why has the bicycle been less popular as a means of transportation in the U.S. than in other nations?

    II. Why did the *vélocipède* decline rapidly in popularity in nineteenth-century England?

III. How did the existence of the bicycle encourage the introduction of the automobile?

(A) I only   (B) II only

(C) III only   (D) I and III

(E) I, II, and III

3. Which of the following most accurately states the author's perception of the relationship between the bicycle and the automobile in America?

(A) Their histories are unrelated.

(B) They have always been competing modes of transportation.

(C) The development of gas-powered engines led to the decline of the widespread popularity of the bicycle.

(D) The bicycle will probably supplant the automobile as the primary means of commuting to work.

(E) The bicycle helped create a need that contributed to the development of the automobile.

4. Which of the following is *not,* either explicitly or by implication, mentioned as a weakness of the *célérifère*?

(A) Lack of steering   (B) Lack of comfort

(C) Lack of speed   (D) Lack of safety

(E) Rigidly mounted wheels

5. According to the passage, the Draisienne's chief improvement on the *vélocifère* was

(A) a smoother ride.   (B) steering capability.

(C) greater speed.   (D) increased safety.

(E) armrests.

6. It can be inferred from the passage that the chief use of the *vélocipède* in France and England was

(A) work-related.

(B) for transportation in rural areas.

(C) for the entertainment of children.

(D) as a machine for exercise.

(E) as an adult sport.

7. According to the passage, the immediate forerunner of the bicycle was popular in England for about

(A) five years. (B) 20 years.

(C) 30 years. (D) 50 years.

(E) 80 years.

8. The author probably considers the most important present-day world-wide use of the bicycle to be

(A) an environmentally sound alternative to the automobile.

(B) for the entertainment of children.

(C) as an expression of personal freedom.

(D) for sport.

(E) as a means of transportation.

9. The last two paragraphs are designed chiefly to

(A) explain the continuing improvements in the design of the *vélocipède*.

(B) illustrate the replacement of France by England and America as trendsetters.

(C) extend the author's account of the *vélocipède* to England and the United States.

(D) explain why the *vélocipède* was replaced by the bicycle.

(E) show the influence of French technology on the rest of Europe and America.

Francis William Aston, British physicist and chemist, invented the mass spectrograph, which made possible the separation of heavier and lighter atoms and proved that almost all elements are composed of mixtures of various isotopes. He was born in Harborne, England, on September 1, 1877, and died in Cambridge on November 20, 1945.

A bright student who finished high school at the top of his class, Aston attended Malvern College and the University of Birmingham. His training was in chemistry, and in 1909 he became an assistant to J. J. Thomson at Cambridge University.

World War I interrupted the work that the two were conducting on neon gas and for four years Aston served in the British armed forces. Then he returned to Thomson's laboratory and redesigned Thomson's positive ray deflection apparatus into his own mass spectrograph. For his mass spectrograph and the knowledge he gained from it, he won the 1922 Nobel Prize in chemistry.

In the mass spectrograph the electric and magnetic fields were arranged so that all particles having the same mass were brought to a focus that produced a fine line on photographic film. Each line indicated the presence of atoms or molecules of a particular mass. With this apparatus Aston confirmed that two forms of neon existed with atomic masses of 20 and 22. From the comparative darkness of the lines he decided that the ions of the mass 20 were ten times as numerous as those of 22. If put together all the ions would have an average mass of 20.2, which was the actual atomic weight of neon.

Working on chlorine, Aston came to similar conclusions about its atomic weight. He formulated his whole number rule: Atomic weights of the isotopes of elements are very close to integers (whole numbers) if the mass of hydrogen is taken as one. The fractional atomic weights are due to the presence of two or more isotopes, or mixtures of different atoms of different integral weights in one element.

Aston continued to measure the exact masses of isotopes, and with a refined mass spectrograph was able to show that the atomic mass of individual isotopes on the atomic weight scale was slightly different from integers, sometimes just a little higher or lower, but these slight differences turned out to represent the energy that went into binding the component parts of the nuclei together.

Aston discovered 212 out of 287 naturally occurring isotopes. His work in measuring more precisely the exact masses of the isotopes was indispensable to progress in mid-twentieth-century atomic research. Aston developed the mass spectrograph, which J. J. Thompson "invented," into a refined instrument capable of making accurate measurements of atomic masses.

10. The main purpose of the passage is to

    (A) explain how the mass spectrograph works.

    (B) define terms useful in one branch of chemistry.

    (C) analyze the influence of background and training on professional achievement.

    (D) summarize the achievements of one scientist.

    (E) set the record straight by giving credit to a scientist whose work is sometimes partially credited to another.

11. The passage most likely appeared in

    (A) a scholarly scientific journal.

    (B) a weekly news magazine.

    (C) an encyclopedia of science.

    (D) a chemistry textbook.

    (E) a dictionary of scientific terms.

12. The passage contains information that answers which of the following questions?

    I.   Was there any continuity between the work Aston performed before and after World War I?

    II. Why didn't Aston discover all of the naturally occurring isotopes?

    III. Which mid-twentieth-century discoveries in atomic research depend on Aston's previous work?

    (A) I only   (B) II only

    (C) III only   (D) I and II

    (E) I, II, and III

13. According to the passage, Aston's mass spectrograph

    (A) revolutionized the study of subatomic particles.

    (B) was wholly original.

    (C) led to the discovery of previously unknown elements.

(D) first made use of electric and magnetic fields in atomic research.

(E) was a refinement of an instrument invented by a colleague at Cambridge.

14. According to the passage, Aston's mass spectrograph first accomplished all of the following EXCEPT the

(A) discovery of isotopes.

(B) separation of heavier and lighter atoms.

(C) formulation of the "whole number rule."

(D) deflection of positively charged particles.

(E) accurate measurement of atomic masses

15. The passage defines which of the following?

I. Ion

II. Atom

III. Integer

(A) I only   (B) II only

(C) III only   (D) II and III

(E) I, II, and III

16. Aston formulated his whole number rule chiefly by experimenting with

(A) neon only.

(B) neon and hydrogen.

(C) chlorine and hydrogen.

(D) neon and chlorine.

(E) chlorine only.

17. It can be inferred from the passage that Aston's work with neon helped prove that

(A) elements are composed of mixtures of isotopes.

(B) the previously accepted atomic weight of neon was incorrect.

(C) the atomic weight of elements can only be established if their isotopes are separated.

(D) lighter ions always outnumber heavier ions.

(E) energy used to bind nuclei distorts the accurate measurement of atomic masses.

Title VII of the Civil Rights Act of 1964 is the principal law that protects workers from discrimination in employment. The act makes it unlawful to discriminate on the basis of sex, race, color, religion, or national origin in hiring or firing; wages; fringe benefits; classifying; referring, assigning, or promoting employees; extending or assigning facilities; training; retraining; apprenticeships; or any other terms, conditions, or privileges of employment.

The Equal Employment Opportunity Commission (EEOC) has primary responsibility for enforcement of Title VII. Under EEOC guidelines on sex discrimination, it is a violation of Title VII to refuse to hire an individual based on stereotyped characteristics of the sexes or preferences of co-workers, the employer, clients, or customers; to label jobs as "men's jobs" and "women's jobs" or to indicate a preference or limitation based on sex in a help-wanted advertisement, unless sex is a bona fide occupational qualification (BFOQ) for the job. Sex is rarely a BFOQ.

If you think you have been treated unfairly in an employment situation and the reason for the action was your sex, race, color, religion, or national origin, you may file a complaint or charge with the Equal Employment Opportunity Commission. The complaint form asks for your name and address; the name and address and other information about the employer, union, or employment agency; and a brief description of the discriminatory practice or action. You must file the complaint within 180 days of the action you are complaining about. If there is a state or city fair employment practices (FEP) law offering comparable protection (most states have such FEP laws), the EEOC will send a copy of the complaint to the agency that enforces the state or local law. If the state agency does not complete action on the complaint within 60 days, EEOC may proceed to process the charge. If you send the complaint to the state agency first, the deadline for filing with EEOC is 300 days from the date of the unlawful act, or within 30 days of a notice that the state agency has finished its proceedings, whichever happens first. Some actions may be continuing violations of Title VII, and are not then subject to the usual time limits.

Title VII of the Civil Rights Act of 1964 also protects workers against discrimination on the basis of sex, race, color, religion, or national origin in most on-the-job aspects of employment. Employers must recruit, train, and promote persons in all job classifications without discrimination. Promotion decisions must be made according to valid requirements. Training and apprenticeship opportunities must be offered in accord with equal employment opportunity principles. Employers may not discriminate against individuals in any terms or conditions or privileges of employment.

Title VII of the Civil Rights Act of 1964, as amended in 1978, specifically prohibits discrimination because of pregnancy. Employers cannot refuse to employ a woman because of pregnancy or terminate her, force her to go on leave at an arbitrary point during pregnancy, or penalize her because of pregnancy in reinstatement rights—including credit for previous service, accrued retirement benefits, and accumulated seniority.

18. The primary purpose of this article is to

 (A) predict the outcome of several recent amendments to Title VII.

 (B) criticize the amendments to Title VII.

 (C) propose amendments to Title VII.

 (D) present Title VII and some of its amendments in abbreviated form.

 (E) call attention to the conflicting aspects of Title VII and some of its amendments.

19. The author states that Title VII is part of the

 (A) state or city FEP law.

 (B) Equal Employment Opportunity Commission.

 (C) Fair Labor Standards Act.

 (D) BFOQ.

 (E) Civil Rights Act.

20. Which of the following situations is most applicable for remediation under the section for sex discrimination covered in Title VII?

 (A) Betty Hall, 47 years old, was denied a job as a teller because she was not between the ages of 21 and 24.

 (B) Waitresses at a Marriott restaurant averaged more than the minimum wage in tips, and management paid any difference if the tips fell below the minimum wage.

(C) Cheryl A. McNeely was discharged, at least in part, for discussing her salary with another clerical employee.

(D) A valve manufacturer promoted only men to managerial positions, although women working in the plant had been applying for, but not granted, managerial positions.

(E) A group of seamstresses refused to work until they were permitted access to their personnel files.

21. Which of the following best describes the author's attitude in the statement that sex is rarely classified as a bona fide occupational qualification?

(A) Objectively neutral   (B) Warmly approving

(C) Mildly amused   (D) Bitterly disappointed

(E) Profoundly shocked

22. The passage implies which of the following concerning the filing of complaints?

(A) Whenever a complaint is filed, it must be documented on a fairly complex form so that all details are recorded accurately.

(B) Even if some actions are viewed as continuing violations, there are certain time limits which must be observed.

(C) Because time is crucial in the Title VII cases, it is important to contact the EEOC soon after the discriminatory action occurs.

(D) The EEOC will file suit for someone if it is found that there is reasonable cause to believe that discrimination has occurred.

(E) The federal agency under whose jurisdiction the complaint falls supersedes the state or city fair employment practice guidelines.

23. The passage provides information that would indicate which of the following as examples of discrimination according to Title VII?

I. A restaurant hires both females and males and assigns bartending and hostess training depending on personality and attitude.

II.   A glass manufacturer pays 21 cents an hour more for male selec-
      tor-packers on the basis that men perform extra duties such as
      lifting and stacking cartons.

III. A dress designer hires only females, ages 14 to 17, to model
      "junior miss" designer fashions.

(A) I only   (B) II only

(C) III only   (D) I and II

(E) II and III

STOP

If time remains, you may go back and check your work.
When the time allotted is up, you may go on to the next section.

Section 7

ANALYSIS OF AN ISSUE ESSAY TOPIC

TIME: 30 Minutes

DIRECTIONS: In an essay, develop a position on the issue below by investigating the different angles of the issue, and explaining your thoughts on the topic. Remember, there is no one "correct" response to the essay topic.

Before starting, read the essay topic and its question(s). You may make preliminary notes in your test booklet before writing the actual essay. Be sure to write your essay on the lined pages provided at the back of the book.

Many educators believe that the approaching twenty-first century should usher in the year-round public school. Statistics showing the educational backsliding of many minority students from June to September and crime reports claiming increased teen activity during summer months are used to support this idea. Local administrators often oppose the wall-to-wall calendar on the basis of current funding inadequacies, while teachers cite their disciplinary problems with vacation-starved students.

Which captures your interest, the projected benefits of year-round public education or the reasons against it? Defend your position, citing relevent reasons and/or examples taken from your own experience, reading, or personal observations.

STOP

Do not go on until you are instructed to do so. Use any remaining time to check your work on this portion of the test.

ANALYSIS OF AN ARGUMENT ESSAY TOPIC

TIME: 30 Minutes

DIRECTIONS: In essay form, prepare a review on the position of the argument provided below. Before taking your own position on the argument's standpoint, it may be helpful to determine the method of thinking behind the argument itself. For example, consider alternative explanations to any assumptions the argument might make, and any evidence or examples that may strengthen or weaken the argument. Remember, there is no one "correct" response to the essay topic.

Before starting, read the essay topic and its question(s). You may make preliminary notes in your test booklet before writing the actual essay. Be sure to write your essay on the lined pages provided at the back of the book.

While the prohibition of liquor failed America in the 1920s, it may now be time to license the consumption of alcohol. Our culture's advocacy of drinking causes many to leave unexamined the role of alcohol in their lives. Alcohol is a major factor in our national health care crisis, and statistics show that liquor is the leading accomplice to violent crimes. The consumption license could be revoked after alcohol-related crimes and accidents. Its written examination would require drinkers to become educated about alcohol's devastating effects on the human body and our society as a whole.

Discuss the degree to which you find this argument logically persuasive. In presenting your perspective, be certain to analyze the argument's use of evidence and line of reasoning. Also discuss what, if anything, would make the argument more solid and convincing or would assist you to better judge its conclusion.

STOP

If time remains, you may go back and check your work.

PRACTICE TEST 2

ANSWER KEY

Section 1 — Data Sufficiency

1.	(A)	6.	(C)	11.	(E)	16.	(B)
2.	(E)	7.	(C)	12.	(E)	17.	(A)
3.	(C)	8.	(E)	13.	(C)	18.	(D)
4.	(C)	9.	(C)	14.	(D)	19.	(C)
5.	(C)	10.	(C)	15.	(C)	20.	(C)

Section 2 — Sentence Correction

1.	(B)	7.	(A)	13.	(D)	19.	(D)
2.	(E)	8.	(B)	14.	(B)	20.	(E)
3.	(C)	9.	(A)	15.	(B)	21.	(B)
4.	(C)	10.	(E)	16.	(A)	22.	(A)
5.	(E)	11.	(E)	17.	(C)		
6.	(D)	12.	(A)	18.	(C)		

Section 3 — Problem Solving

1.	(A)	5.	(C)	9.	(A)	13.	(C)
2.	(E)	6.	(B)	10.	(E)	14.	(D)
3.	(E)	7.	(D)	11.	(E)	15.	(A)
4.	(D)	8.	(A)	12.	(B)	16.	(A)

Section 4 — Critical Reasoning

1.	(E)	5.	(C)	9.	(D)	13.	(C)
2.	(A)	6.	(B)	10.	(E)	14.	(D)
3.	(D)	7.	(E)	11.	(C)	15.	(A)
4.	(A)	8.	(C)	12.	(D)	16.	(D)

Section 5 — Problem Solving

1.	(B)	5.	(C)	9.	(A)	13.	(B)
2.	(D)	6.	(E)	10.	(D)	14.	(D)
3.	(B)	7.	(A)	11.	(B)	15.	(D)
4.	(B)	8.	(E)	12.	(E)	16.	(B)

Section 6 — Reading Comprehension

1.	(C)	7.	(A)	13.	(E)	19.	(E)
2.	(C)	8.	(E)	14.	(D)	20.	(D)
3.	(E)	9.	(C)	15.	(C)	21.	(A)
4.	(D)	10.	(D)	16.	(D)	22.	(C)
5.	(B)	11.	(C)	17.	(A)	23.	(B)
6.	(E)	12.	(A)	18.	(D)		

DETAILED EXPLANATIONS OF ANSWERS

Section 1–Data Sufficiency

1. **(A)**
From Statement (1) *BC* (the hypotenuse) is two times the length of *AC* since it is opposite the 30° angle. Therefore, Statement (1) is sufficient to find the length of *BC*. From Statement (2) no information about *BC* can be obtained and therefore is not sufficient to find the length of *BC*. Choice (A) is correct.

2. **(E)**
From Statement (1) or Statement (2) there is not enough information to find the value of *x*. The correct choice, therefore, is (E).

3. **(C)**
Statement (1) just gives us the 5% interest on the unpaid part of the loan. Since Statement (1) does not give us the amount the debtor has to pay each year, it is not sufficient, by itself, to find the duration of the payment. According to Statement (2), $400 million has to be paid every year. Since Statement (2) does not specify the interest, it alone is not sufficient to figure out the time it takes to finish payment. But, using Statements (1) and (2) together, one can see that the debtor will never be able to finish paying, since the amount to be paid equals the interest.

4. **(C)**
Let the fraction be x/y. According to Statement (1), if the numerator of x/y is increased by 2, the fraction is $1/4$. That is, we will have

$$\frac{x+2}{y} = \frac{1}{4}.$$

After cross-multiplicationn we will get $y = 4x + 8$; i.e.,

$$4x - y + 8 = 0.$$

Since Statement (1) does not give additional conditions on *x* or *y*, we cannot identify the fraction using Statement (1) alone. Similarly, from Statement (2), we only know that

$$\frac{x}{y-6} = \frac{1}{6}, \text{ i.e.,}$$

$$6x = y - 6 \text{ or } 6x - y + 6 = 0,$$

after cross-multiplication and simplifying. Since Statement (2) does not specify x or y, we cannot find the fraction using (2) alone. However, since Statement (1) resulted in the equation

$$4x - y + 8 = 0$$

and we got

$$6x - y + 6 = 0$$

from Statement (2), by putting these two equations together we can solve for x and y.

5. **(C)**
    By Statement (1), one million people have died during the war; therefore, the pre-war population of Iran was 50 million. Since (1) does not give the post-war population, it alone is not sufficient. According to Statement (2), the population right after the war is 103% of the pre-war population. Since (2) does not give the pre-war population, it, by itself, is not sufficient to answer the question. However, using (1) and (2) together, we can figure out the population right after the war. (103% of 50 million = 51.5 million.)

6. **(C)**
    According to Statement (1), $0 \le y < 3$. Since 0, 1, and 2 are integers less than 3 but greater than or equal to 0, Statement (1) alone is not sufficient to determine the value of y. According to Statement (2), $3x + y$ is divisible by 3; therefore, y can be any multiple of 3. So, Statement (2) alone is not sufficient to decide what the value of y should be. But, using Statements (1) and (2), we see that $3x + 1$ and $3x + 2$ are not divisible by 3 while $3x + 0$ is divisible by 3. Hence, (1) and (2) together are sufficient.

7. **(C)**
    By Statement (1), $x + y = 2,500$, which is the total price for the $\$x$-a-plate dinner and the $\$y$-a-plate dinner. Since Statement (1) does not tell us the value of x or y, we cannot determine the values of x and y using (1) by itself. According to Statement (2), $300x = 200y$, i.e., $y = \frac{3}{2}x$. Since Statement (2) does not give other information about x and y, it alone is not sufficient to find the values of x and y. However, using (1) and (2) together,

we have the two equations $x + y = 2,500$ and $y = {}^3/_2x$, from which we can solve for x and y.

8.   (E)
   According to Statement (1), there are 14 tennis balls in the two boxes together. According to Statement (2), there are 5 basketballs and 4 soccer balls in Box B. Since neither Statement (1) nor Statement (2) tells us the number of tennis balls in Box B, we cannot figure out the number of tennis balls in Box A using Statements (1) and (2) together.

9.   (C)
   According to Statement (1), the student population grew by 6% in 1987; therefore, the population in 1987 was 26,500. But Statement (1) does not tell us the student population in 1988; therefore, we cannot tell the student population growth in 1988 using Statement (1) alone. According to Statement (2) there were 28,620 students in 1988. Since Statement (2) does not give the student population in 1987, we cannot find the student population growth in 1988 using (2) alone. However, using (1) and (2) together we can find the growth in 1988.

10.   (C)
   According to Statement (1), six of the companies made equal after-tax profit in the first quarter and doubled this profit in the second quarter. Since Statement (1) does not tell us about the other four companies, we cannot answer the question using (1) alone. Similarly, Statement (2) just tells us that four of the companies made equal profits in the first and second quarters. But if it does not give information about the other six companies, it alone is not sufficient to answer the equation. Using (1) and (2) together we can answer the question: If we let x be the profit each of the six companies made in the first quarter and y be the profit each of the four companies made in the first quarter, then we get the simultaneous equations

$$6x + y = 60 \text{ percent of } \$1.64 \text{ billion}$$

and $$12x + 4y = \$1.64 \text{ billion,}$$

which we can solve for x and y.

11.   (E)
   According to Statement (1), the average income of the ten people in 1987 is $80,000. Therefore, their combined income in 1987 is $800,000. According to Statement (2), five of the people have doubled their income in 1988 while the other five had the same income in 1987 and 1988. Since

neither Statement (1) nor Statement (2) tells us what the incomes of these people were in 1988, we cannot determine the average using Statements (1) and (2) together.

12. **(E)**

According to Statement (1), x, y, and z are consecutive integers; therefore, x and z are even and y is odd, or x and z are odd and y is even, and in both cases $x^2 + z^2$ is even. This shows us that the information in Statement (2) follows from Statement (1), and that $x^2 + y^2 + z^2$ can be even or odd. Hence, (1) and (2) together are not sufficient.

13. **(C)**

According to Statement (1), $AF = 5$. Since Statement (1) does not suggest the length of EF, you cannot find the area using Statement (1) alone. According to Statement (2), $AC = 6$; $DE = 3$. Since the information in (2) helps to find neither AF nor EF, Statement (2) alone is not sufficient. However, since $\triangle ACF$ is similar to $\triangle EFD$, using (1) and (2) together we get

$$\frac{AF}{DE} = \frac{AC}{EF}$$

from which we can determine the value of EF.

14. **(D)**

Let x be the number of people who had tea, y be the number of people who had coffee, and z be the number of people who had soda. According to (1) and from what is given in the statement of the problem:

$$\begin{cases} z = x + y, x + y + z = 12 \text{ and} \\ 0.65x + 0.8y + 0.9z = 9.75, \text{ that is} \end{cases}$$

$$\begin{cases} 2(x + y) = 12 \text{ and} \\ 0.65x + 0.8y + 0.9(x + y) = 9.75; \end{cases}$$

therefore, Statement (1) alone is sufficient. Moreover, since according to Statement (2), $z = 6$ and from the fact that $x + y + z = 12$, we get $x + y = 6$ and therefore Statement (2) and (1) are the same. So Statement (2) alone is also sufficient.

15. **(C)**

According to Statement (1), Liz works Monday through Saturday. Since Statement (1) does not specify the number of hours she works every day, it is not sufficient to answer the question. Statement (2) tells us only that she works one hour less than the preceding day. Since Statement (2) does not tell us the number of days she works, it alone is not sufficient. However, if we let x be the number of hours Liz works on Mondays, by Statements (1) and (2) we have that

$$x + (x - 1) + (x - 2) + (x - 3) + (x - 4) + (x - 5) = 60, \text{ i.e.,}$$

$$6x - 15 = 60.$$

Therefore, (1) and (2) together are sufficient.

16. **(B)**
According to Statement (1), $x^2 - 3x + 2 = 0$; therefore,

$$(x - 2)(x - 1) = 0, \text{ i.e., } x = 2 \text{ or } x = 1.$$

So, Statement (1) alone is not sufficient. According to Statement (2),

$$\begin{cases} x + y - 3 = 0 \\ 2x - y = 0. \end{cases}$$

Solving this system, we get $x = 1, y = 2$, i.e., we see that x has to be 1. Therefore, Statement (2) alone is sufficient.

17. **(A)**
According to Statement (1), $x^2 + y^2$ is odd. Since x and y are integers, then one of x^2 and y^2 is odd while the other is even, i.e., one of x and y is odd and the other is even. Therefore, the product of xy is even. (1) alone is sufficient. However, according to Statement (2), $x + y$ is even; therefore, both x and y are odd. Both x and y are even. So, Statement (2) is not conclusive.

18. **(D)**
According to (1),

$$\frac{2}{1 + |x|} - 1 < 0;$$

therefore,

$$\frac{2 - 1 - |x|}{1 + |x|} < 0,$$

i.e.,

$$\frac{1 - |x|}{1 + |x|} < 0.$$

Since $1 + |x| > 0$, then $1 - |x| < 0$, i.e., $1 < |x|$. So, (1) alone is sufficient.

According to Statement (2) ,

$$\frac{1}{x} - \frac{1}{x+1} < 0;$$

therefore .

$$\frac{x+1-x}{x(x+1)} < 0,$$

i.e.,

$$\frac{1}{x(x+1)} < 0.$$

But $x(x + 1) < 0$ only if $-1 < x < 0$. Therefore, Statement (2) alone is also sufficient.

19. **(C)**

According to Statement (1), the airfare from Paris to Belgrade is $200. Since Statement (1) does not give the airfare from Rome to Belgrade, you cannot find the airfare from Paris to Rome using Statement (1) by itself. According to Statement (2), the train ticket from Rome to Belgrade costs $40 less than the airfare from Paris to Rome. Since Statement (2) does not give the amount the train ticket from Rome to Belgrade costs, Statement (2) alone is not sufficient. Using (1) and (2) together the airfare from Paris to Rome can be figured out as follows: By Statement (1) the airfare from Paris to Belgrade is $200. It is given that taking a plane from Paris to Rome and then taking a train from Rome to Belgrade costs 60% of this $200, i.e., $120. If the airfare from Paris to Rome is x, by Statement (2) the train ticket from Rome to Belgrade is $x - $40. But we have found above that

$$\$x + \$x - 40 = \$120,$$

i.e., 60% of $200. Therefore, 2 $x - 40 = $120 and $x = $80.

20. **(C)**

From Statement (1) the store's cost for a pair of shoes can be found, but this is not sufficient on its own to answer the question. By using Statement (2) the final sale price can be calculated, but this is not sufficient on its own. Statement (1) and Statement (2) together provide enough information to find the profit from five pairs of shoes sold by the store. (C) is the correct choice.

Section 2–Sentence Correction

1. **(B)**
Choice (B) is parallel to the wording in the first part of the sentence. The subject is ESSENTIALS, the verb is INCLUDE, and the compound direct objects are ADDRESSING and KEEPING. There is no need for a comma or any other mark of punctuation before the final AND, so choices (A), (C), and (D) all contain unnecessary punctuation. In choice (A) the infinitive TO KEEP is not parallel with the gerund ADDRESSING. Choice (C) incorrectly makes a gerund out of INCLUDING. Choice (D) creates an independent clause, and choice (E) has another infinitive.

2. **(E)**
Because a gerund is a noun form, a possessive form must be used before a gerund. The sentence must read, JOHN'S BEING INVOLVED, so choices (A), (B), and (C) are incorrect. Choices (A), (B), and (D) all incorrectly include A with the expression, THAT KIND. Choice (E) is the only one correctly using both grammatical constructions.

3. **(C)**
This sentence asks the reader to see a cause-and-effect relationship. Choice (C) correctly indicates this relationship by starting the sentence with BECAUSE. Also, choice (C) uses SENT BY ACCIDENT instead of the incorrect, SENT ON ACCIDENT. Choice (A) has the cause-and-effect relationship, but the phrase BEING THAT is incorrect in standard usage. Choices (D) and (E) do not indicate a cause-and-effect relationship. Choice (B) begins with BECAUSE but uses ON ACCIDENT.

4. **(C)**
Choice (C) is the clearest, most concise statement of the meaning of this sentence. Choices (A) and (B) are entirely too wordy in their attempt at formality. Choice (D) erroneously indicates that movie audiences would be composed of something other than human beings. Choice (E) implies that all people in an audience would have the same tastes, and that there are different types of these single-interest audiences.

5. **(E)**
Choice (E) correctly uses the possessive before the gerund and begins the sentence with REGARDLESS. There is no such expression as IRREGARDLESS. The word REGARDLESS already has a prefix mean-

ing *not*, so to add another prefix also meaning *not* (ir) would be to create a double negative. Choices (A) and (B) can therefore be eliminated. Choice (C) does not make a coherent sentence. Choice (D) changes the meaning of the sentence.

6.　**(D)**

Choice (D) corrects the ambiguous modifier and retains the correct verb tense. The modifying phrase ON MONDAY is called a SQUINTING MODIFIER because it is placed directly between two things it could modify; thus, the meaning of the sentence is not clear. Does ON MONDAY modify when the newspaper reported the story, or does it modify when Paul Radous would receive the scholarship? Choices (A), (B), and (E) do not correct this problem. Choice (C) corrects the SQUINTING MODIFIER, but the verb tense is erroneously changed.

7.　**(A)**

Choice (A) uses the correct verb tense. The sentence contains two past-tense actions, one taking place before the other in time. Past perfect is used for the previous of two past actions, HAD SEEN. Choice (B) is simple past tense, and choice (E) is present tense. Choices (C) and (D) both use WOULD HAVE. The verb of the second half of the sentence, WOULD HAVE BEEN SURPRISED, precludes another usage of that tense in the first half of the sentence. In IF CLAUSES expressing the prior of two past actions, the past perfect tense must be used.

8.　**(B)**

The participle phrase DEVELOPING OVER A PERIOD OF YEARS obviously refers to the novel, not to Cindy Molina or to the publishers. In order to avoid a dangling participle phrase, the main clause must begin with NOVEL. Choices (A) and (D) sound as if Cindy Molina developed over a period of years; choice (C) sounds as if the publishers developed over a period of years. Choice (E) has Cindy Molina illogically presenting a published novel to the publishers.

9.　**(A)**

Choice (A) shows the correct sequence of events in time and the correct wording, NO SOONER...THAN.... Choice (B) inserts the superfluous word WHEN. Choices (C) and (D) do not show the correct idea of the sentence. Choice (E) is the wrong wording.

10.　**(E)**

Choice (E) completes the parallelism, DRILL TEAM GIRLS ALSO

PARTICIPATED, of the subject-verb combinations in the first two independent clauses. Choice (A) uses inverted wording, PARTICIPATING WERE THE GIRLS. Choice (B) changes the form of the verb to WERE PARTICIPATING. Choices (C) and (D) sound as if there are people other than girls on the drill team.

11. **(E)**

Choice (E) is the clearest statement of the five choices. Choices (A) and (D) use the wording, WALKING PARTICIPANTS. Therefore, these two sentences might be read to mean that only the participants who walked in the parade could be seen, indicating that participants who rode cars or horses were not to be seen. Choices (B) and (C) contain an error in subject-verb agreement, PARTICIPANTS...WAS.

12. **(A)**

Choice (A) correctly indicates the idea that we were surprised when we read that statistic. The wording of choice (B) would indicate that we surprised ourselves. Choice (C) indicates that we were surprised before we read the statistic. Choice (D) is hopelessly wordy. Choice (E) indicates that we read the statistic in order to surprise ourselves.

13. **(D)**

Choice (D) correctly places the modifier ONLY before ONCE. Choice (A), ONLY EMBEZZLED, is a misplaced modifier having as its meaning that embezzling is not serious. Choice (B), ONLY SHE, also has a misplaced modifier and means that Connie was alone when she embezzled. Choice (C) uses the wrong tense, WOULD EMBEZZLE, as well as not correcting the placement of ONLY. Choice (E), although it correctly places ONLY, does not logically fit into the context of the sentence.

14. **(B)**

Choice (B) is the most concise wording. The correct usage is WOULD HAVE; WOULD OF, although sometimes used in informal conversations, is not standard English usage; therefore, choices (A) and (C) are incorrect. Choice (D) unnecessarily changes the tense of WISH to WISHED. Choice (E) produces a fragment.

15. **(B)**

The first part of this sentence contains an independent clause followed by a subordinate clause, so that pattern needs to be repeated in the second half in order to produce a balanced sentence. Also, the subordinate clause must state the reason for the activity in the independent clause.

Choice (B) is the only one with the independent clause, HE LEFT, followed by a subordinate clause giving a reason for the activity, BECAUSE HE WAS CONCERNED ABOUT BEING LATE. Choice (A) does not complete the balanced structure. Choices (A) and (C) contain the informal usage, GOING TO BE OR REALIZED ABOUT BEING. The wording of (D) creates a fragment. Choice (E), although moderately acceptable, uses an awkward phrase, REALIZING HIS LATENESS, instead of a subordinate clause.

16. **(A)**
ONE ANOTHER is used when referring to three or more people; EACH OTHER is used when referring to two people. Choices (C) and (D) incorrectly use ONE ANOTHER. Choices (B) and (E) use another incorrect phrase, ONE FOR THE OTHER.

17. **(C)**
The expression THE FORMER can only be used in a series of two. Choices (A) and (B) are incorrect because they use THE FORMER with a series of three. Choice (D) contains the awkward phrasing FOR THE NUMBER ONE. The word serving as a conjunction introducing the last part of the sentence, ALTHOUGH, implies a condition. Choice (E) uses the wrong conjunction FOR; choices (B) and (D) use the wrong conjunction AND.

18. **(C)**
Choice (C) correctly uses a phrase beginning with an infinitive, TO EXTEND. The linking verb, IS, must be followed by a noun form, which is the infinitive phrase. An adverb clause cannot follow a linking verb, so choices (A) and (D) are incorrect. Choices (B) and (E) are prepositional phrases and cannot serve as nouns to complete the linking verb.

19. **(D)**
Choice (D) completes the parallelism with a single-word noun: STANDING, FLUENCY, and INVOLVEMENT. Choice (A) is an infinitive phrase, not a single-word noun. Choices (B), (C), and (E) are verb forms, not nouns.

20. **(E)**
Choice (E) clearly states the condition that must be met before the parent will consider buying a new car. Choice (A) contains poor phrasing, OF NEED DUE TO. Choice (B) uses the passive voice. Choice (C) begins

with the awkward phrase IN ORDER TO HAVE NEED, and what the son needs is unclear in this choice. Choice (D) sounds as if the son himself has mechanical problems.

21. **(B)**
    There is a pronoun reference problem in this sentence. The first part of the sentence describes problems with the roof and the paint, but these are plural problems. There is no antecedent for IT in the sentence as it appears in choice (A) because, clearly, a person would not sell his roof or his paint. The obvious intent is that the roof and the paint problems must be fixed before the house can be sold. Therefore, choice (B) adds the missing word HOUSE in order to clear up the sentence. Choice (C) clarifies what will be repaired but still does not clarify IT. Choice (D) makes it sound as if the roof and the paint will be sold. Choice (E) corrects the first IT but not the second one.

22. **(A)**
    This sentence shows a clear cause-and-effect meaning. Choice (A) begins with BECAUSE, a subordinating conjunction that shows the cause for stopping at the dress store. Choices (B) and (C) would be used to show the effect, not the cause. Although choices (D) and (E) can be heard in everyday speech, they are both incorrect in standard English usage.

Section 3–Problem Solving

1. **(A)**
    The formula to use to find the percent is

    $$\frac{\text{original price} - \text{sale price}}{\text{original price}} \times 100\%$$

    $$\frac{125 - 100}{125} \times 100\% = \frac{25}{125} \times 100\% = 20\%$$

2. **(E)**

    If X is the number, then $.15X = 60$. Therefore, $X = \dfrac{60}{.15} = 400$.

3. **(E)**
    Rearrange

    $$2x + 3y = 0 \text{ to } 2x = -3y, \ y = -\frac{2}{3}x$$

    Substitute in the first equation

    $$x - (-\frac{2}{3}x) = 10$$

    $$1\frac{2}{3}x = 10$$

    $$x = 6$$

4. **(D)**
    Label the room *ABCDEF*. Extend the line at *D* to divide the area into two rectangles, one 5 × 7 and one 20 × 8.

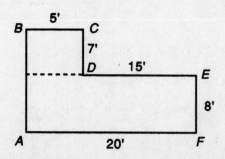

Area of a rectangle = length × width

Area = 5 × 7 + 20 × 8

$\quad\quad$ = 35 + 160

$\quad\quad$ = 195 sq. ft.

5. **(C)**

Let x = the number of pounds of coffee B at \$12/lb.

$(x + 2)\,(12.50) = x(12) + 2(14)$

$12.50x + 25 = 12x + 28$

$.50x = 3$

$x = 6$ pounds of coffee B

6. **(B)**

Let s = score of the final test.

$\dfrac{3(87) + x}{4} = 85$

$261 + x = 85(4)$

$x = 79$

7. **(D)**

Make a diagram from the given information to see that the distance from Joan's house to Dave's house is the hypotenuse of the right triangle.

d = the distance from Joan's
house to Dave's house

$6^2 + 8^2 = d^2$

$36 + 64 = d^2$

$100 = d^2$

$d = 10$

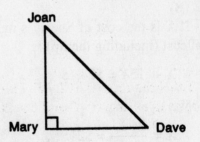

8. **(A)**

If $X + Y = 8$ and $3X + Y = 12$, then

$3(X + Y) - (X + Y) = 12 - 8.$

Therefore, $2X = 4$, $X = 2$, and $Y = 8 - X = 6$. Hence,

$2X - Y = 4 - 6 = -2.$

9. **(A)**

Since the sum of measures of the interior angles of a triangle is 180°, the measure of $\angle ACB$ is

$$180 - (75 + 75) = 30°.$$

This is also the measure of $\angle DCE$. Therefore, the sum of measures of angles D and E is $180 - 30 = 150°$.

10. **(E)**

The number of students at XYZ University is

$$750 + 1{,}600 + 1{,}200 + 450 = 4{,}000.$$

Of these there are

$$1{,}600 + 1{,}200 = 2{,}800$$

that are 19 and 20 years old. Therefore, the 19 and 20 year olds form

$$\frac{2{,}800}{4{,}000} \times 100 = 70\% \text{ of all students.}$$

11. **(E)**

If Mr. Wheeler chooses to pay $50 down and $35 each in 12 monthly payments, his total cost is

$$50 + 12(35) = \$470.$$

Since the cash price is $395, the cost of credit is

$$\$(470 - 395) = \$75.$$

12. **(B)**

If X is the cost of Sherry's meal, then her tip is $.15X$. Thus, her total meal cost (including the tip) is

$$X + .15X = \$24.15$$

so that

$$X = \frac{24.15}{1.15} = \$21.$$

13. **(C)**

If Cyndi invests $X in the certificate of deposit at 9% interest and $(2,000 − X) in the passbook savings account at 5% interest, then

$$.09X + .05(2{,}000 - X) = 148.$$

This is equivalent to

$$.04X + 100 = 148,$$

or $.04X = 48$, which gives $X = 1,200$.

14. **(D)**

The 26 gallon mixture contains 20 gallons of water and 6 gallons of acid. When 4 gallons of acid are added, we have a new mixture of 30 gallons that contains 10 gallons of acid. Therefore, the percentage of water in the new mixture is

$$\frac{20}{30} \times 100 = 66.7.$$

15. **(A)**

Let x = amount at 8%

y = amount at 7%

then $x = 3y$

The interest equation is $.08x + .07y = 930$. Multiplying each term by 100 gives $8x + 7y = 93,000$ and substituting $x = 3y$ in for x gives $24y + 7y = 93,000$ or $31y = 93,000$, then $y = 3,000$ so $x = 9,000$. Choices (B) and (C) come from the mistake of letting $y = 3x$, then the equation becomes $29x = 93,000$ or $x = 3,207$ (rounded to nearest dollar) and $y = 9,621$ (also, rounded). Choice (D) is the amount at 7%, which was not asked for.

16. **(A)**

The total of 12 test scores is

$$12(55) = 660.$$

When the two highest and the two lowest test scores are dropped, the total of the remaining 8 test scores is

$$8(50) = 400.$$

Hence, the total of the 4 dropped scores is

$$660 - 400 = 260,$$

and the average of scores dropped is

$$\frac{260}{4} = 65.$$

Section 4—Critical Reasoning

1. **(E)**
     No direct claim is made in the ad for the superiority of either cotton or rayon; (A) is not the best answer. Joining the bandwagon is not the overwhelming reason that most persons would buy Swabbies after reading this advertisement. Most people are not doctors, so the advertisement does not imply that most people use Swabbies, thus (B) is a poor choice. The advertisement does not sound like one usually found in a medical journal. From the information given, the reader has no idea if it is placed where those with a high degree of education and status would read it, so (C) is not the best choice. No direct statement or implication suggests that Swabbies helped the doctors attain their professional status; therefore, (D) is not the best choice. (E) is the best choice. Most readers would purchase the cotton swabs because of the transfer propaganda technique. "If a doctor recommends it, it must be right," they might conclude.

2. **(A)**
     Since allocations for lighting tend to benefit individuals as well as businesses, (A) is the correct choice. No suggestion is made in the passage that decreased profits are likely to result from the installation of adequate night lighting; (B) is incorrect. The passage does not suggest that businesses may decline to locate in new areas without lighting. Businesses may in fact install their own lighting, thus (C) is incorrect. Economic recession is not always the result of inadequate night lighting; (D) is not the best choice. The passage does not go so far as to suggest that night lighting can result in increased productivity for the nation as a whole. (E) is not the correct choice since it stretches the point made in the article.

3. **(D)**
     One cannot tell from the information given if Lorenzo is older than Nedino. One knows that Lorenzo is older than Martin, but he could still be younger than Nedino. On the other hand, he could be older than Nedino, so (A) is not the best choice. One knows that Lorenzo is older than Martin, but one does not know how Lorenzo ranks in relation to Juarez. (C) also cannot be stated as truth. One knows that Korrie and Nedino are twins. One also knows that Martin is younger than Nedino and that Lorenzo is older than Martin. The reader, however, is not told for sure how Lorenzo ranks in relation to the others. (D) is the right choice. Juarez is older than Korrie; Korrie and Nedino are twins. Since Martin is younger than

Nedino, he is also younger than Korrie. Since the reader is told that Martin is younger than Nedino and since Korrie and Nedino are twins, Martin is younger than Korrie. (E), however, states that Korrie is younger than Martin and is incorrect.

4.   **(A)**
(A) is the best choice; in the U.S. most people want freedom with as little control as possible from the government. (B) is not the best conclusion to draw from the statements; in the U.S. individuals want liberty with firm limits being given to government. It is not predicted that private government will give way to public government; (C) is not the best choice. The above passage was written about America; (D) is a false statement and should not be selected. The passage is typical of America so (E) should not be chosen.

5.   **(C)**
Modifying the language so that words are sounded the way they are spelled would actually be an aid to people who do not speak the language and are trying to learn; therefore, (A) is incorrect. There is no indication that the type on typewriters would have to be changed. (B) is incorrect. (C) is the most serious disadvantage to modifying the language. If a word is pronounced differently in different localities, who is to decide which is right? (D) is not the best choice. Many advocates have worked out complete plans for modifying the alphabet. (E) is not the best choice since young children who are learning to read could certainly be helped, not hindered, by a method which has the words written as they sound.

6.   **(B)**
The opponents of the sight word method did not directly attack the school personnel; (A) is not the best choice. The opponents of the sight word method did suggest that the increase in numbers in remedial reading classes coincided with the advent of the sight word method; (B) is the best choice. The opponents did not suggest that more than one method implied a dilemma. They stated emphatically that the only method to use is the phonics method, thus (C) is not the correct choice. The opponents did not attempt to show in the relatively short passage that the sight word method leads to an absurd conclusion; (D) is not the best choice. The passage does not really try to prove which method is used most readily by students in the school. It suggests, however, that the phonics method is best. Perhaps it is best because it includes word attack skills, so (E) is not the best choice.

7.   **(E)**

The expertise of those employing the method would probably not answer the arguments by opponents of the sight word method; (A) is not the best choice. Opponents of the sight word method did not attack the morals or capabilities of the professionals using the sight word method. Responding with moral uprightness and references to capabilities would not be the best tactic; (B) should not be chosen. The passage makes no references to other reading methods or that they attribute to remedial reading students; (C) is not the best choice. A dilemma being posed by Flesch's claims is not the most logical tactic to take in defending the sight word method of teaching reading; (D) is not the best choice. Showing that there were other reasons for the increase in remedial reading classes would be the best ploy for the advocates of the sight word method to use. Therefore, (E) is the best choice.

8.   **(C)**

(A) is not a correct choice. Cotton is still important to Georgia. It is still grown in Georgia (though not as widely as it once was) and it is still manufactured there. (B) should not be selected since there is no evidence in the passage to suggest that the growth of cotton in Georgia has been unusually high in the past few years. (C) is the correct choice. Farming is still important to Georgia as is evidenced by the emphasis placed on peanuts, pecans, tobacco, and peaches in the passage. (D) is not the best choice. The initial cost of switching from farming to manufacturing was expensive for the state. The cotton growers did not usually build or operate the manufacturing plants, but the expense was there for someone. (E) is incorrect; profits from farming are still important to the state of Georgia.

9.   **(D)**

It is unlikely that anyone foresaw just how important manufacturing would become for the state; (A) is incorrect. The initial cost in switching from tenant farming to working in a factory was probably minimal; therefore (B), is not the correct answer. Supplies of farm products are not low in the state of Georgia. It is the nation's leading producer of peanuts, for instance; (C) is incorrect. Changing from growing cotton to manufacturing was a wise move. If the switch had not been made, Georgia would not be the center of manufacturing it is today. Hence, (D) is the correct choice. There is no evidence to suggest that manufacturing may cease to become important to Georgia; (E) is incorrect.

10.   **(E)**

Finding a skeleton 1.6 million years old which so closely resembles the human form confirms that the human form is *quite* old. Hence, (A) is incorrect. There is no evidence that the remains may have confused two different time periods; (B) is incorrect. No evidence suggests that the body fell down a gerbil hole, so (C) is incorrect. The passage makes no mention of religious groups using human sacrifices; (D) is incorrect. (E) is the correct choice. This body confirms the antiquity of the human form.

11. **(C)**
    (A) is not the best choice. Most scientists believed that humans existed 1.6 million years ago; they were not sure that these humans looked as much like humans today as the skeletal remains indicated. (B) should not be selected; there was no magic date like 100 B.C., according to the passage, when humans looked like humans. (C) is the best choice. It was a surprise to most scientists that the skeletal remains for a child were the size and proportion that they were. The discovery seems to indicate that humans reached their present size more than a million and a half years ago; the smaller size was a result of populations in poor areas. (D) is not the best choice; the discovery *abolished* the belief that humans have grown larger through time. (E) should not be chosen since the passage does not support the belief that human life began on the continent of Europe.

12. **(D)**
    If the case were proven that the weather, not the sport, causes the temper flare-ups, then it would not prove it was the sport which attracted the aggressive fans; (A) is incorrect. If the fans were aware of the testing, it might affect the results. If both groups knew of the testing, however, the results would be less likely skewed in favor of one group or the other; (B) is not a logical answer. If both groups of fans were actually the same people, then the argument that one group is more aggressive than the other would not be valid and (C) is incorrect. Showing that not only are there more incidents of violence but also that there are more incidents per game would strengthen the argument that baseball attracts more aggressive fans, so (D) is the right choice. The inclusion of college athletes who participated in both sports is irrelevant; (E) is not a good choice.

13. **(C)**
    Perhaps the fact that Sammie cites only a single observed case is a weak point in Sammie's claim, but it is not the point on which Johnnie focuses; (A) is not the correct choice. The upturn in grades might be temporary, but, again, it is not the point on which Johnnie focuses, so (B) is incorrect. (C) is the point on which Johnnie's response focuses. Johnnie

cites that the grades came after treatment for diabetes – not after the transfer to a different school. (D) is not correct; certainly Sammie does not make mention of schools which have been public and then gone private, but this is not the point on which Johnnie focuses. No figures are given from Jane's permanent record, but this is not the point upon which Johnnie focuses, thus (E) is not the best choice.

14. **(D)**

(A) is incorrect since the passage is not designed to indicate that other disorders are not serious. The purpose of the article seems to be to suggest the importance of depression. (B) is incorrect; the passage does not suggest prevention or cure of mental disorders. No suggestion is made in the passage that emphysema is psychosomatic; therefore, (C) is incorrect. (D) is the main point of the article, which tries to emphasize that depression is a very costly affliction. Since the passage makes no mention of whether sick benefits should or should not be assigned for depression, (E) is incorrect. (The author seems, however, to be sympathetic toward those who are depressed.)

15. **(A)**

(A) comes closest of the five statements in refuting the claim. (B) is an example of culling a program if individuals have to assume responsibility for services normally paid for by the federal budget. (C) is an example of the claim; it certainly does not refute the claim if some programs – even with a limited number of constituents – were discontinued. (D) is another example of the claim; since it does not refute the claim, it should not be selected as the correct choice. (E) also does not refute the claim and should not be selected as the correct choice.

16. **(D)**

With savings and investments encouraged by a drop in the capital gains tax, the legislators could not use (A) as a reason for not supporting the repeal. (B) is not the best choice because consumption is already more economically attractive than saving because of the capital gains tax. (C) is not an appropriate choice. The U.S. now has to borrow from other nations because of the capital gains tax. Many individuals are not investing but are consuming because of it. (D) is the reason that many legislators are hesitant to support the capital gains tax. They are afraid that they will appear to their constituents as favoring the rich over the middle income or the poor. (E) is incorrect. Currently, spending is cheaper than paying gains on capital. Repealing the measure would change this.

Section 5–Problem Solving

1. **(B)**
    The shaded region = the area of the square – the area of the circle

    $$A = 4^2 - \pi 2^2$$

    $$= 16 - 4\pi$$

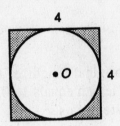

2. **(D)**
    The roots of $3x^2 + 3x - 6 = 0$ can be found by factoring the equation:

    $$(3x + 6)(x - 1) = 0$$

    giving the roots – 2 and 1. Therefore, the product of the roots is – 2.

3. **(B)**
    For two successive months to have the same date of the month be on the same day of the week, the first month must have a multiple of 7 days. Since February is the only month that has (usually) a multiple of 7 days, the first month must be February.

4. **(B)**
    The area of the walls

    $$= 2(15 \times 9 + 20 \times 9)$$

    $$= 2(135 + 180)$$

    $$= 630 \text{ sq. ft.}$$

    Since the area needs two coats of paint, you need an amount of paint to cover 1,260 sq. ft.
    To find the number of gallons, divide by 400 sq. ft. per gallon to equal a little over three gallons. But since you have to buy whole gallons, you therefore need to raise it to four gallons.

5. **(C)**
   Let Jim's age = x and Betty's age = y.

   $$x = 2y \text{ and } x + y = 18$$

   $$2y + y = 18$$

   $$3y = 18$$

   $$y = 6$$

6. **(E)**
   Let 1 equal the original length of the side of the square. After the 40% increase, the new length equals 1.40.
   The area of a square equals s^2.

   $$s^2 = (1.40)(1.40)$$

   $$= 1.96$$

   The percent increase is

   $$\frac{1.96 - 1}{1} \times 100\% = 96\%$$

7. **(A)**

   $$2x - (3y + x) + 5(x - y) = 2x - 3y - x + 5x - 5y$$

   $$= 6x - 8y$$

8. **(E)**
   It would take four 6 inch by 6 inch tiles to cover each square foot of floor space. The area of the room is 72 square feet and $4 \times 72 = 288$.

9. **(A)**

   $$x^{64} = (x^{32})^2$$

   $$x^{64} = 64$$

   $$(x^{32})^2 = 64$$

   Since the only two numbers whose square is 64 are 8 and -8, $x^{32} = 8$ or $x^{32} = -8$.

10. **(D)**

$$\frac{4 \times 4 + 2 \times 5 + 5 \times 6 + 2 \times 7 + 5 \times 8 + 2 \times 9}{20}$$

$$= \frac{16 + 10 + 30 + 14 + 40 + 18}{20}$$

$$= \frac{128}{20}$$

$$= 6.4$$

11. **(B)**

The shaded portion of square *ABCD* together with the shaded portion of square *ADEF* would cover a 10 cm by 10 cm square.

12. **(E)**

Since

$$\sqrt{x-1} = (x-1)^{1/2}$$

and since

$$\left[(x-1)^{1/2} \right]^4 = (x-1)^2$$

$$\left(\sqrt{x-1} \right)^4 = 2^4$$

or $\qquad (x-1)^2 = 16.$

13. **(B)**

$$\frac{16^2 \times 8^3}{2^{19}} = \frac{(2^4)^2 \times (2^3)^3}{2^{19}}$$

$$= \frac{2^8 \times 2^9}{2^{19}}$$

$$= \frac{2^{17}}{2^{19}}$$

$$= 2^{-2}$$

14. **(D)**

Note that 24 ounces is $1\frac{1}{2}$ pounds and $3 \times 1.80 = 5.40$.

15. **(D)**

Let x = the man's pay for the first day, then

$$\frac{3}{2}x, \frac{3}{2} \times \frac{3}{2}x, \frac{3}{2} \times \frac{3}{2} \times \frac{3}{2}x, \text{ and } \frac{3}{2} \times \frac{3}{2} \times \frac{3}{2} \times \frac{3}{2}x$$

is this man's pay for the second, third, fourth, and fifth days, respectively.

$$x + \frac{3}{2}x + \frac{3}{2} \times \frac{3}{2}x + \frac{3}{2} \times \frac{3}{2} \times \frac{3}{2}x + \frac{3}{2} \times \frac{3}{2} \times \frac{3}{2} \times \frac{3}{2}x = 422$$

$$x + \frac{3}{2}x + \frac{9}{4}x + \frac{27}{8}x + \frac{81}{16}x = 422$$

$$\frac{211}{16}x = 422$$

$$x = 32$$

Thus, his first day's pay was \$32. Since $^3/_2 \times 32 = 48$, his second day's pay was \$48.

16. **(B)**

Let a, b, and c be the weights of the smallest, middle-sized, and largest child, respectively. Then

$$a + b = 71$$

$$b + c = 96$$

$$a + c = 87$$

$$(a + b) + (b + c) + (a + c) = 71 + 96 + 87$$

$$2a + 2b + 2c = 254$$

$$a + b + c = 127$$

Section 6–Reading Comprehension

1. **(C)**
    The passage traces the early history of the bicycle from its introduction in France in 1791, including improvements and uses in France, England, and the U.S. in the early nineteenth century. It is not significantly concerned with broader issues of industrialization or European influence on America, nor is it concerned with recent improvements. The author believes that the bicycle may be more widely used in America in the future, but the passage makes no concerted attempt to argue for such use.

2. **(C)**
    The first paragraph indicates that the bicycle facilitated the introduction of the automobile by creating a demand for independent personal transportation. The passage indicates that the *vélocipède*'s popularity declined rapidly and that the bicycle has been less popular as a means of transportation in the U.S. than in some parts of the world, but does not provide reasons in either case.

3. **(E)**
    Their histories are related insofar as the bicycle's demonstration of the possibilities of independent personal transportation created a demand the automobile filled. The passage suggests that the bicycle may become more popular, not that it will supplant the automobile. The passage does not indicate why the bicycle declined in popularity; it did so before the automobile was invented.

4. **(D)**
    The author does not mention lack of safety in the *célérifère*, but says it had rigidly mounted wheels and could not be steered. He implies that its ride was slow and uncomfortable since the improvements in the *vélocifère* addressed both of these problems.

5. **(B)**
    Baron von Drais added a padded saddle and an armrest, but his "revolutionary improvement" was a front wheel capable of being steered.

6. **(E)**
    The examples of use provided by the author are "the sporting set of

Paris," and "riding academies" and many riders in London's streets and parks pursuing this "pastime."

7. **(A)**

The *vélocipède* was the immediate forerunner of the bicycle. It was patented in 1818, almost immediately migrated to England and gained popularity, but was rarely seen after the early 1820s.

8. **(E)**

The author indicates that the bicycle is widely used throughout the world as a means of work-related transportation, not chiefly for sport or personal expression or by children. There is no basis in the passage for speculating about the author's view of the bicycle as an environmentally sound alternative to the automobile.

9. **(C)**

The last two paragraphs continue the author's history of the early use and development of the bicycle by extending the discussion to England (paragraph five) and the U.S. (paragraph six). The next best choice is (A), but it focuses on a secondary consideration and does not account for much of the content in the last two paragraphs. (B) and (E) distort the purposes of the passage, and (D) is mistaken.

10. **(D)**

(D) most fully accounts for the contents of the passage. The passage seeks to enumerate and explain Aston's scientific achievements. Other choices either focus on matters that are secondary to this primary purpose (A), distort the passage's emphasis (E), or stress matters that are not significantly addressed in the passage (B) and (C).

11. **(C)**

The best choice is (C) since the passage's content and organization suggest an encyclopedic entry – brief biography and summary of major achievements. It is not chiefly concerned with definitions of terms (E), it details too much background knowledge for a news magazine (B), and the content (especially the biographical introduction) and organization make (A) and (D) unlikely choices.

12. **(A)**

Aston worked on neon gas before and after the war and "redesigned" Thomson's positive ray deflection apparatus after the war, having worked with Thomson before the war. The passage does not tell us *why* Aston did not discover all naturally occurring isotopes, only that he discovered 212 of 287. Similarly, the passage tells us that later research depended on Aston's work, but not *which* research.

13. **(E)**
Aston's mass spectrograph was a refinement of J. J. Thomson's earlier apparatus. Important as it was, it did not deal with unknown elements or *sub*atomic particles, nor was it the first machine to use electric and magnetic fields in atomic research.

14. **(D)**
Thomson's apparatus deflected positively charged particles. All of the other achievements are mentioned in the passage.

15. **(C)**
An integer is defined as a whole number. Ions and atoms are discussed, but not defined.

16. **(D)**
Aston's whole number rule was derived from the similarity of his conclusions in working with the atomic masses of neon and then chlorine (see paragraphs four and five).

17. **(A)**
By showing that two forms of neon existed with different atomic masses, Aston contributed proof that elements can be composed of mixtures of isotopes. His work indicated that there are two forms of neon with different masses, not that the previously accepted atomic weight of neon was incorrect (B) or that isotopes must be separated to establish the atomic weight of elements (C). The passage does not assert that lighter ions outnumber heavier ones (D). Energy used to bind nuclei affects the atomic mass of individual isotopes in relation to integers, but does not distort accurate measurement of mass (E).

18. **(D)**
The primary purpose of the article is to summarize briefly the law called Title VII and some of its amendments. The author discusses the conditions of Title VII, but there are no predictions made as to the outcome of amendments (A). Since the article is a summary, there is no criticism (B), or suggestions for further amendments (C). There is no discussion of conflicting aspects (E).

19. **(E)**

Title VII is part of the Civil Rights Act of 1964. FEP (A) refers to the fair employment practices law. The EEOC (B) is charged with enforcing Title VII. The Fair Labor Standards Act (C) is not mentioned in the article. BFOQ (D) stands for a bona fide occupational qualification.

20. **(D)**

Choice (D) presents a situation in which men seem to be chosen for managerial positions, although there might be one or more women qualified for placement, so it is the situation most likely to fall under the jurisdiction of Title VII. Choice (A) is an example of discrimination based on age, not sex. Choice (B) deals with setting fair wages for employees. Choice (C) has to do with an employee engaging in concerted activities for mutual aid or protection. Choice (E) covers an employee's right to view his or her own files.

21. **(A)**

The tone of the entire article is objectively neutral. It is a given fact that sex would rarely be a bona fide occupational qualification. The article does not approve (B) or disapprove (C), and the author is neither amused (C) nor shocked (E).

22. **(C)**

Several deadlines for filing are stated in this article. As the statutes seem clearly limited—filing within 180 days, for example—it is apparent that complaints filed after that time limit could not be considered. Therefore, time is crucial to Title VII complaints, so the sooner the complaint is filed, the better. The article presents the complaint form (A) as a rather simplified paper, even though it would be important to capture details fully and accurately in the narrative portion of the form. The article states clearly that continuing violations (B) are not "subject to the usual time limits." The EEOC will examine a complaint, but the article does not indicate that the EEOC is responsible for filing a lawsuit (D) of any nature. The article indicates that the complaintant may file first with a state agency, and that if there is an applicable state agency, the EEOC will forward a copy of the complaint, but it is not evident that any state agency supersedes a federal agency (E).

23. **(B)**

The glass company should not pay men more than women for lifting and stacking cartons because women are probably also able to perform such activities; hence, this would be the most likely form of sexual discrimination in pay. The example of a restaurant hiring males and females and assigning them to positions deemed best by managerial staff appears to be an acceptable practice. If all the women were posted as hostesses and all the men as bartenders, then that would be discrimination as described in Title VII. A dress designer who wishes to hire young women to model "junior miss" dresses would certainly appear to have a bona fide occupational qualification, since young men to not wear "junior miss" dresses and would look ridiculous modeling them.

Section 7–Analytical Writing Assessment

ANALYSIS OF AN ISSUE ESSAY TOPIC

Sample Essay Response Scoring 5 to 6

As a carry-over from an agricultural based society, the "summers off" school calendar seems currently arbitrary and ripe to be eliminated. However, this calendar, by virtue of its constancy, has spawned various major and minor economies and social systems. Just as "no man is an island," the school calendar cannot be considered properly without noting the way in which it affects other aspects of society.

In an era self-conscious of "quality time" spent between and among family members, the classic family vacation is not to be shrugged off. Vacations in all industries and businesses are crowded into gaps in the school calendar, obviously favoring the summer months which allow each mom and dad their turn. This social convention affords quality time without requiring children to miss school. Without children's synchronized vacation, a significant portion of classroom time would be spent in repetition for the benefit of returning children—an inevitability which would undermine the purposes of the year-round calendar. Even if summer vacation were reduced to one month, many industries would groan over the effort to function efficiently with such a great percentage of their workers scrambling for time off within the same month.

Other economic issues related to family vacations are seasonal home rentals and food services at popular vacation areas. Often entire towns depend upon tourist's beach badges and the rental money that justifies high property taxes. Many of those who tread water in tourists' service industries like restaurants and hotels have difficulty in the current calendar. These industries need a reliable season in order to properly adjust the size of their staffs to meet the demands made by patrons.

Not every family is part of the tourist equation, though, because some cannot afford the traditional family vacation. However, these families may depend upon their older children's opportunity to find work during these boom months, as waiters, temporary vacation relief in non-skilled factory positions, and amusement park attendants. In the absence of a "summers off" calendar, such families would be deprived of this needed income. Similarly, economic status would divide student peers based on who took the most time off for vacation. Poorer students whose parents have limited vacation time would feel punished that they are in school more than their peers. This would create a negative image of school for these youngsters. In today's calendar, "How I spent my summer vacation" inevitably varies along socio-economic lines, but the number of days is an undeniable equalizer.

Another factor which must be considered is that some forms of education can only occur outside of the school year. While it is a stigma in itself, summer school provides many students the needed opportunity to catch up and to avoid the greater stigma of repeating an entire school year. Other forms of education are less academic in nature. Many consider a summer job to be a valuable supplement to the year's book work. Similarly, summer camps provide unique experiences in relation to exploring nature, developing physical skills, being away from home, and interacting with peers in a situation of cohabitation.

With today's school budgets, the feasibility of the year-round school calendar is obviously doubtful. When one considers the economic and sociological problems that it would create, its advantages are also called into question. The simple fact is that the "summers off" calendar employs people in various direct and indirect ways. In addition, it provides opportunities for learning experiences beyond the range of the classroom, including such simplicities as intra-family interaction.

Analysis of Sample Essay Scoring 5 to 6

This response would rate a six because it displays a command of the English language, is well organized, selects a firm position, and argues it persuasively and insightfully. The essay introduces its two lines of argument, social and economic, and has a smooth transition between them in the body. The observations that families require the summer season for quality time and for older children's monetary contributions are both probing and convincing. It was important that the essay pointed out the economic effect on all industries, not merely the tourist-oriented, seasonal and location-specific ones. Another significant point made by the essay was that not all learning occurs in the classroom.

ANALYSIS OF AN ARGUMENT ESSAY TOPIC

Sample Essay Response Scoring 5 to 6

The proposal of an alcohol consumption license is a plan to force education on adults, but for most drugs (even illegal ones) education is simply offered, and made known to be available. While the proposal attempts to distance itself from Prohibition, it too would make alcohol a "controlled substance." The status of limited control is meant to give a certain leverage, actually creating the ability to force the education.

The author suggests that the gap between drinking and non-drinking is this education. He argues that the privileged status of alcohol places it in a cultural blind spot. Whether or not this is true is distinct from whether the government has the right to impose an educational agenda on adults. An adult has the same right to remain ignorant of any subject he or she chooses as he or she has the right to pursue an education. Tobacco users have no desire to be force-fed cancer statistics, just as egg lovers cannot be bothered to learn their cholesterol count.

The strongest points made by the author were his references to health care and violent crime. These issues bring drinking beyond the realm of individual concern to a position where a person's choice to drink can affect others physically and financially. However, by referring to alcohol as an "accomplice" to crime, the author characterized alcohol as an independent agent willfully assisting violence. This statement weakens the argument by overextending alcohol's role in violent crime. While the presence of the health care and crime issues justify an effort to educate the public about the consequences of alcohol consumption, it does not justify the proposed enforcement of education.

By making reference to a "written examination" the proposal takes a significant turn. The consumption license is not a counterpart to a liquor license, but a parallel to a driver's license. It is a license to operate an inebriated biological machine. This implied metaphor is a major weakness in the argument. Driver's tests do not require one to operate a vehicle with defective steering, inadequate headlights, and a blaring radio—nor does it allow a quiet radio. Driving is a complicated system of situations and corresponding rules, and thus requires tests. Drinking alcohol simply impairs one's judgment while one is in society's system of situations and corresponding rules, which each of us has studied firsthand throughout our lives.

To be an effective argument, this proposal needs to demonstrate that drinking creates an entirely new set of circumstances compared to sobriety. It does not. Drinking simply impairs judgment—within familiar circumstances it alters one's perspective. The goal of the written examination is obviously to teach people frightening information that would influence them not to drink. The goal of a driver's test is to teach people to drive.

Analysis of Sample Essay Scoring 5 to 6

This response would rate a six because it effectively analyzes and critiques the main points of the argument in strong, persuasive English. The author identified the argument's attempt to liken its proposed license to a driver's license and he proceeded to discredit this alleged parallel. The author does not challenge the proposal's evidence, but points out the intended means of delivery, described as by "force." The response contains varying sentence lengths which alternate and effectively accentuate certain points.

GMAT CAT

Graduate Management Admission Test
Computer-Adaptive Test

Practice
Test 3

NOTE:

The following practice test contains more questions than the actual GMAT CAT. This is necessary to provide a score that is roughly comparable to the shorter computer-adaptive test. Although the format is different, this test will give you an accurate idea of your strengths and weaknesses, and provide guidance for further study.

PRACTICE TEST 3

Section 1

(Answer sheets appear in the back of the book.)

TIME: 25 Minutes
22 Questions

> **DIRECTIONS:** In each of the following sentences, some part of the sentence or the entire sentence is underlined. The five answer choices give various ways of phrasing the underlined part. The first choice repeats the given sentence. Pay attention to grammar, choice of words, and sentence construction in order to select the best version of the sentence. Choose (A) if you think the given sentence is correct.

1. <u>There are many reports of wrongdoing</u> in the policies and procedures of the Department of Housing and Urban Development, officials in that government agency deny any responsibility or knowledge.

   (A) There are many reports of wrongdoing

   (B) Reports of wrongdoing

   (C) In reporting wrongdoing

   (D) Because many people have reported discrepancies

   (E) Although there are many reports of wrongdoing

2. <u>Exercise, if properly done and carefully monitored,</u> can help fight a variety of ailments such as heart disease and depression.

   (A) Exercise, if properly done and carefully monitored,

   (B) Properly doing it, carefully monitored exercise

   (C) Properly done exercise that is carefully monitored

   (D) Properly and carefully done, monitored exercise

   (E) If properly done, exercise, carefully monitored

3. <u>I agreed on the next day to show him how to improve his tennis serve</u>.

   (A) I agreed on the next day to show him how to improve his tennis serve.

   (B) I, agreeing on the next day, to show him how to improve his tennis serve.

   (C) I agreed to show him how to improve his tennis serve on the next day.

   (D) I, on the next day, agreed to show him how to improve his tennis serve.

   (E) I agreed to, on the next day, show him how to improve his tennis serve.

4. <u>We saw many of, though not nearly all, the mosques</u> in the city of Cairo.

   (A) We saw many of, though not nearly all, the mosques

   (B) We saw many, though not nearly all, of the mosques

   (C) Seeing many, though not nearly all, of the mosques

   (D) Having seen many of, though not nearly all, the mosques

   (E) Many of, though not nearly all, the existing mosques we saw

5. The legislature, in a special summer session, passed a number of bills into law, such as the legalization of minibars in hotel rooms and <u>an increase in penalties for illegal fishing</u> techniques.

   (A) an increase in penalties for illegal fishing

   (B) the increasing penalties for illegal fishing

   (C) being increased penalties for illegal fishing

   (D) illegal fishing being increased by penalties

   (E) in illegal fishing an increase in penalties

6. The Ayatollah Ruhollah Khomeini, <u>of whom much has been written</u>, died in 1989.

   (A) of whom much has been written

   (B) of who much has been written

(C) of whom much has been written about

(D) about him much has been written

(E) much having been written about him

7. The traveller in Egypt wanted to know <u>where Abu Simbel is at and
    what it was famous for</u>.

(A) where Abu Simbel is at and what it was famous for

(B) where Abu Simbel is at and for what it is famous

(C) where Abu Simbel is located and why it is famous

(D) at where Abu Simbel is and for what it was famous

(E) the location and claim to fame of Abu Simbel

8. Doctors and dermatologists <u>cannot help but criticize</u> the fact that
    there are few states with laws governing tanning parlors.

(A) cannot help but criticize

(B) can help but criticize

(C) cannot help criticizing

(D) cannot help and criticize

(E) can help and criticize

9. Becoming familiar with people's religious and political views <u>will
    often provide an insight to</u> their personalities and behaviors.

(A) will often provide an insight to

(B) will often provide an insight into

(C) will often provide an insight for

(D) will provide often an insight for

(E) often will provide an insight with

10. When the delivery truck arrived, Mr. Lee, together with his wife,
    directed the delivery men to <u>put the sofa in the living room they had
    just bought</u>.

(A) put the sofa in the living room they had just bought.

(B) put in the sofa to the living room they had just bought.

(C) put into the living room they had just bought the sofa.

(D) put the sofa they had just bought into the living room.

(E) put the sofa newly-purchased into the living room they had just bought.

11. The way some countries are disarming, some experts <u>are afraid Europeans may end up with not enough protection</u>.

(A) are afraid Europeans may end up with not enough protection

(B) being afraid Europeans may end up with not enough protection

(C) afraid not that Europeans may end up with protection

(D) afraid protection may end in Europe

(E) fear Europeans may be insufficiently protected

12. <u>Whether caffeine is a dangerous drug or not</u> is still a debatable issue, but experts do agree that caffeine is the most widely-used psychoactive drug.

(A) Whether caffeine is a dangerous drug or not

(B) That caffeine is a dangerous drug

(C) That caffeine may have been a dangerous drug

(D) Whether caffeine may be a dangerous drug or it may be not

(E) Whether or not caffeine is or is not a dangerous drug

13. <u>People who drink too much are likely to develop</u> a bad hangover.

(A) People who drink too much are likely to develop

(B) People's drinking too much are likely to develop

(C) When people drink too much, likely to develop

(D) That people drink too much is likely to develop

(E) Drinking too much is likely to develop for people

14. The museum has a special exhibit of Egyptian artifacts, <u>and the Scouts went to see it on display</u>.

    (A) and the Scouts went to see it on display

    (B) and seeing it were the Scouts on a field trip

    (C) when the Scouts took a field trip to see it

    (D) which the Scouts took a field trip to see

    (E) where the Scouts took their field trip to see it

15. <u>When he goes to the coast, he plans flying</u> as a means of transportation.

    (A) When he goes to the coast, he plans flying

    (B) When going to the coast, he plans flying

    (C) Upon going to the coast, he is flying

    (D) Upon flying to the coast, he plans going

    (E) When he goes to the coast, he plans to fly

16. <u>Having liked the creative and independence</u> of being her own boss, Helen Li decided to expand her business.

    (A) Having liked the creative and independence

    (B) Liking creative and independence

    (C) Because she liked the creativity and independence

    (D) Having creative and independent likes

    (E) Having the likes of creative and independent

17. <u>Marvin decided there was hardly any reason for our denying him</u> a larger sales territory.

    (A) Marvin decided there was hardly any reason for our denying him

    (B) Marvin, deciding there was hardly any reason for our denying him,

    (C) Deciding there was hardly any reason, we denied Marvin

    (D) Marvin decided there were none of the reasons for our denying him

    (E) Marvin's decision for us to deny him

18. At this time it is difficult <u>for me agreeing with your evaluation</u> of Ramiro's job performance.

    (A) for me agreeing with your evaluation

    (B) for me to agree with your evaluation

    (C) for me to agree or to evaluate

    (D) in my agreeing with an evaluation you have made

    (E) that I should agree with your evaluation

19. The lawn maintenance service <u>agreed to completely mow and edge inside of two hours</u>.

    (A) agreed to completely mow and edge inside of two hours

    (B) agreed to complete mowing and edging within two hours

    (C) completely agreed to mow and edge inside of two hours

    (D) completely agreeing to mow and edge inside two hours

    (E) are agreeable to mowing and edging completely within two hours

20. If professional ballplayers are superior athletes, <u>they should be financially rewarded for it</u>; however, there is a salary cap on professional teams.

    (A) they should be financially rewarded for it

    (B) they should receive monetary remuneration for it

    (C) their abilities should be recognized financially with plenty of money

    (D) finances in abundance should be the reward for their talent

    (E) they should be financially rewarded for their talent

21. The new chief of the town's volunteer fire department has proved himself <u>to be not only optimistic and organized but also a man who is good</u> at managing the budget.

    (A) to be not only optimistic and organized but also a man who is good

    (B) not only to be optimistic or organized but also a man who is good

    (C) not only being optimistic or organized but also being a man who is good

    (D) to be not only optimistic and organized but also good

    (E) to be not only optimistic and organized but also a good man

22. <u>We did not object to him joining our team</u>, provided that he is willing to learn the plays quickly and to get along well with the other players.

    (A) We did not object to him joining our team

    (B) His joining our team was not an objection

    (C) For him to join our team is not an objection

    (D) We do not object to him joining our team

    (E) We do not object to his joining our team

STOP

If time remains, you may go back and check your work.
When the time allotted is up, you may go on to the next section.

Section 2

TIME: 25 Minutes
16 Questions

DIRECTIONS: Solve each problem using space on the page for scratchwork. Indicate the best answer from the choices given.

NUMBERS: All numbers used are real numbers.

FIGURES: Figures accompanying problems in this section provide information useful in solving the problems. They are drawn as accurately as possible; however, when a figure is not drawn to scale, more information will be provided. It is given that all figures lie in a plane unless otherwise stated.

1. Which is the largest fraction: $\dfrac{1}{5}, \dfrac{2}{9}, \dfrac{2}{11}, \dfrac{4}{19}, \dfrac{4}{17}$?

   (A) $\dfrac{1}{5}$ (B) $\dfrac{2}{9}$

   (C) $\dfrac{2}{11}$ (D) $\dfrac{4}{19}$

   (E) $\dfrac{4}{17}$

2. At \$6.75 per hour, the minimum number of hours that Joel needs to work to earn \$150 is

   (A) 20.   (B) 22.

   (C) 23.   (D) 24.

   (E) 25.

3. A new car depreciates 20% after the first year. The value of a car is \$13,120 at the end of the first year. How much did it cost new?

   (A) \$9,506   (B) \$10,496

   (C) \$13,200   (D) \$14,600

   (E) \$16,400

4. A student has test grades of 91, 86, and 85, What must be her next test grade in order to have a 90 average?

    (A) 100   (B) 98

    (C) 96   (D) 94

    (E) 90

5. A wheel on a bike has the diameter of 18 inches. How many revolutions does the wheel make in a mile trip? (1 mile = 5,280 feet)

    (A) $\dfrac{5,280}{\pi}$ (B) 3,520

    (C) $\dfrac{3,520}{\pi}$ (D) 1,760

    (E) $\dfrac{1,760}{\pi}$

6. One of the roots of $10x^2 - 7x - 12 = 0$ is

    (A) $-\dfrac{3}{2}$.   (B) 0.

    (C) $\dfrac{5}{4}$.   (D) $\dfrac{3}{2}$.

    (E) $\dfrac{4}{5}$.

7. A 35% alcohol solution contains 21 gallons of alcohol. How many gallons of the solution are there?

    (A) 21   (B) 32

    (C) 39   (D) 40

    (E) 60

8. If $x + 2y = 10$ and $x/y = 3$, then $x =$

    (A) -2.   (B) 2.

    (C) 4.   (D) 6.

    (E) 8.

9. If X is the least positive integer for which $3X$ is both an even integer and equal to the square of an integer, then $X =$

(A) 2.   (B) 3.

(C) 6.   (D) 10.

(E) 12.

10. A computer is marked up 50 percent and then later marked down 30 percent. If the final price is $3,360, the original price was

(A) $2,240.   (B) $3,200.

(C) $4,200.   (D) $4,800.

(E) $5,600.

11. How many of the scores 10, 20, 30, 35, 55 are larger than their arithmetic mean score?

(A) None   (B) One

(C) Two   (D) Three

(E) Four

12. The area of this right-angled plane figure is

(A) 250.
(B) 162.
(C) 160.
(D) 150.
(E) 140.

3

4

10

6

25

13. The measures of the lengths of two sides of an isosceles triangle are x and $2x + 1$. The perimeter of the triangle is

(A) $4x$.   (B) $4x + 1$.

(C) $5x + 1$.   (D) $5x + 2$.

(E) None of the above

14. John's beginning six-month salary was $15,000. At the end of each six-month period, his salary was increased by $500. His annual salary during his fourth year of employment was

    (A) $18,500.   (B) $19,000.

    (C) $33,500.   (D) $35,500.

    (E) $36,500.

15. If the area of a circle increases by 96 percent, then the radius of the circle increases by

    (A) 14%.   (B) 40%.

    (C) 56%.   (D) 96%.

    (E) 140%.

16. In a discount bookstore all paperbacks are discounted 20%. In a promotion sale the store offers a further discount of 10%. What is the effective discount on a paperback bought at the promotion sale?

    (A) 20%   (B) 22%

    (C) 25%   (D) 28%

    (E) 30%

STOP

If time remains, you may go back and check your work.
When the time allotted is up, you may go on to the next section.

Section 3

TIME: 25 Minutes
16 Questions

DIRECTIONS: For each question in this section, select the best answer.

1. *Driver's News* rated our newest sports coupe number one for performance and road-handling. Come test drive the Rocket turbo and see for yourself!

   This advertisement would lead logically to the conclusion that you should consider buying the car if you already held which of the following assumptions?

   (A) *Driver's News* is a reliable, informed, and objective source of information about automobiles.

   (B) Buying an expensive car is a good investment since it will last longer than a cheaper car.

   (C) Most people buy a car for its style, not for its durability.

   (D) The best buy is the car that gets the most miles per gallon.

   (E) Other people will tend to judge your character according to the kind of car that you drive.

2. A more aggressive prosecution of anti-trust cases is needed in order to reduce monopolistic tendencies in some industries. Even when no one company enjoys a total monopoly, still a tendency toward monopoly results in decreased competition. This reduces production and increases prices. Thus, a tendency toward monopoly is a principal cause of inflation.

   Which of the following conclusions can most properly be drawn from the above assumptions?

   (A) Anti-trust prosecution only benefits foreign competition.

   (B) Anti-trust prosecution reduces inflation.

   (C) Anti-trust prosecution results in a decrease in production.

(D) Anti-trust prosecution causes unemployment.

(E) Foreign competition causes unemployment.

3. George makes less money than Alice.

Fred and Alice make the same amount of money.

Sally makes more money than Fred.

Henry makes more money than George.

Assuming that the above statements are true, which of the following must also be true?

(A) Henry makes more money than Fred.

(B) Henry makes more money than Sally.

(C) Alice makes less money than Henry.

(D) Fred makes less money than George.

(E) Sally makes more money than George.

4. Demographic studies indicate the number of elderly is increasing, and that therefore the total cost of caring for the elderly is also increasing. At the same time, the number of wage earners is not increasing as rapidly. The funds to care for the elderly will have to come from taxes paid by the wage earners.

Which of the following inferences can properly be drawn from the statements above?

(A) Unless average income increases sufficiently, the percentage of each person's income that must go to caring for the elderly will increase.

(B) The elderly will not receive adequate care.

(C) Only the rich will be able to afford care in their later years.

(D) Younger people will vote against the increase in taxes needed to care for the growing numbers of elderly.

(E) Citizens should save their own money now to take care of their own needs during retirement, instead of depending on younger people to take care of them.

5. Opponents of a sales tax argue that it is a regressive tax: a flat tax of, let us say, 5% across the board might be, as a percentage of income, close to or at 5% for a poor person, but will usually be, relative to income, much lower than that for a rich person.

    If the example in the statement above is accurate, which of the following can be most reliably inferred from it?

    (A) Rich people pay more taxes than poor people.

    (B) Most of the money collected as taxes is taken from the incomes of poor people.

    (C) Rich people can afford to pay high-priced accountants to find ways for them to avoid paying taxes.

    (D) Poor people spend a larger percentage of their income than rich people.

    (E) Rich people should pay higher taxes because they can afford to.

6. George: I've got a great insurance policy. It pays for everything.

    Martha: That's terrible. That's not insurance; that's just a very expensive bill-paying service.

    Which of the following statements could be inferred from the above conversation to best represent Martha's philosophy on insurance?

    (A) Life insurance is not worth it, since you cannot spend the money when you are dead.

    (B) Insurance premiums are too high and should be subject to government regulation.

    (C) Don't insure anything you can afford to lose.

    (D) Insurance is a racket because insurance companies never pay for all of the costs.

    (E) Insurance companies make money because they study very carefully the probabilities involved.

Questions 7–8 are based on the following.

Since the planets revolve around the sun in orbits like the paths of electrons revolving around the nucleus of an atom, why couldn't our whole solar system just be an atom in the tail of a dog wagging in some much larger universe?

7. The author bases his argument for a "larger universe" on

   (A) an implied analogy between the universe and an atom.

   (B) evidence of life on other planets.

   (C) the theory of the expanding universe.

   (D) an implied analogy between the solar system and an atom.

   (E) the fact that the sun is the ultimate source of all energy on the Earth.

8. A major weakness in the author's argument for a "larger universe" would be that

   (A) there is no real evidence of life on other planets.

   (B) the only similarity between the solar system and an atom is one of superficial form.

   (C) no one can actually see an atom, so no one really knows what atoms look like.

   (D) no one has yet travelled further away than the moon, so we do not yet know much about the solar system.

   (E) there is no reason to believe that a "larger universe" would be inhabited by a dog.

9. Research indicates that individuals who have served in the Peace Corps tend to be more liberal politically than other citizens of the same age. Obviously, the experience of serving in the Peace Corps had a radicalizing influence on these individuals.

   Which of the following, if true, would most strengthen the conclusion?

   (A) Individuals who volunteer for the Peace Corps are more knowledgeable than other citizens on questions of geography.

   (B) Individuals who have served in the Peace Corps are more tolerant of ethnic and cultural differences than are other citizens.

   (C) The research also indicated that those who did not serve in the Peace Corps were more interested in making money.

   (D) Peace Corps volunteers, but not the other individuals, probably realized that the questions they were asked related to the political influence of the Peace Corps experience.

(E) Individuals who volunteer for the Peace Corps are not more radical than other citizens prior to serving in the Peace Corps.

10. Jack: Increases in the enrollment at Wilson College can be credited to the dynamic leadership of Dr. Smith, who became president last year. The previous president lacked the leadership qualities needed to attract bright young people to the institution.

   Jill: I disagree. Enrollment reached a low point four years ago. This coincided, according to demographic information, with a low point in the number of high school graduates. As the number of high school graduates has increased, so has the enrollment at Wilson College. This, not the personality of the president, is the probable cause of the increasing enrollment.

   Which of the following best describes the weakness in Jack's argument which Jill attacks?

   (A) The enrollment may decline next year in spite of Dr. Smith's dynamic leadership.

   (B) The enrollment actually started increasing before Dr. Smith became president.

   (C) Jack's estimate of the personalities of Dr. Smith and the previous president is purely subjective.

   (D) Jack exaggerates the effect that a single individual can have on the success of an institution.

   (E) Jack fails to consider the specific programs offered at Wilson College that may have attracted the students to the institution.

11. The mayor of Jonesville opposes any increase this year in the salaries of police officers, pointing out that these salaries have increased 10% over the last five years.

   Which of the following, if true, would most seriously weaken the mayor's argument?

   (A) The rate of inflation during this five-year period was 3% annually.

   (B) The salaries of the police officers are the same as the salaries of the fire fighters.

(C) The city budget shows a predicted surplus that would be more than enough to pay for a substantial increase in the salaries of police officers.

(D) A survey of public opinion shows that crime is the number one concern of the citizens of Jonesville.

(E) The mayor was accused of political corruption and nepotism in the recent election.

12. Institutional policies should be designed to help everyone associated with the institution. Groups within an institution, however, often favor policies that are helpful to them alone without taking into consideration the possibility that such policies may hurt another group within the institution. The administration of a hospital, university, or government must seek to balance these conflicting interests.

Which of the following statements provides support for the claim above?

I.   An increase in faculty salaries resulted in an increase in tuition.

II. A decrease in hospital fees resulted in a decrease in wages paid to the nursing staff.

III. Additional appointments to the fund-raising staff resulted in an increase in money available for scholarships.

(A) I and III, but not II

(B) II, but not I and not III

(C) I and II, but not III

(D) II and III, but not I

(E) I, II, and III

13. Nutritionists and dentists offer contradictory advice to parents with regard to the eating of Halloween candy. Nutritionists advise parents to make their children eat a small amount of candy each day over a long period of time. Dentists advise parents to let their children eat all the candy at once.

Assuming that the above passage is accurate, which of the following statements can be inferred from it?

(A) The dentists and the nutritionists cannot both be right; only further research will determine which advice is best.

(B) Since experts disagree, it is obvious that they do not know as much as they claim to.

(C) Dentists and nutritionists disagree because they are concerned about completely different health problems.

(D) Eating all the candy at once causes more cavities than eating the same amount of candy over a longer period of time.

(E) The dentists are more scientific in their approach to the problem.

Questions 14 – 15 are based on the following.

Due to an oil embargo, the price of heating oil in the United States soared. In order to cut heating costs, some people invested in insulation for their homes. Then, as a result of new exploration and increased conservation, the price of oil went back down again.

14. Which of the following can be inferred from the passage?

(A) The government should give a tax credit for insulation and other energy-saving improvements.

(B) As a result of new sources of oil and decreased demand, there was no longer a shortage of supply.

(C) The government should stockpile oil in case of a military emergency.

(D) The government should subsidize solar energy.

(E) Nuclear power is the only alternative to dependence on foreign sources of energy.

15. Given the lower price of oil, some homeowners concluded that the money spent on insulation was not a good investment. This conclusion, however, is probably unwarranted because it can be inferred from the passage that

(A) the price of oil may rise again.

(B) sooner or later we will deplete all of the earth's oil supply.

(C) without such conservation measures the price would not have come back down.

(D) the oil producing countries cannot stick together in enforcing an embargo.

(E) nuclear energy is not a safe alternative.

16. Fifty volunteers from local churches operate a soup kitchen in Sawyer's Falls, a city of 100,000. The volunteers have found that the number of individuals showing up for free soup varies in proportion to the unemployment rate. At the moment, unemployment is at 5% and 350 people show up every day. The soup kitchen is funded through donations from local churches. Recent inflation has increased the cost of food, but the volunteers are asking for increased donations so that they can not only maintain the present program but offer a complete meal — not just soup. Which of the following changes in these factors would help the volunteers to carry out their plan?

(A) An increase in unemployment from 5% to 6%.

(B) An increase in inflation from 4% to 5%.

(C) A decrease in the donations.

(D) An increase in the number of volunteers from 50 to 100.

(E) A decrease in unemployment from 5% to 4%.

STOP

If time remains, you may go back and check your work.
When the time allotted is up, you may go on to the next section.

Section 4

TIME: 25 Minutes
20 Questions

DIRECTIONS: Each of the data sufficiency problems below contains a question and two statements, labeled (1) and (2), in which certain data are given. Decide whether the data given in the statements are sufficient for answering the question. Using the data given in the statements plus your knowledge of mathematics and everyday facts choose:

(A) if Statement (1) ALONE is sufficient, but Statement (2) alone is not sufficient to answer the question asked;

(B) if Statement (2) ALONE is sufficient, but Statement (1) alone is not sufficient to answer the question asked;

(C) if BOTH Statements (1) and (2) TOGETHER are sufficient to answer the question asked, but NEITHER statement ALONE is sufficient;

(D) if EACH statement ALONE is sufficient to answer the question asked;

(E) if Statements (1) and (2) TOGETHER are NOT sufficient to answer the questions asked, and additional data specific to the problem are needed.

NUMBERS: All numbers are real numbers.

FIGURES: A figure in this section will conform to the information given, but will not necessarily conform to the additional information given in the numbered Statements (1) and (2).

NOTES: Lines are straight if shown as straight, and angle measures are greater than zero.

The position of points, angles, regions, etc., exist in the order shown.

All figures lie in a plane unless otherwise stated.

_____

Sample Question:

In the figure, the two circles are concentric (have the same center O) with radius x and y, where $x < y$. What is the area of the shaded region?

(1)   The sum of the two radii is 11 units.

(2)   The area of the smaller circle is $^1/_2$ of the area of the larger one.

Sample Explanation:

(C)   By Statement (1), $x + y = 11$. Since, Statement (1) gives no other information about x and y, you cannot find the areas of the two circles. Since the area of the shaded region is the difference of the two areas, statement (1) alone is not sufficient. According to Statement (2), $\pi y^2 = 2\pi x^2$; therefore, the area of the region is $2\pi x^2 - \pi x^2 = \pi x^2$. Since (2) does not give the value of x, it is not possible to find the area of the shaded region using (2) alone. However, if we use (1) and (2) together, we get the two equations

$$y = 11 - x \text{ and } \pi y^2 = 2\pi x^2$$

from which we can solve for x by writing the single equation $\pi(11 - x)^2 = 2\pi x^2$.

1. In the figure shown what is the value of *x*?

    (1) $\angle ACD = 100°$

    (2) $x - y = 20$

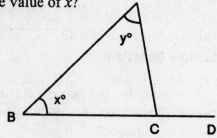

2. Philip first lived in Apartment A with a six-month lease. He then had a one-year lease for Apartment B. What was the monthly rent for each apartment?

    (1) His 18 months' rent was $4,200.

    (2) Apartment B cost him $50 more each month.

3. What is the volume of the cylinder?

    (1) The height is three times the diameter.

    (2) The area of the base is 4π.

4. Helen and Tony finished typing, without interruption, the same story at 11 a.m. When did Helen start typing?

    (1) It took Tony 1 hour and 40 minutes.

    (2) Helen types 10 wpm faster than Tony.

5. What is the value of *y*?

    (1) $3 + 4x - 2y = 0$ and $\dfrac{3}{2} + 2x - y = 0$

    (2) $1 - \dfrac{1}{3}x - y = 0$ and $3 + x - 3y = 0$

6. In 1987 20% of the AT&T employees were executives. What percent of the employees have executive jobs in 1988?

    (1) There were 10 less executives in 1988 than in 1987.

    (2) There were 10 more non-executive jobs in 1988 than there were in 1987.

7. A certain food storage container has a cylindrical base and a hemispherical dome as shown in the figure. What is its capacity?

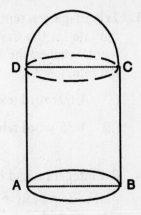

   (1) $AB = 100$ ft.

   (2) $BC = 120$ ft.

8. A college student has a work-study scholarship that pays \$3.50 per hour. He also makes \$3 per hour babysitting. How many hours per week does he spend on each of the two jobs?

   (1) He has a total of $23^{1}/_{2}$ hours of employment every week.

   (2) His weekly income from the two jobs is \$78.

9. The average age of passengers on a certain bus trip, at departure, was 60. While halfway on the trip two passengers were added, which changed the average age to 59. If one of the new passengers was 20 years older than the other, how old were the two?

   (1) There were 30 passengers at departure.

   (2) The sum of the ages of the passengers at departure was 1800.

10. In $\{a, 3, b, a + b\}$, what is the value of a and b?

   (1) $a + b$ is a common prime divisor of 56 and 112.

   (2) a and b are prime numbers.

11. Is $x^2 + y + 1$ an even integer?

   (1) x is odd.

   (2) The square of y is even.

12. If $x \neq 0$, is $x|x| > 0$?

   (1) $x + |x| = 0$

   (2) $x^2 < 1$

13. Telegrams are sent from City A to City B. If all charges consist of a flat rate for the first 12 words plus a fixed amount for each additional word, what is the cost for an additional word and how much is the flat rate?

 (1) A 60-word telegram costs $2.95.

 (2) A 35-word telegram costs $1.70.

14. For integers a and b, if $a - 2b \neq 0$, is $\dfrac{a^2 - 4b^2}{2a - 4b}$ an integer?

 (1) a is odd.

 (2) a is even.

15. In $\triangle ABC$ what is the length of AB?

 (1) $AE = \dfrac{5}{2}$

 (2) $BD = \dfrac{3}{2}$

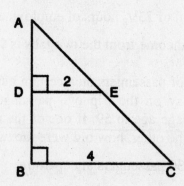

16. Dave opened a savings account with a constant annual rate by depositing $1,000. What was the annual interest rate?

 (1) Two years later his savings were $1,060.90.

 (2) He neither withdrew from nor made additional deposits to the account in the first two years and the bank does not charge for service.

17. If $y = \dfrac{1}{x} + 1$, what is the value of $x - y$?

 (1) $y > x$

 (2) $x - \dfrac{1}{x} = 0$

18. Is x an integer?

    (1) $|3x + 1| = 10$

    (2) $-4 < x < 4$

19. Is a quadrilateral *ABCD* a rectangle?

    (1) $AB = CD$

    (2) $\angle ABC = \angle BCD$

20. If c is a positive integer less than 8, and $D = 3,563 - c$, what is the value of D?

    (1) D is a multiple of 4.

    (2) D is a multiple of 5.

STOP

If time remains, you may go back and check your work.
When the time allotted is up, you may go on to the next section.

Section 5

TIME: 25 Minutes
23 Questions

DIRECTIONS: Each passage is followed by questions based on its content. After reading the passage, choose the best answer to each question. Answer all questions based on what is indicated or implied in that passage.

In recent years, there has been a dramatic increase in the occurrence of cumulative trauma disorders (CTDs), or repetitive motion disorders, and other work-related injuries and illnesses due to ergonomic hazards. As a result, the number of penalties issued against companies for these types of ergonomics-related safety and health violations has increased.

A form of CTD that has received increased attention in recent years is *carpal tunnel syndrome* (CTS), which affects the hands and wrists. CTS is the compression and entrapment of the median nerve where it passes through the wrist into the hand—in the carpal tunnel. The median nerve is the main nerve that extends down the arm to the hand and provides the sense of touch in the thumb, index finger, middle finger, and half of the fourth, or ring, finger. When irritated, tendons housed inside the narrow carpal tunnel swell and press against the nearby median nerve. The pressure causes tingling, numbness, or severe pain in the wrist and hand—often felt at night. Also, the pressure results in a lack of strength in the hand and an inability to make a fist, hold objects or perform other manual tasks. If the pressure continues, it can damage the nerve, causing permanent loss of sensation and even partial paralysis.

CTS develops in the hands and wrists from repetitive and/or forceful manual tasks performed over a period of time. For example, the meatpacking industry is considered one of the most hazardous industries in the United States because workers can make as many as 10,000 repetitive motions per day in assembly line processes, such as deboning meats, with no variation in motion. Consequently, stress and strain are placed on the wrists and hands, which can result in CTS.

In manufacturing, garment makers, who often perform fast-paced piecework operations involving excessive repetitive tasks, increase their risk of developing CTS. (Other garment workers, who are required to push large amounts of materials through machinery, often sustain disabling wrist, back, and leg injuries.)

Today, more than half of all U.S. workers are susceptible to developing CTS. Anyone whose job demands a lot of repetitive wrist, hand, and arm motion, which need not always be forceful or strenuous, might be a potential victim of CTS.

In addition, employees are often unaware of the causes of CTS and what to do about them. They do not associate their pain with their work. When workers finally seek medical help, they may be given the wrong diagnosis and find the road to recovery takes more time and money than they had anticipated.

1. The author is primarily concerned with

    (A) discussing the effects and causes of CTS.

    (B) proving that employers are negligent in considering the health problems of their workers.

    (C) establishing that there are many causes of CTS.

    (D) criticizing the lack of research done on CTS to date.

    (E) analyzing the importance of reviewing the workplace for possible hazards to worker health.

2. The passage contains information that would answer which of the following questions about carpal tunnel syndrome?

    I.   How many people are affected by CTS each year?

    II. What are the symptoms of CTS?

    III. Are the effects of CTS permanent or temporary?

    (A) I only   (B) III only

    (C) II and III only   (D) I and III only

    (E) I, II, and III

3. The passage suggests that scientists think the workers most likely to experience CTS often perform fast-paced repetitive tasks, as in which of the following jobs?

    (A) welders   (B) truck drivers

    (C) carpenters   (D) poultry workers

    (E) boiler makers

4. According to the author, which of the following statements supplies a correct perception of CTS?

   (A) Carpal tunnel syndrome is associated with noise-induced hearing loss.

   (B) Carpal tunnel syndrome occurs more frequently when cold temperatures affect a worker's coordination and manual dexterity.

   (C) Carpal tunnel syndrome is a phenomenon which is occurring with increasing frequency.

   (D) Carpal tunnel syndrome accompanies eyestrain, headaches, and excessive fatigue, as well as severe pain in the wrist and hand.

   (E) Carpal tunnel syndrome affects more than half the workers in the U.S.

5. According to the article, what is the main problem in the early treatment of CTS?

   (A) Resistance of workers to being educated on CTS

   (B) Reluctance on the part of workers to report physical ailments

   (C) Lack of published information on the problem

   (D) Length of time needed to certify that CTS is actually present

   (E) Failure of workers to associate their symptoms with the motions performed on the job

6. In order to facilitate an affected worker's return to the job, the author would probably recommend which of the following?

   I. Conservative treatment and restricted job duties when necessary

   II. Access to health care workers with systematic evaluation and referral

   III. Adequate monitoring which includes periodic workplace walk-throughs

   (A) I only   (B) II only

   (C) III only   (D) I and III only

   (E) I, II, and III

7. The passage contains information which suggests that medical personnel give the wrong diagnosis for carpal tunnel syndrome because

(A) there is no information available in clinics at job sites.

(B) companies are refusing to disseminate medical information to their employees.

(C) doctors are not yet familiar enough with the syndrome and its symptoms.

(D) its many facets are easily confused with other similar medical problems.

(E) patients are unable to describe their symptoms accurately to their physicians.

8. The author states that carpal tunnel syndrome has all of the following symptoms EXCEPT

(A) tingling of the wrist.

(B) back pain.

(C) lack of strength in the hand.

(D) permanent loss of sensation in the fingers.

(E) partial paralysis.

9. The author would most likely disagree with which of the following statements about the workplace?

(A) Adapting the job to fit the worker can help reduce potential disorders.

(B) Excessive vibration and noise are often significant factors in work-related problems.

(C) Ergonomics should include restructuring the workplace to reduce stressors such as poor lighting.

(D) Major causes of current problems are technological advances such as more specialized tasks.

(E) Special guidelines for tool design should be made mandatory for all companies to reduce CTS.

Horse owners who plan to breed one or more mares should have a working knowledge of heredity and know how to care for breeding animals and foals. The number of mares bred that actually conceive varies from about 40 to 85 percent, with the average running less than 50 percent. Some mares that do conceive fail to produce living foals. This means that, on the average, two mares are kept a whole year to produce one foal, and even then, some foals are disappointments from the standpoint of quality.

The gene is the unit that determines heredity. In the body cells of horses there are many chromosomes. In turn, the chromosomes carry pairs of minute particles, called genes, which are the basic hereditary material. The nucleus of each body cell of horses contains 32 pairs of chromosomes, or a total of 64; whereas there are thousands of pairs of genes.

When a sex cell (a sperm or an egg) is formed, only one chromosome and one gene of each pair goes into it. Then, when mating and fertilization occur, the 32 single chromosomes from the germ cell of each parent unite to form new pairs, and the chromosomes with their genes are again present in duplicate, in the body cells of the embryo. Thus, with all possible combinations of 32 pairs of chromosomes and the genes that they bear, it is not strange that full sisters (except identical twins from a single egg split after fertilization) are so different. Actually we can marvel that they bear as much resemblance to each other as they do.

Because of this situation, the mating of a mare with a fine track record to a stallion that transmits good performance characteristics will not always produce a foal of a merit equal to its parents. The foal could be markedly poorer than the parents or, in some cases, it could be better than either parent.

Simple-and multiple-gene inheritance occurs in horses, as in all animals. In simple-gene inheritance, only one pair of genes is involved; thus, a pair of genes may be responsible for some one specific trait in horses. However, most characteristics, such as speed, are due to many genes; hence, they are called multiple-gene characteristics.

For most characteristics, many pairs of genes are involved. For example, growth rate in foals is affected by (1) appetite and feed consumption, (2) the proportion of the feed eaten that is absorbed, and (3) the use to which the nutrients are put—whether they are used for growth or fattening, and each in turn is probably affected by different genes. Because multiple characteristics show all manner of gradation from high to low performance, they are sometimes referred to as quantitative traits. Thus, quantitative inheritance refers to the degree to which a characteristic is inherited. For example, all racehorses can run and all inherit some ability to run, but it is the degree to which they inherit the ability that is important.

10. The primary purpose of the passage is to

    (A) dispell misconceptions about heredity in horse breeding.

    (B) warn horse owners of the potential problems in breeding.

    (C) propose minimum standards in horse breeding.

    (D) provide a working knowledge of heredity for horse breeders.

    (E) analyze sources of disagreement regarding heredity in horses.

11. The passage contains information that answers which of the following questions?

    I.   How many chromosomes are there in the body cells of an embryo?

    II. What are the specific odds of a stallion and mare with good track records producing a foal of equal merit?

    III. Are most characteristics in horses simple-gene or multiple-gene characteristics?

    (A) I only   (B) III only

    (C) I and III only   (D) II and III only

    (E) I, II, and III

12. According to the passage, it is usually necessary to keep two mares for a year to produce one foal because

    I.   the conception rate among bred mares averages less than 50 percent.

    II. some conceptions do not produce living offspring.

    III. some foals are disappointments.

    (A) I only   (B) II only

    (C) I and II only   (D) I and III only

    (E) I, II, and III

13. According to the passage, the body cells of an embryo differ from a sex cell chiefly in

    (A) the number of chromosomes and genes present.

    (B) the manner in which chromosomes are paired.

(C) the absence of quantitative trait genes in the body cells of an embryo.

(D) the presence of only 16 chromosomes in a sex cell compared to 32 in the body cells of an embryo.

(E) the proliferation of genes in the body cells of an embryo and their complete absence before fertilization in a sex cell.

14. According to the passage, growth rate in horses results from inheriting

(A) a single gene.

(B) multiple genes.

(C) a single chromosome.

(D) multiple chromosomes.

(E) a single gene and multiple chromosomes.

15. According to the passage, speed in horses

(A) can be either a single gene or multiple characteristic.

(B) is a single-gene characteristic only.

(C) is both a single gene and quantitative characteristic.

(D) is a multiple but not a quantitative characteristic.

(E) is both a multiple and quantitative characteristic.

16. The author would probably agree with which of the following statements?

(A) Breeding for specific traits is easier than most horse owners imagine.

(B) It is futile to try to breed for any quantitative traits.

(C) If breeders know enough about heredity, they can almost certainly achieve any desired result in horse breeding.

(D) One can never be assured of success in breeding for specific traits, but the undertaking should not be viewed as hopeless.

(E) Breeders should concentrate on breeding for single-gene characteristics to increase the odds of producing successful race-horses.

17. According to the author, what would represent "quality" (line 8) in a foal?

    (A) Good genetic background

    (B) Appetite and feed consumption

    (C) Having similar parental characteristics

    (D) Number of chromosomes

    (E) Simple-gene inheritance

The United States is destined either to surmount the gorgeous history of feudalism, or else prove the most tremendous failure of time. Nor the least doubtful am I on any prospects of their material success. The triumphant future of their business, geographic and productive departments, on larger scales and in more varieties than ever, is certain. In those respects the republic must soon (if she does not already) outstrip all examples hitherto afforded, and dominate the world.

Admitting all this, with the priceless value of our political institutions, general suffrage (and fully acknowledging the latest, widest opening of the doors), I say that, far deeper than these, what finally and only is to make of our Western world a nationality superior to any hither known, and outtopping the past, must be vigorous, yet unsuspected Literatures, perfect personalities and sociologies, original, transcendental, and expressing (what, in highest sense, are not yet expressed at all) democracy and the modern. With these, and out of these, I promulgate new races of Teachers, and of perfect Women, indispensable to endow the birth-stock of a New World. For feudalism, caste, the ecclesiastic traditions, though palpably retreating from political institutions, still hold essentially, by their spirit, even in this country, entire possession of the more important fields, indeed the very subsoil, of education, and of social standards and literature.

I say that democracy can never prove itself beyond cavil, until it founds and luxuriantly grows its own forms of art, poems, schools, theology, displacing all that exists, or that has been produced anywhere in the past, under opposite influences. It is curious to me that while so many voices, pens, minds, in the press, lecture rooms, in our Congress, etc., are discussing intellectual topics, pecuniary dangers, legislative problems, the suffrage, tariff and labor questions, and the various business and benevolent needs of America, with propositions, remedies, often worth deep attention, there is one need, a hiatus the profoundest, that no eye seems to perceive, no voice to state. Our fundamental want today in the United States, with closest, amplest reference to present conditions, and to the future, is of a class and the clear idea of a class, of native authors, literatures, far different, far higher in grade, than any yet known, sacerdotal, modern, fit to cope with our occasions, lands, permeating the whole mass of American mentality, taste, belief, breathing into it a new breath of life, giving it decision, affecting politics far more than the popular superficial suffrage, with results inside and underneath the elections of Presidents or Congresses—radiating, begetting appropriate teachers, schools, manners, and, as its grandest result, accomplishing (what neither the schools nor the churches and their clergy have hitherto accomplished, and without which this nation will no more stand, permanently, soundly, than a house will stand without a sub-stratum), a religious and moral character beneath the political and productive and intellectual bases of the States.

18. The primary purpose of the passage is to

(A) prove that the western world is still dominated by medieval ideals and traditions.

(B) educate the reader regarding the variety and nature of arts available in western civilization.

(C) announce the triumph of literature and character in the United States of America.

(D) convince the reader of the need to create a new social class of authors and teachers.

(E) celebrate the victory of democracy and its political institutions over feudalism.

19. According to the passage, the relationship of the United States to other nations in the near future will be

(A) more and more complex as the years pass.

(B) one of material superiority over other nations.

(C) one of increasing dependency upon other nations.

(D) a cooperative arrangement for mutual aid and benefit.

(E) increasingly hostile and suspicious.

20. Compared to the effects of literature and the arts on society, the passage states that the effect of democracy is

(A) less.   (B) more.

(C) sufficient.   (D) insufficient.

(E) overwhelming.

21. The author apparently feels that, besides himself,

   (A) everyone agrees that foreign diplomacy is extremely important for the nation.

   (B) no one wants the masses to be ruled by an elite, educated minority.

   (C) no one sees one of the greatest problems facing the United States.

   (D) everyone is proud of what the schools and churches have accomplished in the western world.

   (E) everyone agrees that authors are already a sacred and privileged class.

22. From the entire context of paragraph 2, the term "cavil" is most likely intended to mean

   (A) political intrigue.   (B) experimentation.

   (C) unjustified boasting.   (D) servile imitation.

   (E) trivial issues.

23. What influence, according to the author, do feudalistic traditions have on the United States in this time?

   (A) None

   (B) They provide the models for our own political institutions.

   (C) They provide a stark contrast to our political institutions.

   (D) They provide a sound substratum for our civilization.

   (E) They still control education and literature.

STOP

If time remains, you may go back and check your work.
When the time allotted is up, you may go on to the next section.

Section 6

TIME: 25 Minutes
16 Questions

DIRECTIONS: Solve each problem using space on the page for scratchwork. Indicate the best answer from the choices given.

NUMBERS: All numbers used are real numbers.

FIGURES: Figures accompanying problems in this section provide information useful in solving the problems. They are drawn as accurately as possible; however, when a figure is not drawn to scale, more information will be provided. It is given that all figures lie in a plane unless otherwise stated.

---

1. A woman owns a small, cash-only business in a state that requires her to charge a 6% sales tax on each item she sells. At the beginning of the day she has $250 in the cash register. At the end of the day she has $1,204 in the register. How much money should she send to the state government for the sales tax she collected?

    (A) $72.24   (B) $57.24

    (C) $346.25   (D) $572.40

    (E) $54

2. Five-sixths of an iceberg is submerged below the surface of the ocean. If 130 tons of the iceberg are above the water, how many tons are below the water?

    (A) 780   (B) $108.\overline{3}$
    (C) 156   (D) 650

    (E) 420

3. SPLINT, a "we try harder" telephone company advertises that it charges 51 cents for the first minute and 34 cents for each additional minute for a long-distance call from New Jersey to New York. If the number of additional minutes after the first minute is x and the cost, in cents, is y, then the equation representing the total cost of the call is $y = 34x + 51$. AC&C, its competitor, has a cost equation for the

same call of the form $y = 31x + 60$. After how many additional minutes will the two companies charge an equal amount?

(A) 9   (B) 3

(C) 2   (D) 4

(E) The two companies will never charge an equal amount because SPLINT is always cheaper than AC&C.

4. The combined ages of Mr. & Mrs. Massey are more than 80 years and less than 100 years. If Mr. Massey is 4 years older than Mrs. Massey, and the age of each is a prime number, how old is Mr. Massey?

(A) 41   (B) 43

(C) 47   (D) 53

(E) 57

5. Find the single discount equal to successive discounts of 20% and 5%.

(A) $22^1/_2\%$ (B) 25%

(C) 24%   (D) 23%

(E) $24^1/_2\%$

6. If at a given place the longest day exceeds the shortest night by 9 hours, what is the length of the shortest night?

(A) $6^1/_2$ (B) 8

(C) $8^1/_2$ (D) 7

(E) $7^1/_2$

7. In a state with 6% sales tax, John bought books for his business class totalling $159.53. How much were the books without sales tax?

(A) $141.47   (B) $153.53

(C) $150.50   (D) $165.53

(E) $169.10

8. The diameter of an automobile tire is 24". How many revolutions does the tire make in traveling a mile? (1 mile = 5,280 feet)

(A) $\dfrac{220}{\pi}$ (B) 2,640p

(C) $\dfrac{2,640}{\pi}$ (D) $\dfrac{440}{\pi}$

(E) 440π

9. An engineer had her monthly wages increased by 8% and then by 10%. If she now receives $2,376, find her wages before the first increase.

(A) $2,013.60   (B) $1,900

(C) $2,010.50   (D) $1,998

(E) $2,000

10. Two men drove from Hartford to Boston (100 miles) leaving at the same time. Mr. Clifford averaged 30 miles an hour for the first 20 miles, and 40 miles an hour the rest of the way. Mr. Sherman drove at a steady speed. They arrived at the same time. What was Mr. Sherman's average speed?

(A) $35\frac{1}{2}$ (B) $24\frac{1}{2}$

(C) 25   (D) $37\frac{1}{2}$

(E) 35

11. Several people rented a van for $30, sharing the cost equally. If there had been one more person in the group, it would have cost each $1 less. How many people were there in the group originally?

(A) 10   (B) 12

(C) 29   (D) 5

(E) 6

12. If the length of a rectangle is increased by 25 percent, by what percent must the width be decreased if the area is to remain the same?

(A) 20%   (B) 25%

(C) 50%   (D) 4%

(E) 10%

13. If $3x - 2y = 6$ and $x - y = 1$ then $x + y =$

    (A) 7.   (B) 13.

    (C) – 7.   (D) – 13.

    (E) 19.

14. Evaluate $(2^{1-\sqrt{3}})^{1+\sqrt{3}}$

    (A) 4   (B) – 4

    (C) 16   (D) $\dfrac{1}{2}$

    (E) $\dfrac{1}{4}$

15. If $8^{x-1} = \left(\dfrac{1}{4}\right)^{1-x}$ then $x =$

    (A) 2.   (B) 0.

    (C) 1.   (D) – 1.

    (E) No solution

16. Find the area of the shaded portion in the following figure. (The heavy dot represents the center of the circle.)

    (A) $100\pi - 96$

    (B) $400\pi - 96$

    (C) $400\pi - 192$

    (D) $100\pi - 192$

    (E) $256\pi - 192$

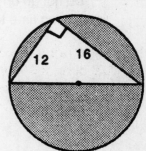

STOP

If time remains, you may go back and check your work.
When the time allotted is up, you may go on to the next section.

Section 7

ANALYSIS OF AN ISSUE ESSAY TOPIC

TIME: 30 Minutes

DIRECTIONS: In an essay, develop a position on the issue below by investigating the different angles of the issue, and explaining your thoughts on the topic. Remember, there is no one "correct" response to the essay topic.

Before starting, read the essay topic and its question(s). You may make preliminary notes in your test booklet before writing the actual essay. Be sure to write your essay on the lined pages provided at the back of the book.

Many people maintain that women are not as likely to be successful in the world of business as men are.

Do you think this is true? Why or why not?

STOP

Do not go on until you are instructed to do so. Use any remaining time to check your work on this portion of the test.

ANALYSIS OF AN ARGUMENT ESSAY TOPIC

TIME: 30 Minutes

DIRECTIONS: In essay form, prepare a review on the position of the argument provided below. Before taking your own position on the argument's standpoint, it may be helpful to determine the method of thinking behind the argument itself. For example, consider alternative explanations to any assumptions the argument might make, and any evidence or examples that may strengthen or weaken the argument. Remember, there is no one "correct" response to the essay topic.

Before starting, read the essay topic and its question(s). You may make preliminary notes in your test booklet before writing the actual essay. Be sure to write your essay on the lined pages provided at the back of the book.

"The turn of the century brought about a sudden shift in values in America. Industrialization and urbanization caused a movement from small towns to big cities, from personal to impersonal, from the individual to the crowd. Morally, there was a shift from values directed and governed from within to more of a concern with appearances. The growth of consumer culture was accompanied by a growth in advertising, and it suddenly became necessary for the individual to sell him or herself as a product."

What is the main point of this argument? Is this argument convincing? Why or why not? Can you tell how the author felt about the subject in the passage? Are the changes discussed in a positive or negative light? What would make this argument more convincing?

STOP

If time remains, you may go back and check your work.

PRACTICE TEST 3

ANSWER KEY

Section 1 — Sentence Correction

1.	(E)	7.	(C)	13.	(A)	19.	(B)
2.	(A)	8.	(C)	14.	(D)	20.	(E)
3.	(C)	9.	(B)	15.	(E)	21.	(D)
4.	(B)	10.	(D)	16.	(C)	22.	(E)
5.	(A)	11.	(E)	17.	(A)		
6.	(A)	12.	(B)	18.	(B)		

Section 2 — Problem Solving

1.	(E)	5.	(C)	9.	(E)	13.	(D)
2.	(C)	6.	(D)	10.	(B)	14.	(E)
3.	(E)	7.	(E)	11.	(C)	15.	(B)
4.	(B)	8.	(D)	12.	(B)	16.	(D)

Section 3 — Critical Reasoning

1.	(A)	5.	(D)	9.	(E)	13.	(C)
2.	(B)	6.	(C)	10.	(B)	14.	(B)
3.	(E)	7.	(D)	11.	(A)	15.	(C)
4.	(A)	8.	(B)	12.	(C)	16.	(E)

Section 4 — Data Sufficiency

1.	(C)	6.	(E)	11.	(C)	16.	(C)
2.	(C)	7.	(C)	12.	(A)	17.	(B)
3.	(C)	8.	(C)	13.	(C)	18.	(E)
4.	(E)	9.	(D)	14.	(D)	19.	(E)
5.	(B)	10.	(C)	15.	(D)	20.	(B)

Section 5 — Reading Comprehension

1.	(A)	7.	(C)	13.	(A)	19.	(B)
2.	(C)	8.	(B)	14.	(B)	20.	(A)
3.	(D)	9.	(E)	15.	(E)	21.	(C)
4.	(C)	10.	(D)	16.	(D)	22.	(E)
5.	(E)	11.	(C)	17.	(C)	23.	(E)
6.	(A)	12.	(C)	18.	(D)		

Section 6 — Problem Solving

1.	(E)	5.	(C)	9.	(E)	13.	(A)
2.	(D)	6.	(E)	10.	(D)	14.	(E)
3.	(B)	7.	(C)	11.	(D)	15.	(C)
4.	(C)	8.	(C)	12.	(A)	16.	(A)

DETAILED EXPLANATIONS OF ANSWERS

Section 1–Sentence Correction

1. **(E)**
Choice (E) is the only one that makes a complete, coherent sentence. The contrast between what is reported and what the agency officials say is made clear with ALTHOUGH. Choice (A) creates a run-on sentence. Choice (B) has no connector between the first half and the second half of the sentence. Choice (C) sounds as if the officials themselves have reported the wrongdoing, a fact clearly contradicted by the second half of the sentence. In order to make sense, choice (D) should eliminate HAVE as part of its verb.

2. **(A)**
This sentence contains two basic conditions for exercise, PROPERLY DONE and CAREFULLY MONITORED. These two parallel adverb + past participle combinations modify EXERCISE. None of the other sentences are parallel and have the concepts properly worded. Choice (B) contains no subject for PROPERLY DOING IT because exercise cannot properly do anything. Choice (C) would be correct with commas to set off the interrupting phrase, but it still is not as succinctly worded as choice (A). Choice (D) completely twists the meaning of the sentence, and choice (E) is choppy and hard to understand.

3. **(C)**
The phrase, ON THE NEXT DAY, is called a *squinting modifier* because it is unclear if it modifies I AGREED or TO SHOW HIM HOW. Choice (A) has the SQUINTING MODIFIER. Choices (B) and (E) do not clarify what ON THE NEXT DAY modifies. Choice (B) is a fragment. Choice (D) unnecessarily splits the subject and the verb, and choice (E) incorrectly splits the infinitive.

4. **(B)**
The interrupter, THOUGH NOT NEARLY ALL, should be placed so it does not split important parts of the sentence. Choices (A), (D), and (E)

are incorrect because the interrupter splits a preposition and its subject. Choices (C) and (D) will produce a fragment because the subject WE is missing.

5. **(A)**
     Choice (A) correctly uses a noun form, AN INCREASE, to be parallel to the other noun form, THE LEGALIZATION. None of the other choices contain parallel article adjective + noun. Choice (B) erroneously indicates that the law already contained increasing penalties. Choice (C) is unclear about what is BEING. Choice (D) places emphasis on ILLEGAL FISHING instead of the increased penalties. Choice (E) is unclear in meaning.

6. **(A)**
     Choice (A) correctly uses the objective case pronoun WHOM as the object of the preposition OF. Choice (B) incorrectly uses the nominative case pronoun. Choice (C) inserts the extraneous preposition ABOUT that has no object. Choice (D) is awkward wording. Choice (E) is also poor wording, especially with the pronoun HIM so far away from its antecedent.

7. **(C)**
     Choice (C) deals clearly and simply with the location and reputation of Abu Simbel. Choices (A) and (B) use the incorrect phrase, WHERE ... IS AT (AT is redundant). Choice (A) ends with a preposition, but the rewording in choice (B) is awkward and stilted. Choice (D) retains AT and has even worse wording. Choice (E) is unacceptable because it uses the cliche, CLAIM TO FAME.

8. **(C)**
     The phrase, CANNOT HELP, should be followed by a gerund, not by BUT. Choice (C) follows CANNOT HELP with CRITICIZING. Choices (A) and (B) are incorrect because they follow CANNOT HELP with BUT. Choice (D) incorrectly uses AND to follow CANNOT HELP. Choice (E) changes the meaning of the sentence.

9. **(B)**
     The correct idiom is to have an insight into a situation or person. While TO in choice (A) is close in meaning, it is not exact; FOR and WITH of choices (C), (D), and (E) are unacceptable. The location of OFTEN in choice (D) is weak, and its location in choice (E) makes no significant change.

10. **(D)**

It is obvious that the Lees have just purchased a sofa: WHEN THE DELIVERY TRUCK ARRIVED. The modifying clause, THEY HAD JUST BOUGHT, should be carefully placed where it clearly modifies SOFA and not LIVING ROOM. Choice (D) has the clause next to SOFA, so the meaning is clear. Choices (A), (B), and (C) sound as if they had just bought the living room. Choice (E) uses the single-word modifier NEWLY-PURCHASED in the wrong position, after SOFA, and creates redundancy by retaining THEY HAD JUST BOUGHT.

11. **(E)**

The construction, TO END UP WITH, is not acceptable in standard English usage. Choices (A), (B), and (C) use TO END UP WITH. Choices (B) and (D) produce a fragment. Choice (D) changes the meaning of the sentence to mean that there will be no protection in Europe.

12. **(B)**

Choice (B) clearly and precisely states the topic of the debate. The correlative conjunctions, WHETHER … OR, should be followed by parallel structures. Choice (A) follows WHETHER with a subject-verb combination not seen after NOT. Choice (C) is eliminated because it uses the wrong tense. Choice (D) uses MAY BE and produces awkward wording. Choice (E) has WHETHER OR NOT run together and uses poor wording.

13. **(A)**

Choice (A) has both correct agreement of subject and verb and clear reference. Choice (B) has a subject-verb agreement problem, DRINKING … ARE. Choice (C) produces a fragment. It is unclear in choice (D) who will have a bad hangover. The wording of choice (E) has the obvious subject PEOPLE as the object of a prepositional phrase.

14. **(D)**

Choice (D) correctly presents the Scouts' field trip in a subordinate clause modifying EXHIBIT. Choices (A) and (B) have the coordinating conjunction AND, but the first part of the sentence is not equal in meaning or importance to the last part. Choice (C) introduces WHEN with no antecedent. Choice (E) uses WHERE as the subordinating conjunction, but it is too far away from its antecedent and is not the important idea of the sentence.

15. **(E)**

In choice (E) the present infinitive is correctly used to express an action following another action: PLANS TO FLY. Choices (A) and (B) use the wrong form, the present participle FLYING. Choice (C) uses the wrong tense, IS FLYING. Choice (D) incorrectly uses the participle GOING to follow PLANS.

16. **(C)**

Choice (C) shows proper cause-and-effect of the two major ideas in the sentence. Choice (A) correctly uses the past participle LIKED after HAVING, and the tense sequence between the first and second parts of the sentence is correct; however, CREATIVE and INDEPENDENCE are not parallel. Choice (B) also lacks parallelism. Choices (D) and (E) incorrectly use LIKES to follow HAVING.

17. **(A)**

Choice (A) has clear wording. Choice (B) produces a fragment because it puts the verb in a nonessential phrase. Choice (E) also produces a fragment by changing the verb to a noun. Choices (C) and (D) produce twisted wording, and choice (C) changes the meaning of the sentence.

18. **(B)**

Choice (B) produces the clearest, smoothest sentence. Choice (A) has the awkward construction, DIFFICULT FOR ME AGREEING. Choice (C) changes the meaning of the sentence by making TO EVALUATE parallel with TO AGREE. Choice (D) is hopelessly wordy. Choice (E) inserts a different shade of meaning by using SHOULD AGREE, a phrase which implies a certain coercion involved.

19. **(B)**

Choice (B) avoids the split infinitive and substitutes the incorrect expression INSIDE OF with the correct preposition WITHIN. Choice (A) splits the infinitive TO MOW with the adverb COMPLETELY. Choices (C) and (D) erroneously place COMPLETELY before AGREED or AGREEING, and thereby change the meaning of the sentence. In choice (E) the phrase, ARE AGREEABLE is not acceptable in standard English usage.

20. **(E)**

The pronoun IT has no antecedent in choices (A) and (B). The antecedent of a pronoun cannot be something that is understood; the noun to which the pronoun refers must be clearly stated in the sentence. IT obviously refers to the players' talent. Choice (C) is too wordy and a bit unclear, RECOGNIZED FINANCIALLY. Choice (D) is incorrect because everyone has FINANCES, and finances are certainly not a reward. However, players may be FINANCIALLY REWARDED FOR THEIR TALENT, as in choice (E).

21. **(D)**

The conjunction NOT ONLY ... BUT ALSO must be properly placed to indicate which qualities are being discussed and to maintain proper parallelism. Choice (D) contains three adjectives following the verb TO BE: OPTIMISTIC AND ORGANIZED and GOOD. Choices (A), (B), (C), and (E) have the first two adjectives combined with the noun MAN. In addition, choices (B) and (C) place the verb TO BE after the conjunction NOT ONLY, so these would need a verb following BUT ALSO to make them structurally correct.

22. **(E)**

Choice (E) correctly uses present tense DO, and possessive before a gerund, HIS JOINING. The verbs in the last part of the sentence are in the present tense, and the verb in the first half must match since all action is obviously taking place at the same time. Choices (A) and (B) use the past tense DID. Choice (C) uses unnecessarily formal and convoluted wording. Choices (A) and (D) use the objective case pronoun HIM before the gerund JOINING.

Section 2–Problem Solving

1. **(E)**
   Since $\frac{1}{5} = \frac{2}{10}$, $\frac{2}{9}$ is larger than either $\frac{1}{5}$ or $\frac{2}{11}$. Also $\frac{4}{17}$ is larger than $\frac{4}{19}$. Now $\frac{2}{9} = \frac{4}{18}$ so that $\frac{4}{17}$ is larger than the two.

2. **(C)**
   If Joel works x hours at \$6.75 per hour, he earns \$$(6.75)x$. Therefore, we want to find the smallest integer x such that $6.75x \geq 150$, or,

   $$x \geq \frac{150}{6.75} = 150\left(\frac{4}{27}\right) = \frac{200}{9}.$$

   Thus x must be 23.

3. **(E)**
   Let x = the value of the new car.

   $$x(.80) = \$13{,}120$$

   $$x = \$16{,}400$$

4. **(B)**
   If x is her test grade on the next test, then

   $$\frac{91 + 86 + 85 + x}{4} = 90.$$

   Therefore,

   $$262 + x = 360,$$

   or $\qquad x = 360 - 262 = 98.$

5. **(C)**

   The number of revolutions = $\dfrac{\text{Distance}}{\text{Circumference of the Wheel}}$

   Circumference = $\pi d = \dfrac{\pi 3}{2}$ feet

   Distance = 1 mile = 5,280 feet

   The number of revolutions = $\dfrac{5{,}280}{(\pi 3/2)} = \dfrac{3{,}520}{\pi}$

6. **(D)**

$$10x^2 - 7x - 12 = 0$$

$$(2x - 3)(5x + 4) = 0$$

Factor the quadratic equation. Solve each factor for zero.

$$2x - 3 = 0 \qquad\qquad 5x + 4 = 0$$

$$2x = 3 \qquad\qquad 5x = -4$$

$$x = \frac{3}{2} \qquad\qquad x = -\frac{4}{5}$$

7. **(E)**

If x = number of gallons of the solution, then $.35x = 21$. Therefore,

$$x = \frac{21}{.35} = 60.$$

8. **(D)**

If $x/y = 3$, then $x = 3y$. Substituting $x = 3y$ in

$$x + 2y = 10$$

we get

$$3y + 2y = 10,$$

or, $y = 2$. Since $x = 3y$, $x = 3(2) = 6$.

9. **(E)**

The answer cannot be B since $3X$ has to be an even integer. Since $3X$ has to equal the square of an integer, X must be 12. Check:

$$3 \times 12 = 36 = (6)^2.$$

10. **(B)**

If x is the original price, then the 50 percent mark-up price is $(1.5)x$. Since this price is marked down by 30%, the final price is $(.7)(1.5)x = 1.05x$. Therefore

$$1.05x = 3,360,$$

or, $\qquad x = \dfrac{3,360}{1.05}$

= $3,200.

11. **(C)**

The arithmetic mean of the scores is

$$\frac{10 + 20 + 30 + 35 + 55}{5} = \frac{150}{5} = 30.$$

Since only two scores, namely, 35 and 55 are larger than 30, the answer is (C).

12. **(B)**

Complete the diagram as shown to give two rectangles. The smaller rectangle has sides 3 and 4 and the larger has sides 6 and 25. The area of the figure

$$= 3 \times 4 + 6 \times 25$$

$$= 162.$$

13. **(D)**

The sum of measures of lengths of any two sides of a triangle must be greater than the measure of length of the third side. Since the triangle is isosceles, the only possibility is a triangle with length of sides x, $2x + 1$, $2x + 1$ which has perimeter

$$x + (2x + 1) + (2x + 1) = 5x + 2.$$

14. **(E)**

During the first year John earns

$$15,000 + 15,500 = \$30,500.$$

During the second year he earns

$$16,000 + 16,500 = \$32,500.$$

During the third year he earns

$$17,000 + 17,500 = \$34,500.$$

During the fourth year he earns

$$18,000 + 18,500 = \$36,500.$$

15. **(B)**

The area of a circle with radius r is πr^2. If this area is increased by 96%, then the area of the bigger circle is

$$(1 + .96)\pi\, r^2 = \pi(1.96r^2)$$

$$= \pi(1.4r)^2.$$

In other words, the radius of the bigger circle is 1.4 times that of the smaller circle. Thus the radius is increased by $(1.4 - 1)100 = 40\%$.

16. **(D)**

If x is the list price of a paperback, then $(1 - .2)x = .8x$ is the discounted price. Since this price is discounted further by 10% in the promotion sale, the selling price is

$$(1 - .1)(.8x) = (.9)(.8)X = .72x.$$

Hence, the effective discount is

$$\$(x - .72x) = \$(.28)x$$

which is 28% off the list price.

Section 3–Critical Reasoning

1.   **(A)**
     A logical argument must follow from assumptions. The argument is valid if it is logical in form, that is, if the conclusions would follow from those assumptions. The assumptions may be granted for the sake of argument, but frequently as in this case the argument is based on a tacit assumption, something assumed but not explicitly stated. The problem is to figure out which of the five statements provides a premise for the argument that would lead, if true, to the desired conclusion. The rating of the automobile by *Driver's News* leads to the conclusion that the automobile is worth buying only if the consumer believes that *Driver's News* is a reliable source of information. The other four statements may or may not also be true. They do not necessarily contradict the argument, but neither are they necessary for it. If the car in question is expensive, then (B) for example would lead you to buy it. The advertisement does not say, however, whether the car is relatively expensive or not. Statement (C) is about consumer preference. This might influence the design and sale of cars, but it is not a necessary assumption for the consumer. Statement (D) would be important if mileage were an issue. Since the advertisement does not discuss mileage, statement (D) is not relevant. The advertisement does not specify a type of character associated with the car, so statement (E) is not a necessary assumption for the argument. Thus, each statement must be examined as a part of a logical argument. Only (A) provides a premise from which the advertisement leads to the conclusion.

2.   **(B)**
     The structure of this argument can be analyzed: *a* causes *b, b* causes *c*, and therefore *a* causes *c*. In this particular example, *a* is more aggressive antitrust prosecution, *b* is increased competition, and *c* is reduced inflation. Thus, the correct answer is (B) "Antitrust prosecution reduced inflation" or in terms of the abstract structure *a* causes *c*. The understanding of the logic of the argument depends on a perception of this structure, not on agreement with the content of the argument. Thus (A), (D), and (E) are irrelevant, whether they are true or false. They involve factors that are not part of the argument: foreign competition and unemployment. Conclusions on these topics do not follow logically from the assumptions because these topics are not part of the assumptions. It would be as if to conclude that since *a* causes *b* and *b* causes *c*, therefore *d* causes *f*. The relationship between *d* and *f* is not implied by this argument. As for (D), "Antitrust

prosecution results in a decrease in production," again whether true or false, it is flatly contradicted by the assumptions. In this argument, increased production is one of the consequences of antitrust prosecution. Given these assumptions, (D) cannot follow logically.

3.   **(E)**

This problem can be analyzed as having the basic form: 3 is more than 2, 2 is more than 1; therefore, 3 is more than 1. In the problem, Sally's income is 3. It is greater than 2, which corresponds to the individual incomes of Fred and Alice. This amount in turn is greater than 1, the income of George. From this information, it follows that (E) "Sally makes more money than George," or in terms of the basic form of the argument, 3 is greater than 1. Choice (D) is flatly contradicted by the information. We know that Fred and Alice make the same amount (2). Since what George makes (1) is less than what Alice makes (2) and since Alice and Fred make the same amount (2), George must make less than Fred. To assert (D) is to say in effect that 1 is greater than 2, contradicting the given information. Choices (A), (B), and (C) all deal with Henry and this raises a different kind of problem. All that we know about Henry is that he makes more than George, but we do not know how much more. Nothing follows from this information. We also know that Sally, Fred, and Alice make more than George, but again we do not know how much more. Therefore, we can not know, from the information given, the relationship between Henry's income and the income of Sally, Fred, and Alice.

4.   **(A)**

In the opening statement we are told that the number of elderly is increasing more rapidly than the number of wage earners, and the cost of caring for the elderly will have to come from the incomes of the wage earners. Since the ratio of elderly to wage earners is increasing, it follows that, other things being equal, each wage earner will have to pay a higher percentage of his or her income for care of the elderly. This assumes that average income does not increase enough to make up the difference.

The other answers are all possibilities, but they do not follow directly from the information given. Thus (B), (C), and (E) are contingent upon (D). Whether the elderly receive adequate care, whether only the rich receive adequate care, and whether citizens would be advised to start saving their own funds to provide for their own needs all depend at least in part on the willingness of future wage earners to pay the taxes needed to care for the elderly. There is nothing in the statement that implies that voters in the future will or will not vote for such taxes.

5. **(D)**

If for the poor person the 5% sales tax is equivalent to an income tax "close to or at 5%," then it follows that the poor person spends all or almost all of his or her income. If, on the other hand, for the rich person the same sales tax is equivalent to a much lower percentage of his or her income, then it follows that the rich person spends a much lower percentage of his or her income. Presumably the rich person saves more than the poor person, both absolutely and as a percentage of income. Thus we can infer (D) "Poor people spend a larger percentage of income than rich people" from the passage.

As for the other statements, they cannot be inferred directly from the passage. One might assume (A), but it is not necessarily implied. One must first assume that the rich person is spending at least as much as the poor person. This seems like a reasonable assumption, but it is not stated or implied in the passage. (B) also depends on additional information. The truth of (B) would depend on the definitions of "rich" and "poor" and the total numbers falling into each category. None of this information is given in the passage. (C) is a notion extraneous to the passage. Nothing is said or implied about finding ways to avoid paying taxes. (E) is a quasi-moral judgment about who should pay what. The assumption that calling a sales tax "regressive" is a criticism implies that the tax should be at least flat: an equal percentage of income. Thus (E) is compatible with the argument as a whole but it is not implied by the specific example. The question asks for a statement implied by the passage. Furthermore, the passage assumes that a regressive tax is undesirable, but does not state or imply *why* it is undesirable. Thus (E) is consistent with, but not implied by, the passage.

6. **(C)**

We can infer from George's statement that he has a policy with no deductibles. In other words, the insurance company pays all of his losses. Martha objects to this. She considers such a policy to be "a very expensive bill-paying service." In other words, George is paying the insurance company a high fee to pay bills that he could just as easily pay himself. To Martha such a policy is at best an expensive convenience. Since Martha disapproves, we can infer that she believes insurance should not be used to pay for losses that the insured could afford to pay for. Thus we can infer from the conversation that Martha would endorse (C): "Don't insure anything you can afford to lose."

As for the other choices, (A) and (B) are irrelevant, (D) is contradicted by the evidence, and (E) is consistent with but not limited to Martha's point of view.

7. **(D)**

The question asks the reader to identify the kind of argument being used. The comparison between the atom and the solar system is correctly identified as an analogy. Whether or not there is life on other planets, whether or not the sun is the source of all energy, and whether or not the universe is expanding are all extraneous to this argument. Choice (A) correctly identifies the argument as an analogy, but incorrectly identifies the terms of the comparison. The argument compares the atom, not with the universe as a whole, but only with the solar system. Thus, (D) is the correct choice, identifying the argument as an analogy and identifying the terms of the analogy as an atom and the solar system.

8. **(B)**

Arguments by analogy stress the similarity of two things that may otherwise be quite unlike. Such is the case in this particular argument. Although the form of the atom and the form of the solar system are similar, there seems to be no other basis for the comparison and therefore no reason to assume any further similarities. Whether or not there is life on other planets (A) is irrelevant to the argument. What we know about the world is not limited to our immediate visual field so (C) would not weaken the argument. Similarly, what we know about the solar system is not limited simply by human space travel so (D) is not an issue. The example of the dog's tail is just an entertaining image not necessary to the argument itself. In the absence of dogs, some other example would serve just as well. Thus the problem is to identify the essential weakness of the argument. This essential weakness is expressed in (B): the comparison focuses entirely on one superficial similarity while ignoring many basic differences.

9. **(E)**

The problem with the argument is that the conclusion may follow, but does not necessarily follow, from the evidence. The evidence shows a difference between two groups of people: Peace Corps and non-Peace Corps. The former are more radical than the latter. The conclusion *assumes* that this difference is a result of serving in the Peace Corps. It might not be. Perhaps the Peace Corps volunteers were more radical to start with and that is why they volunteered. This possibility would be ruled out by (E), and therefore (E) would strengthen the conclusion. The other arguments are irrelevant. Knowledge of geography, tolerance of ethnic and cultural differences, and a desire or lack of desire to make money might be acquired through Peace Corps service or might be already present in the volunteers before their service. In any case, it is not clear just how these factors would relate to a radical political point of view. They might or they might not. As for (D), this would certainly weaken the argument rather than strengthen it, since it would suggest a contamination of the evidence. If one group realized that they were being tested and the other group did not, then this awareness might affect the answers given.

10. **(B)**
Although Jack's argument appears plausible, it is fundamentally weak in that he fails to consider other possible causes of the increased enrollment. Even if Dr. Smith's leadership were a factor, it might not be the only factor or even the most important factor. Jill, however, further weakens Jack's argument by pointing out that (B) the increase had already started three years before Dr. Smith became president. This implies that something else is causing the increase. That the lowest enrollment coincided with the lowest number of high school graduates suggests a factor that Jack has apparently overlooked. In any case, Dr. Smith's leadership could not have caused the increase in enrollment that preceded his presidency.

(A), (C), (D), and (E) may or may not be true, but they are not weaknesses attacked by Jill. If enrollment declines next year (A) even though Dr. Smith continues as president, this would further weaken Jack's argument. There is no indication, however, that it will decline. On the basis of her argument, Jill might predict such a decline if the number of high school graduates had declined. Since we have no information to that effect, we have no reason to suppose that such a decline is likely. Although one might consider Jack's estimation of the two presidents' personalities to be subjective (C), this is not the weakness that Jill attacks. Whether or not Jack has exaggerated the effect that one individual can have (D) is simply not discussed. It may be that dynamic leadership could have the effect that Jack ascribes to it and it may be that Jill would agree to that, and yet Jack could be wrong about the qualities of Dr. Smith's leadership. Jill never comments on this. Likewise, the importance of the programs as a factor (E) is not discussed.

11. **(A)**
Choice (E) is irrelevant. A mere accusation proves nothing, and in any case the mayor's political virtue has no bearing on the merits of the argument. If the accusations were proven true we might question the character of the mayor and his fitness to serve, but this is an attack on the arguer not the argument. The other statements may have some bearing on the question. Choice (D) indicates the importance of crime as an issue. We do not know from this, however, whether raising the salaries of the police

will have any effect on crime. Choice (C) indicates that an increase is financially feasible, but not that it is necessarily appropriate. The surplus might just as well be spent on something else or returned to the taxpayers. The significance of Choice (B) depends on the relative value to be placed on the different jobs of police officers and fire fighters. This is certainly a matter of potential debate, but not one that could be resolved without further information. With nothing more to go on, we have no reason to assume that the salaries should be different.

When we turn, however, to choice (A), we see that it has a direct bearing on the mayor's argument. The mayor refers to a 10% increase over the last five years. What this means is directly affected by the information in statement (A). A 3% annual rate of inflation adds up to a 15% rate of inflation over the five-year period. Thus the real income of the police officers, the buying power of their salaries, has actually been decreasing. In light of this information, the mayor's argument is not very persuasive, and an increase in salaries would seem to be appropriate.

12. (C)

The problem here is to grasp the basic idea expressed in the opening statement and then determine how this general notion applies to the specific examples in the three statements I, II, and III. The basic idea is that a particular institutional policy may help one group associated with the institution while hurting another group associated with the institution. Statement (I) illustrates the idea in that the increase in faculty salaries helps one group, the faculty, but hurts another group, the students, because it results in an increase in tuition. Statement (II) illustrates the idea in that the policy, a decrease in fees, helps one group, the patients, but hurts another group, the nurses, because it results in lower wages for the nursing staff. Statement (III) does not illustrate the idea. Adding to the fund-raising staff results, according to the statement, in an increase in money available for scholarships. Since the added fund-raising effort increases the total amount of money available to the institution, it does not take from one group in order to give to another group. Thus, in terms of the institution, no one is hurt by the policy. The correct choice is thus (C). Statements I and II support the claim, while statement III does not.

13. (C)

The advice is apparently contradictory, but there is an implicit explanation. The dentists offer good advice for avoiding cavities; the nutritionists offer good advice for the overall diet. Thus, the correct choice is (C). The passage implies the opposite of (D). Since the dentists advise eating all the candy at once, we can infer that this causes fewer, not more, cavities. Nothing in the passage implies (E), that one group is more scientific in their approach than the other. Nothing in the passage implies (B), since there is no indication of what either group claims to know. In any case, the advice is consistent with the particular areas of expertise, and there is no evidence that either the dentists or the nutritionists are claiming any additional expertise. At first glance, (A) might appear to be correct since there is an obvious contradiction. There is no indication, however, that further research could resolve this contradiction since it is based not on a lack of knowledge, but on a difference in ultimate concerns.

14. **(B)**
     The key to solving this kind of problem lies in the final words of the question: "...can be inferred from the passage." Among the various possible answers there may be statements that are true, statements that one could agree with, statements even that are consistent with the given information. They do not, however, follow from that given information. The problem, then, is to find the one statement that is logically implied by the given information. In this case the answer is (B) because an increase in exploration and conservation resulting in a lower price implies an increase in supply. The other answers are all statements of policy. With these statements one might reasonably agree or disagree, but the statements are not directly implied by the information given. Many other factors may be relevant to these issues. A tax credit for conservation, a strategic stockpile of oil, a subsidy for solar energy, and a reliance on nuclear energy are complex issues. These issues are certainly related to the information given, but the information given does not in and of itself imply a particular position on these issues one way or the other.

15. **(C)**
     Basic to the solving of this problem is the recognition that the conservation measures themselves have contributed to the reduction in price. Of course, an individual might argue that he or she could save money by not insulating and letting everyone else insulate. Since the total amount of insulating would still be about the same, the net effect on the price of oil would still be about the same. It would not work, however, if everyone took that approach. Then, in the absence of conservation, the price would not go down. The other choices may or may not be true, but in any case they cannot be inferred from the passage. Nothing in the passage implies that (A) "the price of oil may rise back up again." As for (B), we may assume that the oil supply is finite, but this is not implied by the passage. Likewise, (D) and (E) are statements that one might or might not agree with, but that can not be inferred from the passage. Whether or not the oil

producing countries can maintain a unified policy is not implied by the passage. Whether or not nuclear energy is a safe alternative is not implied by the passage.

16. **(E)**

The problem here is to sort out the various factors and determine how each one will affect the outcome. The ability of the volunteers to provide for the needy is determined by the income that the center receives and the costs that the center incurs. If the volunteers are going to provide more, they must either increase the income or lower the costs or both. An increase in unemployment (A) would result, according to the problem, in an increase in costs since there would be more people showing up for soup. An increase in inflation (B) would result in an increase in costs, since it would further increase the cost of buying food. A decrease in donations (C) would decrease the income and, therefore, limit what the volunteers could provide. An increase in the number of volunteers (D) would have no effect since they are not contributing money and they are not paid. Of the five factors listed, only (E) would enable the volunteers to provide more food to each person requesting it. The decrease in unemployment would, according to the problem result in a decrease in the number of people showing up. This would lower the costs, and with lower total costs the volunteers would be able to provide each person with more food.

Section 4—Data Sufficiency

1. **(C)**
    According to Statement (1) $\angle ACD = 100°$; therefore,

    $\angle ACB = 180° - 100° = 80°$.

    Since $x° + y° + \angle ACB = 180°$, $x + y = 100$. But Statement (1) does not give y. So, you cannot determine x by just using (1). Since Statement (2) does not provide y, you cannot solve for x using (2) by itself. However, (1): $x + y = 100$ and (2): $x - y = 20$. By combining these two equations you can find x.

2. **(C)**
    By Statement (1) the combined 18 months' rent was $4,200. Since Statement (1) does not say how much of the $4,200 is paid for Apartment A rent, you cannot answer the question using (1) by itself. If you let x be the monthly rent for Apartment A, then according to Statement (2) the monthly rent for Apartment B is $x + 10$. Since Statement (2) does not give the combined 18 months' rent, you cannot find x. However, by using both (1) and (2) you get the equation

    $6x + 12(x + 50) = \$4,200$,

    from which you can find x.

3. **(C)**
    From Statement (1) the relationship $h = 3d$ or $h = 6r$. From Statement (2) given the area of the base, the radius can be determined. Together the radius and height can be determined to find the volume of a cylinder,

    $V = hr^2\pi$.

4. **(E)**
    Let Tony's typing speed be x wpm; therefore Helen's typing speed is $(x + 10)$ wpm by Statement (2). According to Statement (1) it took Tony 100 minutes to type the story. Since the number of words cannot be figured from the given conditions, you cannot find Tony's speed. Since Tony's speed is unknown, (2) will not help to find Helen's speed. Therefore, although you know when she finished typing you still cannot find when she started using (1) and (2) together.

5. **(B)**

The two equations in Statement (1) are essentially the same:

$$\frac{3}{2} + 2x - y = 0$$

is obtained from

$$3 + 4x - 2y = 0$$

by multiplying each side by $1/2$; therefore Statement (1) is not sufficient to solve for y. However, since the two equations in Statement (2) represent the non-parallel lines, they will intersect. As a result, Statement (2) is sufficient to solve for y.

6. **(E)**

According to (1) and (2) the number of employees in 1988 is the same as the number of employees in 1987. Since we do not know the number of employees, we cannot find the percentage of the executives, i.e., if x is the number of employees in 1987 or 1988, (1) and (2) only say that the percentage of executives is

$$\frac{2x - 10}{x} \times 100.$$

7. **(C)**

By Statement (1), $AB = 100$ ft; therefore, radius of the hemisphere is 50 ft, and we can find the volume of the dome. Since (1) does not give the height of the cylinder, you cannot find the total capacity by using Statement (1) alone. According to Statement (2), the height of the cylinder is 120 ft. Since (2) does not tell us the radius it is not sufficient to find the total capacity of the storage. However, using Statements (1) and (2) you can find the volume of the cylindrical base and the dome.

8. **(C)**

Say the student spends x hours a week on the work-study and y hours babysitting. According to Statement (1),

$$x + y = 23\frac{1}{2}.$$

Since Statement (1) does not give the value of x or y, you cannot answer the question using (1) by itself. Statement (2) can be formulated by the equation

$$3 \times 5x + 3y = 78.$$

Since Statement (2) gives neither x nor y, you cannot find x and y using (2) alone. Using both statements together, you can determine x and y.

9.   **(D)**
     According to Statement (1) there were 30 passengers at departure. Since the average age was 60, using (1), the sum of the ages at departure is 1,800. When two new passengers of age x and $x + 20$ joined the trip, average age is given by the formula

$$\frac{1,800 + x + (x + 20)}{32}.$$

This average equals 59, so you can solve for x. Using just (2) you get the same equation

$$\frac{1,800 + x + (x + 20)}{32} = 59,$$

which also enables you to solve for x.

10.   **(C)**
      According to Statement (1)

$$a + b = 7.$$

Since (1) gives neither a nor b, you cannot find a and b by using (1) alone. Since Statement (2) does not specify the prime numbers it is not sufficient to find a and b. Using both statements together, you can find a and b.

11.   **(C)**
      According to Statement (1) x is odd; therefore x^2 is odd and $x^2 + 1$ is even. Since Statement (1) does not say whether y is even or odd, you cannot answer the question by just using (1). Also, Statement (2) only says that y^2 is even, you cannot figure out what kind of number x is from (2); therefore (2) is not sufficient by itself. Using Statements (1) and (2) together one can answer the question.

12.   **(A)**
      By Statement (1)

$$x + |x| = 0;$$

therefore,

$$|x| = -x.$$

Since $x \neq 0$, x must be negative and therefore (1) is sufficient to answer the question. Since Statement (2) does not indicate the sign of x, (2) alone is not enough to answer the question.

13. **(C)**

Let the flat rate be y, and x is the price for each additional word. By Statement (1),

$$y + 48x = \$2.95.$$

Since (1) does not give the value of x or y you cannot solve for y or x using (1) alone. Similarly, (2) alone only gives the equation

$$y + 23x = \$1.70,$$

and therefore (2) is not sufficient. However, using (1) and (2) simultaneously you can solve for y and x.

14. **(D)**

$$\frac{a^2 - 4b^2}{2a - 4b} = \frac{(a - 2b)(a + 2b)}{2(a - 2b)}$$

Since

$$a - 2b \neq 0, \frac{a^2 - 4b^2}{2a - 4b} = \frac{a + 2b}{2}.$$

Therefore, each statement alone is sufficient for answering the question.

15. **(D)**

Statement (1) says $AE = {}^5/_2$. Since $\triangle ADE$ and $\triangle ABC$ are similar, $AC = 5$. So, we know BC and AE and can find AB from (1) alone. According to (2), $BD = {}^3/_2$. Since the two triangles are similar, we know that $AB = 2AD$. Therefore, $AB = 2({}^3/_2) = 3$. So both alone are sufficient.

16. **(C)**

Statement (1) does not tell us if Dave made an additional deposit or any withdrawals, and therefore (1) alone is not sufficient. By (2) we know that the change in his savings comes from interest alone, but the statement does not say how much that change is. So, (2) alone is not sufficient. If the interest rate is ${}^t/_{100}$, using (1) and (2) together one gets the equation:

$$t^2 + 200\,t - 609 = 0$$

and therefore (C) is the answer.

17. **(B)**

Statement (1) just says $x - y$ is negative. But, there are infinitely many points (x, y) on the graph of $y = {}^1/_x + 1$ for which $x - y < 0$ (i.e.,

$x < y$). So you cannot quite say what the value of $x - y$ should be by just using (1). On the other hand, when $y = \frac{1}{x} + 1$, $x - y = x - \frac{1}{x} - 1$. According to Statement (2), $x - \frac{1}{x} = 0$. So, $x - y = -1$, and the answer is (B).

18. **(E)**

From Statement (1) the value of x can be either $-\frac{11}{3}$ or 3. From Statement (2) x is between -4 and 4, but more information is needed to determine if x is an integer.

19. **(E)**

It is possible to find a non-rectangle quadrilateral which satisfies both Statements (1) and (2). It is also obvious that any rectangle satisfies both statements. Therefore, Statements (1) and (2) together are not sufficient to say whether the quadrilateral is a rectangle or not.

20. **(B)**

From Statement (1) the value of D can be 3,556 or 3,560. From Statement (2) the value of D can only be 3,560. The information from Statement (1) is not necessary.

Section 5–Reading Comprehension

1.   **(A)**
     The primary purpose of this article is to discuss the effects and causes of carpal tunnel syndrome. The author does not discuss employer negligence (B), or analyzing the workplace (E) for possible hazards to worker health. There is only one main cause of CTS mentioned (C), "repetitive and/or forceful manual tasks performed over a period of time." The author does not mention lack of research (D) on CTS to date.

2.   **(C)**
     The article discusses the symptoms and the effects of CTS in the second paragraph; therefore, the only correct answer is (C) because it combines the second and third choices presented. Although the author states, "more than half of all U.S. workers are susceptible to developing CTS," the article mentions no specific statistics on how many people have actually been afflicted with the disorder. Therefore, choices (A), (B), (D), and (E) are invalid.

3.   **(D)**
     The article discusses the meatpacking industry as being considered "one of the most hazardous industries" because workers make "as many as 10,000 repetitive motions a day...such as deboning meat." Poultry workers (D) would fit into this category. Welders (A) and boiler makers (E) have various movements during the day, and their most probable injury would be strained backs, from lifting and fitting heavy pipe and other equipment. Truck drivers (B) perform repetitive tasks in driving, but they are not generally strained or rapid tasks. Carpenters (C) employ a variety of movements, and would most likely be injured from lifting or pushing movements.

4.   **(C)**
     The article begins by stating that cumulative trauma disorders are on the rise; later, the author points out the great likelihood which U.S. employees have of developing CTS. Therefore, it can be inferred that CTS is occurring with increasing frequency. Choices (A), (B), and (D) contain information not mentioned in the article. Choice (E) incorrectly states that over half the workers are affected with CTS, while the article merely states that this percentage of worker are "susceptible" to developing CTS.

5. **(E)**

The greatest problem with early detection and treatment of CTS is that workers do not appear to recognize the symptoms of CTS as being associated with the motions they make on the job, implying that the workers continue in the movements that are aggravating their condition. Choice (C) is the next most likely culprit, as the article states that workers are often unaware of the causes of CTS, but the article does not state there is a lack of published information on CTS. Choice (D) is another contributing factor, because frequently some time passes before accurate diagnosis is made, but it is not indicated that any certain "length of time" must pass before a doctor will certify that CTS is present. There is no evidence in the article to support choices (A) or (B).

6. **(A)**

The only choice that would directly "facilitate an affected worker's return to the job" would have to entail conservative treatment, such as a lengthy rest from duties, and perhaps restricted job duties upon return. Access to health care workers with systematic evaluation and referral would help an employee determine if he or she has a problem or if a job configuration could be modified to prevent CTS. Adequate monitoring with periodic walkthroughs would help to detect problems on the job which could be corrected in order to prevent CTS. Therefore, choices (B), (C), (D), and (E) all deal either partially or totally with detection and prevention, not an employee's return to work after the affliction has been detected and treated.

7. **(C)**

The article states that medical personnel may give the wrong diagnosis, implying that some or many physicians are not familiar enough with CTS and its symptoms because they mistake it for something else. This problem can be solved with education and time. Choice (D) is a logical assumption, and probably quite true since CTS is sometimes misdiagnosed, but it is considered a part of the correct choice (C). Choice (A) is not mentioned in the article, even though it may have some validity at this time. Choice (B) is probably not true because a company would face a damaging suit if it were practiced. Choice (E) may be true to some extent, but probably not in most cases.

8. **(B)**

The article describes all the symptoms except back pain as part of CTS.

9. **(E)**

The author might consider "mandatory" tool design "guidelines" prohibitively expensive for both tool manufacturers and companies that buy them. However, if this was implemented, as it has been in related cases, the government could allow companies to gradually replace old tools as they are phased out naturally from age or breakage. Easier and less costly methods could be implemented, such as (A) or (C). The article does not deal with (B), although vibration and noise certainly are factors in injuries. The author indicates that (D) is probably true, especially in specialized repetitive tasks associated with assembly-line production.

10. **(D)**

The passage provides "a working knowledge of heredity" for horse owners. It does not analyze sources of disagreement (E) or propose standards (C). Horse owners may learn of potential problems (B) and have some misconceptions corrected (A), but these are not the passage's chief purposes.

11. **(C)**

Body cells of an embryo contain 32 pairs of chromosomes. The last paragraph makes clear that most characteristics are multiple-gene. The author offers no statistics on producing offspring equal in merit to parents.

12. **(C)**

Paragraph one explains that conception rates average less than 50 percent and that some conceptions do not produce offspring. Some foals may be disappointing, but that is irrelevant to the question.

13. **(A)**

Sex cells contain a single chromosome and one gene whereas body cells contain pairs of chromosomes and numerous genes. Sex cells contain 16, not 32, single, not paired, chromosomes. Quantitative traits are present in the genes of embryos and body cells.

14. **(B)**

Multiple factors, affected by various genes, account for growth rates in horses (see paragraph six). Heredity is determined by genes, not chromosomes.

15. **(E)**

Speed is due to many genes and is also subject to gradation from high to low performance.

16. **(D)**
    The author makes it clear that full sisters can be very different; nonetheless, knowledge of principles of heredity enhance the chances of achieving desired results.

17. **(C)**
    The author states throughout the passage that parental characteristics, such as speed and performance records, are qualities in a foal that are not necessarily transmitted.

18. **(D)**
    In the sentences containing the phrases "I promulgate new races of Teachers" and "Our fundamental want today...is of a class...of native authors," the author's purpose is set forth, as in (D). There is no attempt at a rigorous train of logic (A) in the passage to prove anything. There is no listing of facts nor a recitation of history in an attempt to educate (B). The author's proposals are intended to bring about the triumph of literature and character (C), so any such announcement would be premature. He complains that feudalism still dominates political institutions (E), so there has been no such victory. From the direct, preaching tone of the passage, the only plausible verb remaining among the answers is "convince."

19. **(B)**
    In paragraph one, the passage expresses great confidence in the material success of the United States and includes the phrase "the republic must soon...dominate the world," as in (B). There is no mention of the complexity of international relationships (A). The implication is that the country will become less and less dependent on others (C). There is no mention of either increasing cooperation (D) or hostility (E).

20. **(A)**
    In paragraph two, the passage claims that literature is "far deeper" than political institutions, implying answer (A). In addition, paragraph three claims that authors affect "politics far more than popular superficial suffrage," also as in (A). Both of these statements indicate the opposite of (B). Any discussion of what is sufficient (C) or insufficient (D) does not address the question asked here about a comparison. If either side were overwhelming (E), it would be literature, not democracy.

21. **(C)**
    Paragraph three contains the statement "there is one need, a hiatus the profoundest, that no eye seems to perceive, no voice to state." There is no

mention in the passage of foreign diplomacy (A). If the author felt that no one besides himself wanted the masses to be ruled by the educated (B), he would be unlikely to propose that very condition. He does not discuss what he believes others feel about the accomplishments of schools and churches (D), only what he feels about them. If (E) were true, he would have no need to write this passage.

22. **(E)**
The first sentence in the paragraph indicates that cavil is something that should be surpassed. This sentence is followed by a list of Congressional issues that the author feels are not extremely important, as in choice (E). Since no mention is made of political intrigue (A) in any other context, it would be strangely alone here. Experimentation (B) is not necessarily something to be surpassed, nor is it mentioned elsewhere. Boasting (C) does not fit the tone or subject of the passage. Imitation (D) might be an appropriate choice if this sentence is considered alone, but it does not match the meaning of the paragraph.

23. **(E)**
The last sentence in paragraph two shows that the author feels they still control important parts of our culture. This sentence is the opposite of choice (A). The beginning of the same sentence asserts that the influence is "palpably" retreating, so the case that they still provide the models (B) while retreating is weak. For the same reason, the transitional period of retreat does not support the notion of stark contrast (C). Paragraph three directly argues that such influence does not provide a sound sub-stratum (D).

Section 6–Problem Solving

1. **(E)**

   Let x = amount of sales, then

   $$x + .06x = 1,204 - 250,$$

   $$1.06x = 954.$$

   Therefore,

   $$x = \frac{954}{1.06} = 900.$$

   Finally,

   $$954 - 900 = 54.$$

   Choice (A) comes from multiplying 1,204 by .06. Choice (B) comes from multiplying $1,204 - 250$ by .06. Choice (C) comes from dividing 954 by 1.6. Choice (D) comes from dividing $1,204 - 250$ by .6.

2. **(D)**

   Let x = tons of iceberg altogether. Then

   $$\frac{1}{6}x = 130,$$

   $$x = 780 \text{ tons}.$$

   The amount of the iceberg below the water is found by

   $$780 - 130 = 650 \text{ tons}.$$

   To check, take $^5/_6$ of $780 = 650$. Choice (A) is the total iceberg tonnage. Choice (B) comes from multiplying 130 by $^5/_6$ and choice (C) comes from $^{780}/_5$.

3. **(B)**

   The solution involves finding the x-coordinate of the point of intersection of the lines $y = 34x + 51$ and $y = 31x + 60$. Setting the equations equal to each other gives

   $$34x + 51 = 31x + 60$$

   $$3x = 9$$

$$x = 3$$

4. **(C)**

Let x = Mrs. Massey's age. Then $x + 4$ = Mr. Massey's age. The sum of their ages is $2x + 4$ and the following inequality holds:

$$80 < 2x + 4 < 100 \quad \text{or} \quad 38 < x < 48.$$

Of the numbers between 38 and 48, only 41, 43 and 47 are prime (only divisible by themselves or 1). Mr. Massey must be 47 in order to be 4 years older than his wife (who is then 43).

5. **(C)**

Let x = cost of an item. Then x would be multiplied by $(.80)(.95)$ to get its discounted value.

$$(.80)(.95) = .76$$

which implies the discount is

$$1.00 - .76 = .24 \text{ or } 24\%.$$

6. **(E)**

Let x = length of longest day and y = length of shortest night. Then

$$x + y = 24$$

and $\qquad x = y + 9.$

Substituting $y + 9$ for x in the first equation gives

$$2y + 9 = 24$$

or $\qquad 2y = 15$

or $\qquad y = 7\frac{1}{2}.$

7. **(C)**

Let x = price of the books.

$$x + .06x = 159.53$$

$$1.06x = 159.53$$

$$x = 150.50$$

8. **(C)**

One mile = 5,280 ft $\times$ 12 in/ft = 63,360 inches.

The circumference of the tire is found by the formula $c = \pi d$ or 24π. Therefore, the number of revolutions is

$$\frac{63,360}{24\pi} = \frac{2,640}{\pi}.$$

9. **(E)**

Let x = amount she made before the raises. The equation is

$$(x + .08x) + .1(x + .08x) = 2,376$$

$$1.08x + .1(1.08x) = 2,376$$

$$1.08x + 0.108x = 2,376$$

$$1.188x = 2,376$$

and

$$x = \frac{2,376}{1.188}$$

$$= 2,000.$$

10. **(D)**

Let x = Mr. Sherman's average speed. Since time is the same for both men, we have

$$\frac{20}{30} + \frac{80}{40} = \frac{100}{x},$$

then reducing gives the equation

$$\frac{2}{3} + 2 = \frac{100}{x}$$

and multiplying by $3x$ gives

$$2x + 6x = 300$$

or

$$8x = 300$$

and

$$x = 37.5.$$

11. **(D)**

Let x = the number of people in the group, then $30/x$ = each person's share of the $30. Therefore, the equation for the solution is

$$\left(\frac{30}{x} - 1\right)(x + 1) = 30$$

$$\left(\frac{30 - x}{x}\right)(x + 1) = 30$$

$$(30 - x)(x + 1) = 30x$$

$$30x - x^2 + 30 - x = 30x$$
$$x^2 - x^2 - 30 = 0$$
$$(x + 6)(x - 5) = 0$$
$$x = -6, 5$$

Disregard the negative number – 6; the answer is 5.

12. **(A)**

Let x = the amount of decrease in the width and L = length of the rectangle, W = width of the rectangle and A = area of the rectangle. Then

$$LW = A,$$

and $(L + .25L)(W - x) = LW$.

Simplifying the equation gives

$$w - x = \frac{LW}{1.25L},$$

or $x = W - \dfrac{W}{1.25} = 0.2W$.

Hence, the width must be decreased by 20%.

13. **(A)**

Solve the system of equations

$$3x - 2y = 6$$

and $x - y = 1$

simultaneously either by the addition or the substitution method. The solution is (4, 3). Therefore,

$$x + y = 7.$$

14. **(E)**

$$(1 - \sqrt{3})(1 + \sqrt{3}) = 1 - 3$$
$$= -2.$$

And $2^{-2} = \dfrac{1}{2^2} = \dfrac{1}{4}$.

Choice (A) comes from adding the exponents

$1 - \sqrt{3} + 1 + \sqrt{3} = 2,$

and $2^2 = 4.$

Choice (B) comes from incorrectly letting

$2^{-2} = -4.$

Choice (C) comes from

$2^{1+3} = 2^4 = 16.$

15. (C)

Solve this as an exponential equation with base 2 because $8 = 2^3$ and $1/_4 = 2^{-2}.$

$$2^{3(x-1)} = 2^{-2(1-x)}$$

$$2^{3x-3} = 2^{-2+2x}$$

$$3x - 3 = -2 + 2x$$

$$x = 1.$$

16. (A)

The triangle is a right triangle because from geometry, an angle in-scribed in a semicircle is a right angle. The hypotenuse of the triangle, which is also the diameter of the circle, is 20 (3, 4, 5 is a Pythagorean triple and this triangle is 4 times 3, 4, 5). The radius of the circle is 10 and the area of the circle is

$$\pi r^2 = 100\pi.$$

The area of the triangle is

$$\frac{1}{2} bh = \frac{1}{2} \ 12(16) = 96$$

so the shaded area is $100\pi - 96$. Choice (B) comes from using the diameter, 20 of the circle, instead of the radius. Choice (C) comes from using 20 for the circle radius and forgetting to take half of 12(16). Choice (D) comes from not taking half of 12(16).

Section 7–Analytical Writing Assessment

ANALYSIS OF AN ISSUE ESSAY TOPIC

Sample Essay Response Scoring 5 to 6

In America, the world of business is largely a public sphere. It was created at a time when men ruled the public world but women were expected to maintain the private. Therefore, for many years, it was rare for women to operate in this realm. After the second world war, however, the distinction between men's and women's roles became less sharply defined. At this point women had to learn to function by the rules of the public sphere as they entered the realm of business. Although it may have been difficult at first to learn these rules, or to gain acceptance from their male colleagues, there is absolutely no reason that women should be less successful than men in the world of business.

To maintain that there are "natural" differences in the personalities of men and women is dangerous. The debate between nature and nurture is a complicated one. It is nearly impossible to determine if personality traits are governed by chemical/biological urges or socially constructed rules. One thing that is certain, however, is that the rules that govern business are not natural. They are imposed from the outside and are completely artificial. Since this is the case, it should be possible for anyone to learn them given the proper exposure.

Some people may argue that women have certain character traits that make them less suited for work in the field of business, and that remains true regardless of whether or not these traits are present from birth or learned throughout life. For instance, some might say that women are not capable of being competitive and aggressive, and that it is irrelevant if this is caused by a hormone deficiency or by a difference in upbringing. In either case, history has proven this supposition to be wrong. Throughout time, the records have offered visions of women who were strong and powerful, who conquered and ruled nations and changed the course of history. Certainly there are some women who are not aggressive, but this is true of men as well. There are a large number of men who are not ruled by cutthroat, aggressive instincts. Thus it is true that certain people are not as likely to succeed in business, but it is not fair to apply this to women alone.

Another argument frequently posited by those who believe women are less likely to be successful in the world of business is that women must carry, deliver, and raise babies. If a woman decides to have a baby, it will take many months out of her life during which time she will be completely unable to work. Once she's had the baby, it will require her constant attention. Even when it is grown to become a toddler or a child, it is still likely to make frequent and unpredictable demands on her time.

Although all of this may be true, it should not stand in the way of women being successful in business. First of all, it is not a given that all women will choose to have children. Childbearing is not necessarily an innate urge that all women must respond to. Many women live full and fulfilled lives and never have children at all. Secondly, even if a woman should choose to have children, this need not necessarily interfere with her career. Pregnant women are still capable people, despite myths of their vulnerability. Furthermore, with constant advances in computers and fax machines, it is frequently possible for women to bring home much of their work. Ideally, having a baby will require as much time from the father as from the mother, yet nobody would suggest this as an excuse to keep men out of business.

There is no natural reason for women to be any less successful in business than men. If, for some reason, they are less accepted by their colleagues, taken less seriously, or paid smaller salaries for the same quality of work, the problem is with the system, and not with the business-women themselves. If the problem is with the system, then it can be changed, and perhaps eventually no one will question the validity of women as professional people.

Analysis of Sample Essay Scoring 5 to 6

The above essay is a "six"-rated or outstanding essay analyzing an issue. From the initial paragraph, the author explores the root of the issue, establishing a historical background for the world of business. In this opening statement, he or she chooses one side of the issue which is then maintained and effectively argued throughout the essay. Although the question is brief, it raises some complex gender issues, and the essayist recognizes this and proceeds to examine these issues in as much depth as the space allows. The organization of the essay is effective; each paragraph identifies a possible argument opposing the essayist's position. The paragraphs also give evidence and examples to disprove the arguments. The essay is written in simple, clear language, which helps to make the subtleties of the issue more easily understood and the position of the essayist more powerful.

ANALYSIS OF AN ARGUMENT ESSAY TOPIC

Sample Essay Response Scoring 5 to 6

The main point of this argument is to describe a turbulent moment in American history and to show how societal changes affected and reflected the nature of individual people. It shows how a society, over a period of time, acts like a piece of woven material in which one strand added or taken away can change the complexion of the whole. Specifically, the focus of the argument is on individual values, and how industrialization and urbanization created a new culture which was both a cause and a result of a new emphasis on appearances and salesmanship. This argument is effective in that it establishes a broad picture of a complex situation in a very short passage.

The greatest strength of this passage is that it manages to connect many different levels of a variegated circumstance in such a way that they seem simple to understand. Broad historical movements such as industrialization and urbanization are very complicated in their own right. They have a great impact on every aspect of a country, from the move removed political and economic domains right down to the most personal, such as diet choices or leisure time entertainment. In this argument, the author manages to choose one specific area in which change occurred and show in a logical sequence how historical events can cause changes in individuals.

The author of the passage goes beyond this to show not only how and why the change in values occurred, but also to show that once the value were different, they began to cause changes as well. This is a further example of how successfully the author crystallizes an involved and difficult situation. It is difficult to say which changes first, a society or what it holds valuable. These things are connected in a cycle of cause and effect in which it becomes impossible to separate the action from the actor. The author of the passage relays the vagaries and complexities of this relationship without making it seem impossibly confusing.

Perhaps, however, this ability to clearly and unequivocally state a case leads to oversimplification. It is one of the weaknesses of the argument that it takes for granted a certain acceptance of the part of the reader and does not fully explore the intricate subtleties of the topic it describes. Words such as "value" and "culture" constantly undergo a process of reevaluation. It is especially necessary in a historical piece to establish a definition for terms such as those found within the context of the historical period under discussion. In this way, the reader would not only have a clearer idea of the climate within which the argument was being made, but would also appreciate the fact that the author had addressed the potential complexities of the situation before he or she decided on a certain interpretation.

Another addition which might make this argument more convincing would be the use of specific examples. If we were given a concrete notion of what makes a culture "consumer," an actual example of contemporary advertisements, or a sense of precisely what had been valued as opposed to what was increasingly becoming valued, it might make the argument seem less vague and therefore more effective.

If the author does have a specific position on the topic, it is not overtly stated. If any judgment is implied, it is one of slight disapproval, but we glean this only from possible negative connotations of certain words and phrases. The most notable of these is the image of an individual selling him or herself, which is difficult to conceive in a positive light. Perhaps this seeming lack of bias is helpful in making the argument more convincing, because it is usually easier to trust the scholarly judgment of someone who is not distracted by a personal agenda.

We witness the strength of this argument because the author sets forth a position in such a way that it appears to be a simple statement of information. The passage deals with complex issues in such a way that they seem simple. It further presents a specific and a singular reading of a historical event as if it were the only possible one. Although these qualities may not produce as thorough a coverage or as unbiased a reading as possible, they are the essential elements of a good argument.

Analysis of Sample Essay Scoring 5 to 6

The above essay analyzing an argument is a "six"-rated or "outstanding" essay. In the first paragraph it effectively recognizes that the main point of the argument is the effect of a historical movement on individual people. It proceeds to show why the argument is convincingly written, citing first how the author expresses a large amount of material in a short space, and secondly how the author crystallizes confusing issues. It then suggests a possible flaw with the argument: it might oversimplify the situation. The next paragraph shows how this problem might be eliminated by the use of concrete examples. The penultimate paragraph explores a more general analysis of whether or not the author of the argument had a specific position on the topic, and this return to the general leads smoothly into the conclusion which ties back to the original paragraph, binding the piece together without restating what has already been said. All of the ideas in the piece are fully developed, carefully organized, and exhibit an understanding of the argument's most important elements.

GMAT CAT

Graduate Management Admission Test
Computer-Adaptive Test

Practice
Test 4

NOTE:

The following practice test contains more questions than the actual GMAT CAT. This is necessary to provide a score that is roughly comparable to the shorter computer-adaptive test. Although the format is different, this test will give you an accurate idea of your strengths and weaknesses, and provide guidance for further study.

PRACTICE TEST 4

Section 1

(Answer sheets appear in the back of the book.)

TIME: 25 Minutes
23 Questions

> **DIRECTIONS:** Each passage is followed by questions based on its content. After reading the passage, choose the best answer to each question. Answer all questions based on what is indicated or implied in that passage.

England became unified late in the 15th century. On Bosworth Field, in 1485, Henry Tudor put an end to the civil strife of the Wars of the Roses and crowned himself Henry VII. Forcefully bringing recalcitrant nobles to heel, he strengthened his authority. For the first time in nearly a century, the country had stability in government and a considerable degree of peace and prosperity. Henry, therefore, could devote his attention to the promotion of commerce. He encouraged English merchants to enter foreign trade, supported the formation of trading companies, and restricted the activities of the foreign merchants in London and Bristol, who had monopolized trade. Columbus even sent his brother to England when he failed to obtain support from the Portuguese or Spanish Kings for his proposal that Cathay could be reached by sailing west across the Atlantic. Henry VII agreed to finance the voyage and urged Columbus to come at once to England. But, before the latter left Spain, the Spanish monarchs experienced a change of heart and supported the voyage that was to give Spain an empire.

Meanwhile, Henry VII never gave up his hope of obtaining for England a share of the rich Eastern trade. British merchants established a trade link with Iceland about 1490. And, encouraged by news of Columbus' voyage, on March 5, 1496, Henry VII granted letters patent to the "well-beloved John Cabot" and his three sons to sail across the Atlantic to Asia. An Italian-born navigator, Cabot had lived in England since 1484. As a youth, he had visited the East, and when he arrived in London he had already decided that an all-water route could be found to the trading centers there. He may have made a few trips to Iceland before the King commissioned his transatlantic voyage.

In May of 1497, Cabot left Bristol with a crew of 18 and, after a voyage of 52 days across the North Atlantic, landed on Cape Breton Island and took possession of the land for Henry VII. From there, he explored several islands in the Gulf of St. Lawrence and in August returned to England and the praise of Henry VII, who granted him new letters patent. When Cabot sailed again, in 1498, he had perhaps 5 or 6 ships, whose crews totaled some 300 men. The King personally financed a substantial portion of the expedition's cost. On his second voyage, Cabot probably explored the North American coast from Newfoundland south to the Delaware or Chesapeake Bays.

Having failed to find the shores of Cathay (China) or Cipango (Japan), the English turned in the opposite direction. Henry VII's son, Henry VIII — better known for his marital involvements and his break with the Pope — enthusiastically began to build "a fleet the like of which the world has never seen." John Cabot's son, Sebastian, became a renowned navigator. After serving Spain for a number of years, he returned to England and opened the northern sea-land route to Moscow. He also helped found the company of Merchant-Adventurers, predecessor of the Muscovy Company, and became its president for life.

Thus, for nearly a century, England's interest was diverted from the New World, and her energies were concentrated on the development of a commercial empire and a merchant fleet that became second to none in Europe. But John Cabot had given England a claim to the northern shores of the New World, and in the course of time the "sea dogs" and other English mariners were to breathe new life into it.

1.   The main purpose of the passage is to

   (A) recount the Cabots' contributions to England's commercial development.

   (B) demonstrate the farsightedness of the Tudor monarchs.

   (C) explain England's early involvement with the New World.

   (D) analyze the late 15th-century competition between England and Spain.

   (E) summarize the voyages of the earliest explorers.

2. Which of the following statements is best supported by information in the passage?

    (A) Henry VIII followed his father's policy of rapid exploration of the New World.

    (B) England's superior merchant fleet was established before her initial voyages to the New World.

    (C) Henry VIII's fame rests mainly on his establishment of a commercial empire.

    (D) Sebastian Cabot established a sea-land route to Moscow during Henry VIII's reign.

    (E) Henry VIII's development of a commercial empire depended on simultaneous exploration of the New World.

3. The author cites Columbus chiefly to

    (A) emphasize the competition between England and Spain.

    (B) illustrate the disloyalty of Spanish navigators.

    (C) demonstrate that England trailed her chief rivals in exploration.

    (D) illustrate Henry VII's interest in promoting commerce.

    (E) illustrate the international nature of late 15th-century exploration.

4. According to the passage, Sebastian Cabot and Christopher Columbus

    (A) competed with each other to find new routes to the New World.

    (B) discovered continents.

    (C) established trading companies.

    (D) worked for Spanish monarchs.

    (E) were born in Italy.

5. The author suggests that Henry VII's interest in navigation was chiefly

    (A) commercial.   (B) military.

    (C) political.   (D) educational.

    (E) adventurous.

6. According to the passage, Henry VII's policies included all of the following EXCEPT

   (A) financing of foreign-born voyagers.

   (B) use of force in subduing English nobles.

   (C) encouragement of foreign merchants in England.

   (D) formation of trading companies.

   (E) personal financing of expeditions.

7. Which of the following statements is best supported by information in the passage?

   (A) Some early voyagers were willing to serve whatever king would finance their expeditions.

   (B) Henry VII wished to reach the New World before Spain did.

   (C) Most early voyagers were not well compensated for their discoveries.

   (D) English monarchs were quick to recognize the importance of the discovery of the New World.

   (E) Patriotism appears to have been a major motivating factor in the lives of the early voyagers.

8. For the purposes of this passage, the end of the Wars of the Roses was important chiefly because

   (A) it established the Tudor dynasty in England.

   (B) it brought a benevolent king to the English throne.

   (C) the English immediately developed military supremacy in Europe.

   (D) it united England, Scotland, and Wales.

   (E) the ensuing peace allowed commercial development.

9. Which of the following statements is best supported by information in the passage? Voyages undertaken in Henry VIII's reign

   (A) increased England's commercial empire and her claim in the New World.

   (B) gave England military supremacy at sea over her chief rivals.

(C) did not strengthen England's claim in the New World, but enhanced her commercial empire.

(D) did not strengthen either England's commercial empire or her claim in the New World, both of which came much later.

(E) gave England both commercial and military supremacy in Europe, but not in the New World.

Over the time period from 1986 to 2000, projections by the U.S. Department of Labor suggest that the number of federal employees will continue to rise in the professional and technical categories while shrinking in the clerical fields. In the white-collar category, 17 out of 22 occupational groups will be adding workers, while among blue-collar jobs, 17 out of 23 will be losing jobs. Overall, there will be 157,000 new jobs in the white-collar group, while blue-collar jobs will shrink by 107,000. Some of the largest and fastest-growing federal occupations include medical personnel (+50,000), legal (+27,000), business and industry (including contracting, procurement, property management, and IRS agents) (+23,000), social scientists (+19,000), and investigators (+14,000). The biggest losers include general services and support (–13,000), mobile equipment operators (–10,000), industrial equipment operators (–10,000), and woodworkers (–7,000).

In 1987, blacks made up 16.8 percent of the federal workforce, far above their 11 percent share of the national workforce. Hispanics, by contrast, were 6.6 percent of the nation's employees, but only 5.1 percent of federal workers. The shares of both groups have been rising steadily over the last decade, and promise to increase further in the years ahead.

Both minority groups are still concentrated in the lowest paying and least-skilled jobs. Blacks are four to five times as likely to staff the lowest-ranking white- and blue-collar jobs as they are to fill high-level slots. Still, progress is occurring across the board, with the greatest gains coming in the middle ranks.

Since blacks will be some 17 percent of the net new entrants into the workforce (compared to their 17 percent share of the current federal workforce), while Hispanics will be nearly 29 percent (compared to their current 5 percent share), it is likely that the greatest increase in minority representation in the federal workforce over the coming decade will be among Hispanics. This should occur despite the considerable number of Hispanic workers who will not be eligible for federal employment because they are not yet U.S. citizens.

The one factor that could constrain the growth of Hispanic and black workers in the federal government may be the rising education and skill requirements of federal jobs. Although blacks within the federal government are better educated than other black workers within the economy, they have fewer years of schooling than white federal workers. Over the period between 1986 and 2000, federal jobs will require skill upgrading even greater than that of the rest of the economy.

10. The primary purpose of the passage is to

   (A) refute the theory that the federal government will continue to grow in an uncontrolled manner.

   (B) present various trends in federal employee composition and employment practices.

   (C) show that in order to compete effectively, federal employees will be forced into other jobs.

   (D) argue that the federal government contains workers that are more highly skilled than those in the general workforce.

   (E) explain the reasons why blacks make up a larger percentage of federal employees than do Hispanics.

11. The passage supplies information that would answer which of the following questions?

   (A) What federal agencies have set goals for hiring minorities?

   (B) To which federal agencies must individuals apply if they wish to be hired?

   (C) How widespread is the use of quotas in hiring minorities in the federal government?

   (D) What is the current educational level of blacks within the federal government?

   (E) How can blacks and Hispanics increase their chances of being federally employed?

12. According to the passage, how can blue-collar workers increase their earning power while in federal employment?

   I.   Apply for a position that is technical or scientific.

   II. Gain further training or education.

III. Become eligible for citizenship.

(A) I only   (B) II only

(C) I and II only   (D) I and III only

(E) I, II, and III

13. It can be inferred from the passage that

(A) federal jobs will comprise a greater percentage of white-collar jobs than found in the economy as a whole.

(B) the number of federal positions overall will be declining.

(C) in the federal government, more white-collar jobs will be lost than blue-collar jobs.

(D) racial discrimination is keeping blacks and Hispanics from holding more upper-level federal jobs.

(E) increases in seniority provide blue-collar workers with a security against losing federal employment.

14. The author would most likely agree that the probable cause for an increase in technical positions and a decrease in clerical positions is

(A) many federal jobs' being located in highly industrialized areas such as New York and Washington, D.C.

(B) the impact of automation in such formerly labor-intensive fields as data processing.

(C) losses of positions by the Selective Service System when the draft ended in 1973.

(D) a workforce that is less dependent on the need for a stable, lifetime occupation.

(E) competition for workers in a growing, globally-competitive market.

15. According to the author, which of the following statements is true?

(A) There is a greater concentration of black workers in the workforce as a whole than in federal jobs.

(B) The percentage of blacks hired in federal positions is expected to grow dramatically.

(C) The percentage of Hispanics applying for federal jobs is expected to decrease as they gain U.S. citizenship.

(D) Because Hispanics have a lower educational level than blacks, Hispanics have greater difficulty obtaining federal positions.

(E) It is expected that more Hispanics than blacks will be represented in the higher levels of federal positions.

16. The statement in the passage that the fastest-growing federal occupations are medical and legal leads to all of the following conclusions EXCEPT

(A) lack of law or medical degrees will decrease as a future applicant's chances of obtaining a federal position.

(B) because minorities do not pursue higher educational levels as consistently as whites, it will be more difficult for the government to hire minorities.

(C) the federal government will be seeking employees with advanced college degrees.

(D) women will have greater difficulty in securing employment with the federal government because they are less educated than all other minority groups.

(E) the aging population of military veterans as well as the increasing complexity and litigiousness of society will require more attention from the federal government.

17. The author of the passage would be most likely to agree with which of the following as the best way to fill the technical positions?

(A) Train existing employees for more complex skills and encourage higher education programs for minorities now in school.

(B) Change classifications and pay scales to whatever levels are necessary to encorage minority recruitment.

(C) Advertise heavily in areas of minority neighborhoods.

(D) Require cover letters, resumes, and related documents from applicants instead of a standard application form.

(E) Shorten the time between application and hiring so more applicants will be encouraged to wait for federal jobs.

18. In the passage, the author is primarily concerned with

    (A) presenting a commonplace idea and its inaccuracies.

    (B) summarizing the achievements of some people.

    (C) proposing a resolution to a conflict.

    (D) predicting a situation and its solutions.

    (E) raising new issues and exploring their implications.

Since the mid-19th century, more than 6 million small windmills, of less than 1 hp each have been built and used in the United States to pump water, generate electricity, and perform similar functions. Over 150,000 are still in operation.

Types commonly used to pump water have metal fan-blades, 12 to 16 feet in diameter, that are mounted on a horizontal shaft and have a tail-vane to keep the rotor facing into the wind. The shaft is connected to a set of gears and a cam that move a connecting rod up and down. This, in turn, operates a pump at the bottom of the tower. A 12-foot diameter rotor of this type develops about 1/6 hp in a 15 mph wind and can pump about 35 gallons of water a minute to a height of about 25 feet.

Small windmills used to generate electricity usually have two or three propeller-type blades that are connected by a shaft and gear train to a DC generator. They usually incorporate some type of energy storage system, often consisting of a bank of batteries.

Many water-pumping windmills are still in use in the western United States for watering stock on ranges in remote areas. However, most of the wind-powered electrical generators were displaced by centralized electric power after the Rural Electrification Administration was instrumental in providing cooperative utilities for most U.S. farms in the 1930s.

The largest operational wind-powered electric system that has been built to date was the Smith-Putnam machine. After a lengthy study in the 1930s, Palmer Putnam concluded that a large machine was required to minimize the cost of the electricity generated. With the assistance of the eminent Cal Tech aerodynamicist Theodore Von Karman, and various members of the MIT staff, he designed a large wind turbine to feed power into the existing electrical network of the Central Vermont Public Service Company. The S. Morgan Smith Company of York, Pennsylvania, constructed and operated the plant in the early 1940s. The two-bladed 175-foot diameter propeller-type rotor weighed 16 tons and operated at a rated speed of 28 rpm to produce 1.25 MW of AC power.

In March 1945, after intermittent operation over a period of several years, one of the blades broke off near the hub where a known weakness had previously been identified but had not been corrected because of wartime material shortages. A comprehensive economic study indicated that the plant, even if repaired, could not compete effectively, at that time, with conventional electrical generation plants, so the project was abandoned.

19. The primary purpose of the passage is to

    (A) show that windmills have no practical uses in modern society.

    (B) trace the decline of electricity-generating windmills in the U.S.

    (C) provide technical data to explain the functioning of windmills.

    (D) provide a brief history of recent windmill usage in the U.S.

    (E) argue for the continued use of windmills in the U.S.

20. The passage provides information that supports which of the following statements?

    I.   Water-pumping windmills require a small generator.

    II. Water-pumping windmills require at least two propeller-type fan-blades.

    III. Water-pumping windmills are currently more common than electricity-generating windmills.

    (A) I only   (B) II only

    (C) III only   (D) I and III only

    (E) I, II, and III

21. According to the passage, the Smith-Putnam project was abandoned chiefly because it

    (A) was mechanically defective.

    (B) was not economically feasible.

    (C) was not in high demand.

    (D) demanded constant maintenance.

    (E) could not produce large amounts of electricity.

22. From the information in the passage, it can be inferred that most of the 150,000 windmills still in operation in the U.S. are

    (A) infrequently used.

    (B) small wind-powered electrical generators.

    (C) owned by the Rural Electrification Administration.

    (D) part of a large, cooperative effort.

    (E) small water-pumping windmills.

23. According to the passage, the provision of cooperative utilities by the Rural Electrification Administration in the 1930s

    (A) led to the demise of all types of small windmills in the U.S.

    (B) made large windmills like the Smith-Putnam machine impractical.

    (C) made small water-pumping windmills obsolete.

    (D) made the Smith-Putnam project feasible.

    (E) resulted in a radical decline in the use of small electricity-generating windmills.

STOP

If time remains, you may go back and check your work.
When the time allotted is up, you may go on to the next section.

Section 2

TIME: 25 Minutes
20 Questions

DIRECTIONS: Each of the data sufficiency problems below contains a question and two statements, labeled (1) and (2), in which certain data are given. Decide whether the data given in the statements are sufficient for answering the question. Using the data given in the statements plus your knowledge of mathematics and everyday facts choose:

(A) if Statement (1) ALONE is sufficient, but Statement (2) alone is not sufficient to answer the question asked;

(B) if Statement (2) ALONE is sufficient, but Statement (1) alone is not sufficient to answer the question asked;

(C) if BOTH Statements (1) and (2) TOGETHER are sufficient to answer the question asked, but NEITHER statement ALONE is sufficient;

(D) if EACH statement ALONE is sufficient to answer the question asked;

(E) if Statements (1) and (2) TOGETHER are NOT sufficient to answer the questions asked, and additional data specific to the problem are needed.

NUMBERS: All numbers are real numbers.

FIGURES: A figure in this section will conform to the information given, but will not necessarily conform to the additional information given in the numbered Statements (1) and (2).

NOTES: Lines are straight if shown as straight, and angle measures are greater than zero.

The position of points, angles, regions, etc., exist in the order shown.

All figures lie in a plane unless otherwise stated.

Sample Question:

In the figure, the two circles are concentric (have the same center O) with radius x and y, where $x < y$. What is the area of the shaded region?

(1)   The sum of the two radii is 11 units.

(2)   The area of the smaller circle is $1/2$ of the area of the larger one.

Sample Explanation:

(C)   By Statement (1), $x + y = 11$. Since, Statement (1) gives no other information about x and y, you cannot find the areas of the two circles. Since the area of the shaded region is the difference of the two areas, Statement (1) alone is not sufficient. According to Statement (2), $\pi y^2 = 2\pi x^2$; therefore, the area of the region is $2\pi x^2 - \pi x^2 = \pi x^2$. Since (2) does not give the value of x, it is not possible to find the area of the shaded region using (2) alone. However, if we use (1) and (2) together, we get the two equations

$$y = 11 - x \text{ and } \pi y^2 = 2\pi x^2$$

from which we can solve for x by writing the single equation $\pi(11 - x)^2 = 2\pi x^2$.

1. What is x and y?

   (1) $\dfrac{x}{y} = \dfrac{x+1}{y+3}$

   (2) $x - 4 = y$

2. How many women work at Company Y?

   (1) 65% of the work force at Company Y are male.

   (2) Company Y employs 10,000 people.

3. What does AC equal?

   (1) $\angle ABC = 30°$

   (2) $AB = 3\sqrt{3}$

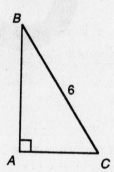

4. Is $\dfrac{x}{y}$ an integer?

   (1) $x + y = 9$

   (2) $2y - x = 0$

5. How many revolutions does a wheel make traveling from point A to point B.

   (1) The distance is 60π feet.

   (2) The diameter of the wheel is 6 feet.

6. Sequences A and B are related in the following manner:

   A. 1, 2, 3, 4, ...

   B. _, 4, _, _, ...

   What are the missing terms in sequence B?

   (1) The nth term of B is the square of the nth term of A.

   (2) The first term of B is 1.

7. A man is cutting his lawn which is in the shape of a rectangle where the width is 60 feet. How many laps around the yard must the man push the lawn mower before the region of the uncut grass is $^1/_2$ the size of the original lawn?

    (1) The width is $^3/_4$ the length.

    (2) The lawn mower cuts a 2 foot swath.

8. "All squares are rhombi" is a true statement. Is figure *A* a square?

    (1) Figure *A* is not a rhombus.

    (2) Figure *A* is a quadrilateral.

9. An observer at point *A* sees an object at point *B*. Asume the circle is the earth with a radius of 4,000 miles. How high is point *B* above the earth?

    (1) Measure of *AX* is 100 feet.

    (2) Measure of *AB* is 100 miles.

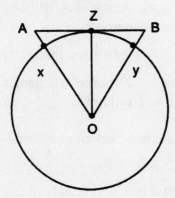

10. If *x* and *y* are real numbers, is $|x-y| = y-x$?

    (1) $y > x$

    (2) $|y| > |x|$

11. A geometric figure has rotational symmetry if it can be rotated through an angle of less than 360 degrees so that it coincides with its original position. Does Figure *A* have rotational symmetry?

    (1) The figure is a quadrilateral with 4 equal angles.

    (2) The figure has 2 sides parallel.

12. x_0 increases by 10 percent in a given year to become x_f. In the same year, y_0 increases by 30 percent to become y_f. What is x_0?

   (1) $x_0 = 2y_0 - 1$

   (2) $x_0 = x_f - 2$

13. A woman buys a stock which appreciates 5% during the first month she owns it. But alas, it depreciates the next month. At this point in time, what is her percent gain or loss?

   (1) The stock cost $100.

   (2) The stock depreciated 5% the second month.

14. The number 14 _ _ 61 has two missing digits. What is the number?

   (1) The sum of the number's digits is 28 and the second missing digit is a perfect square.

   (2) The missing digits differ by two.

15. In his last basketball game Albert shot 10 freethrows. What was the chance he made his first freethrow?

   (1) Albert has made 60 out of his last 80 freethrows.

   (2) Albert has played in 20 basketball games during the last two months and made 60 freethrows.

16. A structure has a square base and an equilateral top. (See the figure.) What is the length of x?

   (1) The distance from E to $\overline{CD}$ is 6 feet.

   (2) The area of the square is $(^4/_3 \sqrt{3})$ times bigger than the area of the triangle.

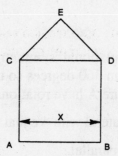

17. In pentagon *ABCDE* what is the value of *x*?

    (1) All sides are equal.

    (2) The measures of the interior angles are in the ratio 2:3:4:5:6 starting with *A*.

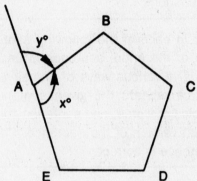

18. Does $y = 4$?

    (1) $y^2 - 16 = 0$

    (2) $y^2 - 2y = 8$

19. "All squares are rhombi" is a true statement. Is figure A a square?

    (1) Figure A is not a rhombus.

    (2) Figure A is a quadrilateral.

20. Consider the path of a ball on a billiard table (no pockets) starting from the lower-left corner and making 45 degree angles with the sides. The ball stops when it strikes any corner. After how many bounces will the ball stop in the upper-right corner?

    (1) The table's sides are of equal length.

    (2) The table's area is 16 feet.

STOP

If time remains, you may go back and check your work.
When the time allotted is up, you may go on to the next section.

Section 3

TIME: 25 Minutes
22 Questions

DIRECTIONS: In each of the following sentences, some part of the sentence or the entire sentence is underlined. The five answer choices give various ways of phrasing the underlined part. The first choice repeats the given sentence. Pay attention to grammar, choice of words, and sentence construction in order to select the best version of the sentence. Choose (A) if you think the given sentence is correct.

---

1. Membership in the United Nations is open to all nations <u>who agree to abide by the conditions</u> in the United Nations Charter.

    (A) who agree to abide by the conditions

    (B) abiding by the conditions

    (C) that agree to abide by the conditions

    (D) with conditions of agreement

    (E) having reached an agreement

2. In England the nineteenth century began on a note of optimism and idealism <u>ending in questioning and indifference</u>.

    (A) ending in questioning and indifference

    (B) ending with questions and some indifference

    (C) and ending in questioning and indifference that some noted

    (D) it was noted that indifferent questioning ended the century

    (E) but ended on a note of questioning and indifference

3. The Lionel Chamber of Commerce <u>has come up with a very original and innovative method</u> of advertising the city's advantages to new businesses.

    (A) has come up with a very original and innovative method

    (B) has come up with an original as well as an innovative method

(C) coming up with an original and innovative method

(D) has come up with an original and innovative method

(E) has coming up a very original and very innovative method

4. <u>In order to qualify for the job, an applicant must be 21 or older, have their own transportation, and pass a simple test.</u>

(A) In order to qualify for the job, an applicant must be 21 or older, have their own transportation, and pass a simple test.

(B) In order to qualify for the job, applicants must be 21 or older, have their own transportation, and pass a simple test.

(C) Qualifications for the job include being 21 or older, having his or her own transportation, and passing a simple test.

(D) Being 21 or older, having your own transportation, and passing a simple test in order to qualify for the job.

(E) Qualifying for the job includes being 21 years of age or older, possessing a means of transportation during period of employment, and taking and passing a simple test.

5. Most of the 25,000 wild species of orchids are <u>hardy, disease-resistant, long-lived plants</u>.

(A) hardy, disease-resistant, long-lived plants

(B) hardy and live a long time

(C) hardy, resist disease, and live a long time

(D) known to be resistant plants with long lives

(E) plants which are known to be hardy, disease-resistant, and long-lived

6. <u>The orchid is one of the most large and varied plant families in the world</u>.

(A) The orchid is one of the most large and varied plant families in the world.

(B) One of the most varied and largest plant families in the world are the orchids.

(C) Orchids are known to be large and varied in their varieties.

(D) One of the most large and most varied plant families in the world are the orchids.

(E) The orchid is one of the largest and most varied plant families in the world.

7. Growing on nearly every continent in the world, <u>most of us think of orchids as only a fragile, tropical flower</u>.

(A) most of us think of orchids as only a fragile, tropical flower.

(B) most of us are thinking of orchids as only a fragile, tropical flower.

(C) most of only think of orchids as only a fragile, tropical flower.

(D) orchids are considered by most of us as only a fragile, tropical flower.

(E) orchids are only thought to be flowers growing in a fragile, tropical climate.

8. People's digging up the Showy Lady's Slipper, a variety of orchid, <u>is destroying wild orchids, in spite of the fact that</u> they are nearly impossible to transplant.

(A) is destroying wild orchids, in spite of the fact that

(B) is destroying wild orchids because

(C) are destroying wild orchids because of the fact that

(D) are in the process of destroying the wild orchids taking into consideration that

(E) have been destroying wild orchids instead of seeing that

9. <u>The age of sixty-five having been reached</u>, Leo decided to retire to his home on Lake Livingston.

(A) The age of sixty-five having been reached

(B) Having reached the age of sixty-five

(C) After reaching age sixty-five

(D) At sixty-five years, reaching the age

(E) The age of sixty-five being reached

10. In the Northwest and upper Midwest United States, the plant purple loosestrife <u>is strangling native vegetation, pushing out wild animals, and clogging open water</u>.

    (A) is strangling native vegetation, pushing out wild animals, and clogging open water.

    (B) has strangled native vegetation, pushed out wild animals, and is clogging open water.

    (C) is strangling native vegetation, is also pushing out wild animals, and is furthermore clogging open water.

    (D) has been strangling, pushing out, and clogging native vegetation, wild animals, and open water, respectively.

    (E) has been strangling native vegetation, as well as pushing out wild animals, and also clogging open water.

11. <u>Purple loosestrife's having the botanical name of</u> *Lythrum salicaria,* from the Greek word meaning blood or gore, symbolic of the flower's magenta color.

    (A) Purple loosestrife's having the botanical name of

    (B) Purple loosestrife's has the botanical name of

    (C) Because purple loosestrife has the botanical name of

    (D) Purple loosestrife, having the botanical name of,

    (E) The botanical name for purple loosestrife is

12. <u>Because it had grown so profuse</u> in major river drainage systems, legislators in the states of Wisconsin, Minnesota, and Illinois have approved laws to control purple loosestrife.

    (A) Because it had grown so profuse

    (B) Because it has grown so profusely

    (C) Seeing as how it had become so profuse

    (D) Profusely growing

    (E) When it is grown profusely

13. <u>Actions to control purple loosestrife include digging up</u> the entire plant, but this method is not realistic.

  (A) Actions to control purple loosestrife include digging up

  (B) Actions to control purple loosestrife includes digging up

  (C) Digging up is one of the actions to control purple loosestrife

  (D) Among the actions to control purple loosestrife include digging up

  (E) Actions include digging up purple loosestrife to achieve a control of

14. <u>If I had had a map and compass,</u> I would have been able to find camp more readily.

  (A) If I had had a map and compass

  (B) If I would have had a map and compass

  (C) Having had a map and compass

  (D) A map and compass having been readily available

  (E) If I had a map and compass

15. <u>They say that the Norman Conquest took place</u> in 1066 when William, Duke of Normandy sailed his army across the English Channel.

  (A) They say that the Norman Conquest took place

  (B) They now say that the Norman Conquest took place

  (C) The Norman Conquest began

  (D) When the Norman Conquest began

  (E) The Norman Conquest beginning

16. The U.S. Department of Agriculture <u>have scientists conducting tests hoping to develop kelp as a food product.</u>

  (A) have scientists conducting tests hoping to develop kelp as a food product.

  (B) have scientists conducting tests that hope to develop kelp as a food product.

  (C) scientists have tests conducting how to develop kelp as a food product.

(D) tests by scientists develop kelp as a food product during tests.

(E) has scientists conducting tests in order to develop kelp as a food product.

17. In the new *Outdoor Sportsman* magazine <u>I read where two of the authors are both</u> instructors at the Colorado Outdoor Leadership School.

(A) I read where two of the authors are both

(B) I read that two of the authors are both

(C) it says that two authors are

(D) I read that two authors are

(E) two authors of are each

18. <u>If you go scuba diving, one should probably</u> not go underwater without a buddy.

(A) If you go scuba diving, one should probably

(B) If you go scuba diving, you probably should

(C) If a person goes scuba diving, they should probably

(D) When going scuba diving, he or she probably should

(E) In case you goes scuba diving, he or she should probably

19. <u>Because the number of licensed hunters in this county has decreased,</u> the deer population has grown.

(A) Because the number of licensed hunters in this county has decreased

(B) Seeing as how the number of deer hunters in this county have decreased

(C) As the number of deer hunters in this county is decreasing

(D) Being that a number of deer hunters in this county is decreasing

(E) In order for the number of deer hunters in this county to have decreased

20. <u>Less hunters mean less concern for potentially weaker government laws governing hunting</u>.

(A) Less hunters mean less concern for potentially weaker government laws governing hunting.

(B) Fewer hunters mean less concern for potentially weaker government laws governing hunting.

(C) Fewer hunters mean less concern for potentially weaker laws governing hunting.

(D) Fewer hunters means fewer concern for potentially weaker laws governing hunting.

(E) Fewer hunters means fewer concerns for laws that could be weaker in governing hunting.

21. It is vital that young hunters take a course that educates them <u>as to how man has always been both a predator and a steward of the resources</u>.

   (A) as to how man has always been both a predator and a steward of the resources.

   (B) in always having been a predator and a steward of the resources.

   (C) about how man is a predator and a steward of the resources.

   (D) in being a predator and always being a steward of the resources.

   (E) about man's always having been both a predator and a steward of the resources.

22. Ethics charges against a former member of a prominent law firm in New York <u>has been considered</u> as part of the ongoing investigations of the government.

   (A) has been considered   (B) is being considered

   (C) to be considered   (D) have been considered

   (E) have considered

STOP

If time remains, you may go back and check your work.
When the time allotted is up, you may go on to the next section.

Section 4

TIME: 25 Minutes
16 Questions

DIRECTIONS: Solve each problem using space on the page for scratchwork. Indicate the best answer from the choices given.

NUMBERS: All numbers used are real numbers.

FIGURES: Figures accompanying problems in this section provide information useful in solving the problems. They are drawn as accurately as possible; however, when a figure is not drawn to scale, more information will be provided. It is given that all figures lie in a plane unless otherwise stated.

---

1. At a certain restaurant the cost of 3 sandwiches, 7 cups of coffee, and 4 pieces of pie is $10.20, while the cost of 4 sandwiches, 8 cups of coffee, and 5 pieces of pie is $12.25. What is the cost of a luncheon consisting of one sandwich, one cup of coffee, and one piece of pie?

    (A) $2.00   (B) $2.05

    (C) $2.10   (D) $2.15

    (E) $2.25

2. A farmer planted corn and oats. The ratio of the number of acres of corn to the number of acres of oats was 3 to 5. He planted 225 acres of oats. How many acres of corn did he plant?

    (A) 135   (B) 150

    (C) 160   (D) 265

    (E) 375

3. If $x + y = 7$ and $x = y - 3$, what is the value of x?

    (A) -5 (B) -2

    (C) 0   (D) 2

    (E) 5

4. If the numbers represented by points C and D are multiplied together, what point best represents the product?

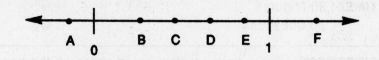

(A) A   (B) B

(C) C   (D) E

(E) F

5. A jug will hold $2/3$ gallon of punch. How much punch is in the jug when it is $3/4$ full?

(A) $5/7$ gallon   (B) $1/2$ gallon

(C) $1/4$ gallon   (D) $2/3$ gallon

(E) $1/12$ gallon

6. How much time is left on the parking meter pictured below?

(A) 8 minutes

(B) 9 minutes

(C) 10 minutes

(D) 12 minutes

(E) 15 minutes

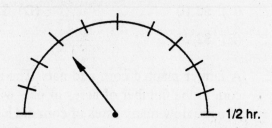

7. Mary has $29^1/_2$ yards of material available to make uniforms. Each uniform requires $3/4$ yard of material. How many uniforms can she make and how much material will she have left?

(A) 39 uniforms with $1/3$ yard left over

(B) 39 uniforms with $1/4$ yard left over

(C) 39 uniforms with $1/2$ yard left over

(D) 27 uniforms with $1/3$ yard left over

(E) 27 uniforms with $1/2$ yard left over

8. Ms. Jones received a 10% salary increase each of the last two years. If her annual salary this year is $41,745, what was her annual salary two years ago?

    (A) $34,500   (B) $33,813.45

    (C) $33,396   (D) $34,000

    (E) $34,750

9. $m(\angle A) + m(\angle C) =$

    (A) $160°$

    (B) $180°$

    (C) $190°$

    (D) $195°$

    (E) $200°$

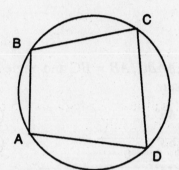

10. If $\dfrac{7a - 5b}{b} = 7$, then $\dfrac{4a + 6b}{2a} =$

    (A) $\dfrac{15}{4}$.   (B) 4.

    (C) $\dfrac{17}{4}$.   (D) 5.

    (E) 6.

11. $\dfrac{2^{100} + 2^{98}}{2^{100} - 2^{98}} =$

    (A) 2^{198} (B) 2^{99}

    (C) 64   (D) 4

    (E) $\dfrac{5}{3}$

12. The area of the shaded region is

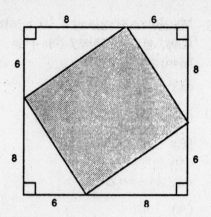

(A) 25 sq. units.

(B) 36 sq. units.

(C) 49 sq. units.

(D) 100 sq. units.

(E) not given.

13. If in $\triangle ABC$, $AB = BC$ and angle A has measure $46°$, then angle B has measure

(A) $46°$.   (B) $92°$.

(C) $88°$.   (D) $56°$.

(E) $23°$.

14. In the figure shown, $\triangle ABC$ is an equilateral triangle. Also, $AC = 3$ and $DB = BE = 1$. Find the perimeter of quadrilateral $ACED$.

(A) 6

(B) $6\frac{1}{2}$

(C) 7

(D) $7\frac{1}{2}$

(E) 8

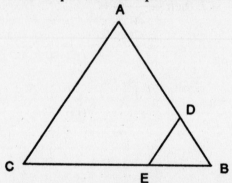

15. Pipe A can fill a tank in 6 hours. Pipe B can fill the same tank in 4 hours. If a drain that can empty the tank in 3 hours is left open, how long will it take to fill the tank using pipes A and B together?

(A) 5 hours   (B) 7 hours

(C) 8 hours   (D) 12 hours

(E) 13 hours

16. Thirty-four students are enrolled in technical writing, statistics, history, or a combination of any two, and no one in technical writing is also taking statistics or enrolled in all three classes. How many are just taking history, if the class size for each class is 15?

    (A) 4   (B) 5

    (C) 6   (D) 9

    (E) 10

STOP

If time remains, you may go back and check your work.
When the time allotted is up, you may go on to the next section.

Section 5

TIME: 25 Minutes
16 Questions

DIRECTIONS: For each question in this section, select the best answer.

---

1. Bill: New math began in the late 1960s. Achievement test scores showed that students were not doing as well with the new math as with old math. The new math had to be removed from the school.

    Jane: Wrong! The tests used measured traditional items, not the thinking skills encouraged with the new math. There are many good remnants of the new math still found in the math currently being taught.

    Which of the following best describes the weak point in Bill's claim on which Jane focuses?

    (A) The time that the new math was taught was a disruptive time in American history.

    (B) Thinking skills were not encouraged with the old math.

    (C) Tests used were not valid since they did not measure all the content of the new math.

    (D) New math is out of the schools for good.

    (E) Students are doing better with the new math than with the old math.

2. June weighs more than Kirt.

    Lulu weighs more than Meg.

    Meg weighs less than Nell.

    Kirt weighs the same as Nell.

    If the above information is true, which of the following is also true?

    (A) Lulu weighs more than Nell.

    (B) Lulu weighs more than June.

(C) Kirt weighs less than Lulu.

(D) June weighs more than Meg.

(E) Kirt weighs less than Meg.

3. Which of the following can be inferred from the passage?

Supply and demand can be easily demonstrated with the market for onions as an example. Higher prices encourage farmers to produce more onions; low prices discourage production. The consumers' reaction when the price is low is that they want a great many onions. At high prices, the consumer uses other vegetables instead. Equilibrium is when supply and demand are equal.

(A) If the price is too high, farmers will produce an insufficient quantity of onions for the customers.

(B) Competition among farmers when prices are already high will force the price up.

(C) If the price is too low, consumers will not demand a large quantity of onions.

(D) The saturation of the market with onions will force the price up.

(E) The scarcity of onions will drive the price up.

4. Public governments define certain acts as crimes, govern behavior, regulate businesses, and set standards. Private governments (a corporation, a school, a labor union, a family) may fine, suspend, or expel a disobedient member.

Which of the following can be most reliably inferred from the passage above?

(A) Private governments take their authority from public governments, so in this private governments may be empowered to execute offenders.

(B) Only a public government can legally use force, imprison, or execute an offender.

(C) Private government may legally execute an offender on occasion in our country.

(D) The jurisdiction of private government is all the individuals within a certain geographical area—a nation, a state, a province, a town.

(E) Public government rules only the members of a particular group, like a corporation.

Questions 5 – 6 are based on the following.

Seven former prison inmates testified at the town meeting at the request of town officials. The seven stated that the physical facilities at the local incarceration center were substandard; four presented evidence that the accommodations were so bad that their health was endangered. The former inmates suggested that unless something were done soon, a riot such as one in the neighboring county might result. If better facilities are to be provided, however, taxes may have to be increased. Several local citizens stated that they are concerned about increasing their tax rate solely on the word of convicted felons.

5. The method of attacking the charges of former inmates is to

(A) attack the character of the opponents rather than their claim.

(B) imply an analogy between their demands and the riots in another county.

(C) point out the inmates' claims imply a dilemma.

(D) show that the inmates' claims lead to an absurd conclusion.

(E) show that the prisoners' demands in a neighboring county were not met before the riot.

6. The former inmates could effectively defend their position against the townspeople's strategy by pointing out that

(A) the expertise of those suggesting reform is outstanding.

(B) they are neither inept or immoral.

(C) the practical renovation will not require tax increase.

(D) the riots in the next county were caused by similar concerns and actions.

(E) the fact that riots were caused by similar concerns in one place does not mean that they would necessarily result in this instance.

Questions 7 – 8 are based on the following:

In 1985 eight mummified bodies originally found in the 1970s in Greenland were subjected to careful analysis. The bodies—five in one place, three in another—were found in chambers in the rocks. The bodies were so well-preserved that at first the six-month-old infant was believed to be a doll. The bodies were placed in the chamber about 1475.

7. Which of the following reasons for the bodies being in the caves is best supported by the evidence presented above?

   (A) The people drowned and the bodies washed into the crevices near the sea.

   (B) The people died of starvation in the small caves.

   (C) The people died from smallpox.

   (D) The people had huddled there and had frozen to death.

   (E) The bodies of the dead had probably been placed there by family members.

8. Which of the following theories best explains why the bodies were preserved so well without embalming?

   (A) The hot, dry air of Greenland preserved the bodies.

   (B) Dehydrating winds and low temperatures preserved the bodies.

   (C) The bodies had only recently been placed there.

   (D) The moisture near the shore preserved the bodies.

   (E) Lightning striking the area preserved the corpses.

9. Good Health is the nutritional supplement preferred by the 400 accomplished or professional athletes who subscribe to this paper, the HEALTH BULLETIN. Shouldn't you give their preferred supplement a try?

   A reader who is not a professional athlete would be most likely to purchase the nutritional supplement if he or she drew which of the following questionable conclusions invited by the advertisement?

   (A) Among nutritional supplements, Good Health is the most nutritionally complete.

(B) Professional athletes cannot do their jobs properly without taking Good Health.

(C) The advertisement is placed where those who will be likely to read it are accomplished or professional athletes.

(D) The athletes mentioned were helped to become accomplished or professional athletes by using Good Health.

(E) Only those who will in fact become accomplished or professional will read the advertisement.

10. Psychologists continue to debate the issue of whether people have a dominant side of their brain which controls reasoning and actions or whether both sides of the brain work together. Proponents of the split-brain theory suggest that a right-brained person is creative, intuitive since this individual uses the right hemisphere. On the other hand, they contend that the left-brained individual uses the verbal, language-oriented, logical hemisphere of the brain to control most of their actions/thinking.

Which of the following, if true, would strengthen the position of the opponents to the split-brain theory?

(A) When surgery is performed to disconnect the two sides of the brain, both sides continue to operate well—but not perfectly.

(B) When a patient has right hemisphere damage, no logical disorders are manifested.

(C) Because of the independent functions of the two hemispheres, an activity might engage one hemisphere of the brain and not another.

(D) The hemispheres operate independently because of specialized functions.

(E) It is impossible to educate one side of the brain without educating the other.

11. Health education needs to be instituted into preschool child development programs across our nation. Unless we can begin proper health habits in our citizenry at an early age, we cannot hope to see the health of adults and senior citizens improving in the future. Investing in preschool health education can benefit society as a whole and may result in a financial savings for taxpayers who now support the sick and disabled across the land.

Which of the following conclusions can most properly be drawn from the information above?

(A) Health education for young children tends to benefit these individuals.

(B) Health education for young children is likely to be accompanied by the creation of teaching jobs.

(C) Society should decrease the amount invested in the sick and disabled to encourage them to do what needs to be done on their own.

(D) Failure to provide health education for young children has been a cause of economic recession.

(E) Health education for young children can benefit the children as individuals and society as a whole.

12. Which of the following best completes the passage below?

In many advertisements the public encounters, messages to the subconscious mind are inserted to increase sales. Advertisements which are bright and colorful may appeal to many readers. Auditory stimuli (such as those found in songs and jingles) may appeal to others. Beneath this obvious sensory appeal there is the underlying goal of_____.

(A) making the advertisement colorful

(B) appealing to the auditory senses in magazine ads

(C) also appealing to the subconscious mind

(D) increasing the length of the periodical carrying the advertisement

(E) developing a new audience for the readers

13. Some growers have concluded that the rise in the price of onions means that the switch by some growers from onions to higher priced potatoes left those growers no better off than if none of them had switched; this conclusion, however, is unwarranted because it can be inferred to be likely that

(A) those growers could not have foreseen how high the price of onions would go.

(B) the initial cost involved in switching from onions to potatoes is substantial.

(C) the price of onions would not be as low if those growers had not switched crops.

(D) potato crops are as susceptible to being reduced by bad weather as are onion crops.

(E) as more growers turn to growing potatoes, potato supplies will increase and the price of potatoes will fall precipitously.

14. Concerned about recent news stories, the Department of Energy is encouraging the eleven states which house nuclear facilities (reactors, plants, weapons assembling stations, waste storage operations, and waste treatment processing) to monitor the facilities also.

Which of the following motives is most likely behind the action described above?

(A) Double monitoring is another example of governmental waste.

(B) Additional monitoring is an indication that the federal government does not have expertise in this area.

(C) Double monitoring was instituted to help to create additional jobs for the work force.

(D) Double monitoring is to assure the public and to insure the safety of the people.

(E) The states should not be involved in a federal project.

15. Industrialized nations of the world are said to have the world's highest standard of living. This means more goods are consumed there than in other nations.

Which of the following constitutes the most serious disadvantage in measuring a country on its standard of living alone?

(A) It does not show how people of that country lived prior to that time.

(B) It shows purchases by individuals and whether the items will be used by individuals or families.

(C) It shows how people actually live.

(D) The future may make life more unpleasant for underdeveloped countries.

(E) It does not show how the people actually live and ignores over-crowding and pollution.

16. To figure parents' expected contribution for college, one must consider several things. Parents' income (Andrea's parents earn $23,100), minus expenses (Andrea's parents' expenses are $21,322), plus assets ($26,525 for Andrea's parents) and minus other allowable deductions, of which Andrea's parents have several. Andrea's parents' expected contribution is $256.

Which of the following corrections of a figure appearing in the passage above, if it were the only correction that needed to be made, would most likely yield a new calculation showing that Andrea's parents' expected contribution is less than $256?

(A) Andrea's parents' income is $25,600.

(B) Andrea's parents' expenses are $20,000.

(C) Andrea's parents' assets are $28,000.

(D) Andrea's parents have no allowable deductions.

(E) Andrea's parents have an income of $20,000.

STOP

If time remains, you may go back and check your work.
When the time allotted is up, you may go on to the next section.

Section 6

TIME: 25 Minutes
16 Questions

DIRECTIONS: Solve each problem using space on the page for scratchwork. Indicate the best answer from the choices given.

NUMBERS: All numbers used are real numbers.

FIGURES: Figures accompanying problems in this section provide information useful in solving the problems. They are drawn as accurately as possible; however, when a figure is not drawn to scale, more information will be provided. It is given that all figures lie in a plane unless otherwise stated.

---

1. What number must be added to 28 and 36 to give an average of 29?

   (A) 23   (B) 32
   (C) 21   (D) 4
   (E) 5

2. A miller took $^1/_{10}$ of the wheat he ground as his fee. How much did he grind if a customer had exactly one bushel left after the fee had been subtracted?

   (A) $1^1/_9$ (B) $1^1/_{10}$
   (C) $1^1/_3$ (D) $1^1/_2$
   (E) $1^1/_5$

3. What is the measurement of x?

   (A) 30°
   (B) 60°
   (C) 90°
   (D) 120°
   (E) 150°

4. Carla is paid $5 per day plus $0.60 for each pizza she delivers. How many pizzas did she deliver if she earned $17.00 today?

   (A) 14   (B) 17

   (C) 20   (D) 26

   (E) 30

5. What is the formula for the volume of a rectangular box with square ends if the length is five times the width of the box?

   (A) $7w$ (B) $\dfrac{w^3}{5}$

   (C) $5w^3$ (D) $6w^3$

   (E) $7w^3$

6. If $X = 2.5642$ and $\overline{X}$ is the number obtained by rounding X to the nearest hundredth, then $X - \overline{X} =$

   (A) .0002   (B) .0042

   (C) .0358   (D) .0642

   (E) .5642

7. How many gallons of water must be added to 5 gallons of a 40% solution of solvent to produce a 25% solution of solvent?

   (A) 1.25   (B) 2

   (C) 3   (D) 6

   (E) 8

8. A square has its edge increased by 10%. By what percent is its area increased?

   (A) 21%   (B) 20%

   (C) 10%   (D) 100%

   (E) Cannot be determined

9. A pitcher holds 6 times as much water as a paper drinking cup. Three pitchers hold 39 ounces more than 5 drinking cups. How many ounces does a cup hold?

(A) 6   (B) 5

(C) 4   (D) 3

(E) 2

10. A man has $20,000 to invest. He invests $5,000 at 5% and $7,000 at 7%. In order to have a yearly income of $1,500, he must invest the remainder at

(A) 8%.   (B) 8.5%.

(C) 9%.   (D) 9.5%.

(E) 10%.

11. If $\dfrac{x}{y} = \dfrac{4}{5}$ then, in terms of y, what is $x - \dfrac{1}{y}$?

(A) $\dfrac{3y}{4}$ (B) $\dfrac{3}{4y}$

(C) $\dfrac{5y-1}{4y}$ (D) $\dfrac{4y^2-5}{5y}$

(E) $\dfrac{4y-1}{5y}$

12. If $a = 5^2 - 4^2$ and $b = 10^2 - 8^2$, evaluate $(\sqrt{a} - \sqrt{b})^2$.

(A) -27 (B) 9

(C) 1   (D) -3

(E) 729

13. Find the area of the shaded region in the figure below, given that $\overline{AB}$ = $\overline{CD}$ = 4 and $\overline{BC}$ = 8.

(A) 40π

(B) 32π

(C) 68π

(D) 76π

(E) 36π

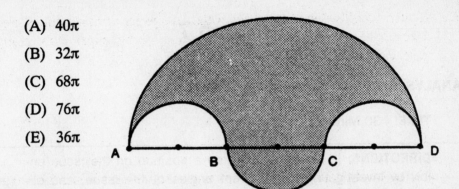

14. Cheryl covered a distance of 50 miles on her first trip. On a later trip she traveled 400 miles going 4 times as fast. Her new time as compared with the old time was

(A) four times as much.

(B) three times as much.

(C) twice as much.

(D) the same.

(E) half as much.

15. John and Mark both drive from one city to another. John drives 90 kph while Mark drives 100 kph. It takes John 40 minutes longer to complete the trip. How many kilometers apart are the cities?

(A) 90   (B) 100

(C) 300   (D) 540

(E) 600

16. At a garage sale, Sarah sold two kitchen gadgets at $2.40 each. Based on the cost her profit on one was 20% and her loss on the other was 20%. On the sale she

(A) gained 8¢.   (B) lost 8¢.

(C) broke even.   (D) gained 20¢.

(E) lost 20¢.

STOP

If time remains, you may go back and check your work.
When the time allotted is up, you may go on to the next section.

Section 7

ANALYSIS OF AN ISSUE ESSAY TOPIC

TIME: 30 Minutes

DIRECTIONS: In an essay, develop a position on the issue below by investigating the different angles of the issue, and explaining your thoughts on the topic. Remember, there is no one "correct" response to the essay topic.

Before starting, read the essay topic and its question(s). You may make preliminary notes in your test booklet before writing the actual essay. Be sure to write your essay on the lined pages provided at the back of the book.

Some publishers complain that the reduced rate at which public libraries buy new books unduly sours the market, and that copyright laws should require libraries to give suitable compensation based on ciculation. These publishers fail to acknowledge the role public libraries play in creating avid readers and therefore the book-buying market.

Which captures your interest, the complaint that libraries sour publishers' markets or the reply given? Defend your position, citing relevant reasons and/or examples taken from your own experience, reading, or personal observations.

STOP

Do not go on until you are instructed to do so. Use any remaining time to check your work on this portion of the test.

ANALYSIS OF AN ARGUMENT ESSAY TOPIC

TIME: 30 Minutes

> **DIRECTIONS:** In essay form, prepare a review on the position of the argument provided below. Before taking your own position on the argument's standpoint, it may be helpful to determine the method of thinking behind the argument itself. For example, consider alternative explanations to any assumptions the argument might make, and any evidence or examples that may strengthen or weaken the argument. Remember, there is no one "correct" response to the essay topic.
>
> Before starting, read the essay topic and its question(s). You may make preliminary notes in your test booklet before writing the actual essay. Be sure to write your essay on the lined pages provided at the back of the book.

Newspaper recycling is a wasteful exercise that should be abandoned. Recollected paper is so abundant that less than ten percent is ever put to a second use, and few dealers can survive the over-supplied market. America's recycling campaign has not prevented newspapers from filling our nation's garbage dumps—it has only made them more neatly stacked, at a cost which most towns must pass on to their citizens.

Discuss the degree to which you find this argument logically persuasive. In presenting your perspective, be certain to analyze the argument's use of evidence and line of reasoning. Also discuss what, if anything, would make the argument more solid and convincing, or would assist you to better judge its conclusion.

STOP

If time remains, you may go back and check your work.

PRACTICE TEST 4

ANSWER KEY

Section 1 — Reading Comprehension

1.	(C)	7.	(A)	13.	(A)	19.	(D)
2.	(D)	8.	(E)	14.	(B)	20.	(C)
3.	(D)	9.	(C)	15.	(E)	21.	(B)
4.	(D)	10.	(B)	16.	(D)	22.	(E)
5.	(A)	11.	(E)	17.	(A)	23.	(E)
6.	(C)	12.	(C)	18.	(D)		

Section 2 — Data Sufficiency

1.	(C)	6.	(A)	11.	(A)	16.	(A)
2.	(C)	7.	(C)	12.	(B)	17.	(B)
3.	(D)	8.	(A)	13.	(B)	18.	(C)
4.	(B)	9.	(C)	14.	(A)	19.	(A)
5.	(C)	10.	(A)	15.	(A)	20.	(A)

Section 3 — Sentence Correction

1.	(C)	7.	(D)	13.	(A)	19.	(A)
2.	(E)	8.	(B)	14.	(A)	20.	(C)
3.	(D)	9.	(C)	15.	(C)	21.	(E)
4.	(B)	10.	(A)	16.	(E)	22.	(D)
5.	(A)	11.	(E)	17.	(D)		
6.	(E)	12.	(B)	18.	(B)		

Section 4 — Problem Solving

1.	(B)	5.	(B)	9.	(B)	13.	(C)
2.	(A)	6.	(B)	10.	(A)	14.	(E)
3.	(D)	7.	(B)	11.	(E)	15.	(D)
4.	(B)	8.	(A)	12.	(D)	16.	(A)

Section 5 — Critical Reasoning

1.	(C)	5.	(A)	9.	(D)	13.	(D)
2.	(D)	6.	(A)	10.	(E)	14.	(D)
3.	(E)	7.	(E)	11.	(E)	15.	(E)
4.	(B)	8.	(B)	12.	(C)	16.	(E)

Section 6 — Problem Solving

1.	(A)	5.	(C)	9.	(D)	13.	(E)
2.	(A)	6.	(B)	10.	(D)	14.	(C)
3.	(B)	7.	(C)	11.	(D)	15.	(E)
4.	(C)	8.	(A)	12.	(B)	16.	(E)

DETAILED EXPLANATIONS OF ANSWERS

Section 1–Reading Comprehension

1. **(C)**

The passage explains how England's earliest involvement with the New World came about and why her claim was neglected for a hundred years. All of the other choices are directly or indirectly touched on in the passage, but none is the central organizing device of the passage.

2. **(D)**

Sebastian Cabot opened a sea-land route to Russia, part of Henry VIII's merchant fleet "the like of which the world has never seen." Henry VIII neglected further exploration of the New World because earlier voyages had not found a route to Asia; he chose to focus on building a commercial empire by looking east. His fame, however, rests more on his break with Rome and on his six marriages.

3. **(D)**

One of the ways Henry VII tried to promote commerce was to finance voyages; hence he agreed to finance Columbus. The author uses Columbus' request to illustrate Henry VII's (and England's) growing interest in commerce, not chiefly to indicate rivalries.

4. **(D)**

Both Columbus and Sebastian Cabot served Spain; later Cabot served England. Cabot's father was born in Italy. Columbus but not Cabot discovered a continent; Cabot but not Columbus established a trading company.

5. **(A)**

Henry VII financed voyages chiefly to promote commerce.

6. **(C)**

Henry VII placed restrictions on the activities of foreign merchants in England.

7. **(A)**

Columbus sought support from Portugal, Spain, and England; Sebastian Cabot served both Spain and England, hence not (E). (B) is incorrect (Henry was unaware of the New World). Whatever the financial status of other voyagers (the passage doesn't say), the Cabots were well-rewarded. English monarchs neglected their claims in the New World for a century.

8. **(E)**

The end of the Wars of the Roses resulted in a relative stability that allowed Henry VII to concentrate on commercial development. It did place the Tudors on the throne, but that is not its chief significance for this passage. It did not unite the three kingdoms, nor did England yet become militarily supreme in Europe. The passage does not indicate that Henry VII was a particularly benevolent monarch (he was not).

9. **(C)**

Voyages undertaken in Henry VIII's reign greatly increased England's commercial empire, but did not strengthen her claim in the New World (the voyages were east, not west). England's military supremacy at sea came later.

10. **(B)**

The primary purpose of this passage is to detail trends in job availability and hiring for the federal government. The passage does not deal with the problem of "uncontrolled" growth in federal government (A), nor is the mode of the passage persuasive. Even though it is stated that federal jobs will require a higher level of education, there is no indication that federal employees will be forced into jobs in the private sector (C). Although the article states that blacks within the federal government are better educated than their counterparts in the general workforce, and thus it may be inferred that federal employees are probably better educated than their counterparts in the general workforce, the main thrust of the article is not to argue this point (D). The article contains no explanation of why blacks make up a larger percentage than Hispanics (E). Despite the mention that many Hispanics are applying for citizenship, this factor should have no bearing on the population that currently hold citizenship, and this is the population underepresented in the federal government.

11. **(E)**

The article goes into some detail about how important an improved educational level is for minorities. The last paragraph, in particular, points out, "federal jobs will require skill upgrading" and that since blacks have fewer years of schooling than white workers, it will be imperative for blacks to get advanced education; the same, of course, can be applied to Hispanics since both minority groups are "concentrated in the lowest-paying and least-skilled jobs." Since there is no specific mention of agencies (for example, the Social Security Administration), choices (A) and (B) cannot be correct; however, the article does name some general professional areas, such as medical and legal. The article does not mention quotas (C), even though affirmative action plans have been in effect for some time. Although (E) blacks in the federal government "are better educated," the article does not give specific grade level or skills level.

12. (C)

The question asks how blue-collar workers can improve their position while employed by the federal government. There are two means—getting further training and applying for a technical or scientific position. Choice (C) contains both these alternatives. Only American citizens may be employed by the federal government, so any answer containing the requirement to gain citizenship must be considered incorrect.

13. (A)

If blacks working for the federal government, for example, are more highly educated than blacks in the workforce as a whole, and if future jobs will require even more education, it follows that a larger percentage of federal government jobs will consist of white-collar jobs than jobs found in the workforce as a whole. It does not appear from the statistics (B) that the number of federal positions will be declining, merely that the composition of these jobs will change. The article presents information to contradict (C), as white-collar jobs will be increasing. Information in the article seems to refute (D). Blacks are employed in greater numbers, but minorities are not; from this one may infer that more blacks than Hispanics are applying for federal jobs. This does not constitute discrimination. Although increases in seniority (E) cannot hurt, this factor alone will not enable a worker to keep a job that will be lost due to blue-collar job attrition.

14. (B)

The most likely reason for an increase in technical positions and a decrease in clerical positions is the increasing role of automation in today's business world. Computers have eliminated the need for a large bank of typists, for example, but have created jobs in the field of computer programming and servicing. Although it is certainly probable that more federal positions are available in Washington and New York (A), and that these areas are urban, changes in business practices and machinery have had more impact on job descriptions than mere location. Although large numbers of positions were certainly lost when the draft was cancelled (C), this event should have little or no bearing on the great shift in types of positions. Perceptions about lifetime employment (D) are changing. People used to anticipate working for one company for a lifetime, and being served for health care and retirement needs by that one company. Now, however, people are forced into changing occupations several times due to changing technologies. These factors do not preclude the need for stable lifetime employment. Indirectly, global competition has created more technology, but there is competition for trained workers (E) due to increased technology, not the other way around.

15. **(E)**
According to the article, it is probable that more Hispanics than blacks will be represented in higher levels of government. This is true because the Hispanics' share of entrants into the workforce will be nearly 29 percent, as compared to the blacks' 17 percent. Even if blacks comprise a greater percentage of federal jobs than statistically appearing in the general workforce, the Hispanic population will grow dramatically, much faster than the blacks' population, and therefore they should still theoretically outnumber blacks in the federal workforce. The article contains information that directly refutes (A); currently, a greater percentage of blacks are represented in federal jobs. Also, the article refutes (B); the level of employment is expected to remain constant at 17 percent. The article states that Hispanics (C) will grow in numbers. The article does not compare the educational levels of blacks and Hispanics (D).

16. **(D)**
The article does not address the educational levels of women. In fact, it is generally acknowledged that women have been entering the workforce in greater numbers, and that trend is expected to continue. Women will have to gain jobs by getting more education. The article states that law and medical positions will be increasing (A), so minorities will be hurt if they do not pursue advanced degrees. The author deals indirectly with the rate at which minorities pursue advanced degrees as compared to their white counterparts (B), and it can be inferred that the statement choice is probably true. In the article, it is stated that advanced degrees (C) will be a requirement for many more jobs. The options in choice (E) are not dealt with directly by the author, but they are logical assumptions one may make.

17. **(A)**

If higher educational and skill levels will be required, then a twofold program of training of existing employees and further education for incoming employees is the best choice. Although increasing pay (B) is helpful, a higher pay scale will also attract more whites to compete for available jobs. Advertising heavily in minority neighborhoods (C) is the next-best answer choice, and must certainly be employed by the federal government. Choice (D) will perhaps help in supplying more data (from resumes), but it is not as good a method as retraining. Shortening the time between application and acceptance (E) will help all job applicants, not just minorities.

18. **(D)**

The author is concerned with predicting a situation (higher standards for federal jobs) and its solutions (better levels of employment for minorities). Choice (A) is erroneous because the article does not deal with inaccuracies. Choice (B) is partially correct, because the article does mention the high percentage of blacks employed by the federal government, but it is not the best choice. Choice (C) does not apply to the article, as no conflicts are mentioned. Choice (E) is a possible correct answer, but the article does more than discuss implications; it presents some courses of action.

19. **(D)**

The passage traces the relatively recent use of windmills in the U.S., including both water-pumping and electricity-generating windmills. Its primary function is to supply information, not to demonstrate a thesis or advance an argument.

20. **(C)**

Water-pumping windmills are still used to water cattle, whereas electricity-generating windmills disappeared with the advent of the REA in the 1930s. Electricity-generating windmills require a generator; water-pumping ones do not, nor do they require more than a single fan.

21. **(B)**

The Smith-Putnam project was abandoned when studies showed it could not compete effectively in the marketplace (see the last paragraph).

22. **(E)**

Since the Smith-Putnam project failed and because small electricity-generating windmills disappeared in the 1930s, it is safe to conclude that the windmills still in use are small water-pumping ones, as the passage suggests in the fourth paragraph.

23. **(E)**
The chief effect of the provision of cooperative utilities was to radically reduce the number of small electricity-generating windmills in use. It did not necessarily influence the use of water-pumping windmills; it may have made large windmill projects feasible, but there is no suggestion of that in the passage.

Section 2–Data Sufficiency

1. **(C)**

   Statement (1) gives us

   $$\frac{x}{y} = \frac{x+1}{y+3}.$$

   Cross-multiplication gives us

   $$xy + 3x = xy + y$$

   or $\quad\quad\quad 3x = y.$

   Hence Statement (1) is insufficient to solve for x and y.

   Statement (2) gives us

   $$x = y + 4$$

   and is also insufficient to solve for x and y.

   Together we get

   $$3x = y$$

   $$x = y + 4.$$

   Substituting the latter into the former

   $$3(y + 4) = y$$

   or $\quad\quad 3y + 12 = y$

   or $\quad\quad\quad\quad y = -6$

   $$x = -2$$

2. **(C)**

   From Statement (1) you can obtain the percentage of women at Company Y. Combined with Statement (2) the number of women working at Company Y can be calculated.

3. **(D)**

   From Statement (1) and use of 30°–60°–90° triangles and the given information, the hypotenuse AC can be found. From Statement (2) the Pythagorean theorem can be used to find AC.

4. **(B)**

From statement (2) one can solve for x in terms of y to determine that x/y is an integer. There is not enough information in Statement (1) to determine if x/y is an integer.

5. **(C)**

From Statement (2) the circumference of the wheel can be determined. With Statement (1) and Statement (2) the number of revolutions the wheel would travel can be determined by dividing the total distance by the circumference (the distance the wheel would travel in one revolution).

6. **(A)**

Statement (1) is sufficient since

$$1^2 = 1, 2^2 = 4, 3^2 = 9, 4^2 = 16, \text{etc.}$$

Statement (2) is insufficient since the nth term, $n > 2$, of sequence B can be any number.

7. **(C)**

The width of the lawn is 60 feet. Statement (1) provides us with a clue to get the length of the lawn. Without this information the total area of the lawn is not known.

Statement (2) gives us the information of how much of the lawn is cut by the lawn mower.

Hence the answer is (C) because without these two separate pieces of data the problem does not have sufficient information.

Statement (1) gives us the following dimensions of the lawn (see the figure below).

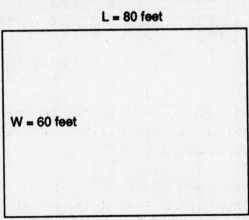

L = 80 feet

W = 60 feet

Area is determined by length times the width. From Statement (1) the original area is 4,800 square feet ($w = \frac{3}{4}l$ implies $60 = \frac{3}{4}l$ implies $l = 80$, and $80 \times 60 = 4,800$). A region $\frac{1}{2}$ the size of the original is 2,400 square feet. Statement (2) now permits us to determine the number of laps to make the new area 2,400 square feet. Each lap removes 4 feet of grass from each the length and width.

Hence, the total area is $60' \times 80' = 4,800$ sq. ft. Statement (2) tells us how much the length l and the width w is reduced by each lap around the yard.

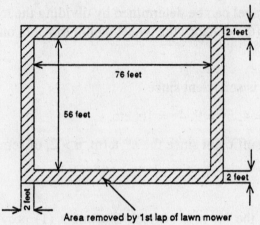

Area removed by 1st lap of lawn mower

After 5 laps we get the following picture:

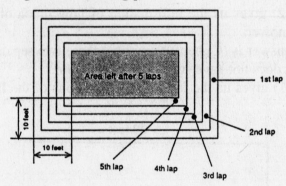

or

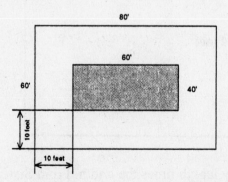

Now, the area left over (shaded) has length 60' and width 40'. Hence, the total left-over area = $60 \times 40 = 2,400$ sq. ft. This is $\frac{1}{2}$ of the original 4,800 sq. ft. Hence, 5 laps is the correct answer.

8. **(A)**   Look at a Venn diagram, where

Q = quadrilaterals

R = rhombi

S = squares

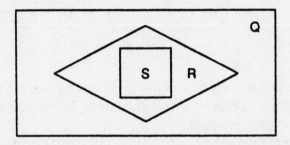

Statement (1) implies that A is not a square. So Statement (1) gives sufficient information to answer the question. Statement (2) only permits one to conclude A is in the set of Q but we cannot answer whether A is a square.

9. **(C)**
Statement (1) gives sufficient information to find the measure of AZ (Pythagorean theorem). The angles at point O are not necessarily equal. Therefore, the measure of BY is not necessarily the same height as AX. By including Statement (2), the measure of BZ can be found by subtracting the measure of AZ from 100 miles and again applying the Pythagorean theorem to find the measure of BY.

With Statement (1) alone we have the following diagram.

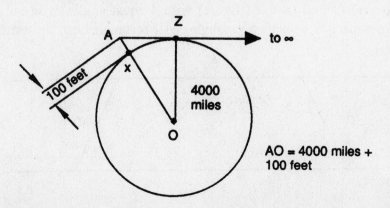

Hence an observer at point A can see an object at B which can lie at any position between Z and ∞ to the right. As the position of B is indeterminate, Statement (1) by itself is not sufficient to solve the problem.

With Statement (2) alone we get the following picture.

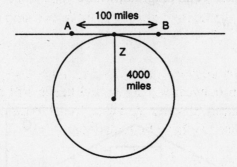

Note that the line AB could be slid to any position along the tangent at Z as long as Z is located between A and B. Hence, Statement (2) alone is not sufficient to solve the problem.

Statement (1) fixes the position of A and then Statement (2) fixes the position B with respect to Z. Hence, a combination of Statements (1) and (2) gives sufficient information to solve the problem.

10. **(A)**

The absolute value of a number is positive. Since $y > x$, $y - x > 0$, so

$$|x - y| = y - x,$$

i.e., Statement (1) alone is sufficient. Statement (2) is insufficient. By counter-example, let $y = -3$ and $x = -2$. Clearly

$$|-3| > |-2|,$$

but $\quad |3 - (-2)| \neq -3 - (-2)$.

11. **(A)**

A quadrilateral (4-sided figure) with 4 equal angles must be a rectangle (a square is a special rectangle). All rectangles can be turned 180

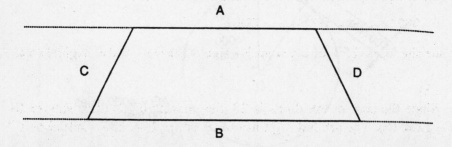

degrees and coincide with their original positions. So Statement (1) alone is sufficient. Statement (2) alone is not sufficient because it contains no information about the other two sides of the quadrilateral. Hence, what we have is a general trapezoid (see the figure below).

Side A is parallel to side B is specified by Statement (2). But we have no information about the relative directions of sides C and D.

12. **(B)**

As x_0 increases by 10% we get $1.1x_0 = x_f$. Also $1.3y_0 = y_f$. Statement (1) gives us a relation between x_0 and y_0 and hence will not solve for x_0. We need another relation between x_0 and x_f to solve for x_0. This is given by Statement (2). Hence, we have two relations:

$$1.1x_0 = x_f \text{ and } x_0 = x_f - 2.$$

Substituting the last equation into the previous equation we get

$$1.1 (x_f - 2) = x_f$$

$$(1.1 - 1)x_f = 2.2$$

$$\text{or } 0.1x_f = 2.2$$

$$\text{or } x_f = 22.$$

Hence,
$$x_0 = x_f - 2$$

$$= 22 - 2$$

$$\text{or } x_0 = 20.$$

13. **(B)**

Interestingly, the question can be answered without knowing the cost of the stock. Think of x as the original cost. Therefore $x + 5\%x$ equals the value of the stock after 1 month. But (Statement (2)) the value after 2 months is

$$(x + 5\%x) - 5\%(x + 5\%x) = .9975x.$$

Now the value after 2 months minus the original cost equals

$$.9975x - x = -.0025x = -.25\%x.$$

We see she loses .25% of the stock's value regardless of the original cost.

14. **(A)**

Since the sum of the digits is 28, the missing digits must sum to 16. $(28 - 12 = 16)$. The second digit has to be either 1, 4, or 9. Only 9 plus 7 equals 16. Hence the number is 147961. There exists no single digit which can be added to 1 or 4 so that the sum is 16. Statement (2) is insufficient. We can deduce that the missing digits are 7 and 9 but there is no way to determine whether the given number is 147961 or 149761.

15. **(A)**

From Statement (1) we know Albert makes 60/80 of his freethrows. Therefore, he has a 75% chance of hitting his next freethrow. Statement (2) claims he is averaging 3 freethrows per game. One might reason (erroneously) that he will make 3 out of 10 freethrows in his last game, or a 30% chance of making his first freethrow. How was anyone to know how many freethrows Albert would try in his last game until after the game?

16. **(A)**

Knowing the distance from E to CD is 6 feet implies that

$$x = 4\sqrt{3}$$
$$(x^2 = 6^2 + [(\tfrac{1}{2})x^2]^2.$$

Statement (2) will always be true for the given figure. But since x depends upon the height of the triangle, we can not find x without knowing the height of the triangle. So, Statement (2) alone is not sufficient.

17. **(B)**

One cannot deduce that all angles are equal when all sides are equal.

18. **(C)**

From Statement (1) $y = -4$ or 4 and from Statement (2) $y = -2$ or 4. Together you can determine that $y = 4$.

19. **(A)**

Look at a Venn diagram, where

Q = quadrilaterals

R = rhombi

S = squares

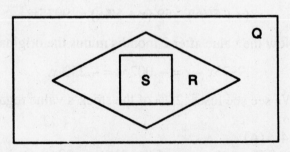

Statement (1) implies that A is not a square. So Statement (1) gives sufficient information to answer the question. Statement (2) only permits one to conclude A is in the set of Q but we can not answer whether A is a square.

20. **(A)**

Given Statement (1) the answer is the first bounce. Statement (2) does not give the length of one side relative to the other, so it cannot help us to determine the solution.

Section 3–Sentence Correction

1. **(C)**
    The pronoun WHO cannot be used to refer to NATIONS; WHO refers to people only. Choice (A) is therefore incorrect. Choice (B) implies that the nations seeking membership in the United Nations are already abiding by the conditions in the charter, a situation that does not necessarily exist. Choices (D) and (E) produce garbled meanings.

2. **(E)**
    Choice (E) is the only choice producing a parallel sentence structure; ENDED ON is parallel to BEGAN ON and QUESTIONING AND IN-DIFFERENCE is parallel to OPTIMISM AND IDEALISM. Also, choice (E) uses a conjunction showing contrast. Choices (A) and (B) lack a conjunction necessary to complete the meaning of the sentence. Choice (C) is awkwardly worded and uses an inappropriate conjunction for contrast. Choice (D) results in a run-on sentence.

3. **(D)**
    ORIGINAL already embodies the idea of VERY and to use this adverb with a word such as ORIGINAL or UNIQUE is incorrect. There-fore, choices (A) and (E) are incorrect, and choice (E) compounds the problem by using VERY before both adjectives. Choice (B) is unnecessarily wordy in using AS WELL AS. Choice (C) produces a sentence fragment.

4. **(B)**
    There is an error in pronoun and antecedent agreement in choice (A): AN APPLICANT is singular, so the plural pronoun THEIR does not agree with its antecedent. Choice (B) changes the noun to the plural form, so the pronoun agrees with the antecedent. Choice (C) contains the awkward wording of HIS OR HER. While this wording is acceptable in common usage, there is no identifiable noun antecedent in choice (C) for the pro-nouns HIS OR HER. Choice (D) is a fragment. Choice (E) is entirely too wordy.

5. **(A)**
    Choice (A) has correct parallel structure because it uses two adjec-tives before the noun PLANTS. Choice (B) omits an important concept of being disease-resistant. Choice (C) pairs the adjective HARDY with two

verbs, RESIST and LIVE, so the sentence is not parallel. Choice (D) leaves out the concept of HARDY. Choice (E) contains PLANTS KNOWN TO BE, thereby making the sentence too wordy and redundant; it is common information that orchids are plants, so it is not necessary to include that information in the sentence.

6.   **(E)**

One problem in this sentence is adjective usage. Although most comparative and superlative degrees are formed by adding MORE or MOST before the adjective, LARGE is irregular. LARGEST and MOST VARIED are the correct forms. Choices (A) and (D) use incorrect forms. Choices (B) and (D) have an error in subject-verb agreement: the subject is the singular pronoun ONE and the verb is the plural ARE. Choice (C) is weak wording, not as clear as (E).

7.   **(D)**

Choices (A), (B), and (C) have dangling participles. The phrase, GROWING ON NEARLY EVERY CONTINENT IN THE WORLD is clearly meant to modify ORCHIDS, not MOST OF US. The sentence should be reworded to put the correct subject next to the modifying participial phrase. Choices (C) and (E) misplace the modifier ONLY, a word which should modify the noun FLOWERS, not the verb THINK or THOUGHT.

8.   **(B)**

This sentence contains a cause-and-effect relationship: the wild orchids are being destroyed because they are nearly impossible to transplant. Choice (B) is the only one to state the relationship in clear terms. Choice (A) contains IN SPITE OF THE FACT THAT and shows the wrong logic. Choices (A) and (C) insert the unnecessary and wordy OF THE FACT THAT. Choices (C) and (D) contain an error in subject and verb agreement. The gerund DIGGING UP is considered a singular subject. While it is appropriate to use the possessive form before a gerund, PEOPLE'S is a modifier, not the subject; Choices (C) and (D) both incorrectly use the plural verb ARE. Choice (E) also uses a plural verb form HAVE BEEN and changes the meaning of the sentence slightly.

9.   **(C)**

This sentence contains both a time sequence and a cause-and-effect relationship. THE AGE OF SIXTY-FIVE HAVING BEEN REACHED is wordy and unnecessary. It is not necessary to use HAVING to indicate a person's age. Choices (A), (B), and (E) use this poor wording. Choice (D) is the worst choice of all because it does not make sense with the rest of the sentence.

10. **(A)**

Choice (A) uses correct parallel structure. All three verbs are present progressive: STRANGLING, PUSHING, and CLOGGING. Choice (B) changes the verb tenses slightly so that the first two actions are in the past, while the third action is ongoing. Choices (C) and (E) use too many transition words. Choice (D) is difficult to read because the actions are separated from their objects; use of RESPECTIVELY is stilted and not necessary when the sentence is correctly phrased.

11. **(E)**

Even though choice (A) correctly uses the possessive PURPLE LOOSESTRIFE'S before the gerund form HAVING, it is a fragment. The gerund is the subject, but there is no verb before the complement SYMBOLIC. Choice (B) incorrectly retains the possessive because there is no gerund form. Choice (C) does not contain a clearly worded cause-and-effect relationship and is a fragment. Choice (D) is also a fragment.

12. **(B)**

The adverb PROFUSELY modifies the verb GROWN. Choice (A) incorrectly uses the adjective form PROFUSE to modify a verb. Choice (B) uses PROFUSELY and contains an appropriate tense sequence: HAS GROWN and HAVE APPROVED. Choices (A) and (C) contain the wrong verb tense, HAD GROWN. In addition, choice (C) uses the wordy phrase, SEEING AS HOW. Choice (D) contains a dangling modifier and sounds as if the legislators are profusely growing. Choice (E) changes the meaning slightly to imply that the plants are being deliberately cultivated, an idea contrary to the meaning of the sentence.

13. **(A)**

The subject is ACTIONS and the verb is INCLUDE. Both of these are plural, so there is proper subject and verb agreement. TO CONTROL PURPLE LOOSESTRIFE is an intervening phrase which does not change the number of the subject. Choice (B) makes the verb singular, INCLUDES, so it erroneously agrees with PURPLE LOOSESTRIFE. Choice (C) produces a garbled sentence. Choice (D) has a redundant choice of words: AMONG and INCLUDE. Choice (E) is not as clearly and concisely worded as choice (A).

14. **(A)**
     Choice (A) correctly uses the past perfect tense to indicate a past action in a clause beginning with IF coming before the verb WOULD HAVE. Choice (B) uses WOULD HAVE in the subordinate clause, an incorrect construction because it creates two WOULD HAVE verbs. Choices (C) and (D) sound as if the person had a map and compass. Choice (E) uses the simple past tense, I HAD, and so is incorrect in this subordinate clause.

15. **(C)**
     The commonly heard expression THEY SAY is used in colloquial or informal speaking but is incorrect in standard usage. Therefore, choices (A) and (B) are incorrect. Choices (D) and (E) would produce fragments when used with the rest of the sentence. Choice (D) creates a subordinate clause beginning with WHEN, and choice (E) lacks the possessive before a gerund. Choice (C) is concise and clear.

16. **(E)**
     An agency is a singular noun, so the verb should be HAS. Choices (A) and (B) incorrectly make the verb agree with the direct object, SCIENTISTS. Choice (C) correctly uses SCIENTISTS as the subject with the plural verb HAVE, but the phrasing CONDUCTING HOW TO DEVELOP is garbled in meaning. Choice (D) sounds as if the tests have already succeeded.

17. **(D)**
     In formal usage it is always incorrect to use, I READ WHERE. This construction should be changed to I READ THAT. Choice (A) is incorrect because it uses I READ WHERE. Similarly, choice (C) uses an expression heard in speaking, but one which is never correct in formal usage: IT SAYS THAT. In choices (A) and (B) the addition of BOTH creates redundancy, as does EACH in choice (E).

18. **(B)**
     Choice (A) has inconsistent pronoun usage. The subordinate clause uses YOU, and the independent clause uses ONE. Choice (E) also has inconsistent pronoun usage and can therefore be eliminated. Choice (B) uses YOU in both places and is appropriate in tone for the subject. Choice (C) has an error in antecedent agreement; A PERSON is singular, so THEY is incorrect and should be changed to HE OR SHE. Choice (D) contains no noun antecedent for the pronouns HE OR SHE.

19. **(A)**

Choice (A) shows the correct cause-and-effect relationship between the decrease in licensed hunters and the resulting growth in deer population. Choice (B) uses the poor phrase, SEEING AS HOW. Choice (C) and choice (D) change the verb tense slightly to IS DECREASING, a change which shifts the time reference slightly. In addition, the phrase BEING THAT is incorrect in formal usage. Choice (E) is totally illogical, as it presents the growing deer population as the cause for there being fewer hunters.

20. **(C)**

The rule states that FEWER must be used before a plural noun, as HUNTERS. LESS must be used before a singular noun, as CONCERN. Choice (A) incorrectly uses LESS HUNTERS, and choice (D) incorrectly uses FEWER CONCERN. Choice (B) is redundant in its use of GOVERNMENT LAWS GOVERNING. In choice (E) the wording of FEWER CONCERNS is weak. The subject, FEWER HUNTERS, could possibly be viewed as a singular concept using a singular verb form, MEANS, but the verb MEAN prevents any confusion.

21. **(E)**

This concept in the course for young hunters includes the idea of the historical relationship between man and animals. Choice (E) clearly indicates the historical perspective and is grammatically correct and clearly stated. Choice (A) uses the awkward phrase, AS TO HOW. Choice (B) is not clear and suggests that the young hunters have always been predators, so the meaning is slightly distorted. Choice (C) and choice (D) also slightly distort the meaning by removing the historical perspective.

22. **(D)**

The subject is CHARGES, and none of the singular nouns in the intervening phrase can be used as the subject. Therefore, choice (D) is correct because it is a plural verb. Choices (A) and (B) are incorrect because they are singular verbs. Choice (C) produces a fragment. Choice (E) sounds as if the charges are considering something—an impossibility.

Section 4–Problem Solving

1. **(B)**
    Let *a, b,* and *c* be the cost of one sandwich, one cup of coffee, and one piece of pie respectively. Then

    $$3a + 7b + 4c = 10.20$$

    $$4a + 8b + 5c = 12.25$$

    $$a + b + c = 2.05$$

2. **(A)**
    Let x = the number of acres of corn planted.

    $$\frac{3}{5} = \frac{x}{225}$$

    $$5x = 675$$

    $$x = 135$$

3. **(D)**
    Substituting $x = y - 3$ into the first equation to obtain

    $$y - 3 + y = 7$$

    $$2y = 10$$

    $$y = 5$$

    Substitute back into the first equation:

    $$x = y - 3$$

    $$x = 5 - 3$$

    $$x = 2$$

4. **(B)**
    Since the numbers represented by points C and D are both between 0 and 1, the product of the two numbers is positive and less than either of those numbers. Then the only reasonable answer is point B.

5. **(B)**
    Since the jug is $^2/_3$ full and the jug holds $^3/_4$ gallon of punch, the jug has $^2/_3$ of $^3/_4$ or $^1/_2$ gallon.

6. **(B)**
    The meter shows that $^3/_{10}$ of the total time on the meter is left. However, this is a $^1/_2$-hour meter. Since

    $$\frac{3}{10} \times \frac{1}{2} = \frac{3}{20},$$

    this means that there is $^3/_{20}$ of an hour left on the meter, and $^3/_{20}$ of an hour is 9 minutes.

7. **(B)**

    $$29\frac{1}{2} \div \frac{3}{4} = \frac{59}{2} \times \frac{4}{3}$$

    $$= 39\frac{1}{3}$$

    Thus, Mary had enough material to make 39 uniforms and enough material left over to "make" $^1/_3$ of a uniform. But

    $$\frac{1}{3} \times \frac{3}{4} = \frac{1}{4},$$

    so she would have $^1/_4$ of a yard left over.

8. **(A)**
    Let x be Ms. Jones' salary two years ago. Then $x + 10\%x$ was her salary last year and $(x + 10\%x) + 10\%(x + 10\%x)$ is an expression for her salary this year.

    $$(x + 10\%x) + 10\%(x + 10\%x) = 41,745$$

    $$1.1x + .11x = 41,745$$

    $$1.21x = 41,745$$

    $$x = 34,500$$

9. **(B)**
    Since $\angle A$ and $\angle C$ are inscribed angles, the measure of each of these angles is half the measure of the intercepted arc. Since the two arcs com-

prise the entire circle, the sum of the measures of these angles is

$$\frac{1}{2} \times 360°.$$

10. **(A)**

$$\frac{7a - 5b}{b} = 7$$

$$\frac{7a}{b} - \frac{5b}{b} = 7$$

$$7 \times \frac{a}{b} - 5 = 7$$

$$7\frac{a}{b} = 12$$

$$\frac{a}{b} = \frac{12}{7}$$

$$\frac{b}{a} = \frac{7}{12}$$

$$\frac{4a + 6b}{2a} = \frac{4a}{2a} + \frac{6b}{2a}$$

$$= 2 + 3 \times \frac{b}{a}$$

$$= 2 + 3 \times \frac{7}{12}$$

$$= \frac{15}{4}$$

11. **(E)**

$$\frac{2^{100} + 2^{98}}{2^{100} - 2^{98}} = \frac{2^{98}(2^2 + 1)}{2^{98}(2^2 - 1)}$$

$$= \frac{2^2 + 1}{2^2 - 1}$$

$$= \frac{5}{3}$$

12. **(D)**
   The four right triangles each have legs of length 6 and 8. Thus, the hypotenuse of each of those triangles is length 10 and the required area is 100 square units.

13. **(C)**
   Since $AB = BC$, angle C has measure 46°. However, the sum of the measures of the angles of a triangle is 180° and

$$180 - (46 + 46) = 88$$

so the measure of angle B is 88°.

14. **(E)**

   In this case

   $$AC = 3, AD = CE = 2, \text{ and } DE = 1.$$

   Thus, the perimeter is 8.

15. **(D)**

   Let t = time it takes to fill the tank.

   $$\frac{t}{6} + \frac{t}{4} - \frac{t}{3} = 1$$

   $$\frac{2t + 3t - 4t}{12} = 1$$

   $$t = 12 \text{ hours}$$

16. **(A)**

   From the Venn diagram below, let the number of students in

   technical writing $= a$

   technical writing and history $= b$

   history $= c$

   history and statistics $= d$

   statistics $= e$

Given that

$$a + b = 15$$

$$b + c + d = 15$$

$$d + e = 15$$

$$a + b + c + d + e = 34$$

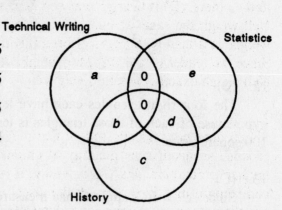

Combine all four equations.

$$15 + c + 15 = 34$$

$$c = 4$$

Section 5–Critical Reasoning

1. **(C)**
    It is true that the 1960s were a disruptive time in the history of America, but the decade was probably no more disruptive than other decades in history. Bill does not focus on the history in his argument, therefore (A) is not the best choice. While it is true that thinking skills were not encouraged as much with the old math as with the new math, this is not the crux of Bill's argument; (B) should not be chosen. It is true that tests which measured traditional math skills were often used to measure students of the new math. Since all the tests were not valid, this may have affected student scores, so (C) is the best answer. New math is not totally out of the schools for good. Remnants of the new math remain; (D) does not relate to Bill's argument. Bill did not state that students were doing better with the new math than with the old math. Neither did Jane go so far as to make this claim, hence (E) is not the correct choice.

2. **(D)**
    One cannot tell from the information given if Lulu weighs more than Nell. One knows that Lulu weighs more than Meg, but the amount she weighs could still be less than Nell. On the other hand, it could be more than Nell, so (A) is not the best answer. The answer cannot be determined for (B) either. One knows that Lulu weighs more than Meg, but one does not know how Lulu ranks in relation to June. (C) also cannot be stated as truth. One knows that Kirt and Nell weigh the same amount. One also knows that Meg weighs less than Nell and that Lulu weighs more than Meg. The reader, however, is not told for sure how Lulu ranks in relation to the others. (D) is the right answer. June weighs more than Kirt; Kirt and Nell weigh the same amount. Since Meg weighs less than Nell, she also weighs less than Kirt. (E) is incorrect, Kirt does not weigh less than Meg. Since the reader is told that Meg weighs less than Nell and since Kirt and Nell weigh exactly the same, Meg weighs less than Kirt.

3. **(E)**
    It does not logically follow that if the price is too high, farmers will produce an insufficient quantity of onions. Normally farmers would step up their production, thus (A) is wrong. If prices are already high, increased competition may in fact lower the price, therefore (B) is incorrect. If the price is too low, consumers may demand a larger quantity of onions; (C) is false. The saturation of the market with onions will force the price of

onions down, not up, so (D) is false. (E) is true. Since a scarcity of a commodity will result in an increase in price, the scarcity of onions will drive the price up.

4. **(B)**

Private governments may not be empowered to execute offenders; (A) is incorrect. (B) is true. A private government, like a school or corporation, could not imprison or execute a person legally. (C) is wrong; even on occasion in our country private government is not able to legally execute an offender. (D) is not a suitable choice. The definition is incorrect, as can be seen by rereading the passage. It is a public government which included all the individuals within a certain geographical area. (E) is incorrect; it is private government which rules the members of a particular group, like a corporation.

5. **(A)**

Since the opponents of prison reform did, in fact, attack the character of the inmates rather than their claims, (A) is the best answer. The opponents of prison reform were not reported to have referred to the analogy; (B) is not the best answer. No dilemma was implied by opponents of the prison reform, (C) is not the best choice. No absurd conclusion was brought out by the opponents, therefore (D) should not be selected. The opponents to prison reform skirted the issue of prison riots in a neighboring county, (E) is not the best choice.

6. **(A)**

Of the choices given, the best defense of the former prison inmates would be to emphasize their expertise and the expertise of those who invited them to the meeting, thus (A) is the best answer. Getting into a discussion of their character would not help the situation; (B) is not the best choice. Denying that changes would cost money which would necessitate a tax increase would be a false argument, so (C) should not be selected. Again, bringing up the riots might sound like a threat; (D) would not defend the inmate's position. There is no point in the former inmates' refuting their own analogy; (E) is not the best choice.

7. **(E)**

If the people had drowned and the bodies washed into the crevices, dirt, sand, and sediment would have been embedded in their clothes; (A) is not the right answer. If the people had died of starvation, there would have been evidence of their gnawing on the animal skins in which they were dressed. (B) is not the correct choice. Since the skins of the people were not disfigured, smallpox would not have been the cause of death; (C) is not the correct choice. Since the bodies had been placed there at different times, the people could not have frozen to death; (D) is not the best choice. The scientists decided that the dead had to have been placed there by family members. (E) is the correct choice.

8. **(B)**
Since Greenland is primarily a cold area, the hot, dry air would not apply; (A) is not correct. (B) is the correct choice. The cold climate and the winds preserved the bodies. (C) is inappropriate. The bodies had not recently been placed there. The passage tells the reader the date of death was around 1475. Moisture from water would not postpone deterioration but would hasten it, therefore (D) is inappropriate. The bodies were so perfectly preserved it is unlikely that lightning would have struck the bodies. If lightning had struck the bodies, they would have been damaged. Evidence also indicated death had come at different times. (E) is incorrect.

9. **(D)**
No claim is made in the advertisement that Good Health is the most nutritionally complete; (A) is incorrect. Although reference is made to the fact that accomplished or professional athletes reading the *Bulletin* prefer Good Health, (B) is not the most obvious claim. Since health is a concern of all people, there is nothing in the ad to suggest that only accomplished or professional athletes would read the *Bulletin*, therefore (C) is incorrect. (D) is probably the reason that most persons who are not accomplished or professional would choose the product—to receive the help (implied in the ad) which helped the athletes to become accomplished or professional. (E) is not the best choice. No suggestion is made that only those who will become accomplished or professional subscribe to the *Bulletin* or will read the ad.

10. **(E)**
If surgery to disconnect the two sides of the brain results in both sides of the brain working well, the theory that the two sides work together would not necessarily be substantiated. Hence, (A) would not strengthen their argument and should not be selected. Since the right hemisphere is not believed to control logic, damage to it would not result in logical disorders being manifested, (B) would not strengthen the position of opponents to the split-brain theory. Opponents of the split-brain theory contend that both hemispheres of the brain work together; hence, an activity would generally engage both hemispheres of the brain—not just one as (C) implies. The hemispheres, opponents of the split brain theory argue, work

together—not independently as (D) implies. Opponents of the split-brain theory *would* argue that it is impossible to educate one side of the brain without educating the other, making (E) the best choice.

11. **(E)**

(A) is a good answer, but it is not the *best* answer. It is true that health education does benefit young children, but it does much more than that. (B) is also not the best choice. There is no suggestion that health education for young children is likely to create new teaching jobs. It is assumed that current teachers in the child development centers would teach the health curriculum. (C) is not the best choice; it would be very difficult to decrease the amount given to the sick and disabled to "teach them a lesson" or to *make* them do what needs to be done. Most people do not choose to be sick. The passage makes no reference to eliminating benefits for those who are sick or disabled. (D) should not be chosen; no analogy was drawn between economic recession and failure to provide health education. The best choice is (E). The passage suggests that health education for preschoolers can also benefit society as a whole.

12. **(C)**

Making the advertisement colorful is part of the obvious sensory appeal. It is not a part of the underlying goal that reference is made to in choice (A). It is normally very difficult to appeal to auditory senses through magazine ads. Since this statement does not fit logically into the blank, (B) is not the best choice. Appealing to the subconscious mind is the underlying goal of many advertisements featuring obvious sensory appeal, therefore (C) is the best choice. The goal of most advertisements themselves is not merely to make the periodicals longer; (D) is not the best choice. The goal of most advertisements is not to develop a new audience for the readers. Choice (E) does not fit logically into the sentence.

13. **(D)**

It is unlikely that growers could foresee how high the price of onions would go; (A) is not the best choice. There would be little initial cost involved in planting potatoes instead of onions, therefore (B) is incorrect. The price of onions is not low at this time; (C) is a poor choice. (D) is the best choice. Both potato and onion crops are susceptible to being reduced by bad weather. (E) is incorrect; if the supply increases, the price of potatoes to the consumer will have to fall, which supports the original conclusion.

14. **(D)**

Double monitoring seems to have a purpose here and could not be, at this point, considered governmental waste, so (A) should not be chosen. There is no evidence in the passage to suggest that the federal government does not have expertise in this area; (B) is not the best choice. The passage does not suggest that the reason for double monitoring is to provide jobs, since the job of the Department of Energy is not directly related to economics. Hence, (C) is not the best choice. Double monitoring is to assure the public and to insure the safety of the people; (D) is correct. The federal government is trying to get the states involved in the project, not keep them on the sidelines; (E) is incorrect.

15. **(E)**

Referring only to the standard of living does not tell how the people of that country lived before. Most people who wish this information would consult historical references and not the standard of living for this information, therefore (A) is not the best choice. The standard of living index shows purchases but there is no indication as to whether the items are to be used by a single individual or by a family. This is a weakness in the standard of living index. Since the answer states that the information used in computing a standard of living indicates if purchases are to be used by an individual or by a family, (B) should not be selected. The standard of living does not show how people actually live. (C) is incorrect. Since the standard of living does not project the future, (D) is not the best choice. The standard of living does not show overcrowding and pollution; it cannot really show how people live. (E) is the most serious disadvantage of using the standard of living to measure a country.

16. **(E)**

If Andrea's parents' income is increased to $25,600, the chances are, that all other things being equal, their expected contribution would be increased—not decreased from the $256, so (A) is not the best choice. If Andrea's parents' expenses are decreased to $20,000, the likelihood of their expected contribution being decreased (provided all other figures remain constant) is nil; (B) is not the best choice. An increase in Andrea's parents' assets from $26,525, would likely result in an increase in their expected contribution if all else remained constant, therefore (C) is a poor choice. With *no* allowable deductions there will be nothing to subtract. The result will probably be an increase (not a decrease) in expected contributions and (D) should not be chosen. With the income of Andrea's parents' being decreased, the chances are that their expected contribution would also be decreased provided all other factors remain constant, thus (E) is the best choice.

Section 6–Problem Solving

1. **(A)**

$$\frac{28 + 36 + x}{3} = 29$$

$$64 + x = 3(29)$$

$$x = 23$$

Choice (B) comes from adding 28 and 36 and dividing by 2. Choice (C) comes from adding and dividing by 3.

2. **(A)**

Let x = amount of wheat originally. Then $x - \frac{1}{10}x = 1$ bushel. Multiply each term by 10:

$$10x - x = 10$$

or

$$9x = 10$$

and

$$x = 1\frac{1}{9} \text{ bushels.}$$

3. **(B)**

From the properties of a straight line

$$\angle y + 150° = 180°$$

$$\angle y = 30°$$

You should also know that

$$\angle A = \angle x$$

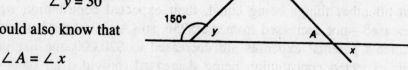

from vertical angles being equal.
The sum of the angles of a triangle equal 180°.

$$\angle x + \angle y + 90° = 180°$$

$$\angle x + 30° + 90° = 180°$$

$$\angle x = 60°$$

4. **(C)**

Let x = the number of pizzas Carla delivers.

$$x(.60) + 5 = 17$$

$$.6x = 12$$

$$x = 20$$

5. **(C)**
    Draw a diagram of the box.

    Volume = $w(w)(5w)$

    $$= 5w^3$$

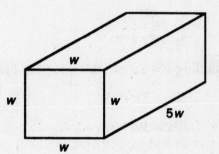

6. **(B)**
    When $X = 2.5642$ is rounded off to the nearest hundredth, we get $X = 2.56$. Therefore,

    $$X - X = 2.5642 - 2.56 = .0042.$$

7. **(C)**
    Set up a diagram as shown.

	amount of solution	strength	amount of solvent
Original solution	5	40%	2.0
Amount of water	x	0%	0
New Solution	$5 + x$	25%	$.25(5 + x)$

    Amount of solvent does not change from original solution to new solution.

    $$2.0 = .25(5 + x)$$

    $$2.0 = 1.25 + .25x$$

    $$.75 = .25x$$

    $$3 = x$$

8. **(A)**

    $$A = s^2, A = (s + .1s)^2 = (1.1s)^2,$$

    $$1.1^2 = 1.21 \Rightarrow 21\% \text{ increase}$$

Choice (B) comes from adding 10% and 10%. Choice (D) comes from squaring 10, 10(10) = 100%.

9. **(D)**
   Let x = drink cup and y = pitcher, then

$$y = 6x$$

and $\quad 3y = 5x + 39.$

Substituting $y = 6x$ into this equation gives

$$18x = 5x + 39$$

or $\quad 13x = 39,$

so that $\quad x = 3.$

10. **(D)**
    Of the 20,000 he has to invest, the man invests 5,000 at 5% giving him $5,000(.05) = 250$ in interest. He invests 7,000 at 7% giving him

$$7,000(.07) = 490$$

in interest. The remaining amount of interest needed to reach 1,500 a year is, therefore,

$$1,500 - 740 = 760.$$

The remaining amount of principal is

$$20,000 - 12,000 = 8,000,$$

so that letting x be the rate of interest, we have $8,000x = 760$ or

$$\frac{760}{8,000} = .095 = 9.5\%.$$

11. **(D)**
    $5x = 4y$ and $x = \frac{4}{5}y.$

$$x - \frac{1}{y} = \frac{4}{5}y - \frac{1}{y},$$

LCD = $5y$, so that

$$\frac{4y^2 - 5}{5y}.$$

Choice (A) comes from

$$\frac{4}{5}y - \frac{1}{y} = \frac{3}{4}y.$$

Choice (B) comes from

$$\frac{4}{5}y - \frac{1}{y} = \frac{3}{4y}.$$

Choice (C) comes from solving the original proportion incorrectly as $4x = 5y$; then,

$$x = \frac{5}{4}y, \ \frac{5}{4}y - \frac{1}{y} = \frac{5y-1}{4y}.$$

Choice (E) comes from

$$\frac{4}{5}y - \frac{1}{y} = \frac{4y-1}{5y}.$$

12. **(B)**

$a = 25 - 16 = 9, b = 100 - 64 = 36$

$$(\sqrt{9} - \sqrt{36})^2 = (3 - 6)^2 = (-3)^2 = 9$$

Choice (A) comes from

$$(\sqrt{a} - \sqrt{b})^2 = a - b = 9 - 36 = -27.$$

Choices (C) and (D) come from an initial error of letting

$$a = 5^2 - 4^2 = 1^2 = 1 \text{ and } b = 10^2 - 8^2 = 2^2 = 4.$$

Then (C) is found as follows:

$$(\sqrt{a} - \sqrt{b})^2 = (1 - 2)^2 = (-1)^2 = 1$$

and (D) is found by:

$$(\sqrt{a} - \sqrt{b})^2 = a - b = 1 - 4 = -3.$$

Choice (E) comes from

$$(9 - 36)^2 = (-27)^2 = 729.$$

13. **(E)**

Diameter $\overline{AD}$ of the large circle is 16, therefore, the area of semi-circle is

$$\frac{\pi r^2}{2} = \frac{\pi 8^2}{2} = 32\pi.$$

The area of "cut-out" small circles is

$$2\left(\frac{1}{2}\pi \times 2^2\right) = 2(2\pi) = 4\pi.$$

The area of the semicircle located below the diameter of the large semi-circles is

$$\frac{1}{2}\pi \times 4^2 = 8\pi.$$

Therefore, the area of shaded region is

$$32\pi + 8\pi - 4\pi = 36\pi.$$

Choice (A) comes from not deleting 2 small circles, i.e., $32\pi + 8\pi$. Choice (B) comes from not taking half of the area of the small semicircles, i.e., $32\pi + 8\pi - 8\pi$. Choice (C) comes from not taking half of the large semicircle, i.e., $64\pi + 8\pi - 4\pi$. Choice (D) comes from not taking half of both of the larger semicircles, i.e., $64\pi + 16\pi - 4\pi$.

14. **(C)**

$t = \dfrac{d}{r}$, let t_1 be her old time and t_2 be her new time so that

$$t_1 = \frac{50}{r}$$

and

$$t_2 = \frac{400}{4r} = \frac{100}{r}.$$

Therefore, comparing, we see that $t_2 = 2 \times t_1$.

15. **(E)**

Know that Distance = rate × time.

Let t = the time it takes Mark to complete the trip

$$90\left(t + \frac{40}{60}\right) = 100t$$

$$90t + 60 = 100t$$

$$10t = 60$$

$$t = 6$$

$$6 \times 100 = 600,$$

the distance between the two cities.

16. **(E)**

Let x = cost of the gadget whose profit was 20% and let y = cost of the other gadget. Then

$$x + .20x = 2.40$$

or $\qquad 1.20x = 2.40$

and $\qquad x = 2.00$

or her profit is 40¢. The other gadget:

$$y - .20y = 2.40$$

or $\qquad .8y = 2.40$

and $\qquad y = 3.00$

or her loss is 60¢. Therefore, her total loss is

$$60 - 40 = 20¢.$$

Choice (A) comes from $2.40(.2) = .48$ or 8¢.

Section 7–Analytical Writing Assessment

ANALYSIS OF AN ISSUE ESSAY TOPIC

Sample Essay Response Scoring 5 to 6

The role which libraries play in educating individuals and entire communities is far too important to be overlooked during a discussion of money. Libraries waken and nurture a love of reading in so many more people than the number of books the institutions can afford to buy. In their busy process of educating the world, libraries daily accidently spill their patrons into bookstores.

Every community scrambles to give itself a library, and every library scrambles for a slightly bigger budget, and every budget committee scrambles to squeeze in that extra book. That extra book is so important to libraries because it is about something or by someone they have never read before, and they cannot wait to see it awaken a new interest in their communities. All this scrambling should tell you how precarious a library's situation is, especially in smaller towns. Libraries invariably sweat over their underbudgeting. To eliminate their purchasing discount or to effectively do so by charging copyright fees could close many libraries, or reduce them to merely updating encyclopedias and periodicals. This would not only destroy the direct market which is the libraries themselves, but it would also paralyze their most significant functions.

Consider the scholarly use of libraries. These institutions provide a location and atmosphere for research and learning. Without the ability to purchase new books as they become available, libraries would fail the needs of their erudite patrons. Such a purchasing system would single-handedly impede the advance of technology, multicultural understanding, artistic insight, and economic relief. In the age of the information highway, raw data travels at the speed of electricity. Studies, reports and theories must also travel from scholar to peer and student as quickly as possible, and not become mired in copyright restrictions. To be able to compete in tomorrow's instantaneous world, today's students must learn to keep abreast in the current torrent of the printed word.

In order to fully appreciate the intergenerational impact of threatening the library system, one must consider that libraries turn bored children into little readers. Many families would not be able to afford to keep up with the reading appetite of their children if libraries were not available. This would greatly affect the eldest children who may lack hand-me-down books, and who, in turn, would set a non-reading example for younger siblings. The weighty opinions of psychologists and sociologists and even the doctrines of political correctness have reached into the children's sections of our libraries to mark as "inappropriate" various classics which were written at less informed and less sensitive times. Thus, libraries are more dependent on new books to meet the needs of young readers than any other age group. From meeting these needs we gain a more intelligent and well-adjusted future generation who will not only be lawmakers and teachers, but book-buyers as well.

In short, the library system must be allowed to flourish because it creates the book-buying public. From opening the minds of children to putting scholars in communication with one another, libraries produce a mindset where reading is doing, where reading is how lives are spent. The fact that a literary market exists alongside libraries proves that readers do buy books. They buy the books that are worth keeping, and buy for loved ones books they wish them to own.

Analysis of Sample Scoring 5 to 6

This response would rate a six because it is well organized, contains few writing flaws, demonstrates a strong command of diction and syntactic variety, and is firmly centered over a persuasive position on the issue. The response begins with the idea that reading begins in libraries. After depicting the familiar scenario of library budgets, it threatens the destruction of libraries. The role of libraries in creating readers and a demand for books is creatively explored.

ANALYSIS OF AN ARGUMENT ESSAY TOPIC

Sample Essay Response Scoring 5 to 6

The very idea that recycling may be a myth, even if only for one resource, is very captivating. Once suggested, it must be explored. A drive through any town on "newspaper day" certainly leaves one open to the suggestion that an over-abundance of recyclable newspaper is possible and even likely. The argument's reference to dealers in these recyclable goods sends one's mind to explore how these markets can work. While bottles and aluminum cans are easy to imagine being melted down and put to use again, limitations suggest themselves in the recycling of paper. Also, many households can go for days without producing an empty can or bottle. How can one effectively sell used paper when seemingly every daily newspaper in America is being turned in for recycling?

Despite these suggestions generated by the argument, a more analytical look at the essay finds ready flaws. The phrase "less than ten percent" is far too vague to be convincing. Ten is a round number and yet the real world is never smooth or perfectly square. A more specific number, even "10.0", is required to convince today's statistic-saturated public. Yet even with a figure of two decimal places this statistic requires a source, and, more importantly, a timeframe to which it applies. This time issue relates to the argument's failure to acknowledge advances in technology which makes use of the recycled paper—a likelihood if this resource is reportedly so cheap.

The argument ends with a persuasive picture in which newspapers land in our dumps anyway, "neatly stacked" at the cost of the taxpayer. While emotionally influential, this image should be backed by statistics demonstrating a minimal effect of recycling on garbage dump influx. Waste disposal locations are required to keep tonnage records which note sources and characterize content, such as household or industrial. If the claims of the argument are true, the data would be available to show significant deposits of newspapers from "recycling" municipalities. This absence of hard data undermines the strong emotional impact of this claim.

The argument's line of reasoning equates the absence of extensive recycling with a need to discontinue paper collection. Such a position fails to realize the significance of "recycling" as a philosophy and an ideal. Establishing the habit of reuse is more than half the battle in learning to insure a cleaner tomorrow, even when that reuse is a fiction. The practice of collecting recyclables is valuable before recycling is possible, because it conditions the public to accept the chore. More importantly, the premature recycling makes the resource readily available, inviting industry to find a use for it.

To be more successful, the argument should have provided support for its evidence. The claim that only ten percent of paper is actually recycled required more detail and sources which would reinforce its credibility. The lack of pictures and statistics minimized the impact of the allegation that most newspapers still retire to garbage dumps. In support of its line of reasoning, the author should have anticipated and discredited the idea that the recycling may have a value beyond whether or not all or most of the paper ever sees a second use. On the whole, the argument was reasonable but hollow.

Analysis of Sample Essay Scoring 5 to 6

This analysis would rate a six because it organizes its ideas logically and intelligently with smooth transitions, it distinctly identifies and sharply analyzes the crucial points of the argument, and it demonstrates a strong command of the English language with at worst minor flaws. This analysis explores the initial effectiveness of the argument to demonstrate its strengths. Afterward, the analysis points out the lack of depth of the main points and their wounding lack of credited source references. Finally, the line of reasoning was creatively and legitimately challenged. This format provided a smooth and well-organized format for the analysis.

GMAT CAT

Graduate Management Admission Test
Computer-Adaptive Test

Practice
Test 5

NOTE:

The following practice test contains more questions than the actual GMAT CAT. This is necessary to provide a score that is roughly comparable to the shorter computer-adaptive test. Although the format is different, this test will give you an accurate idea of your strengths and weaknesses, and provide guidance for further study.

PRACTICE TEST 5

Section 1

(Answer sheets appear in the back of the book.)

TIME: 25 Minutes
16 Questions

DIRECTIONS: For each question in this section, select the best answer.

---

1. Prior to a recent free-trade pact between Canada and the United States, logging mills in the northwest United States argued that without protection they would be driven out of business by Canadian competition.

    Which of the following arguments would best support the pact?

    (A) Ecological concerns require a reduction in logging in both the United States and Canada.

    (B) Increases in unemployment tend to correlate with increases in health problems, crime, and divorce.

    (C) If the workers in the mills would accept a substantial cut in wages, the mills would be more competitive.

    (D) The capital and labor employed at the mills could be redirected into businesses in which the United States is more competitive to the ultimate benefit of both the United States and Canada.

    (E) Canada is an ally of the United States.

2. Hospital administrators, facing a shortage of trained nurses, are considering two possible solutions: either give some of the work previously done by nurses to paramedics or else raise the salaries now paid to nurses.

    Which of the following can be most reliably inferred from the above information?

(A) Raising their salaries will increase the supply of nurses.

(B) Nurses are generally opposed to having some of their duties reassigned to paramedics.

(C) The shortage of nurses will cause hospital costs to increase.

(D) Paramedics would be just as competent as nurses in doing most of the work now being done by nurses.

(E) If some of the work now assigned to nurses was reassigned to paramedics, the nurses would have more time to attend to patients.

3. Supporters of Governor Smith point to the statewide decline in crime that has occurred since his election to the statehouse. Obviously, they claim, Governor Smith's "Let's Get Tough on Crime" program has had an effect.

    Which of the following, if true, would most seriously weaken the conclusion drawn above?

    (A) Since Governor Smith's election, there has been a decrease in the number of males aged 15-30, the group in the population that commits most of the crimes.

    (B) During the previous administration, that of Governor Jones, there was also an anti-crime program.

    (C) Governor Smith's "Let's Get Tough on Crime" program has been characterized as "just another public relations gimmick" by the opposing party.

    (D) The legislature only voted for half of the funding originally requested by Governor Smith when he first presented his anti-crime program.

    (E) Although the number of crimes overall has decreased, the number of drug-related crimes has actually increased.

Questions 4 – 5 are based on the following.

Because of an apparent surplus of college teachers, many college students majoring in the Humanities decided to go to law school instead of pursuing a Ph.D. Upon graduating three years later from law school many of them discovered, to their surprise, that it was suddenly much more difficult to find a job as a lawyer than it had been previously.

4. Which of the following can be inferred from the passage?

   (A) Lawyers make more money than college teachers.

   (B) Practicing law requires a more rigorous graduate program than college teaching.

   (C) On-the-job training is more important than graduate study in learning how to practice law.

   (D) When the students in question graduated from law school there was a surplus of lawyers.

   (E) Majoring in the Humanities is not a good preparation for law school.

5. Some of the law school graduates who could not find employment right away concluded that they would have been better off studying for a Ph.D. and becoming college teachers. This conclusion, however, was unwarranted because it can be inferred to be likely that

   (A) no one can accurately predict three years in advance which professions will be oversupplied with job candidates.

   (B) it is difficult to get a job no matter how much education you have.

   (C) if all of these students had studied in Ph.D. programs there would not have been enough job openings for them in college teaching.

   (D) a graduate-degree program is just a meaningless hurdle that keeps people out of the job market.

   (E) lawyers can always make money by encouraging people to sue each other.

6. Bill owns more shares of AT&T than Sue.

   Gordon owns more shares of AT&T than Henry.

   Henry owns fewer shares of AT&T than George.

   Sue and George own the same number of shares of AT&T.

   If the above information is true, which of the following information must also be true?

   (A) Gordon owns more shares of AT&T than George.

    (B) Gordon owns more shares of AT&T than Bill.

    (C) Sue owns fewer shares of AT&T than Gordon.

    (D) Bill owns more shares of AT&T than Henry.

    (E) Sue owns fewer shares of AT&T than Henry.

7.   Alvin is trying to choose between an inexpensive, two-door subcompact and a roomier, more stylish car that costs several thousand dollars more. He is probably going to buy the subcompact. It gets much better mileage, and there has been a recent increase in the cost of gasoline. Given Alvin's present salary, after taxes and living expenses, he can budget about $300 for car payments. The finance company is offering Alvin a five-year loan at five percent with $1,000 down. At that rate he would not be able to make the payments on the more expensive car. In addition, Alvin must consider insurance. He could reduce the premiums by opting for a policy with high deductibles, but after making the downpayment he would not have enough money in his savings account to cover the deductibles in case of an accident.

Which of the following changes would make it easier for Alvin to afford the more expensive car?

    (A) The state increases the amount of liability insurance every car owner is required to carry.

    (B) Alvin chooses the insurance policy with the lowest deductibles.

    (C) Alvin chooses to pay the lowest possible downpayment.

    (D) The finance company lowers the interest rate on Alvin's car loan.

    (E) The mileage claimed for the cars by the manufacturer is higher than the actual mileage Alvin will get driving to work.

Questions 8 – 9 are based on the following.

    Contrary to the charges made by his critics, the actions taken by President X in an effort to preserve his own political power during the recent scandal were well within the traditions of the American presidency. The critics should remember that, during the political crisis of the Civil War, even Abraham Lincoln took actions that many now consider to have been "unconstitutional."

8. The author's method of attacking the critics of President X is to

   (A) show that Lincoln was also involved in a scandal.

   (B) point out the contradictions inherent in the charges against President X.

   (C) imply an analogy between the actions taken by President X and the actions taken by Lincoln.

   (D) suggest that the critics are motivated by self-interest.

   (E) question the factual basis of the charges against President X.

9. The critics could effectively defend their position against the author's strategy by pointing out that

   (A) the critics are all experts in constitutional law.

   (B) the author is also motivated by self-interest.

   (C) given the extensive Congressional testimony about the scandal, the facts are a matter of record.

   (D) most people consider Lincoln to have been much the greater president.

   (E) the situations are not comparable because Lincoln was trying to save the Union while President X was just trying to save his own administration.

10. Nine out of ten doctors interviewed said that if they were on a space trip to the moon and had a bad cold, they would prefer "Numbs" aspirin to any other cold remedy!

    Which of the following assumptions would you have to hold in order for this advertisement to lead you logically to the conclusion that you should buy "Numbs" aspirin when you have a cold?

    (A) "Numbs" aspirin is cheaper than other cold remedies.

    (B) Aspirin only treats the symptoms of a cold, not the underlying causes.

    (C) "Numbs" aspirin works faster than other cold remedies.

    (D) Doctors are reliable and informed sources of information concerning the relative value of different brands of non-prescription drugs.

    (E) All aspirin is the same, regardless of the claims made in advertisements.

11. Some Shakespearean scholars have argued that certain passages in *Macbeth*, the witches' songs, for example, could not have been written by Shakespeare because they are inferior in quality to anything that Shakespeare wrote.

Which of the following statements points out the most serious logical flaw in the above argument?

(A) It is impossible to determine the quality of everything that Shakespeare wrote prior to determining whether the passages in question were written by Shakespeare.

(B) Shakespeare had a reputation for writing very quickly without taking the time to revise.

(C) Some people believe that all of the plays said to have been written by Shakespeare were actually written by someone else.

(D) Shakespeare probably included the witches in order to please James I who had a keen interest in the subject.

(E) Other critics have voiced exactly the opposite opinion of the quality of the passages in question.

12. Recent polls indicate that voters under 40 are more conservative than voters who are over 40 and have the same education, and voters who finished college but did not go to graduate school are more conservative than voters of the same age who have only a high school education or who have graduate degrees.

If the above facts are true, which of the following statements can be inferred?

(A) Voters over 40 with graduate degrees are more conservative than voters over 40 with only a high school education.

(B) Voters over 40 with graduate degrees are more conservative than voters under 40 with graduate degrees.

(C) Voters under forty with only a high school education are more conservative than voters under 40 who finished college but did not go to graduate school.

(D) Voters under 40 with only a high school education are less conservative than voters under 40 who finished college but did not go to graduate school.

(E) Voters under 40 with only a high school education are less conservative than voters under 40 with a graduate degree.

13. Public policies that are aimed at helping one group often inadvertently cause harm to another group.

    Which of the following statements provides support for the claim above?

    I.   The minimum wage results in increased teenage unemployment.

    II. Dairy subsidies cause higher milk prices.

    III. The space program resulted in advances in computer technology.

    (A) I only.

    (B) II only.

    (C) I and II only.

    (D) II and III only.

    (E) I, II, and III.

14. Some research indicates that aluminum may be a cause of Alzheimer's Disease, a disease that afflicts older people and that is characterized by a progressive loss of memory. According to one explanation, aluminum cookware could be the principal source of the aluminum causing the disease.

    Which of the following, if true, would tend to weaken the above explanation?

    (A) Aluminum cookware is not the only possible source of aluminum in the immediate environment.

    (B) It is not always possible to know whether a patient is suffering from Alzheimer's Disease or stroke.

    (C) There is no known cure for Alzheimer's Disease.

    (D) According to some research there is a genetic factor that contributes to Alzheimer's Disease.

    (E) Alzheimer's Disease occurs as frequently among those who have not used aluminum cookware as it does among those who have used aluminum cookware.

15. During the summer of 1988, there was very little rainfall throughout the grain-producing states. The low rainfall resulted in an unusually low yield of bushels per acre. The low yield resulted in higher grain prices. The high prices of grain resulted in higher feeding costs for livestock owners. The high feeding costs resulted in higher meat prices at the supermarket.

Which of the following conclusions can most properly be drawn from the information above?

(A) Concern about heart disease is causing people to eat less meat.

(B) The drought was caused by the "greenhouse effect," an increase in carbon dioxide in the atmosphere.

(C) Increased productivity in agriculture has resulted in fewer and fewer farmers being able to feed more and more people.

(D) Given the population explosion and threat of world famine, people should eat an ecologically more efficient source of calories, grain, rather than the ecologically less efficient meat.

(E) An increase in rainfall would result in lower meat prices.

16. George: This year's increase in profits at our company is obviously the result of the new advertising campaign that we started recently. This is clear evidence that advertising is the key to business success.

Martha: Wrong. Look at the facts George. There was a general increase in consumer spending throughout the economy this year. The advertising campaign started last month, while profits have been increasing all year long as consumer spending increased.

Which of the following best describes the weak point in George's claim on which Martha's response focuses?

(A) George talks in very general terms about an increase in profits without giving exact figures for sales, profits, and the cost of the advertising campaign.

(B) George bases his whole argument on just one example.

(C) The situation as described by George does not preclude the possibility that the effect preceded the supposed cause.

(D) George does not discuss any examples of companies that did not undertake an advertising campaign.

(E) The increase in profits may prove to be only a temporary phenomenon.

STOP

If time remains, you may go back and check your work.
When the time allotted is up, you may go on to the next section.

Section 2

TIME: 25 Minutes

16 Questions

DIRECTIONS: Solve each problem using space on the page for scratchwork. Indicate the best answer from the choices given.

NUMBERS: All numbers used are real numbers.

FIGURES: Figures accompanying problems in this section provide information useful in solving the problems. They are drawn as accurately as possible; however, when a figure is not drawn to scale, more information will be provided. It is given that all figures lie in a plane unless otherwise stated.

---

1. If $z = \dfrac{xy}{x+y}$, then $x =$

   (A) $\dfrac{zy}{y-z}$.

   (B) $\dfrac{zy}{z-y}$.

   (C) $\dfrac{y-z}{zy}$.

   (D) $\dfrac{z-y}{zy}$.

   (E) $\dfrac{z-y}{y}$.

2. For any integer n, which of the following must be an even integer?

   I. $2n + 1$

   II. $2n + 2$

   III. $2n - 1$

   (A) I only.

   (B) II only.

   (C) III only.

   (D) I and II only.

   (E) II and III only.

3. John wishes to contribute $2,500 to his favorite charities A and B in the ratio of 2 to 3. The amount he should contribute to charity A is

   (A) $500.   (B) $1,000.

   (C) $1,250.   (D) $1,500.

   (E) $2,000.

4. A loan of $150 is made at a simple annual interest rate of 12 percent. The amount that the borrower owes at the end of 10 months is

   (A) $3.   (B) $15.

   (C) $18.   (D) $165.

   (E) $168.

5. Jill buys 20 shares of Unit Corporation at $25 each, 20 shares at $30 each, and 35 shares at $20 each. Her average per share cost is

   (A) $20.   (B) $24.

   (C) $25.   (D) $27.50.

   (E) $30.

6. If the sum of four consecutive integers is 226, then the smallest of these numbers is

   (A) 55.   (B) 56.

   (C) 57.   (D) 58.

   (E) 59.

7. Of the freshmen at a college, 24 percent failed remedial mathematics. If 360 students failed remedial mathematics, how many freshmen are enrolled at the college?

   (A) 500   (B) 1,200

   (C) 1,500   (D) 1,600

   (E) 1,800

8. If $2X + Y = 2$ and $X + 3Y > 6$, then

   (A) $Y \geq 2.$ (B) $Y > 2.$

(C) $Y < 2$.

(D) $Y \leq 2$.

(E) $Y = 2$.

9. On a line segment joining 2.6 to 2.9 what is the number whose distance from 2.6 equals $^1/_4$ of the distance from 2.6 to 2.9?

(A) 2.525

(B) 2.675

(C) 2.75

(D) 2.825

(E) 2.975

10. In the figure shown, the area of the inscribed circle is A. What is the length of a side of the square?

(A) $\sqrt{A/\pi}$

(B) $\sqrt{2A/\pi}$

(C) A/π

(D) $2\sqrt{A/\pi}$

(E) $2A/\pi$

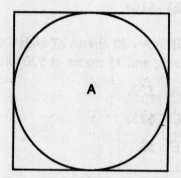

11. In a class of 200 students, 36 received A's. If 15 percent of the men and 20 percent of women received an A, then the number of men students in the class is

(A) 80.

(B) 90.

(C) 100.

(D) 120.

(E) 150.

12. Solve for x: $\dfrac{5}{x} = \dfrac{2}{x-1} + \dfrac{1}{x(x-1)}$.

(A) -1

(B) 0

(C) 1

(D) 2

(E) 3

13. Find the larger side of a rectangle whose area is 24 and whose perimeter is 22.

    (A) 8   (B) 6

    (C) 4   (D) 3

    (E) 2

14. If the diameters of two soup cans are in the ratio 1:2 and the heights are in the ratio 2:1, then their volumes are in the ratio

    (A) 1:1.   (B) 1:2.

    (C) 1:4.   (D) 1:8.

    (E) 8:1.

15. Julie holds 100 shares each of Companies *A*, *B*, and *C*. On January 1, the prices per share, respectively, were $10, $12, and $18. Shares of Company *B* split 2 for 1 and those of Company *C* split 3 for 2. On December 31, the prices per share of Companies *A*, *B*, and *C*, respectively, were $12, $6, and $16. There were no dividends. What was the annual return on Julie's portfolio of stocks?

    (A) 16.7%   (B) 20%

    (C) 25%   (D) 30%

    (E) 33.3%

16. Solve for x, $\dfrac{1}{4} + \dfrac{9}{x} = 1$.

    (A) 4   (B) 6

    (C) 8   (D) 12

    (E) 18

STOP

If time remains, you may go back and check your work.
When the time allotted is up, you may go on to the next section.

Section 3

TIME: 25 Minutes
23 Questions

DIRECTIONS: Each passage is followed by questions based on its content. After reading the passage, choose the best answer to each question. Answer all questions based on what is indicated or implied in that passage.

The decorative dripstone features are called speleothems (from the Greek **spelaion** for cave and **thema** for deposit). When these structures are highlighted by lanterns or electric lights, they transform a cave into a natural wonderland.

The most familiar speleothems are **stalactites** and **stalagmites**. Stalactites hang downward from the ceiling and are formed as drop after drop of water slowly trickles through cracks in the cave roof. As each drop of water hangs from the ceiling, it loses carbon dioxide and deposits a film of calcite. Successive drops add ring below ring, the water dripping through the hollow center of the rings, until a pendant cylinder forms. Tubular or "soda straw" stalactites grow in this way; most are fragile and have the diameter of a drop of water, but some reach a length of perhaps a yard or more. The large cone-shaped stalactites begin as these fragile tubes and then enlarge to cones when enough water accumulates to flow along the outside of the soda straws. Deposition of calcite on the outside of the tubes, most of which are near the ceiling and taper downward, results in the familiar cone shapes.

Stalagmites grow upward from the floor of the cave generally as a result of water dripping from overhanging stalactites. A "column" forms when a stalactite and a stalagmite grow until they join. A "curtain" or "drapery" begins to form on an inclined ceiling when the drops of water trickle along a slope. Gradually a thin sheet of calcite grows downward from the ceiling and hangs in decorative folds like a drape. Sheets of calcite that are deposited on the walls or floor by flowing water are called **flowstone**. **Rimstone dams** are raised fencelike deposits of calcite on the cave floor that form around pools of water.

Helictites are curious twisted or spiraling cylinders or needles. They apparently develop when water seeps through the ceiling so slowly that slight chemical or physical changes can cause reorientation of the crystal structure of the calcite or gypsum. **Cave corals**, also formed by slowly seeping water, are small clusters of individual knobs.

Most cave passages contain deposits of material that have been washed into the cave. This material, known as cave **fill,** varies from sand and clay to stratified gravel. The pebbles in these deposits often are highly polished or frosted and sometimes are as large as six inches in diameter. Cave fills are particularly noteworthy because they contain materials that reflect a geologic history and a record of past climates of the surrounding area.

Rock material produced by the collapse of the ceiling or walls of a cave is called **breakdown** and may range in size from plates and chips to massive blocks. Most breakdown present in caves today appears to have occurred thousands of years ago. It is generally associated with the early history of cave development.

1. The primary purpose of the passage is to

    (A) analyze a situation.

    (B) define phenomena.

    (C) propose a theory.

    (D) correct a misconception.

    (E) describe a specific place.

2. The information in the passage is most relevant to which field of study?

    (A) geography   (B) archaeology

    (C) physics   (D) geology

    (E) biochemistry

3. Which of the following statements best describes the organization of the passage?

    (A) All six paragraphs discuss various kinds of cave features, from dripstone to breakdown.

    (B) Paragraphs one through four describe speleothems, while five and six discuss external matter brought into caves from the outside.

    (C) The first three paragraphs form a unit, but the last three are extraneous to the principal topic of the passage.

(D) Paragraphs one through four describe phenomena caused by water, whereas five and six describe phenomena caused by other means.

(E) The first three paragraphs discuss typical cave features, and the last three discuss atypical ones.

4. According to the passage, all of the following are caused by dripping water EXCEPT

(A) stalactites.   (B) stalagmites.

(C) columns.   (D) rimstones.

(E) curtains.

5. According to the passage, all of the following are formed when water loses carbon dioxide and deposits calcite EXCEPT

(A) drapery.   (B) columns.

(C) helicites.   (D) stalagmites.

(E) rimstones.

6. The passage provides information that answers which of the following questions?

I.   Do cone-shaped stalactites begin as tubular stalactites?

II. Are stalactites or stalagmites longer when they join to form columns?

III. Do stalagmites, stalactites, and flowstone contain calcite?

(A) I only.   (B) I and II only.

(C) I and III only.   (D) II and III only.

(E) I, II, and III.

7. It can be inferred from the passage that which of the following is the most geologically useful?

(A) Breakdown   (B) Fill

(C) Stalactites   (D) Helicites

(E) Columns

8. It can be inferred from the passage that which of the following is LEAST likely to contain calcite?

    (A) Columns (B) Curtains

    (C) Helicites (D) Cave corals

    (E) Fill

Merchant Robert Morris was a man of many distinctions. One of the wealthiest individuals in the Colonies and an economic wizard, he won the accolade "Financier of the Revolution," yet died penniless and forgotten. He and Roger Sherman were the only signers of all three of the Nation's basic documents: the Declaration of Independence, Articles of Confederation, and Constitution. Morris, who turned down appointment as the first Secretary of the Treasury, also served as a Senator in the First Congress.

Morris was born in or near Liverpool, England, in 1734. At the age of 13, he emigrated to Maryland to join his father, a tobacco exporter at Oxford, Maryland. After brief schooling at Philadelphia, the youth obtained employment with Thomas and Charles Willing's well-known shipping firm. In 1754 he became a partner, and for almost four decades was one of the company's directors as well as one of Philadelphia's most influential citizens. Marrying in 1769 at the age of 35, he fathered five sons and two daughters.

During the Stamp Act turmoil in 1765, Morris had joined other merchants in protest, but not until the outbreak of hostilities a decade hence did he fully commit himself to the Revolution. In 1775 the Continental Congress contracted with his firm to import arms and ammunition; and he was elected to the Pennsylvania council of safety (1775-76), the committee of correspondence, the provincial assembly (1775-76), the State legislature (1776-78), and the Continental Congress (1775-78). In the latter body, on July 1, 1776, he voted against independence, which he personally considered premature, but the next day purposely absented himself to facilitate an affirmative ballot by his State.

Morris, a key Member of Congress, specialized in financial affairs and military procurement. Although he and his firm profited handsomely, had it not been for his assiduous labors the Continental Army would probably have needed to demobilize. He worked closely with General Washington, wheedled money and supplies from the States, borrowed money in the face of overwhelming difficulties, and on occasion even obtained personal loans to further the war cause. Immediately following his congressional service, Morris sat for two more terms in the Pennsylvania legislature in the period between 1778 and 1781. During this time, Thomas Paine and others attacked him for profiteering in Congress, which investigated his accounts and vindicated him. Nevertheless, his reputation slipped.

Morris embarked on the most dramatic phase of his career by accepting the office of Superintendent of Finance (1781-84) under the Articles of Confederation. Congress, recognizing the perilous state of the Nation's finances and its impotence to remedy it, granted him dictatorial powers and acquiesced to his condition that he be allowed to continue his private commercial enterprises. He slashed all governmental and military expenditures, personally purchased Army and Navy supplies, tightened accounting procedures, prodded the States to fulfill quotas of money and supplies, and when necessary strained his personal credit by issuing notes over his own signature or borrowing from friends.

To finance Washington's Yorktown campaign in 1781, in addition to the above techniques Morris obtained a sizable loan from France. He used part of it, along with some of his own fortune, to organize the Bank of North America, chartered that December. The first Government-incorporated bank in the United States, it aided war financing.

9. The passage most likely appeared in

    (A) a U.S. history textbook.

    (B) a biographical dictionary.

    (C) a finance magazine.

    (D) a scholarly political science book.

    (E) an eighteenth-century military history.

10. According to the passage, Morris' career encompassed which of the following fields?

    I.   Economics

    II. Politics

    III. Finance

    (A) I only.   (B) I and II only.

    (C) I and III only.   (D) II and III only.

    (E) I, II, and III.

11. Based on information in the passage, which of the following state-
    ments best expresses what seems to have been Morris' attitude to-
    ward personal wealth?

    (A) It was clearly the most important thing in his life.

    (B) He appears to have amassed great personal wealth by ignoring
        his own principles.

    (C) It was clearly of considerable importance to him, but he was
        willing to risk it to benefit others.

    (D) The need to support his family interfered with his desire to be
        philanthropic.

    (E) All things considered, it appears to have been of little conse-
        quence to him.

12. According to the passage, Morris profited from the Revolution

    I.   through government military contracts.

    II. by borrowing money at favorable rates.

    III. by using loans made to the government for personal purposes.

    (A) I only.   (B) II only.

    (C) III only.   (D) I and II only.

    (E) I, II, and III only.

13. Congress' faith in Morris' financial genius is perhaps best attested to
    by

    (A) awarding contracts to his firm.

    (B) chartering the Bank of North America.

    (C) allowing him to borrow money from France.

    (D) trusting him to work closely with George Washington.

    (E) granting him dictatorial powers as Superintendent of Finance.

14. According to the passage, Morris did all of the following in support
    of the war EXCEPT

    (A) procure personal loans.

    (B) borrow money from France.

(C) import arms and ammunition.

(D) serve in the Continental Army.

(E) induce states to contribute supplies.

15. According to the passage, after Tom Paine's attack on Morris, Congress

I. cleared him of Paine's charges.

II. restored his public credibility.

III. granted him unusual power in managing the nation's financial affairs.

(A) I only.   (B) I and II only.

(C) I and III only.   (D) II and III only.

(E) I, II, and III.

16. The passage contains information that answers which of the following questions?

I. How was Morris able to handle the dilemma of personally opposing independence but not actually opposing the Declaration of Independence?

II. How accurate were Tom Paine's charges of profiteering?

III. Why was Congress unable to remedy the nation's financial problems in 1781?

(A) I only.   (B) I and II only.

(C) I and III only.   (D) II and III only.

(E) I, II, and III.

17. Which of the following statements best describes the organization of the first four paragraphs?

(A) The ordering is essentially chronological, from early to later events in Morris' life.

(B) The organization is cause-and-effect; one paragraph introduces an event and the next discusses the results of that event.

(C) Each paragraph introduces an aspect of Morris' life and the rest of the paragraph elaborates on it.

(D) The first two paragraphs deal with Morris' activities at the local or regional level, whereas the next two discuss his participation in national events.

(E) Each paragraph deals with progressively more significant events in Morris' life.

In September 1872, to the great delight of the Chiricahuas, General Howard had Tom Jeffords named as their agent. A realist, Jeffords recognized that his charges had not been conquered and would continue to do just about as they pleased. But he also believed that, as long as he issued rations and did not interfere in their affairs, they would keep the peace. Cochise worked quietly with the agent to make reservation life succeed. The friendship between the two and the chief's great powers of leadership kept the Indians under restraint. Arizona settlers voiced amazement that Cochise actually kept his word. In Arizona he did keep the peace, but in Mexico he did not. For generations Chiricahuas had raided in Mexico, and they did not intend to stop now simply because they had a reservation and an agent.

Early in 1874 Cochise fell ill, and on June 8 he died. The Chiricahuas selected his son, Taza, as their new chief.

Friction with his superiors increasingly troubled Jeffords. The Indian Bureau wanted the Indians governed rigidly, made self-supporting, and started on the road to "civilization." Jeffords knew such aims to be visionary and continued the loose management he had adopted in 1872. The Indian Bureau withheld cooperation and support. At times Jeffords had to buy supplies for the Indians with his own money. The Bureau also disliked the location of the Chiricahua Reservation. Resting on the international boundary, it not only encouraged and facilitated Chiricahua raids into Mexico but also attracted other Apaches who used it as a base for their own raids. And the Bureau had a new policy of bringing all Apaches together on a single reservation, San Carlos, in the parched bottoms of the Gila River some 121 kilometers to the north. By 1876, officials in Washington merely awaited an excuse both to rid themselves of Jeffords and to move the Chiricahuas to San Carlos.

The Apaches themselves provided the excuse. Because of short rations in the spring of 1876, Jeffords let the Indians hunt in the Dragoon Mountains. While camped there, they fell to quarreling. Taza took most of the people back to Apache Pass, but Skinya and about 12 families remained in the Dragoon Mountains. While intoxicated, Skinya's brother, Pionsenay, killed two of his sisters, then killed a whisky-seller and his partner when denied more whisky. With other malcontents, Pionsenay next embarked on a raid in the San Pedro Valley.

At once Jeffords declared all Indians west of the Chiricahua Mountains hostile—Pionsenay and his followers—but the damage had been done. The governor of Arizona Territory denounced all Chiricahuas and their agent and demanded their removal.

18. The passage is most probably an excerpt from

   (A) the memoirs of an Indian descendant of Cochise.

   (B) the journal of Tom Jeffords.

   (C) a modern novel depicting the Old West.

   (D) an essay contrasting Indian and white ways of life.

   (E) a book written about American history.

19. Which of the following situations most accurately describes how the Indians felt about Tom Jeffords?

   (A) They liked him because he understood them.

   (B) They liked him because they could take advantage of him.

   (C) They felt he was basically a good man who did not view them as individuals.

   (D) They had no respect for him because he could not get his superiors to fulfill their agreements.

   (E) They wanted to cause trouble for the restrictive policies of the government and regretted that he got in their way.

20. According to information in the passage, Tom Jeffords was a realist who knew that

   (A) the Indians could not keep the peace for long.

   (B) the Indians could be taught to become agrarian if given enough time.

   (C) it was just a matter of time before he was deposed by the Indian Bureau.

   (D) the Indians could not be expected to be confined according to white laws.

   (E) Washington had no intention of keeping faith with the Indians.

21. According to information in the passage, Cochise's best quality was which of the following?

    (A) While he lived, he was able to keep his son Taza under control.

    (B) No one knew that he was leading his people in raids across the border.

    (C) He was a strong leader among his own people.

    (D) The peace was kept in Arizona, even though raids crossed into Mexico.

    (E) His long life provided a lengthy period of peace.

22. Which of the following best describes the attitude of the author toward the Indian Bureau described in paragraph three?

    (A) Approving   (B) Sympathetic

    (C) Disapproving   (D) Disdainful

    (E) Shocked

23. The passage implies that the main reason for trouble between whites and Indians lay with which of the following?

    (A) Fault for problems could be laid directly at the feet of a few renegade Indians bent on causing trouble.

    (B) Duplicitous behavior on the part of the whites caused the Indians to lose faith.

    (C) Failure of the whites to make their objectives clear to the Indian community caused misunderstandings.

    (D) Lack of leadership within the Indian community created a fractionalized situation.

    (E) Trouble came from conflicting currents found within each culture.

STOP

If time remains, you may go back and check your work.
When the time allotted is up, you may go on to the next section.

Section 4

TIME: 25 Minutes
20 Questions

DIRECTIONS: Each of the data sufficiency problems below contains a question and two statements, labeled (1) and (2), in which certain data are given. Decide whether the data given in the statements are sufficient for answering the question. Using the data given in the statements plus your knowledge of mathematics and everyday facts choose:

(A) if Statement (1) ALONE is sufficient, but Statement (2) alone is not sufficient to answer the question asked;

(B) if Statement (2) ALONE is sufficient, but Statement (1) alone is not sufficient to answer the question asked;

(C) if BOTH Statements (1) and (2) TOGETHER are sufficient to answer the question asked, but NEITHER statement ALONE is sufficient;

(D) if EACH statement ALONE is sufficient to answer the question asked;

(E) if Statements (1) and (2) TOGETHER are NOT sufficient to answer the questions asked, and additional data specific to the problem are needed.

NUMBERS: All numbers are real numbers.

FIGURES: A figure in this section will conform to the information given, but will not necessarily conform to the additional information given in the numbered Statements (1) and (2).

NOTES: Lines are straight if shown as straight, and angle measures are greater than zero.

The position of points, angles, regions, etc., exist in the order shown.

All figures lie in a plane unless otherwise stated.

Sample Question:

In the figure, the two circles are concentric (have the same center O) with radius x and y, where $x < y$. What is the area of the shaded region?

(1) The sum of the two radii is 11 units.

(2) The area of the smaller circle is $^1/_2$ of the area of the larger one.

Sample Explanation:

(C) By Statement (1), $x + y = 11$. Since, Statement (1) gives no other information about x and y, you cannot find the areas of the two circles. Since the area of the shaded region is the difference of the two areas, Statement (1) alone is not sufficient. According to Statement (2), $\pi y^2 = 2\pi x^2$; therefore, the area of the region is $2\pi x^2 - \pi x^2 = \pi x^2$. Since (2) does not give the value of x, it is not possible to find the area of the shaded region using (2) alone. However, if we use (1) and (2) together, we get the two equations

$$y = 11 - x \text{ and } \pi y^2 = 2\pi x^2$$

from which we can solve for x by writing the single equation $\pi(11 - x)^2 = 2\pi x^2$.

1. Does *BC* pass through the center of the circle?

    (1) ∠ *BAC* is a right angle.

    (2) *AB* = 3, *AC* = 4, and *BC* = 5.

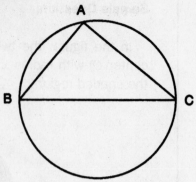

2. Profit, for a particular company, varies directly with income. What is the profit if the income is $95,000?

    (1) Profit is 10 cents on the dollar.

    (2) Profit on $64,500 is $6,450.

3. Is the positive integer, *x*, a factor of 12?

    (1) *x* is an even prime number.

    (2) *x* < 6.

4. The price of a photograph is based on its area. What is the price of picture A?

    (1) Picture A is 7" by 9".

    (2) A 3" by 5" picture costs $15.

5. Is *x* a positive number?

    (1) 2*x* > 12.

    (2) 5 − *x* < 1.

6. ∠ *ABC* = right angle. What is *y*?

    (1) *x* = 30°.

    (2) ∠ *BDC* is a right angle.

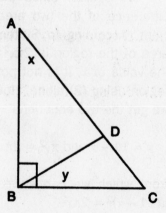

7. *ABCD* is a rectangle and *E* and *F* are centers of the circles. What is the area of the figure?

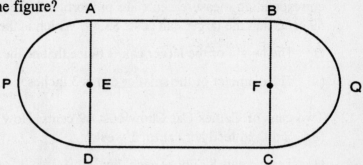

(1) The radius of the circle is 1.

(2) *DC = 2BC*.

8. Jane is twice as old as George. How old is George?

(1) Next year Jane will be three years older than Mary.

(2) George is younger than Mary.

9. What is the length of *AB*?

(1) *ABCDEF* is a hexagon.

(2) The length of the arc *AB* is π.

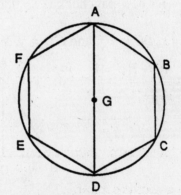

10. *ABCD* is a rectangle. What is the length of *PS*?

(1) $QB = \sqrt{8}$.

(2) *RS* is parallel to *BC*.

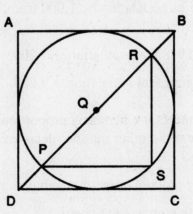

11. Two cans of the same kind of green beans are similar in shape, i.e., corresponding measurements are proportional. The smaller can costs 49 cents and the larger can costs $3.49. Which is the better buy?

    (1) The height of the larger can is twice that of the smaller can.

    (2) The diameter of the smaller can is 3 inches.

12. Two cans of Catties Cat Chow cost 49 cents. How much will it cost Mrs. Smith to feed her cat for 1 week?

    (1) The cat eats 8 ounces each day.

    (2) If more than 10 cans are purchased at any one time, a 10 percent discount is given.

13. An employee receives a 10 percent salary increase. How many times a year is she paid?

    (1) Her old salary was $27,600.

    (2) Her new paycheck is $3,036.

14. $AC = x$, $BC = 1/y$, and $CD = y$. What is x? (See the following figure.)

    (1) $AC + BC = 1$.

    (2) $xy = 1$.

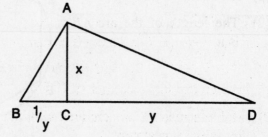

15. A city doubles its population every 10 years. How long does it take to increase its population by 1,000 from its present size? (Assume linear increase.)

    (1) In 1900 the population was 200.

    (2) The present population is 2,000.

16. Two numbers are inversely proportional. When one number increases 25 percent the other number decreases 20 percent. What are the two numbers?

    (1) The product of the two numbers is 16.

    (2) Both numbers are positive.

17. If $| x(x - 2) / (x - 2) | < k$, what are the values of x which make the statement true?

    (1) $|k| = k$.

    (2) $k = 4$.

18. Profit varies directly as selling price of an item and inversely as the cost of materials. Fixed costs are such that only $2 profit can be made on an item which costs $5 for materials and which sells for $100. What annual profit can this company expect if the selling price for the given items increases 10 percent?

    (1) The cost of materials does not change.

    (2) 100,000 items are sold.

19. A fishpole is to be encased in a rectangular box with a square base. The box is shorter than the pole. What are the minimum dimensions of the box?

    (1) The area of the base of the box is 5.5 square feet.

    (2) The pole is 6 feet and the box is 5 feet.

20. Mable invested 10 percent of her annual income in a mutual fund. Later she received dividends that were 10 percent of her initial investment. What interest rate did she receive?

    (1) Mable's annual income is $50,000.

    (2) Mable's account was credited with the dividend six months after her initial investment.

STOP

If time remains, you may go back and check your work.
When the time allotted is up, you may go on to the next section.

Section 5

TIME: 25 Minutes
16 Questions

DIRECTIONS: Solve each problem using space on the page for scratchwork. Indicate the best answer from the choices given.

NUMBERS: All numbers used are real numbers.

FIGURES: Figures accompanying problems in this section provide information useful in solving the problems. They are drawn as accurately as possible; however, when a figure is not drawn to scale, more information will be provided. It is given that all figures lie in a plane unless otherwise stated.

---

1. Solve for x: $\dfrac{x}{0.5} - \dfrac{x}{4} - \dfrac{7}{1.6} = 0$.

   (A) 1

   (B) $\dfrac{7}{20}$

   (C) 0

   (D) $\dfrac{5}{2}$

   (E) $\dfrac{14}{25}$

2. $1 + 2 + 3 + 4 + \ldots + 99 =$

   (A) 4,700

   (B) 4,750

   (C) 4,850

   (D) 4,900

   (E) 4,950

3. The mean distance from Mars to the sun is 1.41×10^8 miles and the mean distance from Earth to the sun is 9.3×10^7 miles. How much closer to the sun is Earth than Mars?

   (A) 4.8×10^7

   (B) 4.8×10^8

   (C) 7.89×10^7

   (D) 7.89×10^8

   (E) 7.89×10^{10}

4. If 6 oranges can be purchased for x cents, how many oranges can be purchased with y dollars?

(A) $\dfrac{y}{6x}$

(B) $\dfrac{6y}{x}$

(C) $\dfrac{y}{600x}$

(D) $\dfrac{100y}{6x}$

(E) $\dfrac{600y}{x}$

5. A rectangle is 3 feet long and 6 feet wide. The number of squares with sides 3 inches long that are needed to cover the rectangle is

(A) 6.

(B) 72.

(C) 144.

(D) 288.

(E) 864.

6. If x is 25% greater than y, what percent is y of x?

(A) 75%

(B) 125%

(C) 20%

(D) 80%

(E) 50%

7. How many ounces of a metal other than gold must be added to 56 ounces of pure gold to make a composition 70 percent gold?

(A) 39.2

(B) 16.8

(C) 9.8

(D) 56

(E) 24

8. If $x + y = {}^1/_k$ and $x - y = k$, what is the value of $x^2 - y^2$?

(A) 4

(B) 1

(C) 0

(D) k^2

(E) $\dfrac{1}{k^2}$

9. The fraction

$$\frac{7x - 11}{x^2 - 2x - 15}$$

was obtained by adding the two fractions

$$\frac{A}{x - 5} + \frac{B}{x + 3}.$$

The values of A and B are

(A) $A = 7x, B = 11$.   (B) $A = -11, B = 7x$.

(C) $A = 3, B = 4$.   (D) $A = 5, B = -3$.

(E) $A = -5, B = 3$.

10. A large cube has a surface of 216 square inches. What is the total surface area of two smaller cubes whose edges are half as long as those of the large cube?

(A) 108   (B) 216

(C) 54   (D) 30

(E) 72

11. If the hypotenuse of a right triangle is $X + 1$ and one of the legs is X, then the other leg is

(A) $\sqrt{2x + 1}$.   (B) $\sqrt{2x} + 1$.

(C) $\sqrt{x^2 + (x + 1)^2}$.   (D) 1.

(E) $2x + 1$.

12. The expression $(x + y)^2 + (x - y)^2$ is equivalent to

(A) $2x^2$.   (B) $4x^2$.

(C) $2(x^2 + y^2)$.   (D) $2x^2 + y^2$.

(E) $x^2 + 2y^2$.

13. If $1 - x^{-1}$ is divided by $1 - x$, the quotient is

(A) 1.   (B) $-\dfrac{1}{x}$.

(C) $-\dfrac{1}{x^2}$.

(D) $\dfrac{1}{x}$.

(E) $\dfrac{1}{1-x}$.

14. When x is decreased by 129 and then that number is multiplied by 129, the result is 129. What is the value of x?

(A) 130

(B) 129

(C) 2

(D) 3

(E) 16,770

15. A 6 meter rope is cut into four pieces with each piece twice as long as the previous one. How long is the longest piece?

(A) .4 m

(B) 1 m

(C) 3 m

(D) 3.2 m

(E) 4 m

16. A book that is 7.5 inches by 9.5 inches has a 1 inch top margin, .75 inch bottom margin and right side margin, and 2 inch left side margin. What is the area of the printed part of the page?

(A) 35.625

(B) 36

(C) 36.8125

(D) 38.8125

(E) 39

STOP

If time remains, you may go back and check your work.
When the time allotted is up, you may go on to the next section.

Section 6

TIME: 25 Minutes
22 Questions

DIRECTIONS: In each of the following sentences, some part of the sentence or the entire sentence is underlined. The five answer choices give various ways of phrasing the underlined part. The first choice repeats the given sentence. Pay attention to grammar, choice of words, and sentence construction in order to select the best version of the sentence. Choose (A) if you think the given sentence is correct.

---

1. Among the seven warning symptoms of cancer are a sore that does not heal, a change in bowel or bladder habits, <u>a coughing or hoarseness that is persistent</u>, and a change in a wart or mole.

   (A) a coughing or hoarsness that is persistent

   (B) a persistent coughing or hoarseness

   (C) a cough that is persistent

   (D) a persistent cough or hoarseness

   (E) a continually persistent coughing or hoarseness

2. Marguerite Bourke-White was a photographer <u>during the Great Depression and World War II which has enabled young Americans to experience events through pictures</u>.

   (A) during the Great Depression and World War II which has enabled young Americans to experience events through pictures.

   (B) during the Great Depression and World War II which has through pictures enabled young Americans to experience events.

   (C) which has through pictures during the Great Depression and World War II enabled young Americans to experience events.

   (D) who has enabled young Americans to experience events during the Great Depression and World War II through pictures.

   (E) who has enabled young Americans during the Great Depression and World War II to experience events.

3. The debate was <u>among those who opposed the use of plastic bags</u> and those who believed that plastic bags were necessary to save the trees.

    (A) among those who opposed the use of plastic bags

    (B) among those opposing the use of plastic bags

    (C) between those opposing the use of plastic bags

    (D) among those who were opposed to the use of plastic bags

    (E) between those who opposed the use of plastic bags

4. In the digestive tracts of termites are certain flagellates which digest the cellulose of the wood which the termites swallow and supply <u>in effect the digestive products for energy to the arthropod and itself</u>.

    (A) in effect the digestive products for energy to the arthropod and itself.

    (B) effectively the digestive product for energy to the arthropod and itself.

    (C) in effect the digestive products for energy to the arthropods and themselves.

    (D) in affect the digestive products for energy to the arthropod and itself.

    (E) in affect the digestive products for energy to the arthropods and themselves.

5. Many biologists believe that the extinction of the dinosaur was not the result of epidemics of diseases <u>but rather was the result from</u> climatic change from perpetual summers to contrasting seasons of warm and cold.

    (A) but rather was the result from

    (B) but instead was the result from

    (C) being rather the result of

    (D) and rather result of

    (E) but rather was the result of

6. Through amniocentesis a needle is inserted into the pregnant uterus and a sample of the amniotic fluid is withdrawn; through <u>the lab specialists examining</u> the fluid, they can determine the sex of the baby.

(A) the lab specialists examining

(B) the examination by the lab specialist

(C) the lab specialists' examining

(D) examination of

(E) the lab specialist's examination of

7. The new rule prohibits <u>smoking by the employee's</u> inside the building.

(A) smoking by the employee's

(B) employees who smoke

(C) all employee's smoking

(D) employees' smoking

(E) that there be smoking by an employee

8. The hurricane was reported as a storm which was <u>apt to hard hit the coast of South Carolina</u>.

(A) apt to hard hit the coast of South Carolina.

(B) inclined to hit hard the coast of South Carolina.

(C) liable to hard hit the coast of South Carolina.

(D) likely to hit hard the coast of South Carolina.

(E) likely to hard hit the coast of South Carolina.

9. Owning nearly 20 percent of all U.S. bank assets, <u>as well as nearly 3 million Americans being employed by foreign-controlled companies</u>, illustrates the tremendous impact of foreign investors on America.

(A) as well as nearly 3 million Americans being employed by foreign-controlled companies

(B) in addition to nearly 3 million Americans being employed by foreign-controlled companies

(C) as well as the fact that they are able to employ 3 million Americans

(D) and employing 3 million Americans in foreign-controlled companies

(E) and being able to engage in the employment of 3 million Americans in their companies

10. The restrictive diet prohibited the inclusion of animal fats, salt, <u>nor any dairy products</u>.

   (A) nor any dairy products.

   (B) neither any dairy products.

   (C) nor also any dairy products.

   (D) or any dairy products.

   (E) or any product classified as dairy.

11. <u>What individuals and business give up in spending to pay taxes, and to consequently reduce their total spending</u>, will be used by the government; since the total spending in the economy will remain the same, a balanced budget tends to have a neutral effect on the economy.

   (A) What individuals and business give up in spending to pay taxes, and to consequently reduce their total spending,

   (B) What individuals and businesses give up in spending to pay taxes and consequently to reduce their total spending,

   (C) What individuals and businesses give up in spending to pay taxes and to moreover reduce their total spending,

   (D) What individuals and businesses give up in spending to pay taxes not only to reduce their total spending,

   (E) What individuals and businesses give up in spending to pay to not only reduce their total spending,

12. The climate of the small island is <u>quite variable and the most unique of any place in the world</u>.

   (A) quite variable and the most unique of any place in the world.

   (B) quite variable and the uniquest of any place in the world.

    (C) variable and the most unique of any place in the world.

    (D) variable and unique to any place in the world.

    (E) variable and the most unique to any place in the world.

13. Australia is noted <u>for their unique animals: koalas, platypus, kanga-roo, and emu</u>.

    (A) for their unique animals: koalas, platypus, kangaroo, and emu.

    (B) for its unique animals: koalas, platypuses, kangaroo, and emus.

    (C) for their unique animals: koalas, platypuses, kangaroos, and emus.

    (D) for its unique animals: koalas, platypuses, kangaroos, and emus.

    (E) for its unique animals: koalas, platypus, kangaroos, and emus.

14. <u>Preparing for the tax season, the leisure time of many young people is lost until after April 15</u>.

    (A) Preparing for the tax season, the leisure time of many young people is lost until after April 15.

    (B) To prepare for the tax season, takes up the leisure time of many young people until after April 15.

    (C) Preparing for the tax season, takes up the leisure time of many young people until after April 15.

    (D) Taking up the leisure time of many young people until after April 15, is the preparation for the tax season.

    (E) Preparing for the tax season takes up the leisure time of many young people until after April 15.

15. All day share prices were <u>lower, that sent bond prices down and interest rates up</u>.

    (A) lower, that sent bond prices down and interest rates up.

    (B) lower, sending bond prices down and interest rates up.

    (C) lower, resulting in bond prices dropping and interest rates which went up.

    (D) lower, resulting in the dropping of bond prices and interest rates which went up.

(E) lower; sending bond prices down and interest rates up.

16. Proponents of the split-brain theory suggest that a right-brained person is creative, intuitive since <u>they use the right hemisphere; they contend the left-brained individual uses</u> the verbal, language-oriented, logical hemisphere of the brain.

  (A) they use the right hemisphere; they contend the left-brained individual uses

  (B) the individuals use the right hemisphere; they contend that left-brained individuals use

  (C) the individuals uses the right hemisphere; they contend that left-brained individuals use

  (D) the individual uses the right hemisphere; they contend that the left-brained individual uses

  (E) the individual uses the right hemisphere, nevertheless the left-brained individual uses

17. Eleven states out of 50 <u>housing nuclear facilities which must be monitored</u> by the Department of Energy.

  (A) housing nuclear facilities which must be monitored

  (B) having been selected to house nuclear facilities which must be monitored

  (C) being the location of nuclear facilities which must be monitored

  (D) house nuclear facilities which must be monitored

  (E) since housing nuclear facilities which must be monitored

18. While Governor Rich was in office, the state's budget increased by an average of 5 percent per year while inflation averaged 25 percent per year; <u>obviously the austere budgets during Governor Rich's term did not contribute greatly to inflation.</u>

  (A) obviously the austere budgets during Governor Rich's term did not contribute greatly to inflation.

  (B) obviously a result of Governor Rich's austere budgets.

  (C) austere budgets causing the slowdown.

(D) causing a slowdown in the growth of state spending because of Governor Rich's austere budgets.

(E) austere budgets during Governor Rich's term caused the inflation.

19. Economics can teach <u>a person to effectively manage their own affairs and be a contributing member</u> of society.

(A) a person to effectively manage their own affairs and be a contributing member

(B) a person to manage effectively their own affairs and to be a contributing member

(C) people to manage effectively their own affairs and to be a contributing member

(D) people to effectively manage their own affairs and to be contributing members

(E) people to manage effectively their own affairs and to be contributing members

20. The reason for structural inflation <u>is because there is a substantial shift</u> in demand to the products of one industry and away from the products of another industry.

(A) is because there is a substantial shift

(B) a substantial shifting

(C) is because of the fact that there is a substantial shift

(D) can probably, but not necessarily always, be attributed to the result of a substantial shift

(E) is the substantial shift

21. <u>The amount of unemployed workers reached 6.6 million in September of 1989</u>.

(A) The amount of unemployed workers reached 6.6 million in September of 1989.

(B) In September of 1989 the amount of unemployed workers reached 6.6 million.

(C) The number in September of 1989 of unemployed workers reaching 6.6 million.

(D) The amount in September of 1989 of unemployed workers reached 6.6 million.

(E) In September of 1989 the number of unemployed workers reached 6.6 million.

22. Due to the fact that the benefits of the recent economic expansion went to the wealthiest Americans, 32 million Americans still lived in poverty in 1988.

   (A) Due to the fact that the benefits of the recent economic expansion went to the wealthiest Americans,

   (B) Because the benefits of the recent economic expansion went to the wealthiest Americans,

   (C) Due to the fact of the benefits of the recent economic expansion going to the wealthiest Americans,

   (D) Since the benefits of the recent economic expansion is going to the wealthiest of the Americans,

   (E) Due to benefits going to the wealthiest Americans,

STOP

If time remains, you may go back and check your work.
When the time allotted is up, you may go on to the next section.

Section 7

ANALYSIS OF AN ISSUE ESSAY TOPIC

TIME: 30 Minutes

DIRECTIONS: In an essay, develop a position on the issue below by investigating the different angles of the issue, and explaining your thoughts on the topic. Remember, there is no one "correct" response to the essay topic.

Before starting, read the essay topic and its question(s). You may make preliminary notes in your test booklet before writing the actual essay. Be sure to write your essay on the lined pages provided at the back of the book.

Many non-smokers feel that secondhand smoke is hazardous to their health; recent medical research supports their allegations. Smokers feel that they have a right to enjoy this pastime, and that it would be a violation of their constitutional rights to deny them this privilege. The first group wants smoking made illegal, while the second group feels that they are being treating unfairly.

With whom do you agree: the smokers or the non-smokers? Using your own experience, reading, and observations, fully explain the reasons for your opinion.

STOP

Do not go on until you are instructed to do so. Use any remaining time to check your work on this portion of the test.

ANALYSIS OF AN ARGUMENT ESSAY TOPIC

TIME: 30 Minutes

DIRECTIONS: In essay form, prepare a review on the position of the argument provided below. Before taking your own position on the argument's standpoint, it may be helpful to determine the method of thinking behind the argument itself. For example, consider alternative explanations to any assumptions the argument might make, and any evidence or examples that may strengthen or weaken the argument. Remember, there is no one "correct" response to the essay topic.

Before starting, read the essay topic and its question(s). You may make preliminary notes in your test booklet before writing the actual essay. Be sure to write your essay on the lined pages provided at the back of the book.

The following appeared as part of an advertisement in a monthly magazine:

A new dog collar is available with a new special feature—an underground electrical barrier which works with a receiver on your dog's collar. It beeps your dog when he nears the boundary and gives him a small electrical correction if he tries to cross it. It keeps your dog safe and out of trouble without having to resort to expensive fences, run ropes or chains that could injure your pet.

Discuss how logical and/or convincing you find this argument. Be sure to analyze the reasoning and the use of any evidence in the argument. Include suggestions that would make the argument more acceptable and persuasive, and that would allow you to evaluate its conclusion more readily.

STOP

If time remains, you may go back and check your work.

PRACTICE TEST 5

ANSWER KEY

Section 1 — Critical Reasoning

1.	(D)	5.	(C)	9.	(E)	13.	(C)
2.	(A)	6.	(D)	10.	(D)	14.	(E)
3.	(A)	7.	(D)	11.	(A)	15.	(E)
4.	(D)	8.	(C)	12.	(D)	16.	(C)

Section 2 — Problem Solving

1.	(A)	5.	(B)	9.	(B)	13.	(A)
2.	(B)	6.	(A)	10.	(D)	14.	(B)
3.	(B)	7.	(C)	11.	(A)	15.	(B)
4.	(D)	8.	(B)	12.	(D)	16.	(D)

Section 3 — Reading Comprehension

1.	(B)	7.	(B)	13.	(E)	19.	(A)
2.	(D)	8.	(E)	14.	(D)	20.	(D)
3.	(A)	9.	(B)	15.	(C)	21.	(C)
4.	(D)	10.	(E)	16.	(A)	22.	(C)
5.	(C)	11.	(C)	17.	(A)	23.	(E)
6.	(C)	12.	(A)	18.	(E)		

Section 4 — Data Sufficiency

1.	(D)	6.	(C)	11.	(A)	16.	(E)
2.	(D)	7.	(C)	12.	(E)	17.	(B)
3.	(A)	8.	(E)	13.	(C)	18.	(C)
4.	(C)	9.	(C)	14.	(C)	19.	(B)
5.	(D)	10.	(C)	15.	(B)	20.	(B)

Section 5 — Problem Solving

1. (D)	5. (D)	9. (C)	13. (B)
2. (E)	6. (D)	10. (A)	14. (A)
3. (A)	7. (E)	11. (A)	15. (D)
4. (E)	8. (B)	12. (C)	16. (C)

Section 6 — Sentence Correction

1. (D)	7. (D)	13. (D)	19. (E)
2. (D)	8. (D)	14. (E)	20. (E)
3. (E)	9. (D)	15. (B)	21. (E)
4. (C)	10. (D)	16. (D)	22. (B)
5. (E)	11. (B)	17. (D)	
6. (C)	12. (D)	18. (A)	

DETAILED EXPLANATIONS OF ANSWERS

Section 1–Critical Reasoning

1. **(D)**
    Choice (A) is not a good argument for the pact because there is no indication that there would be any reduction in logging overall, only that Canadian competition would replace the output of the United States mills. Choice (B) is not an argument for the pact. It would be, if anything, an argument against it since unemployment would probably be one of the consequences at least in the short run. Choice (C) is not an argument for the pact in the absence of any other considerations since there is no apparent benefit offsetting the disadvantage of lower wages. As for choice (E), the alliance in and of itself does not justify closing the mills. It is not clear from this argument what reciprocal benefits might be expected on the basis of the alliance.

    The best choice is (D). It is the only choice that indicates a long-term benefit to accrue from the pact. It appears from (D) that this long-term benefit is not merely a compensation that occurs in spite of the short-term losses, but that it is part of a process that includes these losses.

2. **(A)**
    All of the choices are plausible and may be true. The problem is to determine which of the choices is implied by the given information. It may well be, as stated in (B), that "Nurses are opposed to having some of their duties reassigned to paramedics." Such opposition would be understandable if the reassignment of duties was perceived as an alternative to higher salaries. Nothing in the passage, however, either states or implies that nurses are opposed to the reassignment of some of their duties to paramedics. Choice (C) is also plausible. If administrators are forced to increase the salaries paid to nurses, then it is likely that this will cause an increase in hospital costs. According to the information given, however, increasing the salaries is only one option. The shortage might be dealt with in a way that did not increase costs, that is, by increasing the work done by paramedics. The validity of choice (D) would depend on information not available in the passage. Nothing in the information given either states or

implies that the paramedics are or are not as competent as nurses in most of the work now assigned to nurses. The passage merely states that *some* of the work would be reassigned and does not say whether the paramedics would be competent to do even that work. Choice (E) is an argument that might be used to support reassignment of duties. Presumably the nurses would not have additional time since the problem is a shortage of nurses to begin with. Tasks would be reassigned to paramedics only in so far as the shortage of nurses required. Whether the remaining work that could only be done by nurses can be characterized as "attending to patients" is neither stated nor implied.

Returning to choice (A), we see that this answer, unlike the others, is in fact implied by the passage. Both options are presented as "solutions" to the problem. For the raising of salaries to be properly called a solution, it must result in an increased supply of nurses. Thus, choice (A) is implied by the information given.

3.   **(A)**
The opening claim is of a cause-and-effect relationship between the program and the decrease in crime. The claim could be weakened by showing that the cause in question could not be the cause or that something else is a more significant factor.

In this example, choice (A) suggests another possible factor and thus weakens the claim that Governor Smith's program deserves credit for the change. According to choice (A), a simple demographic factor might explain the decrease in crime. If there are fewer people in the population in the 15-30 male age group and if this particular subset of the population commits most of the crimes, then it seems reasonable that the total number of crimes would decrease. The assumption here is that the percentage of criminals in the population and the number of crimes each criminal commits remains constant. Thus the number of crimes would have decreased with or without Governor Smith's program. Governor Smith and his supporters then would be taking credit for something that would have happened anyway. This is not to say that Governor Smith's program might not also be a factor, but the claim that the program caused the decrease is significantly weakened.

When we look at the other choices, we find that they do not offer arguments that would weaken the claim to the same extent. Choice (B), for example, states that another crime program existed in the previous administration. We are not told whether this program was similar to the new one, whether it was better or worse, or anything else about it. It might be that this was a much better program and that the recent decrease in crime is really due to the long-term effects of this older program. It might be that the older program was completely ineffective and the decrease in crime only came about through the new, better program. It might be that both programs were about the same and neither program had any significant effect on the number of crimes. In other words, we do not get from choice (B) anything that clearly weakens the opening claim. Choice (C) is also not an effective argument. In the first place, it is merely the opinion of the opposing party. Since they have an obvious motivation for criticizing, they would not be a disinterested judge. Moreover, even if they accurately characterized the governor's own motives, this would not in and of itself imply that the program was ineffective. Choice (D) tells us no more than that the legislature provided less money than the governor asked for. Perhaps the legislature is controlled by the opposition. Perhaps there is a budget crunch. In any case, the program still might be a cause of the decrease in crime, and we could conclude that the number of crimes would have decreased even further had the legislature supported the program more generously. Choice (E) is not a strong argument because it does not directly deny or modify the claim. The program could be completely responsible for the entire decrease in the number of crimes, and yet drug-related crimes could have increased due to other factors. This would suggest perhaps a need to modify the program to deal with drug-related crime in the future, but it would not in any way weaken the claim for the program's effectiveness.

4.   **(D)**
The statement, "...it was suddenly much more difficult to find a job as a lawyer," implies that the relative supply of and demand for lawyers had changed. If people were going to law school who would not have previously, then it is a reasonable assumption that the supply of potential lawyers may have increased. Whether the demand for lawyers had increased, decreased, or stayed the same is not stated or implied. In any case, there was a *surplus* of potential lawyers; that is, the supply was now greater than the demand.

The other choices may or may not be true, but they are not implied by the passage.

5.   **(C)**
According to the passage, there was an "apparent surplus" of college teachers. It was for this reason that the students in question opted for law school. If they had gone instead into Ph.D. programs, they would have aggravated the existing problem by increasing the supply of potential college teachers.

Of course, an individual might have entered a Ph.D. program while all the others went to law school. A single individual would not affect the supply and demand significantly. If, however, the group as a whole had entered Ph.D. programs, then they would not have been any better off looking for jobs as college teachers than they were looking for jobs as lawyers.

The other choices may or may not be true, but they are not implied by the passage.

6. **(D)**
The information does not give us the absolute number of shares owned by anyone, but only the relative numbers. Thus we know that Sue and George own the same number of shares, but not how many. We know that the number of shares that Bill owns is more than the number owned by Sue or George. We know that the number of shares that Henry owns is fewer than the number of shares owned by Sue or George. Since Sue and George own the same number, and since Bill owns more shares and Henry fewer, we can conclude that (D) Bill owns more shares than Henry.

Choice (E) is flatly contradicted by this information, since Sue owns the same number as George and George owns more shares than Henry.

As for Gordon, all that we know is that he owns more shares than Henry, but we do not know how many more. Therefore, we cannot place Gordon's holdings relative to Sue, George, or Bill. All of them own more shares than Henry, but we cannot infer from the information given exactly where Gordon fits into the picture relative to Sue, George, and Bill. Thus (A), (B), and (C) may or may not be correct, but this cannot be determined from the information given.

7. **(D)**
The problem here is to sort out the various factors affecting Alvin's decision. Choices (A) and (B) relate to the cost of insurance. Choice (A), an increase in the liability requirement, would increase the cost of insuring the car and thus make it more difficult for Alvin to afford the more expensive car. Choice (B), choosing the policy with the lowest deductibles, would also make it more expensive to insure the car and therefore would also make it more difficult for Alvin to buy the more expensive car. Choices (C) and (D) relate to the car loan. Choice (C), paying the lowest possible downpayment, would increase the amount of money to be borrowed and thus would increase the monthly payments. This would make it more difficult for Alvin to buy the more expensive car. Choice (D), decreasing the interest rate, would decrease the monthly payments. This would make it easier for Alvin to afford the more expensive car. As for choice (E), this would make both cars more expensive to operate. Since

the subcompact gets better mileage, higher operation costs would make it more difficult for Alvin to afford the more expensive car. Thus only choice (D), lowering "the interest rate on Alvin's car loan," would make it easier for Alvin to afford the more expensive car.

8. **(C)**

The question asks the reader to identify the kind of argument being used. The argument is correctly identified as an analogy. The comparison is not, as suggested by Choice (A), an analogy between two scandals. Instead, it is an analogy, as stated in Choice (C), between actions taken. The actions taken by President X are compared to the actions taken by Lincoln. The author does not point out contradictions in the charges, does not accuse the critics of being motivated by self-interest, and does not question the factual basis of the charges.

9. **(E)**

Arguments by analogy stress the similarities while minimizing the differences. If the situations are similar in all significant aspects, then the argument is persuasive. To attack the argument, it is necessary to show that there are significant differences. Choice (E) effectively attacks the analogy by pointing out the fundamental difference between the situation faced by Lincoln and the situation faced by President X. The other Choices are not effective because they do not attack the analogy. The expertise of the critics (A), the motivation of the author (B), the factual basis of the charges (C), and Lincoln's reputation (D) have no direct bearing on the analogy. Therefore, Choices (A), (B), (C), and (D) do not effectively undermine the author's argument. Only choice (E) attacks the analogy directly.

10. **(D)**

Advertisements frequently persuade through psychological association and other rhetorical tricks that are not strictly speaking "logical." For the argument in question to be logical, it must follow from the given assumptions. The problem is to determine which of the five statements provides an underlying assumption that, if true, would lead to the conclusion. The opinion of nine out of ten doctors concerning "Numbs" leads logically to the conclusion that "Numbs" is the aspirin to buy only if the consumer believes that (D) doctors are "reliable and informed sources of information" on this topic. The other four choices may or may not also be true, but they do not contribute to the logical argument. They do not provide the necessary logical link between the ad and the desired conclusion. Believing that "Numbs" is (A) cheaper or (C) faster would be *addi-*

tional reasons to buy the product, but would not combine directly with the ad in order to form a logical train of thought. Choice (B), that aspirin "only treats the symptoms," may also be true, but does not directly affect the argument one way or the other. Choice (E), from leading to the conclusion, would seem to negate it by suggesting that it really does not matter which brand the consumer buys. Thus, only (D) provides the logical bridge from ad to conclusion.

11. **(A)**
The question asks the reader to identify a *logical* flaw in the argument. Choice (A) points out a logical flaw by showing that the argument begs the question. In other words, the conclusion that the argument would demonstrate turns out to be one of the assumptions on which the argument is based. The conclusion is that Shakespeare did not write certain passages of low quality. The assumption is that Shakespeare only wrote passages of high quality. The assumption is true *only* if the conclusion is true. The conclusion is true *only* if the assumption is true. In effect, the conclusion is merely a restatement of the assumption, and the argument is merely a tautology.

Choices (B) and (E) might weaken the argument, but they would do so by questioning the truth of the assumptions, not the logical form of the argument. Choice (B) provides a possible biographical explanation for some variation in the quality of the text. It undermines the assumption that Shakespeare only wrote passages of high quality. Choice (E) questions the judgment of the critics. It undermines the assumption that the passage is inferior. Choice (C) is irrelevant since if none of the text is by Shakespeare, then the whole argument is pointless. Choice (D) is also irrelevant since it would apply as well to any other writer of the period as to Shakespeare. In any case, all of these answers introduce questions of fact, only (A) points out a *logical* weakness in the argument.

12. **(D)**
Choices (B) and (C) are flatly contradicted by the evidence. Choice (B) is contradicted by the evidence with regard to age. Voters over 40 would be less, not more, conservative than voters under 40 with the same education. Choice (C) is contradicted by the evidence with regard to education. Voters with only a high school education would be less, not more, conservative than voters of the same age who finished college but did not go on to graduate school. As for choices (A) and (E), the evidence does not imply anything one way or the other. The variable is education. We know that voters with only a college education are more conservative than those with less or more education, but we do not know how those with

only a high school education compare with those who have graduate degrees. Nothing is either stated or implied as to whether those with only a high school education are more conservative or less conservative than those with graduate degrees.

Choice (D), on the other hand, is a restatement in effect of the evidence with regard to education. According to the evidence: "Voters who finished college but did not go to graduate school are more conservative than voters of the same age who have only a high school education." This is the same thing as saying that the voters who only finished high school are *less* conservative than the voters of the same age who finished college but did not go to graduate school.

13. **(C)**

The problem here is to see the connection between the general idea in the opening claim and the specific examples in the three statements (I, II, and III). The student must determine which statements *in and of themselves* help to support the general idea. In this case, the general idea is that a public policy designed to help one group may nevertheless be harmful to another group. The first statement (I) supports the general idea. The minimum wage helps those who find employment by keeping their wage above a certain level. At the same time, it may be harmful to others who cannot find employment because at that wage it would not be profitable for employers to hire them. Thus the minimum wage would be helping one group (the employed) while harming another group (the unemployed). As for the second statement (II), it also supports the general idea. The dairy subsidy helps the dairy farmers by giving them a higher price for their products. At the same time, it hurts the consumers who must pay more for a gallon of milk. When we turn to the third statement (III), we see that this statement does *not* support the general idea. The fact that the space program results in advances in computer technology is not necessarily in and of itself harmful to anyone. One could argue that the space program, by taking funds away from other programs, in effect harms those who would have been helped by those programs, but this is beyond the scope of this particular statement. Such an argument has nothing to do with "advances in computer technology." Possibly the advances in technology might be harmful to someone who had invested in the older technology, but again this would depend on assumptions outside the scope of the statement.

Thus, the correct choice is (C); we see that statements I and II give examples of the general idea and therefore support the claim.

14. **(E)**

Of the five statements, (E) is the one that tends to weaken the explanation because it provides evidence that using aluminum cookware is not a significant factor in the occurrence of the disease. Since people are just as likely, according to (E), to get the disease whether they have used aluminum cookware or not, we can conclude that using aluminum cookware does not make any difference and therefore the "explanation" does not explain anything.

Choice (A) suggests that we may be looking at the wrong source. It does not, however, *by itself* weaken the given explanation. The aluminum-cookware theory could still be valid even though there are other potential sources.

Choices (B) and (C) are irrelevant. The difficulty of diagnosing the disease might of course contaminate the evidence. If we do not know who has the disease, then we will have difficulty gathering data on the factors causing the disease. This does not, however, weaken the explanation. Aluminum cookware could still be the principal factor.

Choice (D) suggests that aluminum cookware might not be the *only* factor. In this case, we would need to modify our explanation to account for a more complex interaction of factors, genetic as well as environmental. This kind of interaction of factors is commonplace. It modifies the explanation, but does not negate it. There is no particular reason why a given condition might not be influenced by many factors.

15. **(E)**

This argument follows the pattern: *a* causes *b*; *b* causes *c*; therefore, *a* causes *c*. In this case, *a* is low rainfall, *c* is high meat prices, and *b* is all the steps in between. If we can infer from the passage that low rainfall causes higher meat prices, then we can also infer (E): "An increase in rainfall would result in lower meat prices." This would be true, other things being equal.

The other answers all explore side issues that are essentially irrelevant to the argument. Choices (A) and (D), for example, suggest reasons why people either are or ought to be eating less meat. Neither is related, however, to the chain of events outlined in the passage. (C) discusses agricultural productivity in general, also a separate topic. (A) concerns the cause of the drought. This cannot be inferred from the passage since the passage deals only with the consequences of the drought.

16. **(C)**

George presents an argument of cause and effect. His thesis is that the advertising campaign caused the increase in profits. There are many ways in which Martha might attack such a thesis. In this case, Martha attacks the chronology. She argues that *a* did not cause *b* because *b* preceded *a*. The underlying premise is that the future cannot cause the past. Thus, the correct choice is (C). The "weak point...on which Martha's response focuses" is (C) "...the possibility that the effect preceded the supposed cause."

George's argument might be criticized on other points as well. Choices (A), (B), and (D) are all valid criticisms of George's argument. It is true that he cites only one example, that he does not consider what happened in companies that did not advertise, and that he does not provide exact figures. While these are all weaknesses in George's argument, they are not, however, the particular weak point in George's claim on which Martha's response focuses. They are also not enough in and of themselves to demolish George's argument. George might be able to strengthen his argument with exact figures and additional examples. In the absence of these, he could still be right. He cannot, however, be right if "the effect preceded the supposed cause."

As for choice (E), it is a speculation that is essentially irrelevant to the argument. The increase in profits could be caused by the advertising campaign and still be temporary for other reasons since many factors might be involved. It is not, in any case, the weakness that Martha focuses on. Martha argues that the increase in profits was caused by "an increase in consumer spending." She does not say whether this might prove to be temporary or not.

matter how many passengers are aboard. The only way the airline can increase profit is by maximizing the use of each flight.

The other choices do not provide an underlying principle common to both policies. Neither policy increases safety (A). Neither policy eliminates "inessential services" (D). As for (B), "satisfying the needs of traveling business executives," or (E) "encouraging more people to fly," neither policy would do either because both policies involve potential inconveniences: not being able to fly on a scheduled flight because it is overbooked and having to change planes.

Section 2–Problem Solving

1. **(A)**
    If

    $$z = \frac{xy}{x+y},$$

    then $z(x + y) = xy$, or $zx + zy = xy$. Thus, $zy = xy - zx$, or $x(y - z) = zy$, giving $x = zy/(y - z)$.

2. **(B)**
    For any integer n, $2n + 1$ as well as $2n - 1$ must always be odd integers and

    $$2n + 2 = 2(n + 1)$$

    must be an even integer. Therefore, the correct answer is (B).

3. **(B)**
    If John contributes $2X$ to A and $3X$ to B, then his contributions to A and B will be in the ratio of 2 to 3. Then

    $$2X + 3X = 2,500,$$

    or $X = 500$. Therefore, he should contribute $2(500) = \$1,000$ to charity A.

4. **(D)**
    At 12 percent annual interest, the interest on a \$150 loan at the end of 12 months =

    $$\$150 \times 12\% = \$18.$$

    Since 12 percent is the simple interest rate, the interest on a \$150 loan at the end of 10 months =

    $$\$18 \times (10/12) = \$15.$$

    Hence, the borrower owes

    $$\$150 + \$15 = \$165$$

    at the end of 10 months.

5. **(B)**

It cost Jill $(20 \times 25) = \$500$ to buy 20 shares at $25 each, $(20 \times 30) = \$600$ to buy 20 shares at $30 each, and $(35 \times 20) = \$700$ to buy 35 shares at $20 each. Therefore, it cost her $(500 + 600 + 700) = \$1,800$ to buy $20 + 20 + 35 = 75$ shares of Unit Corporation. Her average per share cost is $(1,800/75) = \$24$.

6. **(A)**

If the smallest number is X, then

$$X + (X + 1) + (X + 2) + (X + 3) = 226,$$

giving $4X + 6 = 226$. Therefore, $4X = 220$, or $X = 55$.

7. **(C)**

If X is the number of freshmen at the college, then

$$(.24)X = 360.$$

Therefore, $X = 360/(.24) = 1,500$.

8. **(B)**

If $2X + Y = 2$, then $2X = 2 - Y$, or $X = 1 - Y/2$. Substituting in $X + 3Y > 6$, we get

$$1 - Y/2 + 3Y > 6.$$

Thus, $5Y/2 > 5$, or $Y > 2$.

9. **(B)**

The distance from 2.6 to 2.9 equals

$$2.9 - 2.6 = .3$$

and 1/4 of this distance is $.3/4 = .075$. Hence, the number that is 1/4 of the distance from 2.6 to 2.9 is

$$2.6 + .075 = 2.675.$$

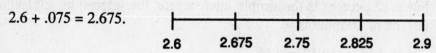

| 2.6 | 2.675 | 2.75 | 2.825 | 2.9 |

10. **(D)**

If r is the radius of a circle, then the length of a side of the square is $2r$. Since

$$A = \pi r^2,$$

$$r = \sqrt{A / \pi}$$

and $\quad 2r = 2\sqrt{A / \pi}.$

11. **(A)**

If X represents the number of men in the class, then the number of women in the class is $200 - X$. Since 15 percent of the men and 20 percent of the women received A's, the number of students receiving an A is

$$.15X + .20(200 - X) = 40 - .05X.$$

Therefore, $40 - .05X = 36$, or $X = 4 \div .05 = 80$.

12. **(D)**

If

$$\frac{5}{x} = \frac{2}{x-1} + \frac{1}{x(x-1)}$$

then $x \neq 0$, $x \neq 1$ and we can multiply both sides by $x(x - 1)$ to get

$$5(x - 1) = 2x + 1.$$

Equivalently, $5x - 5 = 2x + 1$, or $3x = 6$. Thus, $x = 2$.

13. **(A)**

$$A = LW, LW = 24$$

so that $L = {}^{24}/_W$. Now,

$$P = 2L + 2W = 22$$

and substiuting $L = {}^{24}/_W$ we have

$$2 \times {}^{24}/_W + 2W = 22,$$

$${}^{48}/_W + 2W = 22$$

now multiplying every term by W gives

$$48 + 2W^2 = 22W$$

$$2W^2 - 22W + 48 = 0,$$

or $\quad W^2 - 11W + 24 = 0$

$$(W-8)(W-3) = 0$$

so that $W = 8$ and 3. Choose 8 as the larger side.

14. **(B)**

Let r and $2r$ be the radii of the two soup cans and $2h$ and h be their respective heights. Then their respective volumes are $\pi r^2(2h)$ and $\pi(2r)^2 h$ which are in the ratio

$$2\pi r^2 h : 4\pi r^2 h,$$

or 1:2.

15. **(B)**

Julie's portfolio of stocks on January 1 has a total market value of

$$\$[100(10) + 100(12) + 100(18)] = \$4,000.$$

On December 31, she has 100 shares of A, 200 shares of B, and 150 shares of C with a market value of

$$\$[100(12) + 200(6) + 150(16)] = \$4,800.$$

Therefore, her return for the year was

$$\left(\frac{4,800}{4,000} - 1\right) \times 100 = 20\%.$$

16. **(D)**

$$\frac{1}{4} + \frac{9}{x} = 1$$
$$x + 36 = 4x$$
$$36 = 3x$$
$$12 = x$$

Section 3–Reading Comprehension

1. **(B)**
    The passage defines cave features (in general, not a specific cave). It is neither theoretical nor analytical.

2. **(D)**
    Geology is the study of the origin, history, and structure of the earth. This passage focuses on the origin, history, and structure of cave features.

3. **(A)**
    All six paragraphs of the passage examine a range of cave features, from dripstone through breakdown. (B) is incorrect because breakdown is of internal matter. (D) is incorrect because fill is also caused by water. (E) is incorrect because most caves contain fill.

4. **(D)**
    Rimstones are formed by standing water.

5. **(C)**
    Helicites result from reorientation of the crystal structure of calcite or gypsum.

6. **(C)**
    Paragraph two explains that cone-shaped stalactites begin in tubular form; paragraphs two and three indicate that stalagmites, stalactites, and flowstone are all composed of calcite. The passage does not indicate whether stalactites or stalagmites are longer when they join to form columns.

7. **(B)**
    Fill contains deposits that enter caves over periods of time; hence, they reveal much about geologic history.

8. **(E)**
    Columns, curtains, helicites, and corals all contain calcite. Fill may, but it need not since it was washed into the cave.

9. **(B)**
    The passage is essentially a brief biography, beginning with Morris'

birth and continuing through his public career. (A) is perhaps the next best choice, but the structure, especially the opening biographical detail, makes it a less satisfactory choice, as does the passage's emphasis on Morris rather than on U.S. history. The passage is not focused on political science or military history.

10. **(E)**
Morris helped finance the Revolution, helped right the nation's economy, and occupied political offices.

11. **(C)**
Personal wealth was clearly important to him, judging from the conditions he imposed before becoming Superintendent of Finance, but the passage also makes it clear that he often took personal financial risks to further the war and to help the country.

12. **(A)**
Morris' firm had government contracts to import arms and ammunition, from which "he and his firm profited handsomely." There is no indication he received unusually favorable rates in borrowing money. He did use money borrowed from France to organize the Bank of North America, but not for "personal purposes."

13. **(E)**
The clearest signal of Congress' faith in Morris' financial genius is the granting of dictatorial power to enable him to salvage the nation's finances. The awarding of contracts to his firm is a straight business arrangement. There is no indication that Morris had to apply to Congress to borrow money from France or for a bank charter, and certainly not to work closely with Washington.

14. **(D)**
Morris financed the Continental Army, but the passage does not indicate that he served in it.

15. **(C)**
Although Congress vindicated him and entrusted him with power, "his reputation slipped." That was beyond Congress' control.

16. **(A)**
Paragraph two explains that he voted against independence but absented himself so his state could cast an affirmative ballot. Morris later

signed the Declaration of Independence. The passage does not indicate whether Paine's charges were accurate, nor does it explain why Congress was unable to solve the nation's financial problems.

17. **(A)**
The passage has a straight chronological progression. (D) would be a reasonable choice except that Morris' activities in the Continental Congress (paragraph two) are on the national level.

18. **(E)**
This passage is most probably an excerpt from a history book. If it were memoirs of Cochise's descendant (A), it would most likely contain material more favorable to Indians, or at least have more details about the Indian point of view. It cannot be a journal entry (B) because it is not written in the first person point-of-view. The events in this passage are not detailed enough, and characterization is not developed enough, for the passage to qualify as an excerpt from a novel (C). Choice (D) is possible, but not the best choice because the passage would probably contain more opinion if it were an essay.

19. **(A)**
The Indians liked Tom Jeffords because he understood them and did not expect them to change all their ways; also, he expected them to uphold their part of the bargain, peace with Americans. Although some members took advantage of his lax management (B), generally the Indians respected Tom Jeffords, as evidenced by the leadership of Cochise. There is no evidence to support (C) or (E). Tom Jeffords could not always get his superiors to fulfill their (E) agreements, but the article does not deal with the Indians' view of him as a result of that policy.

20. **(D)**
In the opening sentence of the passage, the author states, "Jeffords realized that his charges had not been conquered and would do just about what they pleased." Also, later in the passage the author discusses Jeffords' view that the government's desires for the Indians to be "governed rigidly...and started on the road to 'civilization'" was "visionary." Choice (A) is contradicted by the evidence that Jeffords expected the Indians to keep the peace. The author does not discuss trying to make the Indians agrarian (B), only the government's wish to make them self-supporting. Although the author indicates that the government was looking for an excuse, and that "friction with his superiors troubled Jeffords," the author does not give evidence to the effect that Jeffords knew he was in

danger of being removed (C). Choice (E) seems self-evident, but it is not contained within the scope of this article.

21. **(C)**
   The author states, "Cochise worked quietly with the agent" and mentions the "chief's great powers of leadership." These qualities helped Cochise lead his people and have them keep peace with whites in America, so they can be considered his strongest traits. Choice (A) is probable, and a strong consideration, but not the best choice. Choice (B) is refuted by evidence in the article; indeed, the raids into Mexico (D) were probably a way Cochise was able to maintain control of his people in the United States. The article does not state how long Cochise lived (E), and according to the article he was a leader during settled times for only about two years.

22. **(C)**
   The Indian Bureau clearly was trying to make the Indians be something they were not and did not want to be—"civilized." Also, it appears the Bureau wished to remove the Indians from this land, where it was easy for the Indians to stage raids into Mexico, to a less valuable property—the "parched bottoms of the Gila River," where the Indians would have a difficult time either hunting or farming. Finally, the Bureau withheld "co-operation and support" and Jeffords had to buy food for the Indians with "his own money." The tone is not at all approving (A), nor is it sympathetic (B) in the main, in spite of the continued raids of the Indians. The author does not express disdain (D) or shock (E), as the Bureau certainly had a legitimate complaint that the Indian raids into Mexico were certain to have created friction with that neighboring nation.

23. **(E)**
   Obviously, both whites and Indians were partly betrayed and partly deceiving. While Cochise was able to exert control over his people (D), they continued doing some of what they pleased, and Taza was not able to control individual Indians (A) such as Skinya and Pionsenay, as well as his father. While Jeffords was a realist, his government (B) as represented by the Indian Bureau had a different agenda. The least probable choice is (C) because the Indians had almost certainly figured out the government's desires by that time.

Section 4–Data Sufficiency

1. **(D)**

Statement (1) tells us that $\angle BAC = 90°$. There is a well-known geometry theorem which says that BC must be a diameter of the circle. Hence, BC passes through the center of the circle.

Statement (2) gives the following relation between the sides

$$AB^2 + AC^2 = BC^2$$

$$3^2 + 4^2 = 5^2$$

which is well-known. Hence, $\triangle ABC$ is a right triangle with $\angle A = 90°$. Hence, BC must pass through the center of the circle.

2. **(D)**

Ten cents on the dollar means 10% of income is profit. Therefore, 10% of $95,000 is $9,500. Likewise from Statement (2) $6,400 compared to $64,500 is 10%. Once again 10% of $95,000 is $9,500.

3. **(A)**

Statement (1) is sufficient since the only even prime number is 2 which is a factor of 12. Statement (2) is not sufficient by itself because $x = $ 1, 2, 3, 4, or 5.

4. **(C)**

To answer the question we need both the size of the picture and the unit price. Statement (1) gives the size and Statement (2) gives the unit price. The area of a 3 by 5 picture is 15 square inches which is equal to $1 per square inch. Hence picture A costs $63. (7 by 9 = 63 square inches @ $1/square inch.) But Statement (1) alone or Statement (2) alone is not sufficient.

5. **(D)**

Either Statement (1) or Statement (2) is sufficient to answer if x is a positive integer.

6. **(C)**

In $\triangle BDC$, to find y we need the values of both $\angle BDC$ and $\angle DCB$. Statement (1) allows us to calculate the

$$\angle DCB = 90 - x = 90 - 30 = 60°.$$

But because $\angle BDC$ is not specified, Statement (1) alone cannot give us the value of y. Statement 2 gives $\angle BDC = 90°$. Statement (2) by itself cannot give us y because we do not know the measurement of $\angle DCB$ of the $\triangle DBC$. Together Statements (1) and (2) solve the problem.

$$y = 90° - \angle DCB$$

$$= 90 - 60°$$

(from Statement (1)

$$y = 30°.$$

7. **(C)**

Statement (1) allows us to calculate the area of the two circular halves.

Area $AEDP$ + Area $BFCQ$

= Area of one complete circle of radius 1

$= \pi(\text{radius})^2 = \pi(1)^2 = \pi$

But Statement (1) fails to give the rectangle's area.

Statement (2) gives us the length DC in terms of width BC so that the area of the rectangle can be calculated. But by itself Statement (2) has no length specification and hence will not solve the problem.

Using Statement (1) we get

$$DC = 2BC = 4BF = 4.$$

Hence, the area of the rectangle =

$$DC \times BC = 4 \times 2 = 8.$$

Therefore, the complete figure has a total area of $\pi + 8$.

8. **(E)**

Not enough information is given to find George's age from either Statement (1) or Statement (2) alone or together.

9. **(C)**

Statement (1) tells us that the sides are equal and that each subtends angle of 60° at the center $(^{360}/_6)$.

As $GA = GB$ = radius of the circle, $\angle GAB = \angle GBA$. Now

$$\angle GAB + \angle GBA + \angle AGB = 180°$$

or $$2\angle GAB + 60° = 180°$$

or $$\angle GAB = 60°$$

Hence, $\triangle AGB$ is an equilateral triangle. $\therefore AB = AG$ = radius of the circle. Unless the radius of the circle is known, Statement (1) is not sufficient to solve for the length of AB.

Statement (2) gives us the arc length AB as π. The circumference cannot be known unless we combine with Statement (1). Then the circumference is 6π which must be equal to π times the diameter.

$$\therefore 6\pi = \pi D \quad \text{or} \quad D = 6 \quad \text{or} \quad \text{radius} = 3$$

As AB = radius from Statement (1), we get $AB = 3$.

10. **(C)**
Statement (1) enables us to calculate the radius of the circle but will not give PS unless the angle PRS is given. Hence, Statement (1) is insufficient to solve the problem of finding PS. As Statement (2) does not contain any lengths we will not be able to use it to calculate PS.

Let us try using both Statements (1) and (2). $ABCD$ is a square and hence

$$BC^2 + DC^2 = DB^2$$

$$2BC^2 = (2QB)^2$$

or $$BC^2 = 2QB^2 = 2(\sqrt{8})^2 = 16$$

or $$BC = 4$$

$\therefore$ radius of circle = $\frac{1}{2} BC = 2$.

Hence, $PR = 2 \times$ radius $QR = 4$.

Given Statement (2), i.e., RS is parallel to BC, PS is parallel to DC because $\angle S$ is $90°$. Hence, $\triangle s\ DBC$ and PRS are similar. Therefore, $RS = PS$. Now

$$PS^2 + RS^2 = PR^2$$

or $$2PS^2 = 4^2 = 16$$

or $\qquad PS = \sqrt{8}$

11. **(A)**

From Statement (1), since the height of the larger can is twice the height of the smaller can, the radii have the same relationship. To determine the better buy we need to know the quantity of beans in each can which is determined by knowing the volume of each can.

$\qquad v(\text{small}) = \pi(r^2)h$

and $\quad v(\text{large}) = \pi(2r)^2(2h) = 8(\pi)r^2h$.

We see that the larger can contains 8 times more beans than the smaller can. Forty-nine cents times 8 equals $3.92. Clearly the larger can is the better buy. So, Statement (1) alone is sufficient.

Statement (2) by itself is not sufficient. We need to know the diameter of the larger can or at least its relationship to 3 inches.

12. **(E)**

To answer this question, we must know how much food the cat eats in one day and how much food is in each can of Catties Cat Chow. This would permit us to calculate the number of cans needed and by multiplying by the price per can we get the weekly cost. But we cannot find the information from Statements (1) or (2); thus, both statements together are not sufficient.

13. **(C)**

Statement (1) allows us to conclude that her new annual salary is

$\qquad \$27,600 + 10\%(\$27,600) = \$30,360.$

By dividing the information from Statement (2) into $30,360 we see she is paid 10 times a year. Statement (1) is necessary to compute her new annual salary. Statement (2) about her new paycheck is also necessary to calculate the number of paychecks she gets per year. Hence, the answer is (C).

14. **(C)**

Statement (1) gives us

$\qquad AC + BC = 1$

$\qquad x + \dfrac{1}{y} = 1$

$\qquad xy + 1 = y$

Without the value of y we cannot compute the value of x and hence Statement (1) is not sufficient to find x.

Statement (2) alone gives us

$$x = \frac{1}{y}$$

and this also does not solve the problem.

Let us try both Statements (1) and (2) together.

$$xy + 1 = y \quad \text{(from Statement (1))}$$

$$xy = 1 \quad \text{(from Statement (2))}$$

Substituting the latter into the former

$$\therefore \quad 1 + 1 = y \text{ or } y = 2.$$

As $xy = 1$ or $2x = 1$, $x = \frac{1}{2}$.

15. **(B)**

Statement (1) is redundant and will not solve the problem. Statement (2) gives us the present population as 2,000. Because it increases by 2,000 in 10 years; it takes the present population to increase by 1,000 in 5 years.

16. **(E)**

Let the two numbers be x and y. Being inversely proportional means $y = k/x$. Since their product is 16 ($xy = 16$), we know $k = 16$. As x increases, y decreases. Therefore, $y = 16/x$ and $0.80y = 16/1.25x$. But the two equations are dependent, so there are infinitely many solutions to x and y. Thus, two statements together are not sufficient.

17. **(B)**

According to Statement (1), $|k| = k$ or $k > 0$. But it does not help to find the value of x. So Statement (1) alone is not sufficient. From Statement (2) we have

$$|x(x-2)/(x-2)| = |x| < 4$$

as long as $x - 2 \neq 0$ or $x \neq 2$. $|x| < 4$ suggests that $-4 < x < 4$. So the values of x which make the given inequality true are all numbers between 4 and -4, excluding 2. Thus, Statement 2 alone is sufficient.

18. **(C)**

There are two variables on which the profit P depends and what Statement (1) does is to specify that the cost of materials, c, remains constant reducing P to be just varying with selling price, s.

Unless the number of items sold is specified the annual profit cannot be calculated. Hence, the need for Statement (2). Therefore, to solve for annual profit both the statements are necessary.

10% of $100 = $10. $\therefore$ The item sells for $100 + $10 = $110. For $100 item, the profit was $2. Hence, for a $110 item the profit is

$$\frac{\$110}{\$100} \times \$2 = \frac{220}{100} = \$2.20.$$

For 100,000 items we get a profit of 100,000 × $2.20 = $220,000.

19. **(B)**

The diagonal of a rectangular solid is given by

$$\sqrt{l^2 + w^2 + h^2}.$$

We want this number to be the length of the pole. Because the box has a square base, $w = h$. This means the length of the pole, x, must equal

$$\sqrt{l^2 + 2w^2}$$

Therefore to solve for any variable, we must know the other two. Statement (1) says $w = h = 2.3$ feet (area = w times h) which gives insufficient information to answer the question. Statement (2) lets $x = 6$ feet and $l = 5$ feet. Hence, w equals the square root of $x^2 = l^2$ divided by 2, which equals approximately 2.3.

Therefore, the dimensions are 5 feet by 2.3 feet by 2.3 feet. So, Statement (2) alone is sufficient.

20. **(B)**

Statement (1) is insufficient by itself since the rate cannot be determined from the formula

$$I = PRT$$

without knowing time. It is not necessary because $I = .1P$ (10% of investment). Therefore, $.1P = PRT$ which implies $.1 = RT$. Now from Statement (2), $T = \frac{1}{2}$ year. Solving

$$.1 = R(\tfrac{1}{2})$$

for R gives 20%, i.e., Statement (2) alone is sufficient.

Section 5–Problem Solving

1. **(D)**
    Since $0.5 = {}^1/_2$ and $1.6 = 1{}^3/_5 = {}^8/_5$, the equation becomes

    $$2x - \frac{x}{4} - \frac{35}{8} = 0;$$

    multiplying by the LCD 8: $16x - 2x = 35$ or $14x = 35$ and

    $$x = \frac{35}{14} = \frac{5}{2}.$$

    Choice (B) comes from taking a common denominator of $(.5)(4)(1.6) = 3.2$ and then multiplying each term by it and making the mistake of $3.2(4) = 12.8$ on the second term of the equation so that the resulting equation is

    $$1.6x + 12.8x - 5.12 = 0$$
    $$14.4x = 5.12$$
    $$x = 0.35 = \frac{35}{100} = \frac{7}{20}.$$

    Two more errors come from combining the coefficients, including the constant term as follows:

    $$\frac{1}{0.5} - \frac{1}{4} = \frac{1}{1.6} = 2 - .25 - .625 = 1.125.$$

    The choice (C) comes from $1.125x = 0$ or $x = 0$, and choice (E) comes from

    $$1.125x = .625 \text{ or } x = 0.56 \text{ or } \frac{56}{100} = \frac{14}{25}.$$

2. **(E)**

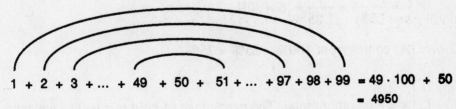

    $$1 + 2 + 3 + \dots + 49 + 50 + 51 + \dots + 97 + 98 + 99 = 49 \cdot 100 + 50$$
    $$= 4950$$

3. **(A)**

$$1.41 \times 10^8 - 9.3 \times 10^7 = 14.1 \times 10^7 - 9.3 \times 10^7$$

$$= (14.1 - 9.3)10^7$$

$$= 4.8 \times 10^7$$

4. **(E)**

Let n = # oranges for y dollars. We know that y dollars = $100y$ cents. Using the proportion

$$\frac{6}{x} = \frac{n}{100y}$$

gives the equation

$$nx = 600y.$$

Solving for n gives

$$n = \frac{600y}{x}.$$

Choice (B) is # dollars divided by the cost in cents, per orange.

5. **(D)**

The area of the rectangle in square inches is

$$(3 \times 12)(6 \times 12)$$

and the area of each square of sides 3 inches is $3 \times 3 = 9$ square inches. If X is the number of 3×3 squares needed to cover the rectangle, then

$$9X = (3 \times 12)(6 \times 12),$$

or $\qquad X = \dfrac{36(72)}{9} = 288$

6. **(D)**

$x = y + .25y = 1.25y$. Comparing y to x:

$$\frac{y}{x} = \frac{y}{1.25y} = \frac{1}{1.25} = .8 = 80\%.$$

Choice (A) comes from $100\% - 25\% = 75\%$.

7. **(E)**

Let x = # oz other metal. The percentage of gold in x is 0 so we get an equation:

$$56 + (0)x = .70(56 + x) \text{ or } 56 = .7(56 + x).$$

Therefore, $56 - 39.2 = .7x$ and $.7x = 16.8$ so that $x = 16.8/.7 = 24$ oz.

Choice (A) comes from

$$56(.70) = 39.2.$$

Choice (B) comes from

$$56(.30) = 16.8.$$

Choice (C) comes from

$$56 + x = .7(x + 56)$$

or $56 + x = .7x + 39.2$

and $1.7x = 16.8$, $x = 9.8$.

Choice (D) comes from

$$1.7x = 95.2 \text{ or } x = 56.$$

8. **(B)**

A very easy solution is $x + y = 1/k$, now substitute for k, its given value:

$$x + y = \frac{1}{x - y};$$

cross-multiplying gives $x^2 - y^2 = 1$. The long way to do this problem (which would have more chance of error): Solve simultaneously, by adding the equations $x + y = 1/k$ and $x - y = k$ getting

$$2x = k + \frac{1}{k} \text{ or } x = \frac{1}{2}k + \frac{1}{2k}.$$

Then squaring both sides:

$$x^2 = \frac{k^2}{4} + \frac{1}{2} + \frac{1}{4k^2}.$$

Finding y from $x + y = 1/k$:

$$y = \frac{1}{k} - \frac{1}{2}k - \frac{1}{2k} = \frac{k}{2} - \frac{1}{2k}.$$

Then squaring both sides:

$$y^2 = \frac{k^2}{4} - \frac{1}{2} + \frac{1}{4k^2}.$$

Therefore, $x^2 - y^2 = \frac{1}{2} - (-\frac{1}{2}) = 1$.

9. **(C)**

$$\frac{A}{x-5} + \frac{B}{x+3} = \frac{7x-11}{(x-5)(x+3)}.$$

On the left side of the equation, add fractions using the LCD in the usual manner, obtaining

$$\frac{Ax + 3A + Bx - 5B}{(x-5)(x+3)}, \quad Ax + 3A + Bx - 5B = 7x - 11;$$

equating coefficients of like terms gives the system

$$A + B = 7$$

$$3A - 5B = -11.$$

Solving simultaneously gives $A = 3$ and $B = 4$. Check:

$$\frac{3}{x-5} + \frac{4}{x+3} = \frac{3x + 9 + 4x - 20}{(x-5)(x+3)}$$

$$= \frac{7x-11}{(x-5)(x+3)}.$$

10. **(A)**

Let x = edge of large cube, then surface area is $6x^2 = 216$ or $x = 6$. Edges of small cubes are 3 and their surface areas are $6(9) = 54$ each and multiplying by 2 gives 108.

Choice (B) comes from not working out the problem but thinking that the edge of the smaller two cubes are each half as long on a side so since there are two of them, the answer equals the value of the larger, 216.

Choice (C) comes from taking the surface area of only one of the small cubes.

Choice (D) comes from

$$\sqrt{216} \approx 15 \times 2 = 30.$$

Choice (E) comes from

$$\sqrt[3]{216} = 6, 6^2 = 36 \times 2 = 72.$$

11. **(A)**

By Pythagorus' theorem the square of the length of the hypotenuse is equal to the sum of the squares of the lengths of the legs. Therefore, if Y is the length of the other leg then

$$(X + 1)^2 = X^2 + Y^2,$$

or $\quad Y^2 = (X + 1)^2 - X^2 = 2X + 1.$

Hence, $Y = \sqrt{2X + 1}$.

12. **(C)**

$$x^2 + 2xy + y^2 + x^2 - 2xy + y^2 = 2x^2 + 2y^2 = 2(x^2 + y^2).$$

Choice (A) is from a common mistake: Note that

$$(x + y)^2 \neq x^2 + y^2 \text{ and } (x - y)^2 \neq x^2 - y^2.$$

Using this mistaken idea gives

$$x^2 + y^2 + x^2 - y^2 = 2x^2.$$

Choice (B) comes from putting both expressions together in a parentheses:

$$(x + y + x - y)^2 = (2x)^2 = 4x^2.$$

Choice (D) comes from incorrect use of the distributive law:

$$2(x^2 + y^2) \neq 2x^2 + y^2.$$

13. **(B)**

Remembering that $x^{-1} = 1/x$ so that

$$1 - x^{-1} = 1 - \frac{1}{x} = \frac{x - 1}{x};$$

now divide by $1 - x$:

$$\frac{x - 1}{x} + 1 - x = \frac{x - 1}{x} \times \frac{1}{1 - x}$$

$$= \frac{x - 1}{x} \times \frac{-1}{x - 1}$$

$$= \frac{-1}{x}$$

14. **(A)**

Let $x - 129 = y$, then $129y = 129$ or $y = 1$. Substituting $y = 1$ in $x - 129 = y$, gives $x - 129 = 1$ and $x = 130$. An alternate solution is $129(x - 129) = 129$; dividing both sides of the equation by 129, gives $x - 129 = 1$, or $x = 130$.

Choice (B) adds 129 instead of multiplying by 129:

$$129 + x - 129 = 129 \text{ or } x = 129.$$

Choice (C) sets up the wrong equation by omitting the parentheses:

$$129x - 129 = 129 \text{ or } 129x = 2(129) \text{ or } x = 2.$$

Choice (D) comes from

$$129x - 129 - 129 = 129, \ 129x - 258 = 129, \ 129x = 387$$

which gives $x = 3$. Choice (E) comes from omitting parentheses

$$x - 129(129) = 129.$$

Then

$$x - 16{,}641 = 129, \ x = 16{,}641 + 129 = 16{,}770.$$

15. **(D)**

Let

$$A = \text{the first piece}$$

$$2A = \text{the second piece}$$

$$4A = \text{the third piece}$$

$$8A = \text{the fourth piece}$$

$$A + 2A + 4A + 8A = 6$$

$$15A = 6$$

$$A = .4 \text{ meters}$$

The longest piece is $8A = .4(8) = 3.2$ meters.

16. **(C)**

Draw a picture of the page with the given measurements.

The width equals

$$7.5 - 2 - .75 = 4.75$$

The length equals

$9.5 - 1 - .75 = 7.75$

Area = width × length

$= 4.75 \times 7.75$

$= 36.8125$

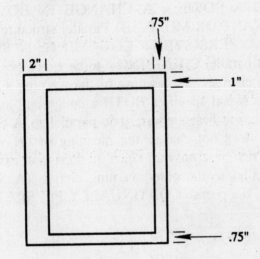

Section 6—Sentence Correction

1. **(D)**

(A) is not the correct answer. A COUGHING does not exhibit structure parallel with A SORE..., A CHANGE IN BOWEL..., or A CHANGE IN A WART OR MOLE. (B) Parallel structure is not present with the choice A PERSISTENT COUGHING; A SORE...and A CHANGE...do not parallel COUGHING—to be exact. (B) should not be selected. Since (C) changes the meaning of the warning signal, it should not be selected; the signal specifies BOTH a cough and hoarseness—not just a cough. (D) is the best answer; it is parallel to A SORE...and A CHANGE...and it does not change the meaning of the warning signal given. (E) is not the best answer since it does not exhibit structure (COUGHING) parallel to the other warning signals (A SORE...and A CHANGE...); also, the phrase CONTINUALLY PERSISTENT is redundant.

2. **(D)**

(A) is not the best answer since there is a misplaced modifier; WHICH HAS ENABLED...does not modify WORLD WAR II. (B) is not the best answer; the phrase WHICH WAS THROUGH PICTURES...does not describe WORLD WAR II. Since there is a misplaced modifier, (B) should not be selected. (C) WHICH HAS THROUGH PICTURES...is not the best way to describe PHOTOGRAPHER. Perhaps substituting the word WHO in place of the word WHICH would make the phrase more logical. (C) should not be selected. (D) is the best answer. There are no misplaced modifiers to cause confusion to the reader; the word WHO is used instead of the word WHICH (encountered in an earlier answer choice) and should make the passage clear to the reader. (E) is not the best answer since DURING THE GREAT DEPRESSION AND WORLD WAR II comes after AMERICANS. To the casual reader this misplaced modifier might imply that the photographs were only useful to young Americans during these time periods.

3. **(E)**

(A) Since the debate was BETWEEN two adversaries, AMONG is not the best word. The word AMONG implies a disagreement involving *several* points of view, not just the two mentioned in the passage. Since (B) uses the word AMONG and BETWEEN is more appropriate for a debate between two factions and since the word OPPOSING is used (a word which does not parallel the term BELIEVED), (B) is not the best answer. (C) does use the word BETWEEN which is a better choice than the word AMONG, but the term OPPOSING is not parallel to the word BELIEVED. (C) is not the best choice. (D) The verb form WERE OP-POSED does not parallel the verb form BELIEVED. (D) is not the best answer. (E) is the best answer. It uses the word BETWEEN for the dispute between two factions; the verb form OPPOSED is parallel with the word BELIEVED.

4. **(C)**
    (A) Since the term ITSELF is used to refer to the FLAGELLATES, (A) is not the best answer. A singular pronoun should not refer to a plural noun. (B) Besides the fact that EFFECTIVELY does not make sense in the sentence, the word ITSELF is used to refer to a plural noun FLAGEL-LATES. (B) is not the best choice. (C) is the best answer. The pronoun agrees with the noun and the meaning is clear. (D) AFFECT is a verb form; it is not the correct word to use here where a noun is required. Also, the pronoun ITSELF does not agree with the noun FLAGELLATES. (D) is not the best answer. (E) The word AFFECT does not fit the sentence where a noun, not a verb, is needed. (E) is not the best answer.

5. **(E)**
    (A) The word OF regularly follows the word RESULT; the word FROM is not appropriate. (A) should not be selected. (B) Again, the word FROM does not regularly follow the word RESULT; (B) is not the best choice. (C) The awkward expression BEING RATHER is used. (C) is not the correct answer. (D) The rather awkward expression AND RATHER is used, (D) is not the best choice. (E) is the correct answer. It uses the more logical word OF after the word RESULT rather than the word FROM in the preceding passage.

6. **(C)**
    (A) Since EXAMINING is a gerund, the possessive of SPECIAL-ISTS must be used. Answer (A) does not employ the possessive and should, therefore, not be selected. (B) The phrase THE EXAMINATION BY THE LAB SPECIALIST does make sense, but when coupled with the words THE FLUID, (B) is clearly not the best choice. (C) is the best choice; it employs the use of the possessive and agrees with the pronoun THEY used later in the sentence. (D) Although this phrase does make sense in the sentence, the word SPECIALISTS' must be used since a pronoun refers to it later. Without the word SPECIALISTS', there will be no antecedent for the word THEY. (D) is not the best choice. (E) LAB

SPECIALIST'S cannot be used correctly since the word THEY (a plural pronoun) refers to this antecedent. Since THEY is a plural pronoun, the antecedent must also be plural. (E) is not the best choice.

7. **(D)**

(A) The possessive form of a noun is not needed in this sentence; no ownership is implied. (A) is an incorrect choice. (B) The rule does not exclude EMPLOYEES WHO SMOKE from the building; rather it prohibits employees who are smoking from entering the building. (B) is not the best answer. (C) The word ALL implies a plural noun will follow. The word EMPLOYEE, however, is singular. (C) is not the best choice. (D) is the correct answer. SMOKING is a gerund and needs the possessive before it; EMPLOYEES' is a plural noun showing possession. Since (E) is wordy, it is not the best choice and should not be chosen.

8. **(D)**

(A) APT does make sense in this sentence, but if one checks the shades of meaning, one finds that APT usually implies a fitness, a suitability, a habitually tending; it appears then that APT is not the best choice for a sentence about a hurricane. Also there is a split infinitive, TO HARD HIT, which makes the sentence grammatically incorrect and choice (A) not acceptable. (B) Since INCLINED implies a bias, it is not the best choice for the passage. (C) The split infinitive prevents one from choosing (C) as the best choice. (D) This is the correct answer since there is no split infinitive. (E) The split infinitive should prevent the test taker from selecting (E).

9. **(D)**

(A) Parallel structure is not present here. OWNING is a gerund and the phrase set off by commas should supposedly have a gerund used also. Since this is not the case, (A) is not the best choice. (B) This wordy phrase does not have the *-ing* word which would give parallelism and coherence to the passage. (B) is not the best answer. (C) Besides non-parallelism, the phrase uses the word THESE, the antecedent of which is unclear. (C) is an incorrect choice. (D) is the best answer. It contains parallelism (EMPLOYING corresponds to OWNING) and is short and to the point. (E) Besides being wordy, this phrase does not use a word to parallel OWNING. (E) is incorrect.

10. **(D)**

(A) The negative NOR is not needed here since the words PROHIBITED THE INCLUSION already imply a negativism. The word NOR is a word which must be used with the word NEITHER—which is not used in the passage. (B) Since the word NOR is not used in this passage, use of the word NEITHER is not appropriate. (B) is not the best choice. (C) The word NOR is not appropriate since the word NEITHER is not used. (C) should not be selected. (D) is the best answer. The word OR is superior to the word NOR since the word NEITHER is not used in the passage. (E) is a grammatically correct answer, but the fact that it is wordy makes it a less suitable choice than answer (D). (E) should not be selected.

11. **(B)**
(A) Since there is a split infinitive TO CONSEQUENTLY REDUCE in answer (A), this is not the best choice. (B) is the best answer. There are no split infinitives and the answer is coherent. (C) The split infinitive (TO MOREOVER REDUCE) makes answer (C) an unacceptable answer. Answer (D) is not a logically structured phrase. (D) should not be selected. (E) Not only does answer (E) have a split infinitive but also it is not clearly written. (E) is not the best answer.

12. **(D)**
(A) UNIQUE is a word which does not have degrees of comparison. An answer like (A) which includes a comparison like MOST UNIQUE cannot be selected. (B) UNIQUE is a word which cannot be compared; UNIQUEST is a word which can best be described as nonsense. (B) is not the best choice. (C) MOST UNIQUE is a nonsense comparison since the word UNIQUE has no degrees of comparison. (C) is not the best answer. (D) is the best answer. It does not include comparisons of the word UNIQUE. (E) Since there is no comparison to the word UNIQUE, MOST UNIQUE is an inappropriate choice.

13. **(D)**
(A) Since AUSTRALIA is a singular noun, the pronoun which refers to it must be singular also; THEIR is plural so answer (A) is inappropriate. The number of the animals must also be considered. Since the words ANIMALS and KOALAS are plural, the other terms must also be plural; neither EMU nor PLATYPUS are plural. Answer (A) should not be chosen. (B) Since ANIMALS, KOALAS, PLATYPUSES, and EMUS are plural, KANGAROOS should be contained in the sentence rather than KANGAROO. Answer (B) should not be selected. (C) The pronoun THEIR is plural, yet it refers to a singular noun AUSTRALIA. Answer (C) has an error and should not be selected. (D) is the correct answer; nouns and pronouns are in agreement and the animals agree in number.

(E) Since PLATYPUS is singular in number, answer (E) should not be selected.

14. **(E)**

(A) PREPARING FOR THE TAX SEASON is a dangling modifier. It is placed beside THE LEISURE TIME which it does not describe. Answer (A) should not be selected. (B) TO PREPARE FOR THE TAX SEASON serves as the subject of the sentence. It should not be followed by a comma. (B) is an incorrect answer. (C) PREPARING FOR THE TAX SEASON serves as the subject of the sentence. It should not be separated from the verb by a comma. Answer (C) should not be selected. (D) TAKING UP THE LEISURE TIME OF MANY YOUNG PEOPLE UNTIL AFTER APRIL 15 is the subject of the sentence; it should not be separated from the verb by a comma. (D) is an incorrect choice. Answer (E) is the correct one. The sentence does not have any misplaced modifiers and the subject is not split from the verb.

15. **(B)**

(A) is a run-on sentence. THAT SENT BOND PRICES DOWN AND INTEREST RATES UP is a complete sentence and should not be joined to the first part of the sentence with just a comma. (B) is the correct answer. The phrase SENDING BOND PRICES DOWN AND INTEREST RATES UP follows the adjective LOWER and includes a comma to separate it and make reading easy. (C) Parallel construction is not evident in answer (C). If the words BOND PRICES DROPPING are to be chosen, the INTEREST RATES RISING should be selected over INTEREST RATES WHICH WENT UP. (C) should not be chosen. (D) should not be chosen because even though the sentence makes sense, it is not of the best grammatical construction. DROPPING OF BOND PRICES is not in parallel construction to INTEREST RATES WHICH WENT UP. If INTEREST RATES WHICH WENT UP is selected as an appropriate phrase, the BOND PRICES WHICH DROPPED should be used. (E) SENDING BOND PRICES DOWN AND INTEREST RATES UP is a phrase and should not be set apart from the rest of the sentence with a semicolon. SENDING BOND PRICES DOWN AND INTEREST RATES UP is not a sentence and cannot stand alone with the semicolon.

16. **(D)**

(A) The antecedent or the noun that the pronoun THEY refers to in the phrase THEY USE THE RIGHT HEMISPHERE is the noun PERSON—not the word PROPONENTS. A singular pronoun is needed and not the plural THEY. Answer (A) should not be selected. (B) Since the sentence uses the words A RIGHT-BRAINED PERSON, THE INDI-VIDUALS USE THE RIGHT HEMISPHERE is not an appropriate selection; INDIVIDUALS is plural, while A RIGHT-BRAINED PERSON is singular. (B) should not be selected. (C) is not an appropriate answer. In the phrase THE INDIVIDUALS USES there is a lack of agreement in number between INDIVIDUALS and USES. (C) should not be selected. (D) is the best answer. The construction is parallel, all verbs and nouns are in agreement. (E) is a run-on sentence. NEVERTHELESS THE LEFT-BRAINED INDIVIDUAL USES and the words that follow should not be joined to the previous sentence with just a comma. (E) should not be chosen.

17. **(D)**
  (A) should not be selected since this makes the statement a sentence fragment and not a complete sentence. (A) should not be selected. (B) the inclusion of HAVING BEEN SELECTED TO HOUSE…makes the statement a sentence fragment and not a complete sentence. Answer (B) is not an appropriate one. (C) Adding BEING THE LOCATION…makes the statement not a complete sentence but a fragment. (C) is not the best answer. (D) Since HOUSE NUCLEAR FACILITIES WHICH MUST BE MONITORED provides a predicate to the sentence, answer (D) is the best answer. (E) The words SINCE HOUSING NUCLEAR FACILITIES WHICH MUST BE MONITORED do not make a logical, complete sentence; (E) is not the best answer.

18. **(A)**
  (A) is a logically constructed, understandable sentence which fits well in the context. (A) is the right answer. Answer (B) is not a complete sentence. With the use of the semicolon a complete sentence is needed. (B) is not the best answer. (C) AUSTERE BUDGETS CAUSING THE SLOWDOWN is not a complete sentence and should not be selected. Since answer (D) is not a complete sentence and should not follow the semicolon, it is not an appropriate choice for the right answer. Answer (E) is a complete sentence but it does not make sense here. If the Governor's budget increased by only 5 percent per year while inflation averaged 15 percent it is not likely that the budget caused the inflation. (E) should not be chosen.

19. **(E)**
  (A) Since A PERSON is singular, the pronoun which refers to it should also be singular. THEIR is plural. Because of this disagreement, (A) is not appropriate. It should also be noted that TO EFFECTIVELY

MANAGE is a split infinitive and incorrect grammatically. (B) A PERSON is singular; THEIR is plural. (B) is not correct grammatically. (C) PEOPLE and THEIR are plural; A CONTRIBUTING MEMBER is singular. Because of this disconsonance in number, (C) is not the best answer. (D) TO EFFECTIVELY MANAGE is a split infinitive; (D) is not the best answer. (E) is the best answer. There are agreements in numbers, no split infinitives, and sense in the construction.

20. **(E)**

Answer (A) makes sense, but it is wordy. The words BECAUSE THERE IS could be eliminated without disturbing the meaning. (A) is not the best answer. (B) A SUBSTANTIAL SHIFTING would make the statement a sentence fragment; (B) should not be selected. Answer (C) is a wordy statement. Although it makes sense, it is not the best choice. The wordy answer (D) is not the best choice. All the qualifiers (PROBABLY, BUT NOT NECESSARILY ALWAYS) are not needed in the definition of the term STRUCTURAL INFLATION. (E) is concise and to the point. It is the best answer.

21. **(E)**

(A) The use of 6.6 MILLION necessitates the use of the word NUMBER, rather than AMOUNT. (A) is not the best answer. (B) Again, the use of 6.6 MILLION necessitates the use of the word NUMBER, rather than AMOUNT. (B) is not the best answer. (C) This sentence fragment should not be selected as the best answer. (D) With the use of 6.6 MILLION, the term NUMBER, not AMOUNT, should be used. (D) is not the best answer. (E) is the best answer; it is a complete sentence and uses the term NUMBER, not AMOUNT.

22. **(B)**

(A) DUE TO THE FACT is wordy and not accepted as correct usage by most guides. (A) is not the best answer. (B) is the best answer; it is concise and not wordy. Answer (C) is wordy and not the best choice. Again the use of DUE TO also makes this not an appropriate choice. (D) BENEFITS is plural; the verb IS GOING is singular. (D) is incorrect grammatically and should not be selected. (E) The words DUE TO make answer (E) not the best choice.

Section 7–Analytical Writing Assessment

ANALYSIS OF AN ISSUE ESSAY TOPIC

Sample Essay Response Scoring 5 to 6

Having known a heavy smoker, I can understand how difficult it is to break this habit. The chronic smoker continually asserts the enjoyment that he or she derives from smoking, but smokers often ignore the harmful effects that result for themselves and others around them. I realize that smoking is a powerful addiction, but why should others need to suffer the consequences of another's medical problem? I agree that smoking should be made illegal.

I have witnessed children wheeze after their parents smoked in the same room with them for several hours. I myself have often choked in a smoke-filled room, even though I was not the smoker. The odor of a cigarette smoker's clothes precedes him or her into every place that he or she goes. It becomes uncomfortable to visit a friend's home when it has the peculiar odor of old smoke; this makes it difficult for me to breathe freely.

Until cigarettes are classified as the dangerous, addictive drug that they are, smokers will not seek the help they need. They must realize they are harming not only themselves, but the health of those with whom they come into daily contact (car pools, apartment houses, restaurants, etc.) We have come a long way from viewing smoking as romantic, but now it seems that only smokers are blind to the dangers of this habit. Smokers are "in denial." It is the responsibility of the non-smokers to show this to them by making smoking illegal and offering smokers the health they deserve.

As for the help that smoking addicts need, we should concentrate on nicotine addiction in the same manner that we treat other drug addictions. There are always the personal, private clinics, but these are not affordable to everyone. City and state run clinics can service the rest of the smoking population. Perhaps government agencies could accept Medicare and Medicaid to offset the expense. Anti-smoking patches, psychotherapy, support groups and even cigarette surrogates such as chewing gum could be offered free of charge.

If smoking were to be declared illegal because of its endangerment to everyone's health, then we could not abandon addicted people to their own devices. This would simply lead to an illegal, dangerous "smokers' market," similar to today's drug market. It is our responsibility to make certain that this does not happen; the addicted smoker forced into this position might be your mother, father, brother, sister, or even your child.

If I were a smoker, I think that I would feel desperate and lie to myself that I was not harming anyone. No amount of reading newspaper articles about the rise in lung cancer deaths would convince me this is unhealthy to myself and those around me. It would be like reading the Surgeon General's warning on the side of a cigarette box; I would know that something was there, but I would never fully understand its significance. It is a kind of unawareness that lets smokers practice their addiction near little children, invalids, and animals who have no say in the matter. I firmly agree that smoking should be made illegal, but we must provide for those former smokers who are suddenly left empty-handed and addicted.

Analysis of Sample Essay Response Scoring 5 to 6

This paper earns a rating of 6 because it deals with the complexities of the issue: the health hazards of secondhand smoke, the smokers' unawareness of the damage that he or she is causing, the possible position of an addicted smoker if smoker were made illegal, and ways to rejuvenate the addicted smoker. The examples using children, animals, and family members persuasively appeal to the reader's emotions. The suggestion of smokers' clinics is well developed and insightful. The essay is clearly organized, separating the smokers' issues from those of the non-smokers. The language, including diction and syntactic variety, is clear and controlled. The technical forms of sentence structure, grammar, spelling, and punctuation are satisfactory throughout the essay.

ANALYSIS OF AN ARGUMENT ESSAY TOPIC

Sample Essay Response Scoring 5 to 6

This argument is logical on the surface, because of an electrical "correction" would stop a dog (or any species, for that matter) from continuing the same action which caused the "correction." Repeated doses of "correction" would eventually convince the dog to change direction. It is also feasible that an electrical barrier could be connected to a receiver on the dog's collar. However, there is a flaw in the argument's overall logic. Because "correction" means shock, one must wonder why a pet owner would subject his or her dog to continuous electrical shocks. How logical can it be to keep your dog "safe" by subjecting him to electrical shocks, which are not necessarily safe.

Sustained doses of electrical shock can jar the molecules in your body. Electric shock therapy is used in cases of mentally ill people in an attempt to reorganize their thinking. Who is to say that the same will not happen to dogs? I would like to see sufficient proof that the dog was not being harmed before I would even consider looking at such a product. I am convinced the product will perform as expected, but at what cost to the poor dog?

I would also like to see several veterinarians' evaluations of this product. How much current is supplied in that electrical "correction"? How will this affect the dog? In what ways? Upon what research are the answers to these questions based? That raises another issue. If veterinarians take an oath to protect animals, how can they conduct this research at all? I cannot be convinced until I see the results of veterinarians' research that proves this product will not harm dogs. Yet they should not conduct research which may harm dogs. The problem is circular.

I also feel the company that produces this product should be able to provide some verifiable research that explains how the product works. Some significant information that might be provided includes the following: 1) the specific electrical current for each "correction"; 2) how often a "correction" can be administered before it permanently damages the animal; 3) the person who decides on the guidelines for each of the numbers provided as well as his or her qualifications.

Furthermore, I would like to read some testimonials from long-term users of this product; I would also like their telephone numbers, so that I might call them and personally verify that there was no ill effect on the dog.

What I find the most illogical and unconvincing aspect of this argument is the use of the word "safe" in conjunction with "electrical corrections." While the scientific reasoning makes sense, this segment of the argument is a paradox; it seems to invalidate the straightforward scientific explanation with a lot of shading, some of it apparently designed to mislead the reader.

Analysis of Sample Essay Scoring 5 to 6

This essay earns a rating of 6: It clearly opposes the argument that this product should be used instead of chains, ropes, or fences to keep dogs within a certain boundary. A counter-argument is raised that makes the product appear unsafe. The essay's ideas are developed cogently, organized logically, and connected by smooth transitions. This can be seen in the paper's persuasive reliance on emotional and moral criteria that answer the coldly scientific argument for the use of this product. While there are minor flaws, the writer demonstrates superior control over language, including diction, syntactic variety, and the conventions of standard written English.

GMAT CAT

Graduate Management Admission Test
Computer-Adaptive Test

Practice
Test 6

NOTE:

The following practice test contains more questions than the actual GMAT CAT. This is necessary to provide a score that is roughly comparable to the shorter computer-adaptive test. Although the format is different, this test will give you an accurate idea of your strengths and weaknesses, and provide guidance for further study.

PRACTICE TEST 6

Section 1

(Answer sheets appear in the back of the book.)

TIME: 25 Minutes
16 Questions

DIRECTIONS: Solve each problem using space on the page for scratchwork. Indicate the best answer from the choices given.

NUMBERS: All numbers used are real numbers.

FIGURES: Figures accompanying problems in this section provide information useful in solving the problems. They are drawn as accurately as possible; however, when a figure is not drawn to scale, more information will be provided. It is given that all figures lie in a plane unless otherwise stated.

---

1. $4\% \times 4\% =$

    (A) 0.0016%   (B) 0.16%

    (C) 1.6%   (D) 16%

    (E) 160%

2. January 1, 1989 was on a Sunday. What day of the week will January 1, 1990 be?

    (A) Sunday   (B) Monday

    (C) Tuesday   (D) Thursday

    (E) Friday

3. Which of the following numbers is not between $.8\overline{5}$ and $.\overline{86}$?

    (A) $.\overline{851}$ (B) $.8\overline{59}$

    (C) $.859$ (D) $.\overline{861}$

    (E) $.861$

591

4. What is the measure of the angle made by the minute and hour hand of a clock at 3:30?

(A) 60°   (B) 75°

(C) 90°   (D) 115°

(E) 120°

5. $15,561 \div 25 + 9,439 \div 25 =$

(A) 997   (B) 1,000

(C) 1,002   (D) 1,005

(E) 1,005.08

6. A box of 61 pieces of candy was passed around a classroom and each student took one piece of candy. The box was passed around again in the same way, and again each student took one piece. This process was continued until there was no candy left. A particular child got the first and last piece. Which of the following is a FALSE sentence?

(A) There could have been 15 students in class.

(B) There could have been 12 students in class.

(C) There could have been 10 students in class.

(D) There could have been 7 students in class.

(E) There could have been 6 students in class.

7. During the one-hour period between 5:00 and 6:00, how many minutes is exactly one "2" displayed on an electronic digital clock?

(A) 12   (B) 13

(C) 14   (D) 15

(E) 16

8. For the triangle pictured below, the degree measure of the three angles are x, $3x$, and $3x + 5$. Find x.

(A) 25

(B) 27

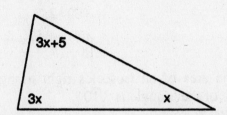

(C) 28

(D) 28.3

(E) 29

9. A rectangular parking lot is 400 feet by 300 feet. How many feet can be saved by walking across the diagonal from A to B rather than going along the outer edge from A to B?

(A) 200

(B) 300

(C) 400

(D) 500

(E) 700

In Problem 10, the formulas $V(\text{cylinder}) = \pi r^2 h$ and $V(\text{cone}) = \frac{1}{3}\pi r^2 h$ may be helpful.

10. A cone of radius 3 inches and a cylinder of radius 4 inches have equal volumes. Find the ratio of the height of the cone to that of the cylinder.

(A) $\dfrac{16}{9}$ (B) $\dfrac{16}{3}$

(C) $\dfrac{9}{16}$ (D) $\dfrac{3}{4}$

(E) $\dfrac{3}{16}$

11. If $x + y = 12$ and $x^2 + y^2 = 126$, then $xy =$

(A) 9. (B) 10.

(C) 11. (D) 13.

(E) 16.

12. If $3^{a-b} = \frac{1}{9}$ and $3^{a+b} = 9$, then $a =$

(A) -2.   (B) 0.

(C) 1.   (D) 2.

(E) 3.

13. What is the area of an isosceles right triangle if the length of the hypotenuse of the triangle is $\sqrt{10}$?

(A) $\frac{5}{2}$ sq. units   (B) 3 sq. units

(C) $\sqrt{10}$ sq. units   (D) 4 sq. units

(E) 5 sq. units

14. The solution of the equation $x^{-2} + x^{-1} - 6 = 0$ is

(A) $x = -\frac{1}{3}$ and $x = \frac{1}{2}$.

(B) $x = -6$.

(C) $x = 3$ and $x = -2$.

(D) $x = -\frac{1}{6}$.

(E) $x = \frac{1}{3}$ and $x = -\frac{1}{2}$.

15. $4^{x-3} = \left(\sqrt{2}\right)^x$ The value of x is

(A) 0   (B) 5

(C) 4   (D) $\frac{1}{2}$

(E) 3

16. A company was forced out of business by its competitor. It was able to pay 25 cents on the dollar, but had the company been able to collect a certain debt of $800, it could have paid 30 cents on the dollar. How much did the company owe at the time of its closing?

(A) $1,600   (B) $160,000

(C) $16,000   (D) $1,455

(E) $14,550

STOP

If time remains, you may go back and check your work.
When the time allotted is up, you may go on to the next section.

25

Section 2

TIME: 25 Minutes
20 Questions

DIRECTIONS: Each of the data sufficiency problems below contains a question and two statements, labeled (1) and (2), in which certain data are given. Decide whether the data given in the statements are sufficient for answering the question. Using the data given in the statements plus your knowledge of mathematics and everyday facts choose:

(A) if Statement (1) ALONE is sufficient, but Statement (2) alone is not sufficient to answer the question asked;

(B) if Statement (2) ALONE is sufficient, but Statement (1) alone is not sufficient to answer the question asked;

(C) if BOTH Statements (1) and (2) TOGETHER are sufficient to answer the question asked, but NEITHER statement ALONE is sufficient;

(D) if EACH statement ALONE is sufficient to answer the question asked;

(E) if Statements (1) and (2) TOGETHER are NOT sufficient to answer the questions asked, and additional data specific to the problem are needed.

NUMBERS: All numbers are real numbers.

FIGURES: A figure in this section will conform to the information given, but will not necessarily conform to the additional information given in the numbered Statements (1) and (2).

NOTES: Lines are straight if shown as straight, and angle measures are greater than zero.

The position of points, angles, regions, etc., exist in the order shown.

All figures lie in a plane unless otherwise stated.

Sample Question:

In the figure, the two circles are concentric (have the same center O) with radius x and y, where $x < y$. What is the area of the shaded region?

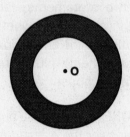

(1) The sum of the two radii is 11 units.

(2) The area of the smaller circle is $1/2$ of the area of the larger one.

Sample Explanation:

(C) By Statement (1), $x + y = 11$. Since, Statement (1) gives no other information about x and y, you cannot find the areas of the two circles. Since the area of the shaded region is the difference of the two areas, Statement (1) alone is not sufficient. According to Statement (2), $\pi y^2 = 2\pi x^2$; therefore, the area of the region is $2\pi x^2 - \pi x^2 = \pi x^2$. Since (2) does not give the value of x, it is not possible to find the area of the shaded region using (2) alone. However, if we use (1) and (2) together, we get the two equations

$y = 11 - x$ and $\pi y^2 = 2\pi x^2$

from which we can solve for x by writing the single equation $\pi(11 - x)^2 = 2\pi x^2$.

1. Tanya's salary is based on a 30% commission on sales plus a base pay of $500 a month. How much did she make last month?

   (1) Her sales were up 25% from the month before.

   (2) She made $6,000 in sales last month.

2. $\sqrt{x} = a$ and $\sqrt{y} = b$. What is xy?

   (1) $a = 2$ and $b = 3$.

   (2) $a > 0$ and $b > 0$.

3. What is the middle term of a consecutive set of three numbers.

   (1) The sum of the first and third numbers is 50.

   (2) Twice the tens value equals the units value of the first integer.

4. What is $\angle b$?

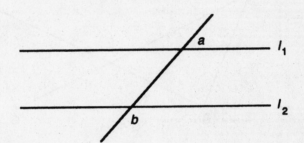

   (1) $l_1 \parallel l_2$
   (2) $\angle a = 55°$

5. What is the cost of 4 doughnuts?

   (1) 1 dozen doughnuts equal $2.40.

   (2) A cup of coffee and one doughnut equals $.80.

6. What is $x > 0$?

   (1) $x + y = 4$

   (2) $x - y = 0$

7. How much does Troy pay for his lunch?

   (1) He spent $1/4$ more than Dan.

   (2) Dan spent $1/2$ of the money he carried that day.

8. An estate is left to three heirs according to the following instructions: the second heir is to receive twice as much as the first heir and the third heir is to receive 50% more than the second heir. How much does the second heir receive?

    (1) The ratio of the amounts received is 1:2:3.

    (2) The estate is $600,000.

9. Let $(a + b)^2 = 1$ and $(a - b)^2 = 25$. What are the numbers a and b?

    (1) a and b are integers.

    (2) $a = 2$

10. In the figure below what is the measure of angle A?

    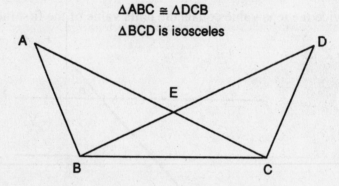

    $\triangle ABC \cong \triangle DCB$

    $\triangle BCD$ is isosceles

    (1) The measure of angle $BCD = 120$ degrees.

    (2) The measure of angle $BCE = 30$ degrees.

11. What is the length of AC?

    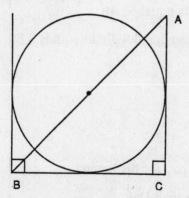

    (1) The radius of the circle is 20.

    (2) AB passes through the center of the circle.

12. Find the value of k so that $1/(x-1) > k \geq 2$.

    (1) $1 < x < \dfrac{3}{2}$

    (2) $k > 0$

13. There were 7 people in the elevator, whose weight averaged up to 145 lbs. when the elevator left the first floor. What is the maximum capacity of the elevator in pounds? (You can assume that whatever the passengers are carrying is included in their weight.)

    (1) The elevator reached its capacity when six more people whose weights ranged from 120 lbs. to 150 lbs. entered at the next stop.

    (2) It reached its capacity when three people whose weights averaged 115 lbs. left the elevator, while 5 people whose weights averaged 166 lbs. entered the elevator on its next stop.

14. In the figure, if A is the center of the circle, what is the perimeter of $\triangle ABC$?

    (1) $|AB| = 4$ and $|BC| = |AC|$.

    (2) $|AB| = 4$ and $\angle BAC = 60°$.

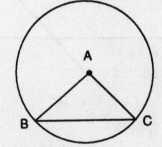

15. A year ago Sam invested in two different investments. At the present time investment A has doubled in value while investment B lost 25%. What is the total percent gain or loss of Sam's two investments?

    (1) Sam invested x dollars in A and twice that amount in B.

    (2) $5,000 was invested in A.

16. A cylinder contains three tennis balls making it completely full. How much space inside the cylinder is not being used by the balls?

    (1) Each ball has a 3 inch diameter.

    (2) The area of the base of the cylinder is approximately 7.07 square inches.

17. Mary wants to invest in two different investments, one paying 8% and the other 12% per year. She wants these investments to produce $600 per month. How much money must she invest in each investment?

    (1) She wants to invest 40% of her money in the 12% investment.

    (2) She has $75,000 to invest.

18. For the equation $y = 1/x^2$, y is less than what number?

    (1) $\dfrac{1}{2} < x < \dfrac{3}{2}$

    (2) $y < (2x + 1)(x - 3) - (2x^2 - 4) + (5x + 3)$

19. What does $\angle x$ equal?

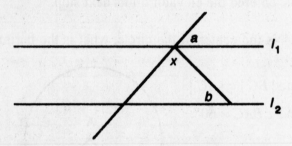

    (1) $\angle a + \angle b = 110°$

    (2) $l_1 \parallel l_2$

20. A copier originally cost $1,050. How much will it be worth when it is salvaged?

    (1) The rate of depreciation is $120 per year.

    (2) The copier is salvaged at the end of 8 years.

STOP

If time remains, you may go back and check your work.
When the time allotted is up, you may go on to the next section.

Section 3

TIME: 25 Minutes
22 Questions

DIRECTIONS: In each of the following sentences, some part of the sentence or the entire sentence is underlined. The five answer choices give various ways of phrasing the underlined part. The first choice repeats the given sentence. Pay attention to grammar, choice of words, and sentence construction in order to select the best version of the sentence. Choose (A) if you think the given sentence is correct.

---

1. Having the best record of attendance, <u>many of the Senators showed her their esteem by a standing ovation</u>.

    (A) many of the Senators showed her their esteem by a standing ovation.

    (B) the Senate showed its esteem by a standing ovation.

    (C) she was given a standing ovation by many of the Senators.

    (D) she was shown the esteem of the Senate by its giving her a standing ovation.

    (E) many of the Senators by a standing ovation showed their esteem.

2. A founder of the National Association for the Advancement of Colored People, James Weldon Johnson was the first black admitted to the Florida bar, a successful musical-comedy writer, and <u>served as a United States Consul to Venezuela and Nicaragua from 1906 to 1916</u>.

    (A) served as a United States Consul to Venezuela and Nicaragua from 1906 to 1916.

    (B) a United States Consul to Venezuela and Nicaragua from 1906 to 1916.

    (C) represented the United States as a consul to Venezuela and Nicaragua from 1906 to 1916.

    (D) from 1906 to 1916 served as a United States Consul to Venezuela and Nicaragua.

(E) was a United States consul to Venezuela and Nicaragua from 1906 to 1916.

3. Persons who use mainly the auditory modality for learning often find it difficult to understand visual stimuli, prefer to express themselves orally, like studying with others, and do not prefer to read silently.

(A) like studying with others, and do not prefer to read silently.

(B) like to study with others, and do not prefer reading silently.

(C) like to study with others, and do not prefer silent reading.

(D) like studying with others, and dislike reading silently.

(E) dislike to read silently, and like to study with others.

4. In the Renaissance artist's studio where there might be orders for a painting, a crucifix, a carved chest, and a silver urn, the artist was an engineer and the engineer was an artist.

(A) where there might be orders for a painting, a crucifix, a carved chest, and a silver urn,

(B) through which there might be orders for a painting, a crucifix, a carved chest, and a silver urn,

(C) where there was orders for a painting, a crucifix, a carved chest, and a silver urn,

(D) for the reception of orders like a painting, a crucifix, a carved chest, and a silver urn,

(E) there was orders for a painting, a crucifix, a carved chest, and a silver urn,

5. In a bear market one not only must face the possibility of fabulous growth stock becoming unsalable merchandise but demoralization must be faced.

(A) one not only must face the possibility of fabulous growth stock becoming unsalable merchandise but demoralization must be faced.

(B) not only must one face the possibility of fabulous growth stock becoming unsalable merchandise but facing demoralization is necessary.

(C) not only must facing the possibility of fabulous growth stock becoming unsalable merchandise become a necessity but demoralization must also be considered.

(D) not only must one face the possibility of fabulous growth stock becoming unsalable merchandise but facing demoralization is a possibility at times.

(E) one must face not only the possibility of fabulous growth stock becoming unsalable merchandise but also the demoralization which occurs at times.

6. <u>Three timeless themes appear in traditional literature: reversal of fortune, survival of the unfittest, and the picaresque (travel) theme</u>.

(A) Three timeless themes appear in traditional literature: reversal of fortune, survival of the unfittest, and the picaresque (travel) theme.

(B) In traditional literature three timeless themes appear: reversal of fortune, survival of the unfittest, and the picaresque (travel) theme.

(C) In traditional literature appear three timeless themes: reversing fortune, survival of the unfittest, and the picaresque (travel) theme.

(D) In traditional literature appear three timeless themes: reversal of fortune, survival of the unfittest, and the picaresque (travel) theme.

(E) The appearance of three timeless themes in traditional literature: reversal of fortune, survival of the unfittest, and the picaresque (travel) theme.

7. <u>Like Abraham Lincoln,</u> John F. Kennedy died from a gunshot wound in the head.

(A) Like Abraham Lincoln,

(B) Like Abraham Lincoln's death,

(C) Just like Abraham Lincoln died,

(D) Similar to Abraham Lincoln,

(E) As did Lincoln,

8. One of every two students in the class <u>say that they have used mari-juana</u>.

    (A) say that they have used marijuana.

    (B) admit to having used marijuana.

    (C) admit the use of marijuana.

    (D) says that they have used marijuana.

    (E) concedes the use of marijuana.

9. The use of alcohol and other intoxicating drugs <u>extend back past the European settlement of the New World</u>.

    (A) extend back past the European settlement of the New World.

    (B) begin before the European settlement of the New World.

    (C) had their origin before the European settlement of the New World.

    (D) had its origin before the European settlement of the New World.

    (E) extend before the European settlement of the New World.

10. Most teachers claim that girls participate and are called on in class as often as boys; a three-year study reports the boys <u>participating in more interactions than girls, were more assertive while the girls sat patiently with hands raised, and were calling out answers eight times more than were the girls</u>.

    (A) participating in more interactions than girls, were more assertive while the girls sat patiently with hands raised, and were calling out answers eight times more than were the girls.

    (B) participating in more interactions than girls, asserting themselves while the girls sat patiently with hands raised, and were calling out answers eight times more than were the girls.

    (C) were participating in more interactions than girls, were asserting themselves while the girls sat patiently with hands raised, and were calling out answers eight times more than were the girls.

    (D) participated in more interactions than girls, were more assertive as the girls sat patiently with hands raised, and were calling out answers eight times more than were the girls.

(E) participated in more interactions than girls, asserted themselves more often while the girls sat patiently with hands raised, and called out answers eight times more than did the girls.

11. Costing local school boards and the federal government about $500 million a year, <u>the schools are attempting to teach non-English-speaking children below high school age in their own language — bilingual education</u>.

(A) the schools are attempting to teach non-English-speaking children below high school age in their own language — bilingual education.

(B) instructors are attempting to teach non-English-speaking children below high school age in their own language — bilingual education.

(C) materials are used to teach non-English-speaking children below high school age in their own language — bilingual education.

(D) bilingual education attempts to teach non-English-speaking children below high school age in their own language.

(E) bilingual education for teaching non-English-speaking children below high school age in their own language.

12. <u>Through the voucher system the government allocates a certain amount of money for each child's education; the parents can then send their child to their choice of any public, private, or parochial school; 44% of the nation favors this system, while 41% opposes it.</u>

(A) Through the voucher system the government allocates a certain amount of money for each child's education; the parents can then send their child to their choice of any public, private, or parochial school; 44% of the nation favors this system, while 41% opposes it.

(B) The government allocates a certain amount of money for each child's education and the parents choose a public, private, or parochial school with the voucher system; 44% of the nation favors this system, while 41% opposes it.

(C) As the government allocates money through the voucher system for each child's education, the parents choose a public, private, or parochial school; 44% of the nation favors this system, while 41% opposes it.

(D) Forty-four percent of the nation favors the voucher system while 41% oppose the government allocating a certain amount of money for each child's education and the parent choosing a parochial, private, or public school.

(E) Through the voucher system the government allocates a certain amount of money for each child's education; the parents can choose a public, private, or parochial school; 44 percent of the nation favors the voucher system and 41 percent opposes it.

13. Political forces today are working for middle-aged and older people in the competition for resources since the proportion of voters with school-age or younger children has shrunk.

(A) Political forces today are working for middle-aged and older people in the competition for resources since the proportion of voters with school-age or younger children has shrunk.

(B) As political forces today are working for middle-aged and older people in the competition for resources, the proportion of voters with school-age or younger children has shrunk.

(C) Political forces today are working for middle-aged and older people in the competition for resources; since the proportion of voters with school-age or younger children has shrunk.

(D) Since political forces today are working for middle-aged and older people in the competition for resources, the proportion of voters with school-age or younger children has shrunk.

(E) A political force working for middle-aged and older people today in the competition for resources and not present for children since the proportion of voters with school-age or younger children has shrunk.

14. When the work week declines to 32 hours, employment will rise by 25%.

(A) When the work week declines to 32 hours, employment will rise by 25%.

(B) Employment rising by 25% resulting from a work week decline of 32 hours per week.

(C) When the work week declines to 32 hours, employment has risen by 25%.

(D) Declining the work week to 32 hours, the figures for employ-ment will rise by 25%.

(E) To raise the employment figures by 25%, you must decline the work week to 32 hours.

15. In *Brown vs. Board of Education* (1954) the Supreme Court ruled that <u>school systems are forbidden to intentionally segregate the races by law or practice</u>.

(A) school systems are forbidden to intentionally segregate the races by law or practice.

(B) for school systems to intentionally segregate the races by law or practice is forbidden.

(C) segregation of the races by law or practice is forbidden.

(D) forbidding the school systems to intentionally segregate the races by law or practice is illegal.

(E) school systems are forbidden to segregate intentionally the races by law or practice.

16. <u>If one was to compare the number of female parents out of 10 who worked in 1969 with the number who worked in 1977,</u> the number would have increased from 1 in 10 to 4 in 10.

(A) If one was to compare the number of female parents out of 10 who worked in 1969 with the number who worked in 1977,

(B) Comparing the number of female parents who worked in 1969 with the number who worked in 1977,

(C) If one was to compare the number of female parents who worked in 1977 with 1969,

(D) If one was to compare the number of female parents out of 10 who worked in 1969 with the number who worked in 1977;

(E) If one were to compare the number of female parents out of 10 who worked in 1969 with the number out of 10 who worked in 1977,

17. Working as an artist and later trained as a teacher, <u>Erik Erickson found his niche after completing psychoanalytic training with Anna Freud</u>.

(A) Erik Erickson found his niche after completing psychoanalytic training with Anna Freud.

(B) the niche for Erik Erickson was found after completing psycho-analytic training with Anna Freud.

(C) Anna Freud trained Erik Erickson in psychoanalysis.

(D) psychoanalytic training proved to be the niche for Erik Erickson.

(E) training in psychoanalysis with Anna Freud helped Erik Erickson find his niche.

18. When one is given lithium, <u>you often become more reflective and have fewer violent episodes</u>.

(A) you often become more reflective and have fewer violent episodes.

(B) they often become more reflective and have fewer violent episodes.

(C) they often were more reflective and had fewer violent episodes.

(D) he or she often becomes more reflective and may have fewer violent episodes.

(E) they became more reflective and had fewer violent episodes.

19. <u>The Senate passing it's measures marked the end of the last day of the congressional session</u>.

(A) The Senate passing it's measures marked the end of the last day of the congressional session.

(B) The Senate passing its measure marked the end of the last day of the congressional session.

(C) The Senate's passing it's measures marked the end of the last day of the congressional session.

(D) The Senate's passing its measures marked the end of the last day of the congressional session.

(E) The Senate passing its measures marked the end of the last day of the Congressional session.

20. <u>Growth stocks are when stocks are expected to increase in market value over a period of years</u>.

(A) Growth stocks are when stocks are expected to increase in market value over a period of years.

(B) Growth stocks are where stocks are expected to increase in market value over a period of years.

(C) Growth stocks are that expected to increase in market value over a period of years.

(D) Growth stocks are expecting to increase in market value over a period of years.

(E) Growth stocks are those expected to increase in market value over a period of years.

21. By using its general controls, the Federal Reserve can influence the total amount and flow of credit and money, which do little, however, to encourage or restrict the use of money for specific purposes.

    (A) money, which do little, however, to encourage or restrict the use of money for specific purposes.

    (B) money, it does little, however, to encourage or restrict the use of money for specific purposes.

    (C) money; these controls do little, however, to encourage or restrict the use of money for specific purposes.

    (D) money, these controls do little, however, to encourage or restrict the use of money for specific purposes.

    (E) money, the flow of credit and money does little, however, to encourage or restrict the use of money for specific purposes.

22. Either revenue or protection are the purposes of tariffs.

    (A) Either revenue or protection are the purposes of tariffs.

    (B) Either revenue or protection are the purposes of levying a tariff.

    (C) A tariff for protection or revenues are levied by a country.

    (D) The purposes of a tariff is revenue and protection.

    (E) Either revenue or protection is the purpose of a tariff.

STOP

If time remains, you may go back and check your work.
When the time allotted is up, you may go on to the next section.

Section 4

TIME: 25 Minutes

16 Questions

DIRECTIONS: Solve each problem using space on the page for scratchwork. Indicate the best answer from the choices given.

NUMBERS: All numbers used are real numbers.

FIGURES: Figures accompanying problems in this section provide information useful in solving the problems. They are drawn as accurately as possible; however, when a figure is not drawn to scale, more information will be provided. It is given that all figures lie in a plane unless otherwise stated.

---

1. If a measurement of 2.25 inches on a map represents 50 miles, what distance does a measurement of 18 inches on the map represent?

    (A) 350 miles   (B) 375 miles

    (C) 400 miles   (D) 425 miles

    (E) 450 miles

2. A teacher earns $25,000 a year and receives a 4% cost of living increase in salary, and a $275 merit increase. His salary increased by

    (A) 4.5%.   (B) 4.9%.

    (C) 5.0%.   (D) 5.1%.

    (E) 5.2%.

3. If $\dfrac{3}{x-1} = \dfrac{2}{x+1}$, then $x =$

    (A) -5.   (B) -1.

    (C) 0.   (D) 1.

    (E) 5.

4. Ball point pens cost $1.50 a dozen for the first 200 dozen a store buys from a wholesaler and $1.25 a dozen for those bought in addition to the first 200 dozen. If the store buys 250 dozen pens from the wholesaler, then its average cost of ball point pens per dozen is

(A) $1.50.　　　　　　　　(B) $1.45.

(C) $1.38.　　　　　　　　(D) $1.30.

(E) $1.25.

Use the following table for question 5.

ANNUAL INCOME BY SEX OF HEAD OF THE HOUSEHOLD

| Sex | Number of heads of households with income | | | |
	Less than $15,000	$15,000 – $35,000	$35,000 – $50,000	$50,000 and above
Male	12	25	35	8
Female	22	10	6	2

5. What percent of the males earn less than $35,000?

(A) 31　　　　　　　　(B) $46^1/_4$

(C) $57^1/_2$　　　　　　(D) 60

(E) 90

6. If $2x + y = 4$ and $2x - y = 8$, then $3x - y =$

(A) 11.　　　　　　　　(B) 7.

(C) 3.　　　　　　　　(D) – 3.

(E) – 9.

7. In the figure shown (not drawn to scale) the lines l and m are parallel. Then $x =$

(A) 140.

(B) 120.

(C) 70.

(D) 50.

(E) 40.

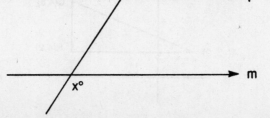

8. If p and q are prime numbers, each greater than 2, which of the following must be true?

   I. pq is an even integer.

   II. $p + q$ is an even integer.

   III. pq is an odd integer.

   (A) I only   (B) II only

   (C) III only   (D) I and II only

   (E) II and III only

9. Rachel has 30 pounds of a mixture of candy that sells for $1.00/lb. Candy A sells for .95/lb and Candy B sells for $1.10/lb. How many pounds of Candy A is in the mixture?

   (A) 5   (B) 10

   (C) 15   (D) 20

   (E) 35

10. In $\triangle ABC$, $AB = 6$, $BC = 4$, and $AC = 3$. What kind of a triangle is it?

   (A) Right and scalene   (B) Obtuse and scalene

   (C) Acute and scalene   (D) Right and isosceles

   (E) Obtuse and isosceles

11. If the product of two numbers is 14 and one of the numbers is $3\frac{1}{2}$ times the other, then the sum of the two numbers is

   (A) 2.   (B) 5.

   (C) 7.   (D) 9.

   (E) 14.

12. In the given figure, the area of the triangle ABC is

   (A) 65.

   (B) 40.

   (C) 28.

   (D) 16.

   (E) 14.

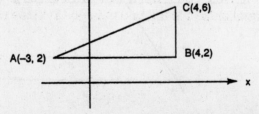

13. The sum of three consecutive even integers is 270. What is the largest integer?

(A) 86

(B) 88

(C) 90

(D) 92

(E) 94

14. A 2,000 foot long fence will be used to enclose a rectangular field that is three times as long as it is wide. The length of the field is

(A) 250 feet.

(B) 400 feet.

(C) 500 feet.

(D) 600 feet.

(E) 750 feet.

15. In the figure shown the right-angled figure is a square of length r, and the circular region on top of the square has radius r. The perimeter of the figure is

(A) $4r + 2\pi r$.

(B) $2r + \pi r/3$.

(C) $3r + 2\pi r$.

(D) $3r + \pi r/3$.

(E) $3r + 5\pi r/3$.

16. In a chess match, a win counts 1 point, a draw counts $1/2$ point, and a loss counts 0 points. After 15 games, the winner was 4 points ahead of the loser. How many points did the loser have?

(A) $4\frac{1}{2}$

(B) $5\frac{1}{2}$

(C) 6

(D) 7

(E) 9

STOP

If time remains, you may go back and check your work.
When the time allotted is up, you may go on to the next section.

Section 5

TIME: 25 Minutes
16 Questions

DIRECTIONS: For each question in this section, select the best answer.

---

1. Mrs. S is extremely jealous with regard to the activities of her husband, a seven foot, 250 pound professional wrestler. One day, while shopping at the mall, she sees a seven foot, 250 pound man going into a movie theater with a young lady. Mrs. S. follows them into the theater and in the darkness of the theater attacks the man with her handbag. She is mortified when, her eyes adapting gradually to the darkness, she realizes that the man is not in fact her husband.

    Which of the following statements points out the logical flaw in Mrs. S's thinking?

    (A) Jealousy is an irrational emotion.

    (B) Mrs. S. should have hired a detective to follow her husband.

    (C) Not every seven foot, 250 pound man is Mrs. S's husband.

    (D) She should have waited until she saw her husband at home and discussed the matter with him in private instead of making a public scene.

    (E) If she were more self-confident, she would not be so jealous.

2. A child, whose parents were hearing impaired and used sign language, could hear normally. Because the child had asthma, he had to stay indoors and was therefore not exposed to normal speakers of language. All of the friends and other visitors to the home were also hearing impaired and communicated to the parents in sign language. The parents kept the television on so that the child could hear language and learn to speak. Although the child learned sign language from his parents, he did not learn to speak and understand spoken language.

    Which of the following conclusions can most properly be drawn from the information above?

(A) The language a child learns is determined by innate factors inherited from his parents.

(B) The language used on television is not correct usage.

(C) A young child would not understand the subject matter of television programs.

(D) Interaction is necessary in order to learn a language.

(E) Children do not learn correct usage until they go to school.

3. Jack: George and Martha's divorce last year is clear evidence of the importance of economic factors in personal relationships. Didn't George also lose his job last year? That's what probably led to the breakup of the marriage.

   Jill: You're wrong, Jack. George and Martha separated in August. George lost his job in September. What led up to the big breakup was George's affair with Betsy in July. It was after she found out about the affair that Martha kicked George out of the house.

Which of the following best describes the weakness in Jack's claim on which Jill focuses?

(A) Jack only considers the economic factors influencing the situation and thus misses some of the other important factors, especially the psychological aspects of the relationship.

(B) It is quite possible that George and Martha will get back together again.

(C) The personal problems leading to the divorce began prior to George's losing his job.

(D) Jack ignores the many examples of couples who did not get divorced even though the husband or the wife lost his or her job.

(E) Jack ignores the possibility that George has found a new and even better job.

4. An increase in the interest rate results in fewer people being able to afford to borrow money. With fewer people being able to afford to borrow money, there are fewer mortgages. With fewer mortgages, there is less demand for new houses. With less demand for new houses, there is a decrease in construction work and a decrease in the

demand for building materials like lumber. With a decrease in construction and a decrease in demand for lumber, there is increased unemployment in the construction and lumber industries.

Which of the following conclusions can most properly be drawn from the information above?

(A) The Federal Reserve increases the interest rates charged to banks in response to a perceived threat of inflation.

(B) Homelessness is a major social problem today.

(C) An increase in unemployment causes a decrease in the demand for construction.

(D) An increase in unemployment causes an increase in crime.

(E) An increase in interest rates causes an increase in unemployment.

5.   Which of the following best completes the passage below?

It is the national policy of the "Superburger" fast food franchise that all employees be courteous and efficient while dealing with customers. The employee greets the customer with a smile and a polite, "May I help you?" As the customer leaves, the employee smiles and says, "Please come again." It is also the national policy of the "Superburger" fast food chain that the decor be designed to make customers vaguely uncomfortable. Bright and clashing colors are chosen so that the ambience is not soothing or restful. The aim of this policy is to keep customers from lingering. Although the two policies, polite and efficient service on the one hand and an uncomfortable decor on the other, might seem to be at odds, in fact they both serve the underlying strategic goal of _____

(A) making the customer feel important.

(B) increasing profits by cutting costs.

(C) maintaining quality control by standardizing the product.

(D) increasing productivity by raising the morale of the work force.

(E) serving as many customers as possible as quickly and efficiently as possible.

6. George paid more for his condo than did Chris.

    Jeff paid more for his condo than did Dave.

    Dave paid less for his condo than did Frank.

    Chris paid the same amount for her condo as did Frank.

    If the information above is true, which of the following must also be true?

    (A) Dave paid less for his condo than did George.

    (B) Jeff paid more for his condo than did Dave.

    (C) Jeff paid more for his condo than did Frank.

    (D) Chris paid less for her condo than did Jeff.

    (E) Chris paid less for her condo than did Dave.

7. For many years, a noted astronomer studied what he believed to be a double star. The companion star was not visible in photographs taken through the telescope, but he inferred its existence by comparing many photographs showing slight variations in the path of the first star, variations supposedly caused by the gravitational force exerted by the companion star. A recent researcher, using a radio telescope, has found no evidence of the companion star and has dismissed the earlier evidence as the effect of atmospheric distortion, variations in the visual image caused by haze and smoke in the vicinity of the telescope used for the photographs.

    Which of the following conclusions can most properly be drawn from the information above?

    (A) The noted astronomer and the recent researcher cannot both be right.

    (B) Radio telescopes are also affected by atmospheric distortion caused by haze and smoke.

    (C) Since you cannot see the companion star, it probably does not exist.

    (D) Air pollution is much worse now than it used to be.

    (E) The two theories are completely relative and depend entirely on the subjective point of view of the observers, each theory being "true" for the person who believes it.

617

8. The median income of subscribers to BIZ WHIZ magazine is $500,000. Shouldn't your company be advertising in BIZ WHIZ?

    A reader would be most likely to act in accordance with the advertisement's suggestion if he or she held which of the following assumptions?

    (A) The subscribers mentioned have reached an average income of $500,000 as a result in part of what they learn from reading BIZ WHIZ.

    (B) If you subscribe to BIZ WHIZ, other people will think that you are rich even if you are not.

    (C) If a company advertises its products in BIZ WHIZ, people will think that the company is extremely successful.

    (D) The company makes a luxury product that is likely to appeal to people with an average income of $500,000.

    (E) The more people you can reach with an advertisement, the more money you can make in sales.

9. According to a recent psychological study, members of an audience at a boxing match have a greater tendency toward violent action than do members of an audience at a tennis match. The study concludes that the contrasting environments, the boxing match and the tennis match, have a contrasting effect on the audiences. The boxing match stimulates more violent action than does the tennis match. This conclusion is not, however, warranted. It may be that the people in the audience at the boxing match are more inclined to violent action to start with than are the people in the audience at the tennis match. According to this line of reasoning, people who are more inclined to violent action to start with would be more inclined to go to a boxing match than to a tennis match.

    Which of the following, if true, would most strengthen the conclusion reached by the psychological study?

    (A) People in the audience at a boxing match become more violent after the match, while there is no corresponding increase in violence among people who have attended a tennis match.

    (B) Members of the audience at a boxing match are more likely than members of an audience at a tennis match to have a criminal record.

(C) The average income of the audience at a tennis match is higher than the average income of the audience at a boxing match.

(D) Additional research indicates that the members of the audience at a tennis match have more respect for authority than do the members of the audience at a boxing match.

(E) Of the five members of the research team doing the study, four played tennis, but none had ever boxed or been previously to a boxing match.

10. According to some classicists, the archaeological discovery of ruins at Ancient Troy lends credence to the legends concerning the Trojan War as described in such works of Ancient Greek literature as Homer's *Iliad*. If as the ruins suggest there really was a city at Troy in the 12th century B.C., then, argue the classicists, the events referred to by Homer, the abduction of Helen, the battles between the Greeks and the Trojans, the wooden horse, are fact and not fiction.

Which of the following points would tend most to weaken the classicists' argument?

(A) Although the legend, if true, would imply a city at Troy, the contrary does not follow: a city at Troy by no means implies all of the details of the legend.

(B) The Greeks did not borrow their alphabet from the Phoenicians until the 8th century B.C.

(C) At the traditional site of Troy archaeologists have found layers of cities from many centuries, and the archaeologists are not in agreement as to which layer is the city referred to by Homer.

(D) 19th-century archaeological methods were so crude that the first archaeologists destroyed most of the evidence in the process of discovering it.

(E) In Ancient Greek literature, the pagan dieties like Ares, the god of war, and Poseidon, the god of the sea, take an active part in the battles.

11. Everyone tends to favor constitutional rights in the abstract and in isolation. The question becomes considerably more complicated, however, when we consider real situations in which rights are in conflict. We are forced to choose one right over another.

Which of the following statements provides an example supporting the above general claim?

I.   The right of free speech is limited by the rights of others when it comes to yelling "Fire!" in a public theater.

II. It is not clear where the freedom of the press leaves off and the rights of others begin when a reporter refuses to divulge his sources of information at a trial.

III. Legal scholars disagree as to whether the constitution should be interpreted according to what its original framers meant or according to the circumstances of modern society.

(A) I and II, but not III

(B) I, but not II and not III

(C) III, but not I and not II

(D) II and III, but not I

(E) I, II, and III

Questions 12 – 13 are based on the following.

The United States should withdraw from NATO and abandon all foreign bases. The United States should focus all of its military energy on just defending its own borders and not get mixed up in conflicts anywhere else in the world. Getting involved in alliances with other countries just leads to trouble. Those who would characterize such isolationism as "sticking one's head in the sand" should remember that, in his farewell address, the first president, George Washington, advised us against "entangling alliances." Washington was concerned that the new country would get caught up in pointless conflicts between decadent European powers. It was good advice then, and it is good advice now.

12. The author's method of defending his opinion against the charges of certain of his opponents is to

(A) imply that the opponents are disreputable characters.

(B) cite George Washington as an authority and imply an analogy between the present and Washington's time.

(C) question the patriotism of the opponents.

(D) show that the opponents' argument leads to a logical contradiction.

(E) emphasize the difference between the present and Washington's time.

13. The opponents could effectively defend their position against the author's strategy by pointing out that

   (A) their own position is supported by some of the most experienced diplomats and foreign policy experts.

   (B) being opposed to isolationism is not in itself evidence for a lack of patriotism.

   (C) it is the author's argument, not their own, that leads to a logical contradiction.

   (D) history is likely to repeat itself unless we can learn from the past.

   (E) the fact that isolationism was a good policy in Washington's time does not make it a good policy now since the situations are very different.

Questions 14 – 15 are based on the following.

As a result of public protest, ZAP Power Co. was forced to close its Big Bang nuclear power plant. The company predicted a power shortage during the following summer and urged consumers to adopt voluntary restraints to conserve electricity by setting thermostats higher during the day. As it turned out, no power outage occurred.

14. Which of the following can be inferred from the passage?

   (A) Nuclear power is inherently unsafe.

   (B) Nobody wants a nuclear power plant "in their own backyard."

   (C) Power companies are only interested in profits and cannot be expected to respond adequately to issues of public safety.

   (D) Demand for electricity peaks during the daylight hours in the summer.

   (E) Solar power is a safe and inexpensive alternative to nuclear power.

15. Some consumers concluded that, since no power outage occurred, they probably could have set their thermostats lower and enjoyed a more comfortable summer without any adverse consequences; this

conclusion, however, is unwarranted because it can be inferred to be likely that

(A) with the nuclear power plant in operation, sooner or later there would be a nuclear disaster.

(B) if the weather had been cooler, there would have been less demand for electricity.

(C) in the absence of these conservation efforts, there would have been a power outage.

(D) the ecological effects of burning coal may be just as bad in the long run as nuclear power.

(E) if the weather had been hotter, there would have been a power outage.

16. The ratings of TV shows are important to sponsors as an indication of how many people are reached by the commercials. The ratings are based on TV-watching schedules filled in by a sampling of the public. Recent research indicates, however, that this method of gathering information is not reliable. Survey companies are trying to devise a new method of gathering data; for example, a camera that turns on when the TV is on and scans the actual audience.

Which of the following conclusions can most properly be inferred from the above passage?

(A) TV sponsors are susceptible to the influence of special interest groups organizing boycotts of their products.

(B) Television violence is probably a major cause of violence in our society.

(C) A significant number of people claimed to watch programs that they did not actually watch or watched programs they did not admit to watching.

(D) Television is a very passive form of entertainment.

(E) Parents should be responsible for monitoring what their children watch on TV.

STOP

If time remains, you may go back and check your work.
When the time allotted is up, you may go on to the next section.

Section 6

TIME: 25 Minutes
23 Questions

DIRECTIONS: Each passage is followed by questions based on its content. After reading the passage, choose the best answer to each question. Answer all questions based on what is indicated or implied in that passage.

Early in the 19th century, Napoleon sat across a chessboard from a robot swathed in the robes of a Turk. Napoleon moved his chessmen into battle; the Turk did the same. Then, when Napoleon blundered three times in succession, the audacious machine swept the board clean with an iron hand.

The chess-playing Turk had been constructed by Baron Von Kempelen; it took on all comers until Edgar Allan Poe deduced that beneath the Turk's chess table resided a diminutive chess expert who manipulated the various controls that gave life to the machine. Those were the innocent times when man believed that technology could build anything — not the least of which was a chess-playing robot.

Indeed, man has always been fascinated by *robots* — machines that do his work and often look like him. He is scarcely less intrigued by machines that seem to think like him (*computers*) and those machines that control themselves (*automatons*). Many are the basement inventors who have built machines that walk and talk like men, but these crude machines did not think or control themselves intelligently. It is in science fiction that the ultimate robots dwell. These sleek robots (often called *androids)* are computerized and thus have some ability to think. They are also autonomous; that is, they need not be controlled directly by man. The ultimate robot of fiction, superior in physical strength and mental capacity, runs the world for his human creators. In many wild tales these arrogant machines take over the planet (or the universe) completely.

Stimulating as science fiction is, it is not reality; the ultimate robot is a long way off. However, this fact should not dissuade us from building machines that can help man: machines that can take the place of men on the bottom of the sea, in dangerous coal mines, in mind-dulling industrial jobs, in all the dirty and dangerous tasks that still must be done by *somebody* or *something*.

1. Which of the following statements is best supported by information in the passage?

   (A) It is not likely that androids will be perfected.

   (B) The development of robots poses a threat to man's independence.

   (C) The dangers of robot technology outweigh its potential benefits.

   (D) Robots can play important roles in industrialized nations.

   (E) Science fiction has impeded the development of legitimate robots.

2. The author uses the Napoleon anecdote chiefly to

   (A) discredit the inflated claims of 19th-century technology.

   (B) demonstrate man's gullibility.

   (C) illustrate man's faith in technology.

   (D) show the ease with which technology can be abused.

   (E) argue that genuine automatons are an impossibility.

3. It can be inferred from the passage that the author believes robots should be used chiefly for

   (A) labor.   (B) entertainment.

   (C) management.   (D) military operations.

   (E) research.

4. According to the passage, androids differ from computers in that the former

   (A) resemble man in appearance.

   (B) are autonomous.

   (C) think like men.

   (D) have superior mental capacity.

   (E) have some ability to think.

5. According to the passage, the machines built by "basement inventors" are

    (A) computerized but not autonomous.

    (B) autonomous but not computerized.

    (C) computerized and autonomous.

    (D) neither computerized nor autonomous.

    (E) autonomous but not capable of thought.

6. The "Turk" can best be classified as

    (A) a robot.   (B) a computer.

    (C) an automaton.   (D) an android.

    (E) none of the above.

7. The author discusses science fiction chiefly to illustrate

    (A) the dangers inherent in technological advances.

    (B) the current limits of robot technology.

    (C) man's desire to control his environment.

    (D) the potential uses to which technology can be put.

    (E) man's fascination with robots.

Not long after the founding of Virginia, other Englishmen established another colony to the north. In 1620, a shipload of religious dissenters, later known as Pilgrims, debarked from the *Mayflower* on the western shore of Cape Cod Bay, on the coast of Massachusetts. The nucleus of the group were Puritan separatists, part of a congregation of nonconformists of Scrooby parish in Nottinghamshire, England. Because of the strict enforcement of the religious laws by James I, in 1608-9 the entire congregation of about 100 had moved to Holland seeking toleration. In 1620, they received permission from the Crown and financial backing from the London Company to migrate to Virginia. About 35 members of the congregation chose to do so; they first traveled to England, where they joined another group of dissenters. The *Mayflower* carried 101 passengers and a crew of 48. They were the first Englishmen — but by no means the last — to escape Stuart persecution in the New World.

The religious situation in England had grown complicated since Henry VIII separated the established church from Rome and placed himself at its head. In the last years of his reign, pressure from Protestant reformers forced him to modify much of the ecclesiastical code. After his death, the regents of his young son stimulated the Protestant movement. Mary then had attempted to reverse the tide, but Elizabeth wisely chose a middle course. She instituted moderate reforms in the Church of England and, though not disposed to tolerance of Protestants, did not rigorously enforce the regulations that restricted them.

A large group arose that wanted to continue the process of reform. Gradually they came to be called Puritans. Those Anglicans who would "purify" the church from within were known as conforming Puritans; those favoring stronger measures, as nonconformists, dissenters, or separatists. Religious disputation was the rage of the day, when translations of the Bible were first beginning to reach the hands of the people, who were also stimulated by the controversies that the Reformation had fostered. Interestingly enough, the version on which the Scrooby Pilgrims based their dissent was probably the Bishops' Bible, not the King James translation used today by most Protestant sects.

By authorizing this magnificent translation, James I undoubtedly hoped to put an end to dissent; instead, he only quickened it. His other religious policies, which grew harsher toward the end of his reign, were also designed to stamp out the heresy that was budding all over England. The King increased the pressure on nonconformists and separatists, and churchmen grew more and more intolerant, even of the conforming Puritans. But the more vigorous the pruning, the healthier the plant became. After James died, in 1625, his son Charles I (1625 – 49) proved to be even less tolerant. A bloody revolution cost Charles his throne and his life, and the Puritan colonies in New England grew rapidly.

8. The main purpose of the passage is to

   (A) provide a brief outline of 17th-century English history.

   (B) summarize the chief political problems in the reign of James I.

   (C) define the various terms applied to Protestant dissenters.

   (D) provide background information elucidating the authorization of the King James Bible.

   (E) provide a context for understanding the establishment of Massachusetts settlements.

9. The passage provides information that would answer which of the following questions?

    I.   Why did the Pilgrims settle in Massachusetts rather than Virginia?

    II. Why didn't the Scrooby Puritans seek reform within the Church of England?

    III. Why did the Scrooby nonconformists leave England?

    (A) I only   (B) II only

    (C) III only   (D) II and III only

    (E) I, II, and III

10. The author suggests that

    (A) Henry VIII welcomed revision of the ecclesiastical code.

    (B) the Reformation weakened the fabric of intellectual life in England.

    (C) the Scrooby Pilgrims left Holland chiefly for economic reasons.

    (D) James I had at least some political motives in authorizing a new translation of the Bible.

    (E) the controversies fostered by the Reformation led to a new spirit of increased tolerance in the Church of England.

11. It can be inferred from the passage that which of the following was most politically astute in dealing with religious dissent?

    (A) James I   (B) Charles I

    (C) Henry VIII   (D) Mary

    (E) Elizabeth

12. In the metaphor in the penultimate sentence, "the plant" refers to

    (A) the colonies.

    (B) religious dissent.

    (C) the Reformation in general.

    (D) the Church of England.

    (E) James I.

13. According to the passage, the chief difference between conforming and nonconforming Puritans was that

(A) the former were Anglicans whereas the latter were not.

(B) they held different views of the Protestant Reformation.

(C) they endorsed different versions of the Bible.

(D) the former sought change within the Church of England whereas the latter sought to leave it.

(E) the former did not encounter intolerance, but the latter did.

14. According to the passage, the King James Bible

I. unwittingly fostered further dissent.

II. was the chief Bible used by the Pilgrims.

III. was regretted by James I before his death.

(A) I only   (B) II only

(C) I and II only   (D) I and III only

(E) I, II, and III

15. It can be inferred from the passage that the power of the Puritans reached its apex during the reign of

(A) Henry VIII.   (B) Mary.

(C) Elizabeth.   (D) James I.

(E) Charles I.

16. Which of the following statements most accurately describes the second paragraph?

(A) It describes the "persecution" alluded to in the last sentence of the first paragraph.

(B) It describes the religious situation in England in the years prior to the events discussed in the first paragraph.

(C) It places English religious dissent in the context of the European Reformation.

(D) It makes clear that the Pilgrims began a movement that was becoming more influential in England.

(E) It outlines the Church of England's position in regard to dissenting sects.

17. The third paragraph

I. provides a context that enables the reader to classify more precisely the Massachusetts settlers.

II. provides some explanation for the spread of religious dissent.

III. explains why separatists sought to leave the Church of England.

(A) II only   (B) III only

(C) I and II only   (D) II and III only

(E) I, II, and III

Joseph John Thomson, British physicist and discoverer of the electron, was born at Cheetham Hall near Manchester on December 18, 1856, and he died in Cambridge on August 30, 1940.

Thomson entered college at the age of 14. When he was only 27 years old, he succeeded Lord Rayleigh as Professor of Physics at Cambridge University. He became head of the Cavendish Laboratory and guided it into leadership in the field of subatomic physics for over 30 years. In 1908 he was knighted. He was a gifted leader, and seven of his research assistants were themselves awarded Nobel Prizes, as well as his son and pupil, Sir George Paget Thomson, who won the Nobel Prize in physics in 1937.

Thomson died just before World War II and was buried near Isaac Newton in Westminster Abbey.

In 1895 Thomson began to investigate the mysterious rays that occurred when electricity was passed through a vacuum in a glass tube. Because they seemed to come from the cathode, the negative electrical pole in the tube, they were called cathode rays. No one had succeeded in deflecting them by an electric field. Other scientists believed that cathode rays were like light waves, but Thomson believed that they were tiny particles of matter.

He built a special cathode-ray tube in which the rays became visible as dots on a fluorescent screen inside the tube. He measured the deflections in magnetic and electrical fields and showed that they were negatively charged particles; thereafter cathode rays were accepted as tiny particles just as Thomson believed them to be.

Then he measured the ratio of the charge of the cathode-ray particles to their mass. He concluded that if the charge was equal to the minimum charge on ions using Faraday's laws of electrochemistry, then the mass of the particles was only a small fraction of that of hydrogen atoms, and the cathode-ray particles were smaller than atoms. Thomson had opened the door to research on subatomic particles.

He had proved the existence of electron particles in cathode rays. For this discovery of the electron he was awarded the 1906 Nobel Prize in physics.

He believed the electron was a universal component of matter and suggested a theory as to the internal structure of the atom.

Thomson engaged in another important discovery with his work on "channel rays," which are streams of positively charged ions that he called positive rays. He deflected these rays by magnetic and electric fields and found that ions of neon gas fell on two different spots of a photographic plate, as though they were a mixture of two types that differed in charge or mass or both. This was his first indication that ordinary elements might also exist as isotopes, which are atomic varieties of a single element differing only in their mass.

18. The primary purpose of the passage is to

    (A) provide a historical context for understanding Thomson's achievements.

    (B) define and explain electrons and "channel rays."

    (C) outline the state of subatomic physics at the turn of the century.

    (D) provide a brief biography and outline the subject's principal achievements.

    (E) examine a scientific discovery in light of its discoverer's character.

19. The passage most likely appeared in a

    (A) physics textbook.

    (B) dictionary of scientific terms.

    (C) popular scientific magazine.

    (D) *Who's Who in Science.*

    (E) scholarly physics journal.

20. According to the passage, Thomson's cathode-ray tube demonstrated

    (A) the existence of electrons.

    (B) that cathode rays are particles.

    (C) that cathode rays are negatively charged rather than positively charged.

    (D) that a fluorescent screen could deflect cathode rays.

    (E) that cathode rays could be deflected by electric but not magnetic fields.

21. According to the passage, Thomson opened the door to subatomic physics by

    (A) proving the existence of electrons.

    (B) showing that ordinary elements exist as isotopes.

    (C) using an electric field to deflect cathode rays.

    (D) studying the ions of hydrogen atoms.

    (E) suggesting a theory about the structure of atoms.

22. Thomson's work on "channel rays" and cathode rays was similar in that both involved

    (A) the discovery of new isotopes.

    (B) negatively and positively charged ions.

    (C) separations of elements on photographic plates.

    (D) deflections in magnetic and electric fields.

    (E) the observation of previously unknown subatomic particles.

23. The passage provides information that would answer which of the following questions? What was the reaction of the scientific community to Thomson's

    I.   discovery of electron particles?

    II.   theory as to the internal structure of the atom?

    III. work on channel rays?

    (A) I only   (B) III only

(C) I and II only   (D) I and III only

(E) I, II, and III

STOP

If time remains, you may go back and check your work.
When the time allotted is up, you may go on to the next section.

Section 7

ANALYSIS OF AN ISSUE ESSAY TOPIC

TIME: 30 Minutes

DIRECTIONS: In an essay, develop a position on the issue below by investigating the different angles of the issue, and explaining your thoughts on the topic. Remember, there is no one "correct" response to the essay topic.

Before starting, read the essay topic and its question(s). You may make preliminary notes in your test booklet before writing the actual essay. Be sure to write your essay on the lined pages provided at the back of the book.

Filmmaking has become an industry. Many millions of dollars are spent making movies in Hollywood each year in the hope that millions of people will spend money to see the movies. Some film makers argue that this has caused film to become more of a commercial product than an art.

Do you feel this is true? If so, is this a positive or negative change?

STOP

Do not go until you are instructed to so. Use any remaining time to check your work on this portion of the test.

ANALYSIS OF AN ARGUMENT ESSAY TOPIC

TIME: 30 Minutes

DIRECTIONS: In essay form, prepare a review on the position of the argument provided below. Before taking your own position on the argument's standpoint, it may be helpful to determine the method of thinking behind the argument itself. For example, consider alternative explanations to any assumptions the argument might make, and any evidence or examples that may strengthen or weaken the argument. Remember, there is no one "correct" response to the essay topic.

Before starting, read the essay topic and its question(s). You may make preliminary notes in your test booklet before writing the actual essay. Be sure to write your essay on the lined pages provided at the back of the book.

An a composer, I was beginning to wonder what went on in the head of the average Englishman. For several years I had been trying to get in touch with normal people. One time I was in a small town near Oxford. As an elite artist, I found it difficult to relate to the regular population. There was only one concert house in town. It was owned by foreigners and they performed mostly folk music from their own country, wherever that was— really low brow, common music. I found that a lot of the music people that pay to hear is written by people who aren't even from this country. I don't even know what that means.

What is the main point of this argument? What was the author's purpose in writing it? Is it an effective argument? Why or why not?

STOP

If time remains, you may go back and check your work.

PRACTICE TEST 6

ANSWER KEY

Section 1 — Problem Solving

1.	(B)	5.	(B)	9.	(A)	13.	(A)
2.	(B)	6.	(D)	10.	(B)	14.	(A)
3.	(A)	7.	(C)	11.	(A)	15.	(C)
4.	(B)	8.	(A)	12.	(B)	16.	(C)

Section 2 — Data Sufficiency

1.	(B)	6.	(C)	11.	(C)	16.	(D)
2.	(A)	7.	(E)	12.	(A)	17.	(D)
3.	(A)	8.	(B)	13.	(B)	18.	(D)
4.	(C)	9.	(B)	14.	(D)	19.	(C)
5.	(A)	10.	(D)	15.	(A)	20.	(C)

Section 3 — Sentence Correction

1.	(C)	7.	(A)	13.	(A)	19.	(D)
2.	(B)	8.	(D)	14.	(A)	20.	(E)
3.	(E)	9.	(D)	15.	(E)	21.	(C)
4.	(A)	10.	(E)	16.	(E)	22.	(E)
5.	(E)	11.	(D)	17.	(A)		
6.	(D)	12.	(B)	18.	(D)		

Section 4 — Problem Solving

1.	(C)	5.	(B)	9.	(D)	13.	(D)
2.	(D)	6.	(A)	10.	(B)	14.	(E)
3.	(A)	7.	(A)	11.	(D)	15.	(E)
4.	(B)	8.	(E)	12.	(E)	16.	(B)

Section 5 — Critical Reasoning

1.	(C)	5.	(E)	9.	(A)	13.	(E)
2.	(D)	6.	(A)	10.	(A)	14.	(D)
3.	(C)	7.	(A)	11.	(A)	15.	(C)
4.	(E)	8.	(D)	12.	(B)	16.	(C)

Section 6 — Reading Comprehension

1.	(D)	7.	(E)	13.	(D)	19.	(D)
2.	(C)	8.	(E)	14.	(A)	20.	(C)
3.	(A)	9.	(C)	15.	(E)	21.	(A)
4.	(B)	10.	(D)	16.	(B)	22.	(D)
5.	(D)	11.	(E)	17.	(C)	23.	(A)
6.	(E)	12.	(B)	18.	(D)		

DETAILED EXPLANATIONS OF ANSWERS

Section 1–Problem Solving

1. **(B)**

$$4\% \times 4\% = .04 \times .04$$
$$= .0016$$
$$= .16\%$$

2. **(B)**
Since January 1, 1989 was on Sunday, the 7th, 14th, 21st, 28th, ... and 364th days of that year will be on Saturday. Thus, the last day of the year will be on Sunday and the first day of 1990 will be on Monday.

3. **(A)**

Since $.\overline{85} = .858585 \ldots$

and $.\overline{851} = .851851851 \ldots ,$

$$.\overline{851} < .\overline{85} < .\overline{86}$$

4. **(B)**
At 3:30 the hands of the clock will be as shown below. The angle has measure 75°.

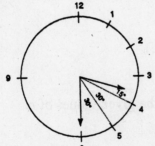

5. **(B)**
When $c \neq 0$

$$a \div c + b \div c = (a + b) \div c.$$

Thus,

$$15,561 \div 25 + 9,439 \div 25 = (15,561 + 9,439) \div 25$$
$$= 25,000 \div 25$$
$$= 1,000$$

6. **(D)**

Since $4 \times 15 = 60$, $5 \times 12 = 60$, $6 \times 10 = 60$, and $10 \times 6 = 60$, if there were 15, 12, 10, or 6 students in the group, the first student would get the last piece of candy.

7. **(C)**

Exactly one "2" will be on the clock at 5:02, 5:12, 5:20, 5:21, 5:23, 5:24, 5:25, 5:26, 5:27, 5:28, 5:29, 5:32, 5:42, and 5:52.

8. **(A)**

$$3x + 5 + 3x + x = 180$$
$$7x = 175$$
$$x = 25$$

9. **(A)**

The distance from A to B along the outer edge =

$300 + 400 = 700$ feet.

Use the Pythagorean theorem to find the diagonal from A to B

$$300^2 + 400^2 = c^2$$
$$250,000 = c^2$$
$$500 = c$$

The difference in distance $= 700 - 500 = 200$ feet.

10. **(B)**

Set V (cylinder) $= V$ (cone).

$$\pi r_1^2 h_1 = \tfrac{1}{3}\pi r_2^2 h_2$$

Cancel the pi's and substitute the given values of r:

$$16h_1 = \frac{1}{3}9h_2$$
$$16h_1 = 3h_2$$
$$\frac{16}{3}h_1 = h_2$$

so that

$$\frac{16}{3} = \frac{h_2}{h_1}.$$

Choice (A) comes from not taking $\frac{1}{3}$ of the cone radius. Choice (C) comes from the mistake in part (A) and also, taking the ratio of the cylinder to the cone. Choice (D) comes from taking the ratio of the radii. Choice (E) has the correct numbers but is the ratio of the height of the cylinder to the height of the cone.

11. **(A)**

$$x + y = 12$$

$$(x + y)^2 = 12^2$$

$$x^2 + 2xy + y^2 = 144$$

$$x^2 + y^2 = 126$$

$$2xy = 18$$

$$xy = 9$$

12. **(B)**

$$(3^{a+b})(3^{a-b}) = 9 \times \frac{1}{9}$$

$$3^{2a} = 1$$

$$3^{2a} = 3^0 \qquad (\text{since } 3^0 = 1)$$

$$2a = 0$$

$$a = 0$$

13. **(A)**
Let x be the length of each leg of the isosceles right triangle. Then

$$x^2 + x^2 = 10$$

$$x^2 = 5$$

$$x = \sqrt{5}$$

$$A = \frac{1}{2}\sqrt{5} \times \sqrt{5}$$

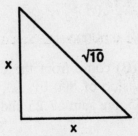

$$= \frac{5}{2}$$

14. **(A)**

$$x^{-2} + x^{-1} - 6 = 0$$

$$(x^{-1} + 3)(x^{-1} - 2) = 0$$

$$x^{-1} + 3 = 0, \ x^{-1} - 2 = 0$$

$$x^{-1} = -3, \quad x^{-1} = 2$$

$$x = -\frac{1}{3}, \quad x = \frac{1}{2}.$$

15. **(C)**

$$4^{x-3} = \left(\sqrt{2}\right)^{x}$$

is equivalent to (since $\sqrt{2} = 2^{\frac{1}{2}}$)

$$2^{2(x-3)} = 2^{\frac{x}{2}}$$

$$2^{2x-6} = 2^{\frac{x}{2}}$$

since the bases are equal, we have $2x - 6 = {}^{x}/_{2}$, multiplying each term by 2 to clear the fraction gives $4x - 12 = x$, $+ x = 4$.

16. **(C)**

Let x = the number of dollars the company owed. Then

$$.25x + 800 = .30x$$

$$800 = .05x$$

$$x = \frac{800}{.05}$$

$$= 16,000$$

Choices (A) and (B) come from the correct set-up but a decimal point mistake in the division of 800 by .05. Choices (D) and (E) come from dividing 800 by .55, the sum of .25 and .30. Choice (D) does the division incorrectly.

Section 2–Data Sufficiency

1. **(B)**
    From Statement (1) there is not enough information to solve the problem because no sales information is given. From Statement (2) Tanya's monthly salary can be determined since it is given her salary is 30% of $6,000 plus $500.

2. **(A)**
    From $\sqrt{x} = a$ and $\sqrt{y} = b$, by definition $a > 0$ and $b > 0$. Also by definition $\sqrt{x} = a$ implies $x = a^2$. Likewise $y = b^2$. Now Statement (1) suggests $x = 4$ and $y = 9$. Therefore $xy = 36$, i.e., Statement (1) alone is sufficient.
    Statement (2) gives no new information, so Statement (2) alone is not sufficient.

3. **(A)**
    From Statement (1) and the given information, the middle term can be determined. Let x = first term and $x + 2$ = the third term. Then, from Statement (1)

    $$x + x + 2 = 50$$

    and the middle term can be calculated to be 25. More information is needed for Statement (2), since from the information given the first term could be 24, 36, or 48.

4. **(C)**
    From Statement (1) and Statement (2) $\angle b$ can be determined from the properties of parallel lines.

5. **(A)**
    From Statement (1) the cost of one doughnut can be determined by dividing the cost of a dozen doughnuts by 12. Then the cost of one doughnut can be multiplied by four to solve for the cost. From Statement (2) the cost cannot be determined without more information about the cost of the cup of coffee.

6. **(C)**
    Neither Statement (1) nor Statement (2) are enough to determine the

value of x. Together there is enough information to solve for x by using the two linear equations to solve for the value of x.

7. **(E)**

Together Statement (1) and Statement (2) do not provide enough information to calculate the amount Troy spent on his lunch.

8. **(B)**

Statement (1) is just another way of stating the instructions of the will, so, Statement (1) alone is not sufficient. Let x equal the amount the first heir receives; therefore $2x$ and $3x$ are the amounts the second and third heirs receive respectively. (Note: $3x = 50\%$ more than $2x$.) We now have

$$x + 2x + 3x = \$600,000$$

which implies $x = \$100,000$ and $2x = \$200,000$. So, Statement (2) alone is sufficient.

9. **(B)**

Given $(a + b)^2 = 1$ and $(a - b)^2 = 25$:

$$a^2 + 2ab + b^2 = 1 \tag{1}$$

$$a^2 - 2ab + b^2 = 25 \tag{2}$$

$$(2) - (1) \quad ab = -6$$

According to Statement (1), a and b are integers, they can be $(2, -3)$, $(-2, 3)$, $(1, -6)$, etc. So, Statement (1) alone is not sufficient. By Statement (2), $a = 2$. Then by equation $ab = -6$, $a = 2$, $b = -3$. Therefore, Statement (2) alone is sufficient.

10. **(D)**

Statement (1) gives the angle BCD at $120°$. It is given that $\triangle BCA$ is similar to $\triangle BCD$ and hence $\angle ABC = 120°$ also. It is also given that $\triangle ABC$ is isosceles and so $\angle BAC = \angle BCA$. Now in $\triangle ABC$

$$\angle ABC + \angle BAC + \angle BCA = 180°$$

or
$$120° + 2\angle BAC = 180°$$

or
$$2\angle BAC = 180° - 120°$$

or
$$\angle BAC = {}^{60}\!/_2 = 30°$$

$$\therefore \ \angle A = 30°$$

Statement (2) tells us that $\angle BCE = 30° = \angle BCA$. As $\triangle BCA$ is isosceles $\angle BAC = \angle BCA = 30°$ $\therefore \angle A = 30°$; hence, the problem can be solved either with Statement (1) or Statement (2).

11. **(C)**

From Statement (1) we can deduce

$$BC = 2 \times \text{radius} = 40.$$

But this is not sufficient to find AC because point A could be anywhere.

Statement (2) is not sufficient by itself because it does not have any length specified. Together with Statement (1) the length of AC can be found. Because AB passes through the center of the circle

$$AC = BC = 40.$$

12. **(A)**

According to Statement (1),

$$1 < x < \frac{3}{2} \text{ or } 0 < x - 1 < \frac{1}{2}$$

so $\dfrac{1}{x-1} > 2,$

thus $k = 2$. Statement (1) is sufficient. But from Statement (2) alone, we only know $k > 0$, so it is not sufficient.

13. **(B)**

According to Statement (1) the elevator is loaded to capacity when six more people whose weights range from 120 lbs. to 150 lbs. entered at the next stop. Since (1) does not give the specific weights of these six people, (1) alone is not sufficient to determine the maximum capacity of the elevator. According to Statement (2), three people whose weights average 115 lbs. left and five people whose weights average 166 lbs. entered at the next stop and as a result the elevator was loaded to capacity; therefore, the maximum capacity can be figured by the formula

$$(7 \times 145 - 3 \times 115 + 5 \times 166) \text{ lbs.}$$

Hence, (2) alone is sufficient to find the maximum capacity of the elevator in pounds.

14. **(D)**

According to Statement (1) $|AB| = 4$ and $|BC| = |AC|$. Since A is the center of the circle, $|AB| = |AC|$ = the radius of the circle, i.e., 4 units. Since $|BC| = |AC|$, then $|AB| = |AC| = |BC| = 4$ units. So, (1) alone is sufficient. According to Statement (2) $|AB| = 4$ and $\angle BAC = 60°$. Since A is the center $|AB| = |AC|$; therefore, $|AC| = 4$. But, if $|AB| = |AC|$, then $\angle ABC = \angle ACB$. Moreover,

$$\angle ABC + \angle ACB + \angle BAC = 180° \text{ and } \angle BAC = 60°.$$

Therefore,

$$\angle ABC = \angle ACB = \angle BAC = 60°,$$

i.e., ΔABC is an equilateral triangle with side 4 units, and the perimeter is 12 units. Hence, (2) alone is also sufficient.

15. **(A)**
Investment A doubles in value which gives its value as $2x$. Investment B, which starts with $2x$ loses 25%. Hence its new value is

$$.75(2x) = 1.5x.$$

The change in value compared to original value times 100% gives the percent change. Computing:

$$[(3.5x - 3x)/3x]\,100\% = (.5x/3x)\,100\% = 16.7\% \text{ gain.}$$

Clearly Statement (1) is sufficient. Statement (2) does not give the amount invested in B. Therefore, by itself, the question cannot be answered.

16. **(D)**
The process is to subtract the volume of the three balls from the volume of the cylinder. By Statement (1) the height of the can is 9 inches and the diameter of the base is 3 inches. Therefore the volume of the can is 63.63 (volume = πr^2 times height) and volume of the 3 balls is

$$3(4/3\pi)\,(1.5^3) = 42.41.$$

(Note: radius of each base is 1.5 inches.) Clearly the unused space is 21.22 square inches. Knowing the base area (Statement (2)) we can deduce the radius of the ball and can.

$$a = 7.07 = \pi r^2$$

which implies that

$$r = \sqrt{7.07/\pi} = 1.5 \text{ inches.}$$

From the previous argument we can again determine the wasted space.

17. **(D)**
Mary wants an income of $600 per month which is $7,200 per year. Let k represent the total amount to be separated into the two investments. According to Statement (1) 40%k and 60%k are the amounts for each investment. Therefore,

$$8\%(60\%k) + 12\%(40\%k) = \$7,200.$$

This gives $k = \$75,000$ and Mary needs to put $45,000 in the 8% investment and $30,000 in the 12% investment. So, Statement (1) alone is sufficient.
Statement (2) gives the total investment. Let x be the amount invested at 8% and $\$75,000 - x$ the amount invested at 12%. Computing:

$$8\%x + 12\%(\$75,000 - x) = \$7,200$$

shows that $x = \$45,000$ and $\$75,000 - x = \$30,000$. So, Statement (2) alone is also sufficient.

18. **(D)**
From Statement (1) $\frac{4}{9} < y < 4$. Hence $y < 4$ for all x, such that $\frac{1}{2} < x < \frac{3}{2}$. Simplifying the right side of Statement (2) gives $y < 4$, which is the range of the equation

$$y = \frac{1}{x^2}.$$

So, each statement alone is sufficient.

19. **(C)**
The two statements together can be used to determine $\angle x$. Since the two lines are parallel,

$$\angle a = \angle a'.$$

Then $\angle x$ can be determined since the interior angles of a triangle equal 180°.

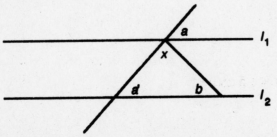

20. **(C)**

Statement (1) can be used to obtain the salvage equation

$$1,050 - 120x$$

where x is the number of years before the machine is salvaged. With Statement (2), the salvage life, the salvage cost can be determined.

Section 3–Sentence Correction

1. **(C)**
    The noun which follows the modifier HAVING THE BEST RECORD OF ATTENDANCE must be the word the phrase modifies. The word MANY is not the word which it describes so the sentence has a dangling modifier. (A) is not grammatically correct. THE SENATE is not the noun which HAVING THE BEST RECORD OF ATTENDANCE modifies. The sentence, then, has a dangling modifier and is not grammatically correct. (B) is not the best answer. (C) is the best answer. The meaning is the same as that in the sample and the sentence is grammatically correct, without misplaced modifiers. (D) is not the best answer. The entire Senate did not give her a standing ovation; only MANY OF THE SENATORS stood for the ovation. (E) is not the best answer. The use of the word MANY following HAVING THE BEST RECORD OF ATTENDANCE gives the sentence a misplaced modifier since HAVING THE BEST RECORD modifies SHE.

2. **(B)**
    After the verb WAS are two predicate nominatives: BLACK and WRITER. SERVED does not give the parallel structure needed. (A) is not the best answer. (B) is the best answer. UNITED STATES CONSUL is a proper noun which fits well as a predicate nominative in the sentence. (C) is not the best answer. REPRESENTED does not give the parallel structure needed. (D) is not the best answer. SERVED does not give the parallel structure needed. (E) is not the best answer. The verb WAS has already been given once before the two predicate nominatives BLACK and WRITER. There is no need to repeat it before the third predicate nominative UNITED STATES CONSUL. The word CONSUL should be capitalized; since it is not, there is an error in capitalization in the sentence.

3. **(E)**
    Two infinitives (TO UNDERSTAND, TO EXPRESS) precede the suggested phrase. Since infinitives were used in the series, parallel structure would demand that the other items in the series also be infinitives. Since STUDYING does not follow the previous structure, (A) is not the best answer. READING does not follow the previous structure, (B) is not the best answer. Since READING does not follow the previous structure, (C) is not the best answer. STUDYING and READING do not fit the form of the phrases which precede them in the sentence. Both of the other

phrases were infinitives (TO UNDERSTAND, TO EXPRESS). (D) should not be chosen. (E) is the best answer. Parallel structure is used (TO UNDERSTAND, TO EXPRESS, TO READ, TO STUDY) and no grammatical errors exist in the sentence.

4. **(A)**

The sentence is correct as given. (A) is the best answer. THROUGH WHICH is wordy. The use of the word WHERE would be preferred. (B) should not be selected. The sentence as written suggests that there MIGHT be orders for several objects, but it did not mean that there necessarily were orders for those items at all times. (C) changes the meaning of the sentence. Using answer (D) would not result in a logical, coherent sentence. (E) should not be selected. There is no agreement between ORDERS and WAS.

5. **(E)**

With the words NOT ONLY, one must also use BUT ALSO. These words were omitted from the sentence. (A) is not the best answer. The logical, parallel structure is not present in (B) either. The words BUT ALSO which provide parallel structure and give the sentence coherence are not present in choice (C). Since the words BUT ALSO, which must necessarily follow NOT ONLY, are omitted, (D) is not the best answer. There is no coherence and no logic to the sentence structure. (E) is the best answer. The coordinate conjunctions are used and the sentence is a logical one.

6. **(D)**

The three types of themes do not follow the word THEME and a colon; instead the three types follow the word LITERATURE. Since they do not follow the proper word, choice (A) should not be used. The three types of themes do not come after a word like ARE and a colon or the words AS FOLLOW and a colon. Instead the three types of themes come after the word APPEAR, which does not imply the themes follow. (B) is not the best answer. The three themes do come after the word THEME with a colon, but the themes are not presented in similar form. It would be better not to use -ING after REVERSE. (C) is not the best answer. (D) is the best answer. The themes are given after the word THEMES and they are stated in parallel form. (E) is not a complete sentence.

7. **(A)**

The sentence is correct as given. The noun DEATH used as the object of the preposition LIKE does not fit well into the sentence. There is no word which the prepositional phrase can modify logically. (B) should not be selected. If choice (C) is selected, a grammatical error has been chosen. LIKE is a preposition and ABRAHAM LINCOLN DIED can not logically follow the preposition. The phrase should read JUST AS ABRAHAM LINCOLN DIED. SIMILAR TO ABRAHAM LINCOLN is awkward construction. (D) is not the best answer. To have parallel structure SO DID KENNEDY must follow AS DID LINCOLN. Since these words are not present, (E) is not the best answer and should not be selected.

8. **(D)**
     ONE is the subject of the sentence. SAY is the verb. The two do not agree in number. (A) is not the best answer. ONE is the subject of the sentence; STUDENTS is the object of the preposition OF and not the subject. The verb is ADMIT; ONE and ADMIT do not agree in number. (B) should not be selected as the correct answer because of the error in subject-verb agreement. (C) cannot be selected as the correct answer since ONE (the subject) and ADMIT (the verb) do not agree in number. (D) is the correct answer. ONE and SAYS agree in number. (E) is not the best answer. The meaning of the sentence has been changed by the use of the word CONCEDES.

9. **(D)**
     Since USE is the subject of the sentence, the verb needs to be singular; EXTEND is plural. Besides this error, EXTEND BACK PAST is an awkward statement. (A) is not the best answer. (B) Since USE is the subject of the sentence, the verb needs to be singular; BEGIN is plural. (B) is not the best choice selection. (C) USE is the subject. HAD is the verb. ORIGIN is the direct object. Since USE is singular, the possessive pronoun before ORIGIN should be singular. (USE HAD ORIGIN, not ALCOHOL and DRUGS HAD ORIGIN.) Rather than having the pronoun ITS, the passage has the pronoun THEIR. (D) is the correct answer. There is agreement in number between the subject and verb and between the pronoun and noun. (E) is not the best choice. The use of BEFORE is probably superior to BACK PAST used in (A), but there is no agreement in number between the subject USE (singular) and the verb EXTEND (plural).

10. **(E)**
     After the word BOYS one finds the actions of the boys. They are PARTICIPATING, WERE, and WERE CALLING. Since these three actions are not in similar form and are not parallel, (A) is not the best

answer. Even though the first two actions of the BOYS are parallel (PAR-TICIPATING and ASSERTING), the third action WERE CALLING is not. (B) should not be selected as the correct answer because of its awkward sentence structure. Parallel structure does not exist in sentence (C). The actions of the BOYS are WERE PARTICIPATING, ASSERTED, and WERE CALLING. Because of the awkward sentence structure, (C) is not the best answer. The actions of the BOYS are PARTICIPATED and WERE CALLING. Because of the awkward sentence structure, (D) is not the best answer. (E) is the best answer. Parallel actions (PARTICIPATED, ASSERTED, and CALLED) are used.

11. **(D)**

It is not THE SCHOOLS which are COSTING LOCAL SCHOOL BOARDS AND THE FEDERAL GOVERNMENT ABOUT $500 MILLION A YEAR; it is BILINGUAL EDUCATION. The way the sentence is worded there is a dangling modifier since SCHOOLS follows the phrase beginning with COSTING. (A) is not the best answer. It is not the IN-STRUCTORS who are COSTING LOCAL SCHOOL BOARDS AND THE FEDERAL GOVERNMENT ABOUT $500 MILLION A YEAR; it is BILINGUAL EDUCATION. The way the sentence is worded there is a dangling modifier since INSTRUCTORS follows the phrase beginning with COSTING. (B) is not the best answer. It is not the MATERIALS which are COSTING LOCAL SCHOOL BOARDS AND THE FEDERAL GOVERNMENT ABOUT $500 MILLION A YEAR; it is BILINGUAL EDUCATION. The way the sentence is worded there is a dangling modifier since MATERIALS follows the phrase beginning with COSTING. (C) is not the best answer. Since it is BILINGUAL EDUCATION which is COSTING LOCAL SCHOOL BOARDS AND THE FEDERAL GOV-ERNMENT ABOUT $500 MILLION A YEAR, the sentence structure for choice (D) is correct. (D) contains no misplaced modifiers, as do the other choices. Since answer (E) is a sentence fragment, it should not be chosen.

12. **(B)**

Joining three sentences not similar in sentence structure together with semicolons is not the best way to construct a passage. (A) should not be chosen. (B) is a logical, coherent sentence without errors in grammar or punctuation and is the best answer. AS is a weak connector. It could mean when, after, as a result of, or may have some other meaning. (C) should not be selected. The possessive of GOVERNMENT should precede AL-LOCATING; since there is no possessive, (D) contains an error and should not be chosen. There is also inconsistency in the sentence. At one point 41 percent is followed by the plural verb OPPOSE; 44 percent is followed by the singular verb FAVORS. (D) is not the best answer. Joining three sentences together with semicolons is not the best way to write a passage. (E) is not the best answer.

13. **(A)**
The sentence is logical and coherent as written. There are no grammatical or punctuation errors. (A) is the best answer. The weak conjunction AS does not make the sentence logical. (B) is not the best answer. A semicolon should not be used before SINCE because the last words of the sentence are not independent. (C) is not the best answer. The reason that THE PROPORTION OF VOTERS WITH SCHOOL-AGE OR YOUNGER CHILDREN HAS SHRUNK is not because POLITICAL FORCES ARE WORKING FOR MIDDLE-AGED AND OLDER PEOPLE. The way choice (D) is worded is very misleading. (E) is not a complete sentence, nor is it a logical statement.

14. **(A)**
(A) is the best of the choices given. (B) is a sentence fragment and should not be selected. The verb tense HAS RISEN does not logically follow the phrase WHEN THE WORK WEEK DECLINES. (C) should not be selected. Statement (D) is an awkward one. It is not logically constructed and should not be selected. (E) is not the best answer. The second person pronoun YOU does not fit logically into the formal statement. REDUCE is a word which would be a better selection than DECLINE.

15. **(E)**
(A) is not the best answer since there is a split infinitive in the sentence. The split infinitive is TO INTENTIONALLY SEGREGATE. (B) is not the best answer since the same split infinitive is in the sentence. Choice (C) changes the meaning of the court case. *Brown vs. Board of Education* dealt only with school segregation; choice (C) broadens the meaning of the decision and makes the answer untrue. Not only is the meaning of (D) incorrect, but there is a split infinitive (TO INTENTIONALLY SEGREGATE). (E) is the best answer. The meaning of the court case is not distorted and there are no split infinitives.

16. **(E)**
With the subjunctive mood, the verb WERE should follow ONE rather than the word WAS. (A) is not the best answer. There is a dangling modifier in choice (B). COMPARING does not modify THE NUMBER which follows it. Besides not being a completely structured phrase, (C)

contains the word WAS instead of the word WERE which should be used with ONE in the subjunctive mood. Again in (D), the word WAS is used when the word WERE should follow ONE; the word IF helps the reader to know that the subjunctive mood should be used. (E) is the best choice.

17. **(A)**

(A) is the best answer. (B) is incorrect since THE NICHE is the noun coming after the phrase WORKING AS AN ARTIST AND LATER TRAINED AS A TEACHER, the reader can easily locate a dangling modifier in choice (C) WORKING modifies ERIK ERICKSON, not NICHE. Since ANNA FREUD is the noun coming after the phrase WORKING AS AN ARTIST AND LATER TRAINED AS A TEACHER, the reader can easily locate a dangling modifier in choice (C). WORKING modifies ERIK ERICKSON, not ANNA FREUD. The reader can easily locate a dangling modifier in choice (D). WORKING modifies ERIK ERICKSON, not TRAINING. (E) is an incorrect choice, the reader can easily locate a dangling modifier in the sentence. WORKING modifies ERIK ERICKSON, not TRAINING.

18. **(D)**

The introductory phrase uses the third person pronoun ONE. Since choice (A) uses the word YOU, the reader should not select choice (A). A shift in person from third person to second person within the sentence is not advisable. Since choice (B) uses the word THEY, the reader should not select choice (B). A shift from singular to plural within the sentence is not advisable. Since choice (C) uses the word THEY, the reader should not select choice (C). In addition, the verb form is not logical; if they are GIVEN LITHIUM, they WERE MORE REFLECTIVE does not logically follow. (D) is the best answer. The verb forms are logical and the pronouns agree in number. Since choice (E) uses the word THEY, the reader should not select choice (E). In addition, the verb form is not logical; if they are GIVEN LITHIUM, they BECAME MORE REFLECTIVE does not logically follow.

19. **(D)**

Two errors are found in choice (A). SENATE should be possessive; ITS, not IT'S, should be used. Choice (B) contains one mistake: SENATE should be possessive. Choice (C) contains one mistake: ITS, not IT'S, should be used. Choice (D) is correct and the answer to be chosen. Two errors are found in choice (E). SENATE should be possessive; CONGRESSIONAL should not be capitalized.

20. **(E)**
    The use of the word WHEN is not needed in the definition of the word GROWTH STOCKS. (A) should not be chosen. The use of the word WHERE is not needed in the definition of the word GROWTH STOCKS. (B) should not be chosen. Since the word THAT does not logically refer to the plural word GROWTH STOCKS, (C) is not the best answer. GROWTH STOCKS is a word which does not logically need the active voice; (D) is not the best answer. (E) is the best answer. There is agreement between THOSE and STOCKS and the sentence is not wordy.

21. **(C)**
    This sentence is awkward. WHICH follows the words CREDIT and MONEY, but the word does not refer to CREDIT and MONEY. (A) is not the best answer. Choice (B) is actually a run-on sentence. The part of the sentence which begins with IT DOES LITTLE is actually a complete sentence and should not be joined with the other complete thought with just a comma. (C) is the best answer. There are no pronouns whose antecedent is unclear. The punctuation is good. Since choices (D) and (E) are run-on sentences, they should not be selected as the correct answer.

22. **(E)**
    After EITHER REVENUE OR PROTECTION a singular verb should be chosen. Since ARE is plural, the agreement needed is not there. (A) is not the best answer. (B) is not the best answer by the same reasoning. A TARIFF (a singular subject) should be followed by a singular verb. Instead, choice (C) uses a plural verb ARE. PURPOSES, the subject of the sentence, is plural; the verb IS is not in agreement, however, since it is singular. (D) should not be chosen as the correct answer since it is not grammatically correct. (E) is the best answer and should be selected. There are no subject/verb disagreements and the sentence is logical and coherent.

Section 4–Problem Solving

1. **(C)**

    Since 2.25 inches on the map represent 50 miles, each one inch on the map represents 50/2.25 miles. Therefore, 18 inches represent

    $$\frac{18(50)}{2.25} = 400 \text{ miles.}$$

2. **(D)**

    Cost of living increase on

    $$\$25,000 = 25,000(.04) = 1,000.$$

    Hence, total increase in salary

    $$= 1,000 + 275 = 1,275$$

    and the percent increase

    $$= \frac{1,275}{25,000}(100) = 5.1.$$

3. **(A)**

    Multiplying both sides by $(x - 1)(x + 1)$ we get

    $$3(x + 1) = 2(x - 1),$$

    or $\qquad 3x + 3 = 2x - 2.$

    Therefore, $\qquad x = -5.$

4. **(B)**

    The cost of the first 200 dozen pens is

    $$(\$1.50)200 = \$300,$$

    and that of the remaining 50 dozen pens is

    $$\$(1.25)50 = \$62.50.$$

    Thus, the store paid

    $$\$300 + \$62.50 = \$362.50$$

for 250 dozen pens at an average (per dozen) cost of

$$\frac{362.50}{250} = \$1.45.$$

5. **(B)**
The number of males

$$= 12 + 25 + 35 + 8 = 80.$$

Of these

$$12 + 25 = 37$$

earn less than \$35,000. Therefore, the percent of males earning less than \$35,000 is $(^{37}/_{80})100 = 46^1/_4$.

6. **(A)**
If $2x + y = 4$ and $2x - y = 8$, then in adding the two we get $4x = 12$, or $x = 3$. Substituting $x = 3$ in $2x + y = 4$ gives $6 + y = 4$, or $y = -2$. Hence,

$$3x - y = 9 - (-2) = 11.$$

7. **(A)**
Since lines l and m are parallel, the 40° angle and the angle x are supplementary. Hence $40 + x = 180$, or $x = 140°$.

8. **(E)**
If p and q are both greater than 2, and both p and q are prime numbers then both p and q are odd integers. Therefore pq must be odd and $p + q$ must be even.

9. **(D)**
Let x = amount of candy A. $30 - x$ = amount of candy B.

$$.95(x) + 1.10(30 - x) = 1.00(30)$$

$$.95x + 33 - 1.1x = 30$$

$$.15x = 3$$

$$x = 20$$

10. **(B)**
Since all the sides are of different lengths, the triangle is scalene. A triangle with sides of lengths 3, 4, and 5 is a right triangle. Thus, a triangle

with sides of lengths 3, 4, and 6 is an obtuse triangle.

11. **(D)**

   If x and y denote the two numbers such that $xy = 14$ and

   $$x = \left(3\frac{1}{2}\right)y,$$

   then $\left(\frac{7}{2}y\right)(y) = 14.$

   Thus, $y^2 = 4$, $y = 2$, and

   $$x = \left(\frac{7}{2}\right)(y) = 7.$$

   Therefore, $x + y = 9$.

12. **(E)**

   Since BC is parallel to the vertical axis and AB is parallel to the horizontal axis, CB is perpendicular to AB. Hence, length of $BC =$ height of triangle

   $$ABC = 6 - 2 = 4$$

   and base = length of

   $$AB = 4 - (-3) = 7.$$

   Therefore, area of triangle

   $$ABC = (^1/_2)(4)(7) = 14.$$

13. **(D)**

   Let $x =$ the first integer

   $x + 2 =$ the second integer

   $x + 4 =$ the third integer

   $x + x + 2 + x + 4 = 270$

   $3x + 6 = 270$

   $3x = 264$

   $x = 88$

The largest integer $= x + 4 = 88 + 4 = 92$.

14. **(E)**

If width is x, then length of the field is $3x$ and the perimeter is

$$2(x + 3x) = 8x.$$

Therefore, $8x = 2,000$ and $x = 250$. It follows that the length of the field is

$$3(250) = 750 \text{ feet.}$$

15. **(E)**

Since the radius of the circular region is r, the angle subtended by the top side of the square at the center of the circle is $60°$. Therefore, only $^{60}/_{360} = {}^1/_6$ of the circumference of the circle is excluded from the perimeter of the figure. The perimeter is equal to

$$3r + \frac{5}{6}(2\pi r) = 3r + \frac{5\pi r}{3}.$$

16. **(B)**

A total of 1 point is accumulated for each game. Thus in 15 games, 15 points are accumulated. Let x be the number of points for the loser. Then $x + 4$ is the number of points for the winner, and

$$x + (x + 4) = 15$$
$$2x = 11$$
$$x = 5^1/_2.$$

Section 5–Critical Reasoning

1. **(C)**

We are given the information that Mrs. S's husband is seven feet tall and weighs 250 pounds. We could deduce from this, for example, that if she saw someone five feet tall going into a movie, it could not have been her husband. The man going into the movie could only be her husband if he fit the given description. It does not follow, however, that it is *necessarily* her husband. There are undoubtedly other seven foot, 250 pound men in addition to Mrs. S's husband. Thus, (C) points out the logical flaw in her thinking.

Choices (A) and (E) are psychological observations. They may or may not be valid psychologically, but they do not refer to mistakes in logic. Choices (B) and (D) offer points of general advice. Again, they may or may not be valid as advice, but they do not in any case refer to mistakes in logic.

2. **(D)**

Since the child learned sign language from his parents, but did not learn spoken language from the television, the conclusion to be drawn would be based on the apparent difference between the two sources: parents and television. If (A) were true, it would follow that you would learn the language of your parents and not the language of a TV set. It does not follow, however, that (A) is necessarily true. Since he has not been isolated from his parents by, for example, adoption, there is no evidence that he inherited sign language rather than learning sign language from watching his parents and communicating with them. Although we might consider the possibility of innate factors, the information gives us no evidence one way or the other. Choices (B) and (E) are irrelevant since the evidence involves the acquisition of any language at all, not the learning of correct usage. There is no evidence from the passage to support the notion that the language on television is particularly correct or incorrect. There is no evidence from the passage to support the notion that correct usage can only be learned at school. Whether correct language is heard on television or whether it is only learned at school are topics that have no bearing on this case because this child did not speak *any* language, correct or incorrect. Although (C) offers a plausible explanation, it is not supported by the evidence one way or the other. We do not know from the evidence whether or not the child could understand the subject matter. Finally, the best answer is (D) because it is the most obvious difference between the two sources. The child probably interacted with his parents on a daily basis. With regard to the television he could be, at best, only a passive receiver of language. Apparently, this was not enough. Thus, the conclusion that "can most properly be drawn" is that "Interaction is necessary in order to learn a language."

3. **(C)**

Jack presents an argument of cause and effect. He claims that the loss of employment caused the divorce. The weakness that Jill focuses on is the chronology of the events. Jill argues that the loss of employment did not cause the divorce because the separation leading to the divorce preceded the loss of employment. Thus, the correct answer is (C): "The personal problems leading to the divorce began prior to George's losing his job."

The other choices do not correctly identify "the weakness . . . on which Jill focuses." Choice (A), for example, identifies a possible weakness in Jack's argument, that he only considers economic factors. This is not, however, the weakness that Jill chooses to attack. Similarly, choice (D) implies that Jack, in order to draw general conclusions about economic factors influencing personal relationships, ought to consider more than just one example. That would be a valid criticism, but again it is not the weakness on which Jill focuses. The relevance of choices (B) and (E) is less clear. There is nothing in the given information to suggest that George and Martha either will or will not get back together again. Similarly, there is nothing to suggest that George either has or has not found a new and better job. Even if they did get back together again or even if he did find a new and better job, it is not clear from the context how this would affect Jack's argument. His argument could still be valid. The divorce might have been caused by economic factors even if they did get back together again or even if George found a new and better job. The point is that neither issue is part of Jill's criticism.

4. **(E)**

The information given in the passage establishes a chain of events linked by cause and effect: *a* causes *b*, *b* causes *c*, *c* causes *d*, *d* causes *e*. Among those conclusions that could "most properly be drawn from the information" is the implication that *a* causes *e*. Thus, the correct answer is (E): "An increase in interest rates causes an increase in unemployment."

The other choices involve terms outside of the given sequence. Choice (A), for example, related to the cause of the first terms in the sequence. Since the sequence starts with an increase in interest rates, whatever causes that increase is outside of the sequence and therefore cannot be derived from the given information. Choice (B), "Homelessness is a major social problem today," may be true and it is related to the supply of and demand for housing. It is not, however, one of the terms of the sequence. How it is related to the sequence cannot be determined from the information given. It is outside of the sequence. Both choices (C) and (D) are related to the consequences of the final term of the sequence. Choice (C) reverses the cause-and-effect sequence. According to the given information, a decrease in the demand for construction causes an increase in unemployment (x causes y). It does not follow that y also causes x. It might or it might not. Whether a decrease in the demand for construction, or anything else for that matter, is a consequence of unemployment cannot "be drawn from the information." Nothing concerning the consequences of the final term can be inferred because these consequences are outside of the sequence. Choice (D), "An increase in unemployment causes an increase in crime," also relates to the consequences of the final term in the sequence. Again, these consequences are outside of the sequence. Therefore, they cannot be derived from the given information.

5.　(E)

The problem is to find an underlying principle that reconciles an apparent contradiction. The policy of giving polite and efficient service would seem to be at odds with a policy of having a decor that makes the customer feel ill at ease. Of the five choices, only (E) provides a principle that could reconcile this apparent contradiction: "serving as many customers as possible as quickly and efficiently as possible." The service is polite and efficient in order to avoid conflict with the customer, in order to avoid keeping the customer waiting, and in order to encourage the customer to return. On the other hand, the decor discourages the customer from lingering and thus taking up table space that could be used by a new customer. The underlying goal is productivity: serving as many as possible. Each added customer is added revenue. This principle, then, resolves the apparent conflict in strategy.

The other choices are possible goals, but they do *not* resolve the apparent contradiction. Polite and efficient service might make the customer feel important, but the decor does not serve this purpose. All businesses would attempt to cut costs, but these policies may involve the additional costs of training personnel to be polite and designing a special decor. These strategies would have to prove cost-effective. They are not, merely on the face of it, reductions in cost. It is true that the fast food industry maintains quality control by standardizing the product, but that is not the issue here. The passage concerns the service and the decor, not the food itself. Finally, the morale of the work force may affect productivity, but again this is not the issue under consideration. Polite and efficient service might depend on the morale of the work force, but a decor that makes one feel ill at ease would probably have the same effect on the work force as on the customers.

6. **(A)**

The information ranks four condos from most expensive to least expensive, but does not give the actual prices. In this hierarchy, Chris and Frank have condos that cost exactly the same, George has a more expensive condo, and Dave has a less expensive condo. Thus, we have the following ranking from most to least expensive: 1) George, 2) Chris and Frank, 3) Dave. From the information, it follows that (A) "Dave paid less for his condo than George."

The main difficulty occurs with regard to Jeff. We know that his condo cost more than Dave's, but we do not know how much more. Therefore, we can not rank it with regard to anyone else's condo. We do not know from the given information whether it was more or less expensive than Chris's, Frank's, or George's. Thus, choices (B), (C), and (D) can not be derived from the given information. They might be true, but there is no way to determine from this information whether or not they are true. As for choice (E), this is actually contradicted by the information. Since Chris paid the same amount as Frank and since Frank paid more than Dave, we know that Chris did *not* pay less than Dave.

7. **(A)**

Since the noted astronomer and the recent researcher disagree about a simple matter of fact, the existence of the companion star, they "cannot both be right." Either the companion star exists or does not exist. Therefore, (A) is the correct answer.

As for the other answers, (B) is contradicted by the passage. That the recent researcher dismisses the photographic evidence as "the effect of atmospheric distortion" implies that the evidence gathered using the radio telescope is to be preferred because it would be free of any such distortion. The passage does not imply (C). A source emitting only radio waves could not be seen either and yet the waves would imply a source emitting waves at that wavelength. We infer the existence of many things that we cannot see. The researcher did not argue that the companion star had to be seen to exist, and the passage does not imply this. As for (D), it is irrelevant. Presumably the air pollution affecting the astronomer's observations must not be just a recent phenomenon since he had been making his observations over a period of "many years." That the air pollution has in fact gotten worse is quite possible, but this cannot be inferred from the passage. Choice (E), that "the two theories are completely relative," implies that they are subjective judgments, matters of opinion or taste depending on one's "subjective point of view." This is not implied by the passage. The existence of the companion star cannot depend on the observer. It is independent of the observer.

8. **(D)**

The problem is to determine which of the statements, when combined with the information given, forms a logical argument leading to the conclusion: advertise in BIZ WHIZ. (D) is the correct answer because the information that the subscribers have a $500,000 median income, when combined with the assumption that the company makes a luxury product that would appeal to this income group, leads to the conclusion that the company should be advertising in this magazine. The other choices do not combine with the information given to form a logical argument leading to this conclusion. It does not matter what the subscribers learn from reading BIZ WHIZ (A). If the company does not make a luxury product, there will be no point in advertising in the magazine no matter how useful the magazine may be to the subscribers. It does not matter what other people think about you if you subscribe to (B) or if you advertise in (C) BIZ WHIZ. What other people think of the subscribers does not directly affect the company one way or the other. What other people think of the company might be important, but having people think that company is successful would not be as important as actually making the company successful. If the company reaches the right audience with its publicity, then it stands a chance of actually being successful regardless of what people think. As for (E), this might be generally true, but would not seem to be relevant in this particular case. Here the point is that the advertisement reaches a rather select and limited audience. The assumption has to be that the product is especially suited for such an audience.

9. **(A)**

The research study claims a cause-and-effect relationship between the environment of the sporting event and the degree of violent behavior exhibited by the audience. The study argues that the environment of the boxing match causes violent behavior in the audience. This argument is consistent with the evidence, but it is not the *only* possible explanation. As suggested in the criticism in the study, this tendency toward violent behavior may be there to start with. The tendency toward violent behavior may be one of the reasons why some people decide to go to boxing matches. Thus, the relationship between cause and effect may be reversed. Instead of the boxing match causing violent behavior, it may be the tendency toward violent behavior that causes someone to be in the audience at a boxing match.

To determine whether or not the study's conclusion was the right explanation, the researchers would have to show that the audience became more violent as a result of attending the boxing match. Choice (A) would support this conclusion by showing that an audience's tendency toward violence increases after a boxing match but not after a tennis match. In this case, there still might be more of a tendency toward violence in one group than in the other, but the environments of the sporting events would appear to be at least a factor in subsequent behavior.

The other choices do not strengthen the study's conclusion because they do not address the criticism. Choice (B), for example, that members of an audience at a boxing match would be more likely to have criminal records, could indicate that members of the audience at a boxing match were more violent to start with. Choice (D), that members of the audience at a tennis match have more respect for authority, would also fail to strengthen the argument since this would be consistent with the criticism that the two audiences were different to start with. As for choice (C), without additional information or assumptions, it is unclear how the difference in average income would bear on the issue. It would not, in any case, strengthen the study's conclusion since once again it would suggest differences in the audiences prior to the experience of the sporting event. Choice (E) implies some doubt as to the objectivity of the researchers in dealing with the two sports. If four of them played tennis and none ever boxed or went previously to a boxing match, then perhaps they are more sympathetic to one sport than the other. In any case, this would not strengthen their argument, but on the contrary it would tend to weaken the validity of their findings by suggesting an underlying bias influencing the research.

10. **(A)**
    The problem with the classicists' argument is that they are starting with an assumption (the legend) and are looking for evidence to support it (the ruins). The proper deductive method is to consider the evidence free of any previous assumptions and devise the simplest possible explanation. In other words, one should consider only what the evidence implies and no more. If one starts with the legend, it should not be too difficult to find *some* evidence that is at least consistent with it. If, on the other hand, one starts with the evidence, it is doubtful that one would ever hit upon the legend. Thus, choice (A) tends "most to weaken the classicists' argument" because it indicates the fundamental flaw of arguing from theory to evidence.

The other choices introduce questions of fact that are not particularly detrimental to the argument. That the alphabet was not borrowed until the eighth century does not matter much since the story could be handed down from generation to generation in an oral tradition. As for (C), one would have to select a particular layer before one could consider the evidence in any detail, but it would not be necessary to persuade all the other archeologists to agree. Choice (D), the destruction of evidence, suggests that the implications of the evidence may be limited in any case. Whether there was much or little evidence, however, one would still need to restrict oneself to the implications of the evidence. As for (E), presumably the religious beliefs of the Ancient Greeks are not at issue here. The classicists are arguing for the validity of the narrative events and not for the validity of the Greek religious beliefs.

11. **(A)**

The problem here is to see the connection between the general idea in the opening claim and the specific examples in the three statements (I, II, and III). The reader must determine which statements provide "an example supporting the above general claim."

The general idea is that complicated constitutional issues may involve a conflict between constitutional rights. The first statement (I) illustrates this by showing how the right of free speech can be limited by the rights of others. Thus, the right of free speech is not interpreted to include irresponsibly shouting "Fire!" in a public theater in the absence of an actual conflagration because this might cause a panic and would violate the rights of others. The second statement (II) illustrates the general idea by showing how the rights of the press may come into conflict with rights of others at a trial. The newspaper reporter's freedom may depend on the confidentiality of his or her sources. At the same time, the rights of those involved in the trial may depend on the testimony of the reporter or the testimony of the source. Thus, both statements I and II illustrate the general idea.

The third statement (III) does not illustrate the general idea because it does not illustrate a conflict of rights. The question of "strict interpretation" is an important constitutional issue, but it is not a conflict between competing rights. For this reason, it does not illustrate the general idea. Thus, the correct answer is (A): "I and II, but not III."

12. **(B)**

The question asks the reader to identify the kind of argument being used. Choice (B) correctly identifies the argument as one of citing an authority and implying an analogy. The authority in this case is Washington, and the analogy is the similarity between the two arguments and, by implication, the similarity between the two situations. The personal characters of the opponents (A) and the patriotism of the opponents (C) are not at issue. Neither is mentioned in the passage, and neither is relevant to the argument. The author does not concern himself with the logical form of the opponents' argument as suggested in (D). As for (E), the author's method is exactly the opposite. He stresses the similarity, not the difference, between the present and Washington's time.

13. **(E)**
Since the argument is correctly identified as implying an analogy, an effective way to defend against this argument would be to attack the analogy. Thus (E), arguing that "the situations are very different," is the correct answer. That an argument may be supported by experts (A) does not in itself demonstrate the validity of the argument. Although choice (B) may be true enough, it is irrelevant since patriotism is not an issue and patriotism would not in and of itself determine the validity of the argument. Like expertise, patriotism would be an attribute of the people arguing and not an attribute of the argument. Neither the author nor the opponents focus on the logical form of the argument (C) so this is not an issue. Choice (D) may or may not be true, but it would seem to do more to support the author's view than to oppose it since it would seem to imply the possibility of a similarity between the past and the present. To attack the analogy, the opponents should do just the opposite.

14. **(D)**
The problem is to determine which of the answers "can be inferred from the passage." Choices (A), (B), (C), and (E) may be consistent with the passage, but they are not implied by it. Apparently, enough people felt that nuclear power was unsafe to force the company to close the plant. It does not follow from this, however, that nuclear power necessarily is unsafe. It is true that people in the area did not want a nuclear power plant, but it does not necessarily follow that "nobody" wanted the nuclear power plant or that nobody ever wants *any* nuclear power plant in their own neighborhood. Even if this were true, it would not be implied by this passage. As for the motives of the power company, it may be true that the company is "only interested in profits" or it may not be true. Again, this cannot be inferred from this passage. It may be true that solar power is a safe and inexpensive alternative, or it may not be true. None of these answers is explicitly denied by the passage, nor is it implied.

Choice (D), on the other hand, is implied by the passage. Since the power company predicted a shortage during the summer, we can assume that demand peaks during the summer. Since the company urged consumers to conserve by setting thermostats higher during the day, we can assume that demand peaks during the day in the summer.

15. **(C)**

We are not told explicitly why the outage did not occur. It is possible that the weather was cooler than usual or that the power company incorrectly estimated the demand. We do know, however, that the company did urge consumers to conserve electricity by raising their thermostats. We can infer that this may have been a contributing factor. If a power outage was a possibility, then these conservation measures may have been instrumental in averting it. Of course, an individual could have lowered his or her thermostat without having a significant effect on the demand for electricity, but if all of those who tried to conserve electricity had decided not to do so, then one of the factors helping to avert an outage would have been removed. Since the power company *urged* consumers to set their thermostats higher, we may infer that this was a decisive factor. If that is the case, then (C) "in the absence of these conservation efforts, there would have been a power outage."

Whether operating the nuclear plant would have led to a disaster or not (A) is irrelevant to this discussion since the nuclear plant had already been shut down. Presumably, it would not have been started up again anyway. Cooler or hotter weather would affect demand, but neither (B) nor (E) would render the conclusion unwarranted. Both are hypothetical situations not included one way or the other in the reasoning leading to the conclusion. The question of the long-term ecological effects of burning coal (D) was also not part of the reasoning leading to the conclusion.

16. **(C)**

The passage states that the old method was found to be unreliable, but does not explicitly state *why* it was unreliable. The new method, however, implies that more reliable information could be obtained from a camera scanning "the actual audience." The difference between the two methods implies that the old method was unreliable because the people were not actually there watching TV when they said they were or because the people were there watching TV when they said they were not.

As for the other choices, they may or may not be true, but they are not implied by the passage. Whether the sponsors would be influenced by a special interest group (A) cannot be inferred from the passage. According to the passage, the sponsors are influenced by the total number of viewers. The sponsors might also be influenced by an energetic and organized minority, or they might not. Thus, choice (A) is not implied by the passage. Choice (B) is irrelevant. Nothing can be inferred from the passage about the influence of TV on general behavior. Such a conclusion would depend on research into a correlation between watching violent programs and acting violently. The passage offers no information on that topic. Choice (D) may be true, but it is not implied by the passage. Nothing in the passage contradicts the possibility that watching TV might be extremely active: perhaps TV watchers do jazzercise exercises or throw beer bottles at the screen. Choice (E), that parents should monitor what their children watch would depend on assumptions about parental responsibility neither stated nor implied in the passage.

Section 6–Reading Comprehension

1. **(D)**
The author indicates that robots can perform "dirty and dangerous" tasks now performed by men. Androids may or may not be perfected. The author does not suggest that robots pose threats or are dangerous, nor does he indicate that science fiction has been an impediment.

2. **(C)**
As the author states, in those days "man believed that technology could build anything." The passage as a whole asserts that man has always been fascinated by robots; the Napoleon episode is only one example. The author's intent is not to discredit man's faith in technology or to show that technology can be abused.

3. **(A)**
The potential uses the author lists all relate to physical labor.

4. **(B)**
Both androids and computers can "think," but androids are also autonomous (they "need not be controlled directly by man"). Androids need not look like men.

5. **(D)**
These machines "did not think or control themselves intelligently."

6. **(E)**
The "Turk" was actually a mechanical device (dummy) controlled by a man under a table.

7. **(E)**
The author uses science fiction chiefly as another example of man's fascination with robots, not as a means of measuring the current status of actual robot technology or to warn readers of possible abuses.

8. **(E)**
The passage is "about" the Massachusetts settlements; it gives us background information, especially dealing with religion, that enables us to view the settlements in a more comprehensive framework. The passage is not chiefly concerned with English history, the reign of James I, or

differences in dissenting sects per se, although these are part of the larger story.

9. **(C)**
The Scrooby nonconformists sought greater toleration. The passage does not explain why the Pilgrims settled in Massachusetts rather than Virginia or why they left the Church of England.

10. **(D)**
James hoped to end dissent by authorizing the King James Bible. Henry VIII was pressured into changing the ecclesiastical code; the Reformation stirred lively debate, which led to greater intolerance in the church.

11. **(E)**
Elizabeth instituted moderate reforms in the Church of England and was lenient in enforcing laws restricting dissenters.

12. **(B)**
As repression increased, so did dissent.

13. **(D)**
See paragraph three.

14. **(A)**
Contrary to intent, the King James Bible fostered dissent. The passage does not say James I regretted authorizing it. The Pilgrims probably used the Bishops' Bible.

15. **(E)**
Charles I was forced from his throne and executed during a revolution or civil war. Prior to the reign of Charles I, Puritan factions were not strong enough to successfully challenge a reigning monarch.

16. **(B)**
The second paragraph summarizes religious history in England in the years prior to the Massachusetts settlements.

17. **(C)**
The third paragraph explains distinctions among dissenting sects (without explaining why separatists sought to leave the Church of England), and attributes the spread of dissent to such factors as widespread availability of translations of the Bible and controversies engendered by the Reformation.

18. **(D)**

The passage summarizes Thomson's life and principal accomplishments. The other choices are either too narrow (B), mistaken (C), or misrepresent the passage's emphasis (A), (E).

19. **(D)**

The biography and explanation of achievements suggest a *Who's Who*. It is not significantly concerned with defining or popularizing, and the content, organization, and format do not suggest a textbook or scholarly article.

20. **(C)**

See paragraph five; Thomson demonstrated that they are negatively charged particles.

21. **(A)**

Thomson proved the existence of electron particles in cathode rays. These are smaller than atoms; hence he opened the door to subatomic physics.

22. **(D)**

Thomson subjected both cathode rays and channel rays to deflections in magnetic and electric fields. Cathode ray particles are negatively charged; channel rays are streams of positively charged ions. His work on cathode rays revealed subatomic particles; his work on channel rays indicated that ordinary elements might exist as isotopes (not subatomic particles). The former work involved a cathode ray tube, the latter a photographic plate.

23. **(A)**

Cathode rays were accepted as particles, and he was awarded a Nobel Prize in physics for his discovery of the electron. The passage does not tell us the scientific community's reaction to his work on channel rays or his theory of the internal structure of atoms.

Section 7–Analytical Writing Assessment

ANALYSIS OF AN ISSUE ESSAY TOPIC

Sample Essay Response Scoring 5 to 6

Filmmaking in America has become a multimillion dollar industry. Every film produced in Hollywood has a phenomenally large budget. Every aspect of the process is expensive, from the stock upon which the film is printed to the salary of the stars whose presence is necessary to ensure the commercial success of the film. The amount of money spent on films in some ways adds to their appeal. It is part of the glamour which makes the world of stars and directors separate and fascinating. It often seems, however, that this glamour, which is an insubstantial facade, is bought at the price of integrity and artistic value.

This issue raises some very important questions such as whether or not film is an art and whether or not an artist is accountable to his or her audience. I think the answer to the first question is that film is sometimes an art, and that this situation exists when the person or people making the film give thought to both the form and content of their work. A film is made up of many different images and an artistic filmmaker must think of both the composition of each frame and the way in which the frames are edited together. Beyond this, I believe that the artist must give serious consideration to the content of the work. He or she must have some message to relate or some story to tell motivated by a genuine desire to communicate. If the sole creational motivation is to make a profit, a loss of integrity is sure to follow: the filmmaker will be saying what he or she feels people will want to hear, but not what he or she feels inspired to say. A film created under such circumstances lacks integrity, and will not be a work of art.

This issue leads directly to the second question, that of whether or not an artist should be accountable to his or her audience. The current situation in the film industry requires that a filmmaker be completely financially dependent on the audience. The fact that Hollywood films are so extravagantly expensive means that a certain audience size must be guaranteed in order for a specific film to be considered a worthwhile project. This system, in which the production and distribution are so closely linked, inevitably requires sacrifices. Frequently, films will be shown to preview audiences during production and the story will be changed to meet audience demand. Similarly, since Hollywood is built firmly on a "star system," certain actors or actresses will be chosen for a part not because they are best suited for it, but because they are capable of drawing the biggest crowd at the box office. This is not to suggest that an artist creates in a vacuum entirely unaware of the response their work will receive. The sense of having a message to relate to a specific audience is powerful and valid. When the accountability is purely financial and commercial, however, the film is likely to lose its status as a work of art.

Throughout the history of film there have been people who have believed passionately in film as an art. They have been entranced by the magical quality of flickering lights and shadows, and by the uncanny suitability of the medium for relating stories. These people have always devoted intense thought to the potential of film, delighting in experimenting with new narrative and technological advances. As film becomes more and more of an expensive industry, and as the glamorous world of film becomes increasingly separated from our daily lives, it becomes more and more difficult to create an "independent" film. In order to create a film based on an artistic vision rather than audience demand, one must seek alternative forms of funding, which are scarce. Even if a filmmaker succeeds in finding the money to produce a film, distribution remains a difficult challenge. Frequently such films are made on a very low budget, and the resulting unusual technical style or story may appeal to only a very small audience, and may only be released in a few smaller theaters or "art houses."

Some Hollywood films are enormously entertaining. Technological advances are constantly being made to enhance the beauty of film images and increase the ability of film to tell a story. It is a sad fact, however, that these skills and techniques are available only to a select group of people working within a closed system. In the ongoing race to compose commercially popular films, the big Hollywood studios will continue to produce sequel after sequel, or stale imitations of the most popular film. Ultimately, this is insulting to the audience, who will grow tired of spending money to see films they recognize as all sparkle and no substance. In the fervor to please everyone, the filmmakers will end up pleasing no one at all.

Analysis of Sample Essay Scoring 5 to 6

The above essay analyzing an issue is a "six"-rated or outstanding essay. The essayist takes a strong stance arguing one position on the issue and defends this position in a cohesive, well-organized essay. In discussing many different aspects of the film industry, the author shows a firm grasp of the complexities of the argument. This is further illustrated when he or she suggests that the original question about the commercialization of film gives rise to other questions, such as the nature of film as an art and the role of an artist. These are complicated queries with no clear answers, and the author maintains this sense while engaging in a thorough and clearly written analysis of the issue.

ANALYSIS OF AN ARGUMENT ESSAY TOPIC

Sample Essay Response Scoring 5 to 6

The author of this passage is a composer who states that the purpose of his work is to understand the people of England. That does not, however, seem to be the purpose of this particular passage. It is difficult to tell exactly what the main point of this argument is. The author discusses music and its paying audience, but it is unclear what motivates this discussion. This lack of clear focal point is one of several problems which detract from the effectiveness of this argument. Although the passage seems to be written from a genuine emotion, and though it seems that the composer himself feels that he has something important to say, the writing is at best vague, and at worst contradictory, and this results in a generally ineffective argument.

Since the author takes the time to state a specific agenda, an expectation is raised that the passage will in some way explore this stated topic. Perhaps the initial problem is that the topic is so vague. He mentions that he wants to "...get in touch with the people of England." England is an enormous country comprising millions of people and the phrase "get in touch with" does not clearly describe a pragmatic process for understanding them. The author proceeds to jump from subject to subject, only occasionally touching upon one that might be conceived as understanding Englishmen (and only in regards to music) in a poorly organized and distracting manner.

Because the author mentions getting in touch with all of England, we would expect to see evidence of a broad and searching study. However, the author mentions only one place—"a small town." Any findings made here are surely not representative of a majority of English citizens. Furthermore, within this context, he describes only one concert house there, and his reaction to what is performed in this place is from a very personal bias.

This biased tone is one of the major flaws of this passage. The author makes no attempt to record neutral observations, but speaks with a judgmental voice. This might be appropriate in an editorial piece, but not in one in which the purpose is to try to understand the thoughts and feelings of an entire population. It is difficult to imagine someone earnestly trying to gauge the public opinion for any other than selfish purposes if he considers himself separated from them because he is part of an artistic "elite." For him to judge the music of others using such words as "low brow" and "common" makes him sound opinionated and arrogant, and reduces his argument's credence considerably.

Another aspect of this judgmental tone which is completely out of place is his mention of "foreigners." To disparage the music performed in a concert house owned by "foreigners" is irrelevant and unnecessary, and could cause the reader to believe that the writer is prejudiced and there-fore less credible. If his purpose is to evaluate English culture, why does he explore this tangent? He even raises the issue that most of the concert halls where music are performed are owned by people not of his own country, and then inconclusively trails off with "I don't even know what this means."

One gets the sense, in reading this passage, that the author is genuinely searching for something. It is a saving grace that even the judgmental tone and the lack of organization lend this piece a sense of honesty and fervor, as if the author was so caught up in his search that he could not write coolly and clearly. In general, however, the tone tends to be pretentious and lacks focus, and these qualities do not fit well in an effective argument.

Analysis of Sample Essay Scoring 5 to 6

The above essay analyzing an argument is a "six"-rated or "outstand-ing" essay. The argument itself is written by a composer who claims to have a specific purpose, but does not execute that purpose in the writing of the essay. The essayist correctly judges that the writing has no clear focal point, is poorly organized, and arrogantly written. He or she backs up these observations with specific examples and even quotes from the work. The essay is organized in such a way that each negative aspect of the argument is discussed in detail, and each paragraph leads smoothly into the next. The essayist does not dismiss the argument altogether, but shows how it might be written more effectively.

GMAT CAT

Graduate Management Admission Test
Computer-Adaptive Test

Answer
Sheets

GMAT – Test 1
ANSWER SHEET

SECTION 1

1. Ⓐ Ⓑ Ⓒ Ⓓ Ⓔ
2. Ⓐ Ⓑ Ⓒ Ⓓ Ⓔ
3. Ⓐ Ⓑ Ⓒ Ⓓ Ⓔ
4. Ⓐ Ⓑ Ⓒ Ⓓ Ⓔ
5. Ⓐ Ⓑ Ⓒ Ⓓ Ⓔ
6. Ⓐ Ⓑ Ⓒ Ⓓ Ⓔ
7. Ⓐ Ⓑ Ⓒ Ⓓ Ⓔ
8. Ⓐ Ⓑ Ⓒ Ⓓ Ⓔ
9. Ⓐ Ⓑ Ⓒ Ⓓ Ⓔ
10. Ⓐ Ⓑ Ⓒ Ⓓ Ⓔ
11. Ⓐ Ⓑ Ⓒ Ⓓ Ⓔ
12. Ⓐ Ⓑ Ⓒ Ⓓ Ⓔ
13. Ⓐ Ⓑ Ⓒ Ⓓ Ⓔ
14. Ⓐ Ⓑ Ⓒ Ⓓ Ⓔ
15. Ⓐ Ⓑ Ⓒ Ⓓ Ⓔ
16. Ⓐ Ⓑ Ⓒ Ⓓ Ⓔ

SECTION 2

1. Ⓐ Ⓑ Ⓒ Ⓓ Ⓔ
2. Ⓐ Ⓑ Ⓒ Ⓓ Ⓔ
3. Ⓐ Ⓑ Ⓒ Ⓓ Ⓔ
4. Ⓐ Ⓑ Ⓒ Ⓓ Ⓔ
5. Ⓐ Ⓑ Ⓒ Ⓓ Ⓔ
6. Ⓐ Ⓑ Ⓒ Ⓓ Ⓔ
7. Ⓐ Ⓑ Ⓒ Ⓓ Ⓔ
8. Ⓐ Ⓑ Ⓒ Ⓓ Ⓔ
9. Ⓐ Ⓑ Ⓒ Ⓓ Ⓔ
10. Ⓐ Ⓑ Ⓒ Ⓓ Ⓔ
11. Ⓐ Ⓑ Ⓒ Ⓓ Ⓔ
12. Ⓐ Ⓑ Ⓒ Ⓓ Ⓔ
13. Ⓐ Ⓑ Ⓒ Ⓓ Ⓔ
14. Ⓐ Ⓑ Ⓒ Ⓓ Ⓔ
15. Ⓐ Ⓑ Ⓒ Ⓓ Ⓔ
16. Ⓐ Ⓑ Ⓒ Ⓓ Ⓔ
17. Ⓐ Ⓑ Ⓒ Ⓓ Ⓔ
18. Ⓐ Ⓑ Ⓒ Ⓓ Ⓔ
19. Ⓐ Ⓑ Ⓒ Ⓓ Ⓔ
20. Ⓐ Ⓑ Ⓒ Ⓓ Ⓔ
21. Ⓐ Ⓑ Ⓒ Ⓓ Ⓔ
22. Ⓐ Ⓑ Ⓒ Ⓓ Ⓔ
23. Ⓐ Ⓑ Ⓒ Ⓓ Ⓔ

SECTION 3

1. Ⓐ Ⓑ Ⓒ Ⓓ Ⓔ
2. Ⓐ Ⓑ Ⓒ Ⓓ Ⓔ
3. Ⓐ Ⓑ Ⓒ Ⓓ Ⓔ
4. Ⓐ Ⓑ Ⓒ Ⓓ Ⓔ
5. Ⓐ Ⓑ Ⓒ Ⓓ Ⓔ
6. Ⓐ Ⓑ Ⓒ Ⓓ Ⓔ
7. Ⓐ Ⓑ Ⓒ Ⓓ Ⓔ
8. Ⓐ Ⓑ Ⓒ Ⓓ Ⓔ
9. Ⓐ Ⓑ Ⓒ Ⓓ Ⓔ
10. Ⓐ Ⓑ Ⓒ Ⓓ Ⓔ
11. Ⓐ Ⓑ Ⓒ Ⓓ Ⓔ
12. Ⓐ Ⓑ Ⓒ Ⓓ Ⓔ
13. Ⓐ Ⓑ Ⓒ Ⓓ Ⓔ
14. Ⓐ Ⓑ Ⓒ Ⓓ Ⓔ
15. Ⓐ Ⓑ Ⓒ Ⓓ Ⓔ
16. Ⓐ Ⓑ Ⓒ Ⓓ Ⓔ
17. Ⓐ Ⓑ Ⓒ Ⓓ Ⓔ
18. Ⓐ Ⓑ Ⓒ Ⓓ Ⓔ
19. Ⓐ Ⓑ Ⓒ Ⓓ Ⓔ
20. Ⓐ Ⓑ Ⓒ Ⓓ Ⓔ

SECTION 4

1. Ⓐ Ⓑ Ⓒ Ⓓ Ⓔ
2. Ⓐ Ⓑ Ⓒ Ⓓ Ⓔ
3. Ⓐ Ⓑ Ⓒ Ⓓ Ⓔ
4. Ⓐ Ⓑ Ⓒ Ⓓ Ⓔ
5. Ⓐ Ⓑ Ⓒ Ⓓ Ⓔ
6. Ⓐ Ⓑ Ⓒ Ⓓ Ⓔ
7. Ⓐ Ⓑ Ⓒ Ⓓ Ⓔ
8. Ⓐ Ⓑ Ⓒ Ⓓ Ⓔ
9. Ⓐ Ⓑ Ⓒ Ⓓ Ⓔ
10. Ⓐ Ⓑ Ⓒ Ⓓ Ⓔ
11. Ⓐ Ⓑ Ⓒ Ⓓ Ⓔ
12. Ⓐ Ⓑ Ⓒ Ⓓ Ⓔ
13. Ⓐ Ⓑ Ⓒ Ⓓ Ⓔ
14. Ⓐ Ⓑ Ⓒ Ⓓ Ⓔ
15. Ⓐ Ⓑ Ⓒ Ⓓ Ⓔ
16. Ⓐ Ⓑ Ⓒ Ⓓ Ⓔ
17. Ⓐ Ⓑ Ⓒ Ⓓ Ⓔ
18. Ⓐ Ⓑ Ⓒ Ⓓ Ⓔ
19. Ⓐ Ⓑ Ⓒ Ⓓ Ⓔ
20. Ⓐ Ⓑ Ⓒ Ⓓ Ⓔ
21. Ⓐ Ⓑ Ⓒ Ⓓ Ⓔ
22. Ⓐ Ⓑ Ⓒ Ⓓ Ⓔ

SECTION 5

1. Ⓐ Ⓑ Ⓒ Ⓓ Ⓔ
2. Ⓐ Ⓑ Ⓒ Ⓓ Ⓔ
3. Ⓐ Ⓑ Ⓒ Ⓓ Ⓔ
4. Ⓐ Ⓑ Ⓒ Ⓓ Ⓔ
5. Ⓐ Ⓑ Ⓒ Ⓓ Ⓔ
6. Ⓐ Ⓑ Ⓒ Ⓓ Ⓔ
7. Ⓐ Ⓑ Ⓒ Ⓓ Ⓔ
8. Ⓐ Ⓑ Ⓒ Ⓓ Ⓔ
9. Ⓐ Ⓑ Ⓒ Ⓓ Ⓔ
10. Ⓐ Ⓑ Ⓒ Ⓓ Ⓔ
11. Ⓐ Ⓑ Ⓒ Ⓓ Ⓔ
12. Ⓐ Ⓑ Ⓒ Ⓓ Ⓔ
13. Ⓐ Ⓑ Ⓒ Ⓓ Ⓔ
14. Ⓐ Ⓑ Ⓒ Ⓓ Ⓔ
15. Ⓐ Ⓑ Ⓒ Ⓓ Ⓔ
16. Ⓐ Ⓑ Ⓒ Ⓓ Ⓔ

SECTION 6

1. Ⓐ Ⓑ Ⓒ Ⓓ Ⓔ
2. Ⓐ Ⓑ Ⓒ Ⓓ Ⓔ
3. Ⓐ Ⓑ Ⓒ Ⓓ Ⓔ
4. Ⓐ Ⓑ Ⓒ Ⓓ Ⓔ
5. Ⓐ Ⓑ Ⓒ Ⓓ Ⓔ
6. Ⓐ Ⓑ Ⓒ Ⓓ Ⓔ
7. Ⓐ Ⓑ Ⓒ Ⓓ Ⓔ
8. Ⓐ Ⓑ Ⓒ Ⓓ Ⓔ
9. Ⓐ Ⓑ Ⓒ Ⓓ Ⓔ
10. Ⓐ Ⓑ Ⓒ Ⓓ Ⓔ
11. Ⓐ Ⓑ Ⓒ Ⓓ Ⓔ
12. Ⓐ Ⓑ Ⓒ Ⓓ Ⓔ
13. Ⓐ Ⓑ Ⓒ Ⓓ Ⓔ
14. Ⓐ Ⓑ Ⓒ Ⓓ Ⓔ
15. Ⓐ Ⓑ Ⓒ Ⓓ Ⓔ
16. Ⓐ Ⓑ Ⓒ Ⓓ Ⓔ

GMAT – Test 2
ANSWER SHEET

SECTION 1

1. Ⓐ Ⓑ Ⓒ Ⓓ Ⓔ
2. Ⓐ Ⓑ Ⓒ Ⓓ Ⓔ
3. Ⓐ Ⓑ Ⓒ Ⓓ Ⓔ
4. Ⓐ Ⓑ Ⓒ Ⓓ Ⓔ
5. Ⓐ Ⓑ Ⓒ Ⓓ Ⓔ
6. Ⓐ Ⓑ Ⓒ Ⓓ Ⓔ
7. Ⓐ Ⓑ Ⓒ Ⓓ Ⓔ
8. Ⓐ Ⓑ Ⓒ Ⓓ Ⓔ
9. Ⓐ Ⓑ Ⓒ Ⓓ Ⓔ
10. Ⓐ Ⓑ Ⓒ Ⓓ Ⓔ
11. Ⓐ Ⓑ Ⓒ Ⓓ Ⓔ
12. Ⓐ Ⓑ Ⓒ Ⓓ Ⓔ
13. Ⓐ Ⓑ Ⓒ Ⓓ Ⓔ
14. Ⓐ Ⓑ Ⓒ Ⓓ Ⓔ
15. Ⓐ Ⓑ Ⓒ Ⓓ Ⓔ
16. Ⓐ Ⓑ Ⓒ Ⓓ Ⓔ
17. Ⓐ Ⓑ Ⓒ Ⓓ Ⓔ
18. Ⓐ Ⓑ Ⓒ Ⓓ Ⓔ
19. Ⓐ Ⓑ Ⓒ Ⓓ Ⓔ
20. Ⓐ Ⓑ Ⓒ Ⓓ Ⓔ

SECTION 2

1. Ⓐ Ⓑ Ⓒ Ⓓ Ⓔ
2. Ⓐ Ⓑ Ⓒ Ⓓ Ⓔ
3. Ⓐ Ⓑ Ⓒ Ⓓ Ⓔ
4. Ⓐ Ⓑ Ⓒ Ⓓ Ⓔ
5. Ⓐ Ⓑ Ⓒ Ⓓ Ⓔ
6. Ⓐ Ⓑ Ⓒ Ⓓ Ⓔ
7. Ⓐ Ⓑ Ⓒ Ⓓ Ⓔ
8. Ⓐ Ⓑ Ⓒ Ⓓ Ⓔ
9. Ⓐ Ⓑ Ⓒ Ⓓ Ⓔ
10. Ⓐ Ⓑ Ⓒ Ⓓ Ⓔ
11. Ⓐ Ⓑ Ⓒ Ⓓ Ⓔ
12. Ⓐ Ⓑ Ⓒ Ⓓ Ⓔ
13. Ⓐ Ⓑ Ⓒ Ⓓ Ⓔ
14. Ⓐ Ⓑ Ⓒ Ⓓ Ⓔ
15. Ⓐ Ⓑ Ⓒ Ⓓ Ⓔ
16. Ⓐ Ⓑ Ⓒ Ⓓ Ⓔ
17. Ⓐ Ⓑ Ⓒ Ⓓ Ⓔ
18. Ⓐ Ⓑ Ⓒ Ⓓ Ⓔ
19. Ⓐ Ⓑ Ⓒ Ⓓ Ⓔ
20. Ⓐ Ⓑ Ⓒ Ⓓ Ⓔ
21. Ⓐ Ⓑ Ⓒ Ⓓ Ⓔ
22. Ⓐ Ⓑ Ⓒ Ⓓ Ⓔ

SECTION 3

1. Ⓐ Ⓑ Ⓒ Ⓓ Ⓔ
2. Ⓐ Ⓑ Ⓒ Ⓓ Ⓔ
3. Ⓐ Ⓑ Ⓒ Ⓓ Ⓔ
4. Ⓐ Ⓑ Ⓒ Ⓓ Ⓔ
5. Ⓐ Ⓑ Ⓒ Ⓓ Ⓔ
6. Ⓐ Ⓑ Ⓒ Ⓓ Ⓔ
7. Ⓐ Ⓑ Ⓒ Ⓓ Ⓔ
8. Ⓐ Ⓑ Ⓒ Ⓓ Ⓔ
9. Ⓐ Ⓑ Ⓒ Ⓓ Ⓔ
10. Ⓐ Ⓑ Ⓒ Ⓓ Ⓔ
11. Ⓐ Ⓑ Ⓒ Ⓓ Ⓔ
12. Ⓐ Ⓑ Ⓒ Ⓓ Ⓔ
13. Ⓐ Ⓑ Ⓒ Ⓓ Ⓔ
14. Ⓐ Ⓑ Ⓒ Ⓓ Ⓔ
15. Ⓐ Ⓑ Ⓒ Ⓓ Ⓔ
16. Ⓐ Ⓑ Ⓒ Ⓓ Ⓔ

SECTION 4

1. Ⓐ Ⓑ Ⓒ Ⓓ Ⓔ
2. Ⓐ Ⓑ Ⓒ Ⓓ Ⓔ
3. Ⓐ Ⓑ Ⓒ Ⓓ Ⓔ
4. Ⓐ Ⓑ Ⓒ Ⓓ Ⓔ
5. Ⓐ Ⓑ Ⓒ Ⓓ Ⓔ
6. Ⓐ Ⓑ Ⓒ Ⓓ Ⓔ
7. Ⓐ Ⓑ Ⓒ Ⓓ Ⓔ
8. Ⓐ Ⓑ Ⓒ Ⓓ Ⓔ
9. Ⓐ Ⓑ Ⓒ Ⓓ Ⓔ
10. Ⓐ Ⓑ Ⓒ Ⓓ Ⓔ
11. Ⓐ Ⓑ Ⓒ Ⓓ Ⓔ
12. Ⓐ Ⓑ Ⓒ Ⓓ Ⓔ
13. Ⓐ Ⓑ Ⓒ Ⓓ Ⓔ
14. Ⓐ Ⓑ Ⓒ Ⓓ Ⓔ
15. Ⓐ Ⓑ Ⓒ Ⓓ Ⓔ
16. Ⓐ Ⓑ Ⓒ Ⓓ Ⓔ

SECTION 5

1. Ⓐ Ⓑ Ⓒ Ⓓ Ⓔ
2. Ⓐ Ⓑ Ⓒ Ⓓ Ⓔ
3. Ⓐ Ⓑ Ⓒ Ⓓ Ⓔ
4. Ⓐ Ⓑ Ⓒ Ⓓ Ⓔ
5. Ⓐ Ⓑ Ⓒ Ⓓ Ⓔ
6. Ⓐ Ⓑ Ⓒ Ⓓ Ⓔ
7. Ⓐ Ⓑ Ⓒ Ⓓ Ⓔ
8. Ⓐ Ⓑ Ⓒ Ⓓ Ⓔ
9. Ⓐ Ⓑ Ⓒ Ⓓ Ⓔ
10. Ⓐ Ⓑ Ⓒ Ⓓ Ⓔ
11. Ⓐ Ⓑ Ⓒ Ⓓ Ⓔ
12. Ⓐ Ⓑ Ⓒ Ⓓ Ⓔ
13. Ⓐ Ⓑ Ⓒ Ⓓ Ⓔ
14. Ⓐ Ⓑ Ⓒ Ⓓ Ⓔ
15. Ⓐ Ⓑ Ⓒ Ⓓ Ⓔ
16. Ⓐ Ⓑ Ⓒ Ⓓ Ⓔ

SECTION 6

1. Ⓐ Ⓑ Ⓒ Ⓓ Ⓔ
2. Ⓐ Ⓑ Ⓒ Ⓓ Ⓔ
3. Ⓐ Ⓑ Ⓒ Ⓓ Ⓔ
4. Ⓐ Ⓑ Ⓒ Ⓓ Ⓔ
5. Ⓐ Ⓑ Ⓒ Ⓓ Ⓔ
6. Ⓐ Ⓑ Ⓒ Ⓓ Ⓔ
7. Ⓐ Ⓑ Ⓒ Ⓓ Ⓔ
8. Ⓐ Ⓑ Ⓒ Ⓓ Ⓔ
9. Ⓐ Ⓑ Ⓒ Ⓓ Ⓔ
10. Ⓐ Ⓑ Ⓒ Ⓓ Ⓔ
11. Ⓐ Ⓑ Ⓒ Ⓓ Ⓔ
12. Ⓐ Ⓑ Ⓒ Ⓓ Ⓔ
13. Ⓐ Ⓑ Ⓒ Ⓓ Ⓔ
14. Ⓐ Ⓑ Ⓒ Ⓓ Ⓔ
15. Ⓐ Ⓑ Ⓒ Ⓓ Ⓔ
16. Ⓐ Ⓑ Ⓒ Ⓓ Ⓔ
17. Ⓐ Ⓑ Ⓒ Ⓓ Ⓔ
18. Ⓐ Ⓑ Ⓒ Ⓓ Ⓔ
19. Ⓐ Ⓑ Ⓒ Ⓓ Ⓔ
20. Ⓐ Ⓑ Ⓒ Ⓓ Ⓔ
21. Ⓐ Ⓑ Ⓒ Ⓓ Ⓔ
22. Ⓐ Ⓑ Ⓒ Ⓓ Ⓔ
23. Ⓐ Ⓑ Ⓒ Ⓓ Ⓔ

GMAT – Test 3
ANSWER SHEET

SECTION 1	SECTION 2	SECTION 3
1. Ⓐ Ⓑ Ⓒ Ⓓ Ⓔ	1. Ⓐ Ⓑ Ⓒ Ⓓ Ⓔ	1. Ⓐ Ⓑ Ⓒ Ⓓ Ⓔ
2. Ⓐ Ⓑ Ⓒ Ⓓ Ⓔ	2. Ⓐ Ⓑ Ⓒ Ⓓ Ⓔ	2. Ⓐ Ⓑ Ⓒ Ⓓ Ⓔ
3. Ⓐ Ⓑ Ⓒ Ⓓ Ⓔ	3. Ⓐ Ⓑ Ⓒ Ⓓ Ⓔ	3. Ⓐ Ⓑ Ⓒ Ⓓ Ⓔ
4. Ⓐ Ⓑ Ⓒ Ⓓ Ⓔ	4. Ⓐ Ⓑ Ⓒ Ⓓ Ⓔ	4. Ⓐ Ⓑ Ⓒ Ⓓ Ⓔ
5. Ⓐ Ⓑ Ⓒ Ⓓ Ⓔ	5. Ⓐ Ⓑ Ⓒ Ⓓ Ⓔ	5. Ⓐ Ⓑ Ⓒ Ⓓ Ⓔ
6. Ⓐ Ⓑ Ⓒ Ⓓ Ⓔ	6. Ⓐ Ⓑ Ⓒ Ⓓ Ⓔ	6. Ⓐ Ⓑ Ⓒ Ⓓ Ⓔ
7. Ⓐ Ⓑ Ⓒ Ⓓ Ⓔ	7. Ⓐ Ⓑ Ⓒ Ⓓ Ⓔ	7. Ⓐ Ⓑ Ⓒ Ⓓ Ⓔ
8. Ⓐ Ⓑ Ⓒ Ⓓ Ⓔ	8. Ⓐ Ⓑ Ⓒ Ⓓ Ⓔ	8. Ⓐ Ⓑ Ⓒ Ⓓ Ⓔ
9. Ⓐ Ⓑ Ⓒ Ⓓ Ⓔ	9. Ⓐ Ⓑ Ⓒ Ⓓ Ⓔ	9. Ⓐ Ⓑ Ⓒ Ⓓ Ⓔ
10. Ⓐ Ⓑ Ⓒ Ⓓ Ⓔ	10. Ⓐ Ⓑ Ⓒ Ⓓ Ⓔ	10. Ⓐ Ⓑ Ⓒ Ⓓ Ⓔ
11. Ⓐ Ⓑ Ⓒ Ⓓ Ⓔ	11. Ⓐ Ⓑ Ⓒ Ⓓ Ⓔ	11. Ⓐ Ⓑ Ⓒ Ⓓ Ⓔ
12. Ⓐ Ⓑ Ⓒ Ⓓ Ⓔ	12. Ⓐ Ⓑ Ⓒ Ⓓ Ⓔ	12. Ⓐ Ⓑ Ⓒ Ⓓ Ⓔ
13. Ⓐ Ⓑ Ⓒ Ⓓ Ⓔ	13. Ⓐ Ⓑ Ⓒ Ⓓ Ⓔ	13. Ⓐ Ⓑ Ⓒ Ⓓ Ⓔ
14. Ⓐ Ⓑ Ⓒ Ⓓ Ⓔ	14. Ⓐ Ⓑ Ⓒ Ⓓ Ⓔ	14. Ⓐ Ⓑ Ⓒ Ⓓ Ⓔ
15. Ⓐ Ⓑ Ⓒ Ⓓ Ⓔ	15. Ⓐ Ⓑ Ⓒ Ⓓ Ⓔ	15. Ⓐ Ⓑ Ⓒ Ⓓ Ⓔ
16. Ⓐ Ⓑ Ⓒ Ⓓ Ⓔ	16. Ⓐ Ⓑ Ⓒ Ⓓ Ⓔ	16. Ⓐ Ⓑ Ⓒ Ⓓ Ⓔ
17. Ⓐ Ⓑ Ⓒ Ⓓ Ⓔ		
18. Ⓐ Ⓑ Ⓒ Ⓓ Ⓔ		
19. Ⓐ Ⓑ Ⓒ Ⓓ Ⓔ		
20. Ⓐ Ⓑ Ⓒ Ⓓ Ⓔ		
21. Ⓐ Ⓑ Ⓒ Ⓓ Ⓔ		
22. Ⓐ Ⓑ Ⓒ Ⓓ Ⓔ		

SECTION 4

1. (A) (B) (C) (D) (E)
2. (A) (B) (C) (D) (E)
3. (A) (B) (C) (D) (E)
4. (A) (B) (C) (D) (E)
5. (A) (B) (C) (D) (E)
6. (A) (B) (C) (D) (E)
7. (A) (B) (C) (D) (E)
8. (A) (B) (C) (D) (E)
9. (A) (B) (C) (D) (E)
10. (A) (B) (C) (D) (E)
11. (A) (B) (C) (D) (E)
12. (A) (B) (C) (D) (E)
13. (A) (B) (C) (D) (E)
14. (A) (B) (C) (D) (E)
15. (A) (B) (C) (D) (E)
16. (A) (B) (C) (D) (E)
17. (A) (B) (C) (D) (E)
18. (A) (B) (C) (D) (E)
19. (A) (B) (C) (D) (E)
20. (A) (B) (C) (D) (E)

SECTION 5

1. (A) (B) (C) (D) (E)
2. (A) (B) (C) (D) (E)
3. (A) (B) (C) (D) (E)
4. (A) (B) (C) (D) (E)
5. (A) (B) (C) (D) (E)
6. (A) (B) (C) (D) (E)
7. (A) (B) (C) (D) (E)
8. (A) (B) (C) (D) (E)
9. (A) (B) (C) (D) (E)
10. (A) (B) (C) (D) (E)
11. (A) (B) (C) (D) (E)
12. (A) (B) (C) (D) (E)
13. (A) (B) (C) (D) (E)
14. (A) (B) (C) (D) (E)
15. (A) (B) (C) (D) (E)
16. (A) (B) (C) (D) (E)
17. (A) (B) (C) (D) (E)
18. (A) (B) (C) (D) (E)
19. (A) (B) (C) (D) (E)
20. (A) (B) (C) (D) (E)
21. (A) (B) (C) (D) (E)
22. (A) (B) (C) (D) (E)
23. (A) (B) (C) (D) (E)

SECTION 6

1. (A) (B) (C) (D) (E)
2. (A) (B) (C) (D) (E)
3. (A) (B) (C) (D) (E)
4. (A) (B) (C) (D) (E)
5. (A) (B) (C) (D) (E)
6. (A) (B) (C) (D) (E)
7. (A) (B) (C) (D) (E)
8. (A) (B) (C) (D) (E)
9. (A) (B) (C) (D) (E)
10. (A) (B) (C) (D) (E)
11. (A) (B) (C) (D) (E)
12. (A) (B) (C) (D) (E)
13. (A) (B) (C) (D) (E)
14. (A) (B) (C) (D) (E)
15. (A) (B) (C) (D) (E)
16. (A) (B) (C) (D) (E)

GMAT – Test 4
ANSWER SHEET

SECTION 1

1. (A) (B) (C) (D) (E)
2. (A) (B) (C) (D) (E)
3. (A) (B) (C) (D) (E)
4. (A) (B) (C) (D) (E)
5. (A) (B) (C) (D) (E)
6. (A) (B) (C) (D) (E)
7. (A) (B) (C) (D) (E)
8. (A) (B) (C) (D) (E)
9. (A) (B) (C) (D) (E)
10. (A) (B) (C) (D) (E)
11. (A) (B) (C) (D) (E)
12. (A) (B) (C) (D) (E)
13. (A) (B) (C) (D) (E)
14. (A) (B) (C) (D) (E)
15. (A) (B) (C) (D) (E)
16. (A) (B) (C) (D) (E)
17. (A) (B) (C) (D) (E)
18. (A) (B) (C) (D) (E)
19. (A) (B) (C) (D) (E)
20. (A) (B) (C) (D) (E)
21. (A) (B) (C) (D) (E)
22. (A) (B) (C) (D) (E)
23. (A) (B) (C) (D) (E)

SECTION 2

1. (A) (B) (C) (D) (E)
2. (A) (B) (C) (D) (E)
3. (A) (B) (C) (D) (E)
4. (A) (B) (C) (D) (E)
5. (A) (B) (C) (D) (E)
6. (A) (B) (C) (D) (E)
7. (A) (B) (C) (D) (E)
8. (A) (B) (C) (D) (E)
9. (A) (B) (C) (D) (E)
10. (A) (B) (C) (D) (E)
11. (A) (B) (C) (D) (E)
12. (A) (B) (C) (D) (E)
13. (A) (B) (C) (D) (E)
14. (A) (B) (C) (D) (E)
15. (A) (B) (C) (D) (E)
16. (A) (B) (C) (D) (E)
17. (A) (B) (C) (D) (E)
18. (A) (B) (C) (D) (E)
19. (A) (B) (C) (D) (E)
20. (A) (B) (C) (D) (E)

SECTION 3

1. (A) (B) (C) (D) (E)
2. (A) (B) (C) (D) (E)
3. (A) (B) (C) (D) (E)
4. (A) (B) (C) (D) (E)
5. (A) (B) (C) (D) (E)
6. (A) (B) (C) (D) (E)
7. (A) (B) (C) (D) (E)
8. (A) (B) (C) (D) (E)
9. (A) (B) (C) (D) (E)
10. (A) (B) (C) (D) (E)
11. (A) (B) (C) (D) (E)
12. (A) (B) (C) (D) (E)
13. (A) (B) (C) (D) (E)
14. (A) (B) (C) (D) (E)
15. (A) (B) (C) (D) (E)
16. (A) (B) (C) (D) (E)
17. (A) (B) (C) (D) (E)
18. (A) (B) (C) (D) (E)
19. (A) (B) (C) (D) (E)
20. (A) (B) (C) (D) (E)
21. (A) (B) (C) (D) (E)
22. (A) (B) (C) (D) (E)

SECTION 4

1. Ⓐ Ⓑ Ⓒ Ⓓ Ⓔ
2. Ⓐ Ⓑ Ⓒ Ⓓ Ⓔ
3. Ⓐ Ⓑ Ⓒ Ⓓ Ⓔ
4. Ⓐ Ⓑ Ⓒ Ⓓ Ⓔ
5. Ⓐ Ⓑ Ⓒ Ⓓ Ⓔ
6. Ⓐ Ⓑ Ⓒ Ⓓ Ⓔ
7. Ⓐ Ⓑ Ⓒ Ⓓ Ⓔ
8. Ⓐ Ⓑ Ⓒ Ⓓ Ⓔ
9. Ⓐ Ⓑ Ⓒ Ⓓ Ⓔ
10. Ⓐ Ⓑ Ⓒ Ⓓ Ⓔ
11. Ⓐ Ⓑ Ⓒ Ⓓ Ⓔ
12. Ⓐ Ⓑ Ⓒ Ⓓ Ⓔ
13. Ⓐ Ⓑ Ⓒ Ⓓ Ⓔ
14. Ⓐ Ⓑ Ⓒ Ⓓ Ⓔ
15. Ⓐ Ⓑ Ⓒ Ⓓ Ⓔ
16. Ⓐ Ⓑ Ⓒ Ⓓ Ⓔ

SECTION 5

1. Ⓐ Ⓑ Ⓒ Ⓓ Ⓔ
2. Ⓐ Ⓑ Ⓒ Ⓓ Ⓔ
3. Ⓐ Ⓑ Ⓒ Ⓓ Ⓔ
4. Ⓐ Ⓑ Ⓒ Ⓓ Ⓔ
5. Ⓐ Ⓑ Ⓒ Ⓓ Ⓔ
6. Ⓐ Ⓑ Ⓒ Ⓓ Ⓔ
7. Ⓐ Ⓑ Ⓒ Ⓓ Ⓔ
8. Ⓐ Ⓑ Ⓒ Ⓓ Ⓔ
9. Ⓐ Ⓑ Ⓒ Ⓓ Ⓔ
10. Ⓐ Ⓑ Ⓒ Ⓓ Ⓔ
11. Ⓐ Ⓑ Ⓒ Ⓓ Ⓔ
12. Ⓐ Ⓑ Ⓒ Ⓓ Ⓔ
13. Ⓐ Ⓑ Ⓒ Ⓓ Ⓔ
14. Ⓐ Ⓑ Ⓒ Ⓓ Ⓔ
15. Ⓐ Ⓑ Ⓒ Ⓓ Ⓔ
16. Ⓐ Ⓑ Ⓒ Ⓓ Ⓔ

SECTION 6

1. Ⓐ Ⓑ Ⓒ Ⓓ Ⓔ
2. Ⓐ Ⓑ Ⓒ Ⓓ Ⓔ
3. Ⓐ Ⓑ Ⓒ Ⓓ Ⓔ
4. Ⓐ Ⓑ Ⓒ Ⓓ Ⓔ
5. Ⓐ Ⓑ Ⓒ Ⓓ Ⓔ
6. Ⓐ Ⓑ Ⓒ Ⓓ Ⓔ
7. Ⓐ Ⓑ Ⓒ Ⓓ Ⓔ
8. Ⓐ Ⓑ Ⓒ Ⓓ Ⓔ
9. Ⓐ Ⓑ Ⓒ Ⓓ Ⓔ
10. Ⓐ Ⓑ Ⓒ Ⓓ Ⓔ
11. Ⓐ Ⓑ Ⓒ Ⓓ Ⓔ
12. Ⓐ Ⓑ Ⓒ Ⓓ Ⓔ
13. Ⓐ Ⓑ Ⓒ Ⓓ Ⓔ
14. Ⓐ Ⓑ Ⓒ Ⓓ Ⓔ
15. Ⓐ Ⓑ Ⓒ Ⓓ Ⓔ
16. Ⓐ Ⓑ Ⓒ Ⓓ Ⓔ

GMAT – Test 5
ANSWER SHEET

SECTION 1

1. Ⓐ Ⓑ Ⓒ Ⓓ Ⓔ
2. Ⓐ Ⓑ Ⓒ Ⓓ Ⓔ
3. Ⓐ Ⓑ Ⓒ Ⓓ Ⓔ
4. Ⓐ Ⓑ Ⓒ Ⓓ Ⓔ
5. Ⓐ Ⓑ Ⓒ Ⓓ Ⓔ
6. Ⓐ Ⓑ Ⓒ Ⓓ Ⓔ
7. Ⓐ Ⓑ Ⓒ Ⓓ Ⓔ
8. Ⓐ Ⓑ Ⓒ Ⓓ Ⓔ
9. Ⓐ Ⓑ Ⓒ Ⓓ Ⓔ
10. Ⓐ Ⓑ Ⓒ Ⓓ Ⓔ
11. Ⓐ Ⓑ Ⓒ Ⓓ Ⓔ
12. Ⓐ Ⓑ Ⓒ Ⓓ Ⓔ
13. Ⓐ Ⓑ Ⓒ Ⓓ Ⓔ
14. Ⓐ Ⓑ Ⓒ Ⓓ Ⓔ
15. Ⓐ Ⓑ Ⓒ Ⓓ Ⓔ
16. Ⓐ Ⓑ Ⓒ Ⓓ Ⓔ

SECTION 2

1. Ⓐ Ⓑ Ⓒ Ⓓ Ⓔ
2. Ⓐ Ⓑ Ⓒ Ⓓ Ⓔ
3. Ⓐ Ⓑ Ⓒ Ⓓ Ⓔ
4. Ⓐ Ⓑ Ⓒ Ⓓ Ⓔ
5. Ⓐ Ⓑ Ⓒ Ⓓ Ⓔ
6. Ⓐ Ⓑ Ⓒ Ⓓ Ⓔ
7. Ⓐ Ⓑ Ⓒ Ⓓ Ⓔ
8. Ⓐ Ⓑ Ⓒ Ⓓ Ⓔ
9. Ⓐ Ⓑ Ⓒ Ⓓ Ⓔ
10. Ⓐ Ⓑ Ⓒ Ⓓ Ⓔ
11. Ⓐ Ⓑ Ⓒ Ⓓ Ⓔ
12. Ⓐ Ⓑ Ⓒ Ⓓ Ⓔ
13. Ⓐ Ⓑ Ⓒ Ⓓ Ⓔ
14. Ⓐ Ⓑ Ⓒ Ⓓ Ⓔ
15. Ⓐ Ⓑ Ⓒ Ⓓ Ⓔ
16. Ⓐ Ⓑ Ⓒ Ⓓ Ⓔ

SECTION 3

1. Ⓐ Ⓑ Ⓒ Ⓓ Ⓔ
2. Ⓐ Ⓑ Ⓒ Ⓓ Ⓔ
3. Ⓐ Ⓑ Ⓒ Ⓓ Ⓔ
4. Ⓐ Ⓑ Ⓒ Ⓓ Ⓔ
5. Ⓐ Ⓑ Ⓒ Ⓓ Ⓔ
6. Ⓐ Ⓑ Ⓒ Ⓓ Ⓔ
7. Ⓐ Ⓑ Ⓒ Ⓓ Ⓔ
8. Ⓐ Ⓑ Ⓒ Ⓓ Ⓔ
9. Ⓐ Ⓑ Ⓒ Ⓓ Ⓔ
10. Ⓐ Ⓑ Ⓒ Ⓓ Ⓔ
11. Ⓐ Ⓑ Ⓒ Ⓓ Ⓔ
12. Ⓐ Ⓑ Ⓒ Ⓓ Ⓔ
13. Ⓐ Ⓑ Ⓒ Ⓓ Ⓔ
14. Ⓐ Ⓑ Ⓒ Ⓓ Ⓔ
15. Ⓐ Ⓑ Ⓒ Ⓓ Ⓔ
16. Ⓐ Ⓑ Ⓒ Ⓓ Ⓔ
17. Ⓐ Ⓑ Ⓒ Ⓓ Ⓔ
18. Ⓐ Ⓑ Ⓒ Ⓓ Ⓔ
19. Ⓐ Ⓑ Ⓒ Ⓓ Ⓔ
20. Ⓐ Ⓑ Ⓒ Ⓓ Ⓔ
21. Ⓐ Ⓑ Ⓒ Ⓓ Ⓔ
22. Ⓐ Ⓑ Ⓒ Ⓓ Ⓔ
23. Ⓐ Ⓑ Ⓒ Ⓓ Ⓔ

SECTION 4	SECTION 5	SECTION 6
1. Ⓐ Ⓑ Ⓒ Ⓓ Ⓔ	1. Ⓐ Ⓑ Ⓒ Ⓓ Ⓔ	1. Ⓐ Ⓑ Ⓒ Ⓓ Ⓔ
2. Ⓐ Ⓑ Ⓒ Ⓓ Ⓔ	2. Ⓐ Ⓑ Ⓒ Ⓓ Ⓔ	2. Ⓐ Ⓑ Ⓒ Ⓓ Ⓔ
3. Ⓐ Ⓑ Ⓒ Ⓓ Ⓔ	3. Ⓐ Ⓑ Ⓒ Ⓓ Ⓔ	3. Ⓐ Ⓑ Ⓒ Ⓓ Ⓔ
4. Ⓐ Ⓑ Ⓒ Ⓓ Ⓔ	4. Ⓐ Ⓑ Ⓒ Ⓓ Ⓔ	4. Ⓐ Ⓑ Ⓒ Ⓓ Ⓔ
5. Ⓐ Ⓑ Ⓒ Ⓓ Ⓔ	5. Ⓐ Ⓑ Ⓒ Ⓓ Ⓔ	5. Ⓐ Ⓑ Ⓒ Ⓓ Ⓔ
6. Ⓐ Ⓑ Ⓒ Ⓓ Ⓔ	6. Ⓐ Ⓑ Ⓒ Ⓓ Ⓔ	6. Ⓐ Ⓑ Ⓒ Ⓓ Ⓔ
7. Ⓐ Ⓑ Ⓒ Ⓓ Ⓔ	7. Ⓐ Ⓑ Ⓒ Ⓓ Ⓔ	7. Ⓐ Ⓑ Ⓒ Ⓓ Ⓔ
8. Ⓐ Ⓑ Ⓒ Ⓓ Ⓔ	8. Ⓐ Ⓑ Ⓒ Ⓓ Ⓔ	8. Ⓐ Ⓑ Ⓒ Ⓓ Ⓔ
9. Ⓐ Ⓑ Ⓒ Ⓓ Ⓔ	9. Ⓐ Ⓑ Ⓒ Ⓓ Ⓔ	9. Ⓐ Ⓑ Ⓒ Ⓓ Ⓔ
10. Ⓐ Ⓑ Ⓒ Ⓓ Ⓔ	10. Ⓐ Ⓑ Ⓒ Ⓓ Ⓔ	10. Ⓐ Ⓑ Ⓒ Ⓓ Ⓔ
11. Ⓐ Ⓑ Ⓒ Ⓓ Ⓔ	11. Ⓐ Ⓑ Ⓒ Ⓓ Ⓔ	11. Ⓐ Ⓑ Ⓒ Ⓓ Ⓔ
12. Ⓐ Ⓑ Ⓒ Ⓓ Ⓔ	12. Ⓐ Ⓑ Ⓒ Ⓓ Ⓔ	12. Ⓐ Ⓑ Ⓒ Ⓓ Ⓔ
13. Ⓐ Ⓑ Ⓒ Ⓓ Ⓔ	13. Ⓐ Ⓑ Ⓒ Ⓓ Ⓔ	13. Ⓐ Ⓑ Ⓒ Ⓓ Ⓔ
14. Ⓐ Ⓑ Ⓒ Ⓓ Ⓔ	14. Ⓐ Ⓑ Ⓒ Ⓓ Ⓔ	14. Ⓐ Ⓑ Ⓒ Ⓓ Ⓔ
15. Ⓐ Ⓑ Ⓒ Ⓓ Ⓔ	15. Ⓐ Ⓑ Ⓒ Ⓓ Ⓔ	15. Ⓐ Ⓑ Ⓒ Ⓓ Ⓔ
16. Ⓐ Ⓑ Ⓒ Ⓓ Ⓔ	16. Ⓐ Ⓑ Ⓒ Ⓓ Ⓔ	16. Ⓐ Ⓑ Ⓒ Ⓓ Ⓔ
17. Ⓐ Ⓑ Ⓒ Ⓓ Ⓔ		17. Ⓐ Ⓑ Ⓒ Ⓓ Ⓔ
18. Ⓐ Ⓑ Ⓒ Ⓓ Ⓔ		18. Ⓐ Ⓑ Ⓒ Ⓓ Ⓔ
19. Ⓐ Ⓑ Ⓒ Ⓓ Ⓔ		19. Ⓐ Ⓑ Ⓒ Ⓓ Ⓔ
20. Ⓐ Ⓑ Ⓒ Ⓓ Ⓔ		20. Ⓐ Ⓑ Ⓒ Ⓓ Ⓔ
		21. Ⓐ Ⓑ Ⓒ Ⓓ Ⓔ
		22. Ⓐ Ⓑ Ⓒ Ⓓ Ⓔ

GMAT – Test 6
ANSWER SHEET

SECTION 1	SECTION 2	SECTION 3
1. (A) (B) (C) (D) (E)	1. (A) (B) (C) (D) (E)	1. (A) (B) (C) (D) (E)
2. (A) (B) (C) (D) (E)	2. (A) (B) (C) (D) (E)	2. (A) (B) (C) (D) (E)
3. (A) (B) (C) (D) (E)	3. (A) (B) (C) (D) (E)	3. (A) (B) (C) (D) (E)
4. (A) (B) (C) (D) (E)	4. (A) (B) (C) (D) (E)	4. (A) (B) (C) (D) (E)
5. (A) (B) (C) (D) (E)	5. (A) (B) (C) (D) (E)	5. (A) (B) (C) (D) (E)
6. (A) (B) (C) (D) (E)	6. (A) (B) (C) (D) (E)	6. (A) (B) (C) (D) (E)
7. (A) (B) (C) (D) (E)	7. (A) (B) (C) (D) (E)	7. (A) (B) (C) (D) (E)
8. (A) (B) (C) (D) (E)	8. (A) (B) (C) (D) (E)	8. (A) (B) (C) (D) (E)
9. (A) (B) (C) (D) (E)	9. (A) (B) (C) (D) (E)	9. (A) (B) (C) (D) (E)
10. (A) (B) (C) (D) (E)	10. (A) (B) (C) (D) (E)	10. (A) (B) (C) (D) (E)
11. (A) (B) (C) (D) (E)	11. (A) (B) (C) (D) (E)	11. (A) (B) (C) (D) (E)
12. (A) (B) (C) (D) (E)	12. (A) (B) (C) (D) (E)	12. (A) (B) (C) (D) (E)
13. (A) (B) (C) (D) (E)	13. (A) (B) (C) (D) (E)	13. (A) (B) (C) (D) (E)
14. (A) (B) (C) (D) (E)	14. (A) (B) (C) (D) (E)	14. (A) (B) (C) (D) (E)
15. (A) (B) (C) (D) (E)	15. (A) (B) (C) (D) (E)	15. (A) (B) (C) (D) (E)
16. (A) (B) (C) (D) (E)	16. (A) (B) (C) (D) (E)	16. (A) (B) (C) (D) (E)
	17. (A) (B) (C) (D) (E)	17. (A) (B) (C) (D) (E)
	18. (A) (B) (C) (D) (E)	18. (A) (B) (C) (D) (E)
	19. (A) (B) (C) (D) (E)	19. (A) (B) (C) (D) (E)
	20. (A) (B) (C) (D) (E)	20. (A) (B) (C) (D) (E)
		21. (A) (B) (C) (D) (E)
		22. (A) (B) (C) (D) (E)

SECTION 4

1. Ⓐ Ⓑ Ⓒ Ⓓ Ⓔ
2. Ⓐ Ⓑ Ⓒ Ⓓ Ⓔ
3. Ⓐ Ⓑ Ⓒ Ⓓ Ⓔ
4. Ⓐ Ⓑ Ⓒ Ⓓ Ⓔ
5. Ⓐ Ⓑ Ⓒ Ⓓ Ⓔ
6. Ⓐ Ⓑ Ⓒ Ⓓ Ⓔ
7. Ⓐ Ⓑ Ⓒ Ⓓ Ⓔ
8. Ⓐ Ⓑ Ⓒ Ⓓ Ⓔ
9. Ⓐ Ⓑ Ⓒ Ⓓ Ⓔ
10. Ⓐ Ⓑ Ⓒ Ⓓ Ⓔ
11. Ⓐ Ⓑ Ⓒ Ⓓ Ⓔ
12. Ⓐ Ⓑ Ⓒ Ⓓ Ⓔ
13. Ⓐ Ⓑ Ⓒ Ⓓ Ⓔ
14. Ⓐ Ⓑ Ⓒ Ⓓ Ⓔ
15. Ⓐ Ⓑ Ⓒ Ⓓ Ⓔ
16. Ⓐ Ⓑ Ⓒ Ⓓ Ⓔ

SECTION 5

1. Ⓐ Ⓑ Ⓒ Ⓓ Ⓔ
2. Ⓐ Ⓑ Ⓒ Ⓓ Ⓔ
3. Ⓐ Ⓑ Ⓒ Ⓓ Ⓔ
4. Ⓐ Ⓑ Ⓒ Ⓓ Ⓔ
5. Ⓐ Ⓑ Ⓒ Ⓓ Ⓔ
6. Ⓐ Ⓑ Ⓒ Ⓓ Ⓔ
7. Ⓐ Ⓑ Ⓒ Ⓓ Ⓔ
8. Ⓐ Ⓑ Ⓒ Ⓓ Ⓔ
9. Ⓐ Ⓑ Ⓒ Ⓓ Ⓔ
10. Ⓐ Ⓑ Ⓒ Ⓓ Ⓔ
11. Ⓐ Ⓑ Ⓒ Ⓓ Ⓔ
12. Ⓐ Ⓑ Ⓒ Ⓓ Ⓔ
13. Ⓐ Ⓑ Ⓒ Ⓓ Ⓔ
14. Ⓐ Ⓑ Ⓒ Ⓓ Ⓔ
15. Ⓐ Ⓑ Ⓒ Ⓓ Ⓔ
16. Ⓐ Ⓑ Ⓒ Ⓓ Ⓔ

SECTION 6

1. Ⓐ Ⓑ Ⓒ Ⓓ Ⓔ
2. Ⓐ Ⓑ Ⓒ Ⓓ Ⓔ
3. Ⓐ Ⓑ Ⓒ Ⓓ Ⓔ
4. Ⓐ Ⓑ Ⓒ Ⓓ Ⓔ
5. Ⓐ Ⓑ Ⓒ Ⓓ Ⓔ
6. Ⓐ Ⓑ Ⓒ Ⓓ Ⓔ
7. Ⓐ Ⓑ Ⓒ Ⓓ Ⓔ
8. Ⓐ Ⓑ Ⓒ Ⓓ Ⓔ
9. Ⓐ Ⓑ Ⓒ Ⓓ Ⓔ
10. Ⓐ Ⓑ Ⓒ Ⓓ Ⓔ
11. Ⓐ Ⓑ Ⓒ Ⓓ Ⓔ
12. Ⓐ Ⓑ Ⓒ Ⓓ Ⓔ
13. Ⓐ Ⓑ Ⓒ Ⓓ Ⓔ
14. Ⓐ Ⓑ Ⓒ Ⓓ Ⓔ
15. Ⓐ Ⓑ Ⓒ Ⓓ Ⓔ
16. Ⓐ Ⓑ Ⓒ Ⓓ Ⓔ
17. Ⓐ Ⓑ Ⓒ Ⓓ Ⓔ
18. Ⓐ Ⓑ Ⓒ Ⓓ Ⓔ
19. Ⓐ Ⓑ Ⓒ Ⓓ Ⓔ
20. Ⓐ Ⓑ Ⓒ Ⓓ Ⓔ
21. Ⓐ Ⓑ Ⓒ Ⓓ Ⓔ
22. Ⓐ Ⓑ Ⓒ Ⓓ Ⓔ
23. Ⓐ Ⓑ Ⓒ Ⓓ Ⓔ

Use these pages on which to write your essays.
If additional pages are needed, use your own lined paper.

REA's *Authoritative Guide* to the

Top 100

BUSINESS
Schools

Complete, detailed, and up-to-date profiles of the top 100 business schools in the U.S.A. and abroad.

Plus in-depth advice on admissions and financing.

 Research & Education Association

Available at your local bookstore or order directly from us by sending in coupon below.

RESEARCH & EDUCATION ASSOCIATION
61 Ethel Road W., Piscataway, New Jersey 08854
Phone: (732) 819-8880   website: www.rea.com

VISA   MasterCard

Charge Card Number

☐ Payment enclosed
☐ Visa   ☐ MasterCard

Expiration Date: _____ / _____
                    Mo   Yr

Please ship **"Top 100 Business Schools"** @ $19.95 plus $4.00 for shipping.

Name _____

Address _____

City _____ State _____ Zip _____

REA's Test Prep Books Are The Best!

(a sample of the <u>hundreds of letters</u> REA receives each year)

" I am writing to congratulate you on preparing an exceptional study guide. In five years of teaching this course I have never encountered a more thorough, comprehensive, concise and realistic preparation for this examination. "

Teacher, Davie, FL

" I have found your publications, *The Best Test Preparation...*, to be exactly that. "

Teacher, Aptos, CA

" I used your *CLEP Introductory Sociology* book and rank it 99% – thank you! "

Student, Jerusalem, Israel

" Your GMAT book greatly helped me on the test. Thank you. "

Student, Oxford, OH

" I recently got the French SAT II Exam book from REA. I congratulate you on first-rate French practice tests. "

Instructor, Los Angeles, CA

" Your AP English Literature and Composition book is most impressive. "

Student, Montgomery, AL

" The REA LSAT Test Preparation guide is a winner! "

Instructor, Spartanburg, SC

(more on front page)